THE MADRAS TERCENTENARY COMMEMORATION VOLUME

THE MADRAS TERCENTENARY COMMEMORATION VOLUME

MADRAS TERCENTENARY
CELEBRATION COMMITTEE

(AUGUST 4, 1939)

GYAN

Published by

Gyan Publishing House
5, Ansari Road
Daryaganj, New Delhi-110002
Phone: 011-47034999, 9811692060
E-mail: books@gyanbooks.com

Distribution Network
gyanbooks.com
India, USA, Canada, UK, Australia, France

ISBN : 978-81-212-4533-3 (HB)
First Published, Madras, 1939

2nd Impression 2020

Printed at: Gyan Press, Delhi.

The Madras Tercentenary Commemoration Volume

EMBARKATION AND DISEMBARKATION AT MADRAS 1837

To face page 213. *—By Courtesy of the Chairman, Madras Port Trust.*

THE MADRAS TERCENTENARY COMMEMORATION VOLUME

Published on the 4th August 1939

For tne Madras Tercentenary Celebration Committee

INDIAN BRANCH

HUMPHREY MILFORD

OXFORD UNIVERSITY PRESS

LONDON BOMBAY CALCUTTA MADRAS

THE MADRAS TERCENTENARY PUBLICATION COMMITTEE

CONTENTS

LIST OF ILLUSTRATIONS

INTRODUCTION

The growth and decline of cities constitutes one of the most fascinating chapters in the political and cultural history of nations and of Empires. The history of India is particularly rich in records of many a famous city which flourished in the distant past and has either completely disappeared now or only provides curious material for the student of Archaeology. Ayodhya and Avantika, Takshasila and Nalanda, Harappa and Mohenjo-Daro, Bijapur and Vijayanagar, Korkai and Gangai-Konda Cholapuram, what an imposing list one could draw up of these vanished cities and how well they illustrate the splendour and antiquity of India's past history and its civilisation! A thousand years before the British founded their settlement on the spit of land to the north of the mouth of the Cooum river, the Pallavas were at the height of their power in South India and ports like Mahabalipuram in the neighbourhood of Madras were gates of adventure for Indian colonists who set sail from them and spread Indian culture in Siam and Cambodia, Malaya and the East Indian Islands. And we hear of the existence of the town of Mylapore, even at the beginning of the Christian era!

Yet this very antiquity of the past history of India lends a peculiar interest to the rise and growth of her cities in the modern period. The circumstances which gave birth to them and the factors which contributed to their expansion and development are vastly different from those of the past, and it is not too optimistic a view to hold that, humanly speaking, the conditions which make for the stability of these cities are far more favourable than those connected with many of the earlier cities of India.

The following pages describe in great detail the remarkable growth and development of the city of Madras and its varied activities during the past three hundred years. When Francis Day obtained a grant of land from the Naik of Poonamalee in August 1639, the English merchants were not very hopeful of the future of their settlement. They were convinced, however, that "this place may prove as good as the best; but all things must have its growth and time." The tercentenary of Madras is a fitting occasion for reviewing what "time and growth" have accomplished for the city.

The history of Madras is full of interest and contains many incidents which deserve to be more widely known than they are at present. A unique distinction of Madras is that twice in its history, the Head of its administration was deposed and imprisoned by his Council—George Foxcroft, the first Governor of Madras in 1665 and Lord Pigot in 1776.

Streynsham Master, one of the early Governors of Madras, did a great deal to organise the town for municipal purposes. He resolved to impose a house-tax and to appoint a scavenger with power to collect this tax and to hire coolies to remove the dirt and filth of the town. The post of scavenger was to be held by a civil servant of senior rank!

In 1687, the Company issued a Charter constituting the Corporation of Madras, consisting of a Mayor, 12 aldermen and 60 burgesses of the town of Fort St. George and City of Madrasapatam. These civic authorities had robes of scarlet serge and white silk gowns, and enjoyed the privilege of having broad umbrellas borne over them.

It was in Madras towards the end of the eighteenth century that the Rev. Andrew Bell inaugurated the monitorial system of instruction known for a long time in Britain as the Madras system of education.

Madras passed through stormy times during the wars between England and France in the eighteenth century and was captured and occupied by the French from 1746 to 1749. Orme, the historian, became a member of the Council in Madras in 1754 and took an active part in the military operations of the period. It was the siege of Madras in 1759 by Lally which led to the development of the Sepoy regiments of the Madras army.

Warren Hastings was a member of the Council in Madras from 1759 to 1762, and it was he who was responsible for the abolition of the post of chief Indian Merchant of the Company, held by a long line of great dubashes from Beri Timmanna to Manali Muthukrishna Mudali. Few people are aware that Madras is historically connected with a famous University in America. Elihu Yale, a native of Boston, was educated in England and joined the East India Company as a clerk. He became Governor of Madras in 1681 and later a Director of the Company. He gave a large donation to the school at Newhaven which in 1745 developed into Yale University. His son, David Yale, lies buried in the old Cemetery of St. Mary's Church, now situated in the High Court grounds. Madras may well be proud of the fact that the trigonometrical and topographical surveys of India had their origin in this Presidency. And it is worthy of record that so early as 1791, the citizens of Madras gave an example of their public spirit by inviting the Government to tax them for the defence of the town and described themselves as "three hundred thousand useful subjects!"

The growth of the city was rapid soon after its foundation. It became the chief factory and the headquarters of the Company on the

Coromandel coast and in 1658 the factories in Bengal were placed under its orders. Manucci, an Italian traveller to Madras in 1686 testifies to the remarkable progress of the British traders in the city. By the end of the seventeenth century, Madras was the chief British settlement in Hindustan and the principal port for European and Indian goods.

The eighteenth century was a period of storm and stress, and saw the foundations of the territorial power of England laid in India. The political importance of Madras suffered, however, by the Regulating Act of 1773 which made Calcutta the seat of the Governor-General.

In the nineteenth century, owing to favourable conditions, Bombay and Calcutta outstripped Madras in industrial and commercial importance, and the city was unkindly described by Kipling as a "withered beldame, brooding on ancient fame." Madras, however, made great progress in many directions during this century. The abolition of the trading privileges of the East India Company in 1833 brought into existence an independent European business community, which has played a great part in the life of Madras. The members of this community have been the pioneers of modern industrial enterprise in South India and have co-operated with their Indian fellow citizens in all matters affecting the welfare of the city. The years between 1835 and 1840 were notable for the foundation of important educational institutions like the Medical College, the Madras Christian College, Pachaiyappa's College, and Presidency College. The establishment of the University of Madras came in 1857. By a charter of 1862, the High Court of Madras was created by the amalgamation of the Supreme and Sudder Courts. The first railway line began to be constructed in 1859 and the Bangalore section was opened in 1864.

The fine promenade appropriately named the Marina was constructed in 1884, and the new Madras Harbour was completed in 1896 and the North-Eastern entrance opened in 1910. No one who reads the following pages can fail to be impressed with the remarkable growth of the city during the past three hundred years and with the great part which its leading men have played in the modern history of India.

The strip of land granted to the East India Company was about 3 miles in length and a mile and a half in width and was occupied by a few fishermen. To-day, the city covers an area of 30 square miles, and its population, if the rate of increase during the decade 1921-1931 is maintained, is likely to approach the million mark by the census of 1941. The city is rapidly outgrowing its boundaries and has a number of residential colonies outside the municipal limits. Madras is a unique and pleasant combination of the urban and the rural, of the old and the new. It has fortunately escaped the fate of Bombay and Calcutta which have been influenced by European modes of housing unsuited to Indian conditions. Owing to modern means of transport, its streets are probably less picturesque than in the old days when people went about in palanquins, and important civic officials had large umbrellas borne over them. Thomas Salmon, who was an Ensign in Madras in 1699, wrote :—

> "Female Choristers make up part of the equipage of a great man when he goes abroad ; for every man of figure in the country, I observed, had a number of these singing women run before him ; even the Governor of Fort St. George was attended by fifty of them, as well as by the country music when he went out ; but some of our late Governors, out of their excessive modesty, have thought fit to dispense with this piece of grandeur."

In spite of the disappearance of these picturesque aspects of public life and the comparative modernisation of the city, the old ways of its people remain essentially unchanged. The scenes round the city's temple tanks and squares are still the same as those witnessed in distant days, the crowds which chaffer in the Kotwal and Triplicane bazaars are little different from their predecessors in earlier years, and the Madras fisherman still goes out in his frail craft to earn a hazardous and precarious living from the sea exactly as his forefathers did many centuries ago.

The city, with its garden houses and palm-groves, its open spaces and fine avenues, has many features of great beauty. But careful planning in regard to its future development would be necessary, if these features are to be preserved. Though the Municipal authorities and the Provincial Government have done a great deal for the improvement of the city in recent years, much yet remains to be done. There is need for a comprehensive housing scheme which will lead to the abolition of the slums of the city, and the inclusion of greater Madras within the municipal limits. It is to be hoped that the city's tercentenary will stimulate civic interest and lead to organised efforts being made to make Madras, in addition to its historic importance, more and more a pleasant and beautiful place to dwell in for all its citizens.

I tender the cordial thanks of the Tercentenary Celebration Committee to all those friends of Madras, near and distant, who have contributed papers to this Commemoration Volume. The thanks of the Committee are also due to the printers, the G. S. Press, Madras, for the prompt and neat execution of their work.

University Buildings,
Chepauk, Madras,
24th July 1939.

S. E. RUNGANADHAN,
President,
Madras Tercentenary Celebration Committee.

SECTION I

Dakshinakulam

A Dream on the Beach in Moonlight

BY

HILTON BROWN.

The Sleeper—

THERE'S nothing old in the world on such a night,
There's nothing new ; I'm in a halt of time,
Caught in a cage of crystal. Time and space
Stand moonstruck. There's immensity perhaps—
The sea contending with the firmament,
The stars contending with the sands, the night
Contending with eternity—but all's
A termless, meaningless and timeless fusion
I am a man half-sleeping on the sands
Yet also I am everyone ; this beach
Is all South India and this moonlight hour
Is twice ten thousand centuries. If gods
Can anywhere exist and anyhow
It must be thus, as one and yet as all . . .
I have counted the moon-diamonds on the sea,
I have summarised the night-winds and the sounds
Of what might be a city—and I have lost
All sequence in the night, a sieve for sand,
A net to hold in water. I am god,
Lonely as god—aloof, apart, without,
Always and now and never, here and absent.
And I've God's vision . . . What, on such a night,
What's thirty years, three hundred or three thousand ?
What's one place or another ? What's Madras,
Bengal, Bombay, Mount Everest, the Poles ?
What but moon-diamonds millioned on the sea
And a night wind full of voices ?

[*Here the Voices Begin.*]

Strophe—

Out of the ocean of milk,
While the gods wondered,
Drawn on that line,

So fine,
So fine as silk,
The round earth blundered.
As long ago was planned,
Forth it was led;
And one, foreseeing, said,
"Here India shall be;
Here shall there be a land
Sun-ridden, hot and dry,
Exacting and unkind,
Where men shall try
Down the long years
Scant sustenance to find—
To draw their pitiful substance from the sand
That shall be fed
Insatiably
With the hearts of men, that shall be nourished
With prisoner hearts and watered with their tears."

A Voice (that may be of an Officer of John Company)—

I took me East to rob and steal,
To make such profit as I could,
And you, my grandson, grind your heel
Upon my turpitude.

You point your finger at me. "Fie!"
You say, "You shameless! Thief and rake!
How very different am I
Who came for India's sake

And laboured all my righteous days
That she might rise in wealth and fame."
Liar! Your ways are but my ways
Under another name.

And if I came to steal and rob,
Was I the worse in India's eyes
Than you, you cold complacent snob,
Who came but to despise

And fashion laws as stiff as stone
And preach a Bible cold as Christ
And walk in arrogance alone
While love was sacrificed?

I stole, I took what I could get;
At least I did not lock my heart

And elevate my nose and set
Mine Excellence apart

And make a scorned inferior thing
Of those whom I was sent to rule . . .
I won a country for my king ;
You lost him it, you fool!

Antistrophe—

So said one, foreseeing ;
But another, wiser still,
As the South came into being,
Stood on God's hill.
"The land shall be hard,"
He said, " and evil-starred,
A harsh and bitter school ;
Ah, yes—but beautiful.
So beautiful that men
When their time comes to die,
Frantic shall cry,
'Let me but see again
The white surf of the Bay,
The palm-trees' gentle sway
And the green of the paddy-field!'"
That wise one said,
Standing above
On the high hill of god,
"This land shall know the rod,
It shall know hardship, misery and regret
And yet
It shall know love ;
It shall steal men's hearts and bury them away
And by love shall it be healed."

Voices (that may be of Pilgrims)—

Down the long road,
The way our fathers showed,
We bear our load.

Through heat and chill
Forward we press until
We see God's Hill.

Its golden height
Hangs in the sun's light ;
We see with fright

How high it stands
Above our suppliant hands
But God commands

We shall ascend,
For where all mountains end
We have a friend.

Till we can hear
His temples chiming near
We must not fear.

Till we espy
His gopuram in the sky
We must not die.

Our feet are slow
But this we surely know—
On we must go.

On yon high crest
God has for ever blest
We shall find rest.

Where Rama trod—
Light-footed, golden-shod—
We shall meet God.

Strophe—

Who shall say what tears are
That are shed in a dream ?
Who shall say what fears are
That are but what they seem ?
Or that now's and then's and days and years are
In the gods' esteem
A solider thing than the wind that passes
Or the fire that scorches the Spring grasses
Or the sunlight on the temple brasses
A moment a-gleam ?

A Voice (which may be of a Ryot at Worship)—

Swami, swami !
I have striven
To give back
What Thou hast given ;
Small my offering,

Poor my gift,
How can I
Make better shift ?
Swami, swami, swami, swami,
Let my troubles lift.

Swami, swami !
Day is done ;
Thou and I
And it are one ;
Grain I harvest,
Seeds I sow,
These and Thou
Are all I know.
Swami, swami, swami, swami,
Let thy servant go.

Antistrophe—

Who shall say what gain is
That is countered by loss ?
Who shall say what pain is
That is under the gloss
Of pleasure ? Or what a blessing and what a bane is
In a world a-toss
Between plus and minus, minus and plus unending
That cancel at last to the ultimate zero, blending
Fortune and wreck—the king to his throne ascending,
The Christ to His Cross ?

A Voice (which may be of an Englishman Gone Home)—

I miss it so—the sunshine and the colour ;
In this grey place
That wears a sullen and a shadowed face
I miss it so.

I miss it so—the dew-bespangled mornings
When the bright day
Rose smiling from the blueness of the Bay ;
I miss it so.

I miss it so—the evenings of the jungle,
Wild things at call
And the gold moon presiding over all ;
I miss it so.

I miss it so—the company of people
Who sought my aid,
Puzzled, confiding, credulous, afraid;
I miss it so.

I miss it so—the crowded days of duty;
In this dull land
Of mind unharnessed and the idle hand
I miss it so.

I miss it so—the golden golden country
That took my youth
And paid for it so princely. Of a truth,
I miss it so.

Strophe—

Now thus did our elders advise;
A man has but one heart
And this is the best—
That he keep it locked and apart,
Not giving
That heart to the living,
The dead or aught that is made
By hands or that may exist
By the bounty of God, however it be arrayed
In the trappings of Paradise,
But shall hold his heart unfluttering in the cist
And the cell of his breast.

Antistrophe—

But what is the thing we see?
Who keepeth his whole heart,
How does he thrive?
He liveth, for all his art,
Unseeing,
Unhearing, his being
Becalmed in a dream that is death;
Barren, he shall forsake
The light of his life and the benefit of his breath;
Not fruitful shall he be
Nor grown nor wise nor accomplishing nor awake
Nor even alive.

Voices (which may be of Old Warriors)—

We who stood fast with the spear or struck home with the sabre
Are met at the last
In the hall where old victories fade and defeats are forgotten
And battles are past;
We who assaulted the *droog* and you who defended
Our quarrels compose;
And—what was the fighting about, *thambi*? Why were we
fighting?
Who knows?

I was a Frenchman perhaps and you were a Moslem,
Or haply again
I was a riever with Sivaji, you bore a musket
With Wellesley's men;
Tippu's was I, for you the bright banner of Gingi
Glowed like a rose;
But—what was the fighting about, *thambi*? Why were we
fighting?
Who knows?

Vijayanagar is dust and Gaganagiri
Flat with the grass;
Over our walls and our battlements only the seasons
Pass and re-pass;
Here we are met and forever, the foot and the horsemen,
Lances and bows;
But—what was the fighting about, *thambi*? Why were we
fighting?
Who knows?

Full Chorus—

Out of the ocean of milk,
Cloud-covered as in silk
And starred and jewelled as a king's daughter,
Dakshinakulam came—
Formless, without name,
A yellow land and washed about with water.
In the night, in the moon, are all things known and remembered.

As the gods, smiling, drew
Patterns the land through,
It rose in beauty and joy for their delighting;
As the gods, jesting, called,

There crept forth and crawled
This man and that—and straightway fell to fighting.
In the night, in the moon, are all things known and remembered.

Fiercely did these engage,
With senseless ruin and rage
They wrought their wars (for what no man discovers);
But were taken in one net,
In this were met—
That the land held them one and all as lovers.
In the night, in the moon, are all things known and remembered.

As it was in the past
And shall be at the last,
To this our land their hearts were pledged and plighted;
Men call them dead,
Say rather, "They are wed,
They lie with their love, in her are they united."
In the night, in the moon, are all things known and remembered.

Ghost upon ghost
Is here, a happy host—
Green forest, diamond coast
And holy hill to cheer them;
Wraith upon wraith
Contented saith,
"There is no death!"
And he that has ears shall hear them.
In the night, in the moon, are all things known and remembered.

[*Here the Voices End.*]

The Sleeper Again—

I have counted the moon-diamonds on the sea,
I have run with the wind, I have climbed with the climbing
stars,
I have been utterly lost. I was a god
And am now a man half-sleeping on the sands.
There's nothing here but the commonplace of night;
A moon, no doubt—a sea, immensity,
Bright sky, the sounding water, the scented breeze.
Paraphernalia! What would you expect? . . .
Was there a spell? I've lost it. I go back
To a dull bed in a dull bungalow—
I that was God and thought I walked with the dead.

I've missed the thing that was offered me. I touched—
'Fore God, I nearly had it! But it's lost . . .
Did I hear voices, choruses, the speech
Of those who would tell me something of grave import?
Did someone say—and credibly as it seemed—
"There is no death"? Did someone say to *me*,
"This land you have loved, that some day you must leave,
You shall *not* leave; nay, you'll for ever linger
A part of it; you'll stay here with the palms,
The singing palms and the Bay—ah! the blue Bay—
Jungle and temple-towers and all the company
That stole your heart"? . . . One said, "Where Rama trod"
(Or so I thought) "We shall find God." It's true!
I've met Himself! . . . One said, "There is no death."
I could believe it! . . . Or is this but the moon—
Moon-magic, witchery, mere lunacy,
Paraphernalia, conjurer's effects,
A trick of mirrors, *maya* upon *maya*? . . .
Did someone say all that to me? What's more,
Is it all true—as for the moment it seemed? . . .
I'd like to think it was . . . Perhaps . . . Perhaps . . .

SECTION II

HISTORY

Government Houses in Madras*

By

A. D. Crombie, C.I.E., I.C.S.

Collector, Vizagapatam

The subject with which I hope to interest the meeting is "Government Houses in Madras," that is to say those at Madras and Guindy. It is of course with the history of these buildings I propose to deal, but I think it will make my address more interesting to you if I commence with an account of the period prior to the acquisition of the site on which the Madras Government House now stands, which was in 1753, so that you may get a picture of the conditions under which the Governor and the servants of the East India Company lived in Madras in the early days.

COMMON TABLE AND RESIDENCE

The Governor of Fort St. George appears to have enjoyed the privilege of free residence from the time of commencement of the English Settlement at Madras, but at first he and all the employees of the Company down to the most junior apprentice lived in common. Their bedrooms were all in one house and they shared a common table. That house of course stood in the Fort. In the course of time the number of employees greatly increased, and as some of the senior officials had wives and children, they were granted permission one by one to live in separate quarters, but the junior employees continued to have a common mess up to the beginning of the 19th century.

Established at the Company's charge and in the interests of order, discipline and economy, the General Table was suspended by Sir William Langhorn (1672-1678) in favour of fixed allowances for diet and lodging, on the plea of inconvenience caused by the messing system to Members of Council and other married officers. The Company however insisted on the immediate revival of the Table for the use of Factors and Writers and a separate Table was maintained for the Governor and public guests. Two orders are quoted in Colonel Love's book. One in 1710 is from the Company:

* An Address delivered before the Madras Rotary Club on 15-3-1935—the subject being "Government Houses in the Presidency," and published in the *Hindu* of that date.

"Wee are Sorry to hear That of late there has not been a Sufficient Decorum kept up among our People, and particularly among the Young Writers and Factors, (and) that there has been Files of Musqueteers Sent for to Keep the Peace at dinner time. This, wee are Sure, casts a very untoward reflection upon the President and Council, and bespeaks them to want Prudence and Conduct. Wee only touch upon it here to caution against the like for the future, for how can it be expected that a due obedience should be paid to Government among all the People when it is affronted by such Youngsters?"

The other is a Fort St. George Consultation of 1712:—

'Severall disorders having been committed at the Generall Table, which we find to be partly occasiond by the absence of those persons in the Service that are of a Superiour Standing, and might awe the young ones into better behaviour, we have thought fit to appoint (here follow several names) and Alexander Bennett, Steward, to take their turns either weekly or monthly, as they shall agree among themselves, to be present at the Table and take care that no indecencys or disorders are committed.'

In 1717 when the Steward, as he was called then but no doubt he would be the Mess Secretary nowadays, was accused of running the bills too high, he pleaded in extenuation that, whereas some four years before no more than nine dishes were allowed for dinner, "now there is fifteen dishes both for dinner and supper!" The explanation also throws an interesting sidelight on the potations of those days. To us Goa Arrack and Batavia Arrack sound very odd, but then we do not indulge in punch. The General Table was finally abolished in 1722.

It may seem that I have somewhat digressed from my subject, but my purpose is to show that gradually the need for a separate house for the Governor was being felt. At the same time a desire for a garden for the recreation of the Company's employees had become manifest.

According to Glyn Barlow's very readable little book on Madras, the first garden was about eight acres in the region of the present Law College and it had a small pavilion in it. It was known as the Company's Old Garden, but the encroachment of the growing town began to make it unpleasant, and what was called the New Garden was established by Streynsham Master (1678-1680), though it is probable that Langhorn had first mooted the idea, as the Company wrote in 1676 "we do give you liberty to build a small Garden House, takeing care that it be no great charge to us." The

Madras Council however "ordered that it be commenced on a handsome plan and large enough to receive phyrmaunds from the King of Golconda and persons of quality." They salved their consciences by adding that it was "yet not to be a great charge to the Company." We are told that in 1681 the Governor "took a general survey of the town and all the fortifications thereof, etc., as also the new garden house and tank and finding the most part almost finished, and the rest brought to such a height that the charge would be more to take them quite down than to finish them, and considering the inconvenience of letting them remain as they are, after having discoursed with the Council about that affair, and asking their opinions, with their advice and approbation, it was resolved that they be finished as was at first designed." Which all goes to show how simple life was in those days when telegraphs and telephones did not exist.

There is some doubt as to the exact site of this garden house, but it must have been on the Cooum river, as the Dutch Governor of Pulicat, who had come to repay a visit, was taken by boat to the garden on 28th July 1688. According to Love, it was on the site of the Medical College, and according to other authorities it was on the Island very near where the Munro statue now stands. In any case the exact position does not much matter for the purpose of this address.

Even when finished the house does not appear to have been the permanent residence of the successive Presidents. On the 29th May 1686 President Gyfford "was taken ill with a violent fit of the stone and wind collic." On account of this and general ill-health he was allowed to live in the Garden House instead of the Fort and was given an allowance of 25 Pagodas for his diet. It is recorded by a visitor to Madras in 1704 when Pitt was Governor that he "during the hot winds retires to the Company's new Garden for refreshment." It had "costly gates, lovely bowling-greens, spacious walks and a teal-pond." It is hardly surprising that the Governor preferred it to the Fort, and gradually the successive Governors seem to have acquired a right to live either in the Garden House or the Fort.

State functions appear to have been conducted in this house from the time it was completed. In 1685 the Persian and Siam Ambassadors were entertained by Governor Gyfford and in the same year there was a grand banquet held here in honour of the proclamation of accession of King James II. Public demonstrations such as fire-works and bonfires had also been held on the occasion. In July 1698 the proclamation at Madras of the peace between England and France, followed as it was by the accession of Mr. Thomas Pitt to the President's chair, was celebrated by a dinner at the new garden to all the Company's servants. In September 1698 the purwannahs obtained from the Nabob and his Diwan were read publicly in the garden. In April 1699, Mortupha Khan, the Foujdar of Poonamallee, was invited to the new garden and entertained. In May 1702, the President and Council and Trainbands celebrated the raising of the blockade by Dawood Khan with a supper at the garden. The proclamation of the accession of Queen Anne was another occasion for celebration. On that occasion "all Europeans of fashion in the City drank the Queen's health and prosperity to Old England."

During the siege of Madras in 1746 the French used the Garden House for big gun emplacements and afterwards while in occupation of the Fort, they pulled down the House lest the English, trying to recapture the Fort, should use it for the same purpose. When therefore the English reoccupied Madras, the Garden House had disappeared. The then Governor Saunders, was naturally restive at having lost his privilege of living outside, so the present site and house belonging to Mr. Madeira were rented for him and within a year (1753) purchased for a sum of 3,500 Pagodas (about Rs. 12,250). The Company considered they had made a good bargain.

We have now brought our story down to the acquisition of the present Government House. In 1756 the grounds were added to by a further purchase of land. In 1758 the French again besieged Madras and their advance guards occupied Government House. They did a considerable amount of damage to it, and when finally two years later Pondicherry was captured and Lally, the leader of the French forces, was brought to Madras "he was lodged in those apartments of the Garden House which had escaped his fury at the Siege of Madras."

The next important step in the history of the house was taken by Lord Clive in 1800. He proposed alterations and additions, which would enable him to dispense with the use of his house in the Fort which could then accommodate the Board of Revenue. He estimated that a saving would thus be involved, but his figures proved very incorrect. Instead of costing 89,500 Pagodas, the alterations actually cost 1,76,350 Pagodas, which called forth an expression of dissatisfaction from the Board of Directors of the Company. Stated in rupees, the alterations to Government House cost more than Rs. 3 lakhs and the Banqueting Hall cost Rs. 2½ lakhs. I think you must all be familiar with the beautiful print of 1807 by Orme which shows both Government House and the Banqueting Hall. A close study of it will show that the main alterations since that date are a third storey and an extension of the porch to the House and a verandah to the Banqueting Hall. It is not easy to say when the improvements to the House were carried out.

THE GOVERNMENT HOUSE, MADRAS

In 1837 there was an estimate for "repairs and additions, etc., to the three stories of the principal building," but in 1859 there is a report that the following work was in progress:—"additional story considered necessary for the accommodation of the Governor and his family and is sanctioned for execution on emergency." As the foundations were underpinned to bear a third storey, we may take it that 1860 was the year when that storey acquired its present form. The Banqueting Hall Verandah and the porch to the house were built in 1895. In the estimate of that time there are mentioned the summer dining room and the monsoon dining room, but even the most senior people of to-day can only remember dining over the porch, a draughty proceedings on a monsoon night, I should think. The present dining room was made by Lady Willingdon out of what had formerly been offices.

The history of Government House, Guindy, can be told much more briefly. It belonged prior to 1813 to one Mr. Gilbert Ricketts of Madras, who in that year applied to the Government Bank for a loan of money on the mortgage of the property described as follows in the records, and it was agreed to lend him a sum of Pagodas 12,000:—

"All that capital messuage, or dwelling house with the outhouses, stables, buildings and erections situate at Guindymoade near the race-stand and St. Thomas' Mount and called or known by the name of Guindy Lodge and also that piece or parcel of ground situate lying and being at Guindymoade aforesaid . . . . . . ".

But no money was actually advanced at the time of the execution of the instrument, it being understood (in conformity with what seems to have been the practice of the Bank) that in consideration of Mr. Ricketts thus executing a bond he was to have a credit with the Bank to the extent of Pagodas 12,000.

Mr. Ricketts subsequently obtained different sums from the Treasurer, and he was at the time of his death indebted to the Bank in the sum of Pagodas 11,911.

Mr. Ricketts died intestate on the 4th December 1817 and the property devolved on the Registrar of the Supreme Court as administrator. The Bank authorities negotiated with the latter officer for the liquidation of the debt due to him and, as the estate was insolvent, took possession of the mortgaged property and tried to sell it by public auction. There was no bid for the property and on the 13th April 1820, the Bank thought it wise to foreclose the transaction by accepting a conveyance of the property at a sum of Pagodas 10,000.

It subsequently transpired that the property had been mortgaged by Mr. Ricketts a second time to one Mr. Griffiths, involving thereby legal complications and proceedings which however ended in favour of the Bank.

Early next year, *i.e.*, in 1821, the Bank offered it to the Government for sale for Pagodas 12,000 urging that the property was to all intents and purposes the property of Government. The premises had been on the Bank's hands a considerable time at great expense from repairs, etc., and difficulty had been experienced in procuring a purchaser at any reduced price.

There was also another piece of land in the neighbourhood of this property mortgaged to the Bank by Mr. Joseph Nazar Shamier, which the Bank proposed to alienate to Government for Pagodas 2,500.

The two properties were accordingly purchased for Rs. 35,000 and Rs. 8,750, respectively, the former being the equivalent of 10,000 Pagodas which was the cost the Government was prepared to pay.

Sir Thomas Munro, who was then Governor, recorded a note under date, the 27th November 1821, pointing out that the necessity of providing the Governor with a country house "where he can transact public business uninterruptedly, now that of the two residences provided for him in Madras, one in the Fort had to be given up with the exception of the Council Chamber, as offices to the Secretaries to Government, while the other house known as the country house or Government Garden, had, from the accumulation of buildings in its vicinity, become a Town House." He accordingly proposed to utilize the Guindy Lodge for his country residence.

It was also proposed to buy up a tract of land separating the Government House from Shamier's land previously purchased.

These proposals were approved in the Consultations of 27th November 1823. By the year 1840, due to various alterations and additions to the main building in the shape of upper rooms and verandahs, the house had acquired its present characteristic features, and I need not weary you with a description of the various additions made since, which for the most part is a catalogue of repairs to the main buildings and increased accommodation in the out-buildings, stables, etc.

Note: Since the above address was given, considerable alterations and improvements have been made both to Madras and Guindy Government Houses, including a new dining-room at Madras.

Madras as a Naval Base

By

Professor Joseph Franco, M.A.,
Presidency College, Madras.

If a few fishing hamlets could attain much celebrity during the last three hundred years—celebrity to the extent of winning a place in the front rank among the cities of the world—it is because of their historical setting even more than the influencing factors of geography, like situation. Geographers of Madras may put forth a plea that geographical factors contributed to the rapid growth of the city. Though one may not totally disagree with their view, one may yet feel with C. N. Parkinson that Madras "owed its birth to historical accident and its survival to strategic necessity."[1] The truth of this statement is seen if we examine the history of Madras from its origin and foundation in 1639 to its full growth in the succeeding years. Madras is situated about the middle point of the Coromandel Coast. A word may be said of 'the Coast' by which name the Coromandel coast was some time known, and how the situation of Madras on that coast gave a sort of fillip as it were to its rise, growth and importance.

The Coromandel coast extends from Cape Comorin to Orissa. The Portuguese called it Choramandala, and the Dutch Choromandel. The derivation of the word has been the subject of some study among scholars and the consensus of opinion is in favour of the word Coromandel being derived from Cholamandalam, considered to be the fifth province of the last Hindu empire, Vijayanagara. Another possible derivation may be that from Karimanal, literally black sand. Karimanal is a small village on this coast on Lake Pulicat. It was almost the first place on this part of the coast seen by the passengers from Europe to Madras in the 16th and 17th centuries. It has been said that it served as a summer resort to European residents of Madras. Yet another name for this place is Kharamandalam, so known in Telugu. Dr. Caldwell thinks that Khara means hot. The more plausible explanation, however, would be to associate the place with the legendary Khara of old. The village exists even to-day but in a much neglected state. But once it was an important place resorted to by Europeans in Madras during the

1 Trade in the Eastern Seas 1793-1813, p. 37 (1937).

hot season.[2] The important ports of the Coromandel coast were Negapatam, Masulipatam, Vizagapatam, Coringa, Tuticorin and Madras; besides Pondicherry, Porto Novo, Tranquebar, Point Calimere and Pulicat. The Portuguese, the Dutch, the English and the French vied with one another in the 17th century and the 18th to secure some suitable factories on this coast, mainly from a commercial point of view. After trying two or three sites both to the north and to the south, the early English factors hit upon the fishing hamlet of Madraspatam as the best under the circumstances. Francis Day who had the courage and foresight to settle at this place did not win the approbation of the authorities; he was indeed censured for incurring heavy and unremunerative expenditure over what might be a bad choice. The authorities of the time little knew that the place was destined to become the fountain-head of a big Presidency. But the natural environment and conditions of Madras in 1639 and 1640 were far from satisfactory. The cautious Directors would not approve of the step taken by the early factors, though things turned out wonderfully beyond expectations. Both Day and his fellow-founder Cogan, were treated harshly and attempts were made to punish them, among other things, for the building of the Fort of Madras.

Firstly there was no natural harbour. In the whole Coromandel coast, Trincomalee was the only place that provided a natural harbour. Others were all ports exposed to the rough surf which would not allow ships to come near the shore, and which had no facilities of a harbour. The choice was between one bad port and another, and ultimately it fell on Madras. The difficulties experienced in landing due to lack of a proper harbour find description in many an account left by visitors to this port. William Hickey for instance narrates how passengers landed and were taken to the South Sea Gate by masulla boats, made of planks sewn together, so as to withstand the breakers. The necessity for a first class harbour was increasingly felt and only in the seventies of the last century the Madras harbour became a *fait accompli*. Though an artificial harbour to-day it provides all facilities which a natural harbour would provide.

Secondly the port of Madras witnessed bad anchorage which could be explained as due to shallow waters. The roadstead was often risky —there were the risk of currents, of a high surf even in the calmest weather and of unexpected gales. Hurricanes and cyclones are a frequent feature of the coast; and M. Martineau, an ex-Governor of Pondicherry, has described in a book the most disastrous cyclones of the last

2. Caldwell: Comparative Grammar: pp. 20-22.

two centuries and more. Large ships had to be in anchorage two miles from the shore, and landing of goods and passengers was by means of masulla boats and catamarans. Sometimes the surf which varied made it impossible for native boats to be safe. The presence of sharks in the waters was a source of perpetual dread alike to the boatman and to the swimmer.

That historical circumstances made Madras what it is to-day, is again borne out by the following fact. Soon after the establishment of Fort St. George, Madras became a naval base for the English to protect the Bay of Bengal from enemy attacks and descent. For the menace from the French brought home to the English the necessity of holding on to this place as their base. The French were in possession of Pondicherry and the English tried to weaken its fortifications whenever opportunity arose. The weakening of Pondicherry meant the strengthening of the English settlement. Indeed Day was offered in the course of his search for a port the choice of the site of Pondicherry.

The military importance of the Madras settlement was more and more realised. It was felt towards the end of the 18th century that even distant Bengal could be defended from Madras. In fact it had been said that the safety of Bengal rested with the secure hold of Madras. Otherwise there would be no effective defence of the Bay of Bengal. If there was an attack by sea on India, especially on the East coast of the country, it was obvious that the naval defence should be based on a port, and Madras eminently suited this purpose. The Bengal River was useless and unhealthy from the defence point of view. Again, if one would read the history of the 18th century Madras from the aspect of defence, one would see that all expeditions to this coast were conducted during the southwest monsoon. Otherwise it would be impossible for ships to reach the Bay of Bengal easily. With the breaking of the southwest monsoon advantage was taken by the European powers to send their expedition to India on the side of Bay of Bengal. History records more than eight naval actions in the seas fought between Madras and Point de Galle, between the English and the French in the 18th century. Most of them were waged in the course of the Anglo-Carnatic wars of 1746-61, in the Second Mysore War of 1780-83, and in the days of Revolutionary and Napoleonic struggles. Admirals La Bourdonnais and Suffren are the most notable on the French side in these ; Boscawen, Watson and Hughes on the English side. And 'it was more than a coincidence that all the fighting should take place between April and September in a strip of water about three hundred miles in length.'

Another fact that cannot be overlooked in this connection is the vast area of hinterland protected from the sea-base of Madras. The extension of its inland territory was to its great advantage in the sense that it enabled to arrest the French from further expansion outside their capital which was at that time Pondicherry. But for this inland territory of Madras, the French would have expanded and the English could not have effectively checked their movements. Thus from military and strategic points of view Madras was of value in the expansion of English power in India.

St. Thome (Mylapore) in the Dutch and English Records

By

A. Galletti, I.C.S. (*Retired*).

The Portuguese had a settlement at St. Thomé or Mylapore from the beginning of the 16th century till 1749—nearly 250 years. It is thus described by the Dutch in 1726:—

"A little further on—from Pulicat, the Dutch headquarters on the Chola coast (Coromandel, C is pronounced ch in Portuguese)—you come to the ruined town of Mylapore or St. Thomé, called after the apostle of that name, who—as they will have it—died there as a martyr. This town, in former times of some importance, was demolished in 1674 by order of the King of Golconda and is now in ruins. .. Not far from this place lies a large hill called by the Portuguese "El grande Monti". The top of this hill is reached by 96 large and broad steps made of stone. It is covered with a nice pavement of small stones. In the centre is a little chapel, which King Emanuel of Portugal built in the year 1514 in honour of St. Thomas. One sees there the apostle and the manner in which, he was beaten to death by a Brahmin while he was praying. There is also a stone cross which—according to those of the Roman persuasion—at times sweats; also a statue of the virgin made—as they say—by the apostle himself. The chapel is small, but very neat, compact and beautiful. It has a small income from Goa and some little offerings from the people, who crawl up and pray here in front of the statue of the saint....Near by lies Madraspatam, a town where the English have established their chief factory."

The Dutch always called Madras Madraspatam, and Sadras Sadraspatam. They had five factories themselves on the Coromandel Coast, of which Sadras on the south and Pulicat on the north were the nearest to Madras. They were surrendered by the Chief in Council of Fort Geldria (Pulicat) to Lord Hobart in Council, Chief of Fort St. George, in 1795. Pulicat was founded in 1610 and Fort Geldria was built there in 1615.

In 1661 the Dutch proposed to take St. Thomé from the Portuguese. Momentous consequences might have ensued if they had—they would almost certainly have driven the English out of Madras. But the King of Golconda intervened, and took St. Thomé under his protection. It was seized by the French in 1672, taken by the Dutch from the French with some assistance from the King of Golconda in September 1674 after a year's siege. The Dutch then suggested to the King that the fort and town should be destroyed, and with some difficulty got him to agree, and in October 1675 some thousands of natives were engaged in the demolition under his orders. There was however still a Portuguese colony there in 1749, when it was occupied by the English Company in spite of Portuguese protests. The Governor in Council explained in a letter home dated 6th August 1751:—

"St. Thomé appears to us a place of very great consequence, its contiguousness to Madras, should it be in other hands, would greatly prejudice us, as it would affect our sea and land customs, investment and private trade, and be an asylum for our military, who would frequently desert. What pretensions the Portuguese can have to it we cannot perceive; it has been under the Moors for many years; they have not had any government, levied customs, nor hoisted colours there, but such as the ecclesiastice made use of to decorate their festivals."

Some Unpublished Letters of Charles Bourchier and George Stratton (1771 to 1802)

By

S. K. Govindaswami, M.A.,
Lecturer, Annamalai University

In a respectable family of Karunikas (hereditary village accountants *siu generis*) at Achalpuram on the estuary of the Coleroon, a valuable collection of letters has been handed down for the last one hundred and fifty years as an inestimable heirloom. The collection consists of twenty-one letters, besides a pathetic memorial datable in or about A.D. 1816. Two of the Governors of Fort St. George Charles Bourchier and George Stratton of the Madras 'Revolution' fame, contribute most of the letters, while two of them come from the pen of James Bourchier. The 'Memorial' is drawn by Venkatachalam an ill-starred member of the family. The dates of these letters range from April 1771 to August 1802. They are addressed to Venkatanarayana Pillai and Venkataranga Pillai. It is not too much to state that these letters throw a flood of light on the politico-social condition of the Carnatic during the period covered by them. I am indebted to my old student, Mr. Venkatanarayana, B.A., Hons, a member of this historic family, for bringing these letters to the knowledge of the scholarly public.

It is not impossible with the help of these records to narrate the history of this family. It originally hailed from Vendalur, now Vandalur, a station on the Villupuram-Madras section of S.I.R. Enterprising members of this family seem to have migrated to Madras where,—to cite a passage from Mr. Venkatachalam's memorial—"they had the honour of being employed upwards of a century, at different times and they behaved to the high regards and full trusts placed in them by gentlemen." Let Venkatachalam relate the story of his forbears:—

"In the year 1687, my great grand-father Venkatadri Pillai served Mr. Elihu Yale, the 4th Governor of Fort St. George; and my grand-father Moota Pillai served in 1740 Mr. N. Morse, the 19th Governor; but unluckily their fortunes and above all, the correspondence that showed the high regards of those gentlemen have been lost in 1746 and '59 during the French War of Admiral De la Bourdonnais and General Lally." What shall we not pay for the recovery of those letters valued so much by Venkatachalam!

In the next generation Venkatanarayana Pillai, endearingly addressed by Charles Bourchier and George Stratton as "My Faithful Venkati," seems to have achieved a great name and fame in the services of the two Governors mentioned above. Referring to his uncle Venkatanarayana, Venkatachalam says, "he had also had the honour of waiting on Mr. Morse, on his return to India, in the service of supplying provisions to the naval forces at Madras, when he was pleased to recommend my said uncle, in the year 1769, to Mr. Warren Hastings, as a Dubash when he was Second in Council at Madras . . . My said uncle, Venkatanarayana Pillai, by his protection gained the good-will and affection of His Highness the old Nabob, Muhamad Ali Khan Bahadur . . . His services were so long and faithful, and regards and trusts of the said great men were so true that we are not known at even this day unless we are called by the name of Bourchier Narayana Pillais' family, under which title we pass these 80 years."

Among other members of this family we must mention Paupa Pillai, the maternal grand-father of Venkatachalam. "He served Marquis Dupleix....and Nabob Chanda Sahib, one of the Moorish lords who fought for the possession of the Carnatic, and managed the Subah of Arcot for some years under them. After Pondicherry was yielded to the British Arms for the first time in the year 1762, he, the said my grand-father came and settled at Madras, and served the Nabob Muhamad Ali Khan Bahadur by managing the affairs of the Honourable Company's Jaghire in the year 1769." This man, who so facilely changed sides, was certainly the agent of Madame Dupleix, on whom Anandaranga Pillai unreasonably heaps invective upon invective in his diary. To quote him: "she (Madame Dupleix) has taken Paupa Pillai and Venkataraman into her service—two cunning fellows, who have been trying to persuade the Madras merchants to come and settle in Pondicherry."[1]

Another notable member of this family was Ranga Pillai who was a dubash of George Stratton.[2] After the precipitate departure of George Stratton to England consequent on the "Revolution" Ranga Pillai entered into the service of Mr. Powney, a civilian of the company when, as a result of the mismanagement of the Zamindari of Ramnad during the rule of Mangaleswari Nachchiar the Company took over the Zamindari, Powney was sent out as the Revenue Collector. Lushing-

1. Ananda Ranga Pillai's 'Diary' IV, pp. 32 and 57.

2. George Stratton. Entered the Company's service in 1751 and was the Second in Council in 1775. He usurped the Government of Madras in 1776 which led to his recall.

ton, the Collector who succeeded Powney, had the following remark to make upon his administration.[3] In a letter dated 21st June 1799, he wrote: "Abuses and irregularities of all kinds were rampant throughout every part of the Zamindary. The late collector's dubash, one Ranga Pillai, had embezzled large sums of money and had cheated the government to a very considerable extent in disposing of the grain collected as land tax and the people were suffering much for want of food." However, Ranga Pillai in his letter to Charles Bourchier dated 30th September 1800 appears to have complained to him about his financial failure at Ramnad. On the receipt of this letter Charles Bourchier in his letter of reply dated 6th March 1801 writes: "I shall be glad to hear that you are more successful in your future undertakings than you say you were in the Ramnad country." In an inventory of house property in the Fort appended to a letter addressed to Lord Clive, by Messrs. Harrington Walts and Company, Ranga Pillai is said to have possessed two houses in Powney's street and one by the Ware House.[4]

Venkatachalam's father was Venkatarama Pillai about whom the son writes as follows:—"My father Venkatarama Pillai had the honour of serving Messrs. James Bourchier,[5] Peter Perring[6] and Robert Barclay,[7] the Councillors of Fort St. George and also was an attorney to Peter Perring and saved a good character."

Venkatachalam Pillai, the Memorialist, "was recommended in 1789 by his patron Mrs. J. D. Porcher to Messrs George Parry[8] and John Jervis.[9] . . . civil gentlemen of the Madras establishment." Later Jervis defrauded him of his money and consequently Venkatachalam was put to great financial difficulties. After wandering from Poona to Ceylon, thanks to Macleod and Major Blackburne, Resident at Tanjore, he was despatched as an emissary to Tranquebar where he distinguished himself. According to his own statement, "I have been from time to time employed in several respectable situations in the

3. *Ramnad Manual*, p. 255.

4. *Vestiges of Old Madras*, III, p. 511.

5. James Bourchier was appointed Commissioner of the Court of Requests in 1753. Served under Cook. He was the brother of Charles Bourchier.
(*Vestiges*, II p. 440 and III, pp. 555 and 556).

6. Peter Perring: *Vestiges*, III, pp. 103, 148 and 200.

7. Robert Barclay: *Vestiges*, p. 315.

8. George Parry—A Civil Servant and Customer.
(*Vestiges*, II, p. 578 and III, p. 429).

9. Jervis was on the Grand Jury in 1794. (*Vestiges*, III, p. 429). On his Ceylon career see *Ceylon under British Rule*, pp. 16 and 22.

public services which I was frequently obliged to resign on account of my ill-health, and was as often employed through the protection of gentlemen, as the state of my health permitted to engage into any active employment. Thus I continued to serve both in Judicial and Revenue line etc. from 1803 to 1816."

"Thus," observes Venkatachalam, "my ancestors had the honour and happiness of growing up with the British Nation on this coast for a considerable length of time."

A welcome and interesting light is shed by the letters in question on the social condition of the Carnatic in the 18th century. I am referring here only to the relations between the company's white servants and their Indian Dubashes. We cannot say that the one wanted sincerely and open-heartedly to understand or meet the other on equal terms. G. P. Spear in "*The Nabobs*" remarks: "In the case of India easy contact was made more difficult by the institutions as well as by the character of the two peoples."[10] The same writer in another place says, regarding individual friendship, that "the seal of social intercourse is personal friendship, and this too had its place in the life of the 18th century."[11]

These letters reveal the feelingful intimacy and sympathetic understanding that existed between the two governors of Madras and their Dubashes, Venkatanarayana and Venkataranga. A century of epistolary contacts on either side is a positive proof of this, though one wonders if some other material interests of the persons concerned would not explain this continuity of correspondence.

Small incidents referred to in the letters suffice to prove the intimate nature of their social relationship. Ranga Pillai asks for the portrait of his old master Charles Bourchier in one of his letters, to which the latter replies: "I could not have declined to comply with your repeated request to send you my portrait; if my being so much employed in matters of more consequence had not occupied most of my time; it is also a tiresome and disagreeable task to sit several times to a limner, for my likeness. I may nevertheless . . . gratify your wishes, and can meet with an experienced limner to perform the task." Many other mutual obligations are on record. For example, George Stratton in his letter dated 6th August 1788 addressed to Venkatanarayana writes: "my bankers tell me that they have received a small bottle of peacock oil which you have been so very obliging to send. I cannot express to you how very sensible I am of the kind attention on your part, for let

10. p. 126. 11. p. 135.

me hope in God it will be of service to my little boy's arm which is greatly contracted."

On the other hand, Venkatanarayana and Venkataranga had some request or other to make to their old masters at England. Sometimes they were given power-of-attorney to attend to appeals in Privy Council from the Mayor's Court of Madras. Charles Bourchier in answer to one such request writes: "I am very sensible you must be very anxious about your suit against Messrs. Taylor and Co., executors to the estate of Mr. Majendie before the King-in-Council. I have again written to Mr. Winterbottom to know how it went on; and his answer was that the Lords have not met since the King's illness and recovery, to decide any causes." James Bourchier promises to buy wall-paper in London for Umdat-ul-Umara, one of the sons of Muhammad Ali. When George Stratton,[12] the nephew of George Stratton, Governor of Madras was appointed as a writer on the Madras Establishment in 1794, the latter commended him to the care and consideration of his old and faithful dubash, Ranga Pillai. "Mr. George Stratton, nephew of mine" says he, "is being appointed a writer........Let me request you will be a warm friend to him on his arrival from Bombay, giving that advice for his conduct that he may not err from falling into improper hands." In the generally demoralised social atmosphere of the times these instances smell sweet like the fragrance of spring flowers.

In this harmonious relationship we sometimes find a discordant note. Instances were not wanting of dubashes who were oppressive and fleecing, and of officers defrauding their Indian servants. Dodwell rightly considers them as representing "not the crimes of unbridled licence, but the perquisites and peccadilloes of a bad system."[13] We had already mentioned the case of Ranga Pillai who diverted the revenue of Ramnad into his pocket. Halliburton in a pamphlet of his warns the officers in the company's service against "the unprincipled audacity" of dubashes, when under the patronage of men in power.[14] Venkatachalam's 'Memorial' is the pathetic story of the foundering

12. George Stratton (Junior) entered the civil service in 1793. He was a member of the Council in 1820 A.D.

(*Vestiges*, III, p. 473).

13. *The Nabobs of Madras*, p. 31.

14. *Journal of Indian History*, V, p. 194. See also *Vestiges*, III, p. 324. Popham in his letter dated 16th Dec. 1785 to the Government of Madras, has the following remark to make on the abuses of "Dubashism", "Dubashes exercise their power for the most oppressive, illegal and unjustifiable purposes........ Is the extirpation of Dubashism such an Hydra of labour that the idea should affright us?"

of his fortunes, thanks to an English civilian whom he trusted. Venkatachalam mortgaged his undivided property at Madras and bought the Nawab of Arcot's Consolidated Bonds in partnership with Mr. Jervis to the tune of 26,000 star pagodas. These are the words of Venkatachalam on the question :—" Mr. Jervis was appointed Head Assistant at Jaffna to Mr. Andrews, the late Resident of Ceylon, went there and got the farm of the Pearl Fishery, where I had proceeded in the hope that he would be able to discharge his debts......But I have been greatly mortified at Mr. Jervis's having given up the lucrative farm of Pearl Fishery." Jervis's choice can be explained in the light of an enquiry conducted by North, Governor of Ceylon, into the Pearl Fisheries, which disclosed "gross and erroneous peculation," causing a loss of 12 lakhs of Pagodas to the Government.[15] This change of fortune, Venkatachalam says, made him " plunge into sorrow and overwhelmed with grief that I wandered so far as Bombay and Poona to linger out the rest of my days in misery and obscurity......I thought my deplorable condition better among strangers than among acquaintances...... I lost Mr. Jervis and all I had in the world."

Another ubiquitous evil was the desire on the part of every servant of the Company as soon as he came to India to amass easy money. From the pages of these letters the irrepressible cry of " Money, More Money," arises in an endless blast. Mervyn Davis observes: " One thing only had brought these Englishmen to India, one thing only held them here 'Money.' "[16] In the letter of George Stratton to Ranga regarding his nephew, he writes : " you will act as faithful a part as your father did by me, telling the black merchants........to show every mark of attention." In another letter he urges upon Ranga " to give him that advice so that he may soon gain a little competence independent of the Company's pay which you know full well he cannot live upon. On you therefore I depend for his prosperity." Charles Bourchier in a reminiscent mood writes in 1872 regarding his investments in private trade with China. I now lament that I did not stay three or four years longer in India, that I might have improved my fortune to have made me more at my ease in this country. Mr. George Smith's scheme of sending broadcloth to China in which you know I was concerned one third with my brother amounting to near 19,000 pagodas. " Very few, (however) managed to carry home a fortune with them "[17] says Dodwell.

It is not unnatural that the letters under consideration here should say something about the political events of the Carnatic in the 18th

15. *Ceylon under the British Rule*, p. 23.
16. *Private Life of Warren Hastings*, p. 20.
17. *The Nabobs of Madras*, p. 34.

century. Learning from Venkatanarayana that the Third Mysore War had broken out, George Stratton, in his letter dated 18th November 1790, wrote, "Sincerely do I wish success to the expedition against Tippoo, though I have my fears, that it will be attended with much trouble and expense will be greater than the company can well support." Judging from the war indemnity of three crores and thirty lakhs of rupees, George Stratton's prophesy appears to have been sound. Again in April 1792 he wrote: "I am obliged to you for the very particular account you sent me of the proceedings of our Armies, and of our success in taking Bangalore. I wish we had been as fortunate against Seringapatam. As it appears that the Nizami troops did us more prejudice than service I know too well from long experience they were never to be depended upon......and that Tippoo may buy any of them with a bribe to betray us and do him service when an opportunity offers. I hope therefore that Lord Cornwallis will keep a strict watch over them." He concludes with a prayer: "I therefore hope that a lucky cannon shot may put (him) out of the world, as some atonement for his numberless people he has at times been the cause of the Death of."

The account so far given may show that the letters have got some value in the study of the history of the Carnatic in the 18th century. These letters contain pungent observations on the trial of Warren Hastings, the Revolution of France, the Napoleonic Wars, the Nawab of Arcot's Debts, etc., which I hope to discuss in my edition of the letters with comment in the near future under the auspices of the Annamalai University. I take this opportunity to request such of the scholars in England interested in this subject to let me know if the letters written by Venkatanarayana and Ranga to the Stratton and Bourchier families in England can be traced out.

Origin of the Word " Madras "

By

Rao Bahadur R. Krishna Rao Bhonsle, I.S.O.

The origin of the word 'Madras' is a tantaliser. In the words of Talboys Wheeler, " the whole English Settlement was known as Madras, but the origin of this name is unknown." There has been much speculation as to the derivation of the word, and many fanciful theories have been suggested. Whatever this may be, it is a fact that a part of the city went by the name Madraspatam. It is remarkable that the firman granted to Sir Francis Day by Venkata of Damil (a village near Conjeevaram), contains the name Madraspatam. Thanks to the Rt. Rev. Monsignor A. M. Teixeira, the clue has been supplied and the mysterious veil on the origin of the name has been lifted.*

In July 1927, Mgr. Teixeira lighted upon a stone while excavating the foundations of a new chapel of St. Lazarus at Mylapore on the site of the old one; it was a fine tombstone bearing a Portuguese inscription It had been embellished by an escutcheon at the top. The following is the English rendering of the inscription :—

> This is the grave of Manuel Madra and of his mother,
> Son of Vincente Madra and of Lucy Brague. They built
> This Church at their own expense in the year 637.

Mgr. Teixeira's comments as published in the *Madras Mail* of the 23rd July 1927 were as under :

" It goes without saying that 637 stands for 1637. Here then we have the most probable origin of the word Madras, it seems to me. The Madra family were evidently rich enough to build a church at their own cost. The members of the Madra family could also boast of some title to nobility, as their Coat-of-Arms reveals. They flourished in these parts towards the end of the 16th century, beyond which we find, if I report correctly, no historic traces of the word Madras. The natural inference to be drawn is that a wealthy Portuguese family, Madra by name, must have settled down somewhere near the present Assumption Church,

* *Vide* also The Madras Guide Book, published by Messrs. Ajita Kumar & Co., Madras, 1927.

which bears two dates namely, 1640 and 1857, and must have given their own name to the locality, or that the people did it, as the custom in India is."

I supported Mgr. Teixeira's view (*vide* the *Madras Mail* of the 28th December 1927), relying, as I did, on the authority of Sir William Foster's "The Founding of Fort St. George, Madras" (1902) and other sources.

In Col. Love's "Vestiges of Old Madras 1640-1800," the following is found recorded :—

> "Writing in 1820, Bundla Ramaswami Nayudu, in a "Memoir on the Internal Revenue System of the Madras Presidency," alluded to a family tradition that his ancestor, Beri Timmappa, acted as intermediary in procuring the grant of territory made to Francis Day, Agent of the East India Company. He says :
>
> 'Mr. Day undertook to erect a factory on the spot where there was a fisherman's 'Coopum', the headman of which was a Christian named Madarasen who had thrown some obstacle in allowing the piece of ground he was in possession of, which was his plantain garden. Beri Timmappa had by his influence obtained that spot, promising him that he would cause the factory, which was then about to be erected, to be called after his name as Madarasenpatnam'."

Authorities like Colonel Love and Sir William Foster, were not able to accept this tradition, with the data they had then before them. But I may state that the discovery of the tombstone of Manuel Madra, throws more light on it and is, therefore, authentic. In the Memoir of Bundla Ramaswami Nayudu, two important things are to be noted :

(1) The name of the headman of the fisherman's 'Coopum' was Madarasen ; and

(2) He was a Christian.

A Hindu whose pious ancestor Timmappa had caused two temples to be built—one for Vishnu (Chenna Kesava Perumal) and the other for Siva (Chenna Malleswara) in Chenna Patnam, should naturally state the facts related to Madarasenpatnam in contrast to Chennapatnam. An orthodox Hindu is not likely to have included in the Memoir an incident relating to a fisherman who happened to be a Christian, if he had not himself believed the veracity of the incident.

It is possible that Madarasen, a convert to Christianity or a convert's son, in grateful remembrance of his indebtedness to the Portuguese merchant's family of 'Madra' who built a church at their own expense, adopted the name of his benefactor's family, with the Indian suffix of

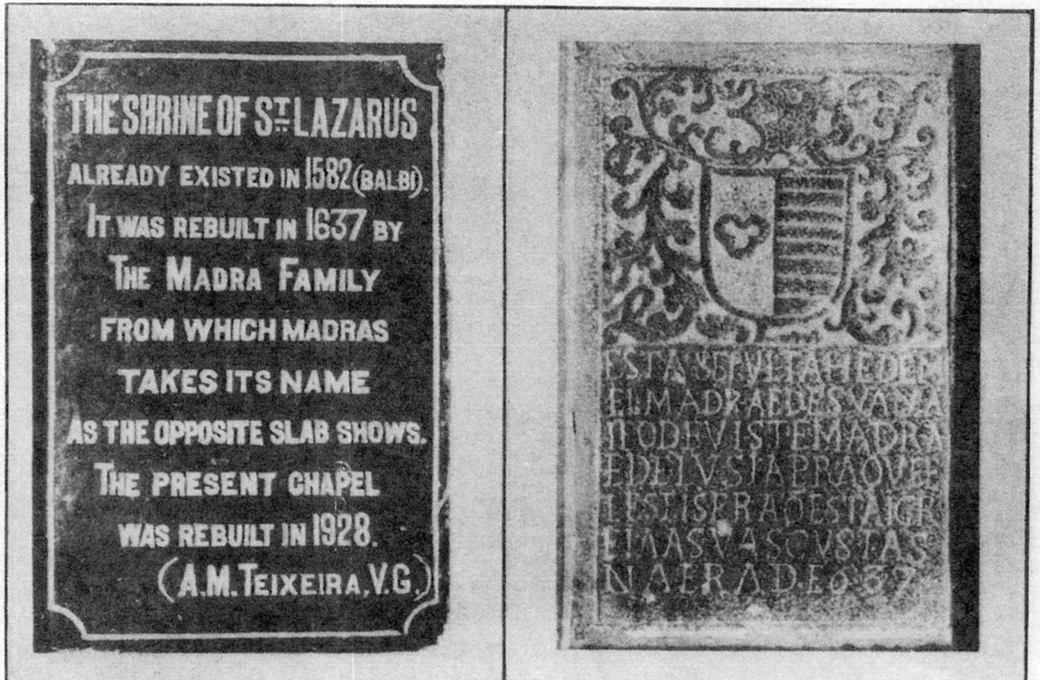

TOMBSTONE AT SAN THOME, RECENTLY DISCOVERED

—*By Courtesy of Rev. Mother Superior, St. Thomas Convent.*

humility—" en "—added to it (as in Gopalen, Gopal), the other letters in the word being to Indianize the whole.

" It is of interest to note that there are those who say that a Mylapore Church gave its name to the City of Madras "—thus states Glyn Barlow in his 'Story of Madras'. It was in this way: The rural village of Madraspatam, where Mr. Francis Day selected a site for the Company's settlement, has been colonized by fisherfolk from the Parish of the Madre-de-Deus Church at San Thomé—the Church of the Mother of God —and the emigrant fisherfolk called their village by the name of their Parish and the name was eventually corrupted into 'Madras'.

I may add that it is not unusual in this country to take European names and Indianize them, e.g., Munrolappa, out of gratitude or respect for individual European benefactors. Sometimes the original European name itself is taken with the family title added to it, e.g., Hume Sastri. Mgr. Teixeira observes, rightly too, that the inherent tendency of the people of India is to affix to localities the names of some important personage or historic fact. Have we not Todhunternagar, Theagarayanagar, Colletpetta, George Town ? The name of my house is " Stone-Gift ", after Sir Henry Stone, C.I.E. So, Beri Timmappa, the clever Dubash, would appear to have thrown the golden bait to Madarasen to call the new place Madarasenpatnam in contrast to Chennapatnam. The loyal Christian must have readily acceded for the reason that by so doing, the name of 'Madra' his benefactor, would be perpetuated for ever, as it has been. I need hardly add that Madarasenpatnam dwindled to Madraspatnam and then dwarfed into Madras, as it was the case with Calcutta, the original of which was Kali-ghat.

The Character and Significance of the Foundation of Madras

By

Dewan Bahadur Dr. S. Krishnaswami Aiyangar, M.A., Ph.D.,

On a day in the August of the year 1639, three centuries since, a document was handed over by Damarla Venkaṭa, "Lord General of the Carnatic," as the European correspondence describes him, to Francis Day, the East India Company's Agent at Pulicat. It was the cowle conveying to the Company a piece of waste land lying between the river Kūvam almost where it debouches itself into the sea and another river, which, in the Company's correspondence figures as the Egmore River. This bit of land is described as an islet caught between the waters of the two streams and the sea, unfit for any useful purpose and described popularly by the name *Narimēḍu,* a Tamil term translatable into "jackal mound." On this piece of waste land was laid the foundations of a fort which developed, in course of time, into Fort St. George, the seat of the Presidency under the East India Company. With the changing vicissitudes of history, it has developed into the capital of Southern India taking the place of the capital of what was at the foundation of the empire, Vijayanagar, which has since ceased to exist. The date, generally taken to be the 22nd August, of this charter while it marks the foundation of Fort St. George undoubtedly marks almost with equal certainty, not the foundation of Madras, but rather its completion as a city worthy of its high destiny in the future as the capital of South India.

The foundation of this city marks the fulfilment of a desideratum which was felt by two sets of people in two different ways. The English East India Company was a private body of merchants whose mission was to carry on trade in the East Indies in spices and such other commodities very much prized in Europe in those days, and gain large profits in return for the risky adventure that it involved. This body after almost a generation of chequered history felt imperatively the need of a sheltered harbour to which ships could come under the protection of an efficient and well affected Indian government, or as the best substitute for it a fort which they could equip with a view to their own defence. The first landing of the Company's servants was on the West Coast at Surat in 1609. Their main purpose was trade in spices in the Eastern Islands where they established themselves in something like a factory at Bantam. The Dutch Company, which was much better provided for the adventure and had the backing of their own Government, were there already before them; and from the very outset of the English venture they had to find means to get on with the Dutch. It could be easily understood that in that disparity of conditions anything like a permanent alliance would be difficult to maintain, and so it proved. The Dutch always had the upper hand and showed themselves constantly active to maintain their dominance as against the English. For facility of this spice trade, they felt the need of a factory in India to purchase Indian goods, particularly cotton cloth, coloured, painted, and plain, to be offered in exchange for the spices that they prized very much for the purpose of the European market. The Dutch had a factory in Masulipatam and the English moved thither also. An English factory was founded there in 1611. In a short time they discovered their position untenable in Masulipatam with a subordinate factory at Pettapoli, some distance away from it, but located in a better place for the purpose of making purchases of the cloth, some miles south of Masulipatam. Masulipatam being the chief port of the government at Golkonda had its own official importance and proved a little too exacting in its demands, official and unofficial, from the Company's servants that the Company's servants responsible for the trade felt it necessary to change over to a better locality. They had been constantly on the look out to change from there and ultimately moved into Armagon, having already been for years under the hospitality of the Dutch at Pulicat. The open roadstead at Armagon proved disadvantageous another way. It was a comparatively unprotected open roadstead, and the country was thrown very soon into a turmoil and proved very inconvenient for the quiet prosecution of trade. Further the district was not one which was conveniently placed either for the manufacture or the dyeing of the cloths, which was the chief commodity of their commerce. In this condition of distress more or less, they were pretty constantly on the look out, and the agent at Armagon, Francis Day, heard a good account of the country further to the south both from Armagon and Pulicat, in the near neighbourhood of the Portuguese factory at Mylapore. The Portuguese neighbourhood would have been no less unwelcome than that of the Dutch; but just about the year 1635 Methwold, the English Agent at Masulipatam went on a mission and came to a friendly understanding with the Portuguese, so that the objection to that neighbourhood was removed. After an inspection, Day found the locality admirably suited his purpose as providing a harbour for entrance of the Company's shipping, the place itself being in the centre of a manufacturing district from which the cloths could be obtained 20 to 30 per cent cheaper than in the locality round Armagon; and, what is more, it was situated in a region under the government of Dāmarla Venkaṭa, which assured efficient protection for a commercial body, which was bound to have large money transactions with the inhabitants of the locality.

On the other side, what we now-a-days call Madras goes in history at least down to the beginning of the Christian era. The port of Mylapore, sometimes written Maliyapur, and known to the Greek geographer Ptolemy as Mylarphon, a corruption of the Tamil name Mailārpu, which was its original name in classical Tamil, was a town of consequence, in which was included the ward of Triplicane which contains the ancient shrine of Triplicane regarded as the foundation of one of the early Toṇḍamāns, and already celebrated in the hymns of one of the early Āḻvārs. Across on the northern side is the famous Śiva shrine of Tiruvottiyūr celebrated as a famous shrine in the Tēvāram hymns; not far from it was the neglected hamlet even in those days of Puḻal, the village on the bund of the Red Hills Tank, which was traditionally the capital of the Toṇḍamaṇḍalam region. Between these two lay scattered within the area of two to three miles from the coast a number of villages carrying, as part of their names, the termination *Pākkam,* which in Tamil is the specific name of a seaside village; Śēlpākkam, (modern Chepauk), Nungambākkam, Purasapākkam, etc. So what we now call Madras is certainly no new foundation, and we might almost say that nobody knows its foundation.

But then coming down to historical times, we do reach a stage at the commencement of the seventeenth century when the foundation of a city was laid in this locality with a purpose which was not altogether dissimilar, although from an entirely different point of view of those of the Agents of the English East India Company. The Portuguese had their factory at Mylapore for some generations. The Dutch acquired the site of Pulicat from Emperor Venkaṭapatirāya in 1606 in the estate of one of his queens, the Gobbūri princess Koṇḍama. The site of Pulicat was granted and a formal agreement was entered into between the Vijayanagar emperor at Chandragiri and the Dutch in 1610, and Pulicat became a factory ever since. The political jealousy between the Protestant Dutch and Catholic Portugual, now a part of the Spanish empire, was carried into their commercial business as well, to add to the commercial jealousy, and made them almost habitual rivals. Mylapore and Pulicat being apart by about 25 miles, happened to be within striking distance, and the particular period with which we are concerned was one in which the Dutch were laying themselves out deliberately, as a matter of policy, to exclude everybody else from the coastal trade. The Portuguese and the Dutch therefore frequently fought on the sea; but often times they carried the war also on land and that proved a source of disturbance to the quiet government of the locality from the point of view of the ruler of the provincial government. This region was included in the government of Wandiwash, the territory included in the division extending from Pulicat southwards to almost Cuddalore in the south. The governor of this large province of Wandiwash at the time was this Dāmarla Venkaṭa of the family of the Kāḷahasti zamindars. He had a brother by name Ayyappah or Aiya, who held a subordinate position in the province with headquarters at Poonamallee. This Tarafdar of Poonamallee, as he would have been later called, felt this constant prosecution of hostility within his territory a nuisance. To prevent them from doing that and, in commemoration of his father Channamanāyaka, he laid the foundations of a small town, properly equipped for the purpose in the locality, which now constitutes the centre of the town of Madras, and called it in the name of the father, Channapaṭṭinam,[1] the city or town of Channa.

Channa or Channappa was the son of a certain Venkaṭappa Nāyaka of Dāmal, according to an inscription.[2] Dāmal is a village next to Conjivaram on the high road to Bangalore. The emperor Venkaṭapatirāya, whose headquarters were at Chandragiri had to move down from there against the rebel Lingama Nāyaka, son of Chinnabomma Nāyaka of Vellore, the enlightened ruler and patron of the great South Indian scholar Appayya Dīkshita. This Channa or Channappa who apparently held office under that Venkaṭa played a distinguished part in this war against the rebel, defeated Lingama at a place called *Munnali,* now the railway station Minnal, a little way from Arakonam, and subdued the rebel. Then the province dependent upon Vellore was brought under imperial government directly as a result of this conquest. This Channa or Channapa was appointed governor of this province after its recovery from the rebel. As memorials of his rule, we have a tank which goes by the name Channasāgaram in the North Arcot District, and this town of Channapaṭṭinam, which is said to be a foundation in honour of the father by his son Aiyappa, who held a subordinate position under his elder brother, Dāmarla Venkaṭa, whose government was the province of Wandiwash, but who actually happened to be the prime minister of the empire, which position both the Dutch and the English describe as that of the "Lord General of the Carnatic." This statement is made in a poem Ushāpariṇayam by one Dāmarla Ankabhūpāla, another of the Dāmarla brothers. Yet another brother Dāmarla Venga or Vengaḷa (properly Venkaṭa) had written another Telugu poem Bahuḷāśva Charitam, which gives details of the family

1. S. K. Aiyangar's *Sources of Vijayanagar History,* Secs. 93 and 95.
2. A. S. R. 1911-1912, S. 192, Note 2.

and its relationship to the neighbouring family of the Velugōṭi Yāchamanāyaka, whose name figures prominently even in the European correspondence, being a brother-in-law (wife's brother) of this Channa or Channappa. Emperor Venkaṭapatirāya remained in Vellore for a number of years after the conquest of the rebel Lingamanāyaka, Chandragiri having been his usual capital heretofore. In the poem ascribed to him, Anka says that the foundation of the town was due to the constant fight between the Dutch at Praḷaya-kāvēri, the Telugu variant for Pulicat (Tamil Paḻavērkkāḍu) and the Portuguese at Mylapore. This foundation could not have been many years earlier than that of Fort St. George as Aiyappa could not have laid the foundations of the town before he came to occupy the official position of governor of the locality.

In regard to this particular foundation, the reasons leading to the actual foundation of the town require to be considered carefully. Two points come out clearly. The local governor found the inconvenience of the European companies fighting between themselves in the territory of the empire, and the sea littoral within the limits of his own particular province. The two companies were fighting both on the sea, carrying their disputes as well on land. The local ruler found that he could do nothing efficient to prevent their fighting on the sea. But he felt at the same time that he could do something to prevent their fighting extending into the land. The foundation of a town whereby to prevent such fights between the two hostile companies was the town of Channapatam. It brings into clear view the want of control over the sea due to the want of an efficient fleet, though they had a large number of commercial craft to carry on their trade, and that trade was constantly exposed to the inroads of these European companies, possessed of more efficient shipping. The Europeans themselves state it that they were often driven to the use of Indian sailors whenever they were in need of them, although they make the complaint that they were less efficient and therefore more costly.[3] That is one weakness which proved detrimental to the empire of Vijayanagar even in her best days. Apart from the military necessity that led to the interposition of a well equipped town between the factories of the two Companies, the foundation of Chennapatam had perhaps other objects in view which come out more prominently in the terms of the cowle that was actually granted to Francis Day by Dāmarla Venkaṭa.

The charter that Francis Day received is set down here *in extenso* with the English modernised for convenience of reading. The original document seems to have been lost, but a certain number of copies, two

3. Eng. Fact. in India, Vol. No. 37, 1641, p. 50.

or three of them, had been preserved, and what is set down here is from one of these marked O.C. 1690 in the India Office records. The "firman granted by Domela Vintatedro Nague unto Mr. Francis Day, Chief for the English in Armagon, in behalf of the Honourable Company, for their trading and fortifying at Madraspatam, to this effect as followeth: Whereas Mr. Francis Day, Captain of the English at Armagon, upon great hopes by reason of our promises often made unto him, hath repaired to our port of Madraspatam and had personal conference with us in behalf of the Company of that nation, concerning their trading in our territories and friendly commerce with our subjects, we, out of our special love and favour to the English do grant unto the said Captain, or whomsoever shall be deputed to manage (*idgitate*) the affairs of that Company by virtue of their firman, power to direct and order the building of a fort and castle in or about Madraspatam, as they shall think most convenient the charges whereof, until fully and wholly finished, to be defrayed by us, but then to be repaid when the said English shall first make their entrance to take possession thereof. And to make more fully expression of our affection to the English nation, (we) do confirm unto the said Mr. Francis Day, or whatsoever other subjects or agents for that Company, full power and authority to govern and dispose of the government of Madraspatam for the term and space of two years next insuing after they shall be seated there and possessed of the said fortifications: and for the future by an equal division to receive half the custom and revenues of that part. Moreover, whatsoever goods or merchandize the English Company shall either import or export, for as much as concerns the duties and customs of Madraspatam, (they) shall, not only for the prementioned two years in which they enjoy the government but for ever after, be custom free. Yet if they shall transport or bring any commodities up into or through my country, then shall they pay half the duties that other merchants pay, whether they buy or sell the said commodities either in my dominions or in those of any other Nague whatsoever. Also that the said English Company shall perpetually enjoy the privileges of mintage, without paying any dues or duties whatsoever, more than the ordinary wages or hire, unto those that shall coin the moneys. If the English first acquaint us before they deliver out any money to the merchants, painters, weavers, etc., which are or shall hereafter reside in our prementioned port or territories, and take our word for their sufficiency and honest dealing, then do we promise, in case those people fail in their performances, to make good (to) the English all such sums of money as shall remain upon their accounts, or else deliver them their persons, if they shall be found in any part of my territories. That whatsoever provision the English shall buy in my country, either for their fort or ships, they shall not be liable to pay any custom or duties for the same. And if any ship or vessel belonging to the English (or to any other country whatsoever which tradeth at that port) shall by misadventure suffer shipwreck and be driven upon any part of my territories, they shall have restitution upon demand of whatsoever can be found remaining of the said wreck." This document makes it clear that it refers to the town or port as it is called of Madraspatam, the sovereign right for which belonged to the empire of Vijayanagar, and consequently placed under the authority of the governor. The purpose of the foundation of the fort is the peaceful prosecution of commerce, for which the English Company wanted a place of safety. The conditions of safety required are guaranteed by the grant of permission to build a fort to be occupied by the Company. The full authority for the port is given to the Company for two years, and thereafter these extraordinary rights were to revert to the governor. In order to encourage them to prosecute their trade, they were given the privilege of bringing goods and sending them out customs free, and of providing themselves with supplies for themselves and their seagoing ships duty free from the country. For facilitating commerce, they were also given the privilege of minting. Further they were promised assistance in regard to the loans and advances that the Company might make for the cotton goods, which formed the chief article of their export trade. If the Company would only give previous intimation, the governor took the responsibility of seeing to it that the country party kept to their promises and engagements, and even to recover whatever monies may be due. They were given the further privilege of restitution of shipping which might suffer shipwreck on the coast of the territories of the Nayak. These conditions make it quite clear that the part of Madras that is concerned in these transactions is the place that is called Madraspatam which is a distinct part, a port if it should be so called, as this document calls it, placed to the south of Chennapatam on the southern margin. To the south of this Madraspatam was the bit of land that was given for the building of the fort. This distinction of Chennapatam, Madraspatam, and what became afterwards Fort St. George, is very carefully maintained in the cowle that this very same Company obtained from Śrīrangarāyalu just about six years later than this, so that it will be seen at once that the grant has reference to the grant of a mere suburb of Chennapatam, and not the whole of it. From the terms of the document it is equally clear that what the English Company desired was nothing more than facilities for the successful prosecution of their trade. These terms are clear so far as the Company is concerned.

Why was the Nāyak so anxious to show the English Company such extraordinary favour and grant them the privileges in the manner detailed above ? What was it that he expected in return ? That is set forth in a letter that the Agent and Council at Masulipatam wrote to the Company on the 25th October 1639, hardly two months after the grant of the privileges. The relevant part of the letter is this:—"They are fair privileges and (it) may be questioned why hee should make us these fair proffers. It is answered by himself: first, he desires his country may flourish and grow rich, which he conceives it will by drawing merchants to him; secondly, he desires (for his money) good horses from Persia; thirdly, that yearly upon our ships he may send a servant into the Bay of Bengalla to buy him hawks, apes, parrotts, and such like bables, and that when he shall have occasion to send a vessel of his own there, or to Persia, a man of ours may proceed upon her; and lastly, the fort, being made substantial and strong, may be able to defend his person on occasion against his insulting neighbours. If Your Worships intend to continue this trade, as we are confident you will (for without this your pepper trade is of small value, especially where you shall buy all for ready moneys), the above said proffers are not to be refused." These terms make it clear that the Nāyak's anxiety was to promote the commerce of his territory for the profits that that would bring. He wishes to have freedom from molestation by others to sail his ships either in the Bay of Bengal or even outwards towards Persia. Thirdly, the condition is important that a fortified port would give him protection, not merely personal protection, as is indicated in the letter, but also the protection that that would imply of keeping that part of the territory guarded against the piratical enterprise of other Companies and peoples. At the same time, there is mention of the superior right of the sovereign retained by him, and of some of these, the privileges, particularly that of trade could be prosecuted by the Company even in the territories of the other Nāyaks, his neighbours, which, as governor, he could hardly guarantee without the knowledge or countenance of the ruling sovereign for the time being, that is, the Vijayanagar emperor, Pedda Venkaṭa, for whom Dāmarla Venkaṭa, was transacting business with the Company, as in fact he was transacting the business of the administration as the chief officer of the empire. The gift of the site of Fort St. George, and of the privileges actually granted on the basis of this cowle and other similar documents which renewed the privileges to the Company, were certainly not sovereign rights guaranteeing the full possession of all the rights to the fortified town to the English Company. That this was so is brought home to us time and again in the course of the Company's correspondence as well as in the disputes that they early got into with the country powers in the course of their trade.

The grant of this document was, as stated before, made under the authority of the emperor Pedda Venkaṭa. He died in the October of the year 1642, and was succeeded by a nephew of his named Śrīranga or Śrīrangarāyalu. The change of succession brought on a number of other changes besides Śrīrangarāyalu had ideas as to the needs of the empire to which he succeeded, and was set upon pursuing a vigorous policy by asserting imperial authority over the viceroys and governors of provinces, and maintaining his own sovereign right intact. Of course that would apply to all the territory then under the empire of Vijayanagar. Almost the first important act of his reign was the dismissal of this Dāmarla Venkaṭa from the chief ministership for the carrying on of the administration on his own account. This he was enabled to do with justice because of Dāmarla Venkaṭa showing himself inclined to turn traitor to the empire by negotiating with the troops of Golkonda which had advanced south, and, lay in the region round about Madras. The advance of Golkonda had begun almost immediately with the treaty dictated by Shah Jahan to the Bahmani states of Bijapur and Golkonda which, while it effectively shut them up from activities to the northward of their territories, gave them almost free reins to carry their conquests into the territories of the Hindu empire to the south. Golkonda showed itself ever ready to take advantage of this possibility and exhibited that readiness ever since the great battle of Rakshasatangaḍi, miscalled Talikota in 1565. The Hindu empire managed to keep Golkonda activities within limits all the while. It began afresh and with much greater activity soon after this treaty of 1636. Śrīrangarāyalu as governor of this northern frontier under the rule of his uncle, his predecessor, had already shown commendable activity in preventing these incursions, and we find him in the Company's correspondence as being actively engaged in turning back the Golkonda troops from the imperial territory as far south as the frontier of Pulicat and Tirupati where we find Śrīranga just the year before the grant of Fort St. George. Pulicat was in the northern frontier of the province of Wandiwash, the territory of which Dāmarla Venkaṭa was the governor, and what took place immediately on Śrīranga's accession would be nothing strange. During the first three years of his reign Śrīranga succeeded in beating back Golkonda and reasserting his authority with so much success that the English Company thought it proper to send a special mission and get a renewal of the charter from him, having regard to the complete change of position of Dāmarla Venkaṭa, through whose good offices they obtained their first charter. A mission was sent to Śrīranga at Vellore composed of Mr. Greenhill and four others. A renewal of the charter was obtained in 1645, the new cowle being generally referred to as the gold cowle. That charter makes it quite clear that the main town was Chennapatam; that Madraspatam was but a small southern suburb, hanging on to which was the bit of land given over for building Fort St. George. Śrīranga went further than the first cowle, and made it a condition that when Fort St. George should be built and fully occupied, it should be called Śrīrangarāyalupaṭṭinam, to be a southern suburb of Madraspatam, itself the southern suburb of Chennapatam. The name Śrīrangarāyalupaṭṭinam, however, did not take on, and, to that extent Śrīranga's efforts in this matter proved abortive. But with 1645, Fort St. George attains to a definite position as a recognised part of Madras, having its own organisation for the management of its business, recognising to the fullest extent the authority of the ruler for the time being, the emperor of Vijayanagar, and the governors of the region.

Śrīranga, however, continued to be emperor for thirty years and more after this date, devoting the whole of his resources to the rehabilitation of the empire of Vijayanagar to something of its former importance; while the struggle was relieved by successes which held out great hopes, the forces against proved ultimately too strong for the attainment of his ambition, and poor Śrīranga had to give up the struggle in despair, and let the history of the empire take its own course. We might mark Sivaji's conquest of Vellore in 1678 at the end of his invasion of the south as providing a landmark in the history of the empire of Vijayanagar, as the capital in this region passed out of the hands of the empire definitely. Śrīranga had therefore to remain in Bēlūr, and we might say definitely that the Carnatic (we are concerned with the eastern part of it, which came to be known in the British History of India as the region of the Carnatic), definitely passed out of his hands. This Carnatic thereafter passed under Muhammadan authority first under the authority of Mir Jumla, who made the conquest of these parts in the name of Golkonda, and ultimately under Golkonda itself. The authority of Golkonda came to be recognised definitely in 1668 when the English in Fort St. George obtained a charter from the Golkonda Nawab Neknam Khan through the local governor of the locality, Chinnapalli Mirza, residing at the time in Tirupati. Just five years after that, that very region passed on to another governor of Golkonda by name Musa Khan as the result of the death of Neknam Khan. The English obtained a charter from him thereby indicating their subordinate position.[4] When however some years later than this, the region passed under the authority of Akkanna, the brother of the chief minister at Golkonda, Mādanna, the territory round Madras actually was under the government of a nephew of these ministers, Podili Linganna at Poonamalle. Disputes as to the political position and relative authority between them were raised, and, after a couple of years of dispute and acts just falling short of war, things were left very much in the same indefinite position as before. This has relation to the period 1780 to 1782 when Streynsham Master was the Agent and Governor.

4. Fort St. George Consultation, dated 25th April 1672, Sir William Langhorn, Governor.

When Golkonda passed under the authority of the Great Mughal Aurangzeb, his general Zulfikar Khan became the Mughal governor of the Carnatic, and, so far as Madras was concerned, he allowed the same arrangements to continue. When he was called away, he left the Carnatic to be governed by his deputee Daud Khan, to whom is due the foundation of what began as a camp, and developed ultimately into the fortified town of Arcot. Just a few years after that he in his turn was called away to take charge of the governorship of Malva, and he left his civil officer, generally known as Sadat-ulla-Khan, to take charge of the government of the Carnatic, and the province thereafter came to be known by the name of Arcot, as Arcot had now become the settled capital of the Carnatic. Things continued in this condition and without incident, when the simultaneous activities of the Mahrattas to enforce the chauth and the Nizam for the possession of this region, brought both of them upon the scene. The province of Arcot was reconstituted, at any rate the Nizam succeeded in appointing a new governor in Anwar-ud-din Khan, and, soon after, the European Companies, both the French and the English began taking active interest in the affairs of the Indian states, chiefly through the influence of the French Governor Dupleix to whom is due the credit of the idea of Europeans taking advantage of the anarchical condition prevailing in India for establishing themselves as something more than trading companies becoming owners of territories. This assumed a definite shape only with the fall of Arcot, and the termination of the wars of which that happened to be an incident. During the next half a century, the tendency in political affairs was more and more for the devolution of authority in the hands of the power which had to do the fighting, and, that happened to be the English Company under Anwar-ud-din's son and successor, Muhammad Ali. It is not the Company's forces and resources alone that played this part, but the British army had to bear not merely a share, but the brunt of the whole affair, till at last Muhammad Ali himself resolved to shift his headquarters from Arcot to Madras. The authority of the Nawab of Arcot passed from Muhammad Ali's successors into the hands of the English. This transformation might be regarded as marking the transformation of the Company's factory in Madras, which had, in the course of its development, come to include, on the authority of an imperial farman, all the villages which now go into the town of modern Madras.

We thus see how, by force of historical circumstances, and by virtue of its geographical position, the mere seaport town of Madras gradually transformed itself into the capital of South India, the political authority in the meanwhile passing by steps from the Hindu emperors of Vijayanagar to the Nawabs of Golkonda, and then to the Mughal emperors. and ultimately to the English East India Company who could put forward a legal title by virtue of the charter which they obtained from the Mughal emperor. This gradual development of the seaport of Madras.

of which the foundation of Fort St. George could, in the actual circumstances of its foundation, be regarded as merely a subordinate part to remedy a defect in Channapatam and make it an efficient seaport, gradually developed to occupy the position of the capital of South India. Even in the best days of the empire of Vijayanagar, the want of sea power was brought home, as a very serious inconvenience to the exercise of the imperial authority, as well as the proper development of the imperial resources, of which one essential feature was the seagoing commerce. Vijayanagar in the best of her days had the revenues of 300 ports within its territory, and that was by far the most lucrative of the material resources of the empire. But the want of this power was brought home much more directly when the activities of the Dutch East India Company and the hostility that this Company early showed to the Portuguese and their position all along the coast. Mir Jumla who was inclined to be friendly to the Dutch at Pulicat was made sore once by the Dutch declining to give him permission to carry on trade in the ports of the southern sea board of the Coromandel Coast including Ceylon. That was a grave inconvenience felt even before the days of Mir Jumla, and was one of the influencing motives for the foundation of the town of Chennapaṭṭinam under Pedda Venkaṭa, the emperor, and Dāmarla Venkaṭa, his minister. The foundation of Fort St. George under the direct management of a foreign Company actually provided what the country rulers wanted, protection of the high seas for the prosecution of commerce. It may be noted in passing here that the Mughal empire was in no better condition, as the early history of the Company at Surat makes it clear. Once that defect was removed, Madras stood out equipped for a higher destiny than that of a mere sea port town. The subsequent history of the region merely brought this to fulfilment. From the point of view of the East India Company it began merely as a trading settlement and gradually worked its way up to be the British capital of South India. But almost as much could be said of it, if the sea-port had continued to be under the aegis of the empire of Vijayanagar, and if the empire had succeeded in beating down its enemies and maintaining itself in full possession of her territories and authority. The transfer from Vellore to Madras of the imperial headquarters might have come about for the reasons that induced Nawab Wallajah to move from Arcot to Madras. That is a piece of historical speculation, which it is hardly necesary we should indulge in. What has need to be pointed out here is the transformation of the Hindu town into the capital of not merely the southern Presidency but of South India as a whole, was due to a process of history in which what was then the foreign English East India Company played a very important and direct part, and when ultimately Madras attained to the fulfilment of its destiny, the authority of the surrounding region had already passed into the hands of the English.

A History of Medical Relief in Madras

By

Dr. A. Lakshmanaswami Mudaliar, M.D., F.R.C.O.G.,
Principal, Madras Medical College.

The East India Company formed in 1599, received a charter from Queen Elizabeth on 31st December 1600. The first voyage to the East Coast of India was made by Captain Anthony Hippan in 1611 in the *Globe*. Soon factories were established at Masulipatam, Pettapolli (now known as Nizampatam), Motupalli and Viravasaram, all in or near the Kistna delta. The first settlement on the Coromondel Coast, Armagon, was founded in 1625. This factory was located at a place called Chenna Kuppam at the northern end of Pulicat lake in Nellore District. In February 1639, Andrew Cogan and Francis Day moved from Armagon to Madraspatam, taking with them the staff of Armagon Factory and founded the settlement of Fort St. George or Madras.

It was generally the practice with the East India Company that whenever a ship was chartered and sent to the East, a surgeon was included in the crew. Most of these surgeons were attached to the ships, but later the need for surgeons in the various factories was felt and the Directors sent them out to look after the settlers in the Coast. The first surgeon on the coast whose name has been recorded is John Clarke appointed to the Fort of Armagon. The first surgeon at Madras whose name has survived was Edward Whiting. In 1676 a second surgeon was allowed and Baskel Sherman was sent to fill this place.

At this time several European surgeons were employed under oriental potentates and not a few of the concessions obtained by the East India trading companies, of the British, Portuguese, French and Dutch settlements were due to the influence of these surgeons with their respective chiefs. The Fort St. George consultations of 1683 record the despatch of a letter to Monsieur Esheimon, surgeon to the King of Golconda, asking his help in procuring them a firman permitting them to coin rupees. The same consultations record a letter from the President of Madras to Johannes Poterliet, an Armenian physician to the Nawab of the Karnatik, who tried to help the English to get a farman from the Emperor at Delhi for free trade on the Coromondel Coast. Haidar Ali and Tippu Sultan had several European medical men in their service. Not infrequently, the surgeon deserted them and came over to the opposite Camp. Jean Martin, a Frenchman deserted Haidar and went over to the English at Vaniambadi on 8th December 1767, the first Mysore War; while in the India Gazette of 31st March 1781, it is stated, "There is a Doctor Lloyd, an English surgeon came over to us from Hyder's camp, who informs us that Hyder is very much distressed for provisions and stores of every sort and that his fighting men do not exceed tenthousand."

Up to the middle of the 18th Century, the Company employed no regular forces, except the small garrisons of their chief factories. Their medical officers were therefore civilians occasionally employed in the desultory fighting which took place from time to time, but for the most part engaged in purely civil duties. The wars in the Karnatik with the French and with various Indian powers from 1745 onwards, necessitated the formation and use of regular bodies of troops, and, as a consequence, the employment of military surgeons. In 1766, little more than two years after its first formal constitution, the medical service was divided into two branches, military and civil. This was not found satisfactory and in 1773, less than seven years later, the military and civil branches or the medical service were again united.

The next stage in the development of the medical administration of the city and the presidency was in 1785 when the Court of Directors sent out orders for the regulation and government of the medical departments of the three presidencies. These regulations were incorporated in Madras G. O. of 8th July 1786. The following extract from the above G.O. defines the pay and prospects of the medical officers employed by the company. "With a view to give every degree of encouragement to men of professional abilities and integrity to prosecute the medical line in our service in India, we hereby direct that at Bengal and Madras there shall be a Physician General as Director of the Hospitals with a salary of £2,500 per annum and a chief surgeon with a salary of £2,000 per annum and the Head Surgeon of every hospital where 8,000 men may be stationed in peace or war, shall have a salary of £1,500 and the Head surgeons of all the other General Hospitals are to receive each £1,000 per annum. "It was also decided that the Governor and Council shall appoint a Hospital Board which was to consist of the Director, chief surgeon and surgeon of the hospitals established at head quarters, for the purpose of directing the necessary regulations and arrangements for all the hospitals of the presidency. This board was required to recommend to the Governor and council the most able and deserving officers to direct and superintend the duties at each hospital and to be responsible for the conduct of those so appointed.

The boards which were thus constituted were originally called Hospital Boards, but the designation was later changed into Medical Board. The first actual use of the new term in Madras appears to have been in

August 1796. The Madras Medical Board was constituted on 14th April 1786 in obedience to the orders conveyed in the court's letter of 21st September 1785. It was composed of James Anderson, Physician General, Colley Lucas, Chief Surgeon and Thomas Davies, Head Surgeon of the Presidency General Hospital.

THE GROWTH OF HOSPITALS IN MADRAS

The first hospital in India appears to have been that at Goa, mentioned in Fryer's *Travels*. The first hospital at Madras was opened about 1664; the establishment of a hospital at Bombay was under discussion in 1670, but apparently it was not actually opened till 1676; the earliest hospital in Calcutta dates from 1707-08, so that Madras may well claim the unique distinction of being the first city in India to have established a hospital.

It is interesting to note that the hospital was opened in anticipation of proper sanction in a rented house. The letter announcing this event is published in Love's 'Vestiges of old Madras' and was written to the Agent, Sir Edward Winter then on tour at Masulipatam by William Gyfford and Jeremy Sambrooke. The letter states "The fresh soldiers which came forth this year taking up their habitations in the bleak wind in the hall fell sick in that four of them are dead, and about ten remain at the time being sick and complain not without reason that the wages are not sufficient to supply them with what is necessary at the time of their sickness. So rather than see English men drop away like dogs in that manner for want of Christian charity towards them, we have thought it very convenient that they might have an house on purpose for them and people appointed to look after them and to see that nothing comes in to them, neither of meat nor drink but what the Doctor alloweth. We have for that purpose rented Mr. Cogan's house at two pagodas per month, which we hope you will so well approve of as to continue it for the future."

The record hospital at Madras was built, between 1679 and 1688 by public subscription at a cost of 838 pagodas, nearly Rs. 3,000. It was a large two-storey building, the property of the Church and Vestry and stood in the Fort near the church and adjoining the company's sorting godown, a situation which was found inconvenient in various ways. In 1688, during the Governorship of Elihu Yale, the Madras Council determined to acquire this hospital building paying its full value to the Vestry, and directed that a new hospital should be built near the river. The third hospital seems to have been erected soon after the Company acquired the second during Yale's term of office and was probably in use by 1690. It stood in Jame's street in the Fort near the north end of the barracks, and, like the barracks, was a handsome building, in the Tuscan style costing about 2500 pagodas. It is interesting to note, in passing, that Elihu Yale was born at Boston, Massachusets, the son of an Englishman David Yale, who had emigrated to the New England Colonies. Elihu Yale, who later became a Director of The East India Company, died in London in 1721. In 1718 he gave a large donation to the school at New Haven which in 1745 developed into a university, now famous as the 'Yale University', after its early benefactor. Madras would thus seem to have more than a passing interest in the University of Yale!

War against France was declared on 21st March 1743 and on the 18th January 1744 it was decided to open a special hospital for the Royal Navy at Madras, which will be referred to later. Madras surrendered to the French, under De La Bourdonnais on 10th September 1746. Peace between England and France was made by the treaty of Aix-la-Chapelle on 7th October 1748 and the city was restored to the English on 21st August, 1749. The hospital appears to have been much overcrowded after the rendition and in 1752 it was converted into a barrack, and twelve houses were converted into a hospital.

In 1757 Captain Brohier the senior Engineer at Madras wrote to Government advocating the demolition of the hospital, " as all the buildings comprising the hospital were on higher ground and their situation of great disadvantage to the fortifications of the place as an enemy would enfilade the greatest part of our north front and greatly perplex the besieged." The hospital and surrounding buildings were pulled down during 1757 and the former transferred to some houses lying further south west, near the site of the present General Hospital, Madras was beseiged by the French from 12th September 1758 to 17th February 1759, when the siege was raised, on the arrival of an English Fleet, under Captain Kempenfelt, who was afterwards lost in the "Royal George" at Spitehead, a tragedy made famous by the poet in the lines,

> " Down went the Royal George
> With all her crew complete."

During the seige the hospital was necessarily transferred into the Fort. In February 1759, it was moved to the site in Armenian Street, occupied by the Capuchin and Armenian Churches, and there remained for some thirteen years.

The General Hospital: The site where these hospitals were located in Armenian Street was found unhealthy and the Board therefore ordered in their despatch dated 28th December, 1762, that a proper building ought as soon as possible be erected by the Engineer in consultation with surgeons to receive and accomodate 500 men and thirty officers. It was not till 1771, however that practical shape was given to the decision of the board, when Col. Patrick Ross, chief engineer submitted his plans for the construction of a double block of buildings to cost with out-offices pagodas 46,500. Tenders were called for and that submitted by John Sullivan, a young writer of six years' service, and 23 years of age, was accepted for 42,000 pagodas. A public despatch to England dated 15th October 1772 reports that the new hospital has been completed and occupied. It consisted of two blocks, perhaps the most westerly of the present buildings. They were of one story only, but were designed to carry another story above, when required.

From the hospital of 1772, the present Madras General Hospital has descended in a direct line. Col. Love in his 'Vestiges of old Madras,' writes " A medallion on the wall of the present General hospital, facing the road, bears the inscription 'Hospital founded 1753'. The legend is misleading. It cannot apply to the Madras hospital irrespective of situation, because the institution in the Fort was established nearly a century earlier. Nor can it serve for the present building or site, because the hospital of 1753 had its position on what is now the north west Esplanade. Another structure nearer the present site, was in use in 1758, but after the si ge the institution was transferred to Muthialpetta, where it remained for several years." From what has been stated above, it will be noted that while 'a General Hospital' was founded as early as 1664, the present General Hospital dates its origin from 1772. By an order dated 12th November 1782, two members of the Council were to visit the General Hospital every week, and report its condition to the Committee and new medical regulations, chiefly on superintendence of medical stores, indents, etc., were passed. By an order dated 28th January 1794, it was laid down that the control of the management of the hospital should be entrusted to the Head surgeon at the Presidency, and that diaries should be kept by every surgeon and assistant surgeon attending the hospital.

Orders issued in the Fort St. George Gazette of 9th December 1814, turned the General Hospital into a Garrison hospital. In 1842 the Madras Medical Board describe the General Hospital as an institution for the reception of sick, both European and Indian, civil and military. The building occupied a space 185 yards long by 145 broad. The main hospital was a pakka one story building, consisting of two parallel ranges connected by a third, in the form of a capital letter H, one half being reserved for the soldiers and the other half for other sick Europeans. In the same enclosure, running its whole length, but detached from the hospital, was a range of tiled buildings, one half of which was set apart for European women and children and the other half for Indians of both sexes, in separate wards. In 1859, the entire building was reconstructed and not only doubled in size, but an upper story was added. The eastern portion was assigned to British troops, while the western was used as a civil general hospital, of which the upper story was occupied by Europeans and Anglo Indians, the lower by Indian sick. Women and children were transferred to a building hired for the purpose in Vepery and twenty years later, in 1881, to the old lying in Hospital. Out patients were first treated in 1862 and a new out-patient department was built in 1884. In 1893 new wards were built on the roof of the western wing, making a third story. In 1895, the western half of the eastern wing or station hospital was handed over to the civil authorities, and became part of the civil general hospital. The patients from the old hospital for women and children at Egmore were then transferred to the General Hospital. In 1899 the remaining portion of the station hospital was handed over; and for the first time in history the whole block of buildings became a purely civil institution.

Staff: From 1841 to 1865 the staff consisted of two officers only, the Surgeon and the assistant surgeon. In 1865 a third called the Senior Medical Officer, was added. In 1878 a fourth was sanctioned, and the staff became, Senior Medical Officer Senior Surgeon, assistant physician and resident surgeon. In 1882 a second surgeon was appointed, and in 1893 an additional medical officer. In 1895, when the Women's and children's hospital was incorporated, the surgeon of the second district joined the staff. In 1899 the staff number seven and in 1901 a further reorganisation took place so that there were 9 officers—the Senior Medical Officer, 4 physicians, 3 surgeons and a resident medical officer with 8 assistant surgeons working under them.

It is curious that this staff continued till after the Great War. It is only within the last fifteen years, that great changes were introduced, special departments were created, Honorary medical officers and assistants were taken on the staff and the whole of the medical and surgical staff reorganised.

Side by side with the reorganisation of the staff, the scheme for the remodelling of the General Hospital was taken up in 1928 during the Governorship of Lord Goshen and is nearing completion. A modern and up-to-date hospital equipped with the latest medical and surgical accessories and with a new Radiological institute now presents as an inspiring pile of buildings, of which Madras may well be proud and which delights the eye of every professional visitor to this city.

The Monegar Choultry hospital: The older citizens in Madras may recall the dilapidated building in Monegar choultry road at the end of Popham's Broadway, which was for long the only institution available for the poor sick of North Madras. This institution owes its existence to an assistant surgeon of the Company, John Underwood by name. In 1797

THE MONIGAR CHOULTRY

Underwood applied for a piece of ground at Pursawalkum as a site for a hospital for indigent Indian sick. The superintendent of the Company's lands objected to the site mentioned, whereupon Underwood applied for any piece of waste ground for a site. The "Native Infirmary" so founded in 1799 was combined in 1809 with the "Native Hospital and Poor Fund" in the institution known as the Monegar Choultry. This institution not only served the needs of the indigent sick but was utilised for teaching purposes for the students of the medical school adjacent. During the War, the Monegar Choultry Hospital was gradually demolished and on its site was built the present Royapuram Hospital providing accomodation for over 500 patients and comparing favourably with the General Hospital in its facilities and equipment.

The Naval Hospital: A naval hospital was established at Madras in 1745 and was used as such up to 1790. In 1784 the Madras Government ordered the erection of a new naval hospital and a site was chosen, but no further steps were taken for twenty four years. In 1790 the sailors who were till then accommodated in the naval hospital, were transferred to the Garrison hospital which continued to receive the sick from the fleet for eighteen years. In 1808 a new naval hospital was built, on the site chosen in 1784, and this hospital was used upto 1831, when the buildings were turned a gun-carriage factory and the sick from the fleet, who were now too few in number to require a separate hospital, were finally transferred to the military hospital. The road where the naval hospital was situated is still called the Naval Hospital Road; the gun-carriage factory having been closed down, the site and the buildings are now used to locate the medical store depot of the Government and are situated in Vepery on the Poonamalle High Road.

The Opthalmic Hospital: This is one of the oldest institutions of its kind and was founded in 1819. It is situated in Marshalls Road, Egmore.

The Leper Asylum: A Madras Public letter dated 26th Sept. 1816, reports that a hospital for lepers had been completed at a cost of 983 pagodas. This hospital, later known as the Madras Government Leper Hospital, was situated in Washermanpet opposite the Monegar Choultry. It received lepers of all races and of both sexes. Under orders issued in 1889, leper convicts from jails in Madras Presidency were transferred to this hospital. During the Governership of Lord Willingdon in 1921, the scheme for a leper settlement was taken on hand; finally the hospital at Washermanpet was closed and the Willingdon Leper Settlement was opened near Chengleput under the management of a mission agency.

The Lunatic Asylum: In 1793 Assistant Surgeon V. Conolly put forward proposals for the establishment of a Lunatic Asylum at Madras.

These proposals were accepted by the Government and the Asylum was opened on 1st Oct. 1794. This asylum appears to have been built by Conolly and to have remained his property until he sold it to Dalton, Government paying a rent of 825 rupees a month for its use. Dalton rebuilt the whole asylum, enlarging the accomodation and this property appears to have been in possession of Dalton's heirs, being rented by Government till the new asylum was occupied in 1871.

It was for long known as Dalton's Madhouse and was situated in Kilpauk in the site now known as 'College Park' which was till recently the residence of the Principal and staff of the Madras Christian College, and which is now the residence of the students of the Madras Medical College in the Hostels built for them at the site.

In 1867 the Madras Government sanctioned the construction of a new lunatic asylum, about a mile to the north west of the old institution in Locock's Garden. The new buildings were occupied on 15th May 1871, the cost being a little over two lakhs. Considerable additions have been made since that date. In 1892 the criminal lunatics of the Presidency who were till then kept in jails were transferred to the asylum now known as the Mental Hospital.

The Women and Children Hospital at Egmore, formerly known as the Lying-in Hospital and later as the Government Maternity Hospital was opened in May 1844 and was originally situated in the compound adjoining the S. I. Ry and facing the Cooum, now occupied by a training school next to 'White Hall' the habitation of the Anglo Indian Association. It was later transferred to its present site in Pantheon Road, adjacent to the Museum in 1882. Beginning with a total confinement of under 50 in the first year, its popularity and usefulness have increased and in 1938, the total confinements exceeded 4,500, which represents the total number of births in a city like Trichinopoly. The hospital like other medical institutions in the city has had improvements effected from time to time, the last of which however was in 1921.

The Royal Victoria Caste and Gosha Hospital for women was founded in 1885 under the presidency of Lady Grant Duff, patients being admitted for the first time on 15th December 1885. The Raja of Venkatagiri contributed a lakh, and the Maharaja of Vizianagaram Rs. 62,000 towards the cost. It is worthwhile recording with gratitude the many munificient donations that have been made to medical institutions in the city and the presidency by the Zemindars of the northern and central districts of the presidency, from time to time.

Other Hospitals: Space forbids recording in detail the other hospitals that have come into existence within the last thirty years. Pro-

MEDICAL SCHOOL BUILDINGS 1836

—By Courtesy of the Principal, Medical College.

minent among these are the Kalyani Hospital at Mylapore, the Rainy Hospital at Royapuram and the Tuberculosis Dispensary and Hospital situated at Spur Tank in Egmore and Tambaram respectively.

MEDICAL EDUCATION

This paper would be incomplete without a reference to the growth and spread of medical education and research in the city and the institutions founded for this purpose. The Madras Medical College was founded as a medical school by the Rt. Hon. Sir Frederick Adam K.C.B., by general order of Government, dated 13th February 1835 and the school began its session on the 1st of July, 1835, the classes assembling for instruction at first in the rooms adjoining the quarters of the surgeon of the General Hospital. The object of opening the medical School was to render the medical subordinates more efficient in the performance of their professional duties. The medical school opened with 10 medical apprentices and 11 Indian medical pupils, and was first located in temporary rooms, but as the accommodation was insufficient, a building consisting of 4 apartments, a theatre, lecture room, a museum and a library at a cost of nearly ten thousand rupees was constituted. The teaching staff consisted of Surgeon Mortimer, assistant surgeon George Hardinge with two assistants, a warrant officer assistant apothecary D'Beaux and dresser P. S. Muthuswami Mudaliar.

The course extended over two years, which was extended to three years in 1846. On the recommendation of the school council, supported by the medical board, Government sanctioned the change of name and from the 1st October 1850, the institution has been known as the Madras Medical College. Its first Principal was Dr. James Shaw. In 1855-56 the course of instruction given at Madras was recognised by the Royal College of Surgeons, London. In 1863, the Madras University which had been constituted by Act 27 of 1857, claimed the exclusive right to give medical degrees and diplomas, and the power of granting diplomas was withdrawn from the Medical College, except as regards students already under instruction.

It was in 1875 that the portals of this institution were thrown open to women students at a time when even in Great Britain the admission of women into many of the Medical Colleges was a very controversial subject. The Hospital assistant department of the college was moved over to the auxiliary medical school in Royapuram in the year 1882 and continued working there till 1897. It was again shifted to the College in September 1897, while the clinical training of this class was carried out in the Monegar Choultry hospital.

During 1888-89 several improvements were made in the buildings, and the laboratories and lecture halls being augmented. The Hospital assistant department was again transferred to the Medical School at Royapuram on the 1st April 1903, from which date this school was functioning till it was raised to the status of a college—The Stanley Medical College—in July 1938.

The Government sanctioned in 1907 the construction of the Hygiene and Physiology laboratories, which were completed in 1911. The Great War saw many of the alumni of this great institution in the many war fronts, taking their due share and filling the roll of honor as befits members of a great institution. The most substantial additions to the college were sanctioned in 1929 and the present massive structure—a three storeyed building known as the Pathology block—was completed and opened for use on 1st July 1935. Together with the remodelled General Hospital which is almost in continuation of the college building, the new buildings provide great facilities for study and research, which it is hoped the alumni of the college would fully avail themselves of.

Madras can now feel proud of its two medical colleges like the sister cities of Calcutta and Bombay, and together with another fine institution at Vizagapatam, it may be said with confidence that the needs of medical education are fully provided for in this presidency.

The centenary of the Medical College was celebrated with great eclat in 1935, and let us hope when the next centenary of the city is celebrated many more bright chapters chronicling the records of the alumni of the colleges in the city would be recorded by the historian of the future.

DR. JAMES SHAW, FIRST PRINCIPAL, MEDICAL COLLEGE,
18TH NOV. 1858 TO 28TH FEB. 1863.
—*By Courtesy of the Principal of the Madras Medical College.*

The Grange, Adyar and Some Notable Madrassis

By

Percy Macqueen, I.C.S.,

Collector, Nilgiris

During recent years the north bank of the Adyar has been rapidly developing into a teeming suburb. It was formerly a quiet resort of the wealthy Europeans, who lived in a few large mansions surrounded by wide lawns and big trees which recalled the features of an English park. The mansions still remain but the parks are rapidly disappearing under a load of bricks and mortar. A typical example of this process of peaceful penetration is that of 'the Grange' which stands in marked contrast to the modernist bungalows recently erected within its spacious compound. It is itself one of the old, though not the oldest of the 'garden houses' built on the banks of the Adyar. To fix its date we must turn to the old maps of Madras City. The first map of the City which includes the suburb of Adyar was drafted in 1798, when the Court of the Recorder was established in order to fix the limits of the City. It indicates the building which is now the Adyar Club and that of Brodie Castle. But the site of the Grange appears as an empty meadow, bounded on the north by a stream which runs into the Adyar at the eastern corner and follows approximately the line of road which now leads to the Elphinstone Bridge. The map of 1822 shows a few native houses in the east of the compound but still no bungalow. The house was, in fact, not built till 1853, though the history of the changes in the ownership of the land before that date is not without interest.

From a report to the Collector of Madras in 1806 we learn something of the site and its original owners. It was enclosed in 1803 and its area, as described in the quaint notation which we still use, was 46 cawnies, 9 grounds and 495 square yards. The soil was sandy and the villagers nearby held the right to pick leaves from the palm trees which grew on it. The owner of the land is described as 'the temples of Kadari and Kumeswara.' Two temples and a chavadi stood on the land. One Venkatachellapati laid claim to the management of this endowment and in 1807 Government admitted this claim, making him a 'maniam' or tax-free grant for the maintenance of the temple flower garden. Behind this transaction stood one Alanda Narayanaswami Nayak, who, as 'dharmakarta' or manager of the endowment, handled such profits as might arise from leasing the pasturage or the right to cut cadjans from the palm trees. He appears to have been a rich man and at one time to have held all the land on the north bank of the Adyar. But by 1821 pearl fishing in the Gulf of Manaar, with other speculations, had swallowed up his fortune, the Sheriff had sold up his lands on the Adyar and the compound of the Grange thus came for the first time into European hands. One of the principal creditors of the Nayak was the Honourable Leveson Grenville Keith Murray who served in the Indian Civil Service from 1792 to 1831. He belonged to a junior branch of the Murrays of Atholl and his father was the fourth Earl of Dunmore, the last British Governor of Virginia, U.S.A. On the failure of Narayanaswami Nayak, Mr. Murray bought in the maniam and the lands adjoining and when he retired he gave the land to Mr. E. F. Elliott, son of the Right Hon. Hugh Elliott who was Governor of Madras from 1814 to 1820. Mr. Elliott in turn gave or sold a portion of the maniam and surrounding land to Mr. Joseph Pugh of Messrs Pugh and Breithaupt, whence it passed successively by sale to Mr. Acworth, to Mr. William Ambrose Searle, Registrar of the Supreme Court in 1852, and finally in the same year to Mr. John Bruce Norton.

'Gee Ess' (Mr. G. S. White, late Registrar of the Madras High Court) has published two interesting articles on the Norton family in Madras. The first of the name to achieve reputation in Madras was George Norton who was appointed Advocate General in 1827. He introduced a scheme for the high class education of high class Indians. The principles which he advocated produced such great public servants as Sir T. Madhava Rao, Diwan of Travancore, Sir A. Seshiah Sastri, Diwan of Travancore and Pudukotah, C. Ranganatha Sastri grandfather of Sir C. V. Kumarasami Sastri, Rama Ayyangar and Sir T. Mutthusami Ayyar, the first Indian to be promoted to the Bench of the High Court. It was George Norton also who first obtained the sanction of the Supreme Court to the scheme which he prepared for carrying out the trusts of Pachaiyappa's will and his portrait hangs in Pachaiyappa's hall. He died in England in 1877 at the age of 85. This gentleman was not, apparently, a relation of John David Norton who came to Madras as a judge of the Supreme Court at the age of 54. John Norton started his career in the Royal Artillery but soon exchanged the fuse for the forum. Later in life he was appointed to the Supreme Court Madras in 1841 and landed in 1842. His work in India was very brief for he died on a voyage to Malacca in the following year and was buried at sea. But he left behind a son in Madras who had come out with his father in 1842. This was John Bruce Norton, born in 1815, educated at Harrow and Merton College, Oxford, and called to the bar at Lincoln's Inn in 1841. He enjoyed a large practice in Madras, was made Advocate General in 1863 and retired in 1871. He, like his namesake George Norton, took a keen interest in education and was a patron of Pachaiyappa's charities. He was also the author of several works on

THE GRANGE, ADYAR

law and politics. His son Eardley Norton was a well known and successful barrister in Madras, a man of much wit and independence of character.

To return to 'the Grange.' The area of the land which John Bruce Norton purchased in 1852 did not coincide exactly with that of the original maniam. Mr. Pugh had exchanged a piece of sandy ground on the river bank for a plot belonging to the washermen, on which they had houses. They then removed their houses from the vicinity of his bungalow to a site on the river margin. An area of about 18 cawnies was transferred to H. H. Gartumina Begum Sahiba and 6 cawnies and odd was river accretion. So Mr. Norton purchased the maniam property in its modified form, together with some additional land, thus bringing the whole property to an area of 52 cawnies, 2 grounds and 842 square feet. His holding was bounded on the north by the road, on the south by the river, on the east by the land of Lingappan and Venkatesan and the Adyar road and on the west by another piece of land and the river.

He was not to enjoy the site long in peace. When he applied for a grant of the whole extent, one I. C. Narasimhalu Naidu objected that a part of the property had been sold to Mr. Norton by the mirasidars of San Thome, who had no claim to it. After some correspondence, government, who contemplated straightening the course of the river above the Elphinstone bridge, agreed to allow him to hold this portion on condition that he should surrender on demand so much of it as might be required for public purposes. In 1856 Mr. Norton held 55 cawnies, 16 grounds and 242 square feet. Government then discovered that he should have been paying a quit rent for three years previously and presented him with a bill for Rs. 877-1-3. Mr. Norton protested vigorously against this demand and under his skilful handling the dispute began to assume the proportions of a cause celèbre. His main grievance was the fixing of the date from which the arrear was to run. "I am aware", he writes," that the Act gives power to call for arrears for six years. But I apprehend that this arbitrary and anomalous power is only to be exercised where the occupant has been enjoying profits from his property." He then attacks the principle of assessing land at the same rate, whether it is occupied as a garden yielding profit or by a private house and compound. He points out that most of the compound is sand —valueless for cultivation. "It should be remembered," says he, "that the Hon. Sir Henry Montgomery sits on the other side of the Adyar in his large park at a comparatively nominal quit rent," and adds, "I have laid out a very large sum in erecting a house, one of my reasons for so doing was that the land had been immemorially free of quit rent. When Mr. Seymour was here he asked me on this point. I told him that I believed I was at the mercy of government to put what tax they pleased on. He repeated this in the House of Commons, when it was immediately and indignantly denied by Sir James Hogg with some observations not very flattering to myself. The result has shown the truth of Mr. D. Seymour's representation."

Mr. Cunliffe, the Collector of Madras, replied to Mr. Norton's arguments in the following vigorous terms, "When, therefore, Mr. Seymour asked Mr. Norton the amount of land tax to which he was subject, I think that he should have replied in this manner, 'When I purchased the ground, I was told that it paid no land tax, but I did not enquire for what reason it was exempted. I do not know what amount is leviable on it but I could have ascertained the exact rate before 24 hours had passed over my head by a reference to the collector. The government, I dare say might put any rate they liked upon it, but you see that without enquiring the rate, I have such confidence that it will be a fair one when imposed, that I have purchased the land, built this house upon it and the lot is worth some Rs. 30,000. No government title has ever been issued for the land and I have not registered my purchase in the collector's office."

Mr. Norton built the house in 1853 and resided there till he sold it to Mr. Alexander Mackensie, a partner in Messrs Arbuthnot & Co., in 1865. After this time the property changed hands more than once. It seems to have been owned by the Rajah of Vizianagram for a time and in 1917 it was the property of P. Venkatachellam, from whom government bought it at a cost of Rs. 1,56,803-12-5 for the purpose of building a Rajkumar college, a project which, unfortunately, has been finally abandoned. It is interesting to compare its estimated value in 1917 with the cost of acquisition and building 60 years before. Time had enhanced its value by five times.

The name of this property has changed several times. Built in 1853, the first reference to its name is to be found in a letter written by Mr. Mackensie junior to the Board of Revenue in 1861 in which he speaks of it as 'Norton's Gardens'. Next comes the map of Madras in 1864, compiled by Gantz Brothers and issued in 1870. Here it described as 'Mc Kenzie's or Admiralty House.' The reference to the second name is obscure. Col. Love in his 'Vestiges of Old Madras' (Vol. III, p. 116, note 4) refers to "the picturesque riverside residence now called, 'Admiralty House' the property of the Maharaja of Vizianagram" and queries whether Admiral Sir Edward Hughes ever occupied it. The description in the map must, therefore, be in error. The earliest reference to the present name of the house as 'The Grange,' that I can discover, is in the Madras Residents Directory for 1907 against the name of Sir Murray Hammick, of the Hammicks of Torquay, a distinguished civilian who acted as Governor of Madras in 1912.

A Note on Marakkayars in Madras

By

M. G. Muhammad Ali Marakkayar,

Madras

The name Madras sounds very much like the original name Makhras Kuppam. Burhanuddin, author of the Tuzuk-i-Walajahi, writing of the foundation of Madras by the English, thus says:—"The Raja (Chandragiri) according to the recommendations of his diwan (the Zamindar Damarlawar of Kalaastri) complied with the request (of the representative of the East India Company) and granted the place known as Makhras Kuppam in the taluq of Poonamallee. In the year 1049 A.H., the Company laid the foundation for building in the place on the sea-coast and gave it the name of Madras which sounds very like the original name (Makhras Kuppam). After some time they were granted through the kindness of Damarlawar, three other places, viz., Chenam Nayak Kuppam, Arkuppam and Bailpet which were within the taluq of Poonamalle. They settled in Chenam Nayak Kuppam adjacent to Madras and named it Chennapatan which sounds very like the original name' (pp. 98-99 of Dr. S. M. H. Nainar's translation of Part I, Madras 1934). There is every reason to believe that the name was Marakkayars Kuppam as there are several Marakkayar streets, Madrasa Musjids, and Grave yards on the sea coast especially in the Harbour division, Madras. The Arabs who came to the Ma'abar (Coromandel coast) by their ships in the earliest period of the annals of humanity were designated Marakkayars by the natives for they came by their Marakkalam a Tamil name for ship. The word Marakkalam was probably from the Arab Markab a ship. They write tamil in Arabic characters and speak a dialect of Arab tamil in which books have been published. In early days they collected taxes, levied on chank and pearl fisheries, and the salt pans and remitted them to the Central Treasury. In return for this, they were given rent-free lands. The Marakkayars soon established Madras as the centre of their holy business namely, to supply foodstuffs to the pilgrims, Hajis and inhabitants of the holy city Mekka Muazzama and formed Arab-Ma'abar Markab Service which served both the sea and the land communications. They established Madrasa (College) in Markars Kuppum and stationed Marakab Madrasa (Trainingship) on the sea. They also established Maritime ports with Madras, Straits Settlements, Burma, the Archipelago Islands and other parts of the World. In these places, they were known only Chuliars because they belonged to Cholamandalam. The Marakkayars belong to the lineage of Hardrat Ibrahim Khalilullah one of our Prophets. Nawab Amirul Hind Muhammad Ali Walajah belonged to this lineage. He was a friend of the English and helped them very much. It was a custom for Muslim Princes and Merchants of Madras to go on a ziarath (pilgrimage) to Nagore through Shiyali. The writer's family can claim to have had Madras as their place of business for at least five generations and had connection with the Hon'ble East India Company—the chief article of merchandise being handwoven lungis and sarongs. Thus, the Marakkayars have played their own part in the growth of the City of Madras.

Rao Sahib M. Raghava Aiyengar furnishes the following interesting note:—

> The first mention of the name Chennapatnam in Tamil literature occurs in a book Nondinatakam, sung by a poet on Sayyad Zadir otherwise known as Periyatambi Marakkayar, a resident of Kilakkarai town near Ramnad. He flourished towards the end of the seventeenth century. It appears that Sayyad Zadir was a prosperous merchant, and had dealings with the Company's merchants at Madras. On page 7 of Madras Diary and Consultation Book 1690, we are told that Mamun Nayinar a brother of Periyatambi Marakkayar visited Madras to further the cause of his brother's trade and to negotiate on behalf of the Setupati with the East India Company authorities to open a settlement on the Madura coast. It is thus interesting that just fifty years after the foundation of the Fort St. George a Marakkayar merchant from Ramnad had business dealings in Madras. (See also *J. O. R.* 1929 pp. 36-37.)

Some Madras Monuments

By

Dr. S. Muhammad Husayn Nainar, M.A., Ph.D.,
Lecturer, University of Madras.

The fact that Madras is a particularly interesting corner of the world is often forgotten. Many of the people who are aware that Madras has played an important part in the making of India's history, are strangely not interested in its historic remains; they omit to think that Madras is an historical museum where the sight-seer may spend many an hour in streets and in buildings, studying old world exhibits and living for the while in the facinating past. While the story of Madras fills an absorbing page of history, the sights of Madras are worthy of sympathetic interest for all types of people. In the following pages certain events and places connected with the city of Madras are briefly described.

Madras, when Francis Day acquired it in 1639, was within the domain of the decaying Hindu Empire of Vijayanagar and the deed of possession was delivered to the English merchant by the Raja of Chandragiri, the representative of the past magnificent Hindu Empire. Seven years afterwards the Raja of Chandragiri was a refugee in Mysore, driven from his throne by the Sultan of Golkonda who assumed the sovereignty of Haydarabad and the Carnatic. Thus Madras which belongs to the Carnatic came under the sway of the Muslims, and the Company were careful to secure from the new sovereign a confirmation of their possession. The power of Golkonda was destined to fall in its turn, for, Awrangzeb, the Mughal Emperor at Delhi, who desired to bring all India under his rule, waged war against the Sultan of Golkonda and defeated him. The Emperor appointed his representative in the south, who, known as the *wazir* of the Deccan, resided at Haydarabad. But the Carnatic was one of the outlying provinces of the Mughal Empire to which *nazims* were sent from time to time by the imperial court; the *wazir* of the Deccan had no control over them. The earlier *nazims* of the Carnatic who belonged to the Nayit community had their residence at Arcot. After the death of the Emperor Awrangzeb the disintegration of the Empire set in, the *wazir* became independent in the Deccan and so did the *nazims* of the Carnatic. In course of time family feuds among the Nayits in Arcot led to the murder of the *nazim* in power, and the absence of a ruler created confusion in the land. Asaf Jah, then *wazir* of the Deccan, who was waiting for an opportunity to bring the Carnatic under his control found the occasion suitable; he came down from Haydarabad with an army, took possession of Arcot without any opposition and appointed Nawwab Anwarud-Din Khan as the *nazim* of the Carnatic. The new *nazim,*—the founder of the Walajahi dynasty—was a stranger to the country and disliked by the Nayits who were defeated by Asaf Jah. The Nayits tried always to regain their lost power and never missed an opportunity to bring trouble to the new *nazim.* The enmity between the two communities continued without any outward manifestation till the death of Asaf Jah, which coincided with the advent of Husayn Dost Khan (Chanda Sahib) an able man of the Nayit community, till then a captive in the hands of the Mahrattas. Naturally troubles arose in the Deccan and the Carnatic. There were rival claimants to the thrones of the Deccan as well as of the Carnatic. Hidayat Muhiyyud-Din Khan (Muzaffar Jang), the grandson of Asaf Jah claimed the throne of the Deccan against Nasir Jang, the son of Asaf Jah, and Husayn Dost Khan the throne of the Carnatic against Anwarud-Din Khan. The European merchants, prominently the English and the French, had their trade settlements in the various districts of the Carnatic. The French at Pondicherry supported Husayn Dost Khan, while the English at Madras supported Anwarud-Din Khan and on his death at the battle of Ambur, Muhammad Ali Walajah, his son. This was a great opportunity for the English. They triumphed against the French; so that Muhammad Ali Walajah became undisputed Nawwab of the Carnatic.

CHEPAUK PALACE

The intimate association of the Nawwab Muhammad Ali Walajah with the English, prompted him to establish a permanent residence for himself in Madras. The Nawwab writing from Madura in 1764 to Governor Palk says:

"I have been desirous this long time of building a large handsome house within the fort of Madras, that whenever I come there, either on my own or the Company's business, it may serve as a place of residence for me; and in case of an enemy's raising any disturbances in the Carnatic—may God forbid—as a place of safety for my family and dependants also........I could wish therefore that it was made both large and lofty........"[1]

Palk offered ground within the fort and a grant for an area of upwards of 18,000 square yards was accordingly prepared. He also promised that the Engineer would take the work in hand.

1. Military Country Correspondence, Vol. XII, 11th October .764.

THE CHEPAUK PALACE

In 1766 the Nawwab wrote again thus "Last year in the month of June when I had the pleasure of paying you a visit, you were pleased, out of sincere friendship, to pitch upon a piece of ground in the fort or white town of Madras in order to build a house on it on my account and accordingly granted me a *sanad* under the Company seal to the purpose. When a foundation was laid, you were so good as to lay the first brick by your hand and appoint Engineer Call upon that work...................... ....I now hear the said engineer will shortly return to Europe, which induces me to write this to desire you and the Gentlemen of the Council to appoint Mr. Benfield, one of the Company's engineers, he being a person that drew out the plan of the house and presented it to me before, and likewise he has a good skill in beginning and finishing the works of buildings."[2]

Governor Palk agreed to the appointment of Benfield. But the following despatch from the Directors of the Company, which gave a qualified approval to the palace scheme, seems to have prevailed with the Council to withdraw their support:—

"The Nabob's earnest desire to build a palace in the fort for the reception of himself and family in case of a reverse of fortune implies a confidence in our future support. We wish to have such ideas strengthened and encouraged, and upon that principle we approve of the grant you made him of a piece of ground to build on. We hope, at the same time, you have well revolved in your minds all the consequences of such a step, and that, if you saw, or at any time hereafter shall perceive any inconvenience likely to arise, you did, or will whenever they occur take proper and timely measures to obviate them."[3]

Thus the original scheme was set aside, and the records make no further mention of the project. But the name Palace Street, which is still borne by the principal thoroughfare in the Fort, lying to the west of Choultry Gate Street and Charles Street, commemorates the original intention of the Council to build the Nawwab's palace.

In the following year (1767) the Nawwab acquired private property in Chepauk and engaged an English architect to build him a house. Chepauk palace thus came into existence. The details about the erection of the palace have not been traced, but the edifice is depicted on an accurate French map, which does not indicate Black Town Wall. Hence the structure was probably built in 1768. It consisted of two blocks, the southern called the *kalsa mahal* of two floors and the northern of one floor containing the *humayun mahal* and *diwan khana*.

2. Military Country Correspondence, Vol. XIV, 21st March 1766.
3. Public despatches from England, Vol. LXX, 4th March 1767.

The architect is not known, but it is not improbable that it was Benfield for whom Nawwab Muhammad Ali Walajah entertained a predilection.

In 1770 the Nawwab acquired additional ground and built a wall round his property. The enclosure formed many acres including a large part of the grounds of Government House of to-day and a great deal of adjoining land.

The Chepauk palace was the scene of some grand doings in its time. On the 25th May 1770 the President and Council accompanied by the Secretaries and Persian Translator, proceeded to the Nawwab's palace at Chepauk in order to deliver to him the letter from the Honourable Court which was brought by the *Houghton.* They were received by the Nawwab Muhammad Ali Walajah with great pomp and ceremony, and after the delivery of the letter, they were entertained to an 'elegant breakfast.' After the feast the Nawwab presented cash to his guests, one of whom, Warren Hastings, received 1,500 *pagodas.*

When Sir John Lindsay, the naval commander-in-chief arrived at Madras in 1770, he identified himself with the Nawwab in opposition to the Company and Chepauk became a centre of intrigue. In March 1771 he was invested by the Nawwab at Chepauk with the insignia of the Order of the Bath.

The Nawwab Muhammad Ali Walajah died in the year 1795 at the age of seventy-eight and his eldest son Umdatul-Umara succeeded to the throne of the Carnatic. His rule lasted only six years. On the capture of Seringapatam in 1799, papers were brought to light which were held to prove the existence of a treasonable conspiracy between the Nawwab Umdatul-Umara and the Sultan of Mysore. The Governor-General with the approval of the Directors, resolved that the administration of the Carnatic should be assumed by the Company; but the execution of his orders was postponed in consequence of the Nawwab's illness. When the Nawwab expired in 1801, at the age of fifty-three, British troops were ordered to occupy the palace. Lord Clive, camping in its precincts, offered terms to Ali Husayn, son of Nawwab Umdatul-Umara, which were rejected; and Azamud-Dawla, son of Amirul Umara was elevated to the throne. Under an agreement concluded with him the company virtually annexed the Carnatic, comprising the present collectorates of Nellore, North Arcot, South Arcot, Trichinopoly and Tinnevelly.

The Company were now the actual rulers of the Carnatic and the future Nawwabs were styled 'Titular Nawwabs.' On the death of the last Titular Nawwab in 1855 the palace was acquired by the Govern-

MARINE VILLA

ment for a price and was eventually turned into Government offices. The northern block was enlarged and allotted to the Board of Revenue. The central tower was added by the Government architect R. Chisholm.

Thus, Chepauk palace is some thing more than a Government building on the marina, if regarded in relation to its history. The palace, it should be remembered, was the seat of powerful Nawwabs who were great patrons of learning and art. In the building which was buzzing with gay life and a crowd of retainers, we see to-day a multitude of officials and clerks who work out the accounts of the Government of Madras.

MARINE VILLA

Marine Villa (University Buildings). It was originally within the limits of the palace compound at Chepauk, built by Nawwab Muhammad Ali Wallajah who used it as his bathing pavalion. The original name of the building is not known. But a reference to 'Nabob's Octagon' in Madras Courier[4] has led H. D. Love in his Vestiges[5] to suppose that it may probably refer to the building known in later days as Marine Villa at the south end of the Cooum Bar.

Marine Villa was the residence of Lord Clive, Governor of Madras, (1798-1803) when the Governor-general Wellesley stayed in Madras superintending the operations of the last Mysore War (1799). Long after, the Surgeon-general to the Government of Madras used to reside in this building. Later on it was handed to the University of Madras and the offices of the Tamil Lexicon and the Department of Indian History and Archaeology were located there. In the year 1930 it was demolished and on its site the University Library and the Departments of Research are built.

AMIR BAGH

[6]*Amir Bagh* (Spencer's Hotel). This mansion built before 1798, was the property of the Nawwab, who frequently lent it to Governor Clive for public entertainments. At a later date it accommodated the court

4. A melancholy accident happened on Friday last at the barr near the Nabob's Octagon. Too many people having got into the ferry boat to cross over, the boat sunk, and between forty and fifty people were floating on the water, many of whom unable from the strength of the current to reach the shore were drowned. Twelve bodies were found the subsequent day and it has not yet been ascertained how many were by the force of the river, carried into the Sea. (*Madras Courier*, 2nd February, 1792).

5. Love's *Vestiges of Madras*, Vol. III, page 452, *n.*

6. Love's *Vestiges of Madras*, Madras Place-names, p. 561.

of Sadr-i-adalat, and was afterwards used by the Agra Bank. It was the premises of the Elphinstone Hotel and since March 1910 it is the Spencer's Hotel.

UMDA BAGH

[7]*Umda Bagh* (Madrasa-i-Azam and Government Muhammadan College). This imposing mansion, standing on the river bank, is depicted in the survey of 1798. Under grants of 1807 and 1810 (Nos. 1228 and 1320) it became the property of 'Colah Singannah Chitty' whose name is attached to it in the maps of 1816 and 1822. In that of 1837 it is lettered 'Mr. E. S. Moorat.' During the latter part of the nineteenth century it was occupied for rent by Khayrun-Nisa Begam Sahiba, the chief spouse of Nawwab Ghulam Muhammad Ghawth Khan Bahadur Azam, the last titular Nawwab of Carnatic. The building attained a fame in those days and was popular in the mouth of high and low because of the generosity of the Begam Sahiba and her agent Firuz Husayn Khan Bahadur. It was also the resort of distinguished Muslim visitors from the North. Sir Sayyid Ahmad Khan the renowned reformer and the founder of the Aligarh Muslim University, Aligarh, stayed in Umda-bagh when he visited Madras. His Exalted Highness Mir Mahbub Ali Khan Bahadur, the father of the present Nizam of Haydarabad, Deccan, also stayed in the *bagh* as a guest of the Begam Sahiba.

The scene shifts and we hear again about this *bagh* from 1901. In that year the All-India Muslim Educational Conference was held in Madras and as a result of the deliberations in that Conference a proposal was sent to the Government of Madras requesting them to buy the compound for the use of Madrasa-i-Azam which was till then located in Chepauk. The Government agreed to the proposal and the Umda-bagh was bought for a lac of rupees from Diwan Bahadur Govind Doss Mukhandoss. After that a portion of the buildings was demolished and the hostel was erected in the area adjoining the Mount Road and it is now known as the Umda-bagh Hostel. The second floor was put up in the *diwan khana* of the Begam Sahiba's agent to meet the requirements of the Principal's quarters. Big trees in the compounds were cut down to make room for playgrounds. A beautiful mosque in the middle of the compound was built by the Government of Madras in 1909. Thus additions in buildings were made from time to time to meet the needs of a fully developed high school and a growing college. Eventually proposals were sent to the Government to erect a separate building for the College and in 1934 the new buildings of the Government Muhammadan College came into existence in the midst of the spacious compound.

7. Love's *Vestiges of Madras*, Madras Place-names, p. 573.

THE GOVERNMENT MUHAMMADAN COLLEGE, MADRAS-I-AZAM

Famines in the City of Madras

BY

DR. B. V. NARAYANSWAMI NAIDU, M.A. PH.D.,
Professor, Annamalai University.

THE first famine that visited the city of Madras was in 1646, i.e., 7 years after its foundation. It commenced in September of that year. By the beginning of 1647, 'there hath dyed no less than 3000 people out of our little towne.' In the Portuguese colony of San Thome the mortality was reckoned at the incredible figure of 15,000, 'soe that all the painters and weavers are dead.' The ravages of famine were aggravated by war. 'The body of this kingdom was harried by two forreigne nations,' the Muhammadan powers of Golconda and Bijapur, both striving to 'make a prey of this miserable and distracted people.' In five months time 4000 out of an estimated population of 19,000 perished in the English territory alone. There was not 'above 1/3 of the weavers, painters and washers livinge of what were formerly.' Twentyfive English soldiers at the Fort fell a victim to it and about five were continuously sick 'with the misseries of the time.' [1]

The calamity shook the very foundations of the social fabric. At San Thome many wives deserted their husbands and took refuge in the Fort St. George where relief was available. Slaves fled from their masters. These incidents fanned the flame of hatred already smouldering between the Portugese and the English. A quarrel ensued and it was not till the famine had run its course that peace was concluded, wives restored and slaves returned.[2] Men offered themselves as slaves to escape from the clutches of death. A brisk trade in export of slaves sprang up which the European powers turned to the best advantage.

The suffering of the English settlers was also great. The Fort ran short of food supply. No meat was available and rice and water had

1. From Thomas Ivy, George Travell, and William Gurney at Fort St. George to the President and Council at Surat, 21st January 1647. (Original Correspondence Series 2019).

2. Agreement between Agent of Fort St. George and the Governor of St. Thome, 30 December 1651 (O.C. 2238).

become the sole source of sustenance of the Europeans. The Council pathetically appealed to the factory at Masulipatam for an early consignment of 100 hogs or pigs.[3] Finding that Masulipatam turned a deaf ear to their prayers, they proceeded to detail their woes to Surat.

> We have not, nor is here anything to be bought, to relieve any sick person, unless hee will eate carryon beife which wee procure out of the Moores Campp, which we obtain by much favour. This is our missery; yet our friends at Masulipatam will not be sencible of this; notwithstanding our many and earnest requests unto them to send us some provissions from thence to relieve us; and wee are now driven to that pass that we are forced to goe to lowance of rice, and are not able to subsist longer than 5 or 8 daies. Our wants are such that we are ashamed to make it knowne. Wee also intreat you to send us tentie baggs of whaete for our howse expence.[4]

Surat rendered timely aid. On 18th April 1687 the factory there despatched the vessels,[5] *Endeavour* and *Francis* 'full laden with rice.' They arrived 'very seasonably' and 'to the great relief' at Fort St. George on the 22nd of the following month.[6] The vessels were then sent to Armagon 'and a little to the northward thereof' to fetch rice.

The famine had a very depressing effect on the Company's trade. It led to a decline in investments of chintz and other cotton goods which had become 'very deare and scarce...... The reason is multitude of buyers, scarcity of weavers and painters and ruine of the country by war and famine.' The price of cloths rose by 15 percent; but little could be procured even at those prices. Contracts for supply of cotton goods to Pegu became difficult to fulfil.[7] Import trade was also adversely affected. European goods were 'quite unvendible' at the Madras port. The con-

3. From Thomas Ivy, George Travell and William Gurney at Fort St. George to Thomas Winter, etc., at Masulipatam, 4 January 1647 (O.C. 2015).

4. From Thomas Ivy, George Travell, and William Gurney at Fort St. George to the President and Council at Surat, 21 January 1647 (O.C. 2019); also in Factory Records, Surat, Vol. CII A (p. 88).

5. From Thomas Ivy and William Gurney at Fort St. George to the Company, 9 October, 1647 (O.C. 2046).

6. From Agent Greenhill, William Gurney and Martin Bradgate at Fort St. George to the Adventurers in the Fourth Joint Stock, 23 September, 1648 (O.C. 2085).

7. From Thomas Ivy, George Travell and William Gurney at Fort St. George to the President and Council at Surat, 21 January 1647 (O.C. 2019); also Factory Records, Surat, Vol. CII. A. (p. 88).

signment of coral from Bantam could not be disposed of as usual. The Swally Marine Factory hesitated to furnish the Madras agents with the usual money for investment purposes.[8] However, it speaks a volume for the enterprising zeal of the early servants of the Company at Madras to note that they 'managed to provide for Europe a stock of excellent cloth, though at somewhat dear rates, as it was well bought at Madras-patam, where the famine has raised prices considerably.'

The shrewdness of the Madras agents is evident from a further fact. Trade in textiles having proved precarious, they turned to advantage the import trade in rice. They knew, 'no question but the rice will yeald cent percent proffitt.' And it did yield. The Company thus combined profit with philanthropy. The Surat imports enabled a large number of artisans who produced for the Company to live on; and the surplus went to relieve a large number of Indian residents. Supplies also came from inland parts forced by the 'dear time and by reason of Robbers.' Mr. Thomas Ivy, the Agent directed that a third part of this supply 'bee distributed to the Townes people.'

By 1648, the famine had run its course. As early as January of that year Ivy could write with a sigh of relief 'The Warrs doth yet continue in these parts; butt (God bee thanked) the famine is much abated.'[9] But the fear of its recurrence revived in September of that year;[10] and as a precuationery measure it was decided to fill the *Blessing* with rice on her return from Persia and dispatch her to Madras.[11] These fears were short lived. By April 1649 they were set at rest and the project of importing rice by the *Blessing* was abandoned.[12]

The next famine occured in 1658. Its effects were aggravated by the presence of the armies of Golkonda and of Chandragiri. This

8. From President Breton and Messrs. Merry, Knipe, Tash and Pearce at Swally Marine to the Company, 6 January 1648 (O.C. 2067).

9. From Thomas Ivy at Fort St. George to the President and Council at Surat, 17 January, 1648 (O.C. 2066).

10. From Agent Greenhill, William Gurney and Martin Bradgate at Fort St. George to the Adventurers in the Fourth Joint Stock, 23, September 1648 (O.C. 2085).

11. From President Breton and Messrs. Merry, Pearce and Oxenden at Swally Marine to the Adventurers in the Fourth Joint Stock, 31, January 1649 (O.C. 2114).

12. *Ibid.*

famine was protracted and wide-spread. North India suffered much.[13] At this time Masulipatam was also affected.[14] In Madras it was not much more than a temporary scarcity.

In 1686 was the last famine of the 17th century. But it was not the least devastating in its results. It nearly decimated the population of the city of Madras. No less than 35,000 out of an estimated population of 300,000 died. 6000 families emigrated to other parts and people were reduced to great necessity, and poverty;[15] and those who escaped from the Cindrella of famine fell into the Charybedis of fell diseases, which were supposed to proceed from the 'Multitude of Dead Corps that infect the aire: they being so inhumane a people as to Lett them rott where they fall without any Care to bury them.' Death knows no racial distinction; Englishmen shared the fate of Indians; 'From the too common fatality of sickness, having buried within three months 43 English......and many more doubtfully ill of this malignant distemper, a Feavour and Ague; some having sup't merrily and well, and Dead before breakfast'......[16]

Compared with districts to the northward, and particularly Masulipatam, Madras suffered less; for, 'the graine the whole time has been more plentifull and chaeape here than at any place to the Northward of this coast.'[17] Further the Company rose to the occasion and organised relief measures, as will be seen from the following extract:

> In regard so many poor people do daily die in the streets for want of food, Itt is agreed that Pagodas 100 be given on the Right Hon'ble Companys Accountant to buy Rice for them, and that a collection be made among all the English for the same purpose, Severall having already offered very liberally towards itt. And we do appoint the burying Garden to be the place where they are daily to receive their Almes, and Narrand, the Chief Dubass, to get the Rice boiled, and see it distributed to the most necessitous people which, though they are very numerous, yet there may be sufficient to keep them alive till it shall please God to send more plenty, there being no less than two thousand poor creatures ready to

13. Elliot: *History of India*, Vol. VII, pp. 263, 246-7; Dow: *History of Hindoostan*, Vol. III, pp. 310, 341; Scott: *History of Deccan*, Vol. VII, p. 47; Etheridge: Report on past famines in Bombay (text).

14. W. Foster: *Factory Records of the East India Company*, 1661-64, pp. 32, 57, 159

15. From Fort St. George to Surat, 29, September 1687 (O.C. 5621).

16. *Ibid.*

17. *Ibid.*

perish for want, whose sad spectable with the lamentable cries sadly fill and afflict our Town......[18]

The funds raised and the grant given lasted only till December. The famine and the distress did not abate. A further grant of 50 pagodas and another 'general collection' were made at the end of that month.[19]

In the eighteenth century several famines occured. The first was that of 1718. This was not one of those major scourges that racked the country from time to time. Prices of food stuffs rose and Englishmen like Collet, Jennings, Howen and Legg 'by the gift of rice, preserved the lives of several thousand of the poorest inhabitants.'[20]

The famine of 1728 does not appear to have been severe. The factory records were silent on the subject. However, there was discontent among the soldiers. The garrison in the Fort laid down their arms twice. The local authorities attributed it to a mutinous spirit, but the Home authorities took a different view. They were informed of the famine through the 'presentments of the Grand Jury'[21] that want of sufficient rations was the real cause. After all, armies move on their bellies. They, therefore, took the occasion to remind the Madras factory that famine was too great a subject of 'Importance and Signification' to be ignored in their despatches.[22]

The next famine was in 1736 and this seems simply to have been but the climax of the scarcity and high prices that began in 1728. Between the years 1728-33 prices of food grains rose by 100 percent of what they were 20 years previously. Servants' wages also doubled itself and the cost of living, particularly for Europeans, rose abnormally.[23] A protracted drought aggravated the situation. The ravages of the Marathas added fuel to fire. G. M. Pitt, the then Governor of Madras attributed the frequent recurrence of famine to the neglect of irrigation works by the Mogul rulers and to their oppressive mode of land assessment. He wrote:

The tanks are almost choack'd up, and great Part of the Lands lye uncultivated for want of Water......To which if we add the Rapacious Disposition (of) the Mogulls, altogether intent upon

18. Fort St. George Consultations, 19 & 27, August 1686.
19. Fort St. George Consultations, 27, December 1686.
20. Public correspondence, 5, January 1718-19, Vol. L.; Vide Love, Vol. II, p. 179.
21. Public correspondence, 10 October 1729, Vol. LIX.
22. Public Letter from England, 23, January 1729, Vol. XXXI.
23. Public Letter to England, 29, January 1736, Vol. XII.

making the mo(s)t of their Governments while they continue in them, We need not seek far for the Reason why even within these 10 years the Lands which are Tenanted are let f(or) more than double for what they were before.[24]

Matters came to a head in 1736. Hungry vagrants surged into Madras.[25] The council apprehended a famine that would be 'more cruel than any we have felt yet.' The absence and indifference of the Nawab of Arcot encouraged 'frequent Robberys in the Great Towns as well as in the Roads........Confusion and disorder of the country was exceeding great.'[26]

The Company's business received a rude shock. The price of cotton soared to phenomenal heights.[27] The Company's weavers settled at Chintadripet found it impossible to pay back the advances they had received towards buildings, houses, etc., which were repayable within seven years. Further sums had to be given to keep them going.[28]

Very early in the period of drought, the Government took measures to check the abnormal rise of prices. Seeing that the grain merchants combined to exploit the situation, the Government fixed the selling prices of grain. It was declared that any grain purchased at higher rates should be forfeited to the purchaser and his money returned to him. No one was to have in stock more grain than was necessary for his 'usual annual' consumption. Concealment rendered it liable to confiscation.

These regulations, however, were cancelled soon after. It was feared that they would discourage all imports and thus place Madras in a worse situation. The forces of supply and demand were again left to decide the market price. In the next year however 'a grain committee' was constituted. It was entrusted with the task of superintending the sale of grain. Any one who possessed more than 5 garce of rice or paddy was ordered to surrender the surplus on penalty of a severe fine. A reward of Rs. 35 for each case of proved evasion was offered to the informers. Subsequently the hours of sale and prices of grain were regulated.[29]

This famine, however, does not seem to have resulted in any great loss of life.

24. Public Letter to England, 1, January 1733, Vol. X.
25. Col. Love: *Vestiges of Old Madras*, Vol. II, p. 278.
26. Public Letter to England, 29, January 1736, Vol. XII.
27. Love: *op. cit.*, p. 251.
28. *Ibid.*, p. 260.
29. R. A. Dalyell: Memorandum on the Madras Famine of 1866, pp. 10-12.

In 1781 occurred perhaps the most acute famine that Madras had ever experienced. It followed the footsteps of the devastations wrought by Haidar Ally's incursions into the Carnatic, known as Haider's Kalabham. Those were very troubled times for South India. The French, the Dutch, the Mysoreans and the English were fighting with one another and hacking the panic-stricken people to pieces. Crops were burnt, communications were cut off and peaceful cultivation rendered impossible. Food supplies ran short and it was ordered that 10,000 'miserable wretches to be at once struck off from the domestic army list who were thus doomed to perish of famine upon the desolated plains.'

The organisation of relief measures at this critical period was initiated by the Acting Governor, Mr. Charles Smith, a civilian of 27 years standing. Early in 1781, import duties on grain were suspended.[30] Officers in charge of the subordinate settlements were called upon to forward all available grain to Madras.[31] But the war demands pressed hard on the supplies of the civilian population. At the end of March 1781, the stock at Madras did not exceed forty-two days' consumption. A system of rationing was resorted to by which the alien population were got rid of. An order went forth to every family in the Fort and Black Town to deliver immediately to the Superintendent of Police 'an exact Account of their families, as means must be taken of clearing the Black Town of all people who do not belong to the families of those who are actually House-keepers.'[32]

On May 20th following the previous example the 'grain committee' was again constituted to ration grain supply. After a trial of various regulations such as fixing of prices, penalising the concealment of supplies etc., the committee learnt that it was unwise to interfere with the laws of economics. And so the regulations were relaxed. But the committee now took the supply of grain into their own hands. Four hundred bags of rice, a quantity estimated as sufficient to support about 600,000 people, were daily put into their hands from the Company's godowns and were retailed at favourable price.[33] The grain committee functioned very efficiently.[34] Breaches of its regulations were promptly

30. Love: *op. cit.*, Vol. III, p. 195.

31. Dalyell: *op. cit.*

32. Public correspondence, 31, March 1781, Vol. CXXV.

33. Dalyell: *op. cit.*

34. The members of the Committee were Robert Huges, George Mowbray and William Webb (Superintendent of Police). Next year Mr. Alexander Davidson took the place of George Mowbray.

punished. Nallanna, a grain merchant was ordered to 'receive immediately twenty five lashes in the most public manner for his Audacity in so notoriously attempting to controvert Regulations established'.[35]

Lord Macartney, not only continued the measures inaugurated by his predecessor, but also devised other modes of relief. He imported considerable quantities of grain from Bengal, both through the Governor-General and through private traders.[36] Just then a large number of trading vessels from all the parts of the Coromandel Coast had flocked. to the Madras Port laden with rice. The greedy traders demanded unconscionable terms and Lord Macartney had to place an embargo on imports. But the 'vengeance of Heaven seemed to overtake their inhuman proceedings.' A violent storm broke on the coast and no less than seventy vessels were stranded on the shores of Madras in one single night. In December, Madras was left with only six weeks allowance of grain.[37]

The year 1782 opened with intense distress. The relief measures taken by the Government were supplemented by private charities. 'The humanity shown upon this occasion by the gentlemen of the settlement, and likewise the Armenians cannot be sufficiently extolled. Many of these regularly fed hundreds of those miserable creatures of a day at their hospitable doors, and thereby rescued numbers of them from the gripe of death.'[38] But a characteristic feature of this famine was the birth of organised charity, perhaps for the first time in Madras.[39] Early in 1782 a famine relief fund was started at the instance of the Church Wardens of St. Mary's and public subscriptions were collected. At a special vestry held there, the community assembled elected a commitee of 15 for the 'guidance of above charity,'[40] which consisted of 11 Europeans and British Eurasians, 1 Portuguese Eurasian, 1 Armenian and 2 Hindus. This Committee has gone down to history by the lengthy name 'the Committee for the management of the native poor fund in Madras.'

The Europeans subscribed 800 pagodas every month, which the Committee found inadequate. They therefore appealed to Lord

35. Public Correspondence, 14, June 1782, Vol. CXXVII.
36. Public Letter to England, 28, October 1781, Vol. XXIV.
37. Innes Munro: *op. cit.* pp. 296-7.
38. Innes Munro, *op. cit.*, pp. 298-300.
39. S. V. Chari: Famine relief in Madras 150 years ago, in Indian Historical Records Commission, Vol. VI, pp. 78 ff.
40. Public Correspondence, 1, February 1782, Vol. CXXVII.

Macartney to recommend to the Governor-General in Council at Bengal to open a subscription list there. They further requested the Government to give them a free supply of building materials like Palmirahs, 'to enable them to erect a few sheds to cover these miserable wretches from the excessive heat of the sun'; for, the 'dying objects daily met with in the streets require shelter as well as support.'[41]

Lord Macartney readily complied with the Committee's requests. Very soon they received a bill for 5000 Pagodas from Calcutta, being the subscriptions raised among the residents there. The Europeans at Madras were continuing their monthly contribution. But 'these Sums, notwithstanding the exertions of the Committee in the frugal Management of them' were found insufficient. The number receiving relief rose to the figure of 4,000. The Committee was anxious to give them not merely the bare nourishment, but 'comfortable Support.' In May a subscription list was opened among the Indian residents also, but the 'Black Subscribers' were miserly and irregular. The Committee requested the Government to use their influence with Indians to contribute more liberally and more regularly.[42] This appeal did not go in vain. The 'black subscription' of 242½ Pagodas every month, contributed mainly by the Dubashes, Kanakapillais and Sowcars—was now augmented by a sum of 400 Pagodas from the godown merchants. Damerla Venkatapaty Naick, Zamindar of Kalastri descendent of that Venkatappa who made the original grant of Madras, contributed 100 pagodas.[43] Bengal again came to the rescue by a second contribution, but all these were enough to meet only one-third of the sum necessary for the effective relief of the swelling army of the distressed poor. The 'melancholy effects' of the famine were sensibly felt in September, 'instances daily occurring of persons dying in the street for mere want of food.'[44]

More drastic measures, therefore, had to be devised. The famine relief committee suggested that the poor should be transferred to the northern parts of the Madras Presidency which were free from famine. Lord Macartney yielded. 'In the present critical times there is unhappily no alternative. The poor must leave the place or perish.' The subordinate factories in the north were directed to apply to the 'several Zamindars to assign Places of Settlement for the Poor in the Villages of their District, with Orders that they be subsisted at the Company's Expence as economically as possible until they shall be able to gain a

41. Public Correspondence, 1, February 1782, Vol. CXXVII.
42. Fort St. George Consultations, 24, May 1782, Vol. CXXVII.
43. Love: op. cit., Vol. III, p. 231.
44. Public Correspondence, 7, September 1782, Vol. CXXVIII.

Livelihood by their bodily Labour.'[45] Madras was rid of its 'useless people' under a 'Guard of Sepoys beyond the next River to the Northward' in batches of 1000.[46] 9000 people were thus got rid of.

In the meantime the Grain Committee was pursuing a vigorous policy of counteracting the high prices of grain. Early in October of 1782, it was decided to bring the grain trade under Government monopoly, with a view to keep down prices. This raised a storm of protest, particularly from the grain merchants. A public meeting was held in the Town Hall on October 11th, under the Chairmanship of Mr. Edward Garrow. Resolutions were passed condemning the Governmental measures regarding the control of grain supply and recommending the removal of the poor to the northern districts. The Government met these demands half-way. The removal of the poor had already been effected. Regarding the monopoly of grain supply, the Government reserved to itself a major part of the supply, releasing only one-sixth of the cargo to private trade with freedom to sell at any price they liked. By this means, the Government's virtual monopoly was not shaken.

Early in 1783 the famine had run its course.[47] The services rendered by the Grain Committee on the official side and by the Relief Committee on the non-official side were indeed incalculable. It would be of interest to note in this connection that the Monegar Choultry which even today harbours the destitute and the poor was the permanent building obtained by this committee for housing the poor.[48] The Fund started by the committee came to be known as the Native Poor Fund and was administrated by St. Mary's Vestry till the year 1809.[49]

The nineteenth century witnessed similar distresses. The Famine of 1807, centred round Madras, and spread to the neighbouring districts of Nellore and North Arcot. It was the culmination of series of monsoon failures since the year 1804. The heavy death rate for the city of Madras may be seen from the following figures:

Years.	No. of Deaths.[50]
1805	.. 3,225
1806	.. 4,902
1807	.. 17,207

45. Public Correspondence, 28, September 1782, Vol. CXXVIII.
46. Public Correspondence, 12, October, 1782, Vol. CXXVIII.
47. Dalyell: *op. cit.*
48. Military Consultations, 4, April 1783, Vol. LXXXVII; Public Correspondence, 18, August 1807.
49. Rev. Frank Penny: The Church in Madras, Vol. I, pp. 362-63.
50. Dalvell: *op. cit.*, pp. 21-26.

Large crowds of emaciated people flocked into the town of Madras, and besieged the gates of the Monegar Choultry in the expectation of obtaining relief without limit.[51] The Black Town presented a wretched spectacle of misery. Large numbers daily died for want of food and the calamity rapidly spread.[52]

This Famine was the occasion for a learned controversy as to whether it was proper to interfere in the grain market. Lord William Bentinck, the Governor was against such an interference. But in the end the Government agreed to give a guaranteed price to grain importers with a view to encourage them.[53] The Government also imported large quantities and this measure seems to have had the most satisfactory effect in keeping down the price of food.[54]

The Grain Committee was constituted and the committee enquired into certain disturbances that had taken place between the grain dealers and the public. It also managed the grain imports on behalf of the Government. It forwarded consignments to relieve the mofussil places also. The most striking feature of the relief measures during this famine was the starting of public works to employ the able-bodied poor. The Company had now become the suzerain of the whole of South India and it became alive to the increased responsibilities. The Engineering department was instructed to start relief works in the vicinity of Madras. This wise step 'restrained in a great measure emigrations to the presidency town and thousands were usefully and advantageously employed, who must either have perished from want or proved burdensome to the community. The pay which they received while it was adequate to their support, was so far below the ordinary rate of labour as to prove that the benevolence of Government would not be liable to abuse and that those only would avail themselves of its liberality who were objects of compassion and unable to obtain employment elsewhere.'[55]

The starting of public works relieved the strain on the non-official agencies to a great deal. In spite of it, in 1807, 4050 persons were being fed at Monegar Choultry and its vicinity daily. Four branch relief depots were also opened. Lord William Bentinck became the patron of the Poor Fund Committee. Subscriptions were raised. Appeals for funds

51. Maclean: Manual of Administration, Vol. I, p. 299 *n.*

52. Minutes of Mr. Thomas Oakes, Member of the Council, quoted by S. V. Chari, *op. cit.*

53. Dalyell: *op. cit.*

54. *Ibid.*

55. Minute of the Poor Fund Committee, quoted by S. V. Chari, *op. cit.*

were sent to Bombay and Calcutta. A charity sermon was preached at St. Mary's in aid of the Famine Fund. Supplies of grain were requisitioned from the Bengal Government and were brought in the Company's ships. In the month of March alone, 25,867 persons were fed from this fund. Several lakhs were spent on relief operations. Mr. Thomas Oakes, a member of the Council felt that the relief work of the Poor Fund Committee should be supplemented. He pleaded that Government must step in and directly dole out food. He was supported by Lt. General J. F. Cradock, the Commander-in-chief of the Madras Army. According to Cradock much reliance must not be placed on private charity, for, 'what is the business of every person becomes that of no one.' Government should undertake it in a 'spirit of a great and enlightened state.' Bentinck, however, did not agree with them.

The famine seems to have passed away by October 1807 and such of the poor as had survived were returned to their homes.

The famine of 1824 was sweeping in its extent and intensity. Madras city also came under its grip.[56] The scarcity of grain was acutely felt. Only a single shop had grain to sell. A 'grain riot' broke out and the aid of the military had to be invoked. The riot could not be quelled until fire was opened.[57] Mortality was great and distress indescribable.

Relief through public works was opposed on *laissez faire* principles and all restrictions on free trade of grain were removed. Four Relief Depots, managed by the Committee of the Monegar Choultry and supported by Government grant continued to dole out food. Several thousands of people were fed free for months together.

The expenditure came to 1 rupee per head. Relief varied with the capacity to work. Each recipient was provided with a ticket which enabled him to get just the food necessary to keep body and soul together. Of the able-bodied, none was permitted to eat the bread of idleness. With the setting in of the monsoons in October, the famine melted away and relief depots were closed at the end of the year[58]

The "Guntoor Famine" of 1833 affected the city also. The distress was aggravated by 'multitudes that came in search of food,' attracted by generous relief provided here.[59] 'Grain riots' again

56. Maclean: *op. cit.*, Vol. I, pp. 299*n*.
57. Dalyell: *op. cit.*, p. 27.
58. Dalyell: *op. cit.*, pp. 31-32.
59. Captain Best: Madras Journal of Literature & Science, 1844-45.

broke out and were quelled as during the previous famine.[60] Starvation and death stalked naked. In February 1833, 1,500 people were regularly fed at the Monegar Choultry, and by the end of May 12,000 were seeking relief. The number rose to 33,000 in June. About 7000 were employed by the Committee of the Monegar Choultry. Attempts were also made to send back the natives of Northern districts.

The period between 1825-54 was a period of acute depression, punctuated by occasional scarcities as in 1843 and 1854.[61] The subsequent decade witnessed an unprecedented increase in the economic welfare of the Presidency, so that when the "Orissa Famine" broke out in 1866, the Government were in a better position to afford relief. Indeed distress in the city was trifling compared with that in districts like Ganjam, yet prices rose high and suffering followed. The city organised relief not only for itself, but also for the distant northern districts by starting the Ganjam Famine Relief Fund.

Official and non-official relief readily came to succour. Lord Napier, the then Governor, took a prominent part in raising funds. A Famine Relief Committee, consisting of Europeans and Indians, was organised at the instance of the Sheriff of Madras.[62] Subscriptions amounted to Rs. 20,000 and the Government contributed an equivalent sum. Two important test works were commenced in the vicinity of Madras. A move was made by philanthropic men among the Hindus and Muslims to purchase grain and sell it to the poor at low rates.

The sub-committee for the relief of the city held weekly meetings and directed the relief operations. A committee of three managed each relief house. The able-bodied were excluded from the benefits. Such of those who were unable to wait at the doors of the relief house either on account of infirmity or of caste were given money doles. The payments ranged from Rs. 2 to Rs. 4 per mensem. This was the first occasion when the system of money doles was started. The European and Eurasian paupers were also given relief through the Friend-in-need Society.

In addition to the relief houses opened by the committee, four other relief centres were started by charitably inclined persons at Periamet and other localities. The French Consul M. E. Lecot also opened a relief house. The funds for the relief of the city during this period

60. Dalyell: *op. cit.*, pp. 32-41.
61. Thomas and Natarajan: Economic Depression in Madras Presidency, 1820-54.
62. Mr. Dalyell was the Honorary Secretary of this Committee.

amounted to Rs. 39,603-14-2; of this, Rs. 20,834-13-5 came from the General Relief Fund and the rest from local subscriptions.[63]

The next great famine commenced with the failure of the summer monsoons in 1876.[64]

Several charitable men opened relief houses in the town and the suburbs. But that was inadequate. Government had to come to rescue. Besides the Lungerkhana at Triplicane, the Government organised two other relief camps under the superintendence of the Commissioner of Police, one of which was at Triplicane in the premises of Venkataswami Naidu's market. To check the stream of pauper immigration, a third camp was organised at Sathangadas, a village on the Cochrane's canal, about 2 miles to the north of the Municipality under the management of the President of the Municipal Commission. Two small relief works were commenced, giving employment to about 600 men and women. In addition, the Government also contributed a monthly sum equal to the amount spent by private relief organisations.

The relief, being scattered, was found inadequate to meet the needs of the resident poor of the city. The President of the Municipality took efforts to increase the funds.[65] A town Relief Committee was constituted and special arrangements were made to the caste poor. New relief centre were opened by Government in Mylapore, Royapettah, Vepery and Royapuram. The private relief houses supported by Government grant were gradually superseded. Branches of the Town Relief Committee were opened in every division. A Town Relief Fund was also started for which help poured even from England. A Sheriff's meeting was held at the Banqueting Hall on 4th August 1877, at which 'His Grace' the Governor presided. Government sanctioned Rs. 12,000 towards the fund. Money dole relief was also administered successfully. Special care was taken to extend the relief to the poor among Non-caste Hindus and Gosha Muslims.[66] Under this system money doles were given in eight divisions to the extent of Rs. 1,74,290-14-0; and free clothing to the extent of Rs. 29,872. The number relieved was 24,045.

The rest of the famine history can be briefly told. After the famine of 1876, the *laissez faire* policy was definitely given up at least in the sphere of famine administration. Great economic

63. Dalyell: *op. cit.* Appendix.

64. Madras Journal of Literature and Science, 1839-40.

65. From the President of Madras Municipality, to the Government, 10 February 1877.

66. Review of the Madras Famine 1876-78, p. 203, App. F.

changes swept over the country. Gigantic works of productive and protective irrigation were undertaken in many parts of the country. The country was closely knit up by railways. A phenomenal development in roadmaking followed. Peace reigned uninterruptedly. The Famine Relief and Insurance Funds were started. The Famine codes were promulgated. 'In conducting a campaign against famine it must be laid down as a first principle that the object of State intervention is to save life and that all other considerations should be sub-ordinated to this. The success or otherwise of the relief methods at such a crisis cannot be subjected to a financial test, for the bills of mortality will furnish the only true criterion.'[67] These introductory words of the Madras Famine Code mark the begining of a new and far-sighted famine policy on the part of the Government.

There was a famine in 1896-97, a scarcity in 1907-8 and another during the closing period of the Great War. The famines of the 20th century are work famines rather than food famines.[68] The days when 'life was offered for a loaf, but none would buy, rank was to be sold for a cake, but none cared for it; the ever-bounteous hand was stretched out to beg for food; and the feet which had always trodden the way of contentment walked about in search of sustenance',[69] now appear to belong to a bygone dark age.

The story of famines through these three hundred years is indeed, a dismal one. But it is not without its bright spots. The relief measures attempted during these famines, the great public works launched to mitigate their evils and the humanity displayed both by the Government and the people run as a golden thread through this tangled web of misery. The eventual effacing of the miseries of death-dealing famine is an achievement which any Government may justly be proud of.

67. Madras Famine Code; Introduction (1927 Edn.).
68. Sir H. V. Lovett: Cambridge History of India, Vol. VI, p. 31.
69. Elliot: *op. cit.*, Vol. VII, pp. 24-25.

Beginnings of British Justice in Madras

By

K. A. Nilakanta Sastri, M.A.,
Professor, University of Madras.

We are now so used to the amenities of a fairly well-ordered city that it takes an effort to visualise the conditions that obtained in Madras three centuries ago. Then there was no city in existence, and the area of the present city was taken up by a number of adjacent villages hardly to be distinguished from any other rural neighbourhood. Triplicane, Mylapore, Chetput and so on were indeed ancient names, but they were separate villages with no greater consciousness of a common life than villages elsewhere in the land. And we cannot quite tell why or when Madras came to be called by that name;* but of this we are certain that the name was applied at first only to the coastal strip on which stands Fort St. George and the land behind it to the extent of two square miles oı more, corresponding to the Fort and Georgetown of to-day.

Madras in its old and restricted sense was a creation of English merchants and grew round Fort St. George. It grew rapidly; the construction of the Fort began early in 1640 and was completed only several years after; but by the end of 1640 between 300 and 400 families of weavers had immigrated into Madras. Here Englishmen and Indians faced the task of organising the means of carrying on a civilized life for their mutual benefit, in the midst of the growing anarchy caused by the slow dissolution of the last remains of the once famous empire of Vijayanagara.

The preservation of life and property and the punishment of offenders against these, are among the prime requisites of any society. In the city of Madras today we have an elaborate police organisation for the detection of crime and a number of magistrates and courts for the punishment of criminals and settlement of civil disputes. In 1640

* Note, however, that Damerla Venkata's charter already calls the place Madraspatam. There were feudatories under Vijayanagara of the name Madarāju—as in 161 of 1905 dated Ś. 1476 (1554 A.D.). Dr. C. Minakshi tells me that she has evidence of a more conclusive character attesting the existence of the city at an earlier date. I have not seen it. But Mailāpura Mādara, one of the donees of the Bevinahalli grant of Ś. 1473 should, I think, never have been connected with the etymology of the name Madras. Contra EI. xiv, p. 216.

Madras had none of these; it had not even the traditional, if decadent, organisation that obtained in the neighbouring villages where they still managed somehow to preserve the rudiments of governmental order.

The English factors in Madras had in this period, only two sources from which they derived authority over the area under their control, the charter of the Company under which they carried on their operations in India, and the grants from the 'Country powers' which conferred on them lands and privileges from time to time. And in the beginning neither of these sources gave any guidance to the factors as to how they were to deal with crimes or dispense justice. All the earlier charters of the Company seem to have given it power only 'to make laws for its own government and for that of the factors, masters and mariners employed in voyages provided such laws were not repugnant to the laws of England,' and to punish offenders against such laws by imprisonment or fine. It was only in 1661 that the Company first got authority to appoint Governors and Councils in different places who could 'judge all persons living under them in all causes, civil or criminal, according to the laws of England, and to execute judgment.'

The charter granted to Day by Damerla Venkatapati in 1639 on the other hand does indeed contain a provision which at first sight seems to confer the necessary power on the factors of Madras. It reads: 'And to make more full Expression of our affection to the English Nation, wee Doe Confirme into the said Mr. Francis Day, or whatsoever other substitutes or Agents for that Company, full power and authority to governe and dispose of the Government of Madraspatam for the terme and space of two yeares Next Insueing after they shall be seated there and possesst of the said fortifications.' The words 'full power and authority to governe and dispose of the Government of Madraspatam' may well seem to include the judicial power over the inhabitants resident in the area; but this first impression created by these words is proved to be erroneous by two things. *First,* the words quoted above are immediately followed by a clause which restricts considerably the meaning of the general expressions employed earlier: 'and for the future by an Equal Division to receive halfe the custom and revenues of that port.' So that the full power and authority to govern for two years meant really no more than power for the Company's factors to levy customs on the trade of the port and appropriate to the Company the entire proceeds of such levy. *Secondly,* the factors of Fort St. George did not themselves think that they had been granted by the naik the power to administer justice in Madras. This becomes clear from the action they took when a case actually came up before them.

In December 1641 there was a murder of a woman in Madras, and the casual manner in which the crime was detected cannot be better described than in the words of a letter sent to England from Fort St. George in September 1642 : " A few dayes after Andrew Cogan his arrivall as aforesaid, a murther was committed in our towne. Two parriars (pariahs) had kild a common whore for her jewels and throwne the corps into the river ; the discovery of which murther is not unworthy your knowledge. The woeman had byn wanting many dayes, and none but the murtherers coold say where she was. At length somewhat was seene to floate upp and downe the river ; when the partie that murthered her, being amongst divers others, made profer and did swime of to see what it was and bring it ashore. When the corps was ashoare, no wound was perceived, and therefore conceived that she might drowne herselfe ; Whereuppon order was given for her buriall. When then the party that swam of aforesaid was very importunate to have some satisfaction for his pains ; but one of the standers by tould him that he had no reason of all men to require any such thing, for that she had mainteyned him and his consort for a long time together ; uppon which words every mans eye was uppon him, when one amongst the many discovered uppon the cloath he wore some blood ; and being asked how that came, he presently made answere how, but within less than half an hower that tale of his was provd a ly, and in the interim wee found that the cloath that he wore and that uppon the dead corps had byn on intire piece. When then wee layd the murther to his charge ; but he denying it, wee sent, searched his house, and there found all her jewells and cloaths, not any one wanting. So then, when all things appeared so plaine, he confessed the murther. But his consort was gone two or three dayes before ; nevertheless he had not the power to goe out of our command. So wee apprehended him likewise, and notified all the passages to our Naique, who gave us an express command to doe justice uppon the homicides according to the lawes of England ; but if wee would not, then he woold according to the custome of Karnatte ; for, said he in his olio (letter : Tamil *olai,* a palm leaf), if justice be not done, who woold come and trade here, espetially when it shall be reported it was a place of theevs and murtherers ? Which being so, and unwilling to give away our power to those who are too readie to take it, wee did justice on them and hanged them on a gibbet ; where they hung till 'twas the 15 of December ; when then, because the great Naique (i.e. Damarla Venkatappa) cam to visit us for a present, they were cut downe."

So when an actual murder occurred and it somehow came to light, all that the factors could do was to apprehend the culprit on their own and then await instructions from the Naick. And the Naick would fain escape being bothered with it if the English would do justice according to their laws. But who was there to give an authentic declaration of English law ? Evidently the factors had to do the best according to their own lights.

The same letter from Fort St. George gives the story of another murder which took place on the 11th August 1642. Three Portuguese soldiers from San Thomé came to Madras, fell to drinking with a Dane 'in a base arack house' and started a brawl. When two English soldiers were sent to stop it, one of them was stabbed by Anthony Myrando, one of the Portuguese soldiers, and died on the spot. The three Portuguese soldiers fled, but were soon captured; the actual murderer was detained and the others allowed to depart to San Thomé. Thereupon the English found themselves pulled in opposite directions. The Portuguese of San Thomé pressed for the release of their *fidalgo;* the Naick sent some four to five hundred soldiers 'to lye in the towne (not knowing what the Portugalls might attempt to get their man) and order that out of hand he shoold be put to death.' The Madras factors wanted to consult Surat in view of English interests in Goa, 'but the importunitie of our Naique and our people here woold not suffer us longer to deferre it,' and the *fidalgo* was executed on the 13th August by being 'shott to death before our corps du guard.' This forced summary execution seems to have done very well with the Portuguese, for the Madras factors add: 'Since when wee have byn wonderful at ease in respect of the Portugalls, for till then wee were dayly troubled with one or other.' This case differs from the last in two respects. No Indian was involved in it. And though it was primarily a matter between the English and the Portuguese, the Naick felt free to intervene and insist upon justice being done according to his own ideas. Apparently the Portuguese of San Thomé had proved themselves a nuisance for some time to the Naick as well as to the English, and the Naick was ready to vent his spleen on them when he got the chance.

A third case, also of man-slaughter, occurred on the 8th January 1644 and was characterised by the factors of Madras as 'a most unfortunate accident' in a letter to Bantam at the end of the month. The culprit in this case was a Sergeant of the Company called Bradford. Being licensed to sleep in his house outside the fort, Bradford found a man hiding in his house 'at a most unseasonable tyme,' and fatally wounded the man in a scuffle. The sergeant, we are told, 'cutt him over the arme, soe for to give him a marke for to discover and knowe him the next day. And indeed itt proved soe that the man was easily to bee found; for whatt with timerousness and neglect to have his blood stincht, hee proved a corps.' When the factors came to know of the occurrence, they became 'dubious that our masters might suffer somewhat' and sent their surgeon to examine the wounds; but this was useless as the corpse had been interred early in the morning by the parents of the victim 'being ashamed of the act.' And a general meeting held later of the factors and the most sustantial merchants and Komatis of Madras received an oral and written 'Confession' from the father of the victim 'that his sonn received a just guerdon for his offence.' The merchants and Komatis averred and confirmed 'that such was the law and custome of the country.' Still the factors, it seems, would have sent Bradford to Bantam if they had found 'a fit man to have seated in his office,' which, however, could never be, 'so long as wee are to be supplyed by the discretion of masters of shipps.' The inhabitants of the town who saw the victim 'eare his interring' are said to have acknowledged with one voice that he had 'no other wound but only on the armes, which confirmes that there was no intent to take his life.' The factors, however, propose to defer drawing up a consultation on this affair 'some short time to see if there will be any further question thereon,' but 'verily believe there will not.' They also took security against the sergeant escaping meanwhile.

Bradford had been at Fort St. George from its foundation, and was evidently a favourite with the factors. He had got into trouble by 'killing of one of these natives,' and we may suspect that the surgeon of the Fort either did not or would not take a hand in whitewashing the affair, which had to be done independently of him and with the obliging assistance of the merchants and Komatis who were quite ready to help the factors whose presence in Madras brought them so much business and profit. However that may be, we can hardly doubt that the only official record now accessible to us of this matter is a cooked up story. Sergeant Bradford's case must count among the earliest instances of that contempt for native life which till recently formed so marked a feature of the relations between European soldiers and Indians and to some extent even of Anglo-Indian jurisprudence. But the appeal to the opinion of the inhabitants of the locality, howsoever it may have come about, was a new feature in the life of the growing city.

The first occasion on which the Company's factors in Fort St. George gained a definite accession of judicial power in Madras was Oct.-Nov. 1645 when Śrī Ranga Rāyalu, the last Vijayanagar ruler of Karnataka, gave them a grant which surrendered into their hands 'the government and justice of the towne.' There is no direct evidence for it, but it seems probable that it was only from this time that the township of Madras received its own administrative organisation on indigenous lines. The officials bore the common Indian designations of Adigāri, Kaṇakkupiḷḷai,* Peddanaick and Talliar, but from the first they seem to have been appointed by the Council of Fort St. George and responsible to it for the proper conduct of town affairs. The *adigār* had also charge of administration of justice and held his court at the choultry or Town

* This office, however, seems to be mentioned earlier though the officer is also described as Broker.

House. The Peddanaick and his assistants, the Talliars, assisted him in apprehending and confining suspected criminals before they took their trial.

Śrī Ranga's charter soon ceased to be of effect when in 1647 the house of Vijayanagar was finally driven out of the Karnatic which passed thus to Golconda. But as the new Muslim sovereign of Madras confirmed the rights and privileges enjoyed by the British in Madras, the political revolution made no difference to the evolution of the administration of the city.

But this evolution was no peaceful process. The quarrels that broke out between the Right and Left hand castes during the Presidency of Aaron Baker filled Madras with a 'spirit of factious madness' which would not be brought under control by the town authorities or the Council of Fort St. George. Even the Nabob of Golconda to whom the matter was sent up 'would not decide it', and the Right hand castes roundly assert in a Declaration sent to London about April 1655: "This Towne is called the Towne without Government."

The obscure caste disputes pertaining to an alien and complicated social system were not the only source of embarrassment to the Council of Madras; Venkata, the Company's chief Indian merchant, and Kanappa, his brother, who was the Adigar of the town, wielded a great deal of power between them and promoted various intrigues which led to faction among the factors and grave discontent in the city. In March 1653 therefore Kanappa was shorn of his duties relating to the administration of justice, and two members of the Council 'were ordered to sit during alternate weeks at the choultry to administer justice.' Kanappa was required to assist them in a subordinate capacity.

Even after the new arrangement the course of justice did not run smooth. The factors took too much interest in the affairs of their peons and friends and hampered the execution of justice by undue personal influence. Leigh was one of the two councillors ordered to sit in the choultry court, and after narrating the details of a typical case of insolence and defiance of the Court's order on the part of a peon of the President, he justly observes: "If this bee not mighty Oppression...... it will make the English names to stinke amoung this Country People, for they are able to know what is justice and what is Oppression. Besides, if these great oppressions and injustices bee tould the Nabob, hee will then have his desire, for hee may justly take away the Government of the Towne from you, and then what is the ffort worth?" (Dec. 1654).

Fort St. George was reduced to an Agency soon after, and this did not improve the chances of a proper judicial administration. And when in 1665 another murder occurred and the Agent and Council, uncertain of their powers, wrote to London for instructions, the Company took the occasion to put an end to all doubts and difficulties by creating a Governorship of Madras under the terms of the charter of 1661. They not only took legal opinion upon the relevant clause in the charter, but even made their 'addresses unto his Majestie for his speciall allowance and direction.' This was the beginning of modern judicial Administration in Madras.

REFERENCES

Foster—The English Factories in India.
Love—Vestiges of Madras Vol. I.

A Striking Episode in Madras History

BY

SIR FRANK NOYCE, K.C.S.I., C.B.E.

MADRAS has many claims to fame. One probably unique distinction it possesses is that, twice in its history, the Head of its administration has been deposed and imprisoned by his Council. Mr. George Foxcroft, who came out from England as Agent in June, 1665, was arrested by Sir Edward Winter, the Second in Council, in September of that year, and remained in imprisonment until August, 1668, eventually triumphed over his adversaries. He was not only reinstated but was raised to the rank of Governor. A century or so later, Lord Pigot, less fortunate, died in confinement. The brief account of one of the most striking episodes in the history of Madras which is given in the following pages, is based, in the main, on contemporary publications in the writer's possession. But, like all writers on old Madras, he has quarried extensively in that mine of information, Colonel Love's "Vestiges of Old Madras."

Lord Pigot arrived in Madras in December, 1775, as Governor for the second time. He came out to Madras first in 1737 at the age of eighteen, had been made a prisoner of war on the surrender of Fort St. George to the French in 1746 and had returned to India in 1750. In 1754 he was transferred from Vizagapatam to Fort St. David as Deputy Governor with the reversion of the Governorship of Madras to which he succeeded in January, 1775, on the resignation of Mr. Thomas Saunders. His first Governorship, which lasted for as many years as his second did months, was vigorous and successful but of the stirring events which marked it, the capture of Calcutta by Suraj-ud-Daula, the despatch from Madras of a relief expedition under Watson and Clive which recaptured Calcutta and took Chandernagore, the loss of Cuddalore and Fort St. David, the siege of Madras by Lally, the capture of Pondicherry and the expedition to Manila, this is not the place to write. Pigot resigned in November, 1763, was made a baronet in the following year and raised to the peerage of Ireland in 1766.

The troubles which occurred during Pigot's second administration had their origin in the affairs of Tanjore. During his first Governorship, he had compelled the Nawab of Arcot to enter into a treaty with the Raja of Tanjore. The story of the Nawab's debts which eventually formed the subject of an enquiry by Parliament and the theme of an impassioned speech by Edmund Burke in 1785 would require a volume to itself. The influence they enabled the Nawab to exert on the members of the Government of Madras was such that he was able to secure their active assistance in annexing Tanjore to his dominions. Of this reversal of Pigot's policy the Directors of the East India Company sternly disapproved. The Governor, Alexander Wynch, was superseded and his Council severely reprimanded. It is not surprising that the Directors turned to Pigot to ensure that their orders to restore the Raja were carried its effect. Their wisdom ended there and Pigot, on arriving in Madras, found himself saddled with an unwieldy Council of eleven members, many of whom had been responsible for the policy he had been sent out to reverse. That Council consisted, at the outset, of George Stratton, Sir Robert Fletcher, the Commander in Chief, George Dawson, Henry Brooke, Claud Russell, Alexander Dalrymple, John Maxwell Stone, Archdale Palmer, Francis Jourdan and George Mackay. Stratton who, with Fletcher, was to lead the opposition to Pigot, had recently been transferred from Vizagapatam where he had been Chief of the Settlement. Sir Robert Fletcher had started life as a Writer in Madras. He was transferred to the Army as an Ensign in 1757 and became Captain three years later. He had been dismissed from service whilst in command of a brigade in Bengal for his part in the officers' mutiny of 1766. He had persuaded the Directors to reinstate him and came out to Madras in 1772. Three years later, he became Commander in Chief with Colonel Stuart as Second in Command. Russell and Dalrymple, who had been on leave, came out with Pigot and were his loyal supporters throughout as were also Dawson and Stone.

The composition of the Council was such that it was inevitable that faction should display itself almost at once. Pigot lost no time in carrying out his instructions. Colonel Harpur took possession of Tanjore in February, 1776, and restored the Raja. Pigot thereupon went to Tanjore himself but resisted a demand that two Members of Council should be associated with him in his proceedings there though he agreed to be accompanied by Jourdan. The sinister figure of Paul Benfield, "civil servant, engineer, contractor and financier," who, as the solidity of the west front of Fort St. George bears witness, shone to greater advantage in the second of these capacities than in any of the others, now appears on the scene. In an indictment drawn up by Lord Macartney at a later stage of his career, he is described as "a Champion in the cause of faction; who, in the year 1770, was by the Court of Directors dismissed from the Company's service for his factious and inflammatory behaviour; who, after he had, on promise of future good behaviour, been restored to the Service, was for disobedience of orders in 1772 unanimously suspended from the Service, and was, in the year 1774, ordered by the Court of Directors to be reprimanded and mulcted for his offences." Burke speaks of him as a master "of the profession of *soucaring* ; by which a few innocent, inexperienced young Englishmen, without property on which any one would lend to themselves a single shilling, are enabled at once to take provinces in mortgage, to make princes their debtors, and to become creditors for millions." Whilst Pigot was in Tanjore, Benfield put forward claims on its revenues amounting in all to about a quarter of a million pounds. He alleged that these represented loans which had been made to the Nawab for payment of his troops and advances to the inhabitants for cultivation as well as compensation for grain which had been requisitioned by the Company's troops. The magnitude of Benfield's transactions with the Nawab speaks for itself and throws a lurid light on the integrity of the age and on the subsequent happenings in the Madras Council. Pigot promised to lay Benfield's claims before the Government on his return to Madras. He did so and, on May 29th, the Council passed a resolution that it was not in their power to comply with Benfield's requests in any respect, "those claims on individuals which bear the appearance of having no connection with Government not being sufficiently explained to enable the Board to form an opinion thereon; and the assignments of the Nabob not being admissible." This was carried by six votes to five, Pigot, Dalrymple, Russell, Dawson, Stone and Brooke against Stratton, Fletcher, Mackay and Jourdan. The repudiation of his assignments on the Tanjore revenues thoroughly alarmed the Nawab, especially as Pigot was endeavouring strictly to enforce the orders of the Directors that the only channel of communication between the Government and the Nawab should be the Governor. He wrote both to the Government of Bengal and to Sir Edward Hughes, the Admiral in command of the Fleet, charging Pigot with arbitrary acts in Madras and Tanjore. At this juncture, unfortunately for Pigot, Charles Floyer joined both the Council and the opposition and Brooke began to waver in his support. Thus reinforced, the opposition returned to the charge and, on June 14th, motions asserting the validity of the Nawab's claims upon Tanjore and directing the Raja to give Benfield all reasonable assistance in recovering his debts were carried by seven votes to five, the minority consisting of Pigot, Russell, Dalrymple, Dawson and Stone. A motion moved by Pigot himself that all Benfield's claims were a private and not a public concern was negatived by the same majority. Another motion that the letter from the Nawab to Sir Edward Hughes had been written purposely to create animosity between the Members of the Government was carried by Pigot's casting vote, Brooke on this question siding with him as he did on the next motion that "agreeable to the Company's orders, no Member of the Council do henceforth visit or correspond by writing or by message with the Nabob or either of his sons." This was the last of Pigot's triumphs. At this stage, Brooke deserted finally to the opposition and a further motion that the Nawab should be advised to transfer his residence from Madras to Arcot was lost by seven votes to five.

A further cause for dissension now developed. Pigot was anxious to establish a factory at Tanjore with Russell in charge. The opposition was too strong for him but on July 8th it was agreed—by his casting vote, Stratton for some unaccountable reason voting with him—that Russell should be appointed Resident at Tanjore. At this juncture, Dawson proceeded on leave and on the following day it was decided that Stuart, who had been appointed to the command at Vellore should be sent to Tanjore instead, Harpur being recalled to make way for him. In order to ensure that Stuart who was a close friend of Benfield should have a free hand at Tanjore, the opposition now contended that, as Russell and Dalrymple had been appointed by the Company members of the Committee of circuit to investigate the affairs of the Northern Circars, it was their duty to proceed on that work forthwith, and August 31st was fixed for its commencement. Pigot urged that the orders of the Company were that the Committee of Circuit should not begin its work until the affairs of Tanjore had been placed on a satisfactory footing and declared his intention of not allowing any instructions to be given to Stuart unless Russell were allowed to go to Tanjore even if it were only for a short period. On all matters on which a vote was taken after the departure of Dawson, the voting was always seven to four.

Matters were now rapidly approaching a crisis. On August 20th, Pigot refused to take a vote on the question of the instructions to be given to Stuart on the ground that the conduct of the business of the Council lay entirely within his discretion. On the 22nd, the opposition put in a minute declaring that Pigot was bound by the orders of the majority and that, in the event of his refusing to put a question to the vote, it was the duty of the Secretary to the Council to do so. Pigot offered to allow matters to remain as they were until the pleasure of the Company was known but the offer was refused. The opposition now produced the last shot from its locker, a letter directing the Secretary to sign the instructions to Stuart and Harpur. This was signed in the Council Chamber by Stratton and Brooke but before it could be passed further round the table, Pigot, driven to desperation by the tactics of the opposition and having no constitutional weapon for dealing with a refractory Council, directed the two signatories to withdraw—from the Council table, apparently, but not from the room. They were thereupon suspended from office by his casting vote, the voting being Pigot, Russell, Dalrymple and Stone against Mackay, Floyer, Palmer and Jourdan. Fletcher was away ill and Stratton and Brooke were declared ineligible to vote on a matter which affected them personally. The Council then adjourned to the next day for which another meeting was summoned. This was attended by Mr. Richard Lathom who had been brought up from Cuddalore. The opposition absented itself but sent in a protest claiming that they were the only legal representatives of the Company. At this meeting, Floyer, Palmer, Jourdan and Mackay were also suspended and the arrest of Fletcher was ordered, pending a court-martial. By an extraordinary error of judgment which was to prove fatal to him, Pigot entrusted the command of the troops to Stuart. Of all the strange acts of this strange period, nothing is stranger than that Pigot should have placed any faith in a man whose fortunes were as closely bound up with those of his opponents as were Stuart's. He seems to have genuinely believed that Stuart had accepted the command from him and would act accordingly. Stuart subequently maintained that he had told Pigot no more than that, Fletcher being under arrest, the command passed automatically to him. Pigot's awakening did not come until the following evening. By then Stuart who had, as might have been expected, thrown in his lot with the opposition, had had ample time to "complete my plan" to carry out their orders to arrest Pigot. He had, in the meantime, had supper, breakfast and dinner with Pigot and been again invited to supper. Much to his relief, as he explained later, the Governor selected the Garden House, now Government House, for supper that evening as this saved him from what might have been regarded as a breach of military discipline if he had arrested him in the Fort, of which he was *ex-officio* in military as well as civil command. On their way to the Garden House, they were met, by Stuart's prearrangements, by Eidingtoun, the Adjutant General, who told Pigot that he was to consider himself under arrest, transferred him to another carriage which belonged to Benfield, and sent him, in charge of Captain Lysaght, to the Mount, where he was handed over to the custody of Major Horne. On August 25th, the majority issued a proclamation announcing the assumption of the Governorship by Stratton and the suspension of Russell, Dalrymple, Stone and Lathom. The General Order of the Day in which the proclamation was issued contained the significant announcement that "The President and Council being, upon the report of Colonel Stuart, thoroughly satisfied with the conduct of the officers and men comprising the garrison, have empowered him to assure them that they shall meet with a proper gratification."

Both sides appealed to the Governor General and his Council, Clavering, Barwell and Francis, and Pigot, in September, sent a long account of all that happened to the Directors which he entrusted to Captain Robert Wood, the Town Major. Communications with England were so slow that their answer was not received until the following August, three months after Pigot's death. From Warren Hastings, who might have been expected to sympathise with a Governor who had to deal with a refractory Council, and his colleagues Pigot receive cold comfort. He was told that the account of his confinement had filled the

Bengal Government with equal anxiety and surprise but "that the rights and powers of the Governor and Council of any of the Company's Presidencies are vested by their original constitution in the majority of the Board; that the violence committed by your Lordship in excluding two of the Members of the Council of Fort St. George from their places was a violation of the constitution; that the measures taken by the majority to recover the actual Government which of right is vested in them arose from the necessity of the case; and that we shall acknowledge and support the title and authority which they consequently possess." A similar reply was sent to the *de facto* Government. The Supreme Court, of which Impey was Chief Justice and Chambers, Le Maistre and Hyde were Judges, was much more cautious. It refused to express any opinion on the material before it but drily added that "we suppose that the Gentlemen there had fully considered the legality of their conduct in assuming the Government before they executed that measure."

Pigot applied to the Mayor's Court for a writ of *Habeas Corpus* which was refused. He also instituted a suit in that Court claiming damages of £200,000 against Fletcher and Stuart and £50,000 against Eidingtoun and Lysaght. Stratton and his associates, acting as a Court of Appeal, had the fairness to acknowledge that they were themselves virtually parties to the suit and, therefore, unable to try it. The defendants had declared their intention of appealing to the King in Council when Pigot's death put an end to the suit.

In the elaborate defence of their conduct which Stratton and his colleagues subsequently prepared when they themselves were under arrest, they maintained that Pigot was surrounded by every comfort and indeed luxury at the Mount and was treated with all possible respect. But, as early as October 14th, he was complaining to Sir Edward Hughes that he was not getting sufficient exercise and that he was guarded by the Nawab's cavalry instead of by European troops. And, although it was stated in the defence that, after Pigot's arrest, the Mount "became the gayest place on the Coast and, on Christmas Day and New Year's Day as well as Twelfth Night, the balls given by Messrs. Monckton, Russell and Stone were uncommonly splendid" and that Pigot was allowed to build a bath, the construction of which he took much interest in superintending and also to occupy himself in the garden, it was not denied that all the accommodation he was given was a single room and that it was not until his illness that a small adjacent room was allotted for the use of his servants. The evidence given at the inquest also established that he went for a drive only once during his illness when he was taken to a place appropriately named "The Cave of Despair!"

The new Government did not have quite such an easy time with the civil service as with the army. In addition to the four Members of Council (including Lathom), five other civil servants were suspended for refusing to recognise it. Thirty-eight others protested but offered to continue in service until the Company's pleasure was known.

Stratton and his Government could not feel secure as long as Pigot remained near Madras. On August 27th, an attempt was made forcibly to remove him to Chingleput but he resisted so violently that it had to be abandoned. Later on, an offer was made to transfer him to any other settlement on the Coast or to send him to Europe but was refused.

The evidence given at the inquest showed that his imprisonment began to tell on Pigot's health at the beginning of 1777 but it was not until the first week of March that he became seriously ill. In the hope that he would benefit from the change, he was moved from the Mount to the Garden House on April 28th. On May 10th, the Government, evidently greatly disconcerted by the unlooked-for turn of events, announced his release from confinement. By that time Pigot was too ill to know or care. He died at 11 a.m. the following day. Sir Robert Fletcher had predeceased him. He sailed for the Cape on sick leave in October, 1776, but died at Mauritius on Christmas Eve.

An inquest was promptly held by Mr. George Andrew Ram who claimed to be Coroner for Madras. Of the twelve members of the jury, one, John Turing, was a civil servant, one was the Master Attendant and seven were free merchants. Mr. Ram and the jury were obviously deeply impressed by the solemnity of the occasion and did their utmost to rise to it. Fifteen witnesses were examined at great length, including Russell, Stone and Lathom, Sir Edward Hughes, the Hon. Edward Monckton, Pigot's son-in-law, four doctors, Pasley, who subsequently became Surgeon General to the Government of Madras, Anderson, Davis and Mallet, Nutting, Pigot's valet, and Telasingha, his peon. The medical witnesses were agreed that the cause of Pigot's death was bilious fever and congestion of the liver but were much less definite as to whether it could be attributed to his confinement. Pasley, in his evidence before the Coroner, deposed that "His Lordship's situation and the circumstances which attended it contributed to lay the foundation of the disorder of which Lord Pigot died but this Informant cannot say whether in any situation his Lordship might not have been attacked with disorders." In the subsequent proceedings in the Sessions Court, when he was specifically asked whether Pigot's illness was due to his imprisonment, to natural causes or to imprudence, he replied, "The first part of the question I have already answered by ascertaining the causes of his Lordship's disease; as to the second, it was imagined and prophesied by everybody that his Lordship would sooner or later be attacked by some disease, owing to his exposing himself so much to the sun which indeed his friends always remonstrated against."

The Coroner's jury were not so hesitant in pronouncing a definite opinion. In one of the most lengthy charges that can ever have been delivered at an inquest, covering as it does 27 quarto pages, Mr. Ram put four questions to them; whether Lord Pigot died in confinement, whether his confinement was the cause of his death, whether his death was occasioned by rigorous treatment and, if so, what persons were responsible, and whether his confinement was legal or illegal. The verdict was that Stratton and his party and also Stuart, Eidingtoun, Lysaght and Horne, "not having the fear of God before their eyes but being moved and seduced by the instigation of the Devil," "the said George Lord Pigot, in manner and by the means aforesaid, feloniously, voluntarily and of their malice forethought, did kill and murder, against the peace of our said Lord and King his crown and dignity." The verdict was not unanimous as, though it was signed by all the members of the jury, two of them subsequently sent the Coroner qualifying notes. De Fries held the Pigot's death was not due to his confinement and that the offence was, therefore, not murder but manslaughter. Ewing refused to say more than that Pigot's confinement was the cause of his death and that "the seizure and imprisonment was a false and illegal seizure and imprisonment."

The verdict was signed on August 7th, but it is not surprising that Mr. Ram refrained from taking action on it so long as Stratton was in power. He had not long to wait for, on August 31st, after a journey *via* Suez which had taken the record time of 79 days, Mr. John Whitehill arrived with a despatch from the Court of Directors dated June 11th and written, of course, before they had heard of Pigot's death. The despatch restored him to the Governorship but "as his Lordship's proceedings appear to us in several Instances to be reprehensible," he was directed to hand it over to Mr. Thomas Rumbold, who was being sent out to succeed him, and to proceed to England. Stratton and his party were all suspended and recalled as was Benfield. Stuart was suspended for six months and Russell, Dalrymple and Stone were ordered to England.

Pigot, it may be noted, had suffered in a good cause. The Directors, anxious to prevent further scandals of such magnitude, reduced the number of Members of Council, excluding the Governor and the Commander in Chief, to five, forbade the Governor and the Members of Council from engaging in any financial or commercial transactions except on the Company's behalf, prohibited loans by any servant of the Company or any person under its protection "to any of the Country Powers or to any Person or Persons having commissions under or employed by them" and, to place them above temptation, fixed the salary of the Governor at 40,000 pagodas a year and that of the Members of Council at 16,000 pagodas.

Whitehill, on his arrival, found himself the only member of the new Council present in Madras but was allowed to enter into peaceful possession. He immediately summoned to Madras three of the Directors' nominees, Samuel Johnson and Peter Perring from Vizagapatam and Charles Smith from Ganjam, and meanwhile constituted a temporary Council, consisting of himself, Anthony Sadleir and Quintin Crauford, the two senior civil servants immediately available. The Council, in its capacity as a Court of Sessions, proceeded on September 25th to try Stratton and the other members of the late Government who had acted with him. They had been arrested on the Coroner's warrant which, with the jury's verdict, had been delivered in on the previous day. Stratton and his colleagues had a taste of the treatment they had meted out to Pigot but, after a fortnight's confinement, were released on bail. The Sessions Court wisely decided to apply to the Supreme Court of Bengal for advice but, in the meantime, started taking evidence. They had examined five witnesses, Sir Edward Hughes, his Secretary, Captain Marlow of H.M.S. *Coventry*, and the doctors, Pasley and Mallet, before the opinion of the Supreme Court was received. Stratton and his colleagues had also handed in the written defence already mentioned in which they alleged that Pigot's death was due partly to exposure to the sun and partly to "eating remarkably hearty of a turtle, an imprudence all the more remarkable as his Lordship was in general an exceeding moderate man." Stuart, now a Brigadier General, had prepared a separate defence for himself and the Army, the gist of which that everything that he and those under him had done had merely been under the orders of the Commander in Chief and the lawfully constituted Government.

Whitehill and his fellow Justices—in the course of the hearing Sadleir and Crauford had been replaced by Smith and Perring—must have been immensely relieved by the decision of the Supreme Court. That Court held that there was no such officer as a legal Coroner of Madras and, that consequently, the proceedings of the socalled Coroner's Court were null and void. Whilst it was the duty of a Grand Jury to determine whether Pigot's death was due to murder or manslaughter, they could not collect sufficient materials for an indictment either of murder or manslaughter. They added that, if a jury consisted of twelve members, its verdict must be unanimous. Acting on this opinion, the Sessions Court quashed all the proceedings on November 26th and released the prisoners. Stratton and Brooke left immediately for England *via* Anjengo.

The others, before following by sea from Madras, decided to bring a criminal action against Ram and Monckton but, at the earnest solicitation of the Government, were induced to delay and finally to abandon it. The story, so far as Madras is concerned, ends with a report from the Government to the Directors that "since the termination of the above prosecution, your Settlement hath gradually returned to its former tranquility and good order." There was, however, an aftermath in England for, in 1779, the House of Commons, on the motion of Admiral Pigot, Lord Pigot's brother, resolved on an address to the Crown praying for the prosecution of Stratton, Brooke, Floyer and Mackay who were then in England. They were ultimately convicted of misdemeanour and fined £ 1000 each.

A word may perhaps be said in conclusion about the subsequent history of two of the principal actors in this drama, Stuart and Benfield. When Stuart was suspended, the Directors ordered a Court of Enquiry into his conduct and that of Edingtoun, Horne and Lysaght, to be followed by a court martial, if necessary. Much to Stuart's annoyance, for he was anxious to be tried, Sir Hector Munro, who had become Commander in Chief, held that no military offence had been committed as, although Pigot held the chief military command in the Fort, his arrest took place outside it. Stuart remained under suspension throughout Rumbold's administration but, in November, 1780, obtained the court martial he had so ardently desired, was honourably acquitted and restored to his appointment as Second in Command. He lost a leg by a cannon ball at the Battle of Pollilore in August, 1781, but this did not prevent his succeeding Munro as Commander in Chief in 1782. The shade of Pigot must have smiled a smile of ironic satisfaction when, in 1783, he was recalled to Madras by Lord Macartney for systematic disobedience of orders, arrested in his garden house and deported to England. There, in June, 1786, he fought a duel with Macartney at Kensington. One learns with regret that it was Macartney who was seriously wounded.

Benfield, on reaching England, demanded an investigation into his conduct in regard to his loans to the Nawab. He emerged from it successfully and for the third time was restored to the service. According to Burke, he was as successful in boroughmongering as he had been in "soucaring" for, in 1780, he returned not only himself but seven other members to Parliament. He did not, however, take his seat for the pocket borough of Cricklade and the House of Commons did not, therefore, enjoy "the luxury of beholding that minion of the human race and contemplating that visage which has so long reflected the happiness of nations." One can well understand that Benfield preferred to avoid the House of Commons so long as Burke was in it. He came out again to Madras where he stayed until he left India for good in 1788. Ten years later, the firm of Boyd, Benfield and Co. which he had established failed and, like so many eminent financiers, he died in poverty—at Paris in 1810.

GOVERNOR GEORGE PIGOT

—By Courtesy of the Chaplain, St. Mary's Church, Fort St. George.

Notices of Madras in Two Sanskrit Works

By

Dr. V Raghavan, M.A.

Lecturer, University of Madras

I. THE VISVAGUNADARSA CHAMPU

Venkatadhvarin of Arasanippalai near Conjivaram was a well known poet of the latter half of the 17th century A.D. The most originally conceived work of his, the Visvagunadarsa Champu, a poetic composition in prose and verse, holds up the mirror to the universe. Two semi-divine beings of the Gandharva class take off in an aerial car, with a desire to see the whole of India. Krisanu, whose name itself means fire, passes under fire every thing he sees; Visvavasu, on the other hand, extols the virtues in all the things. The two proceed southwards from Badarikasrama. From Badari, they fly over Ayodhya and Kasi; from Kasi they fly to Puri (Jaggannath) on the eastern sea-coast; flying west from there, they scan the Gujara and Mahratta regions; they next criticise and praise respectively the Andhradesa and the Karnatadesa.

Leaving the Andhra and Karnata regions, the two Gandharvas proceed to places which poet Venkatadhvarin definitely considers as falling out of the boundaries of the Andhra desa, that is, places belonging to Dravida desa, which is described next. The first Tamil region which the two Gandharvas describe is Venkatagiri or Tiruppati.

From Tiruppati, the two pass to Ghatikachala, crossing forest tracts. Tiruvallur and God Viraraghava engage them next. Sriperumbudur is the next holy place reviewed by them. From Sriperumbudur, the two Gandharvas fly to Triplicane.

Triplicane or Tiru-alli-k-keni, the sacred lily tank, is called in Sanskrit Kairavini, Kairava meaning lily. The small tank which we now see in front of the Parthasarathi temple is not the Tiruvallikkeni or Kairavini described as the sacred lily tank(एषा कैरविणी विशल्यकरिणी). The Kairavini was there on the south of the present tank and temple, at the place where a new colony of houses called Vedavallipuram has now arisen. On reaching this sacred pond and the shrine of Parthasarathi on its bank, Visvavasu the good extols the place and its residents. Unable to appreciate this praise from his friend, Krisanu, the fault-finder, says:

"Kairavini may be holy, Parthasarathi's shrine more so, and the inhabitants pious, learned and honourable. But the merit of the place is vitiated by its proximity to the "Town" (nagara) which is full of objectionable inhabitants, chiefly white people (Huna) who are intent on destroying the good. Indeed, people more despicable than the white cannot be had. They are merciless; they think low of the Brahmanas but do not realise that their own national vices are beyond words, they being people who do not have the habit of properly washing themselves after answering calls of nature. It is indeed ununderstandable why providence is so perverse as to make these white people affluent." But Visvavasu insists that even in these objectionable white people, the existent virtues must be appreciated. Visvavasu pays an extravagant tribute to the high character of the white who, according to him, do not forcibly and illegally snatch others' wealth, do not speak falsehood, meet out just punishment to the offending and, above all, are capable of achieving wonderful things and manufacturing astonishing objects.

The Town mentioned by Venkatadhvarin as being near to and contaminating Triplicane is the Black Town and the Fort St. George. When through the mouth of Krisanu the poet speaks of the mercilessness of the behaviour of the English, the poet evidently has in mind the military character of their settlement. When he speaks of their insult to the Brahmanas, the poet is certainly thinking of the activities of Christian missionaries who were engaged in criticising Hinduism. In the eulogy of the English coming from Visvavasu's mouth, the feeling of security which people had after the troublous Muslim times of wars is apparent. Since plunder such as the Mohammedan chiefs and their forces did were not the rule with the English, the poet mentions that the English did not forcibly and unlawfully rob others of their possessions. The reference to their administration of justice is to the Choultry Court and the Mayor's court of those days in the Fort, which had already in 1652 settled a caste dispute between the Chettis and Nayudus. The miraculous objects which they are praised as capable of doing are evidently the military machines and other products possessed by them.

II. THE ANANDARANGA VIJAYA CHAMPU

The Anandaranga Vijaya, another Champu Kavya, was composed by poet Srinivasa in A.D. 1752. It celebrates the lives of Tiruvengadam Pillai of Perambur and his son, Anandarangam Pillai.[1]

1. I am preparing an edition of this work on the basis of a paper manuscript in the Madras Government Oriental Mss. Library and a palm-leaf ms. secured by Profs. K. A. Nilakanta Sastry and S. Vaiyapuri Pillai from the house of Anandarangam Pillai himself at Pondicherry.

ANANDARANGAM PILLAI

—*By courtesy of Professor G. J. Dubreuil.*

An ancestor of Aanandaranga named Garbhadharaka (Tamil கருவேந்தன்) was living at a place called Ayanapura. This Ayanapura is Ayanavaram, a village now to the south west of Perambur and south east of Villivakkam and about two miles from Perambur. Hearing of his munificence to poets Kumuda and others who visited him from Golconda, the King of Golconda, Makaranka, invited Garbhadharaka to his court and presented him the place called Vetrapura, i.e., Perambur, now part of Madras (Vetra பிரம்பு). Garbhadharaka moved to Perambur from Ayanavaram. In the Anandarangarat Chandamu[2], a Telugu work on Prosody, by Kasturi Rangayya, dedicated to Anandaranga, Ayanavaram is mentioned as situated in Pattana rajya.

According to the Anandaranga Campu and the Anandarangarat Chandamu, the Golconda king made Garbhadharaka the lord of Vetrapura. Love notes in his Vestiges of Old Madras (I. p. 82) that in, 'Perambore,' before it was granted to the British, *mirasi* right existed. It was the young and newly proclaimed Nawab of Arcot, Sahib jadda renamed Muhammad Sa'id, who, as a return for the British hospitality, granted them in 1742 five villages, one of which was 'Perambore.' (Love, vestiges II, pp. 284-285).

After shifting to Vetrapura or Perambore, Garbhadharaka begot three sons, Colaya (சோலை), Uttara (வடமலை), and Sridhara (திருமலை) Colāya married Alamelumanga and begot Bommaya. To Bommaya and Nayanamma were born twin sons Peda Bomma and China Bomma. The latter had six sons, the first of whom, Bommayya, married Ramanujamma and begot two sons and one daughter. The second son of Bommaya and Ramanujamma is Tiruvenkata, the father of Anandaranga, the hero of the Anandaranga Champu.

The Anandarangarat Chandamu gives a glowing account of Tiruvenkata's literary accomplishments. Tiruvenkata knew several foreign languages, French, English, Dutch, Portugese etc., could tackle any European and beat any 'Padre.' He had studied Christianity and would expound it to Christians. He was greatly efficient in mundane affairs, business and politics.

According to the Diary of Anandarangam Pillai, Tiruvenkata built a choultry at Perambur and founded a Brahmin village by its side. In the Anandaranga Campu, many charities of his and his ancestor, Garbhadharaka, are mentioned. The Campu says that, desirous of a male offspring, Tiruvenkata went on a pilgrimage to Tirupati and in the year Sarvadhari, Phalguna month, Anandaranga was born to him.

2. Edn. Vavilla Press, 1922.

The date of Anandaranga's birth is 30th March 1709. In Vijaya Dhanus, Sukla pratipat, Monday, Tulalagna, a second son named Venkata was born to Tiruvenkata.

Tiruvenkata's wife then died and after living for a time at Perambur, Tiruvenkata moved to *Cenna pattana* with his two sons. There he stayed in the city (Nagari) in the midst of merchants. There the Huna Chief (French-*Pramsu*) met him, and with a contract from him, Tiruvenkata did business on ship-borne articles like silks and spices. He became a favourite of the Huna chief and stayed in Madras for some time like this.

The Champu says that Tiruvenkata lived in town amidst the merchants. The place is evidently the Fort area. In a statement of the private property possessed by merchants within the Fort given in Love, we find three houses in the name of one Ranga Pillai (Vestiges, III, pp. 511), which is evidently Tiruvenkata's son Anandarangam Pillai. It was suggested to the Company that they might pay off compensation in cash to the merchants and make the Fort an entirely military area. This suggestion was turned down, but finally the shifting of some offices from the Fort to the Black Town resulted in the merchants migrating to the Black Town from the Fort. (Vestiges III, pp. 505, 523).

Tiruvenkata's brother-in-law, Nainiya Pillai, was doing trade as the chief native agent of the French at Pondicherry (*Nutana* or *Nava Pura*). At this suggestion and on the invitation of the then French Governor at Pondicherry, M. Hebert, Tiruvenkata, with some merchants of Madras, migrated to Pondicherry. Nainiya and Tiruvenkata made trade flourish at Pondicherry, but Hebert preferred certain charges against Nainiya, threw him into prison where, owing to ill-treatment Nainiya died. Nainiya's son Guruva Pillai or Guru Pillai and Tiruvenkata fled to Madras from where Guru Pillai reached France *via* England. In France, Guru reported about the conduct of Hebert to the regent, Duke of Orleans, and got Hebert home under restraint in 1719. From France Guru returned a Christian and head of the Indian subjects at Pondicherry. Even before he returned, M. de la Prevostiere, Hebert's successor, had induced Tiruvenkata, through a special messenger, to return to Pondicherry. The Champu says that when Tiruvenkata returned to Madras, he did so also because of his desire to see his sons whom he had left in Madras. When Tiruvenkata went to Pondicherry, he took another batch of Madras merchants with him. Guru Pillai died issueless in 1724. Tiruvenkata died in 1726. In 1726, September, M. Lenoir succeeded as Governor of Pondicherry and he appointed Tiruvenkata's son in the place held by his father.

The Champu then speaks elaborately of Anandaranga's marriage, his service under the French at Pondicherry and the part he played in the wars in which he helped Chanda Sahib (*Candra*) of Arcot (*Arkatika*) and Hira of Delhi against Nazir (*Nasara*), son of the Nizam, the Mahrattas and Anavardi Khan (*Anavardhi*); and in recognition of these military services the Delhi King, Ahmed Shah, awarded him the title Vajarata Raya. The Champu takes Anandaranga's life only up to this.

Anandaranga organised the French factory at Porto Novo (*Hunakheta*) and established factories at Lalapettai and Arcot; he was in power during the period of M. Dumas who succeeded in 1735 and M. Dupleix who made Anandaranga his chief Dubash. In 1754, when M. Godeheu succeeded, Anandaranga's influence was on the wane; he was not in office during his last days. He passed away on 12-1-1761.

Leaving Anandaranga's life at Pondicherry and his exploits, let us see what interest in respect of Madras the Champu Anandaranga Vijaya has.

THE NAME CHENNAPATTANA

When the Champu speaks of Tiruvenkata moving to Madras Town from Perambur, the work mentions the Town as Chennapattana.

तिरुवेङ्कटभूपालः कदाचित् चेन्नपट्टणम् ।
दिदृक्षुस्सात्मजः प्रोयाद:स्वसैन्यैरनुद्रुतः ॥

In the beginning of Chapter V the work describes Tiruvenkata's return to Madras from Pondicherry (along wih Guru Pillai), after the imprisonment and death of his brother-in-law Nainiya at Pondicherry. Here the work says that Tiruvenkata returned to *Chenna Kesava pura.*

"— प्रध्वस्तसाध्वसः चेन्नकेशवपुरमेत्य—"

Soon, M. de la Prevostere gets Tiruvenkata back to Pondicherry, sending him a special messenger. When Tiruvenkata goes back to Pondicherry, he takes with him a number of Madras merchants. And here again these Madras merchants are described as merchants of *Chenna Kesava pura.*

न्यायवृत्त्युदितश्रि चिराय स्व निषेवितुमंथो घतमारात्
आनिनाय स पुरं नव मे तत् चेन्नकेशवपुरायकसंघम् ॥

It has been generally supposed that the name Chennapattana borne by Madras commemorates Chennappa Nayudu, father of Damarla Venkatappa Nayudu, who made a gift of the Fort area in Madras to the

English. It is said that the donor desired that the fortified town which the English raised on the land should bear his father's name. It is true some descendants of Venkatappa Nayudu argued in their memorials that the town was named after their ancestor and that the story of the town being named after Chennappa, the donor's father, is found in some of the papers of the Company. But it must be noted that in Cogan's copy dated October 22nd, 1639, of the firman granted by Damarla Venkatendra Naik to Frances Day, the Grant for Madras (O.C. 1690) (William Foster, English Factories in India, 1637-1641, pp. 156-158), the Grant which permits the building of a fort in or about Madraspatam by the English, there is no mention of any desire or stipulation on the part of the donor that the new-built town must be named after his father Chennappa.

Henry Davison Love comes to the following conclusions regarding the name Chennapattana (Vestiges, I, pp. 83-85) :—

1. The Fort region must have had an original name, prior to Venkatappa Naiyaka's gift of the place to the English.

2. This original name may be Chinnapatam.

3. The assigned derivation from Chennappa was evolved later.

4. This designation Chinnapatam is found in the grant of 1644 relating to an endowment (by Naga Pattan) of the *Chenna Kesava Perumal temple.*

This Chennakesava Perumal Temple or the Great Pagoda stood originally in the Fort area, covering part of the site now occupied by the High Court. Records speak of only one temple, for Visnu.[3] It is after this temple of Cenna Kesava that the place was known as Cenna Kesava pattana or Chenna Kesava pura which was abbreviated into Chennapattana. It is therefore after God Chenna Kesava that the place got the name Chenna (Kesava) pattana, and not because, at the instance of Venkatappa, the name was given to the place to commemorate his father Chennappa. This is confirmed by the Anandaranga Champu.

3. This temple was destroyed and in 1762 the Chenna Kesava temple, along with Cenna Mallesvara temple, was rebuilt in its present place in China Bazar.

Some Old Madras Houses

By

M. D. Raghavan, B.A., Dipl. Anth. (Oxon),
Government Museum, Madras.

(i)

THE PANTHEON

Tracing the origin of the existing Museum Buildings on the Pantheon Road, the fact emerges that the original Pantheon, a place for public entertainments, for balls, banquets and theatricals in the days of the Company, was the nucleus from which developed the existing structure for long known as the Museum Old Building, a name which has a better historical association about it than the new name of Rear Buildings by which it is now named in the Museum reports. Known also as the Public Rooms or Assembly Rooms, the Pantheon had for years been the centre of the social life of the European settlement in the City, an association which it may be observed has in some measure been perpetuated down to our own day in the revues, entertainments and theatricals of the Madras Dramatic Society, who hold their performances in the Museum Theatre.

Our first peep into the mysteries of the Public Rooms is from an announcement published in the *Madras Courier* of 21st October 1789[1] which tells us that "the directors of the Female Asylum had unanimously resolved to signify to Sir Paul Jodrell by their Secretary, that it was desired Lady Jodrell should retire from her situation as Principal Directress of the Asylum, and that the Managers of the Public Rooms had also unanimously resolved to require, by their Secretary that Sir Paul Jodrell and his family should absent themselves from the Public Rooms until they vindicated themselves from the reports generally prevalent against them." This reference makes it clear that the Public Rooms must have been well established anterior to 1789. Mention is again made of the Public Rooms in the *Courier* of 18th May 1791[2] when in the course of an appeal for the cultivation of mulberry, Dr. Anderson included the gardens of the Public Rooms among the gardens in which the Board of Revenue should encourage the cultivation of the mulberry tree.

1. Col. H. D. Love: *Vestiges of Old Madras*, Vol. III, p. 362.
2. Col. H. D. Love: *Vestiges of Old Madras*, Vol. III, pp. 407-419.

At the Pantheon were entertained Lord Cornwallis on 10th October 1793, when Madras felicitated him on the success of his operations against Tippu Sultan; and Sir Arthur Wellesley in 1805[3] on his way home after Assaye, when he opened the ball with Lady William Bentinck.

The Pantheon has an interesting history behind the name. At the time when it figured in the pages of the *Madras Courier*, it was the property of Hall Plummer, who is referred to as a civil servant and contractor for Public Works, a combination too strange to comprehend at the present day, to whom the grounds on which the Pantheon was later built, were assigned on 21st August 1778 by Governor Thomas-Rumbold on behalf of the Company.[4] The site bounded on the North-east and North-west by paddy fields and on the South-west and on South-east by roads, now known as the Casamaijor's Road, and the Hall's Road, was no doubt much more extensive than the compound in which the Museum buildings now stand. In 1793 Hall Plummer, who had built a mansion and planted a garden, assigned the property to a number of gentlemen, mostly civil servants and officers of the Army, among whom was James Brodie of Brodie Castle associations. The Pantheon and its grounds again changed hands, certain gentlemen constituting the Pantheon Committee disposing of the property to Mr. Edward Samuel Moorat, a wealthy Armenian merchant whose name is linked with the property now known as the Moorats Gardens, on the other side of the Anderson Bridge.

The document shows that several plots of the original ground had been sold, the residue being substantially the present Museum Compound, bounded on the east by Pantheon Road, on the west by Hall's Road and on the North and South by plots of garden houses. The property which thus passed on to E. S. Moorat on 26th March 1821 was finally purchased from the latter by the Government for Rs. 28,000.[5] Allotted first as the Collector's cutcherry, the Government Central Museum which had by then been formed at the College[6] of the Fort St. George, was moved to it in 1854.

3. Sir James Thomson, *Jour. of the Soc. of Arts*, March 29, 1907, p. 536.

4. Col. H. D. Love: *Vestiges of Old Madras*, Vol. III, p. 419.

5. Col. H. D. Love: *Vestiges of Old Madras*, Vol. III, p. 421.

6. A misleading name, as the College of Fort St. George was for long located in the property which originally belonged to Dr. James Anderson, and who had developed the extensive grounds into a botanical garden which formed part of the site of the present property of Pycroft's Gardens and Tullock's Gardens. The College for junior Civil Servants was later transferred to the 'Old College' building on the purchase of that property from E. S. Moorat in 1827.

We are indebted to that writer of contemporary events, Rev. William Taylor[7] for an illuminating account of the Pantheon, an account which is of particular interest for the attempt it makes to demarcate the outlines of the Pantheon, within the fabric of the Museum building in which it is so inextricably merged. Here is the picture he draws :—

"Soon after being occupied as a Museum, two wings, with two interior spacious apartments were added. To come at the original building you have to remove the colonnade or porticoe, the upper storey, and lastly the two sides, leaving only a small lodge on either side; and then the old building will remain which was once called the Pantheon, a building by no means handsome in exterior appearance, but erected more for use than show. In that state it was once the Land Customs House or Cutcherry. Visiting it in that state, you would have gone up a few steps into a large oblong hall; going out at the end, a narrow platform would conduct you to some steps, leading up to another oblong hall, with a room on the south side to which you would descend by steps. This style of construction was for the purposes of a Theatre. The entrance hall was for the audience; the broken space was filled in by the orchestra, the hall above was for the stage, green room and Manager's apartment."

A description indeed which cannot be improved, but which is not so easy of application, for the building has undergone further changes since Mr. Taylor's days, which no doubt accounts for the fact that his description, not supported by a plan, scarcely enables the reader to feel his way through the present labyrinth, and pick out the Pantheon in its outline. For the origin of the building, Taylor takes us back to the closing days of the eighteenth century, " when Madras was very Grecian in taste, Grecian couches, with chintz covers, printed with uncial Greek letters, Grecian tripods and lampadas; of course plays also. A considerable number of civilians and officers had been smitten in early life with Garrick's and Kemble's performances and were stage-struck themselves. It became necessary to build a theatre, and it was done. A stage Manager was commissioned from England; and a Mr. Rowbotham was imported in that capacity. By his instructions the roof over the stage was laid with iron grooves so that a heavy cannon shot being rolled over them produced a mock thunder."

Glyn Barlow tells us that " the Government lodged the geological specimens in the Collector's Cutcherry—a house which forms part of the Museum buildings of to-day."[8] Adapted for its new function of housing

7. Rev. William Taylor (W. T. Munro), *The Madrasiana*, pages 84-85.
8. Barlow: *The Story of Madras*, page 109.

the Museum and enlarged beyond recognition, the Pantheon is swallowed up in the Museum buildings, and what remains of it is acknowledged to be the centre part of the ground floor of the Old Building. The name of the Pantheon survives in the Pantheon Road which sets a riddle to every one acquainted with it, to find the Pantheon.

(ii)

BRODIE CASTLE

A civil servant of the Company, James Brodie was undoubtedly an outstanding charter in early European society. Like many a fellow servant of the Company, he also engaged himself in business on his own, the name Jarvis and Brodie, apparently denoting the firm under which name he carried on commercial transactions. He figured as one of the many gentlemen to whom Hall Plummer on 1st December 1793 assigned the Pantheon and its grounds, a body of men who later constituted the Pantheon Committee, responsible for the management of the Pantheon, the centre of the social life of the city.

When towards the close of the eighteenth century private trade by public servants was absolutely forbidden, he was one of the civil servants, who was called on to resign the service or withdraw from commercial pursuits. What he elected to do is not known. We are told that his commercial prosperity did not long continue, and his firm failed, though he was still a gentlemen of means and led a comfortable life. We are indebted to Rev. William Taylor for the picture he gives us of the man and his life, which is of particular interest as the account of a contemporary writer. Mr. Taylor speaks of him thus, "I often saw Mr. Brodie, he being a regular attendant on the morning Sunday service at St. Mary's in the Fort. He was rather tall and slender ; with a calm placid countenance, of fine complexion but pale. He wore powdered hair with a *queue* behind, a sky blue coat, with two or three large cloth buttons and a collar with lappets—in the fashion of the close of 1790 odd." He married Miss Ann Storey in 1790, and his daughter Isabella was married to Captain Archibald Patullo of the Madras Cavalry.

On the bank of the Adyar stands the house which bears his name, Brodie Castle, built on a grant of land 11 acres in extent, assigned to him by the Company in 1796 on the Quibble Island, an extensive area originally an island formed by two branches of the Adyar River. The house is large, embanked by sloping walls, with two castellated turrets on the north front and entrance. Following the reverses in his fortune, he let his house on rent, and with the favoured situation it presented on the bank of the river, the house has never been in want of tenants of the highest station in life. Beginning with Sir Thomas Strange the first

THE BRODIE CASTLE, ADYAR

Chief Justice of the Supreme Court, the house has been the residence of a long line of civilians down to the present day among whom number many a member of the Government. Sir Thomas Strange seems to have been followed by Archdeacon Vaughan. In the intervals when the house fell vacant, Brodie went to stay in his house. He could not resist the call of the river and he grew fond of boating. Report has it that his wife one night had an alarming dream, and cautioned him against going out on the river. Brodie did not pay heed to the warning, went out as usual and was drowned. Taylor has an interesting comment on the incident, and inculcates a lesson that a wife's caution to her husband founded on a dream is salutary, and should command respect,—which it perhaps should.

(iii)

LEITH CASTLE

In San Thome to the South-east of the Cathedral stands the house known as Leith Castle, after James Leith, who entering the Army in 1781, became Major-General in 1825, and died in Madras in 1829, after serving as Judge Advocate-General for nearly thirty years. In the grounds of the house may be seen what remains of the San Thome Redoubt, executed in 1751 "as a refuge for the garrison of Mylapore." The erection of small suburban forts or redoubts was part of the Company's plan for the protection of the outlying quarters of the city. Of such suburban fortifications the two largest were the Egmore and San Thome redoubts. Designed as additions to what was called the Moore's Bungalow on the site, the San Thome redoubt cost the Company a large sum of money. Judging from the ruins which consist of a square keep, having walls fifteen feet high and three feet thick, the redoubt must have been a well fortified place, and with a moat forty feet wide, a glacis, and all other appurtenances of a fort, it was indeed no mean fortification.

It was only two years previous to the building of the redoubt that the Company had come into the possession of San Thome, as a result mainly of a clever move on the part of Admiral Boscawen. San Thome which had developed from a seventeenth century Portuguese settlement into a town of considerable size, fell a prey to successive invaders, who ruled over it in different periods of its history. At about the time of the building of the Redoubt, San Thome had become part of the dominions of the Nawab of the Carnatic following the break up of the Mughal empire. After the hostilities between the French and the English were suspended in 1749, Dupleix recognising the strategic importance of the place decided to make a French settlement of it. Admiral Boscawen coming to know of his intentions, struck on the ingenious plan of occupying it in the name of the Nawab Muhammad Ali. The plan succeeded and the Nawab enjoined on all to pay due allegiance to the English. The English flag was hoisted at San Thome on 11th October 1749. The Portuguese lost no time to claim San Thome as the dominion of the King of Portugal, a claim which was disregarded.

That the Company's efforts in fortifying the place were justified is evident from the service it gave during the sixty-seven days of the Siege of Madras by Count De Lally in 1759, and its capacity may be judged from the fact that Captain Preston was directed to stay in the San Thome fort with the Europeans belonging to Chingleput, four companies of sepoys and fifty horse.

Following the siege of Madras, the San Thome Redoubt was not cared for, as is evident from the fact that at the end of the eighteenth century, it was already in ruins when Colonel Brathwaite applied to the Company for a grant of the site, which was accordingly granted. The present residence was apparently built by him. After him, the ownership of the house seems to have been a matter of considerable doubt, for though called after Major Leith, it is marked " Mr. Parry's " in a survey of 1802, the property to the north of it being shown as Major Leith's. while in a map of 1822 the house is marked " Mr. T. Parry's castle,"—presumably Thomas Parry who came out as a free merchant in 1788 and founded the firm now known as Parry & Co. The house no doubt underwent modifications from time to time,—marked circular in 1822, it has become pentagonal as shown in a map of 1837.

(iv)

ADMIRALTY HOUSE

For a student of history fresh from the College to find his lot cast within the four walls of the Fort St. George is not a bad beginning in life. Such was my feeling when on a cold wet morning in November 1913, I found my way to the Fort St. George on appointment as a clerk in the Chief Secretariat. The Secretariat buildings, the old Fort House, occupy perhaps the most commanding position of all buildings in the Fort, flanking the parade ground from north to south, with the flag staff behind, over which flies the Union Jack, with the lofty spire of St. Mary's church raising its head high on the right. The neighbourhood of St. Mary's was gratifying, as during the luncheon interval one could get an occasional glimpse of its beautiful interior with its historic treasures. Any visitor to St. Mary's cannot but be struck as I was, by the high imposing structure that is the Accountant-General's Office, with its beautiful Corinthian capitals, facing St. Mary's. That both the Accountant-General's office and the Secretariat are located in the Fort, is perhaps no mere accident, for the association of the two offices is more intimate than is the case with any other two offices in the City. Auditing and control of accounts go hand in hand with any administration, and the first thing that the Secretariat clerk does is to refer any "current" to the Accountant-General for remarks.

To trace the history of this building which has so much of what the Greeks call the *symmetria prisca* about it, one must delve deep indeed into the early history and development of the Fort. That Robert Clive once occupied the house seems to be fairly well known, but that is almost the only thing known about it. While this association of the house with Lord Clive is sufficient to class it as a historical building, it is not indeed the only interesting or the most interesting fact about it. Tracing the ownership of the building, it is soon revealed to us as one of the buildings which we owe to the Armenians, to whom in 1688 the Company granted special privileges to settle and trade in British towns in India, "on the same terms as English freemen and possess all rights enjoyed by British subjects." The Armenians were not long in reaping the full benefit of this agreement, and the fine building in Charles Street now accommodating the Accountant-General's Office appears to have first been the residence of a wealthy Armenian merchant Nazar Jacob Jan. That the Company did not pursue a uniform policy in regard to the Armenians and other foreigners in White Town is clear, for in 1743 the Council resolved that "considering how large a part of the White Town is already in the possession of foreigners," no persons other than "the natural subjects of the King of Great Britain should in future acquire property within the walls except with the permission of the Government." The house had in the meanwhile passed on to Shawmier Sultan son of Sultan David, and on behalf of his father and himself, Shawmier petitioned that they be permitted to continue in the White Town. In refusing his request the Company directed that "for the future no Armenian whatsoever be allowed to inhabit the White Town; and that such of them as at present possess houses there do forthwith dispose of them to European Protestants". Not longer after, to be precise in November 1749, Shawmier "received instructions from Fort St. David through Stringer Lawrence, to refrain from selling the property as it might be required by the Company." At about this time, the Company having ordered that Fort St. George should be subordinate to Fort St. David, the Council appointed Mr. Richard Prince to be Deputy Governor of Fort St. George, who was thus in residence in the "Great House in Charles Street" during the whole term of his Deputy Governorship.

That the owner had no little difficulty to recover the rent for the occupation of the house from the 17th November 1749 to 10th July 1752, is clear from the number of petitions he had to make, in one of which he lets us into the interesting information that among the persons who occupied it was Colonel Clive. The conclusion is thus drawn that "the building was restored to Shawmier in July 1752 after which he let it to Clive and others." Though the house was ultimately acquired by the Company, there is no record of the date of purchase nor whether he was the immediate seller. The surmise is that in obedience to the Company's orders against Armenian ownership of White Town property, he sold it to David Lopez Fernandes and Samuel De Castro, from whom it was bought, for it is recorded that Pigot's Government bought in the beginning of 1755, a large house in Charles Street to provide for the accommodation and reception of visitors of rank and distinction.

During all these vicissitudes, it was just "the Great House in Charles Street," and had not come to be known as the Admiralty House, by which high sounding name it was later known. The Company having obtained early a charter from King Charles authorising the erection of Courts of Admiralty "to deal with interlopers," a court of Admiralty had been established in 1686 with Sir John Biggs as a Judge-Advocate. The Court apparently functioned for some years "for the trial of fugitives and pirates," after which nothing was heard of until July 1755, when it was "Agreed that a Court of Admiralty be held at the Company's house in Charles Street for the trial of certain mutineers." The house in Charles Street has since come to be styled Admiralty House—, a title first quoted in a return of buildings made by Mr. Call in May 1758. In 1762 the House was fully furnished "for the reception and accommodation of strangers, a house keeper being appointed to superintend the establishment." Though the house has thus become the property of the Company, the latter had not settled the arrears of rent due to Shawmier Sultan, who in 1773 when Alexander Wynch was the Governor once more petitioned "for payment of the rent of the house and godowns in Charles Street, now Admiralty outstanding since 1752." To the great relief, no doubt, of the distressed owner, the Honourable the Court of Directors to whom the petition was forwarded, finding that circumstances appeared strong in favour of his claim, resolved that he be paid the rent charged by him.

As Col. Love concludes, "later in the century the Admiralty house became the Governor's town residence, and in Lord Clive's time (Edward, Lord Clive, Governor of Madras 1799 to 1803) it was used for the celebration of State functions until the present Banqueting Hall was erected." Not only is it now utilised as the office of the Accountant General, it is also labelled as such on the wall in bold black letters, an obtrusive label on a historical building.

The name Admiralty house is also applied to another residence, a large house on the coast road running South from San Thome, towards

THE ICE HOUSE, TRIPLICANE

the Adyar side. Reputed to have been the residence of the Admiral of the East Indian fleet, it is now the property of the Maharaja of Vizianagaram. It was here that Admiral Rainier entertained the Nawab of the Carnatic in 1805.

(v)

THE ICE HOUSE

The visitor to the Marina cannot escape noticing a high circular building enclosed by a high wall. There is nothing very pleasing about the structure altogether different in character from the more modern buildings which grace the Marina. The high walls give it a prison-like look, and many a stranger wonders what purpose it served and what purpose it serves now. This was the old Ice House, after which the road running to the west of it is called, Ice House Road.

In the days when Madras was not favoured by the ice factories that it now has, and refrigerators were unknown, the idea was conceived of importing ship loads of blocks of ice from America. We may be sure that the scheme was a success. A large building was erected close to the sea which then was nearer to the shore than it now is, and the cargo of ice was brought in sailing ships in huge blocks from the West and landed in boats and stored in the Ice House. This seems to have been about 1840, when the Company were well established on the Coromandel Coast. Selling at 4 annas the pound, large quantities of the ice were sold, and the business prospered.

Ice factories were in due course opened, and the need stopped for imported ice. The business of bringing ice in ship loads from overseas thus coming to an end, the Ice House was soon closed. It was later turned into a residence, by whom we do not know, but that it did not find much favour as a residence is obvious, despite the improvements which the purchaser carried out, including the placing of numerous windows in the circular walls. Failing as a house, it was tried as a free hostel or a temporary abode for religious teachers or preachers, who resorted to the city. Not long after, it was again deserted.

At present it fulfils the purpose of a Widow's Home, for which benevolent purpose the Government acquired it. Surely the inmates who pass their lives within it, deserve a better place in life, a place with better warmth and greater cheer than what the dull walls of the Ice House can give them.

A History of Some Place-Names of Madras

By

Professor V. Rangacharya, M.A.,
Madras

I propose to trace in the present paper the historical evolution of the place-names connected with two of the conspicuous areas of Madras, namely, the Mount Road Zone, and Egmore.

Section I.

THE MOUNT ROAD

Historically speaking the Mount Road goes back to pre-British times. It was an ancient thoroughfare leading from the region where Madras was afterwards to rise, but where places like Mylapore, Egmore and Tiruvorriyur had existed for many centuries, to Chingleput and other parts of historic Tondaimandalam. But under the caption *Mount Road* it came to figure in the life-history of Madras from the close of the 17th century when the St. Thomas Mount, already rich in historic associations Hindu, Muslim and Portuguese, became a favourite resort among the early servants of the East India Company. In 1651, Agent Greenhill came to the Mount for hawking. In 1685 the Council purchased a garden house for the sick and disabled who were in need of pure air for recuperation. By 1750 there arose a number of garden houses which belonged to Englishmen, and they found there all the necessary amenities of secular and spiritual life owing to the association of the place with the European life for nearly a century and a half. One of the garden houses at the Mount belonged to Major Lawrence.

From the time when, in the course of the 17th century, the Company came to appreciate the Mount as a sanitorium and health resort, and to acquire sites for residence there, the Mount Road, leading from the Fort to it, became an important thoroughfare. There were, in fact, in those days two well-known highways, one leading from the Fort to Poonamallee, and the other to Chingleput through the Mount. The Company's troops were the first to use them.

Another circumstance which favoured the growth of the Mount Road as a busy centre of British activity was the rise of the Government House at Guindy in the last few years of the 17th century. The real meaning of the term *Guindy* is rather obscure. It had been translated as a basin or depression, and it was apparently a region of gardens in those times. It was Governor Thomas Pitt (1698-1709) that was responsible for the growth of the Government House at Guindy. There were two residences for the Governor then outside the Fort—one on the Cooum sanctioned by Government in 1678, and the other at Guindy. The latter was generally preferred. According to one account Guindy Park, with a residence in it, was got by the Company in 1695 from Chinna Venkatadry, a wealthy merchant who was related to the Company's broker Timmanna and who was also a partner in the firm of Timmanna and Viranna; but "no historical proof has been found that Guindy and Chinna Venkatadry's gift are identical." Thomas Pitt was fond of gardening, and did much for the Guindy Park. Being much more convenient than the Government House at Madras, Guindy became more popular; and it was naturally made accessible by a good system of road-connections with the neighbourhood.

An event which took place in 1726 added one great convenience to the Mount Road as a highway of traffic. Seeing that both the Little Mount and St. Thomas Mount were favourite objects of pilgrimage to the Catholic Christians, Europeans, Eurasian and Indian, the great Armenian merchant Petrus Uschan, who is intimately associated with commercial and religious history of early 18th century Madras, built at his own expense the great bridge over the Adyar between Saidapet and Guindy. It is generally known as the Marmalong Bridge, *Marmalong* being a corruption of *Mambalam,* the suburb of Madras which in those days extended to this area. One of the two pillars flanking the south of the bridge has a tablet in which there is an inscription recording Uscan's construction of the bridge in 1726. Petrus Uschan's name is also connected with the religious history of Mylapore, the Mount and Madras City itself.

CHOULTRY PLAIN AND THE MOUNT ROAD

One of the terms figuring in the records of the East India Company from about 1721 onward on account of the growing expansion of Madras is the Choultry Plain. It is a general name given to the sandy area, spotted here and there with little hamlets, between the sea in the east and the winding course of the Cooum and the Long or Mylapore Tank in the west; and between the Government House Bridge in the north to the Zenotaph Road corner of the Mount Road at Teynampet in the south. The limits are represented by the Government House Bridge, the Long Tank, the Zenotaph Road corner, and the High Road running from the present Walajah Road through Triplicane towards Mylapore. The region included the present area of Puduppakam, East Chintadripet, Rayapettah, Nungambakkam and Teynampet in the main. Egmore, Chepauk and even Triplicane are sometimes included in the term

Choultry Plain, but they had their growth under independent circumstances. In a word, the area on both sides of the Mount Road comprised the Choultry Plain. It had its name from the fact that there was, in those days, an old choultry called *Uddandi* (Woodundy) just opposite to Mackay's Garden.

Like the obscure pathways between the local hamlets, this part of the Mount Road was quiet and eventless till, from about 1740 onward, it became a favourite resort for the construction of Anglo-Indian country houses. The White Town in the Fort had become crowded by that time. The Company's servants needed places for residence where they could have plenty of space, breeze and quietness. There was no beach road then. The nearest road to the Beach was the Triplicane High Road, which was half a mile inland. A few European garden houses had risen in Peddanayakanpet and its vicinity, but the acquisition of the other suburban villages made that area less and less popular. So from about 1740 onward, a group of mansions arose in the plain which stretched south of 'the Triplicane Bridge.' When, in 1752, the Company purchased from Mrs. Madeiros the chief portion of the present Government House, the area traversed by the Mount Road came naturally to be from that time the chief building region of the future.

At the time when the Mount Road began to be busy, its alignment immediately to the south of the Triplicane Bridge as the Government Bridge was then called, was a little different from what it is at the present day. The river itself was at the bridge which, Col. Love suggests, was partly a causeway, in two channels, with a low marshy island in between. The road further south was not direct as at present, but passed the back of the Government Garden House which had just been acquired from Mrs. Madeiros. To the east of the bridge, and before reaching the Governor's Garden, there was a guard-house, with the residence of Mr. Henry Powney close behind. This Henry Powney was the son of Captain John Powney who died in 1740, and whose family vault is seen in the old Black Town Cemetery to the west of the High Court and adjacent to the Law College. Close to the Governor's House, in the south, there was the residence of a Captain John Standard, "a seafaring man who had been in India since 1710, came to Madras from Bombay before 1733," and then owned the house at Chepauk above-mentioned. Captain Standard had settled as a Free Merchant like Mackay and many others who were the pioneers in the great Anglo-Indian scheme of garden houses which have made Madras not only beautiful and healthy but a city of distances. East or south-east of the Government House there was a walled garden with the residence of a Signora Estra Gregorio, occupied probably at this time by Alexander Wynch, a prominent Civil Servant, who was later on Governor from 1773 to 1775. Estra Gregorio's house must have been a little far off from the Mount Road corner; for it has been described as having been in the Mile's end, that is Chepauk. The lady figures in the Company's records for the first time in September 1729, when she was fined for making bad bread. The history of her residence is connected with that of Chepauk.

Another noteworthy point in the alignment of the Mount Road about 1750 was that it passed from the south-western angle of the Government Garden, that is, the spot where the present Walajah Road (which came into existence a few years later) meets the Mount Road, right westward to the site of the present Harris Bridge (which was built a century later, that is, in 1854), and then ran in the south-eastern direction till it joined it in the present junction of General Patter's Road.

PUDUPPAKKAM

An important point to be understood in regard to the development of the Mount Road is the rise of the crowded division called Puduppakkam. It covered the region to the north and west of Tiruvateesvaranpet (which had been just formed) in the angle formed between the High Road leading from that village to the Mount Road, the Mount Road itself, and the White's or Peter's Road in the south. First mentioned in the Company's records in 1673, 'Podupaca' or 'Podupacka' was obtained from the Nawab, after a long period of negotiations, in 1742. Young Nawab Muhammad Sayyid, who had just come to the *gadi* after a period of revolutions and convulsions, gave it, together with several other villages, in gratitude for the Company's sympathy, for a rent of about 105 pagodas. The Killedar of Poonamallee actually handed it over only after 1744. The village then became a favourite site for country residences. Its southern limit was that which was known as Lord Pigot's Road. This designation, points out Col. Love, is no longer in use; and he suggests that it must have been either White's Road or Peter's Road, preferably the former, as it had probably existed as a highway from Triplicane to the Mount Road from early times. It came to be so called at the close of the 18th century from Captain Thomas Peters who died in 1798.

The earliest residence to come into existence at Puduppakkam was Mackay's Garden, which was named after Mr. George Mackay, a Free Merchant, who came to Fort St. George about 1738, became Mayor in 1756, and a contractor for supply and transport to the Army in 1760. From a record of 1758, we find that he asked the President and Council for the lease of a piece of ground for constructing a house, and that it was granted to him on a 99 years' lease on his payment of a fee of 30 pagodas, together with the undertaking to pay a rent of 1 pagoda per annum. At the expiration of the 99 years, the ground, with all buildings and improvements, was to revert to the Company. There are two separate properties in this region called Mackay's Garden, one being to the north of the 'Thousand Lights,' and the other a little further to the north-east off on the Graeme Road which leads to Nungambakkam. The former was the one acquired by George Mackay, as the latter was occupied by paddy-fields till as late as 1798. It may be added that Mr. Mackay went to England in 1761, and returned to Madras in 1766 as the member of Council. He held then the post of Assay-Master as well. In 1776 Mr. Mackay took part in the factions which led to the deposition of Lord Pigot, and was suspended by the Directors, and recalled to England. According to one version he received, like many others, a bribe of a lakh of rupees from Nawab Walajah for his part in the Pigot affair. In 1779, Mackay was, together with four of his colleagues, prosecuted at the instance of Parliament, convicted of misdemeanour, and fined £1,000. George Mackay had acquired the ground for his house before his first departure to England in 1761, and constructed his residence about 1758-9. On his death in England it was occupied by his son, Alexander George Mackay, and he sold it to the Nawab Walajah. The garden occupied in 1798 a much larger space than it does at present, and was occasionally known as Azeembagh. The latter name was obviously due to Nawab Azimu-d-daula, Walajah's grandson (1801-19). The extensive character of the Mackay Gardens, establishment can be gauged from the fact that James Taylor, the executor of Mackay's estate, claimed compensation for the damages caused by its temporary occupation by the army during Haidar's invasions to the extent of 491 pagodas on items like the replacement of 400 reapers in the tile-house, 9 windows in 'the Slave Boys' godowns,' 3 windows in the pigeons' house, etc.

In December 1759, Captain Charles Tod, Town Major and Commandant of the Sepoys, received a lease of ground on the Choultry Plain on the same terms as Mr. George Mackay. The Directors, on this occasion, wrote to Fort St. George to the effect that they did not like such grants, as they were not made for utilitarian purposes but for show and vanity which they did not approve. They were particularly dissatisfied with Mackay's grandeur and expensiveness, and thought that such large-scale luxury was not expected except in the case of the Governor and 'principal persons.' But circumstances were stronger than the Directors' remonstrances, and the number of garden houses rose everywhere. A record of 1774 says that, out of 30 grants of lease grounds during that year, no less than 11 were at Puduppak, the rest being at Veerasanur to the southwest of it, and elsewhere.

Another person who got a lease of six acres for an annual rent of one pagoda was Reynold Adams, a Free Merchant who came in 1764 and who afterwards became Master Attendant. He owned a house in the Fort and another in 'the parish of St. Thomas,' that is, San Thome as well. His Puduppakkam garden was to the north of the east end of Lord Pigot's Road.

A better known figure and owner of a garden at Puduppakkam was Patrick Ross, the celebrated engineer who carried out, in the last quarter of the 18th century, the reconstructions of the Fort in its final form, as well as the General Hospital which has been replaced by later structures. Ross got 10 acres at Puduppakkam on the Choultry plain 'opposite to Pigot's Road,' and probably came thither from a house which he had been occupying in the Luz.

Still another leaseholder was James Taylor, a Civil Servant from 1764, who became in course of time Senior Merchant, Assistant Assay-Master, and Registrar of Mayor's Court. As Assay-Master, Taylor had an allowance of 2,000 pagodas per year; and this was only a small fraction of his earnings. In 1790 Taylor became the acting Justice of the Mayor's Court, and in his time took place an interesting incident in connection with slave traffic. Taylor's resources can be realised from the fact that he lent a lakh of rupees to the Nawab of the Carnatic. He rented 8 acres at Puduppakkam for 2 pagodas per annum in 1773. It is said to have lain "to the southward of the avenue leading from the Mount Road to Mr. Stratton's garden and near the Brick Kilns." James Taylor, Junior, who became Civil Servant in 1795 gave his name to a road at Kilpauk. George Stratton, Thomas Powney, John Holland, Edward Monckton, Colonel Cosby, James West, 'Cawn Saib' (Abdur Rashid Khan), and probably John Sulivan, similarly came to have garden residences.

The rise of numerous houses on either side of the Mount Road and in Puduppakkam led naturally to the perfection of the road from the standpoint of engineering. Col. Sydenham, for example, is said to have 'completed' it in 1788. We have to take 'completed' in the loose sense, and interpret it as 'repaired' and strengthened. Two years earlier, that is, in 1786, a convenience had been added to the road in the form of a bridge over the channel which flowed across it carrying the surplus water of the Long or Mylapore Tank. There is, in front of the Lushington Garden at Saidapet a monument in the form of an obelisk standing on a square basement with inscriptions on four sides—English, Tamil, Latin and Persian. The inscription which is in 23 lines, bears date 1786, and is to this effect:

This bridge erected as a public benefit from a legacy bestowed by M. Adrian Fourbeck, merchant of Madras, is a monument useful as lasting of the good citizen's munificent liberality. It was erected by his executors T. Pelling, J. de Fries, and P. Bodkin from the plan and under the direction of Lieu.-Col. Patrick Ross, Chief Engineer, in the year of Our Lord, 1786. Major General Sir Archibald Campbell, Knight of the Most Hon'ble Order of the Bath, being then Governor of Fort St. George.

Adrian Fourbeck, whose generosity was the cause of the bridge, had an interesting history. He was an old resident of Madras, who died in 1783 and was buried in the Roman Catholic Church in Armenian Street.

An inscription, dated in 1790, on the corner stone of an old building near the Harris Bridge which has 'lately been converted to the use of the Post-Master General,' tells us that it was built in that year. The inscription is in Persian and it is to the effect that when the exalted shadow of God conceived loyally to do good deeds, the data for its foundation was prayed from Khizr the Wise and He answered: *'The bountiful canal of Walajah,'* which, in the numerical value of the letters, means 1790. The bountiful canal was undoubtedly the Cooum, and the beautiful work was apparently the building near the Harris Bridge, which was erected on a piece of land purchased in 1779 as a Persian deed of sale in the Madras Deputy Collector's office indicates, and completed in 1784 as a Tamil version shows. The building was in later days the business place of Messrs. Lewis Milner & Co., then of Messrs. Spencer and Co., and still later the office of the Madras Survey, to be eventually taken over, as has been already said, by the Postal Department. Nawab Walajah who owned as many as 37 houses in different parts of the city, giving rise thereby to considerable legal embarassments, had this building as only one of his properties in the Mount Road.

There was, for example, the Amir Bagh, built by Nawab Walajah and occasionally lent to Governor Clive for public entertainments. It became later on the Court of Suddar Adalat, then Agra Bank and then Elphinstone Hotel. A slightly later building was the Umda Bagh which is mentioned in the survey map of 1798. It was probably named after Umdat-ul-Umara the Nawab (1795-1801). It is the place where the Madrasa-i-azam is now situated. It became, in 1807, the property of Kola Singanna Chetty, a rich and public-spirited business man who owned the Pawney House in the fort, which was worth 10,000 pagodas. Singanna Chetty's name has been perpetuated by a set of three streets and two lanes at Chintadripet and by a short but broad road connecting Sunkuvar Agraharam with Wallers Road in the immediately adjoining part of Tiruvateeswaranpet Division. He left a number of charities which are even now administered by the Accountant General. After 1822, the Umda Bagh became the residence, first of Mr. E. S. Moorat and then of the Begam of the last titular Nawab of the Carnatic, Ghulam Muhammad Ghaus (1825-

55). To this place was shifted after 1901 Madrasa-i-azam, literally the school of Azam named after the Nawab who had the poetic title of Azam. It was the chief Muslim educational institution in South India, and it was taken over by Government under its management in 1859.

In 1795-6 'a reform of the Road' was in progress and, as the records say, a constant stream of carts were under the Chief Engineer's Service. This 'reform' seems to have been only the repairing and gravelling of the road. The author of the *Vestiges* observes: "There could have been little change in the alignment of the ancient highway but the work may perhaps have consisted in refounding, metalling and draining. Colonel Gent proposed the construction of parapet walls 'on the long bridge near the Governor's Garden', but Government intimated that repairs of the old teak railings would suffice.

In 1798 an important diversion of the road was made immediately after the bridge on account of the necessity to improve the Government House. At the instance of Lord Clive not only was provision made for the improvement of the Governor's residence and reception room, but the huts which then existed to the west of the main building and which were a source of great nuisance were removed after payment of compensation to the owners; and the old "crooked alignment which is depicted on the map of 1798, between the Triplicane Bridge and the junction with Peter's Road, was made straight, and a considerable area was thus added to the Government Garden on its west side."

Another improvement of the period was the opening of the Binny's Road, the short thoroughfare connecting the Mount Road with the Commander-in-chief's Bridge, which was then a causeway. It derived its name from John Binny whose residence afterwards became the Imperial Hotel, the Spencer & Co., and the Connemara Hotel. The Binny family had a close connection with the Madras of the 18th century. The earliest was a Charles Binny who came to India in 1769 without license. We do not know anything about him till 1778, when he apparently accompanied Governor Sir Thomas Rumbold (the successor of Lord Pigot) from England as his Secretary. Evidently he had left for England some time earlier than 1778, and then accompanied Sir Thomas as his Secretary. Subsequently, Charles Binny became Secretary to Nawab Walajah, which post he held till 1792. We find him to be one of the prominent citizens who asked the Government of Lord Macartney, in 1781, to regulate the sale of grain among the poorer inhabitants on account of the threatened invasion of Haidar Ali. In 1785 he joined in the agitation for better police arrangements, for which more than 200 citizens memorialised. In 1792 his place as the Nawab's Secretary came to be filled by William Abbott, who had been Deputy Master Attendant. Another Binny, who is mentioned about 1779, was George Binny, Surgeon at Ganjam. Slightly later was Alexander Binny, purser of one of the Nawab's ships. Lastly, there was that John Binny who owned the garden house in the site of the present Spencer and Co., and from whom Binny's Road got its name. John Binny, like the members of his family, entered the Nawab's service about 1797. He was Sheriff of Madras in 1801. He founded a firm known in 1803 as Binny and Dennison but shortly afterwards as Binny & Co.

Just opposite to Binny's Road on the western side of which the premises of Messrs. Spencer and Connemara Hotel have risen, and running from the Mount Road southward to White's Road, is the Patulla Road which arose shortly after. It was named after Captain Patullo of the Madras Horse, who owned a house there called Hicks' Bungalow which now forms part of the Madras Club buildings. Patullo married Isabella, the daughter of James Brodie of the Brodie Road which connects Mylapore with Adyar. Captain Patullo died in 1824 when commanding the Governor's Bodyguard. White's Road to which Patullo's Road leads from the Mount Road, came to be so called from John D. White who received a grant of 9 acres in 1809, and built there 'the house which forms the nucleus of the Madras Club.'

Wood's Road which is nearby, received its name from Edward Wood, Registrar of the Sudder Court in 1811 and Chief Secretary in 1822, who owned there a house which later on came to be called Castle Hotel. A few yards off the junction of the eastern end of White's Road lies the *Amir Mahal*, the new palace of the Nawab of Arcot when, after 1855, he ceased to be the Nawab and became only the Prince of Arcot. He had to go thither, leaving his Chepauk Palace for good.

THE THOUSAND LIGHTS (C. 1800)

A circumstance which led to the further growth of the Mount Road was the rise of the place known in Tamil as *Ayiravilakku* and in Hindustani as *Nakshah* (or picture). It has been named after a building constructed by Nawab Umdat-ul-Umara (1795-1801), for the assemblage of the Shias during the Moharram mournings. It is in the angle formed by the junction of the Mount Road with Peter's Road, a few yards off St. George's Cathedral. Col. Love holds that the current tradition that Umdat-ul-Umara "erected the curious structure called the Thousand Lights in the wedge at the junction of the Mount Road and Peter's Road does not seem well founded, as the earliest map depicting it is 1822." He adds that the building is there marked *Majeed Dowlah*. In a third note he observes: "The compound containing two buildings is first shown in the map of 1816, and is lettered 'Nabob' but the singular window-less edifice, built with insets, which adapts itself to the extreme angle between the Mount Road and Peter's Road, was not created till later. In the map of 1837 the property, containing a Moslem graveyard, is marked "*Thousand Lights.*" Majibu-d-daula, I may add, was the son of Maliku-n-Nisa Begam Sahib *alias* Deria Begam Sahib who was the third daughter of Nawab Walajah by his, 'throne wife.' His real name was Ulan Asad-ulla-Khan. The Begam Sahib, Buddy Begam (literally, the old Begam', the first daughter of Walajah), and other members of the Nawab's family have given rise to a number of streets and houses in this region. Their history, though interesting and not irrelevant, has not been given here for want of space. It is dealt in detail in my forthcoming book, *The Making of Madras.*

THE CORNWALLIS ZENOTAPH

It was just at the time when the Thousands Lights area was becoming a busy part of the Mount Road zone that a fresh stimulus to its attraction was created by the opening of the Cornwallis Zenotaph Road which branches off from the Mount Road at the corner where it turns westward from Teynampet towards Saidapet, and runs towards Adayar. The Zenotaph was later on removed to the North Beach Road and erected opposite to the Port office. There was constructed on oval drive around it, and it was a favourite evening resort of the Madras public till the South Beach Road was opened about 1820. Amidst the noteworthy state functions in the Zenotaph was the reception given to Sir Samuel Auchmuty on his return from the conquest of Java.

THE RISE OF TEYNAMPET

It is to the same period that the crowded village of Teynampet between the Thousand Lights and the Zenotaph corner came to prominence, adding a fresh busy division to the Mount Road zone. The region was, before 1800, an area practically devoted to the cultivation of paddy, betel, plantain, sugarcane and vegetables. A large number of Vellalas and Pallis took advantage of the facilities afforded by the Mount Road and its communications with the neighbouring villages to settle here, and the Vellala and Palli Teynampets thus came into existence. The local people made a name as gardeners and cultivators. The long tank in the west, parallel to which the Mount Road runs, gave them every facility, and the expansion of Madras gave them ample opportunity for marketing their produce.

Just at the time when the Indian part of Teynampet was rising, a number of Anglo-Indians settled on both sides of the road and founded new garden houses. One of these houses was Blacker's Gardens, so called after Lieu.-Col. Valentine Blacker, the famous historian of the Mahratta wars of 1817-19, who was Quartermaster general in 1813. He got a grant of 9 acres on the Mount Road in 1806, and built his house. He ought not to be confounded with that H. Blacker who gave the name to Blacker's Road at Puduppak and who, about 1837, owned a house at the junction of that road with the Mount Road.

Another early residence was the Lushington Garden, founded by S. R. Lushington in the premises of the later Botanical Garden. He was a cousin of that Henry Lushington of the Bengal Service, who served as Clive's Private Secretary in which capacity he prepared the false document which deceived Umachand and died in the Patna massacre. S. R. Lushington built his residence at Teynampet on a piece of land got by him in 1796. He was the private secretary and son-in-law of General Harris, and afterwards Governor of Madras from 1827 to 1835. S. R. Lushington, after retirement, became member of Parliament for Rye and Canterbury and died as late as 1868. His son, James Stephen Lushington, was a civil servant of Bengal service and died of illness at Arcot in the early age of 28 on 12th September 1832. A beautiful statue of his by Flexman exists in St. George Cathedral opened just next to his father's residence at Teynampet. It was his namesake, Charles May Lushington, a civil servant of 1837-8, that, in the opinion of Col. Love, founded the famous house known as the Lushington Gardens opposite to the Veterinary College at Saidapet. Just in front of this residence we have the obelisk commemorating Adrian Fourbeck's construction of the bridge over the Long Tank drainage Channel in 1786. It is next to the same residence that the Morse Choultry, now known under a different name, existed at that time and served not only as a landmark in the Madras Boundary Hedge but also as Dr. Anderson's Nopalry which affords one of the most interesting chapters in the Company's economic enterprise in Madras. The history of Nicholas Morse and of the 'Mootia' family with which he was connected, thereby leading to the adhesion of both their names to the Choultry above-mentioned, is too big to be treated here.

It is not surprising that the movement for founding the celebrated cathedral at Teynampet known after the Patron Saint of England took place in the second decade of the 19th century, and reached fruition in January 1816 when Bishop Middleton opened it. The credit of the design for the grand monument belongs to Col. James Lylliman Caldwell and Major Thomas Fiott de Havilland, R.E. The former of these entered the Madras Engineers in 1789. He served in the Mysore Wars, and became Lieut.-Col. in 1811, and General in 1854. In 1798 he owned the property known as the Royal Hotel, Puduppak, which, some time after 1816, was purchased by a prominent Indian merchant of the day, Ravanapa Chetti. Thomas de Havilland, the Chief Engineer to the Madras Military Board from 1812, was, as Col. Love says, a name to conjure with in this period.

He entered 'the Engineers' in 1793, and rose to the rank of Lieut.-Col. in 1824. During this period he carried out some of the most valuable monuments of Madras. He completed (and possibly planned) the Cathedral, as has been already said, in 1814-5. Besides the Cathedral, he built the magnificent circular temple of St. Andrew's Church in the Poonamalli Road (which is described elsewhere), St. Andrew's Bridge, Wallajah Bridge (by renovation), and the great sea-wall from the southern end of the fort to the northern end of 'the Black Town'. "He fixed the mean sea-level at Madras. In his younger days at Seringapatam, he proposed to bridge the Cauvery with five brick arches, and he built in his garden an arch of 110 feet span, and 11 feet rise, which may still be seen, to prove that his scheme was practicable."[1] (Love's 'Descriptive List of Pictures', p. 88). About 1822, Major Havilland built and occupied the two buildings known as Eastern and Western Castlets, Puduppak, on the Mount Road. He owned not only these castellated buildings, but the Army Clothing Office in their vicinity, and a house in Egmore where the Record Office now stands. Havilland died as late as 1866.

It is not possible to deal here with the architectural features or with the numerous historical sculptures, bas-reliefs, inscriptions and other interesting materials connected with this grand and striking monument, which has deservedly been the metropolitan headquarters of the Church of England. It is enough to draw attention to the enthusiastic statement which Bishop Middleton, who opened the Church on 8 January 1816, makes in his *Diary* regarding its grandeur and its beauty. He writes that the church was more handsome than any other outside London; that no English eye could distinguish its 18 magnificent Ionic columns from marble; and that, with its high and elegant spire, its broad palm-covered grove around, and other features, conveyed a magnificent idea of Christianity in the East. The study of the memorials, inscriptions and other materials in the Cathedral is indispensable for the historian of Madras in all aspects of its many-sided growth.

The completion and consecration of St. George's Cathedral gave a fillip to the growth of this part of the city. New garden houses like *Pugh's Garden*[2] which, from 1816 onward, came to be occupied by the Bishop of Madras, and the Cathedral Gardens which, before its enlargement in 1816, had been the residence of R. A. Maitland, Justice of the Peace, Sheriff, and partner of the firm of Messrs. Abbot and Maitland, came into existence. New roads like the highway to Nungambakkam, and the Yeldam Road to Mylapore 'Luz' connected the Cathedral region

1. Recently the bridge has given way.
2. Joseph Pugh also owned property at Adyar, besides a firm in Parry's Corner.

with the surrounding areas. Yeldam Road was named after Richard Yeldam, a Free merchant, who was Mayor of Madras in 1801, Muster-master of the King's troops in 1803, and Treasurer of the Government Bank in 1811. He acquired 1½ acres of ground at Teynampet, and built the residence called Luz House. He died in 1820. More important still was the grand and avenued Cathedral Road which, with its continuation known as Edward Elliot's Road, leads from the Cathedral to the Beach through Mylapore, and across the equally magnificent Mowbray's Road which was laid out at this time. It was the opening of the two former highways that led to the neglect of the Cornwallis Zenotaph Promenade; for the South Beach became more accessible to the people, and the new attraction was intensified in course of time by the construction of the magnificent Marina in continuation of the North and Fort Beach Roads when M. E. Duff was Governor (1881-6). The Zenotaph Road, however, is even today important for the fact that it connects the Mount Road with the beautiful road system of Adayar which, with its fashionable and magnificent garden houses, had by this time become important in Anglo-Indian life.

The Mount Road was, by this time, the most busy thoroughfare in Madras. It came to be adorned by some of the most handsome buildings, and enriched by some of the most opulent firms. It is unnecessary to deal with them; but mention may be made of the opening of the Botanical Gardens in 1837 in Teynampet; of the Christ Church in the heart of the Mount Road in 1852. Almost all the commercial firms have had interesting history of their own, but integrally they have not contributed to the configuration of the greatest and noblest artery of Madras life. The social life is represented by the Madras Club with its historical associations; commercial life by too many houses to be dealt with; intellectual life by the *Hindu* and the *Madras Mail* offices; and religious life by the Christ Church. The roads and buildings of political, dynastic and military interest are by no means rare; and if there is the Government House to mark its political importance at the most metropolitan part of the metropolis there are not lacking humbler edifices which might be more humble in appearance but not defective in historical interest.

Section 2

EGMORE

The designation of the well-known hamlet of Egmore, which is a corruption of the Tamil Elumbur,[3] is said to be derived from the fact that it originally consisted of seven hamlets, namely,

3. Madras Manual of Administration, Glossary.

1. Elumbur proper,
2. Chintadripet,
3. Komalesvaranpet,
4. Narayan-gaud Paracheri,
5. Sami Reddi Paracheri,
6. Sitapet, and
7. Surammalpet.

It is difficult to say how far this derivation is genuine. Some at least of the above names seem to clearly indicate an element of anachronism in the derivation. In any case, that Elumur existed in very early times can hardly be doubted. An inscription[4] dated on 2, September 1264 at Tiruvorriyur temple says that, in the 15th year of Tribhuvanachakravartin Vijaya Ganda Gopala deva, a certain piece of land was given, for the purpose of feeding the Mahesvaras in a Matha (monastery) at Tiruvorriyur, by a merchant who purchased it from a native of Kattuppakkam in Elumur-Tudarmudinadu. This shows that Elumur was the headquarters of an extensive Nadu in Pulal-kottam or Vikrama-sola-vala-nadu in Jayangonda-sola-mandalam (earlier, Tondamandalam), by which name the whole of Chingleput district was then known. A record of the 16th year of a Sriranganatha Yadavaraya, again, records a similar gift in the same temple by a resident of Serruppedu (Chetpat) in Elumur-Tudarmuni-nadu in the same political division. Egmore, thus, was a political division going at least to the 13th century.

Egmore figures under the Company's records under highly mutilated names like Elambore, Eghumur, Eghambur, Elambur, Yeagamour and Egoomooroo. Being nearly two miles west of the Fort, it was outside the limit granted to the Company in 1639. For more than half a century it was a subject of negotiations with the Muslim rulers till it was acquired by the Company and made 'a home farm' in 1693. Ever since then it became an important seat of military works and garden residences of opulent Anglo-Indians. The local military work was known as the Egmore Redoubt or 'fort'. It was constructed on a high level in the village from which a clear prospect of Madras could be had and signals made for succours from the fort against an advancing enemy. There had been before 1703 an Indian choultry there. Governor Pitt placed it in a state of defence and established a guard house there which could secure the safety of the area between Egmore and Madras from menace. His wisdom was proved by an incident of 1710. A set of 40 Muslim horsemen, then stationed at Periamet by the Nawab's Government, had to be compelled to decamp by

4. See Rangacharya's Topographical List of Madras Inscriptions, Cg. 1107 and Cg. 1111.

a detachment of 20 soldiers who were sent from the Fort to succour the British guards at Egmore. Governor Fraser appointed a Committee consisting of the Pay Master, the Commanding Officer, and the Chief Gunner, to consider and report on the question of developing the post at Egmore. The Committee reported that 'the smooth rising ground at the town's end of this side of Egmore' should be made the seat of a guard room for a defence party of soldiers, and that the lower part of the ground must be entrenched and forced up with brick-work. The guard-house on the Redoubt thus constructed came also to serve the purpose of a convenient residence for sick soldiers, particularly those who had just arrived from England and were in need of good air for their health. Governor Harrison carried out the work of construction. But in February 1713 the Directors felt that the cost had been unduly excessive. They complained that, instead of the original estimate of 925 pagodas, it had already involved the expense of 5060 pagodas, and that an additional sum of 1,500 pagodas was threatened in the future; that the result was, after all, a good 'Mansion House'. The Directors left the task of completing it to the judgment of the Council, but expected the late President Fraser and the six members of the Council to pay the charges beyond what had been previously approved! Harrison's Government completed the work in 1715 at a further cost of 1000 pagodas, and the six Councillors, who acknowledged their error, were warned not to repeat it. In 1746 the hostile Nawab of Arcot occupied the Redoubt for a time in the course of his campaign. In 1752 the Company established a Powder Mill at the Redoubt at a cost of 7,500 pagodas; "and the manufacture of powder was commenced, in August 1754, by a German overseer named John de Roos, who was able to turn out 500 lbs. per day . . . In 1756 Capt. Brohier (the Engineer) complained that the quality of the powder was not equal to that of the European factories." De Roos justified his mode of manufacture by giving details, which made the Council place the Factory under the control of the Committee of Works. The Powder Magazine was then active, and "the surplus powder manufactured was stored temporarily in 'the two Pagodas at Chindadre Pettah" which had been built in 1735. During Lally's siege of Madras, the Powder Mill in Egmore Redoubt was blown up by the French. After the expulsion of the French, "the Committee of Works manufactured gun powder in a temporary shed after native methods, until a disastrous explosion occurred by which many people miserably perished. It was then resolved to restore the factory in the Redoubt pending the erection of the machinery which had been sent out from England several years earlier." (Vestiges, II, p. 453).

In 1793, the Redoubt was a little out of repairs, and Major Maule, the Chief Engineer, reported that its old draw-bridge must be replaced by a new one. "Part of the rampart of this redoubt," says Col. Love, "may still be seen, for the external face-wall along the western side, and about half that on the northern side, were utilized in the construction of buildings which still survive. The face-wall was 6 feet high to the cordon and 3½ feet above, and the rampart, including both external and internal walls, was 12 feet thick. Twelve embrasures are visible in the portions preserved." (Vestiges, III, 437). In a map of 1800 "Egmore fort appeared as a square redoubt with sides measuring about 100 yards." (*Ibid.*, p. 534).

The need for the Redoubt vanished with the fall of the last formidable enemy of the British in South India, Tipu Sultan. There was at this time near the Redoubt the Madras Male Asylum the history of which is traced elsewhere. In 1800 the Redoubt was handed over to the Asylum authorities. These made some quaint alterations in the structure of the Redoubt so that they could have more comfortable quarters. The attempt to convert a military building into a civil one naturally led to queer architectural features. As Mr. Glyn Barlow observes in his interesting little brochure on Madras,[5] "At some date or another the authorities of the Asylum had an upper story added to one of the military buildings, with the result that there is the strange spectacle of a row of windowed chambers on the top of a buttressed and battlemented wall, windowless and grim. The upper story has been built into the battlements in such a manner that the outline of the battlements is still clearly visible, and the building is a composite reminder of old-time war and latter-day peace. The whole of the lower part of the building, with its massive walls and its frowning aspect, is of curious and suggestive interest; and the ground around, which is extensively bricked, is a reminder of the fact that the Redoubt in its original form was large indeed. The place provides interesting material for antiquarian speculation."

The addition of the incongruous but necessary accommodation which Glyn Barlow refers to above was due to the fact that the Male Asylum possessed a press. It was on a small scale at first; but in 1800 a bigger Government Press was established there, from which emanated the famous Asylum Press Almanac. It is curious that a place associated with military defence and manufacture of gun-powder should have come to be utilized for purposes like the Orphanage and the Press.

Nor does the history end here. About 1900 the Asylum Directors sold their property in Egmore to the South Indian Railway authorities, as they removed to new premises in the Poonamalle Road; and the old monument, in its attenuated and unrecognized form, is under the occupa-

5. "The Story of Madras." (Oxford University Press, 1921), pp. 45-6.

tion of some Railway employees. And Mr. Glyn Barlow would indeed have been even more intensive when he made the above reflection on the scope for antiquarian speculation in regard to the locality, had he but a dream of the very possibility of the renouncement of the name Redoubt Road, under strangely radical political influences, to the name Gandhi-Irwin Road!

One of the curious names found in connection with Egmore is the Spur Tank given to its reservoir. It has been said to be so called because 'the tank was like a spur in shape'. Whether it was actually so or not, there is no doubt that it was a spur to the amenities of local life. Situated more than two miles from the fort, Egmore became central to the city when it reached large dimensions in the early 19th century. Bounded on the north by the military trunk road leading to Poonamalle, on the east by the village proper, on the west by Chetput, and on the south by a road called after the tank itself and connecting Egmore with Chetput, the Spur Tank came to be useful in contributing to the health of the neighbouring villages. The growth of the city made the life of the old tank, as in the case of its sisters, often precarious. In the third quarter of the 19th century, for example, proposals were in the air for converting the reservoir, which was fed only for half the year by the monsoons, into a dry bed of building sites. The proposal was fortunately given up for reasons of health, a tangible demonstration of which is afforded by the opening of the T. B. Hospital in a section of its broad breezy expanse; but the danger is not yet over, and, in spite of the craving for broad spaces and fresh breeze in modern Madras, the ever-growing need for residences threatens to swallow the area altogether. Already it is half-suffocated by the buildings which have arisen to its east, north and south; and it is difficult to say how long it will be true to its name and be a spur to the health of the neighbouring people.

SOME ROADS AND GARDEN HOUSES

From the time when Egmore came into the British hands and had its security guaranteed by its Redoubt, it became a favourite area of residential gardens and houses. Endowed with good climate and broad spaces, it became one of the early seats of Anglo-Indian garden bungalows. The construction of the Egmore bridge as early as 1700 made the connection with the Fort easy. About 1715 this bridge was repaired. The earliest garden houses we hear of were those of Richard Horden and Thomas Theobalds, the former of whom was first a civil servant and later on a Free Merchant, and the latter a Free Merchant and School Overseer. Their garden houses were built on grounds leased for a period longer than 20 years, but they sold them to Joseph Walsh and Joshua Draper in 1721. All these persons had interesting careers in the early 18th century.

The Renters of Egmore and allied villages complained, in 1720, of the loss of agricultural lands on account of such grants, but their complaints were regarded as baseless. In 1740, when the Spur Tank is named for the first time, 'a lease of ground near it measuring 200 yards square was granted, with the consent of the Renters, to Mr. Matthew Empson, Junior, a senior merchant who had entered the civil service in 1718 and who married just at the time of the grant, Elizabeth, daughter of William Plumbe, 'a seafaring man'. Empson also rented part of the Three Brothers' Garden near the Kachalesvara Pagoda in Black Town, which had been known as the Four Brothers' Garden in the map of 1733. The Spur garden and house of Empson were subsequently in ruins, and in 1766 purchased by Major Eley. Col. Love identifies this Major Eley with John Elly, 'a sergeant of the Train who was commissioned Lieutenant Fireworker in May 1756'. Major Eley also obtained some additional land to the west of Empson's 'between the garden and the road by the tank side', thus indicating that the Spur Tank Road was already in existence. In 1771 the Nawab owned one of his numerous houses 'near the Spur'. It is now known as Wallajah Bagh.

The growing popularity of Egmore is evident from the fact that in 1774 alone there were, out of a series of 30 grants made by the Council for garden houses, eleven were at Puduppakkam, six at Virasanur, three at Nungambakkam, seven at Egmore, and one at Veperi and San Thome each. The Egmore Grants were these:—

1. William Petrie. 11 acres. Rent of 4 pagodas, between the south-west side of Munro's garden and the river. Petrie was a civil servant. Robert Duncan Munro, the son of Dr. Andrew Munro, was also a civil servant. He married Miss Elizabeth Williamson in 1782.

2. Joseph Smith. 15 acres. Rent 7 pagodas. "Eastward of Mr. Dark's." Charles Darke was a Free Merchant from 1770. His daughter, Rebecca, was the wife of Col. John Floyd in 1791.

3. Eyles Irwin. 11 acres. Rent of 5 pagodas. "Near the village of Erembore to the eastward of the garden belonging to Mr. Charles Darke." Irwin was a civil servant of 1768, who was 'the Superintendent of the Company's Grounds.'

4. Richard Matthews. 11 acres. Rent of 4 pagodas. "To the south-east of Mr. Troutback's garden near the River." Samuel Troutback was "a Free merchant and old resident of Madras" who "was Boatswain of the *King George* when that ship was wrecked near Sadras in 1719."

5. Charles Bromley. 6 acres. Rent, 1 pagoda. 'Near the road leading from Madras to Ellembore, between the Garden House of Col. Jno Wood, and Egmore Fort.' Bromley was an attorney and notary, who married Miss Elizabeth Steward in 1770.
6. James Call. 6 acres. Rent, 1 pagoda. 'Contiguous to Col. Wood's garden on the north side.' James Call was a Civil Servant of 1765, who was Deputy Inspector of Nawab's Accounts and who is believed to have been a younger brother of Col. John Call.
7. George Smith. 11 acres. Rent, 5 pagodas. G. Smith was a free merchant of 1754 and nephew of Dr. Andrew Munro. He married his cousin, Margarate Aurora Munro.

The 1798 Map of Madras gives an idea of Egmore and its connections, as it does of other parts of Madras. "From the Walajah Bridge two roads under double avenues of trees diverged to the west and south-west across the Island, the first leading to Periamet, Egmore Redoubt, and the Poonamallee Road, the second to Triplicane Bridge and the Mount Road . . . The omission of the Little Egmore Bridge, near the General Hospital, is perhaps accidental, but the Old Garden House Bridge to the east of it appears to have been demolished." "In the Poonamallee Road the Naval Hospital occupied the present Gun Carriage Factory premises; the house to the west of it, now called Stove Hall, was Mr. C. B. Dent's; and the building opposite, in the compound now belonging to St. Andrew's Church is believed to have been the Masonic Hall...... In Egmore, south of Vepery, Monteith's and Cosa Major's Road are shown in their present alignment. The Pantheon Road extended from the river past the Pantheon to the open ground near the existing Court of the Presidency Magistrate. Commander-in-Chief's Road started from the river, but had a length of only 300 yards. In this road the houses now known as Ottershaw and Victoria Hotel are represented. In the Pantheon Road a group of 4 large buildings appears, one of which is College Bridge House. The Pantheon is situated in a compound of immense size. Egmore fort appears as a square redoubt, with sides measuring about 100 yards. Cosa Major's Road possessed one house, which, however, does not now exist. The portion of the Poonamallee Road eastward of the Spur Tank appears narrow and ill-defined."

An early and important Road at Egmore is that known as the Pantheon, in which the Central Museum is situated. It is a very long and ancient thoroughfare, and consists of two branches, one from the College Bridge to the Police Commissioner Office Road, a distance of 3,000 feet, and the other from the Western Riverside Road to the same destination, covering a length of 2,000 feet. The main Pantheon Road, took its name from the Pantheon or 'Public Assembly Rooms,' which now forms the main part of the Central Museum. The Pantheon was originally a big landed estate consisting of 43 acres from Cosa Major Road to the Police Commissioner's Road. It was granted in August 1778 by Governor Thomas Rumbold to Hall Plumer, Civil Servant and Contractor. In the original grant the area is described as 'all that piece of ground in Egmore which was bounded on the north-east and north-west by the paddy fields in the south-east by the Road, and in the south-west by Mackay's Garden. This garden seems to have been between the present Cosa Major's Road and the river, and was different from its name-sakes on the Mount Road at Puduppakkam and at Nungambakkam (the latter being later than 1798). In December 1793 Hall Plumer, who had got his estate for 99 years' lease for an annual rent of 18 pagodas and a payment of 30 pagodas every 30 years, assigned the ground, together with a dwelling house and a garden which he had built there, to a set of 24 gentlemen who formed a committee for regulating the public amusements in the city. The committee also included Basil Cochrane, Colonel Henry Malcolm, Colonel Close, Benjamin Sulivan, George Powney, Charles Floyer; Charles Baker, Mark Wilks (the historian of Mysore), and James Brodie (of Brodies Castle at Adyar). In 1821 the gentlemen who formed the Committee disposed of the property to Mr. E. S. Moorat, the well-known Armenian merchant. He received one part, while the other came into the hands of a number of gentlemen of whom the most famous were V. Blaker the historian; Thomas F. D. Havilland, the celebrated Engineer; Thomas Parry; George Arbuthnot; and Hamilton Hall. In March 1830, the whole property was purchased from Mr. Moorat by Government for Rs. 28,000. The building was first made 'the Collector's Cutcherry,' and later on the Central Museum. The Pantheon Road skirts the property. It is a Road which is associated thus historically with a large number of men who have played their parts in British Indian History. Near its eastern terminus was the Presidency Magistrate's Court-house owned in 1816 by J. D. Fries and in 1837 by Mr. Liddle of 'the Old Police.'

Another historic house in the Pantheon Road is the Haliburton Gardens. It was named after David H., appointed Writer in 1770. In 1782-4 he was Persian Translator and a member of the Committee of Assigned Revenue. The Haliburtons in the varied forms of Halyburton and Hallyburton, began to figure earlier than David. John H. of the Civil Service was the earliest. Entering service at the age of 19, he became Resident at Madapollam in 1743-4. He came to Fort St. George in 1746. A fine linguist he played a prominent part in the negotiations with La Bourdonnais. Subsequently he took part in the Fort St. David campaign as a volunteer. During Admiral Boscawen's attack on Pondicherry in 1748 he was murdered by a mutinous sepoy. His tomb is in the

Cemetery in Sonnaga Street, Cuddalore, Old Town. It is dated 27 May 1748, and is as follows:

Here lies
John Hollyburton
An Honest and Brave man
and
A sincere lover of his country
who was basely murdered
on the 27th day of May 1748
By a mutinous sepoy
At the siege of Pondicherry where he served
in quality of a Volunteer
Aged 31 years.

The Marshall Road, which extends from the Commander-in-Chief's Road to Harris Road along a distance of 3,350 feet, owes its name to General Marshall. As early as 1798, it was a thoroughfare. In 1822, Marshall who entered the army in 1790, was Presidency Paymaster, and owner of the house called East Nook. In 1873, he was Major General; and it was from him that the above-mentioned Road has been named.

Another Road in the neighbourhood, the Monteith Road, which extends from Pantheon Road to Marshall's for 1,900 feet, was already in existence in 1800. It came to have its *present* name from the fact that William Monteith of the Madras Engineers built a house there about 1820. Monteith had entered service in 1809. In 1826, he was Lieutenant Colonel, and in 1854 Lieutenant General. "Down to 1816 or later the space between Monteith Road and Commander-in-Chief's Road was occupied by the two compounds of 'College Bridge House' and 'Ottershaw', and a cross road divided those properties. These were owned by Basil Cochrane, the well-known excavator of the Cochrane Canal in 1816, and then by General Hamilton Hall, who also owned the Egmore House in the same locality. Monteith House which absorbed the cross Road, is marked 'Col. Monteith' in the map of 1837."

Hall's Road, which stretches from Cosa Major Road to the Egmore High Road, and is 1,900 feet long, was named after Gen. Hamilton Hall. He entered service in 1781, and rose to the rank of Lt. Col. in 1807. He died at Trichinopoly in 1827 as the Commander of the Southern Division. His tomb is in St. John's Church Cemetery, Trichinopoly and contains this inscription: "Sacred to the memory of Major General Hamilton Hall, who, after a period of 40 years' service in the Honourable East India Company's service, ended an Honourable Career when in Command of the Southern Division of Army on the 12th May 1827, aged 66 years. Simple and unassuming in his manners and unostentatious in his character." General Hall had married Flora Tondeclair at Poonamallee in 1795. She owned, after his death, two houses in this road, called Ottershaw and East Nook. Another historical road in Egmore is named after Cosa Major. It runs from the Spur Tank to the Pantheon Road along a distance of 2,000 feet. It came into existence before 1798, and was connected with the name of James Henry Cosa Major, son of Noah Cosa Major, who entered the Company's service in 1762, and served till after 1811. The Cosa Majors formed an important clan in the Company's service. The first name in the family to come to prominence is the Noah C. above mentioned. He was, in 1732, a super-cargo at Madras, and in the same capacity served in the *Narcissus* which proceeded on an expedition to the Red Sea in 1734. In 1741, he was Assistant Accounts Officer in the Fort, and then obtained a great reputation as one acquainted with the Dutch and French languages as well. In 1744, he became the Registrar of the Mayor's Court. He died in 1746 in his 45th year, and his tombstone is in St. Mary's Church. Noah Cosa Major married Rebecca, the daughter of Captain John Powney, in 1736. He owned a house in the Island opposite the Company's old Garden House. His property had originally been granted to Thomas Cooke, in 1717, for 21 years' lease on a pagoda per annum, with the provision that the lease might be renewed to him in case he paid 100 pagodas. But the house built by Cooke came into others' hands. Mrs. Higginson, the wife of a former Governor of Madras, who accompanied her son Richard to Madras in 1722, got permission from the Directors in 1731 to renew the lease of Cooke's property in her name. But in 1733, it came into the possession of George Drake, and then Captain Alexander Carvalho, who renewed the lease for 51 years in 1738. Soon after, however, it was purchased by Noah Cosa Major. It was in the north-west corner of the Island, between the roads leading to Egmore and Chintadripetta. The latter, in fact, forked beyond Cosa Major's house, one branch leading to Egmore Bridge, and the other to Triplicane Bridge and Chintadripetta. Near it was constructed in the middle of the 18th century a powder-house which, together with Cosa Major's house, is no longer there.

Mrs. Rebecca Cosa Major, the wife of Noah and daughter of Captain John Powney, who became widowed in 1746, ten years after her marriage, inherited from her husband not only the Island house and garden but a house and garden near the Company's garden at Chepauk. In 1746, when the French took Madras, the former property was destroyed, and it was taken over for its own use by the Company and a plot of ground was given in the Black Town in compensation, in 1773, as the result of her application for it. In December 1781 she offered her Chepauk house and garden for sale to Government, and as they were necessary for the convenience and expansion of the Government House, Government took it over for 6000 pagodas. The property in Black Town also had been purchased by the Company a little earlier.

James Henry Cosa Major, the son of Noah C. by Rebecca C., joined the Company's service as a writer in 1762. In 1770 he applied for a grant of land at 'Virasanoor' east of the Mount Road but did not get it. There is a road at Egmore in his name but, as Col. Love points out, there is no record of his acquisition of any landed property there. In 1776 James Henry Cosa Major was Paymaster at Vellore. In 1780 he was chief at Vizagapatam, and then "had a narrow escape from death. The sepoys at that place mutinied on being ordered to embark for Madras, in October 1780. They shot down two of their officers, killed one civilian and wounded another, plundered the place, and threatened to murder Cosa Major and the remaining members of the civil establishment." In June 1782 he left for England and, returning a few years later to Madras, he rose by 1810 to be fourth in Council and the Chief Judge of the Sudder and Faujdari Adalat. Cosa Major made a great name in other fields as well. In 1787 he made an enquiry and report on the riot at Tiruvottiyur; in 1796 he settled a caste dispute in regard to the passage in the Esplanade. In 1788 he was Vice-President of the Female Orphan Asylum, and reported that its funds exceeded 34,500 pagodas. James Henry died in England in 1815. His daughter, Amelia, was married in 1809 to Hon. John Elliot, the son of Lord Minto.

The other Cosa Majors in service were John C. who entered the civil service in 1792 and was member of the Board of Trade in 1810; George James who entered service in 1812 and died at Ootacamond in 1848; and James Archibald who became the servant of the Company in 1801 and was subsequently Collector of Seringapatam.

One of the longest streets in Egmore division is the Langs Garden Road which extends for 3,200 feet from Harris Road to the West Riverside Road. It was evidently named after General Ross Lang who, in 1775, was a Colonel at Vellore. He was a colleague, in the Infantry, with Flint, Baillie and others. In the Second Mysore War, Lang defended Vellore with distinction, and was, after the death of General Coote and the dismissal of General Stuart, appointed to command the army. In 1784 General Lang entertained elegantly all the 1146 Englishmen and 3,000 Sepoys who had been Tippu's prisoners and just set free. Lang was a Company's officer, and his appointment as Commander-in-Chief was regarded with jealousy by the officers of the King's Troops. In May 1785 he retired on a pension of £1,000 a year. In 1773, Lang had married Mrs. Ann Oats, widow of Capt. Thomas Oats and daughter of Mr. Thomas Pelling. He had a son, General Ross Lang Junior. Entering the army in 1787 he became Major-General in 1813, and died in 1822. During that year his name was marked on the house called Fallowfield at Rayapetta.

19

He had married Miss Amelia Pelling in 1792. It was the Senior Lang, apparently, that gave the name to the road and garden of his name.

It is unnecessary to refer to other roads and houses. What has been said is enough to show how rich the field is for the study of the place-names in Egmore ; and this is the case, more or less, with the other parts of Madras. I shall close this article with the notice of the fact that the salubrity of the Egmore climate has not only given rise to good residential houses but to institutions like the Maternity Hospital founded in 1844, the Opthalmic Hospital founded in 1819 and removed here from Royapetta, and the Tuberculosis Hospital. The Museum (1851) and the Connemara Public Library, which were partly developed out of the property of the Madras Literary Society (1812), the Oriental Manuscripts Library the origin of which is interesting, and the Record Office represent the intellectual life of Madras, and the Scotch Kirk, deservedly famous for its architectural grandeur, has contributed to the religious activity of the place ever since its construction in 1821. The South Indian Railway, the Power Station and other institutions represent the commercial growth of the place.

Manucci in Madras

By

Rao Bahadur K. V. Rangaswami Iyangar, M.A.,
Tirupati

One of the distinctions of Madras in the first half-century of the foundation of Fort St. George is that it was for twenty years at least the chosen home of the now famous Niccolao Manucci, the author of the racy *Storia do Mogor.* This important work, whose value as a contemporary authority for the reign of Aurangzebe is now well-recognized, was composed at Madras. Of the five parts of the *Storia,*[1] the first three were written or dictated, between 1699 and 1700, the fourth between 1701 and 1705 and the last between 1706 and 1709. It is unlikely that any section of the *Storia* was composed outside Madras. François Martin, the celebrated Director-Geneıal of the French settlement at Pondicherry (*Puducheri*) was the inspirer of the racy chronicle. Manucci appears to have hoped that it could be laid before Louis XIV and published by royal sanction. The hope was not fulfilled, and the recovery of the genuine *Storia* through the scholarly efforts of the late William Irvine is one of the romances of research.

The adventurous career of Manucci began in 1653, when, at the age of fourteen, he ran away from Venice. He reached Surat in 1656, passed on to Delhi and entered the Mughal artillery under Dara Shikhoh, to whose memory he remained singularly loyal. After serving in various parts of the Mughal empire, and under different masters, he settled down at Lahore in 1670 as a physician. After eight years, he followed Shah Alam to the Dakhan. Tired of his position as a soldier in a camp perpetually on the move, he obtained leave on two occasions to visit Goa, where his savings had been invested. After the second of these visits, he fell under the displeasure of Shah Alam, and was kept under arrest as a deserter. Manucci's escape from the Mughal encampment to the court of King Abul Hassan of Golcondah, against whom the troops of Shah Alam were then moving, reads like a romance. The deserter crept into the favour of the ruler of Golcondah by curing a member of the royal family, and was given what was then the large salary of Rs. 700 a month. Shah Alam's chagrin was increased by the knowledge that the deserter was now a courtier of the King of Golcondah. The Mughal

1. Irvine, *Storia,* I. p. lxxiv.

envoy was therefore instructed to get Manucci back to the Mughal camp by some means or other. In considerable and justifiable alarm, Manucci managed to get sent to the sea-port of Masulipatam, on the pretext of treating another distinguished patient. From Masulipatam escape was easy to the newly founded English settlement of Madras-patam or Fort St. George, then an asylum to many fugitives like the Italian.

Manucci records the welcome he received from the Portuguese at Madras, who remembered his services to their nation, when he was at Goa. But, the new settler did not tarry long at Madras. He repaired to Pondicherry, being " all anxiety " to see his old friend François Martin, who entertained him cordially for several days. Manucci was desirous of going back to Europe. Martin dissuaded him from the enterprise, pointing out that, after his long acclimatisation in India, his health would suffer in Europe. He advised Manucci to marry and settle down in India. He informed the Italian of the existence of an eligible lady in the widow of a Thomas Clarke. Thomas Clarke had died in 1683, and the lady was still young, having been married at an early age. She was the daughter of an English Catholic named Christopher Hartley, President at Masulipatam, and a " country-bred " Portuguese lady named Donna Aguida Pereyra. The maiden name of Mrs. Clarke was Elizabeth Hartley. Clarke had left her a valuable house and garden near the southern end of modern Broadway, somewhere between the present China Bazar Road and the compound of the Law College. Manucci, who was approaching forty, and claims to have escaped the sex-temptations of the Mughal court and camp, resolved to settle down and marry the eligible widow. Two *padres,* in whose judgment he had confidence, reported favourably of the "qualities and virtues" of the lady. The courtship was short, and the marriage was celebrated at Madras on the 28th October 1686. By the marriage Manucci had a son, " but God chose him rather to make him an angel in Paradise rather than leave him to suffer in this world." The union was apparently a happy one. Manucci's character had been above reproach, and his denunciations of the profligacy of the settlement at San Thomè might lead to an inference that he himself trod the narrow and straight path. Manucci's wife died in 1706, when his love for Madras began to decline. He had a recrudescence of his fever for wandering, and in 1712, he agreed to go as an envoy to the court of his old master Shah Alam, who had become Emperor and from whom he had received an invitation to repair to the Imperial Court. What apparently detained him at Madras, after the death of his wife, was the need to complete the *Storia.* The projected journey fell through after the receipt of the news of the death of the Emperor (1712). By that time, Manucci had become an inhabitant of Pondicherry, probably because of the sad associations of his wrecked life at Madras. He kept his property till he died.

The contemporary records of Fort St. George confirm two claims which Manucci makes for himself in his memoirs. His wide knowledge of the Imperial and subsidiary Indian courts was admitted and his advice on relations with the "country powers" was sought and esteemed. His rectitude was unquestioned. He delighted to move with clerics, and at one period of his life at Madras, *viz.*, 1703-1706, he mixed himself in local ecclesiastical disputes and intervened with influential Indian magnates more than once on behalf of persecuted *padres.* It speaks much for the Italian settler that the cautious Englishmen, among whom he chose to live, came to entertain respect for his ability and character.

Manucci resumed at Madras his medical practice, and was apparently in great request among Indians of position for his knowledge of Eastern and Western systems of treatment. His 'Cordials,' for which he claims special excellence, were in great demand. So were "Manooch's Stones", the scrapings of which were used to correct fevers. They are referred to in Lockyer's *Trade in India* (1711) as "highly cryed up for their virtues", and apparently were the *lingam of Siddha-vaidyas* made on a base of mercury. In spite of his practice, Manucci's earnings from his profession could not have been considerable, for there are three official references to his being a poor man. Possibly, the state he felt bound to maintain, as a minor grandee of the Mughal court, might have made it impossible for him to save, as he had been doing when he was in the service of Indian princes. His consequence was made manifest to the other inhabitants of Madras by the communications and visits he continued to receive from Indians of position in his former services. The receipt of an invitation from the Emperor in 1711 shows that he had made up his quarrel with Shah Alam, and his whereabouts were known at Court.

The presence of so useful a man was naturally valued by the English settlement. Governor Gyfford, who desired in 1687, to procure the delivery of letters from Bengal to the Emperor "determined to take the advice of Senor Manouche, an Italian Doctor, inhabitant of this Town, who was formerly in the Mogull's service."[2] Gyfford's confidence in Manucci was not shared by his successors, Elihu Yale (Governor between 1687 and 1692) and Higginson (1692-1698). Thomas Pitt took Manucci into favour, and it was the apprehension of losing his good opinion more than failing eyesight—the ground adduced—which made Manucci refuse an invitation from Sir William Norris, who had come out on behalf of the rival East India Company, to be his interpreter (1700) In 1699, he had pleaded his infirmities and age for not accepting an invitation from Pitt to undertake a mission. The kingdom of Golcondah

2. *Public Consultations*, 7-3-1687 and 19-9-1687.

had fallen in 1687, and Gingee (Senji), about eighty miles south of Madras, which had stood against the Imperial troops fell in 1698. From that date, the Mughal army became active through out the Carnatic. Obeying orders from headquarters, the Mughal General, Daud Khan Panni, made himseif particularly disagreeable to the English. His arrival in the Carnatic stirred up in Fort St. George the hope of obtaining from him a confirmation of privileges, and Manucci was selected as the envoy for this purpose. In referring to him the Council said : " We have selected Signor Nocola Manuch, Venetian, an inhabitant of ours for many years, who was reputed as an honest man. Besides, he has lived in the King's Court for upwards of thirty years, and was servant to one of the Princes, and speaks the Persian language exceedingly well." Manucci was commissioned with the chief Dubash Ramappa to bear the Company's presents to the Nawab. The presents consisted of a consignment of Cordials and French brandy, and the selection perhaps reflects Manucci's personal knowledge of Daud Khan's fondness for strong liquors. The smallness of the presents irritated the Nawab, who sent back Manucci with a threat to appoint a Mughal governor to the Black Town and to develop San Thomè as a rival to Madras.[3] In 1701 Daud Khan appeared at the head of 10,000 men before Madras. His truculence was sensibly reduced by the bold front exhibited by Governor Pitt, possibly after a hint from Manucci. The Nawab accepted a dinner from the English at which he got drunk, and left, to return eight months later to blockade Fort St. George. The siege was raised only on payment of Rs. 25,000. Manucci's personal influence with the Pathan soldier is evidenced by his successful intervention on behalf of persecuted priests in Tanjore, and by his accepting an invitation to spend a night at Manucci's garden house in St. Thomas' Mount (1706)[4].

The house and garden obtained by his marriage were sold to Thomas Clarke in 1675. They were leaseholds. By 1703 the lease had expired. The *Public Consultations* for 1703 show that Manucci was granted that year a renewal of the lease for another 21 years on a yearly payment of sixty pagodas, and that in view of his unaffluent circumstances and his services to the Company on many occasions, the amount was remitted on payment of a nominal annual rent of one pagoda. Even this was reduced in 1711, and the entire property, in which by mistake some freehold property had been wrongly included as leasehold, against Manucci's appeals, was converted on the recommendation of the Governor into an absolute freehold. The grounds for this special treatment, which are set forth to in the President's Minute are interesting. Manucci was about to set for to

3. Irvine, *Storia*, III, pp. 384-393.
4. Irvine, IV., p. 129.

Arcot to meet the Dewan, who had orders to supply him with what was necessary to enable him to proceed to the Imperial Court to which he had been specially commanded. The Governor thought it proper to placate so influential a man, especially as he had been of service to the English on several previous occasions and might be of service again, and would be particularly useful in representing the English case against Surup Singh, the hostile Governor of Gingee.[5]

The death of the Emperor destroyed the chance of Manucci's last considerable journey. He had already removed to Pondicherry, only retaining his freehold property at Madras. He now disappears from history. We do not know when he died and where he died. A survey of old cemetries in South India, particularly in Pondicherry, might reveal his date of death. The tradition that he died in 1717 rests, as Irvine pointed out (*Storia*, I. p. lxvi) on a vague intimation in a Venetian work published in 1752, on the Literature of Venice. This would make him 78 at the time of his death. The date is not improbable in view of Manucci's frequent affirmation of his failing health and powers as early as 1700. There is a record of his having sought and obtained in 1716 permission, which he apparently did not use, to return to Europe, on condition that "his effects be invested in Diamonds and brought hither on the Company's usual terms".[6] The answer of the Madras Council that "when Senr. Manuch desires to come to England, will let him; he never was denied; his effects will ly in little room"—is significant of the continued kindness at Fort St. George to the 'stranger within the gates', who had served his adopted town with fidelity and zeal. But for the reference in the letter of sanction to the conversion of Manucci's property, prior to the voyage to England, into diamonds it may point to his unaffluence. As against this, there is the reference in the list of estates under the administratorship of Father Severini of Madras in 1740 to that of Nicolao Manooch, valued at 30,000 pagodas. The difficulty in reconciling the existence of this estate under administration in 1740, so long after the probable death of Manucci, can be explained by the circumstance that Manucci having no natural heirs, left the estate in trust. If the author of the *Storia* and the owner of this estate be identical, it will be some satisfaction to those who have derived light and entertainment from the perusal of the vivacious narrative of this Pepys of Mughal India, to feel that so good a man did not pass his last days in want.

5. H. D. Love, *Vestiges of Madras*, II, p. 124; Irvine, *Storia*, I., p. lxvi.
6. Irvine, *Storia*, IV, p. 435.

European Tombs and Monuments in Madras

By

C. Sivaramamurti, M.A.,

Curator, Archaeological Section, Government Museum, Madras.

Short donative inscriptions on the rails of early stupas all over India at Bharhut, Sanchi and Amaravati have supplied materials for the social history of the period. Inscribed Sati stones, Hero stones and such other memorials have had their own story to tell of customs that prevailed about a time, of loyalty to the Chieftain that manifested itself in action, bravery that was rewarded by celestial bliss and devotion to the consort that consumed the body in flames too terrible to behold. Epitaphs have also thus helped in the compilation of a nation's history.

European contacts with India have scattered on her soil many a tombstone and monument that chronicle on imperishable material incidents in the life of men and women who had played important roles in the affairs of the country. Though the field for the historian extends all over the land where these relics are found it is outside the scope of this paper to consider the monuments outside Madras. The materials for this paper are from J. J. Cotton's "List of Inscriptions on Tombs and Monuments in Madras."

The earliest European monument in India, centuries after her contact with the Greeks, after the triumphal march and conquest of the Panjab by the young and ambitious Macedonian King, is of 1516 A.D. and it is in Mylapore. It is the foundation stone of the Luz Church, "an ancient looking black stone in one of the outer walls." Tradition has it that the Portuguese when they arrived at this place and wondered where to build their church saw a light which they regarded as a divine beckoning, settled there and built a church on the spot where appeared the light. This was in 1516 and the church is named after Light, Luz. But that was the beginning and Madras has grown since into mighty proportions that scarcely allow us to imagine that the present city had such beginnings.

In the early days when the fort was the chief centre of the trading company the first President and Governor was Aaron Baker. His wife Elizabeth Baker died in August 1652 and a tomb stone bearing a coat of arms in the compound of St. Mary's Church in Fort St. George marks the place of her rest. Six years later died Henry Greenhill who was

Agent of Madras before it was raised to a Presidency under Baker in 1652. Agent Greenhill, an early settler in the Fort, built his own house on the river bank. He died in 1664 and sleeps in St. Mary's.

Many former governors of Madras lie buried in one or other of the churches of Madras and some have splendid memorials worthy of their achievements and eminence.

In St. Mary's cemetery on the Island sleeps Nicholas Morse, once governor of Fort St. George. He was a friend of Clive and it is from his library that the great general acquired all his book learning. In 1746 it was his misfortune to be marched in a triumphal procession through the streets of Pondicherry soon after his surrender of Madras to the French. Yet Morse was a descendent of one of the greatest of English generals, Oliver Cromwell, being the grandson of the Protector's daughter Bridget. Among other governers that lie burried in this City are Sir Henry George Ward who has a statue at Kandy and the Right Honourable Vere Henry Lord Hobart whose life-size bust by Noble in St. Mary's church in the Fort was erected by the public who greatly lamented his demise.

There is scarcely a person in Madras that has not passed through the Island and seen the majestic figure of a horserider just as the Fort is approached. It is a memorial for a great governor of Madras who rose to that position by dint of great merit and the memory of whose 47 years of distinguished career in India was perpetuated by this equestrian statue by Chantrey. It was at Pattikonda near Gooty that he died in July 1827 just on the eve of his retirement and his remains are now in St. Mary's church in the Fort. His portrait by Sir Martin Archer Shee in the Banqueting hall and that of his wife by Lawrence in the Government House perpetuate his association with the home of the governors in the metropolis.

Near and dear to the many governors that carried on the government of this presidency are some, who breathed their last on this soil and have their tombs in this city. Margarette, the wife of Lord Hobart and the mother-in-law of Lord Ripon, both governors of Madras, lies buried in St. Mary's Church along with her child John Hobart whose death hastened the sorrowing mother to the grave. Amelia Boileu the daughter of Sir Frederick Adam sleeps in St. George's Cathedral. A fine marble monument by Flaxman in St. George's Cathedral perpetuates the memory of James Stephen Lushington the son and grandson of governors of Madras.

Military men number largely among those that repose in the churchyards and cemeteries in Madras. The most noted in the early years of the company are generally military officers of all ranks. Sir John Burgoyne Bart, who raised a regiment of light dragoons for service in India, the first European Cavalry in this country, rests in St. Mary's where he was laid in 1785. A monument by Peart showing Britannia crowning a portrait head with laurel is in honour of Lieutenant Colonel Joseph Moorhouse who was killed at the Petta gate of Bangalore in 1791 and immortalised in a picture of the storming of Bangalore by Robert Home. Major General Sir Barry Close who by the treaty of Bassein destroyed ultimately the power of the Maratthas has the finest monument in St. Mary's Church executed in marble by Flaxman. To him was dedicated the History of Mysore by Wilks, one of his very intimate friends. A large marble effigy by Tornouth marks the place where rests Brigadier-General Thomas Henry Somerset popularly known as 'The Soldiers' Friend' being the first to build permanent barracks for the soldiers. A building in Nungambakkam known as Doveton House and also Commander-in-Chief's house belonged to Lieutenant General Sir John Doveton who had charge of Tippu's sons when they were hostages in 1792. To his memory is inscribed a tombstone dated 1847 in St. Mary's. Monuments in marble by Richardson and Walker mark the tombs of two military officers and among the many memorials raised by fellow officers for those that departed this life in the discharge of their duty is a bas relief of a battle-field by Sievier. Wrought by Richardson is the monument for George Broadfort that shows the dead man in military dress attended by a couple of sepoys. But the most famous of the military monuments in Madras is in the Government Museum where it was removed from the Arsenal its original place. It is the monument of victory of the British arms at Manilla and is in honour of the bravery of the land and sea forces under the command of Brigadier General Draper and Admiral Cornish.

Of the military officers who have been laid to rest in this very city are some whose names are perpetuated in street names. Sydenham's Road is after Major General William Sydenham, Commandant of artillery whose monument can be seen at St. Thomas' Mount. General Collins Road is similarly named after Major General Edward Collins who died at Vepery. At Royapetta, Patter's Road and Patter's Gardens take their names after Lieutenant General John Patter. Colonel Peter Whannell has given Egmore Whannell's Road.

Visitors to Mysore may have noticed in Seringapatam a curious looking narrow arch of bricks. This bridge swings when any one climbs and stamps it at the centre with more than ordinary violence. It is a wonder of an arch and is named after Major T. F. de Havilland, a distinguished civil Engineer and architect who proposed a bridge for the

Kaveri composed of five brick arches and surprised the wondering authorities at Mysore by this his experimental arch built in his own garden at Seringapatam. Havilland's hand was at work in Madras also. St. Andrew's church and bridge at Egmore were his creations and the long and meandering sea wall in Royapuram all along the coast that keeps away the billows was executed by de Havilland. In 1818 died his beloved wife Elizebeth and was laid to rest in St. Georges Cathedral Cemetry and de Havilland's associations lend interest to this tomb of his consort. A tablet in St. George's Cathedral keeps alive the memory of Captain Samuel Best, the Engineer who was "the first to carry out a comprehensive scheme of roads for the Madras Presidency."

Many doctors that served the East India Company and cured the ailments of the Nobob of the Carnatic as physicians of His Highness now sleep in the land where they toiled for the benefit of humanity and fitting memorials have been raised over their remains in this city. There is a large granite tomb fenced by an iron railing near the general hospital opposite to the Medical College grounds. It is for Edward Bulkley who is described as "ingenious Dr. Bulkley" in the description of the Hospital given by Lockyer in his Account of Trade in India 1711. To the memory of John Mack, physician to the Durbar of H. H. the Nabob of the Carnatic, who joined his forefathers in 1832 is a tablet in St. George's cathedral showing the sculpture of Hygeia, the goddess of health; and in the same place a portrait medallion by Turnouth commemorates another physician, Thomas Moore Lane, who held a post similar to that of Dr. Mack. There is a portrait in the examination room of the Medical College of a great doctor and linguist Henry Harris, M.D., an authority on Hindi spoken in the Deccan and his tomb can be seen in St. George's Cathedral Cemetery.

Dr. James Anderson M. D., physician-general in Madras whose name is famous among those of the medical line that served in this presidency had a bust and a model of a magnifying glass on his tomb stone which have disappeared but fortunately there is preserved for Madras his excellent figure by Chantrey in St. George's Cathedral. He was a distinguished doctor who was keenly interested in botany and was responsible for the introduction of silk manufacture in Madras. It is interesting to find that another distinguished doctor had the same passion for the science relating to plants. William Griffith of the Madras Medical Service, an eminent scientist and one of the most famous botanists of his day, collected as many as nine thousand species, by far the largest number acquired by the exertions of a single man. In the Botanical gardens at Calcutta is to be seen a monument raised in his honour and in St. George's Cathedral at Madras is a tablet to his me-

ST. GEORGE'S CATHEDRAL

mory. He was barely thirty five when he died in 1845 and his death was a loss to the cause of science as expressed by the Governor-General of India. Another medical man that was a naturalist and botanist was W. S. Mitchell who lies buried in St. Mary's Cemetery.

But scientists were also among those in other walks of life. Another botanist of eminence was a gifted linguist and grammarian. Adjoining the Vepery church is Rottler's lane where a bungalow known as "Rottlers House" keeps on the memory of Rev. John Rottler, an able divine who delighted in the study of plants and words and now sleeps in the churchyard of St. Matthias where he went to rest in 1836. No student of philology can forget the name Bishop Caldwell who has a tablet to his memory in St. George's Cathedral.

The majority of the Flaxman monuments in Madras are for divines. The Missionary activities of Rev. Frederick Christian Swartz are famous. To him the church at Tanjore owes its existence. He was always the friend of the poor and his house two miles east of Tanjore was an asylum for orphans. He was so highly respected as a religious man that Hyder Ali ordered his officers "to permit the Venerable Father Swartz to pass unmolested and show his respect and kindness, for he is a holy man and means no harm to my government." On his death bed, Tuljajee, the Rajah of Tanjore, entrusted his adopted son Serfojee to the care of Father Swartz and his memorial by Flaxman in Tanjore representing him on his deathbed contains verses composed in his honour by that Marattha prince who had deep veneration for him. The monument erected for him by the East India Company is in St. Mary's church in the Fort. An associate of Swartz was the Rev. Christian William Gericke who gave 1500 pagodas and other valuable property for the S.P.C.K. and his monument by Flaxman in St. Mary's represents him in the attitude of preaching. In 1804, close on the death of Rev. Gericke went to rest the Rev. Archdeacon Leslie, Minister of Fort St. George and Flaxman's chisel has shaped for him a monument to mark the place of his burial in St. Mary's Cemetery while a tablet in St. Mary's perpetuates the respect that his parishioners bore to him. A representation of Faith leaning on a cross by Flaxman in St. George's Cathedral is to the memory of Archdeacon John Mousley who held that office soon after it was provided for Madras and Bombay in 1813. Many in Madras are familiar with Bishop Corrie's School. It is named after the Right Rev. Daniel Corrie, Bishop of Madras, to whose memory stands a monument by Weeks in St. George's Cathedral. In the same place is a memorial to Thomas Dealtry, Bishop of Madras erected by his friends in India and executed by Joseph Durham who has represented him in the act of performing the rite of ordination. But among the memorials to the churchmen in Madras, that of Reginald Heber, the second Bishop of Calcutta, who died in Trichinopoly in 1826 when on a visit there, deserves special notice as the monument that is probably described by Southey in his Ode on a Portrait of Heber since he is there represented by Chantrey as described by the poet.

A great astronomer discovered twenty new variable stars and ten new minor planets. Of the latter six were discovered in this city. For thirty years Norman Robert Pogson was government astronomer at Madras and in his work was assisted in his last years by his scholarly daughter who was only next to him in the study of the luminous bodies in the firmament. In 1891 he went to rest and a tablet to his memory is in St. George's Cathedral.

In the days of the Company there was an office known as the Master Attendant. The first European to hold it was George who died in 1799. The remains of this officer who improved the water supply of Black Town and the Fort lie buried in St. Mary's Cemetery. Another Master Attendant who breathed his last in this city and whose tombstone has now disappeared from St. Mary's Cemetery was Hugh Boyd. He was acquainted with Goldsmith, and Pitt believed strongly that was the famous Junius. Among the tablets in St. George's Cathedral is one for Christopher Biden who was for nineteen years Master Attendant of Madras. He founded and endowed the "Biden Home for destitute seamen" at Royapuram which is used for a different purpose to-day.

There is no man in Madras who has not heard of the great lawyer Norton. Even in the nooks of distant villages there are often tales told of how Norton used to argue in the courts and invariably win cases. His father John Bruce Norton whose portrait adorns the Pachayappa's College Hall was Advocate General of Madras for eight years. His father Sir John David Norton who was judge of the High Court for a couple of years died in 1843 and a marble tablet to his memory is to be seen in St. George's Cathedral. Another legal man whose name is still remembered is Stephen Popham who sleeps in St. Mary's Cemetery and after whom Popham's Broadway, now shortened into Broadway, takes its name.

The names of several able civilians of Madras are remembered either through their monuments or those of members of their family. An excellent monument by Flaxman in St. Mary's Church in the fort showing four types of mourners beside a portrait medallion perpetuates the memory of Josiah Webb who was for several years the Chief Secretary to the Government of Madras. A marble monument by Gibson in St. George's Cathedral mentions the name of Anne Antoinett Evelina the wife of Henry Chamier, Chief Secretary to Government. In the same Cathedral is a tablet to the memory of the wife of John Orr, the Collector of Salem, who is still remembered with gratitude as the good man who planted trees to provide shade for sun-scorched travellers on the roadside. John Dent, a distinguished Civilian has a monument by Weekes in St. George's Cathedral showing him at work with his munshi. There is perhaps no one who has visited Adyar and not heard of Brodie's Castle. James Brodie of the Company's Civil service, the name of whose family is so imprinted on the house, was drowned in Adyar and lies buried in St. Mary's Cemetery.

Next to the military officers it is the merchants whose associations with this city are most easily remembered by names that linger here and there in different parts of the city and remind us of an older Madras wherein they all played their parts before some of them were laid to rest in the very place of their activities. Parry's Corner is on the lips of every busy man in George Town. The offices of Parry & Co., are situated even to-day in that same corner; and the place takes its name after William Parry the founder of the firm whose monument by Baily is in St. George's Cathedral. John Binny popularly known as 'Deaf' Binny was for a time a surgeon in the Company's service and has his last resting place in St. George's Cathedral Cemetery. Binny & Co., the firm of which he is the founder, still perpetuates his name more than eleven decades after his death. A member of the family of the merchant Cammiade whose name still lingers in Cammiade gardens, Nungambakkam, and was responsible for the building of Salt Cotaurs sleeps in the Roman Catholic Church, Armenian Street. In the same place lies buried Adrian Fourbeck, a merchant of Madras who should always be remembered as the man who left the legacy that gave a bridge over the Adyar near Lushington's gardens.

Associations with celebrities have made some persons interesting and among such who have found a last resting place in this city are Henry Inman a captain in the Royal Navy who served with Lord Nelson at Copenhagen, Colonel Richard Baird Smith the husband of Florence De Quincy, the second daughter of the celebrated writer, Joseph Garrow whose poetically minded daughter, Theodosia, the sister-in-law of Anthony Trollope, was appreciated by Landor, Sir Samuel Hood, Vice Admiral, through whose wife, Lady Hood, Sir Walter Scott sent a long letter to his brother-in-law, Charles Carpenter, who was a commercial resident at Cuddalore. The tomb stones of the brothers of Addison who died in Madras are, however, unfortunately, missing.

Among the other tombs in the city there are some which are interesting from certain other points of view. The number of years that

Mary Patterson lived to take cognisance of events that happened during a whole century have made her an interesting person. A tomb stone in the Jewish cemetery in Mint Street is interesting as a skyed one, a large tree having lifted it bodily from the ground keeping it in the air all the time. Six of the Powney family lie buried in the High Court enclosure, of whom Captain John Heron is important as "the first to make a chart of the Hoogly river" and as "sojourner in India for 61 years." In the Roman Catholic Cathedral lie buried the remains of Edward Samuel Moorat after whom is named Moorat's gardens, where the office of the Director of Public Instruction is now situated; he is the man who sold the Pantheon about the early thirties of the nineteenth century and here the Madras Museum has had its origin and growth. The only tomb-stone containing a Greek inscription in South India and one earlier than any in Calcutta or Benares is a stone in two pieces with the letters badly worn dated 1727 and mentions one Joannes Constantinus. It is preserved in the Madras Museum. Of the Armenian monuments in Madras the most noteworthy are that of Shameer Sultan who granted the site where the Armenian Church, in which he lies buried, now stands and whose painting in oils, now lost, has supplied the idea of a crest for his family, and that of Petrus Uscan de Coja Pogas the most important Armenian about his time who was a member of the Council for a time. This man was responsible for the Marmalong bridge and the steps up St. Thomas' Mount.

Some Ancient Families and Personalities

BY

K. VENKATASWAMI NAIDU, B.A., B.L.,
Mayor of Madras.

THE history of a nation is the history of its great men and families. These people have, from time to time, shaped the fortunes of the country. Similarly, cities have their own important men and families, whose history is worth studying. No history of a city will be complete without a description of such men and their affairs. When the city of Madras was formed several *desayis* or headmen were appointed each to represent one community. These headmen or *desayis* as they were called, presided over family meetings and decided family disputes. They had special honours and first *tambulam* was always given to them. They had special flags, festoons, trumpets, etc. All the community men had special regard for the headman's words. Some of these persons were big men with the Company, but even apart, they commanded the respect of the community. According to H. D. Love, the leading merchants in 1705 were Kalavay Chetty, Venkata Chetty, Kitti Narayan, Sunkuram and Bala Chetty. Some of these were heads of the castes. These heads of the castes used to be summoned to Fort St. George to decide important civil cases arising in the town. I shall now briefly describe some of these ancient families and personages.

BERI FAMILY

In the early part of the seventeenth century, when the East India Company's Agents were obliged to remove their Factory from Armagon, the Company's Agents at Calcutta, requested the assistance of one of the ancestors of the family named Berry Timmapa, an inhabitant of Palacole, a Dutch factory near Maddipollam, for using his influence with the native princes in this coast in order to establish a Factory. Accordingly, he came out to this part of the country, and procured permission from one Damerla Venkatapa Naick, to build a factory at Madras. But it was found necessary that the sanction of the ruling prince of the Dynasty of Rayalu should be obtained for it previously. Berry Timmapa succeeded in procuring a *Sasanam* or Grant from Sreeranga Rayalu who then reigned at Chandragiri, for three villages, namely, Egmore, Tondavadoo and Poodupauk. Damerla Venkatapa Naick, at Poonamallee, insisted upon building the Town in the name of his father Chennapa Naick. The Dynasty of Rayalu was at that time in a declining state.

Berry Timmapa assisted in building a Town (which was accordingly called Chennapatnam) in the north side of the factory, and in inviting people from different parts of the country, by the aid of a Cowle from the Company's Agents to settle there. Lands for both right and left hand castes were allotted separately. He also caused two pagodas, one of Vishnu, and the other Siva, to be built there, calling the former Chenna Kesava Perumal and the latter Chenna Mallesvara, both after the same name, nearly one hundred and eighty years ago. According to Hamilton's Gazetteer and that of the Fragments of Orme's Hindustan, it was in the year 1639.

Mr. Day, the then Agent, undertook to erect a factory, on the spot, where there was a Fishermen's Kuppam, the headman of which was a Christian named Madarasen. He threw some obstacle in allowing the piece of ground he was in possession of, which was his plantain garden. But Berry Timmapa used his influence to obtain that spot, promising him that he would cause the factory, which was about to be erected, to be called after his name, as Madarasenpatam or commonly called Madraspatam.

Some time after Berry Timmapa had procured a Perwannah from the Sultan of Golconda, for Land Custom, by deputing his dependents Cassah Veerana, and Sunkoo Ram Chetty, and Tumby Chetty, the former of Komati caste and the latter Berry Chetty.

It was stated that Berry Timmapa had held a seat in Council and a salute of five guns was fired, whenever he paid a visit to the Agent or Governor on Pongal days. Besides, six yards of superfine scarlet were presented to him on that occasion. It is interesting to note that the honorary coat and cane of the President were deposited with Berry Timmapa in his house, and taken out to be worn on every Quarter Sessions and the new year's day. This is borne out by the original of a letter written by Mr. Thomas Pitt, in the name of Berry Timmapa, nephew (son of Pedda Venkatadry, first brother to B. Timmapa) to B. Timmapa, No. 1, dated the 19th July 1698, still with the family.

To his son-in-law, Kittunarain, the Governor was pleased to grant a Cowle, for the eminent services he had rendered to the Company, at different times, especially for the assistance to procure investment at Masulipatam and Maddipollam in the year 1700, exempting all manner of customs except the ordinary ones for two generations.

The descendants of B. Timmapa of Percawar caste had the honour of being called *middle caste* at that time, because they were the founders of the City of Madraspatam, and they were allowed to go upon conveyance, and conduct all ceremonies in both right and left hand caste streets, in proof of which there is a copy of an award or agreement, No. 3 between right and left hand castes signed in the presence of the above said middle caste and deposited with them, (in the hands of Goda Ancana), dated 28th October 1728.

B. Timmapa's grandson by Chinna Venkatadry, his second brother, held the rent of paddy fields, and salt pans, one of the oldest possessions of the Company, in the year 1742, for a term of five years. From the Cowle No. 4, it will be seen that the rent of the farm, was held in the family, for a long time since the year 1684.

There is a copper plate grant by Chika Raya Timmia, the prince of Poonganur now in Arcot District, conferring a *Dasavandam*, in the name of Berry Pedda Venkatadry (Timmapa's first brother), Berry Chinna Venkatadry (Timmapa's second brother), Berry Venkatanaranapa Timmapa's eldest son), and Cassah Veerana, his dependent or agent, (whom he had deputed to Hyderabad before) for erecting a tank, named Chennapatanam Chervoo, in the year Shaliwagana 1598 or Nala year, answering to A.D. 1676, nearly 144 years ago, the fruits of which *Dasavandam* are enjoyed by his descendants to this day.

The Mirasee or the right of packing up the Company's Bales, in the export warehouse, was held by Timmapa, and continued in the family ever since. Two or four caste people were also employed in it, not only here, but in all the Company's factories as far as Ganjam.

The descendants of Timmapa still enjoy certain rank and honour at Madras, however obscure it may be. Previous to the commencement of the annual festival, at the Vishnu and Siva Pagodas of the Town Temple, the Pagoda Brahmans, together with all the servants and musicians of the Pagoda, wait on Berry Venkatadry Naick, a descendant of Timmapa, now living, and obtain his formal permission to commence the festival.

Although the churchwardenship of the pagoda was held by different people, there has been a custom in the performance of the daily festivities to offer prayers in the name of Honourable Company and Berry Timmapa, and temple honours such as distributing Parwattan (honouring with a turban), Tirumalai (garland of flowers), Tirtham (the holy water), to the descendants of Timmapa to this day. It is further interesting to note that a special day's festival is being celebrated to this day every year in honour of Timmapa, in the pagoda of Tiruvottiyur, in the Mantapam built by him.

Chinna Venkatadry was the brother of Beri Timmapa, the Company's chief merchant and the first builder and warden of the Town Temple. He succeeded his brother Pedda Venkatadri as the chief merchant and was one of the first Alderman nominated to the Corporation of Madras at its foundation in 1687-88. He gifted away his house and garden near St. Thomas Mount to the Company. They now form a portion of the Government House, Guindy.

In the 18th century, the family of Beri Timmapa continued to be very prominent in Madras and was closely associated with the foundation, growth and prosperity of Chintadripet. Among the first twelve Aldermen of the Corporation, there were three Gentoos, viz., Alangatha Pillai, Muthu Viranna, and Chinna Venkatadry.

BANDLA FAMILY

Let me briefly mention about Bandla Ramaswami Naick of the Bandla family. He played a prominent part in the history of South India. He is a descendant of Beri Chinna Venkatadry. Bandla Ramaswami Naick rose from an ordinary writer's place to that of Head Sheristadar of Tinnevelly and held that place for over seven years. In recognition of his valuable services, which were in the highest degree creditable to the character of Ramaswami Naick, the Hon'ble East India Company granted the Shrotiriyam of Shevaram (Palayaseevaram) in the Zilla (District) of Chingleput. In one of the records it is stated that his allowance of 80 pagodas had been increased to 100 pagodas more on account of his character than for anything else. He was, besides, a man of charitable disposition. He built choultries for feeding the poor at Alwar Tirunagiri, Srivilliputtur and Conjeevaram and endowed properties for the maintenance of said choultries. He also built several temples and Mantapams.

SUNKUVAR FAMILY

The next important family in Madras was the Sunkuvar family. Sunkurama was Company's merchant in 1705. He was the chief man of the Right hand caste (Vaisya or Komatti). Sunkurama was permitted to purchase a house in Gate Street in the White Town for use as cloth godown. The descendants of this family still maintain their old dignity and command respect and influence in the community. Thambu Chetty was a chief merchant in 1724 and he belonged to the Left hand caste and Thambu Chetty Street took its name in Muthialpet from this merchant.

CONCLUSION

There are other families equally ancient which played a great part in the past but it is difficult to get accurate information about them. It is hoped that this paper will stimulate further investigation on this interesting theme.

SECTION III

INSTITUTIONS

The Poligars of Madras

By

Dr. E. Asirvatham, M.A., Ph.D.,

Reader, University of Madras.

The police arrangements of Old Madras were vested in a hereditary official known as the Poligar of Madras. The first of these watchmen, named Pedda Naick, ('senior naik' or 'big peon'), has left his name to a large section of the town, known as Peddanaikpetta. Formerly a suburb of Madras, it is to-day a part of George Town.

The office of the Poligar existed in the village of Madraspatam from very early times, and was recognised by the British from their first settlement. According to one account, the Poligars were the descendants of the Naiks, or chiefs, who had jurisdiction over the southern kingdoms, such as those of Tanjore and Madura, under the general control and supervision of the Rajah of Vijayanagar. In 1646 Poonamallee was owned and managed by the Poligar of the Damarla family. It was this family which ceded certain villages, including Madras Coopam, to the Merchants of the English Company in return for an annual sum of 1200 Madras Pagodas, besides the expenditure involved in supporting the 'Holy Pagodas.'

In the early days of the East India Company, the Poligar's police duties extended to the territory within the "Bound Hedge," outside the Fort, i.e., to the Black Town and the pettahs. After the fashion which prevailed in the villages of the time, the Poligar was responsible for the peace of the town. In return for his services, the Poligar was given certain paddy fields free of rent, and was allowed to levy petty duties on rice, fish, oil, betel-leaf, and betel-nut. He was also allowed to levy small duties on imports and exports. His chief duty was to provide a staff of peons (also known as taliars or watchmen) for the protection of the town. When any crime was committed, it was his business to detect the criminal; failing which he had to make good the losses of those who had suffered robbery. As one writer observes: "the Poligar was thus the prototype of the modern Burglary Insurance Company." The number of Poligar's peons in 1640 was twenty; but as the town grew and the work increased, the number also had to be increased. In 1659 the number was fifty and in 1701 it was raised to a hundred.

Another duty of the Poligar was to provide the Governor of Fort St. George, when called upon to do so, with a bodyguard of 150 peons; and provide escorts for officials. When "our dread Soveraigne King James the Second" was proclaimed King in 1685, the Fort St. George Consultation recorded:—

"The whole Councill, with the Commanders of Ships and the rest of the Rt. Hon'ble Companys servants and English Gentlemen, Inhabitants of the Citty, came to attend the President att the Garden House in a handsome equipage on Horse back. After that came Peddy Nague with his Peons, and the Chief Merchants, with a great number of the Inhabitants of the Gentue Town, all in Armes, bringing with them also Elliphants, Kettle Drums, and all the Country Musik."

At a time of insecurity in 1741, the Company sent the Poligar to escort the Nawab's family into Madras with 200 peons, to the accompaniment of 'country music,' which was probably the precursor of the Governor's Band. On State occasions such as the installation of the Mayor, the Poligar rode at the head of his peons in procession, accompanied by 'country music.' In 1727 the order of the procession was:

"Major John Roach on horseback at the head of a Company of Foot Soldiers, with Kettle drum, Trumpets and other Music.

The Dancing girls with the Country Music.
The Pedda Naigue on horseback at the head of Peons.
The Marshall with his Staff, on horseback
The old Mayor on the right hand and the New on the left.
The Aldermen two and two, all on horseback.
Six halberdiers
The Companys Chief Peon on horseback, with his Peons.
The Sheriff with a white Wand, on horseback.
The Chief Gentry in the Town, on horseback."

In 1699 when Ensign Thomas Salmon, who later became a well-known literary figure and eleven others ran away from Fort St. George garrison, it fell to the lot of the Poligar of Madras to apprehend the deserters and send them back to Madras. The old papers say that the deserters were apprehended sixty miles away from Madras in the interior and were sent back to the Fort a month later under promise of pardon. Notwithstanding the promise, Salmon was committed to prison and a few months later deported to England.

When a man was absconding and his brother was suspected of concealing him, the Poligar, in accordance with the custom of the day, recommended that the brother be "confined in the Choultry" till the man be delivered up; and the Governor gave the necessary sanction.

Watching merchants' goods and merchandise which were imported from abroad formed a part of the duties of the Poligar of Madras. The Poligar was even responsible for watching the company's clothes from being stolen when they were being washed at the washing town.

The Poligars at times served as recruiting officers. In 1698 when the Company's peons were inadequate to cope with the trouble with Daud Khan, the Pedda Naik's Talliars were utilised to supplement the garrison. When hostilities broke out between the French and English in 1745, two hundred peons were engaged from the Poligars in the neighbourhood of Madras. In the following year the Nawab was joined by the Pedda Naik with his peons and a body of Poligars.

The Poligars enjoyed several privileges, one of them being freedom from arrest. In 1736 the Mayor's Court Serjeant arrested a Poligar in a village 1½ miles from the Fort which was out of the Company's bounds, although, according to the Charter, the jurisdiction of the Court extended ten miles. On receipt of this news the Mayor was informed that the Poligars were exempt from arrest, and the man was then set free and compensated. The Fort St. George Consultation issued an order on 19th April, 1736 to the effect that "no Sheriff do serve any warrant of Arrest or Execution upon the Person of the Poligar of Madrass, or any of the Poligars of the Villages, nor upon their dwelling Houses where they keep their Prisoners, nor upon any of the Duties due and payable to them for the Guard and Safety of the Town and Villages."

Another privilege enjoyed by the Poligars was exemption from the payment of Quit Rent. In 1778 Government resolved "that the Pariars in the Parchery, the Poligar and his followers, together with the menial servants and poor Moors, consisting of Peons, Housekeepers, Masalgies, etc., be excused from paying Quit Rent or Scavenger's duty. But with respect to the Washermen, Town Pagodas, Europeans, Armenians and others, who evade it by making objections of various kinds, that the Rental General do proceed to recover it of them."

In 1672, re-affirming earlier orders regarding the Pedda Naik's allowances, Sir William Langhorn, "Governour and Agent for Affairs of the Honourable English East India Company in Fort St. George" ordered that:

"In Paddy Bancksall the former allowance was—Custome for the Gentu Pagoda, for every heape of paddy, one measure; for Peddinagg the watchman, on every greate ox-load of paddy, ¾ measure; for small ox-load, ½ measure.....

"The allowance of seaffish was: for every great nett, 5 ffish to the Hon'ble Company, and to Peddinagg the watchman 10 ffish. And on the ffish they catch with a hooke, one ffish for the Company, and one for Peddinagg the watchman......"

The duties charged of Christians were less than those charged of others, and the Company at one time protested against such discrimination to Fort St. George. In spite of the protest, the "usuall duty to the Pedda Naik" in 1684 was "for all Christians 3/32, and for all Jentues and Moores 5/32 per cent." As an acknowledgment that the Poligar held his place from and under the Company, according to the Cowle issued by Governor Pitt in 1701, the Poligar was required "to bring us in every year Twelve head of Dear in their season, and twelve Wild-hogs in their Season."

Towards the close of the seventeenth century there was a protracted dispute between Timappa Naik and Angarappa Naik for the post of Poligar of Madras and was finally decided by Government in favour of the latter in 1699.

During the siege of Fort St. George between 1758-59 the Poligar of Madras died. After his death it was resolved that his office and the petty taxes levied in support of it "be suspended till further orders." Sepoy guards in the Black Town were substituted for the Poligar's watchmen. But the demand for the Poligar was so great that five years later the old plan was restored and the son of the late Peddanaique was appointed Poligar.

In 1777 Vera Perumal, the Board Overseer of the Markets, recommended "that 25 Sepoys and some of the Polygar's peons attend at the Choultry office to prevent riots, secure the quiet of the bazar and the streets; and at night patrole the streets to pick up disorderly people, or those who can give no proper account of themselves." The Orders of the Board on these proposals were "A Guard and some Polygar's peons to attend at the Choultry office for the purpose here mentioned."

In the last quarter of the eighteenth century there were several complaints of the Poligar's conduct. He was accused of having allowed to escape from his Choultry a notorious robber who had been sentenced by the Court of Quarter Sessions of January 1795, "to be publickly whipped three times, and to be kept to hard labour on the Roads and public Works for the space of two years." The Poligar was deprived of his fees at the sea beach by the Board of Revenue. When he made his "humble representation" against this action, the Government issued the following order in 1796: "The Board are aware that the new regulations established for the collection of customs of this Presidency would deprive the poligar of the fees in question; but neither the utility of his office nor the merit of his conduct entitle him to any exemption from the general rule."

When official protection and patronage were withdrawn, it virtually meant the extinction of the office of Poligar. The inhabitants of the Black Town, however, petitioned the Government to retain his office in order to watch their houses and goods. The petition read:

"That from the Establishment of Madras, Peddanaik the Poligar had continued to receive certain fees from your Petitioners and Merchants for watching their Houses and goods, and held himself responsible for thefts committed at your Petitioners' Houses, and of the said Merchants' Goods and Merchandize......Government having lately ordered the said Poligars fee......[to] be discontinued in consequence of his having incurred your displeasure, thereby the Office of the said Poligar became abolished, and your Petitioners are constantly labouring under great fear and Apprehensions to secure their Properties: therefore may it please your Lordship to order the said Poligar's fees to be paid by your Petitioners and Merchants as usual, in condition of his Answering the thefts Committed at your Petitioners' Houses, which shall induce him to Employ a number of Watchers and thereby to secure your Petitioners' Property's......"

In 1798, in accordance with the recommendation of a police committee, the Governor re-instated the Poligar as "poligar of the Black Town and of the washing town." The Cowl issued by him ran as follows:—

"A *Cowl* granted by the Right Hon'ble Lord Hobart, President and Governor of Fort St. George, and the Council thereof, To Codungone Ungarapah Naig—

"1st. Having constituted and appointed you to be Watchman of the City of Madras and of the washing grounds near the Bound Hedge on the following Terms, you must keep a sufficient Number of good Peons, not less than 100 at least, for the preventing of Robberies and other disorders in the said City; and for their maintenance we allow you the following custom.

"2nd. That for all goods brought into the Land Custom House by all the Native Merchants you shall receive fees as formerly, viz. On Piece Goods as cleared at the Custom House, Seven and one half cash on each Pagoda value; on weighing goods as cleared at the Custom House, twenty Cash on each Pagoda value.

"3rd. That you shall collect from all Goods of all the Merchants, excepting Europeans, paying Duty at the Sea Gate as formerly; Piece

Goods, Raw Silk, Drugs, Grain, Lamp Oil seeds; twenty seven and a half cash on each Pagoda value; on Paddy, Rice, Comboloo......, Timbers, Planks, Palmiras, Reapers and Redwood, seven and a half cash on each Pagoda value.

"4th. That all inhabitants of the Town, excepting Europeans, shall pay you yearly, for a Great House three fanams, and small Houses two fanams.

"5th. The Peons aforementioned are to be always kept and employed for the security and Peace of this City of Madras as the Governor shall direct.

"6th. When any Person paying Custom as aforesaid to you has been robbed, such Person will acquaint you, and if satisfaction is not obtained in due time, in any case not exceeding two months, application shall be made to the Governor or the Justices of the Peace, who will take proper measures to cause you to make good the property.

"7th. The Hon'ble Company will allow you the usual fee of seven and half Cash on each pagoda value of cloth for watching their Cloth at the washing Green, but it is required that you should make good the property that may be robbed."

By the time this Cowl was granted it is probable that the Poligar had come under administrative control. His office was abolished in 1806 and a regular police was formed, which, however, continued the methods and persons of the old system. In 1858 another effort was made at reform, and the police force was remodelled on the same lines as the provincial constabulary.

Mayor and Corporation of Madras

An account of the establishment of the first 'Body Corporate and Politick' by Royal Charter dated 30th December, 1687.

By

A. R. Ingram,

Author of : '*The Gateway to India*'

Municipal affairs in Madras in the early days of the East India Company's settlement involved no great official establishments. The Fort, with its garrison of twenty-five men and the Factory were administered by an Agent and Council of two factors, while the village of Madrassapatam, which was included in the grant of land upon which the fortress was built, was controlled by a staff of native officials. The chief of these were the Headman, the Accountant, and the Watchman, but there were numerous minor functionaries such as the potter, barber, washerman, carpenter, sweeper, etc. All these offices were hereditary, and the earlier occupants had been remunerated by lands held practically free of assessment and by petty fees, which terms were continued by the Company on taking possession. The population was then roughly seven thousand, and, except for the settling of periodical faction fights, their duties were not very onerous. With trade increasing, however, and Madras tending to become the chief market on the Coromandel coast, the village rapidly developed into an important township, and with its greater prosperity the status of the officials gained in dignity. Thus, in 1652, the Agent became 'President,' the Headman, 'Governor of the Town' or 'Adigar', the Accountant 'Town Conicoply', and the Watchman, (now assisted by a number of Talliars) the 'Peddanaigue'.

The Governor of the Town sat at the Choultry, or Town House, as a Justice of the Peace, where he was assisted by the Town Conicoply. The Choultry was a court of petty causes, a custom-house, and a registration office for the recording of sales of real property, and the licensing of slaves. The building was situated at the junction of Market Street with Choultry Street, afterwards called Choultry Gate Street.

The Peddanaigue arrested evil-doers, and confined them in the Choultry jail pending their appearance before the Governor of the Town.

During Streynsham Master's presidency, 1675-81, the Choultry Court was reorganised and the number of Justices increased from two to three, a proviso being made that not less than two should sit for the trial of Causes, and for registration of bills of sale of land and other property.

For some time the need of a superior Court had been felt, so Master's council established a Court of Judicature for the trial by jury of civil and criminal causes. This was, in effect, the formation of a Supreme Court and was held at the Chapel in the fort upon every Wednesday and Saturday; but all causes of small misdemeanour, matters of the peace, and actions of debt of the value of fifty pagodas or less were examined and decided by the Justices of the Choultry as formerly, and also all other causes of a higher or greater value by consent of the parties. Right of appeal to the Court of Judicature was allowed.

Another feature of Master's administration was the initiation of a demand for ground rent from the inhabitants, and the levy of a tax for conservancy. These originated in London, for, on the strength of a *firman* issued in 1674, the Court of Directors considered that they possessed adequate authority to impose taxes other than customs. They accordingly wrote to Fort St. George on 24th December 1675:

"The ffort and Town of Madrassapatam being made over to us by the King of Golcundah, Wee would have you to consider whither we have not a right to a Quitt Rent for the howses in the Town, or what other Improvement may be made, by virtue of that Grant."

This enquiry raised some perturbation in Madras, the Council demurring, and explaining that the native population were "altogether unacquainted with such Customs, and will not be brought to understand and practice them." They suggested as an alternative that all land and property sales should be absolute bargains, each purchaser paying a reasonable rate "to be set." The tax for conservancy appeared to present a lesser problem and was first imposed in 1678, by means of a house-tax. For its purpose the Council created the office of 'Scavenger' whose duty, it should be noted, was to collect the cash, not the sweepings. The earliest incumbent was the 'Scrivan of the Choultry,' but the job was no sinecure as the inhabitants made vociferous objection to a list or roll being taken of the houses in the town, proposing rather to make a voluntary contribution to defray the cost of cleanliness. On being investigated it was found that the objection really amounted to a fear that if such a roll were compiled it would form a ready means to levy other impositions. This suspicion was well founded, for opportunity was soon taken to impress upon the inhabitants that the cost of upkeep of the city walls should be borne by the community in general instead of devolving upon "those poor people that lived next to the walls."

(This is probably an allusion to rent paid for the use of the recesses in, or lean-to sheds against the walls.) The mass response to this suggestion was "that it had never yet been required of them for these forty years, and the Company had thriven well, and were better able to bear it themselves now than ever." The Council's official comment on this native protest was "by this it may be observed how jealous this people are of being imposed upon by new customs." Nevertheless the tax was imposed, the levy ranging from ¼ to 1 fanam per house, the total assessment bringing in 110½ fanams,[1] two-thirds of which was allocated to the cost of four coolies, the remaining third going to the Choultry scrivan for collection and supervision. The tax was levied on 118 houses, in the Christian town and on 75 in the Out town.

Also about this time, weights and measures were regulated according to the 'Standard of the Choultry' which bore the Company's mark; and in August 1678 all tavern-keepers were directed to appear at the Court of Judicature to take out licences. These authorised the holders to sell by retail 'any kind of Wine, Beere, Mum, or other Europe Liquors; Punch, Arrack, or other Indian Liquors; and to keepe a common Victualling house, or house of entertainment.' These licences were farmed for one year at 205 pagodas.

These revenues did not go far towards the expenditure on a growing town which now had a population of three hundred thousand, the influx being due largely to the freedom of religious practice which the settlement offered. Nor did they contribute greatly towards the outlay on the fortifications and other necessary buildings which, at December 1684, had cost the Company £300000 in all. The Directors therefore wrote: "You must never give over contriving easy methods for raising revenue ......until you have arrived at such a measure of constant Income as may sufficiently serve your keeping in repair and enlarging our ffortifications, and the constant maintenance of 500 European Souldiers." From letters received in the interim they had learned of the reactions of the populace of Madras to the quit-rent and conservancy proposals, and returned to the attack in their letter to the Fort dated 16th March 1685: "On the meantime wee are resolved to have our Out Town of Madras walled round and competently fortify'd at the charge of the Inhabitants, whether it displease them or any body else; and therefore wee require you to go about it forthwith, and take Compass enough; and as you proceed, to levy charge therof of and from the Inhabitants by a pound rate, according to the respective value of their houses, which, after this is done, will be worth 3 times what they are now; so that we shall do

1. The value of the fanam varied from 32 to 36 to the pagoda. In 1675 the Company fixed the exchange rate between England and India at 9s. 8d. for the pagoda and 2s. 3d. for the rupee.

them good against their wills, which, when they are older and wiser, they will thank us for."

A problem of another kind then confronted the Company in the departure for Indian ports of a number of English trading vessels, the owners and masters of which were flagrantly contravening their monopoly charter. This was not altogether a new experience, but hitherto the offenders if and when caught, had to be brought to England for trial. The Directors resented this expense and inconvenience, and, so that they might deal with the interlopers at first hand, obtained from King Charles II a new charter authorising the erection of Courts of Admiralty at Madras and Bombay. Advice reached Madras that a 'Judge Advocate' would be sent by an early opportunity 'for the hearing and determining of all Suits and Causes under their government with the assistance of two merchants.' In the interim the President was empowered to act as Judge Advocate and to proceed upon the terms of the charter. This was read as the 'silencing' of the Court of Judicature, but as neither the President nor anyone else knew the procedure of an Admiralty Court the old method was continued. Eventually their difficulties were overcome and the Court was established on 10th July 1686.

The foregoing will acquaint the reader with the early development of Madras so far as the social services, maintenance of law and order, and the protection of its citizens are concerned, and it is significant that defence measures loom largely in the records. There was reason for it, as the Company's servants in the Mogul's dominions had for some time been subjected to insidious persecution and interference from the district officials, so much so that the withdrawal of the Gujerat and Bengal factories was under consideration. The obvious bases for withdrawal were Bombay on the west coast, and Madras on the east, both of which had the advantage of being south of the Mogul's territory, and were held under independent grants. These advantages, however, were more superficial than solid, for war was in the offing, and it was known that the Emperor Aurungzeb had taken the field in person against the Kingdoms of Bijapur, Golconda and Maharashtra. There was, consequently, a grave risk that if his arms prevailed, these havens of refuge, being in the zone of hostilities, might be swept into the Mogul's net. The Company's position therefore became one of extreme difficulty as, though they traded under Royal Charter, they were not in actual sense a State concern and could not depend upon national aid in the event of being attacked. The ready remedy, therefore, was to seek the protection of the British Crown, which was obtained, and the Court of Directors thereupon ordered that both Madras and Bombay should be declared Regencies.

GOVERNOR ELIHU YALE

—*By Courtesy of the Librarian, Connemara Public Library.*

Sensing an emergency, the Directors arranged for the early despatch to Madras of three hundred soldiers, drafted from the King's troops in Ireland, and instructed the factors to see that the city was victualled and otherwise equipped to withstand a six months siege. By way of defining their attitude towards the warring factions, the Court authorised Madras to continue to pay to the King of Golconda the twelve hundred pagodas of quit-rent for the territory round the city, but in the event of his having been worsted in the conflict with the Mogul, then the President was not only to refuse to pay the quit-rent, but to declare the place the property of the Company as delegates of His Majesty the King of Great Britain. The next step taken by the Court of Directors was to ensure that the internal administration of Madras should correspond with its new character of a Regency, so they made application to the King to erect it, by Charter, into a Corporation. When this proposal was discussed in Privy Council, some argument ensued as to whether such Charter should proceed from the King, under the Great Seal, or from the Company, by the exercise of its delegated sovereignty, under its Broad Seal. His Majesty ultimately decreed that the Charter should be under the Company's seal, for reason that 'the Corporation must be always, in some measure, subject to the control of the President and Council.'

Elihu Yale was President at that time, and it was evidently the purpose of the Directors that he should be free from municipal control.

The charter was drawn up in due course and proved a lengthy document, far too detailed to be quoted here in full. However, the following are its principal provisions:

> *Charter granted by the Governor and Company of Merchants Trading into the East Indies to the Mayor, Aldermen and Burgesses of Madras, 30th December, 1687.*
>
> 'We, The said *Governor and Company,* having found by Experience and the Practice of other European Nations in India that the makeing and establishing of Corporations in Citties and Towns that are grown exceedingly populous tends more to the well-governing of such populous Places, and to the Increase of Trade, than the constant Use of the Law Martial in trivial Concerns, We have therefore......for the speedier Determination of small Controversies of little Moment, frequently happening among the unarmed Inhabitants, thought it convenient to make, ordain, and constitute Our Town of *Fort St. George,* commonly called the Christian Town and Citty of Madrassapatam upon the coast of *Choromandel* in *East Indies,* and all the Territorys thereto belonging, not exceeding the Distance of Ten Miles from *Fort St. George,*

to be a Corporation under Us by the Name and Title of the Mayor Aldermen and Burgesses of the Town of *Fort St. George* and Citty of *Madrassapatam*; And therefore We, The said *Governor and Company,* do by these Presents ordain, constitute and appoint that the Inhabitants of *Fort St. George* and *Madrassapatam* aforesaid, or so many of them as shall be hereby nominated......shall be One Body Corporate and Politick in Deed and in Name, by the Name of the Mayor, Aldermen and Burgesses of the Town of *Fort St. George* and Citty of *Madrassapatam* really and fully for ever....'

The Corporation, which was to come into existence from the 29th September 1688, consisted of the Mayor, twelve Aldermen, and sixty or more Burgesses. The Mayor was to hold office for one year, the Aldermen during their lives, or residence in Madras.

'And for the better Execution of Our Intent and Meaning in this Behalf, We do nominate, constitute and make *Nathaniel Higginson,* Second of Our Council of *Fort St. George,* the First and Modern (=current) Mayor of the said Corporation......Also we do assign, nominate and constitute *John Littlton, Thomas Wavell,* and *William Fraser,* three of Our Council of *Fort St. George, Daniel Chardin* French Merchant, *Lucas Lewis de Oliveria* and *Alvaro Capella de Valle,* Portugal Merchants, *Bartholomew Rodrigues, Jaques de Paiva* and *Domingos de Porte,* Hebrew Merchants, *China Vencatadre, Mooda Verona* and *Allingal Pella,* Gentu Merchants, to be the Twelve First and Modern Aldermen.'

Then follows the names of twenty-nine free merchants nominated Burgesses. A new Mayor was to be elected annually from the Aldermen. Any vacancy among the Aldermen was to be filled by election from the Burgesses, subject to the condition that three Aldermen were always to be covenanted servants. The Burgesses, who were not to exceed one hundred and twenty in number, were to be elected by the Mayor and Aldermen.

The Mayor and Aldermen were to be a

'Court of Record within Our Town of *Fort St. George* and City of *Madrassapatam* and the Precincts thereof aforesaid, and the Mayor of the said Corporation for the Time being shall be always One of the Justices of the Peace within the Precincts of the said Corporation and without the Walls of Our said Fort.'

The Mayor and Aldermen might levy a tax

'for the building of a Town Hall or Guild Hall......of a publick Gaol for the detaining in Prison such Criminals or Debtors as

CITY COAT OF ARMS

—*By courtesy of the Corporation of Madras.*

shall be committed to the Custody of some Gaolor to be appointed for that purpose......of a convenient School House or House for the teaching of the Gentues or Native Children to speak, read and write the English Tongue, and to understand Arethmetick and Merchant's Accompts; and for such further Ornaments and Edifices as shall......be thought convenient.'

The Mayor's Court was empowered to try all causes civil or criminal. Right of appeal lay in civil cases when the value of the award exceeded three pagodas, and in criminal cases if the offender was sentenced to lose life or limb.

Two silver-gilt maces were to be carried before the Mayor by two English-born sergeants and a silver oar before the Admiralty Judge. Robes of scarlet serge were ordained for the Mayor and Aldermen, and white silk gowns for the Burgesses. The Mayor and Aldermen might 'enjoy the Honour and Priviledge of wearing Rundellos and Kettysols.[2] born over them, and......may ride on Horseback in the same order as is used by the Lord Mayor and Aldermen of *London,* having their Horses decently furnished with Saddles, Bridles, and other Trimmings after one Form and Manner.'

A rather modern note was sounded in the preliminary stages when Nathaniel Higginson declined the appointment on the grounds of overwork, saying that his duties as Member of Council, Book-keeper and Mintmaster would not allow of his accepting office. His objections were overruled, however, and the installation took place on the date fixed, 29th September 1688. It is recorded that 'The President, the Mayor, Recorder, Aldermen, Burgesses, and Chief of the Inhabitants mett at the Fort Hall, before whom the Rt. Hon'ble Company's Charter for this Corporation was publickly read by the Secretary, after which the President administered Oaths to the Mayor and Recorder for their due performance of their Places, and then the Mayor and Recorder did the like to the Aldermen and Burgesses in their severall manner and formes. Awhile after, went to a Handsome dinner, and about three in the Evening the Whole Corporation march't in their Severall Robes with the Maces before the Mayor, to the Town Hall.'

While the citizens of Madras were thus celebrating the inception of a national settlement, the ancient kingdoms of Bijapur and Golconda had already fallen before the might of the Emperor Aurungzeb, and his troops roamed at large throughout the conquered territory. Then news came through that the Company's servants at Hugli and Surat had been

2. Umbrellas of State.

in conflict with Mogul forces. Whether these clashes represented localised outbreaks or an actual state of war was not yet apparent, but, with a potential enemy almost at their gates, the garrison prepared for a siege. But a greater menace to Mogul domination occupied the Emperor's thoughts to the exclusion of all else and he suddenly struck camp, despatching ten thousand horse southward to deal with the Mahrattas, and so, for the moment, Madras was spared the ordeal of war.

The initial activities of the Corporation centred upon schemes for the paving of the streets, construction of sewers, and the building of bridges, schools, and a Town Hall, but difficulty was encountered in persuading the President to allocate funds or revenues for their purpose. Yale, for some reason or other, failed to enthuse over town development, and consequently lived in constant friction with the officials. Higginson resigned the Mayoralty within six months of his appointment, and went to Bengal, where he traded as a 'free' merchant for three years. He then returned to Madras and was re-employed in his former rank, but sidestepped the civic chair by succeeding Yale as President on 23rd. October 1692. He returned to England for good in the year 1700.

REFERENCES :

Vestiges of Old Madras : by Henry Davison Love.
Annals of the East India Company : by John Bruce.

A History of the Mayoralty of Madras

By

RAO SAHEB C. S. SRINIVASACHARI, M.A.,
Professor Annamalai University

INTRODUCTORY

THE growth of the City of Madras in the first century of its life was all that could be desired. The crowded Indian Town that rose up immediately to the north of Fort St. George soon came to have a population of about 40,000; while the outlying suburbs of Muthialpettah to the north of the Indian Town, Peddunaickenpettah to its west and the more distant villages like Triplicane, Egmore and Purasawakam soon came to be filled with weavers and other castemen whose following was closely bound up with the manufacture of cloth.

Governor Streynsham Master (1678-81) was the first to make a serious attempt at the conservancy of the streets. He proposed to keep the Town, evidently the White Town in the Fort, clean after the manner followed in England by taxing every house at a moderate rate and to appoint a Scavenger to collect the tax and to hire coolies to carry away the dirt and filth from the streets. He desired to appoint a clerk for supervising the great market that lay between the Indian and White Towns and to make arrangements for the perambulation of the bounds of the City during night-time. He would also insist upon the proper licensing of all tavern-keepers, victualling houses and places of entertainment.

When Master proposed to impose a house-tax, in Black Town, the Indian residents stoutly resisted the proposal and said that they would make their arrangements for cleaning the streets. Consequently, the Governor had to drop the proposal of the house-tax for the time being and imposed duties on arrack and paddy and raised that on tobacco in order to meet his conservancy arrangement.

His successor, Governor Gyfford (1685-87), re-organised the Black Town Police which consisted of a number of peons under the control of the Peddanayak. The next Governor, Elihu Yale (1687-92), started the Corporation of Madras under instructions from the Court of Directors; this Corporation is the earliest of its kind in the British India; and its significance has not been sufficiently stressed by historians of British India like Mill and Thornton. The originator of the scheme was Sir Josiah

Child, the masterful and imperious Governor of the Court of Directors, who had already made the fire and vigour of his pen felt often by the Madras Council.

The idea of a municipal government for Madras was taken by Child from the Dutch Government in the East Indies. In the general letter to Madras dated the 28th September 1687, Child detailed a plan for the formation of a Corporation composed of Indians mixed with some Englishmen and equipped with a regular Mayor, Aldermen and Burgesses, a Recorder and a Town Clerk and armed with power to decide petty cases and to levy rates upon the inhabitants for the building of schools, of a Town Hall and a Jail. This elaborate letter is given in extracts below.

" But if you could contrive a form of a Corporation to be established, of the Natives mixed with some English freemen, for aught we know some public use might be made thereof ; and we might give the members some privileges and pre-eminencies by Charter under our seal, that might please them (as all men are naturally with a little power); and we might make a public advantage of them, without abating essentially any part of our dominion when we please to exert it. And it is not unlikely that the heads of the several castes, being made Aldermen and some others Burgesses, with power to choose out of themselves yearly their Mayor, and to tax all the inhabitants for a Town Hall, or any public building for themselves to make use of,—your people would more willingly and liberally disburse five shilling towards the public good, being taxed by themselves, than six pence imposed by our despotical power (notwithstanding they shall submit to when we see cause), were Government to manage such a Society, as to make them proud of their honour and preferment, and yet only ministerial, and subservient to the ends of the Government, which under us is yourselves.

" We direct nothing positively in this, but refer it to your consideration, and, if you think it may redound to the public good, and that you may the better adapt it to the good of the place, and establishing of our absolute power over it, and unto some similitude to the forms of such like Corporations in England where there is always a Governor, a superior power and a garrison, we have thought fit to send you a copy of the later Charter granted by His Majesty to the Borough of Portsmouth, where Sir John Biggs (Judge of the new Court of Admiralty at Madras) was Recorder, and understands well not only that constitution, but the practical way of proceeding it.

" We know this can be no absolute platform for you. You may make great alterations according to the nature of the place and the people, and the difference of laws, customs, and almost everything else, between

England and India; but this will serve as a foundation from whence to begin your considerations and debates concerning this affair; which will require great wisdom and much thinking and foresight, to create such a Corporation in Madras, as will be beneficial to the Company and place, without the least diminution of the sovereign power His Majesty has entrusted us with, and which we are resolved to exercise there during His Majesty's royal pleasure and confidence in us.

" Upon the whole matter, if you think any such constitution beneficial, and shall send us a Charter filled up with the names of the first and modern Mayor, Aldermen and Burgesses,—the proper habits and ornaments we shall enjoin them to wear in the Court House and upon all other solemn occasions,—and what maces, or ensigns of authority, we shall admit to be carried before them by their proper officers or serjeants, —we shall consider of it, and probably return it to you, engrossed under our larger seal, with none or very little alteration.

" We conceive their Court Books must always be kept in the English tongue; and the Town Clerk must always be an Englishman that can speak Portuguese and Gentoo; and their Recorder must be the same. The habit of the Aldermen in that hot country, we think ought to be thin scarlet silk gowns; their number twelve, besides the Mayor; that they may be allowed to have Kettysols over them. The Burgesses to wear black silk gowns; their number to be limited to 60, 80, or 100 as you shall find most convenient. The sergeants attending them, to bear silver maces gilt, not exceeding one yard in length. All officers to be elected by the Mayor and Aldermen, with the approbation of our President, and to be paid by the Corporation such reasonable salaries as the Mayor and Aldermen shall think fit and to have such fees established as shall be settled and appointed by them with the approbation of our President and Council. And to give the Mayor and some of the Aldermen power to be always Justices of the Peace, as in the Portsmouth Charter and to have power to try all causes that shall be brought before them,—to erect a proper prison for the use of the Corporation, and to award judgment and execution in all causes that shall be exhibited before them. The judgment to go always according to the sense of the Mayor and major part of the Aldermen present. But if any party thinks himself injured in a cause exceeding the value of twenty shillings by the sentence of the said Mayor and Aldermen,—the party offended may appeal for a re-hearing to our Judge and Judicature of the Admiralty; who shall determine any cause brought before them by appeal, within two Court days next after the appeal brought; and their determination shall be final. In all civil causes, any party grieved by the sentence of the said Mayor and Aldermen, or any Mayor or Justice of the said Corporation, may appeal to our

President and Council for redress, who shall determine thereof the very next Council day ensuing, to the end that justice be not delayed.

"We think it may be convenient that in the said Court of Aldermen, being twelve beside the Mayor, there should never be above three English freemen, and three Portuguese; the other seven to be Moors and Gentoos. But if you find any inconvenience or inconsistency, in the particulars we have propounded, you may correct or alter them in draught you send us for such a Corporation.

"The Mayor and two Aldermen shall be a quorum for the trial of petty causes; but no duty shall be levied upon the inhabitants for public structures, officers salaries or other ornaments, but with consent of the Mayor and at least six of the Aldermen.

"The Mayor, Aldermen and Burgesses, and all their officers, before they enter upon their respective trusts shall take an oath to be true and faithful to His Majesty, to the Company, and to the Company's General of India for the time being.

"In your nomination of the first Aldermen, and for ever thereafter, you must observe not to make two brothers at the same time Aldermen, nor any that are near kindred; but so mix the heads of all castes in that Court that you may always hold the balance. Many other particulars of this and other kinds, you may find wisely provided for in the Dutch papers before mentioned, which will be worth your studying and frequent perusal.

"Our design in the whole is to set up the Dutch government among the English in the Indies (than which a better cannot be invented) for the good of posterity, and to put us upon an equal footing of power with them to offend or defend, or enlarge the English dominion and unite the strength of our nation under one entire and absolute command subject to us; as we are and ever shall be most dutifully to our own sovereign. But this distinction we will make, that we will always observe our own old English terms, viz., Attorney-General instead of Fiscal, Aldermen instead of Scepin, Burgesses instead of Burghers, Serjeants instead of Bailies, President and Agent instead of Commander, Director or Commissary etc."

Sir Josiah Child was particular that the Court of Aldermen should be representative of the English residents and also of the Portuguese, the Moors and the Hindus of the City. He insisted that the Mayor, Aldermen and Burgesses should take an oath of loyalty to the English King and to the Company. In the elaborate letter above referred to, Child invited the Madras Governor and Council to offer their own suggestions to his draft scheme. But yet within three months of his first letter, he and the Deputy President of the Company had an audience with King James, and it was determined at this audience to send out already-drawn Charter under the Company's seal for the formation of the Madras Corporation.

THE CORPORATION AND THE MAYOR

The Charter was issued by the Company on the 30th of December 1687; and along with it were sent out the Maces* and the Sword together with orders that the Corporation should be immediately started. "Our Town of Fort St. George, commonly called the Christian Town and City of Madrassapatam upon the Coast of Coromandel in the East Indies and all the territories thereunto belonging not exceeding the distance of 10 miles from Fort St. George, to be a Corporation under Us by the name and title of the Mayor, Aldermen and Burgesses of the Town of Fort St. George and City of Madrassapatam," was the heading of the Charter. There were to be twelve Aldermen and sixty Burgesses. Mr. Nathaniel Higginson, Second in Council, was nominated to be the first Mayor. Three other English members of the Council, three Portuguese merchants, three Jewish merchants—there was a fair-sized Jewish colony in Madras at that time—and three Hindus were nominated Aldermen in the Charter itself. These latter were Chinna Venkatadri, the younger brother of Beri Timmana whom he succeeded in the office of Chief Merchant of the Company, Mooda Verona who was also Chief Merchant for some time and Alangatha Pillai who was the builder of the Ekambareswarar Temple in Mint Street. A new Mayor was to be elected on the 29th of September every year; and the Charter itself was to come into force from the 29th September 1688. The Mayor and Aldermen were to be a Court of Record; and the Mayor and the three English Aldermen were to be Justices of the Peace. The Judge of the Supreme Court of Judicature that was created was to be the Recorder of the Corporation and a Town Clerk who was also to be a notary was to be elected.

On the appointed day, 29th September 1688, the Corporation was inaugurated with all due solemnity, the Mayor and others taking their respective oaths. After dinner, towards 3 in the afternoon, the whole Corporation marched in their several robes, the Aldermen in scarlet serge gowns and the Burgesses in white China silk, with the Mace carried before the Mayor in procession, to the Town Hall Two silver-gilt maces were to be carried before the Mayor by two English-born sergeants. Robes of scarlet serge were to be worn by the Mayor and

*The mace and the oars were subsequently lost at the time of the French capture of Madras in 1746; they were said to have been sold.

Aldermen; and white silk-gowns by the Burgesses. The Mayor and Aldermen enjoyed also the privilege of having *rundellos* (broad umbrellas) and *kettysols* (umbrellas made of bamboo and paper imported from China) borne over them. They might ride on horseback in the same manner as was used by the Lord Mayor and Aldermen of London. The Mayor was always to be addressed as 'the Worshipful Mayor.'

Mr. Nathaniel Higginson, the first Mayor of Madras, served only for six months and then resigned; and he was succeeded in his office by Mr. Littleton. The Corporation was empowered, as we saw, to levy a tax for the building of a Town Hall, of a Jail House and of a School House, 'for the teaching of the Gentues or Native children to speak, read and write the English tongue, and to understand Arithmetic and Merchants' Accounts.' But the Mayor soon complained that the Corporation had no revenues or funds for carrying out the tasks expected of them. The Corporation had got the right of collecting the existing petty taxes of paddy-toll, measuring and weigher's duty and brokerage paid by the town brokers. But these sources of revenue were applied to other objects than those which the Corporation was asked to take up.

A quarrel quickly arose between the Governor and the Mayor's Court. The Governor complained of the high-handed action of the Aldermen, some of whom were members of his Council. He objected to the claim put by the Mayor that the decisions of his own Court were final, since under the Charter, there was provided a right of appeal from the Mayor's Court to the Court of Admiralty and the latter had become extinct in 1689. Yale even went to the length of proposing to withdraw the power of collecting petty taxes from the purview of the Corporation.

In 1692, the Company complained that there were, as early as 1690, as many as eight English Aldermen in the Corporation and desired that the body of Aldermen should be composed of the heads of several castes like the Armenians, the Hebrews, the Portuguese, Hindus and Moors. Thus, from the beginning the representation of the different communities resident in the place was a feature of the composition of the Corporation.

REORGANISATION OF THE CORPORATION (1726-27)

In 1721, the procedure was fixed for the election of the Mayor and the Aldermen by a resolution of the Governor in Council. Six years later, came the reorganisation of the Corporation in accordance with the terms of the Royal Charter issued by King George I in 1726, which gave greater judicial powers to that body. This Royal Charter was received in Madras in July 1727 and according to it the body corporate of the

City was to be composed of the Mayor and nine Aldermen, of whom at least seven should be natural-born British subjects. The Mayor was to be elected annually on 20th of December; but the Aldermen, unless removed, were to continue for life and vacancies among them were to be filled up by the Corporation. The Mayor and the Aldermen were to form a Court of Record and were authorised to try all civil causes and an appeal should lie from the Mayor's Court to the Governor and Council whose decisions should be final in all causes up to the limit of 1,000 pagodas. The Mayor's Court was empowered to grant probates and to exercise testamentary jurisdiction also. The Governor and Councillors were to be Justices of the Peace; and they were to hold quarter sessions for the trial of all offences except high treason. Provision was made for the appointment of a Sheriff annually by the Governor and Council; and the Sheriff was to summon both the grand and petty juries to assist in the sessions, while all offenders were to be tried and punished in the same manner as in England or as nearly as was possible. The Mayor's Court was to meet its expenses from the collection of measuring and weighing duties which were assigned to it and from the proceeds of the fines that were imposed. The Sheriff was to execute the processes of the Mayor's Court as well as the sentences of the Justices. The next great step in the modification of the Corporation was in 1753.

Thursday, the 17th August 1727, was the day when the new Mayor and Aldermen were sworn in at the Company's Garden-House in Peddanaickenpettah where the Governor and Councillors were met to receive them. The Mayor and Aldermen proceeded from the parade ground in the Fort through Old Black Town on horse-back with guards, peons and country music in the following manner:—Major John Roach on horse-back at the head of a company of foot-soldiers with kettle-drum, trumpet and other music; the dancing girls with country music; the Peddanayak on horse-back at the head of his peons; the Marshall with his staff on horse-back; the old Mayor on the right hand and the new Mayor on the left; the Aldermen two and two all on horse-back, the Company's chief peon; the Sheriff with a white wand on horse-back; the chief gentry in the town on horse-back.

The Charter contained the names of the first Mayor and Aldermen —"Richard Higginson is appointed to be the 'First and modern Mayor of the said Town or Factory of Madraspatnam,' and 'Edward Croke, Richard Carter, Duncombe Monroe, Robert Woolley, Abraham Wessel, John Powney, Francis Rouse, Luis De Medeiro and Thomas Way, are to be first Aldermen." It is a curious thing that this new first Mayor was the son of Nathaniel Higginson who was the first Mayor under the old Charter of 1687. The Company cautioned the Government that they should not meddle with the laws and customs of the Gentoos and other natives, but allow them to live in full enjoyment of their respective rights. The new Charter of 1727 was delivered to Captain John Powney, who was selected in the place of Richard Higginson, who died before the Charter could be implemented. Powney was thus the first Mayor. He was a free merchant as also Rouse, who was retiring Mayor.

GEORGE II'S CHARTER OF 1753

Owing to the capture and occupation of Madras by the French (1746-49), the continuity of the Municipal Corporation and the Mayor's Court was destroyed, and the charter of 1726 was regarded as surrendered. A fresh charter was issued in 1753, which exempted from the jurisdiction of the Mayor's Court "all suits and actions between Indian Natives only," and directed that all these suits were to be determined among themselves, unless both parties agreed to submit them to the Mayor's Court. This new charter (issued on the 8th January 1753) provided for the revival of the Mayor and the Aldermen. They were nominated, in the first instance, in the Charter itself and included Robert Clive in the list of the first Aldermen. Seven of the nine Aldermen were to be natural born subjects of the King, and only two could be foreign Protestants. The Aldermen were to continue in office for life; and from among them two were to be elected annually by the Corporation, one of whom was to be chosen as the Mayor by the Governor in Council. The Mayor and Aldermen were to form a Court of Record for civil suits, not being between Indians arising in Madras and its subordinate factories. Appeals from decrees up to 1,000 pagodas were to lie to the President and Council, while in judgments for larger sums an appeal might be made to the King-in-Council. There was to be a Court of Requests for the summary decision of petty civil suits by Commissioners appointed by Government. The President and Members of Council were to be the Justices of the Peace for Madras and the subordinate factories, to hold Quarter-Sessions and Oyer and Terminer and General Gaol Delivery and to be a Court of Record dealing with all offences excepting high treason. The mode of trial was to follow English practice, and the Sheriff was to summon persons to serve as Grand and Petty Juries.

In those days it was the practice for the assembled Governor in Council to administer through the Governor the oaths of allegiance and office to the Mayor and also to the Sheriff, who were elected for the succeeding year. It was usual upon this occasion to salute the new Mayor with nine guns. The institution of the office of Mayor lasted effectively till 1798, when the Mayor's Court was absorbed in the Re-

THE MAYORAL CHAIR : PRESENTED BY THE KUMARARAJA OF CHETTINAD TO THE CORPORATION OF MADRAS WHEN HE WAS MAYOR IN 1933

—*By courtesy of the Corporation of Madras.*

corder's Court; and the Mayor and Corporation were abolished in 1801. The Mayor thus disappeared from Madras after an existence of nearly 113 years. He exercised important judicial and magisterial functions; and his office was accompanied with picturesque ceremonial. But he was essentially under the effective control of Government and no wide powers were entrusted to him. The Court of Aldermen remained during all this time primarily a judicial and magisterial body.

The Mayor and Aldermen sat in the Record's Court along with the last mentioned officer from 1798-1801 when the Court itself was merged in the Supreme Court of Judicature. We have a long list of the Mayors of Madraspatam, first, of those, who were appointed on the 29th of September annually under the Company's Charter of 1787; second, of those who were elected under the Charter of George I of 1727, on the 20th of December annually; and third, of those who were elected under the Charter II of 1753 annually on the first Tuesday in December. There was a hiatus in the office of the Mayor and in the institution of the Corporation from September 1746 when the Charter of Charles I lapsed on account of the capture of Madras by the French, till 1753 when the new Charter of George II came into force. From the time of Nathaniel Higginson, Mayor for 1688-89, down to the time of Mr. Richard Yeldham, who was the Mayor for 1801, we have a long list of the holders of that office; and among these were included Robert Raworth, Mr. Richard Benyon, three members of the well-known family of Powney, Mr. Charles Smith, the brothers Hollond and others of greater or lesser fame in the history of Madras.

THE MUNICIPALITY OF MADRAS FROM 1792 to 1919

Municipal action proper proceeded from the Act of Parliament of 1792 (33 Geo. III, Cap. 527) containing a clause making provision "for the good order and Government of the towns of Madras, Calcutta and Bombay." Clause 151 of this Act provided for the appointment of Justices of the Peace, while a succeeding clause empowered them to assemble at general or quarter sessions to make arrangements for the care of the streets.

The Act further provided for the collection of the assessment and for licensing the sale of spirituous liquors in the Presidency town. This is the commencement of the Madras Municipality as such, differing from the Mayor and Corporation who were almost purely judicial functionaries. A Member of the Council presided over the meetings of Justices for municipal purposes. The Justices who thus met were sometimes five, sometimes six and occasionally seven in number; and Government ordered at a later date that the senior Civil Servant among them should preside. There was no quorum for their meetings; and on several occasions, we find only two Justices meeting; while on one occasion we read of only one Justice being present and considering himself competent to transact business.

This Parliamentary Act of 1792 was modified by an Act of 1836 passed by the Governor-General of India in Council to the effect that no assessment made by the Justices for the Presidency of Fort St. George under the Act of 1792 should be imposed without the consent of the Governor-in-Council. Another Act of 1841 sought to give greater liberty of action and a real measure of self-government to the people. According to this Act, the rate-payers of particular sections of the City were given the right to assess, collect and manage the rates of their own divisions, with the consent of Government.

A latter Act of 1856 superseded the existing regulations for the sanitation of the City. It abolished the Bench of Justices and replaced them by three Commissioners, who were called "the Municipal Commissioners for the Town of Madras." They were salaried officials and were empowered to look after the conservancy and improvement of the City and to assess and collect the municipal taxes.

An Act of the Madras Provincial Legislature, of 1865, added to the three paid Commissioners, three honorary Members to be selected from the resident inhabitants of the town. Two years later a radical change was made in the constitution of the Municipality. The City was divided into eight wards, each being represented by four Commissioners appointed by the Government from among the inhabitants of the respective divisions. An Executive Officer presided over the meetings of these 32 Commissioners and became known as the President. This Act defined the way in which municipal funds could be administered. In 1878, an Act of the Legislature provided that 16 out of the 32 Commissioners should be elected from among the rate-payers; it created two new officers, known as the Vice-Presidents, who, along with the President, exercised all the executive powers and control.

In 1884, there was passed the City of Madras Municipal Act, which defined the purposes for which the municipal funds might be spent. These purposes were divided into four categories, public health, public safety, elementary education and poor schools and public convenience. 24 out of the 32 Commissioners were to be elected. This was supplemented by the Act of 1904 which raised the number of Commissioners from 32 to 36 and allowed the representation of institutions on the Council of Commissioners.

THE ACTS OF 1919 AND 1933—REVIVAL OF THE MAYOR AND ALDERMEN

The Madras City Municipality Act of 1919 created in the place of the President, the Vice-President and the Commissioners,

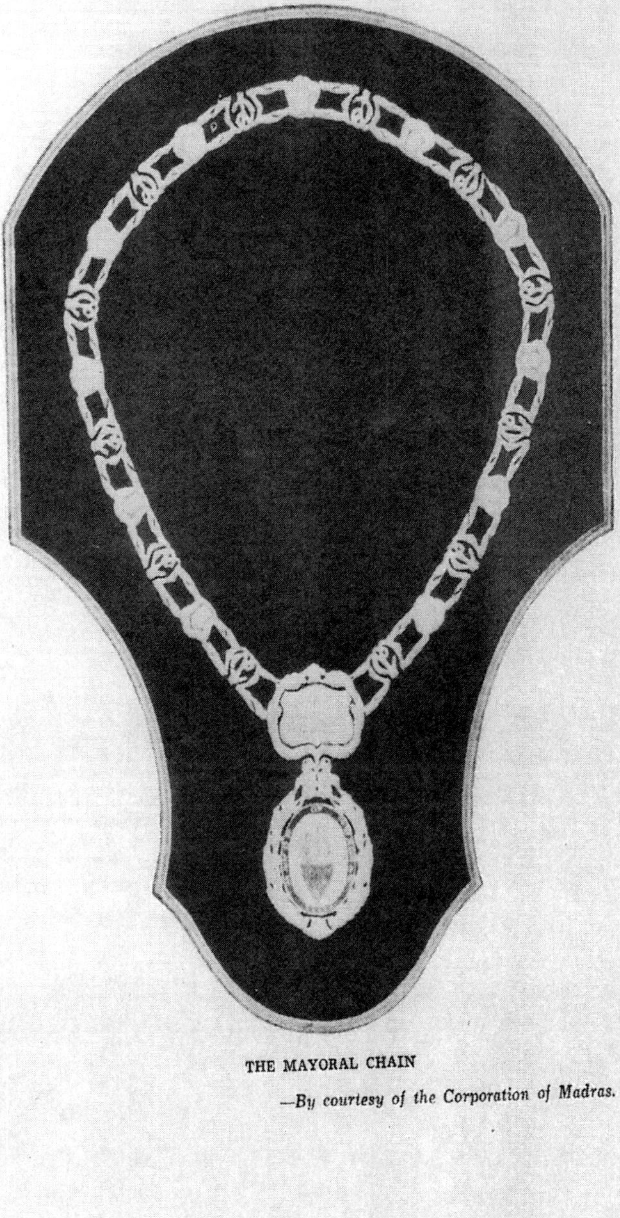

THE MAYORAL CHAIN

—*By courtesy of the Corporation of Madras.*

(a) A Council of 50 Councillors, 30 of them representing the 30 divisions of the City, 11 representing institutions and 9 nominated by Government, with particular reference to the representation of Muhammadans and other minorities;

(b) Four Standing Committees dealing respectively with taxation and finance, works, health and education; and

(c) A Commissioner appointed by Government as the Chief Executive officer.

According to this Act, at their first meeting in November, the Council should elect one of their number to be their President. The Act also gave the Corporation new powers and defined the relations between the President and the Council and the Commissioners. The first elected President was Diwan Bahadur Sir P. Theagaraya Chetty (1919-23), one of the leaders of the Justice Party.

During the Ministry of the Raja of Bobbili and at the instance of the Kumararaja of Chettinad, the son of Raja Sir Annamalai Chettyar of Chettinad, the illustrious Founder of the Annamalai University, who was then President of the Corporation of Madras, a Bill was passed to amend the City Municipal Act so as to create the office of Mayor. A Gazette Extraordinary containing the Bill was issued on the 19th January 1933; it was introduced in the Legislative Council on the 26th following and was passed into law on the same day. The Statement of Objects and Reasons contained the following: "The object of this Bill is to designate the President of the Corporation as the Mayor. The Presidents of most of the civic bodies in England and of the Corporations of Calcutta and Bombay are styled Mayors. It is desirable that the same designation should be adopted in the case of the President of the premier Municipal Corporation of the Presidency.

The Hon'ble Diwan Bahadur S. Kumaraswami Reddiar, Minister, in the absence of the Hon'ble the Raja of Bobbili, Chief Minister, who was in charge of the Bill, observed, in moving that the Bill be passed into law:—" It gives me great pleasure on behalf of this House to offer its most sincere congratulations to my Hon'ble friend, the Kumararaja of Chettinad who will be the first Mayor of Madras. It is a dignity that has been long overdue." Credit for bringing it back to Madras should, in a large measure go to the Kumararaja for his well-directed efforts.

The Bill itself consisted of five clauses:

1. This Act may be called the Madras City Municipal (Amendment) Act, 1933.

2. In Sections 23, 25, 26, 28, 29, 30, 32, 33, 34, 35, 37, 38 and 44 of the Madras City Municipal Act 1919 (hereinafter referred to as the

said Act), and in rule 1, 2, 3, 4, 5, 6, 8 and 15 of Schedule II to the said Act, for the word 'President' wherever it occurs, the word 'Mayor' shall be substituted.

3. In the heading to Section 37 and 38 of the said Act, for the words 'President of the Council' the word 'Mayor' shall be substituted.

4. In rule 16 of Schedule II to the said Act, for the word 'President of the Council,' the word 'Mayor' shall be substituted.

5. Section 413 of the said Act shall be omitted.

The Bill was thus passed by the Legislature. The creation, anew, of the Mayor of Madras by this amendment of the City Municipal Act is a very important measure, because it has reinvested the oldest Municipal Corporation in India with its old dignity, as well as a special status consonant with the position of the city as one of the major urban centres of the Indian Empire.

This office of the Mayor came into official existence on the 7th of March 1933, soon after the bill was passed. A special ceremony was held to invest the then President, Kumararajah M. A. Muthiah Chettiar of Chettinad, with the new dignity of Mayor. He was conducted to the Council Chamber in a procession, when one of the ex-Presidents received him and installed him in his seat. Since then the Mayor has always been preceded by the mace-bearer and ushered in by the Secretary when he enters the Council Chamber, all the members standing till he occupies the chair, after bowing to all sides of the House. Soon afterwards, the Corporation decided to make certain recommendations regarding robes, regalia, etc., for the use of the Mayor, who was empowered to wear court dress on ceremonial occasions and a small badge or insignia of office below the collar. The Council resolved as follows:—

"The Mayor shall have two sets of gowns of the approved pattern; (1) one for ordinary wear during Council meetings and (2) another for special and ceremonial occasions.

"At the time the Mayor attends the Council meetings, he shall wear the ordinary gown made of black silk or material with gold lace border, one inch broad, and white bands.

"The Mayor shall wear on special and ceremonial occasions a gown made of velvet or other suitable material of fuschia shade, with a gold lace border of two inches breadth.

"The head-dress for the Mayor shall be a lace turban of the Hindu or Muslim type, or a three-cornered hat of black velvet with gold braid cloth over it or a tarboosh."

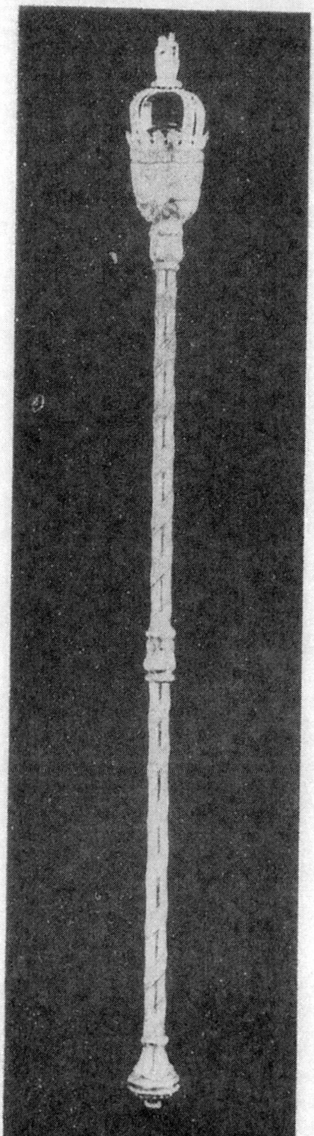

THE MACE

—*By courtesy of the Corporation of Madras.*

The Corporation has provided the Mayor with a gold Mayoral Chain and Badge to be worn by him on special and ceremonial occasions. The Chain consists alternately of the Corporation Monogram and Shield, bearing the City Coat of Arms; the top plaque of the pendant is beautifully enamelled with a picture of the Ripon Buildings (the spacious offices of the Corporation which were opened by Lord Hardinge in 1913) and surrounded by a wreath of thistle; the pendant itself is enamelled with the City Coat of Arms raised in relief and surrounded by a highly embossed wreath of thistles. There has also been provided for the Mayor a Mace of 4 feet and 6 inches in length, consisting of a highly chased spiral design surmounted by a Crown bearing on one side an embossed view of the Ripon Buildings, and on the other the monogram of the Corporation, while on the top of the Crown, there is the City Coat of Arms. A grand and massive Mayoral Chair which was presented to the Corporation by the first Mayor, serves as his seat. It is modelled on the presidential chairs of the Madras and Indian Legislative Assemblies.

It is interesting to know something in detail of the Mayor's dress. 'The robe worn by the Mayor of Madras is almost a replica of that worn by the Lord Mayor of London, but made to suit the conditions of this country. It is made of a specially soft light-weight silk velvet in a rich shade of fuschia, trimmed with gold lace, instead of ermine, and lined with silk.

"The Mayor's full court-dress suits, for both day or evening wear, are made of light-weight black vicuna fully lined with silk, and completely equipped with sword and Mayor's cocked hat."

These dignities attaching to the Mayor have greatly enhanced the social significance of his office and the picturesqueness of the ceremonial functions of the Corporation. It is interesting to note that the present Mayor of Madras, Mr. K. Venkataswamy Naidu, traces his descent from Ketti Narayana, one of the Company's Chief Merchants of the 17th century and an Alderman of the first Corporation of 1687-88. The Institution of Aldermen has also been revived in the amended Madras Municipal Act of 1936, and thus another element of the old Madraspatam Corporation has been restored to life.

It was in 1934-35 when the Kumararaja of Chettinad was the Mayor for a second time that further amendments to the City Municipal Act were taken up; and the present Act is the outcome of the Amending Bill of 1936, in the shaping of which he had a large part, as Chairman of the Select Committee of the Legislative Council. The present constitution of the Council of the Corporation, consisting of 65 members is the result of the above amending act.

The Sheriff in Madras

By

P. R. Srinivasa Aiyangar, M.A., B.L.,
Advocate, Madras.

The office of the Sheriff, called High Sheriff in England, is an ancient and picturesque office coming down from the Anglo-Saxon period. At one time a very big office, at the present day the duties of the office, both administrative and judicial, are still of importance. In the administration of justice and the preservation of the King's peace in the shires and counties the Sheriff in the early days played a very important function and was a prominent figure in the local administration. Maitland in his book *Justice and Police* has put it thus: "The whole history of English justice and police might be brought under this rubric, the decline and fall of the sheriff." As representing the interests of the Crown against the local baronage the Sheriff executed the King's writ and called out in an emergency the *posse comitatus* requiring the help of the local armed force or militia. In the exercise of his judicial functions he presided over the County and the Hundred court and held the sheriff's *tourn* as the King's deputy. In the early days the Sheriff was appointed by popular election but in course of time the right of appointment became vested in the Crown, hereditary offices being abolished finally by 1850. The office is now of an honorary nature, the appointment being an annual one made by the King in Council out of the list of names nominated by the Chancellor of the Exchequer and the Judges of the King's Bench Division. Usually the Magistrate in the county is nominated, Peers, Clergy, officers in active service, practising barristers and solicitors, etc., being exempted. The most important of the administrative duties now falling on the Sheriff is attendance on the Judges at assizes and election petitions, a function attended with old time pomp and ceremony. Besides execution of writs the Sheriff prepares the panel of jurors and nominally has the duty of summoning the *posse comitatus.* His judicial duties now remain in a very attenuated form, the civil jurisdiction having been superseded by that of modern courts and the criminal jurisdiction by the Justices of Peace at the Petty Sessions. His duties as conservator of the King's peace are now discharged by the police.

When the English first established their settlement at Madras they found the indigenous village system established there. Madras, then a small fishing village, had a headman or *Athikari,* an accountant or *Kanakkapillai,* watchman or *Peddanaick.* The *athikari* was the executive head administering justice to the local inhabitants holding his court at the Choultry or Town house, while the *peddanaick* with a number of *talaiaris* or peons under him arrested wrongdoers and made himself generally responsible for the policing of the place. By 1661 under the Charter of that year the office of *athikari* was abolished and the agent became governor with power to administer civil and criminal law, while the *peddanaick's* office continued down to the early part of the 19th century.

For some years prior to the grant of the Charter of 1661 the East India Company felt considerable difficulties in enforcing obedience in all Englishmen and subjects resident within their jurisdiction and punishing the offenders conformably to the laws of England. Under this Charter the Governor and Council constituted themselves as a tribunal to hear and judge all causes, sitting in the Fort Chapel every Wednesday and Saturday, the justices and constables under them executing their orders and apprehending the criminals. In order to provide for appointment of civilians learned in law as assistants in the courts of justice the Charter of 1683 provided for the appointment of a Judge-Advocate. The rapid development and growing importance of the Settlement led to the grant of the Charter 1688 under which the "Town of Fort St. George (commonly called the Christian Town) and the city of Madraspatnam and all the territories thereto belonging not exceeding the distance of ten miles" was constituted a Corporation under the name and title of Mayor and Aldermen and Burgesses. The Mayor and Aldermen became a court of record, while the Mayor and three senior Aldermen became Justices of the Peace. The Mayor's court was reconstituted under the Charter of 1726 which introduced the common and statute law extant at that time in England into the Indian settlements and Presidencies and established a court of Oyer and Terminer with juries consisting of the principal inhabitants of the place. Consequent on the introduction of the English Law and procedure the office of the Sheriff for the city was created.

Under this Charter of George I dated 24th September 1726, received in Madras in July 1727,

"The Governor and the five senior members of Council shall hold Quarter Sessions of the Peace, and shall be a Court of Record, and Commissioners of Oyer and Terminer and Gaol Delivery for trying all offences, except High Treason, committed 'within the said Town of *Madraspatnam, Fort S. George,* or within any of the said Factories subordinate thereto, or within Ten *English* Miles of the same.' Grand

and Petty Juries are to be summoned by the Sheriff and offenders are to be tried and punished in the same manner as in England, or as nearly as may be." (Love: *Vestiges of Old Madras*, Vol. II, p. 241.)

The provisions of the Charter relating to the Sheriff's appointment are reproduced hereunder:

"And Our further will and pleasure is, and We do, for Us, Our heirs and successors, will, nominate and appoint the Junior of the Council of Fort St. George aforesaid at the time of the arrival of this Our Charter, or an exemplification of the same, at that place to be Our Sheriff of Fort St. George and the Town of Madraspatnam and the district aforesaid, and for any space within ten miles of the same; and We will and direct that such Sheriff shall at a time to be appointed for that purpose by the Governor or President or in his absence, the two Senior of the Council at Fort St. George residing there, within thirty days after notice of this Our Charter, take a oath duly to execute his office together with the Oath of Allegiance, which oaths, the said Governor or President or in his absence, the two Senior of the Council, residing within the said Town of Madras-patnam are hereby empowered to administer, and that from the time of taking such oaths, the said Sheriff shall continue in his office for the space of one year, and until another shall be duly elected and sworn into the said office.

"And We do further for Us, Our heirs and successors, will, ordain, direct and appoint that the Governor or President and Council of Fort St. George aforesaid or the major part of them shall yearly on the twentieth day of December, unless the same happens on a Sunday, and then on the next day, assemble themselves, and proceed to the election of a new Sheriff, which Sheriff, when elected, as soon as conveniently may be, shall take the usual Oath of office, and Oath of Allegiance before the said Governor or President, or in his absence the two Senior of the Council (who are hereby authorised to administer the same) and shall continue in such office during the space of one whole year from the time of such swearing and until another shall be duly elected and sworn into the said office, the said Governor, President and Council or the major part of them, shall and may as soon as conveniently assemble and choose another person to be Sheriff in his room who shall be sworn as aforesaid and continue in his office for the remainder of the year; And the said Sheriff hereby appointed and every other to be elected and sworn as aforesaid, shall during his and their continuance in such office respectively have full power and authority to execute and make return of all process of the said Court, and of any other Court, erected by these *Letters Patents* within the district aforesaid.

. . . And it shall and may be lawful to and for the said Justices of Peace Commissioners of Oyer and Terminer and Gaol Delivery respectively to proceed by indictment or by such other ways, and in the same or like manner as is used in that part of Great Britain called England, as near as the condition and circumstances of the place, and inhabitants will admit of, and for that purpose, to issue their Warrant or Precept to the Sheriff of the said district for the time being, commanding him to summon a convenient number of the principal inhabitants within the said district, to serve and attend as a Grand and Petty Jury at the said Courts respectively."

On the 17th August 1727, the Charter was brought into force, and all concerned proceeded in a procession with "kettle drum and the Dancing Girls with the Country Music", etc., from the Parade in the White Town to the Garden House where the President administered the oaths to the New Mayor and Aldermen and delivered the New Charter to the Mayor. Mr. Augustus Buxton, the junior member of Council, was nominated Sheriff in accordance with the provisions of the Charter. As Mr. Buxton was at Fort St. David, Mr. August Nicholas Morse, then junior member, was sworn in as Sheriff on the 22nd August.

A Sessions Court was established later and the Justices of the Peace were made Justices of the Choultry for decision of small causes up to Pags. 20, subject to appeal to the Mayor's Court. In November of the same year the Government decided to set up a separate court for the decision of petty civil causes and accordingly a Sheriff's Court was constituted in which such petty causes should be decided without a right of appeal to the Mayor's Court except in cases involving a sum greater than Pags. 5. To this Court was transferred the registry of slaves and also of houses and lands. This new Court superseding the Choultry Court was not viewed with favour by the Directors and had a short-lived existence. After functioning nearly a year and eight months, the Sheriff's Court was abolished in July 1729, and was replaced by the Justices of the Peace who again sat at the Choultry.

Though the Sheriff's court had only a short lease of life, the power and prestige of the Sheriff did not undergo any change. He continued to enjoy the old power of summoning grand and petty juries and executing and making return of all processes of Courts. It was his privilege to attend the Mayor's procession on horse-back with a white wand. The growth of litigation by the establishment of the new Courts brought in its wake opportunities for friction between the Government and the Mayor's Court. An interesting episode resulting from this disharmony is found in the records of 1735. The Mayor's Court imposed a fine on Torriano as Sheriff, "for inserting in the Bill of Sale of a house a fee paid to the Choultry Justice for certifying the sale." The fact seems to be that such fees had been authorised since early days but they had not been of late claimed. The Sheriff appealed to the President of the Council who observed that the practice of alternative registration before the Mayor's Court or at the Choultry Court lent itself to fraudulent conveyances of property. The Council thereupon resolved in accordance with the Company's standing orders to institute a single registration office for maintaining separate registers for the town, each of the pettahs, and the villages. Two of the Justices of the Peace were nominated to certify conveyances of property. A notification was issued calling upon all persons to produce their title to lands and houses within a period of six months, in default whereof the Company as " Proprietors of the Soil " would resume possession.

The extension of jurisdiction of the Courts to the ten miles radius proved to be a source of trouble and conflict with the adjoining country powers. Early in 1736 it was reported to the President that a Poligar 'in Tiruvatesh (Thiruvateeswaranpet) a village not two miles from the Fort, but out of the Company's bound' had been arrested by the Serjeant of the Mayor's Court. The complaint was that the Poligars as influential overlords having surveillance of villages " would not suffer the Mayor's warrants to pass in their Territories." Orders were sent to the Mayor for the immediate release of the Poligar, as it was held that Poligars were held exempt from arrest. The Poligar was accordingly released and compensated. The following Fort St. George Consultation relating to this incident will be read with interest :

" The ill Consequences which may ensue from the breach of the Old Rules of the Place established for many and very good reasons, induced the Board to come to the following resolutions thereupon :—

" Ordered that no sheriff do serve any Warrant of Arrest or Execution upon the Person of the Poligar of Madras, or any of the Poligars of the Villages ; nor upon their dwelling Houses where they keep their Prisoners, nor upon any of the Duties due and payable to them for the Guard and Safety of the Town and Villages." (Love : *Vestiges of Old Madras* Vol. II p. 275). The above resolution made it abundantly clear that the sheriff could not issue warrants of arrest and imprisonment against the Poligars as such. The Poligar of Madras went by the appellation of the Peddanaigue. The Peddanaigue was the chief of Talaiaris or peons and head of the Police. He arrested wrong-doers, confined them in gaols pending their trial and in case of thefts and robberies had to compensate the losses. Besides this official, there were other Poligars who were responsible for the watch and ward of the parts of the town committed to their charge.

In the same year 1736 towards the end, the Sheriff became involved in executing another warrant issued by the Mayor's Court. The following extract from a communication to the Hon'ble Company will be read with interest as vividly describing the incidents illustrative of the anxious concern for and tolerance of religious rites and ceremonies evinced from the very early days of the English settlement in the country

'The 28th September the President was surpriz'd to see a great Croud of People enter the Fort, Merchants and others, who came with a Complaint that the Mayor's Court had committed to Jail two Merchants named Perrima Moodalare and Ram Chundree for no other Reason but that they had refused to take certain Oaths which, they alledged, were contrary to their religion and the Rules of their Cast. The Crowd and Clamour was so great, and some of them calling out that if such a Power was tolerated they would not continue longer in the Bounds; and knowing besides there was nothing about which these People are so tenacious as that which affects their religious Rites and Ceremonies, the President thought himself under an absolute necessity of doing something immediately which pacify and make them easy. Accordingly he sent for the Mayor and the Sheriff. The first owned to him that the said two Merchants were only imprisoned because they had refused to take certain Oaths at Trivlicane Pagoda...... The President having talked sometime with the Mayor ......, told him in the End...... that he should be very ready to join with the Court in any measures which they shou'd propose that the regular Course of Justice might not be obstructed, provided a due regard was had for Consciences truly scrupulous, and that the Natives might not be disturbed in their religious Rites and Ceremonies; but in the meantime he must desire Mr. Sheriff to release the two Merchants upon their Parole, which he accordingly did; and then the people being satisfied, they dispersed.'

'The President acquainted the Council the next Day with what he had done, with his reasons for the same who approved thereof; but we avoided to mention it upon our Consultations, being unwilling to record anything which might reflect upon the Gentlemen of the Mayor's Court, and hoping also they wou'd have consider'd it again, and have had the Prudence either to drop it or propose some Method not liable to be attended with the Mischiefs this might have been.' (Love: *Vestiges of Old Madras* Vol. II p. 276).

As befitting the dignity and importance of the office the Government sanctioned in 1745 a special seal for the use of the Sheriff. It was directed "that the Device on it be the Maces crossed on the Sword in a Mashle, with *Sheriff of Madraspatnam* in the circle round it."

The years following 1746 were memorable years in the history of the city. The French had captured Madras and remained in occupation till 1749. During their occupation, the Mayor and the Aldermen became dispersed and the Mayor's Court and all the powers and authorities established under the Charter of 1726 were dissolved and came to an end. Consequently it became necessary to set up courts and authorities to function anew. The Charter of 1726 of George I was surrendered and a fresh Charter of George II was granted on 8th January 1753. The Charter of 1726 lapsed in 1746 on the French capture of the city and from 1746 to 1753 there was no nomination of any Sheriff. The provisions in this Charter relating to the appointment of the Sheriff are extracted below:

"And Our further Will and pleasure is, and We do for Us, Our heirs and successors ordain and direct that the person who shall be Sheriff at the time of the arrival of this Our Charter or an exemplification of the same, at Fort St. George aforesaid shall continue to be Our Sheriff of Fort St. George and the Town of Madraspatnam, and the district aforesaid, until another shall be duly elected and sworn into the said office. And we do further, for us, Our heirs and successors will, ordain, direct and appoint that the Governor or President and Council of Fort St. George aforesaid for the time being or the major part of them (whereof the said Governor or President or in his absence, the Senior of the Council then residing at Fort St. George aforesaid to be one) shall yearly, on the first Tuesday in December assemble themselves, and proceed to the election of a new Sheriff for the year ensuing to be computed from the twentieth day of December next after such election; which Sheriff when elected as soon as conveniently may be and before he shall enter upon his said office shall take the usual oath of office, and the Oath of Allegiance before the said Governor or President, or in his absence, before the two Senior of the Council then residing at Fort St. George aforesaid (who are hereby authorised to administer the same) and shall continue in such office during the space of one whole year from the said twentieth day of December, and until another shall be duly elected and sworn into the said office unless his said place shall be avoided in such manner as hereinafter is mentioned. And in case any such Sheriff shall die in his office or shall remove from the said Town of Madraspatnam or be absent from the same by the space of three months (unless for such reasonable cause as the Governor or President and Council or the major part of them shall allow) then the said Governor or President and Council or the major part of them shall and may as soon as conveniently may be after the death, removal or absence of such Sheriff, assemble and choose another person to be Sheriff in his room, who shall be sworn as aforesaid and continue in his office for the remainder of the year.

"And the said Sheriff hereby appointed and every other Sheriff to be elected and sworn as aforesaid shall during his and their continuance in such office respectively, have full power and authority to execute and make return of all processes of the said Court and of any other court erected by these our *Letters Patents* within the district aforesaid; and in case of the absence of any such Sheriff, for such reasonable cause to be allowed as aforesaid, the Deputy or Under Sheriff to be nominated by such Sheriff shall return all processes, and do all Acts in the name and by virtue of the authority of such Sheriff.". Mr. H. D. Love in his invaluable book *Vestiges of Old Madras* has furnished us with a list of the names of the Sheriffs down to year 1807 in an appendix to the third volume.

The appointment of the Sheriff was to be made annually. A record of the year 1759 shows how these nominations were made. On the appointed day the Council assembled as usual. The President would administer oaths of Allegiance and office to the candidates who had been chosen as the Mayor and the Sheriff. The name of Henry Eustace Johnston is mentioned as the Sheriff of the year 1758.

The Sheriff's office in the early days was not always a bed of roses. In the execution of the duties of his office, the Sheriff had to incur personal danger and risk rough handling and illtreatment at the hands of the populace. In 1779 there was a case of assault on the Sheriff by the Nawab's guards. In an action brought before the Mayor's Court against Amir-ul-Umara for non-payment of debt the defendant was *ex parte* and the Court effected a public sale of the defendant's house to one Nathaniel Bacon. On the Sheriff attempting to take possession of it, the incidents that followed will be read with interest in the following extract:

MINUTES OF THE MAYOR'S COURT, 21st SEPTEMBER, 1779

John Allison vs. *Ommeer Ul Umirah Bahadur*

'The Court observe with extreme astonishment and concern the narrative and Proofs of the most flagrant Acts of violence committed upon the person of the Sheriff and his Officers in the Execution of their public Duty, whereby the authority of the King's Court has been grossly insulted, and the Law of the Land opposed. Resolved therefore that the sheriff be directed to proceed immediately in the Execution of his Duty, and that the Register be directed to wait on the Governor and Council with a Copy of this Resolution and Copies of the Informations and Sheriff's Letter to the Register delivered into Court this Day....

JAMES THOMAS,
Registrar.

THE INFORMATION OF THOMAS EVES, SHERIFF'S OFFICER

On Monday the thirteenth day of September......William Jackson, Esq., Sheriff of the town of Madraspatnam, went, accompanied by his Deputy, John Fairney, his Bailiffs Thomas Clifford and Thomas Ives, a

Dubash belonging to Captain Nathaniel Bacon and the Sheriff's Dubash as his Interpreter, to give lawful possession of a House in Trivitation Pettah, commonly called the Ommeer's to, Captain Nathaniel Bacon, who had purchased the same at public Sale.

'About 10 minutes past 12 o'clock of the forenoon of the same Day, the Sheriff, with aforementioned Persons, arrived at the Gate of the Ommeer's House, who, getting out of the Palanquin with his Sword on and his Wand in his hand, he found himself surrounded by a number of Sepoy Officers and Sepoys. The Sheriff asked who they were, and in whose Service. They replied that they were in the Nabobs Service. He then told them that he wanted to go into the house, when they assembled in his way, and the Black Officer put his hands to the Sheriff's breast and told the Sheriff that he should not enter into the house, for they had Orders not to let them in. The Sheriff then demanded Entrance several times in the King's name, when the Subidar who said he belonged to the Nabob replied that he must have the King's Order first, or he, the Sheriff, should not go in unless he, the Sheriff, killed him......

THE NARRATIVE OF WILLIAM JACKSON, SHERIFF

'Finding I could not enter into the aforesaid house, I called upon the *Posse Comitatus* to assist me in the Execution of my Duty and ordered my Interpreter to explain this to the people standing near us, but did not receive the least Assistance. At this instant I saw a man come out of the aforesaid house who by his uniform had the Appearance of a Havildar of Sepoys; he whispered the aforesaid Subidar, and instantly, I, my Deputy and Officers, Interpreter and Palanquins' Boys, were immediately attacked by the Subidar and about Forty Sepoys. Finding it would be in vain for me and my people to oppose so large a Body of soldiers, some being armed with Swords and others with Musquets I ran away, and was pursued by the said Subidar and several Sepoys for some hundred Yards, in the course of which pursuit I lost my Wand; but being at last quite exhausted with running so far in the heat of the Sun, I threw myself into a Botque or Shop, and repeatedly called out for the Assistance of a *Posse Comitatus*, but in vain. In about a minute afterwards the aforesaid Subidar and two or three Sepoys seized me and began beating me in a violent manner as I lay in the Shop. At last they dragged me out and repeated their Blows, insomuch that I was put in fear of my life. A little time afterwards a Sepoy pulled away my Sword and Stole my Hat, and he, with the Assistance of another Sepoy and the said Subidar dragged me by main force towards the aforesaid House; and when they had brought me near the House, I saw a man who had the appearance of a Dubash come out from the aforesaid house in violent hurry, and saying something which I did not understand to the Subidar and Sepoys who were dragging me along, they immediately let me go and told me repeatedly to *Jow*, throwing my Hat and Sword on the Ground, which took up, called for my Palanquin and returned to the Fort....! Love: Vol. III p. 190-191. This led to the Nawab appealing to the Governor to be exempted from the jurisdiction of the Mayor's Court.

The principal duties of the Sheriff were to execute the writs and warrants issued by the Court, effect sales of land in respect of which revenues and dues had fallen in arrears and to keep in custody prisoners who were chiefly debtors. Among the persons of historical importance committed to the charge of the Sheriff were the following: George Stratton, Sir Robert Fletcher, Henry Brooke, Charles Floyer, Archdale Palmer, Francis Jourdan, George Mackay, James Stuart, James Edington, Arthur Lysaght and Mathew Home. At the inquest in 1777 held by the Coroner upon the death of Lord Pigot, Governor of Madras, who died while in confinement in Mount, the Jury found a verdict of wilful murder against the above persons who were kept in confinement pending the hearing of the case at the Quarter Sessions. Another notable prisoner was Rev. John Philip Fabricius who officiated at the marriage of Robert Clive in 1753. This reverend gentleman got himself involved in pecuniary difficulties and was confined in debtor's gaol. It is interesting to find that the problem of imprisonment for non-payment of debts and the iniquity of confining them for long terms for small debts drew the attention of the authorities even in those early days. How they attempted to solve them will be seen from the following extract from a communication sent to the Company in England.

FORT ST. GEORGE TO THE COMPANY

'In consequence of a petition delivered in from the Debtors under confinement at this Presidency representing the sufferings they labour under, we desired the Sheriff to transmit us a list of the Persons under his Custody for Debt, specifying how long they had been in confinement, with the nature of their case, and such other particulars as could afford full information concerning them.

'The Sheriff has complied with our requisition in laying a list of the Prisoners before us; and as it frequently happens that the Debtors are confined for small sums, a great part of which is too often accumulated from the exorbitant Charges of the Attornies of the Mayor's Court, we take the Liberty to expressing our hope that you will be pleased to adopt such measures as may appear to you proper for their releasement after a certain period of confinement, or to have them included in the King's Acts of Grace passed from Time to Time for the relief of Debtors. (Love: Vol. III p. 431.)

As early as 1790 the health and comfort of the prisoners committed to their charge was the subject of anxious consideration. In those days before Howard came with his prison reforms when the old retributory theories of punishment prevailed, the conditions prevailing in gaols were in accordance with the medieval notions of punishment. In 1793 Edward Atkinson (Atkinson Road, Vepery goes after his name), then Sheriff, faced this problem and took steps to ameliorate the lot of debtors and prisoners. He urged the desirableness of enlarging the goal and pleaded for better accomodation for the debtors. The following communication to Sir Charles Oakely in Council speaks for itself:

'I cannot quit this Subject without mentioning to your Hon'ble Board the necessity of building a Commodious Gaol in an open healthy Situation, with a number of small Apartments in it, that a man who may be so unfortunate as to be confined there may have an Opportunity of carrying on his particular business, and may by his industry extricate himself from his embarassments........'

"Mr. Jones, who is confined in the felon's Gaol as a Lunatick, has represented to me his Distressed circumstances. He was pensioned many years ago on fifteen Pagodas per month, which he received regularly until March 1791, when it was ordered by Government to be discontinued. Since that period he has had nothing but the common Gaol Allowance of two fanams a Day, which is not sufficient to find him in victuals...." (Love: Vol. III p. 432.) Ten years later in 1795 the Sheriff of the year Mr. Richard Borough urged the necessity of proper housing of the debtor prisoners and suggested that 'a bastion of Black Town Wall adjacent to the one now used as a Felon's Gaol be suitably altered for the purpose.' But this recommendation was found by the Chief Engineer to be unworkable on account of the insufficiency of space to accommodate the necessary buildings.

By the new Charter proclaimed on the 1st November 1798, the old Courts and judicial institutions were abolished and in the place of the Mayor's Court and the Court of Oyer and Terminer and Gaol delivery, a Recorder's Court was constituted. The new Court was to be called "The Court of the Recorder of Madraspatnam," the principal Judge and the President of the Court being called the Recorder of Madraspatnam, the Mayor and three of the Aldermen n rotation to be assistant judges thereof. Sir Thomas Strange who came out as the first Recorder of the Court and who became later Chief Justice of the Supreme Court of Judicature established on September 4th 1801, in reviewing the work of the officers of the Court suggested to the Government that in view of the increasing work a fixed stipend should be given to the Sheriff. So far it appears that that officer 'has been in practice of retaining one third of the sum allowed for his Bailiffs at

Madras and of drawing for no less than for fourteen others who do not exist, providing in the whole the sum of pagodas 104 per month together with poundage upon sales." The Government generally approved of these proposals. On the establishment of the Supreme Court of Judicature the Sheriff became attached to that Court. In 1838, an important legal point was raised as to whether the Sheriff of Madras under a writ of *Fieri Facias* issued by the Supreme Court to seize and sell 'goods and chattels within the jurisdiction of the Supreme Court,' had jurisdiction to seize and sell lands and chattels in the moffusil. But no opinion was given by the Privy Council. In 1862, the High Court of Judicature was established, in which was merged all the functions of the Sudder Adawlat and Foujdary Adawlat and the Supreme Court, and the High Court administered justice as a Court of Law and Equity, of Oyer and Terminer and General Gaol Delivery, of Ecclesiastical jurisdiction and of Admiralty. The Sheriff since then continued to be attached to the High Court with his Bailiffs and office there.

The Sheriff's office is an annual one, the appointment being made by the Government. The duties attached to the office to be discharged personally are very slight, the principal functions, namely the service of the writs and processes of the High Court being carried out by the Bailiffs and the Deputy Sheriff working under him. Under the Charter of 1752 the Sheriff was authorised to nominate the Deputy or Under Sheriff to act for him in case of absence. The Deputy Sheriff as the nominee of the Sheriff used to change every year along with the Sheriff. Now the term of the office has been made permanent. The first Indian to be nominated as Sheriff was Sir S. Ramaswami Mudaliar, Rao Sahib Kt., C.I.E., who was the Sheriff for the years 1886 and 1887. Dewan Bahadur M. Balasundaram Naidu, C.I.E. was the hundredth Sheriff. The duties of the Sheriff's office now consist in the main of attending on the Judge of the High Court holding the Quarter Sessions of Oyer and Terminer and General Gaol Delivery, of the summoning of the juries for their attendance at the said Courts and of the execution of all writs and processes issued by the High Court. At the opening of each Session the Sheriff dressed in his ceremonial dress preceded by his attendant carrying a White Wand waits on the presiding Judge of the High Court in his Chambers, escorts the Judge to his Court, and sits on the dais along with Judge during the Sessions. Once a year the Sheriff draws up a preliminary roll of persons to act as common and special jurors and submits the same to the Crown office. On important occasions on a requisition of the citizens the Sheriff convenes a public meeting, an act reminiscent of the ancient right to call out the populace in emergencies. The Sheriff's office has now become one of dignity and honour, conferred on the recipient in recognition of his signal services, mainly social and humanitarian, to the public.

SECTION IV

TRADE AND COMMERCE

Port of Madras for Three Hundred Years

By

G. G. Armstrong,
Chairman, Madras Port Trust

I. THE FIRST PORT

If we could take ourselves back to Madras three hundred years ago we should see nothing more than a strip of sandy beach and a few villages, one of which was known as Madraspatam. On the coast further north was a fortified Dutch settlement at Pulicat, and a little to the south was the Portuguese settlement of San Thome; but Madras itself was only a village when Francis Day of the Hon'ble East India Co., came sailing down the coast on a voyage of exploration to find a suitable site for a trading settlement for the Company.

Hitherto the Company's Headquarters on the east coast of India had been at Masulipatam. The town itself did not belong to them, but they had there what was known as a factory; not a factory in the modern sense of the word, but a sort of combined office, godowns and quarters, where the "factors" collected goods from the country merchants, chiefly cloth and muslins, and shipped them to England. Masulipatam was found to be a very inconvenient site for this factory, chiefly owing to the constant payments required by the local Ruler, and the difficulty of getting anything done there, increased by the rivalry of the Dutch factory which was also established at Masulipatam; and at last in 1639 Francis Day was sent to sail southwards and to explore the coast to find a place where the Company might build a fort and settlement of its own and trade without the burden of exactions or rivalry.

It is difficult to see exactly why Day chose Madraspatam, where there was nothing but a perfectly flat strip of beach, with no natural harbour at all. The attraction seems to have been the river, which was not quite the same thing as the modern Cooum. Two streams flowing from the west and north respectively had a common outlet to the sea about a mile south of the village of Madraspatam. The first of these, which was known as the Triplicane river, corresponds roughly to the present Cooum, winding through the villages of Chetpat, Mambalam and Triplicane to the sea. The northern or Elambore River flowed from the north parallel with the coast until it reached the site of the present General Hospital where it curved round to meet the southern river at its outlet to the sea.

It thus ran along the western and southern side of Day's proposed settlement, which, with the sea on the east, was thus reasonably well guarded against attack. On the sand bank thus enclosed, containing only a few fishermen's huts, a little way to the south of the village of Madraspatam, Day proposed to build his fort.

The first step was to get a grant of the site. The country was part of the Dominion of the Raja of Chandragiri, ruled for him by local Naicks. Madras came under Venkatappa, a Naick who ruled the coast from Pulicat to San Thome, and his brother Ayyappa, the Naick of Poonamallee, from whom is descended the present Raja of Kalahasti. Three copies of the Naick's grant still exist, one of which is dated July 1639, permitting the Company to build a fort at "Madraspatam" and trade there, custom free at the port, and paying only half dues on any goods carried up through the Naick's territory.

On the sand bank thus acquired Day and Cogan built the first Fort St. George, a small square with bastions at each corner for defence, containing the Company's offices and godowns; the Company's Officers were lodged at first in huts outside. It seems a very modest affair, but the Company was not pleased; the Directors said that too much money had been spent and the place was not worth it. Nor has posterity been any more grateful; among all the statues and buildings and streets which preserve the names of the makers of Madras those of Day and Cogan appear nowhere at all.

II. GROWTH OF SETTLEMENT

(*a*) *San Thome.*—Madras was thus founded purely as a trading settlement and as such it grew to be, by the end of the seventeenth century, the chief port in India before the development of Calcutta and Bombay. But its early years were not without anxiety. One great source of trouble was the Portuguese settlement of San Thome, only separated from Fort St. George by a few miles, not of modern road but of sand and marshy country. About twenty years after the foundation of Madras, San Thome was besieged and taken by the King of Golconda, one of the five Mohammadan Kings of the south. Ten years later the French took it from him, but it was twice besieged by the Mohammadans during the next four years and the French decided that it was an unsuitable place for trade. They therefore, handed it over to the King of Golconda and went off to found a more peaceful settlement at Pondicherry. All this fighting was most disturbing for the traders at Madras; they persuaded the Mohammadan King to pull down all the fortifications, hoping for no more trouble. But the Portuguese came back and the place became a thorn in the side of the Madras settlement as a refuge for offenders and "interlopers," that is, independent merchants who infringed the Company's monopoly of trade.

(b) *Madras Trade.*—This leads us to consider the methods of trading in the Madras settlement. Now-a-days trade is carried on by a number of firms independent of each other and unconnected with Government. But then the Hon'ble East India Company was everything within its own settlement; it was Government, it administered its own justice, employed its own army and it was also the only legitimate trader. It was ruled by a Board of Directors in London; the Governor was under their orders. The Governor's council consisted of senior merchants, all servants of the Company. The Company had all the expense of keeping up and developing the settlements and objected very strongly to what were called "interlopers," private persons making use of the Company's settlements to trade on their own account. But private trade was very profitable and not only were there interloping ships, private ships which came to the Company's settlements and took goods to sell at home, but the Company's servants bought goods locally on their own account and shipped them home to be sold for their private profit. Descriptions have come down of the excitement in Fort St. George when an interloping vessel was sighted off San Thome and various officials of the Company slipped quietly along the beach of San Thome to take the opportunity of a little private trade.

(c) *Early Landings.*—We must now turn to the Company's own trade at Fort St. George. The arrival of a ship in the seventeenth and eighteenth centuries was an event; ships were not then a regular feature of the place. There was great excitement when one of the Company's ships was sighted; everybody thronged to the beach to see. There was no harbour, not even a pier or jetty; the East Indiamen lay at anchor in the sea off the Fort and in front of them was nothing but a narrow strip of beach. The present expanse of sand in front of the Fort was not there; in stormy weather the sea came right into the Fort moat, and at one time threatened to undermine the foundations to such an extent that the Company seriously considered abandoning the place. But in stormy weather there was no trade; the ships avoided the monsoon months. In fine weather they lay at anchor outside the surf and the goods and passengers were all landed by masula boats through the surf on to the beach. Many descriptions have come down to us of landing at Madras in these boats, how the boatmen waited for a big wave, came in on the crest of it till it was spent, paddled hard to get past the breaking place of the next wave so as to be carried by it right uo the beach. And as they waited outside the surf for a good wave they bargained with their passengers; "their luggage was so heavy they must give extra pay"; and the passenger, thinking his last hour had come, usually paid.

If he did not, or if his luggage looked valuable, a box or two usually fell out into the surf, whence the boatmen salved it at their leisure. Most of the profits were made out of passengers ; possibly the Company's goods were more carefully treated. But there was nowhere to put them ; they were piled anyhow on the sand in front of the Sea Gate at the Fort, where the road now runs, until they could be carried in through the Sea Gate past the Sea Customer whom we now call the Collector of Customs and stored in the Company's godowns in the Fort. The present Officers' Mess in the Fort was then the Commercial Exchange, and we can picture the merchants standing on the verandah and looking on to the beach as the goods were brought in.

(*d*) *Exports.*—In the same way were treated the goods for export to England ; cloths and muslins were bought from local merchants, or made by the Company's weavers in their newly established suburb of Chintadripet. They were washed by the Company's washermen, at first close to the Fort and later, as things became more safe, further away at Washermanpet. They were sorted by the Company's officers and kept in the Company's godowns in the Fort till one of their ships came in ; then the goods were carried through the sea gate to the beach and taken by masula boat through the surf to the ship.

III. THE SECOND PORT

This then was the beginning of the Port of Madras ; the first Harbour offices and godowns were in Fort St. George, which was built for that very purpose. There is a coloured print, dated 1797, "Portrait of an East Indiaman sailing from Madras", showing ships lying at anchor just outside the Fort. But by the end of the eighteenth century the trade had outgrown the premises in the Fort and, as the trade grew, Madras grew. In 1798 the Governor, the second Lord Clive, moved the Sea Customer out of the Fort, first of all to the temporary huts on the beach, and then to "the Paddy Godown on the North-East Beach, lately occupied as a French prison," on the site where the Custom House still is to-day. It is difficult for us to realise what a daring move this was and how much it alarmed the merchants ; goods had of course to be landed where the Custom House was, and it was considered most unsafe to keep them in such an exposed spot, so far from the rest of Madras. For there was no George Town, or very little : Messrs. Parry & Co.'s building was all that existed of the present First Line Beach ; there were gardens along the line of Pophams Broadway : and Madras was still exposed to the raids of Tippu from Mysore. But no harm came of this daring move into the open country, in spite of the protest by the Merchants of Madras that it was "a Place perhaps the most inconvenient to us of any which could be pitched upon for the purpose." Thus from the end

EAST INDIA MAN SAILING FROM MADRAS 1797

—By Courtesy of the Chairman Madras Port Trust.

of the eighteenth century goods were landed on the strip of beach opposite the present Custom House, instead of at the Fort; but it must be remembered that here too the sea came very much further in than it does to-day. First Line Beach really was the line of the beach, as is shown in the coloured prints of "Embarkation and Disembarkation at Madras", dated 1837. The method of landing was the same as it had been at the Fort; goods were still brought ashore in masula boats and piled indiscriminately on the beach, and the boatmen continued to make their profits. Indeed, one of the great objections raised to the first plan of building a harbour was that it would deprive the boatmen class of their means of making a living. On the other hand, the great reason which induced the Chamber of Commerce in 1868 to press for the building of a harbour was the exceedingly good living which these boatmen were making. They had a magnificent monopoly, being a closed caste and quite indispensable, as nothing but a masula boat could live in the surf. They charged what they liked, five, six and even ten times the regulation fare; and they also took a very heavy toll on all goods in the way of damage and pilferage. The loss in this way between ship and shore was estimated at 90% of the loss on the whole voyage, and at 20% of trade profits.

IV. PLANS FOR HARBOUR

For this reason in 1868 the Chamber of Commerce urged on Government the construction of some sort of harbour to protect ships from weather and from the extortions of boatmen. A Committee was appointed to report, which was strongly in favour of building something, but much divided on the question whether it should be a closed harbour, or a long breakwater parallel with the coast, keeping the force of the waves off the ships lying inside it. The majority was "strongly of opinion that no closed harbour at Madras, however ingeniously constructed, could be prevented from shoaling up," nor could they believe that any basin could be kept open by dredging. The President of the Committee, however was of the opinion that no sand whatever would pass the mouth of an enclosed harbour, and that there would be no necessity whatever for dredging. This clash of opinions is characteristic of the early history of the Madras Harbour; experts and boards of experts have reported with the utmost confidence in completely opposite senses, and the Government has steered its way as best as it might between the Scylla and Charybdis of high engineering authority completely unacquainted with the place, and the vehement opposition of local experts.

The first idea was a breakwater, 1200 yards from the shore, extending from opposite the Lighthouse to opposite the Railway Station at Royapuram, with guns mounted on it for defence. After much contradictory reporting by experts, however, they adopted a plan by Mr. Parkes, who had been very successful at Karachi, but had not at that time even seen Madras. He proposed a pair of breakwaters, 3000 feet apart, stretching out seawards parallel to one another for a length of about 3000 feet, and then curving round towards each other till they left an opening of 515 feet between their pier-heads. This work was begun in 1877, but met with much tribulation. First it was in danger from the Viceroy, Lord Lytton, who was strongly of the same opinion as the Directors of the East India Company 230 years before, that Madras was not worth the money that was being spent on it. He wanted the whole thing abandoned at once, but was over-ruled by the Secretary of State, and the work continued. After the Viceroy came the cyclone. In 1881 a storm destroyed a large part of the unfinished work, wrecking much of the piers, rolling the two Titan cranes into the harbour, and sinking the two small ships which lay at anchor inside. This was hardly surprising, as the walls were only designed to be 2½ feet above the surface of the water at ordinary times, and the entrance faced due east, exposing the still unfinished harbour to the full force of the waves.

It was after this storm of 1881 that the question of changing the entrance to the N. E. corner of the harbour was raised. Again the experts girded themselves for battle; a Committee of distinguished engineers at home declared that it would be impossible for a ship to get in and out of the harbour at the north end, as the prevailing wind for two-thirds of the year was from the north; while the captains of the P. & O. and B. I. lines unanimously agreed that it would be perfectly easy, as the prevailing wind was from the south. The Government of Madras, with all the local engineers, pressed strongly for the northern entrance, with a protective arm as at present; but they were over-ruled by the Secretary of State, who insisted that Mr. Parkes should complete his plan, with the entrance on the east; and later recommendations in favour of the north-east corner were met at home with the same refusal.

SIR FRANCIS SPRING

This, then, was the situation when the real maker of the Madras Harbour, Sir Francis Spring, came on the scene in 1904. He has described it himself. "The harbour at this date was formed by the pair of arms already described, curving round so as to leave an entrance on the east side, with full scope for the swell to roll in nearly all the year round, which made the working of vessels slow, difficult and dangerous during many months of the year. The 5-fathom line was about half a mile from the shore forming the west side of the harbour, which consisted of a long flat sandy slope, with surf rolling in on it but little less violently than outside. There was no place for small craft to lie in shelter in dangerous weather, and though a few dozen 10-ton lighters had come into existence alongside of the old surf boats, they were constantly breaking loose during May and November, and, once broken from their moorings, nothing could save them from wreck. Needless to say, this greatly discouraged the provision by capitalists of an adequate tonnage of lighters. Between high water mark and the streets of the town of Madras there were to be found a few confused and unregulated railway sidings and two or three exiguous sheds. The beach was to be seen at all times littered with timber, coal, railway materials, general cargo, machinery, liquors, etc., all in dire confusion. Every packet of dutiable goods landed along the beach, unless too big to be so handled, was obliged to be carried on men's heads to the Government Custom House across the road, while goods arriving over the old screw-pile pier had to be pushed into the same Custom House on lorries. The entire dutiable trade of Madras had to pass in, and the empty lorries to pass out through one 10-foot Custom House gateway. The result was that it was no uncommon thing for a consignee not to get his packages under several weeks or even months. Machinery and railway packages used to be piled up in stacks, sometimes three or four deep, on the beach, and it was constantly happening that before the cargo of one vessel could be delivered to waiting consignees, that of another had perforce, for want of sidings, to be dumped on top of it. In fact, the arrangements were about as bad as they could possibly be." So Sir Francis Spring found the Madras Harbour; there is no need to describe in detail how he left it. To those who know the Harbour as it is today, the best tribute to him is the contrast with this description of the place as it was when he came to it. He saw, too, as indeed the Chamber of Commerce saw in 1868, that it was the lack of harbour facilities which discouraged the trade of Madras, and made it in the nineteenth century such a poor, tenth-rate sort of place. Kipling saw the poverty; he wrote of Madras in 1896:—

> Clive kissed me on the mouth and eyes and brow,
> Wonderful kisses, so that I became
> Crowned above queens; a withered beldame now,
> Brooding on ancient fame.

The withered beldame has taken a new lease of life since, very largely owing to Sir Francis Spring. The Directors in 1640 and the Viceroy and his council in 1878 were all wrong; Madras was worth spending money on. Given decent harbour facilities, the trade would come, and would more than repay the expense, in prosperity for the city. The event proved him abundantly right; but his work was better than he knew; he did not altogether foresee the enormous rate at which the trade would come. He left Madras in 1919, just at the beginning of the great boom, when the trade and prosperity of the city leapt up, and the Harbour again found itself too narrow to cope with it. He estimated that the next big step would have to be taken in twenty, thirty, or even fifty years ; the need for it has begun to be felt in ten.

MADRAS A TRADING CITY

We must never forget that the city of Madras is built on her trade. It was a trading settlement that Francis Day founded in 1639 on the site of the little fishing village ; the Honourable East India Company had no interest whatever in anything else. When in the nineteenth century her trade declined, her importance sank to nothing. As efforts were made to improve her shipping accommodation, her trade began to return and the withered beldame to revive. The more the harbour grew, the more trade and prosperity returned, and for this reason the history of the Port is a vital part of the history of Madras for these three hundred years.

A Short Account of "Development of Road, Transport and Communications in Madras" from 1639 to 1939

By

H. H. Chapman,

Director, Messrs. Simpson & Co., Ltd., Madras.

Three Hundred years is a very short period to the Historian and an infinitesimally short period to the Geologist. Three Hundred years in the development of a City however is a tremendous period, particularly when during that three hundred years saw the commencement of the Mechanical Era and the revolutionary changes which this Era brought about, and that Madras in 1639 was then but a village.

The changes that have occurred in Madras or "Matharas Pattanam" as it was originally known, have been probably without equal in any other part of the world. Very little record is available concerning the first part of the Tercentenary period and it can be safely assumed that Roads and Communications were entirely neglected as we know them to-day and only existed in so far as the road traffic of the times, i.e., the bullock carts, etc., had compacted the earth to permit a comparatively light-laden vehicle to pass. This is, of course, excepting those roads which to-day we call "Strategic."

With the British occupation in 1639 and their permission to build a Fort at Madras the need for Military Roads became essential and these Military Roads naturally enough came under the Military Engineering Department, but even so, the maintenance of such roads depended upon their military significance.

As the British occupation extended, certain Military Roads, being of no further use went into disrepair and others were extended. Certain of the old Military Roads remain to-day, some of them being the original site and direction of some of the Trunk Roads leading out of Madras, to-day.

It was not till the year 1858, more than 200 years after the founding of Madras that Roads became a subject of serious consideration. This is extremely surprising when it is remembered that the original site of Madras was a tiny village which rapidly grew to become a large City and thousands of tons of produce must have been brought into the City for export to Europe.

The honour of the earliest effort at establishing communications seems to go to the Post and Telegraph Department, although, of course, it was something vastly different from the wonderful organisation that we know to-day. The first reference to a regular Postal system is made in the Minutes of Consultation of the East India Company of the 7th July 1736, less than 100 years after the establishment of Madras, and the following are some extracts from the Minutes which seem to indicate how casual were the conditions prevailing even in important business circles in those days :—

" As there have been of late frequent miscarriages of packets to and from Madras without possibility of tracing the cause, not knowing the stages where they do happen, as no advice is ever sent us by the neighbouring Residencies, and as this on any emergency may be attended with the worst consequences, it is agreed to establish the following Rules and communicate to the Presidency of Madras, recommending the same to be circulated to the factories and Residencies subordinate to them, as we shall do to those dependent on Bengal :—

'That the packets henceforward be numbered in regular succession for the present season from this time to the end of the year and in future from the 1st January to the last of December.

'That the day and hour of despatch as well as the number be noted on the tickets affixed to the packets and that on every packet the number and date of the next preceding despatch be noted.

'That in order to have the earliest information of the loss of a packet at any time, the Resident or Chief of a factory shall regularly give advice of the receipt of each packet to the Resident of the stage from whence it came last.

'That when any packets are found to be missing the Chiefs or Residents at the two nearest stages shall immediately make it their business to examine the Dauks or Tappies very particularly, and punish them severely when they do not give a satisfactory account how the packets came to be lost, giving advice in the meantime to each Presidency.' "

Nearly 40 years later in 1774 a Postmaster-General was appointed and postage was charged for the first time on private letters. The carriage of letters from Madras was charged on a mileage basis and copper tickets were struck for public convenience to be solely used for postal purposes,—obviously a precursory of the modern Postage Stamp.

The Post Office having once started its development went ahead rapidly, probably more rapidly than any other branch of communications, and in 1785, revised regulations for the Post Office were issued based on those already in vogue in Bangalore.

In 1786, arrangements were made for a fortnightly Mail Service from Madras to Calcutta and Bombay. But, for the next half century no definite attempt was made to extend or improve the system of Postal communications on what was later termed "Imperial basis."

At the commencement of British Rule the responsibility for Roads came under the Maramut Department, but the date of establishment of this Department is not clear. The Maramut Department worked through the District Collectors and exercised charge of all irrigation work, civil buildings, and roads, and Collectors being responsible, but receiving no professional aid of any kind. The fact that Collectors received no professional aid for such technical subjects is another illustration of how sadly communications were treated in the earlier days.

Later on, Engineering Officers were appointed to assist Collectors and received a designation of "Superintendent of Tank Repairs."

In 1819, the question of communications received some attention and Civil Engineering including Roads came under the control of an Engineer situated in Madras to control the whole Presidency, who was styled "Inspector General of Civil Estimates."

In 1825, the whole Maramut Department was placed under the Board of Revenue and in 1836 the Chief Engineer received a seat at the Board to look after public works interests. The office of the Inspector-General was abolished and the Public Works Department can be said to have been born by the appointment of a Public Works Secretary to the Board of Revenue. But all treatment of communications was, however, very slipshod for many more years. A Commission however was appointed to examine the P. W. D. system and in 1856, the Commission submitted a report, a short extract of which will give an indication of the still scandalous position of the Roads:—

> "We found that in the extensive provinces composing this presidency, having a total area two and a half times that of England and Wales, and a population one fourth more numerous, there is no more than about 3,400 miles of what in the returns is called "made road," and that even of this small extent, a great part has never been made at all, being only tracks where the soil is of so firm a character as to bear a very light traffic in dry weather, without

requiring much repair; and further that another very large portion of the so-called "made road" is very imperfectly provided with bridges, and is therefore still closed for a considerable part of the year. We found that nearly all the most important lines of commerce, being those connecting the Coast Districts with the interior, still remain entirely neglected; and that even of the great Military lines, which have received a larger share of the attention of Government, there are very few in good order; while the greater part are in an utter state of ruin, or more properly speaking have no existence at all as roads, being unmade, unbridged, and intercepted by frequent swamps and ravines."

During this time, that is to say, between 1750 and 1800 the question of the Geography of India was concerning the British Generals and for the first 150 years of the life of Madras little or nothing was known of the exact Geography of the Districts outside of Madras and even as late as 1800, the exact latitude of Madras still remained unknown in any degree of accuracy.

Madrasis will be interested to know that the magnificent undertaking known by the name of "The Great Indian Trigonometrical Survey," consisting of chains of triangles, which extend from Cape Comorin to the borders of Tibet and from Afghanistan to Burma, was commenced about the year 1800, and that the original base line on which all these millions of triangles were based was a straight line drawn roughly along Mount Road, between Madras and St. Thomas Mount, the first base line being approximately seven miles long. The first survey of India, therefore, started in Madras, and it can be assumed that the forthcoming maps provided excellent data for Generals for the development of a road system from Madras into the interior for military purposes.

By 1845, a Trunk Road Department had been formed and Railways had already become inaugurated, although curiously enough, Madras remained for a long time without being directly connected with any of the major Railways. It was not until 1876 that Madras was first connected with the Metre Gauge system of the South Indian Railway, when Madras Park and Tindivanam were connected with railways. Earlier connection had, of course, been made with the M. & S. M. Railway. In 1879, Madras Park was connected with the old Madras Beach Station, a distance of nearly 2 miles; but it was not until 1900 that the old Madras Beach Station was connected to the Madras Beach Junction. From that time right up until 1931 there appears to have little improvement in the Railway Service for the City other than perhaps a slight increase in the number of trains that run.

Throughout the whole of this time, the Postal Department continued to develop excluding a lapse of over half a century, when a fresh era of Postal Development commenced. Railways and the development of good metal roads under the Trunk Road Department assisted the Postal Department, and in 1853, a Railway Mail Service was started from Madras. In 1854, Postage Stamps were first introduced and the whole Department was placed under the control of a Director-General. The Office of the Postmaster-General was separated from that of the Presidency Postmaster, both of which Offices were till then vested in the same Officer. This marked the commencement of the Indian Post Office in its present footing.

By 1864, there were nine Post Offices in Madras, all of which are still in active use to-day, with the exception of one.

In 1871, through railway communication was established between Madras and other Presidencies. This added considerably to the communications of Madras.

During the period 1870-1880, special Postage rates for official letters, V. P. Postage, and Money Orders came into being.

Throughout the earlier history of Madras, one is surprised and interested to learn that although Madras is considered by some to be lagging behind in its development as an important Presidency Town, it will be found that Madras was in many things much ahead of other towns in India and in some things ahead even of the largest City in the world, London.

1881 saw the opening of the first Telephone Exchange, which was situated in a building in Blackers Road, opposite to what is now "Bosotto Hotel." The number of subscribers is not definitely known, but must have been surprisingly small, because by 1910 the number of subscribers had only reached 350. This is not surprising because, between 1881 and 1890 very few cities even in Europe had Telephones.

The first Telephone Switch Board was of the old "Magneto" type. Early in the century of 1900 the Telephone Exchange was shifted to Errabalu Chetty Street, and a later pattern Switch Board was introduced.

It is really from 1890 onwards that the development of communications in Madras really jumps ahead, although the name of Mr. Basil Cochrane is associated with the development of communications in Madras 100 years earlier, when in 1801 he became noted as the projector of the Canal scheme, which today is known as "The Buckingham Canal."

In 1892 the Madras Tramways Company was floated and sanction was given to Messrs. Hutchinson & Co., Ltd., London, with a capital of £100,000 to start a Tramway system. It was, however, not until three years later, (1895) that the first Tramway Section was completed and open for the use of the public. The Madras Electric Tramways were opened in May, 1895, fully six years before Electric Tram Cars were running anywhere else in India and even in London and other large cities in England,—another example of Madras being ahead in its development.

In 1900, the original Tramway Company was obliged to sell the undertaking as the capital was inadequate. The purchasers, "The Electric Construction Co., Ltd.," England, then operated the Tramways in Madras for a period of four years. It was about this time that the first Motor Cars were seen on the roads in Madras, although, the first one that did not have a very successful life was put on the road in 1894 and was driven some distance down Mount Road. Messrs. Simpson and Co., Ltd., played a large part in the development of the early Motor Cars and buses.

In 1904, The Madras Electric Tramways (1904) Ltd., was formed and has been carrying on business ever since. Extensions were made in 1905, 1911, 1919 and to-day the Company has 11 miles of double track and 5¼ miles of single track.

In 1922, presumably due to the impetus of the Great War, the public leaned more kindly towards the Telephone system and the number of subscribers had increased to 1300, and the Madras Telephone Company found it necessary to consider new premises. The "Telephone House" in Esplanade was built in 1925 and in 1926, the Madras Telephone system became automatic and Madras again set a precedent by becoming the first city in India with a fully automatic Exchange and was years ahead of most European Cities in this respect.

Although it was many years before Madras had a properly organised Bus Service, Messrs. Simpson and Co., Ltd., have some interesting catalogues of buses dating back prior to 1910. The type of buses illustrated is essentially similar to the open type of bus still found on the moffusil roads. From 1910 onwards there was seen a steady increase in the number of buses running and owners were badly financed and badly organised and the buses left much to be desired in speed, safety and comfort. The first real attempt at organising the bus transport was undertaken by the Madras Electric Tramways (1904) Ltd., who in the years 1925-27 operated a fleet of 50 Motor Buses. This scheme was abandoned in 1928 owing to the uneconomical competition offered by the unorganised bus owners, and Madras reverted to its unsatisfactory bus system until about 1933.

Madras was still growing rapidly and this encouraged the South Indian Railway to extend the travel facilities offered by them to the Madras public. It must be noted that it took them over 30 years to decide to make a real improvement in railway facilities for the city and they were doubtless attracted by the fact that the more convenient, even if poorly conditioned buses were better patronised than the slow inconvenient and comparatively few steam trains. In 1931, the double line Suburban Electric Train Service was opened alongside the original single track steam main line between Tambaram and Madras Beach. This is a well patronised line equipped with fast, comfortable and safe Electric Trains of the latest design and construction.

Between 1931 and the present day very serious attempts have been made at improving communications within the City. Although the present roads still leave much to be desired, there is to-day a large number of miles of really first-class roads and these are being annually improved. The Bus Services have been completely re-organised in the last three or four years and the City and Suburban routes are now operated by financially sound Companies operating modern Saloon Buses comparable with any other city in the world, bearing in mind the limitations of the routes on which they operate and the climatic requirements of the country.

No mention has been made in this paper of the development of the Telegraph Services due to the fact that the information could not be obtained in time for inclusion; but the Post Office in Madras has always been very progressive and telegraph facilities in Madras have always been on a basis easily comparable with the telegraph facilities offered in other countries. The latest development in Madras is the connecting of certain of the more important Newspaper Offices with direct telegraphic tape connection to the Post Office, and the inauguration of the Madras Flying Club which was founded in 1930 and handled the first Tata Air Mail plane in 1932.

It is also necessary to mention here that there was in 1872-73 a bi-monthly sea-borne Postal Service between Madras and Rangoon. In 1886, a fortnightly service was introduced between Madras and the Ports on the North-Eastern coast, alternately with the fortnightly service between Madras and Rangoon, thus establishing a weekly service in those parts. In February 1888, Mails were sent from Madras direct to Rangoon which brought about a large saving in time and commenced the weekly service between Madras and Burma.

The internal carriage of Mails in the Madras City was by Tongas till 1915, when a Motor Service on a small scale with two Cars was introduced as an addition to the Tonga Service. In 1917-18 the Tonga Service was completely replaced by a Motor Service. The Post Office with its excellent record causes surprise when it is realised that their internal Service in the City still operates a large number of its original Motor Vehicles and the balance of the vehicles are also as antiquated as is the Postal Service excellent.

Madras has on the whole an excellent record of development of Transport and Communications compared with other Cities in India, but reading through this paper and looking back in perspective, one cannot help being impressed by the apparent gross negligence in the development of such essential public requirements as a properly cared for and well-maintained road system for the development of Ryotwari lands and other indigenous enterprises.

The Southern India Chamber of Commerce

BY

THE HON. MR. M. CT. M. CHIDAMBARAM CHETTIAR,
President, S.I.C.C.

THE Southern India Chamber of Commerce was established on the 9th October 1909 under the Presidentship of the late Sir P. Theagaraya Chettiar with a strength of 100 members on the rolls in the premises of the "Ramakoti Buildings" where the Indian Bank was then located. Among those who took the most active part in the formation of the Chamber were Sir P. Theagaraya Chettiar, Dewan Bahadur Govindoss Chathurboojadoss, Khan Bahadur M. A. Kuddus Badsha Sahib, Mr. D. V. Hanumantha Rao and Pandit Vidya Sagar Pandya. The Chamber has had a distinguished career under the guidance of the leading commercial men of Madras who became the presidents of the Chamber in succession for varying periods. They were: Sir M. Ct. Muthiah Chettiar, M. Jamal Mahomed Sahib Esq., Nawab C. Abdul Hakim, Dewan Bahadur Govindoss Chathurboojadoss, and Dewan Bahadur M. Balasundaram Naidu, C.I.E.

On the occasion of the celebration of the Silver Jubilee of the Chamber on the 7th December 1935 His Excellency Lord Erskine, Governor of Madras, summed up the history of the Chamber in the following appreciative words: "There can, I think, be no higher testimony to the value of the services which the Chamber has performed in the interests of the commerce of Southern India than the strength and widely representative character of its membership. Moreover, in matters political and administrative, I would myself like to pay a tribute to the courteous assistance which the Chamber has so frequently rendered to my Government and its officers. There have, I fear, been occasions—perhaps more often than not—when the Chamber failed to see eye to eye with the policy of Government. But a Government that does not welcome responsible criticism is not worth its salt, and it is to organisations such as yours that my Government must look for helpful and constructive advice......Yours is truly a most businesslike address, to which it is a pleasure to respond. And if the work of this Chamber is conducted in the same fashion, I can well understand how it is that, while still in the full bloom of youth, as counted in terms of human years, it has already attained the dignity and discretion of a venerable maturity."

The Chamber has now 482 members on the rolls and as the Provincial Chamber of Commerce, has the following up-country Chambers of Commerce and Associations affiliated to it:—

The Andhra Chamber of Commerce, Madras.
The Central Delta Chamber of Commerce, Amalapuram.
The Godavari Chamber of Commerce, Cocanada.
The Indian Chamber of Commerce, Coimbatore.
The Indian Chamber of Commerce, Tuticorin.
The Malabar Chamber of Commerce, Calicut.
The Madura-Ramnad Chamber of Commerce, Madura.
The Negapatam Chamber of Commerce, Negapatam.
The Rice & Grain Merchants Association, Madras.
The Salem District Chamber of Commerce, Salem.
The South Indian Cine Exhibitors Association, Madras.
The Trichinopoly District Merchants Association, Madras.
The Oilman Stores & Sundry Merchants Association, Madras.

For purposes of All-India business affairs of a commercial and industrial nature the Chamber is associated with the Federation of Indian Chambers of Commerce and Industry, Delhi, and the Chamber is also connected with the International Chamber of Commerce through the Indian National Committee. The Chamber is housed in its own buildings, "The Indian Chamber Buildings", Madras and conducts its monthly journal called "Southern India Commerce." Its subscription has remained at Rs. 24 for city members and Rs. 10 for mufassal members from its very inception and yet the Chamber is among the most affluent commercial bodies in India and in the front rank in point of reputation and standing.

The Chamber has not restricted itself to the interests and grievances of its own members but has always been working on a broader and national basis. In the same spirit it has been always ready to give financial help to any deserving cause. Mention may be made in particular of the prizes given from year to year at the old Government Institute of Commerce, Madras, the Presidency Shorthand Writers Association, Madras, the donations given from time to time for leprosy and tuberculosis relief, for education of the blind, for the Girl Guides Association, for industrial and commercial exhibitions and for organising and ventilating public opinion on general problems like currency, taxation etc. The Chamber from its own funds gave Rs. 1,000 for Bihar Earthquake relief in 1934, Rs. 1,500 for Quetta Earthquake relief in 1935 and Rs. 500 for Indian refugees who returned from Burma during the riots in 1938. The Chamber conducted the Indian Industrial and Commercial Congress in 1927 and donated Rs. 1,000 for the starting of

SOUTHERN INDIA CHAMBER OF COMMERCE BUILDINGS

—By Courtesy of the S. I. C. C.

the Federation of Indian Chambers of Commerce and Industry. The Chamber has long been feeling the necessity for establishing a permanent industrial and commercial museum in Madras which is bound to solve the marketing problems of the province in a most effective and inexpensive manner, and after discussion of the question at a conference with the Hon'ble Ministers at the Chamber in 1937 a scheme was submitted to Government in which the Chamber agreed to undertake the management of the museum and also to make a recurring grant of Rs. 1,000 for the up-keep of the museum and to pay an extra sum of Rs. 1,000 for the initial expenses.

In various statutes and Government notifications the Chamber's co-operation for administration of public institutions has been vouchsafed by the reservation of seats to its representatives. Among the chief institutions where its representatives work in the management are the following: Madras Legislative Assembly, the Madras Port Trust, the Madras Corporation, the Madras and Annamalai Universities, the South Indian Railway and the Madras and Southern Maharatta Railway Advisory Committees, Madras Board of Industries, Madras Board of Communications, Madras Provincial Cotton Committee, Indian Tea Market Expansion Board, Madras Marketing Board, Madras City Excise licensing Board, Government Royapuram Hospital Advisory Committee, Madras University Employment Bureau, Madras Air Raid Precautions Committee, Railway Rates Advisory Committee Panel, and the Madras Income-tax Board of Referees. Various commercial and industrial matters coming before those public bodies affecting the interests of the members of the Chamber are duly discussed in advance and necessary steps taken for protecting the interests of the Indian mercantile community in the administration of those public bodies.

The Chamber is the acknowledged apex of the provincial commercial organisation and through its affiliated bodies educates, organizes and controls commercial opinion in the province. Government and public bodies receive authoritative business opinion on every question of commerce or industry when it is examined by the Chamber, and members of the Indian mercantile community may be sure of their difficulties and grievances being handled in a most effective and efficient manner under the collective authority of the Chamber both by correspondence and by interviews with the authorities concerned. The Chamber has frequent interviews at its own premises with various Officers, both of the Provincial Government and the Central Government, on various matters of interest to the mercantile community. As many problems of merchants come before the public bodies on which the Chamber has representation a vigilant watch is maintained for giving the proper turn to any proposal that may be coming before them so that the interests of the merchants will not be prejudiced. The Chamber supplies authoritative information to members on trade, tariff and industries in India and abroad, brings together buyers and sellers and arranges trade connections and introductions for enquirers. The Chamber registers trade marks, issues certificates of origin to accompany shipments, makes official inspection of shipments with a view to issue certificates on invoices on which banks can rely for advances and credit facilities. The Chamber holds survey of goods under dispute between buyers and sellers, and arranges arbitration between parties whether on their own application or on reference from Courts. Through its official magazine the Chamber keeps contact with the entire mercantile community of the province and educates and mobilises opinion on all current matters of topical interest. Members of the Chamber are entitled to concession rates in all charges, particularly with regard to registration of trade marks, survey, arbitration and certificates.

With a membership of nearly 500 members, with a building of its own, with investments worth about Rs. 35,000, with a well-trained Secretariat, with a coterie of alert representatives on the various public bodies to voice merchants' grievances, with an excellent Library and Reading Room for public use, with a standing connection with other Chambers of Commerce and Associations in the Presidency through their affiliation to this Chamber and with those outside the Presidency through the Federation of Indian Chambers of Commerce and Industry and through the Indian National Committee of the International Chamber of Commerce, Paris, the Chamber bids fair to remain an unfailing authority and bulwark of the Indian mercantile community of this country.

Early Trade Difficulties at Madras

By

Sir Charles Fawcett, I.C.S. (*Retired*),
Editor of the India Office Publication,
'The English Factories in India.'

It is not easy for anyone unacquainted with the past history of Madras to visualise the vicissitudes that hampered trade in the first hundred years after its foundation in 1639. One of the things that induced Francis Day to settle a factory at Madraspatam was his finding that the locality produced "the best paintings" (i.e., printed calicoes), as well as excellent varieties of other cloth, better and cheaper than anywhere else on the Coromandel Coast. It might be thought that, with this good start, progress in the development of its trade would be easy and steady, and that its merchants, weavers, and other workmen, would meet with prosperity rather than adversity. The actual facts show a very different state of affairs.

It was fortunate that the settlement began with the building of Fort St. George. Day had the courage to start this work without waiting for orders from the East India Company, and it was continued in spite of its disapproval. The Fort and its English garrison provided a protection, the absence of which would almost certainly have altered the history of Madras. The surrounding country was then under the arbitrary rule of the Muhammadan King of Golconda, whose officers were adept at extortion and other oppression, so that bribery and injustice were rampant. Trade, which was chiefly in the hands of Hindus, necessarily suffered. Captain Thomas Bowrey, who was in India from 1670 to 1688 and who had a large experience of the countries adjoining the Bay of Bengal and the Coromandel Coast, describes the prevailing conditions as follows:—

> "The merchants, as alsoe most tradesmen, are of the Gentue cast, and live for the most part in admirable [i.e. strange] subjection to the Moors, payinge the King's taxes and duties to the uttermost farthinge, besides many oppressions of taxes the Governor and his Mahometan Councell lay heavily upon them; and, which is more grievous, they are compelled to beare it with the largest extent of patience, by reason little or noe justice is to be acquired where the Mahometans are Lords over them, for if

complaint be made to the High Court of Justice, the Mussleman, as they all themselves, shall certainly carry it (if he appeare in person) onely with one saying, K[y]a Mussleman j[h]ute bolta, Will a true believer lye ?"

Again he says :—

"Some of the richest Indian merchants inhabit upon this coast; but many of them dare not be knowne to be soe, for feare of receivinge injury from the Mahometans, and for some reasons more, the chiefe of which is, if any of them die, their estates in full falls to the Kinge, none of his seed dareinge to claim any of it by right or title, onely lyeth at the mercie and benevolence of the Kinge or Emperour. Theire habit is generally but meane, more like to servants then masters, theire houses very ordinary low and for the most part thatched over, and are for foregoinge reasons forced, for the benefit of theire posterities, to bury the major part of their treasure in the earth."

Dr. Fryer who made a nine days visit to Fort St. George in 1673, similarly speaks of the people in those parts being "under the same bondage" as those at Masulipatam, but says the inhabitant of Madras had this "alleviated by the power of the English, who command as far as their guns reach." This protection involved a drawback, for, to use the words of Charles Lockyer (1711), while it provided a 'sanctuary to the fortunate people living in it', it was also 'a bugbear to the Moods', i.e. its Muhamamdan neighbours. Thus, if quarrels arose—and occasions for these were numerous—the Fort and its dependencies were liable to have their supply of provisions stopped, and their trade hindered by a blockade which sometimes lasted for several months. Bowrey, for instance, says :—

"Our Fort (and towne) of St. George's hath been often molested by some of the inland native forces......I have known an army of some thousands, both horses and foot, come down and pitch theire tents within 2 miles of the walls where they have put a stopp upon all sorts of provisions, and most chiefely the East India Company's goods that were to be sent that monsoone to England, threateninge what strange feats they would play, if in case our Agent and Governour sent them not soe much moneys, 10 or 20,000 pagodes (each value 9s.), but they are generally mistaken in the summe and be satisfied with a farre smaller present, and sometimes with none at all."

These statements are amply corroborated by records of the East India Company. Thus in 1670 Chenupalli Mirza, the commander of the local forces of the King of Golconda, 'besett the towne on all sides' for nearly a month, but failed to secure the 1500 pagodas he tried to extort, as the Governor of Madras succeeded in getting orders from Golconda for his withdrawal. In 1676, 1678 and again in 1681, Lingappa, the Governor of Poonamalee, similarly stopped goods and provisions from coming to the town for considerable periods. It was not easy to get the Golconda authorities to interfere on such occasions, as there was an almost continuous controversy with them about the sufficiency of the rent paid to the King for the town and other matters; nor could anything usually be done without making considerable presents, at which the Company looked askance.

There were more serious dangers. In 1677 Sivaji's incursion into the Carnatic brought him within a few miles of the town; but his memory of the resistance he had met with from the English when he attacked Surat in 1670, and the terms of friendship between him and them, which had been initiated by Gerald Aungier, the Governor and 'founder' of Bombay, induced him to leave Madras alone. On the other hand there were constant rumours that he was about to attack the English and Dutch settlements, which must have interfered with trade. There was more real danger when a French fleet under De La Haye seized the neighbouring Fort of St. Thome in July 1672. The King of Golconda, whose territory had been thus invaded, naturally objected, and his forces besieged the place from September 1672 to March 1673. The situation then became one of great difficulty for the government at Madras, as both sides expected it to help them. It was disadvantageous for the Company to have the French, who were rival traders in India, in such close proximity; but they were allies of England in the war against Holland which had then broken out in Europe, and the request of the King of Golconda to help him to drive them out of St. Thome, had to be refused. On the other hand, Fort St. George could not afford to offend the Golconda ruler, with whom they had recently settled outstanding differences. A policy of non-intervention was accordingly adopted, but constant trouble arose over Golconda complaints that Sir William Langhorn, the Governor of Madras, was surreptitiously helping the French with supplies, and recriminations by De La Haye for not helping him enough. The danger was enhanced when news of the outbreak of war with Holland reached India at the beginning of 1673. The Dutch, with whom Langhorn had meanwhile managed to keep on good terms, became disposed to assist the Golconda forces in their attack on St. Thome. In May they sent 13 ships to its neighbourhood; in August a fight took place between a Dutch fleet and 10 ships the Company had sent out to the Coromandel Coast, in which the latter were badly worsted; and in September the Dutch landed forces at Triplicane and joined Golconda in the siege of St. Thome. After a gallant struggle, the French were forced to surrender to the Dutch on 26 August 1674. Madras then became in imminent danger of being attacked and taken by the Dutch; but this catastrophe was averted by news of peace between England and Holland arriving just after the capitulation of St. Thome; and Langhorn's maintenance of friendly relations with the King of Golconda prevented a similar attack by his forces in spite of some critical disputes, one of which led to Madras being blockaded for a short time.

In 1693-98 Zulfikar Khan, the commander of the Mughal army sent by the Emperor Aurangzeb to the Carnatic, gave considerable trouble to the Fort authorities. In 1696 it was feared he might attack Madras, and the Governor and Council said his conduct had emboldened his officers to "stop and seize our goods, exact unusual customs, and to do all things that tend to the lessening of the trade and destroying our privileges." In 1697, after he had overthrown the King of Golconda, there were renewed alarms, when his forces came in the neighbourhood of Fort St. George.

These are a few among many events that illustrate the interference with trade that so often arose in the seventeenth century. Other facts to be borne in mind are that, though the population of Madras rapidly increased, its trade was largely dependent on supplies of cloth, etc., from up-country; and its merchants and brokers when they travelled abroad were liable to suffer from local oppression. For instance, Bowrey relates how Khemchand, the Company's chief broker at Balasor, was made to disgorge Rs. 50,000 by the Governor of Cuttack; and this is supported by India Office records, which mention his detention as a prisoner and his being mulcted of part of his wealth. Banias who had not the Company's influence to protect them, were an easy prey. Bowrey says:—

> "I remember in the yeare 1674......a new Nabob was sent from Dacca to settle in Cattack [Cuttack]. The new Nabob in his journey took all opportunities to get moneys, in soe much that he lett slipp none whereby he might enrich himselfe......[Near Balasore] he sent for most rich merchants of Gentues [Hindus] and Banjans [Banians] commandinge theire estates, or considerable portion of them, at his owne pleasure. His demands off some were 10, 20, 30, 40, 50 thousand rupees, and of some more, accordinge as they were of abilities (havinge subtle fellows near him that had first pryed into their estates)."

To much the same effect is the following description of the sad state of merchants and weavers given by Langhorn in a letter to the Company, which he wrote in 1676:—

> (He remarks on) "the different stile of these arbitrary and slavish dominions from our Europe countrys, where justice is legally circumscribed. In Europe industry is in favour, and propriety [property] secured, and particularly weavers of all sorts, like our Cloathyers and [? makers of] Italian fabricques, raise themselves vast estates......But here the quite contrary, where they dare not hoord nor increase their estates to any bulk. It's meat for harpys; the merchants who are in some way of getting [money], spend it in a manner all in good workes and plentiful living, where they dare; [owing to the risk of extortion] reserving little else but creditt and a bare stock to carry on business. But the poore weavers, betweene their inbred way of feeding Brahmenys and the extortions of their Avaldars, live meerely from hand to mouth, with hardly a ragg to hide their shame; and seldome able to put a peece upon the loome without the money aforehand; in somuch that rather than starve, some pedling fellow traveling with his ox......may take advantage of their necessity and pick up here and there a little at his own prices. But for great quantitys one must contract with them who deale up in the country, or send up factors and money distributed up and down to deliver out among the weavers, who will not undertake but at market rates, on which report and competition (when more buyers than sellers) have their usuall effects; and the great danger of these poore fellowes dying or running away and other accidents, and charges, make price accordingly."

The last sentence draws attention to another impediment to trade at that time, viz., the difficulty of recovering up-country debts. No doubt there were weavers at Madras from an early date; but their number and skill appear to have been comparatively small. To improve this position, Governor Yale in 1690 induced fifty families of 'fine' weavers to settle there; but it was not till well after beginning of the eighteenth century that a larger immigration of weavers and dyers into Madras took place. That this state of things continued for some time is shown by the following remarks of Captain Alexander Hamilton, whose '*New Account of the East Indies*' was published in 1727:

> "The current trade of Fort St. George runs gradually slower, the traders meeting with disappointment, and sometimes with oppressions, and sometimes the liberty of buying and selling is denied them... The Colony produces very little of its own growth or manufacture for foreign inlets."

On the other hand the sea-borne trade of the town did not suffer to the same extent as that of Bombay, where Malabar pirates and contests between bitter enemies like the Sidi (the admiral of the Mughal fleet) and Sivaji, at the entrance to its harbour were a great impediment to its flourishing. Ordinarily, imports by sea to Madras arrived safely, and were assured of a ready sale, as Charles Lockyer, who was in the Company's service there in 1702-04 testifies in the following passage from his '*Account of Trade in India.*'

> "Trade they drive to all parts eastward of the Cape of Good Hope; that of China is most desired for the gold and fine goods brought thence; but the Company sending directly from England vessels of their own, has quite spoiled it. Manilla, under Armenian Colours, is a profitable voyage; Battavia, and the coasts of Java, Jahore, Malacca, Quedah, Pegu, Arracon, Bengall and all the Coromandell Coast, are yearly visited; with Acheen, Priaman, Indrapore, Bencoolen, Bantall, etc., on the West coast of Sumatra. But of late their greatest ships use the Mocho, Persia and Surat markets with Bengall or China commodities, touching at several ports on the Malabar Coast in their way: especially Callicut for pepper, coco-kernels, coyr, and cardamons, nuxvomica, turmorick, coculus Indi [a poisonous berry] etc., which are all the produce of that part of the coast and turn to good account in any western port they may be bound to. Rice is often a profitable commodity in Mocho and Persia. On her [a ship's] return from a voyage.... the ship and cargo are sold by outcry or auction, at the Sea-Gate; where he that offers most ready money has the lot he bids for. A note is generally put up at the Sea-Gate a week before it begins, informing the sorts, quantities, and time when [the sale will take place] ....whence there's always a great concourse of people, which makes well for a sale.... The women drive as great a trade as the men, and with no less judgment, nay, some are so forward as to have invoices, accounts currant, etc., in their own names tho' their husbands are in being."

There was therefore a bright side as well as a dark one to the state of trade at Madras in those days. But it was not till more settled conditions arose in the latter part of the eighteenth century that a clear path became open for the progress of industrial development to its existing level in the Presidency.

Three Hundred Years of Madras Commerce

By

G. H. Hodgson, M.L.A.,

Director, Messrs. Parry & Co., Ltd., Madras.

Trade and commerce have existed at Madraspatnam ever since the first weaver or potter bartered his wares for the surplus catch of a longshore fisherman.

That, no doubt, takes us back several thousands of years; but commerce, in the full sense of the dictionary definition, that is to say, "the interchange of merchandise on a large scale between nations and individuals", may be said to have been born in Madras only towards the end of the year 1639.

It is from that date that the little village of Madraspatnam, situated on the now vacant piece of land between the High Court and Fort St. George, first appeared on the commercial atlas of the world—even though it is true that an important and efficient hand weaving industry, with its connected trades of spinning and dyeing, and even of printing, was well established there long before that date. For part, at least, of the attraction of this small village to Francis Day when he landed there in 1639 was the fact that it was, in his own words, "the only place for paintings so much desired at southwards*, and likewise great store of long cloath and morrees which is there procurable."

"Paintings" were chintz on which coloured designs were imprinted by wooden blocks, or traced by hand, and "morrees" were, and still are, a plain blue cotton cloth.

Madras dyes were held in high repute in those days, and it was said of them that "they never run and scarcely fade". Added to this was the fact that these paintings and morrees were "better Cheape by 20 per cent than anywhere Else." A Dutch chaplain, writing of Madraspatnam in 1649 said that "their chief Traffic consists in colour'd Stuffs, their Weavers here being famous throughout the Indies, as well as their Dyers". And a Spanish priest in 1670 wrote that "the conveniency of buying clothes is great, all those people living upon it."

* * * * * *

* Pegu, the headquarters in the East of the East India Co., in those days.

And so it was that a factory, which then meant little more than a large warehouse, came to be built on the site of Fort St. George, alongside the village of Madraspatnam, and the products of the local handlooms first penetrated the European markets.

Nevertheless, the trade of the Port of Madras was, for the first few years, comparatively insignificant, the exports for the four years 1640 to 1644 averaging only Rs. 25,000 annually. But more and more weavers and their families were attracted to Madras, and by 1649 the total trade of the Port had increased to Rs. 4,00,000.

The following figures extracted from contemporary estimates indicate how very rapid was the growth of the population of Madras.

1639	.. 7,000
1647	.. 19,000
1674	.. 50,000
1685	.. 300,000
1691	.. 400,000

and it is now over 700,000.

* * * * * *

The procedure in the early years was for the East India Company to send out two or three ships annually from London carrying, amongst other things, £10,000 to 15,000 of gold and of Spanish Dollars. These dollars, called pieces of eight, were at that time current throughout the East and the gold was at once coined into pagodas (worth from eight to nine shillings each) at the mint which had been established at Fort St. George in 1640. This money was then invested, through dubashes, in "paintings", "morrees" and so forth, to be shipped to England on the return voyage.

Thus, in 1660, in the words of Fort St. George, "the *Truro* brought with her sterling 12,500 L. in gold which, with the two chests of Corall, wee tooke ashoare into your Fort, and with what haste wee could, converted her gold into pagodas, to loose noe tyme of goeing in hand with our investments."

In 1675 the Company obtained permission from the King of Golconda "to coyne Silver Rupees", and they fixed the exchange at 2sh. 3d. The pagoda remained the basis of currency in Madras until 1813, when it was replaced by the rupee, and during the whole of that period the exchange value of the rupee exceeded 2sh., rising at times as high as 2sh. 10d.

The steady cash income which thus regularly accrued to the weavers established at Madras naturally led to a large and ever increasing influx of weavers and their families from the interior. And these weavers in their turn attracted others to the city; so that in 1652 reference is made to accountants, silk weavers, leather workers, artisans, metal workers, potters and oilmongers.

Thus the expansion of trade continued, and, by 1704, it had grown, at a "moderate computation" to Rs. 20,00,000 per annum of both exports and imports. It still consisted mainly, if not entirely of piecegoods, and in 1714 the export list is comprised chiefly of "long cloth, selampores, bettelees, chintz, morrees, ginghams, romals fine and dimities," and the import list of "auroras, scarlets, popinjays, fine cloth, embost cloth and long ells".

* * * * * *

By 1728 the East India Co. were sending coral and silver to Madras to be exchanged for diamonds from Golconda, and the trade of the port continued to flourish; but by 1732, following on famine in the interior, resulting in high prices for cotton, and therefore of yarn and cloth, the trade declined considerably, and the directors in London despaired that year of "ever seeing Madrass retrieve its ancient Glory of sending several thousand bales of Calicoes in a Season, which was the constant practice for so many years."

The trade, therefore, temporarily declined below the 1704 level, and even as late as 1754 the total turnover was no more than Rs. 25,00,000.

And so during the first hundred years of our survey the trade and general prosperity of Madras increased with astronomic rapidity. An annual turnover of Rs. 25,000 had been increased a hundredfold to Rs. 25,00,000, and the population had risen from 7,000 to 400,000. But from the middle of the eighteenth century a long period of trade recession set in, and the forward march was, for nearly a century, seriously checked. The main reasons for this are not far to seek, and may be recorded under three main headings.

Firstly, war and misrule in the interior as the result of which many thousands of the tillers of the soil left their villages and fled to the hilly tracts.

Secondly, the industrial revolution in Europe resulting in the gradual introduction of the steam-driven loom, and the growth of the factory system.

Thirdly, the policy of protection which resulted from this "revolution".

One might also add a fourth cause, namely the long drawn out wars in Europe resulting in the struggle for supremacy in India between France and England which centred mainly round Madras.

This combination of adverse circumstances played havoc with the trade of Madras, and by 1,800, she might with truth have been described as " a withered beldame brooding on her ancient fame "—an epithet which the modern businessman would strenuously and rightly resist.

Nevertheless these adverse factors set to work in about 1750, and were at their height during the last decade of the eighteenth century. And so, from 1750 onwards, if there was no permanent recession, it is certain that the pace of advance was seriously checked, and the trade of Madras did not really begin to find its feet again until some years after the peace which followed the battle of Waterloo in 1815.

* * * * * *

As late as 1809 the composition of the trade from Madras bore a very close resemblance to that of 1640. That is to say it was still comprised mainly of piecegoods.

" The Company (1809) exported to Madras, from England, a quantity of woollens, lead, iron, copper and naval stores; this in addition to the supplies for the English community there. From Madras the Company imported piecegoods and little else. It also exported from Madras to China a certain amount of piecegoods, with a little cotton; while sugar and saltpetre passed through Madras on the way to China and England. Altogether, the trade there was not considerable."*

Madras at that time also supplied Bengal with salt, cordage and re-exported naval stores; and Bengal supplied Madras with rice of which there was at that time, for the reasons already given, a constant shortage in the South. With roads and transport comparatively undeveloped, the population of Madras was, apart altogether from the ravages of war, much too large to subsist on the crops grown in the neighbourhood.

As regards cordage, the excellence of Madras rope manufacture had long been acknowledged throughout the East. As early as 1726 the Chief Gunner at Madras begged Government to prohibit the import of coir cables because " these Cables sold to ships in this place, if damaged or not well made, may pass for Madrass Cables, and bring an ill repute on the cables and cordage of this place, which has hitherto the Repute of Laying cables the best of any port in India." And in 1799 reference is made to "a cable of 17 inches, by order of the Admiral, from a species of Aloes that grows wild in this country."

During the early years of the nineteenth century raw cotton and indigo were added for the first time to the Madras export list. The former coming mainly from the Tinnivelly, Ramnad and Ganjam Districts,

* Parkinson: *Trade in the Eastern Seas*, 1793-1813.

and the latter from South Arcot. The indigo trade was eventually killed by the synthetic German product, but raw cotton is still exported in considerable quantities.

* * * * * *

The first we hear of Banking in Madras is in 1682 when the Directors recommended Fort St. George to constitute itself into a Bank for the receipt of fixed deposits; but the notification which followed really amounted to no more than the issue of a Government Loan, and the Governor of Fort St. George resolved on "the raising of a banke of money to the vallue of One hundred Thousand pounds att six per Cent."

More than a century passed before the first joint stock bank was formed in Madras. This was the Carnatic Bank, constituted in 1788 for "the receipt of money, the issue of bills, notes and other securities after the manner of the most respectable Banks in London." The Bank was given power to issue notes to the value of three times its capital of 120,000 star pagodas—the pagoda being then worth Rs. 3-12-0.

Marine insurance was first underwritten in Madras in 1687 when the Company resolved to set up an Insurance Office at Fort St. George "for the furtherance of your trade and our own Customes."

The Company's instructions continued; "To set the wheels a going, we are content to write, by way of assuring, 5,000 L. adventure from India to England upon any our own three decked ships at the praemio of 5 per cent if you apprehend no extraordinary danger."

* * * * * *

In 1805 the first factory of which there is any record was established in Madras in the shape of a tannery started in San Thome by Mr. Thomas Parry. This factory, which after a few years was employing over 300 men, shipped its manufactured products all over the world including England, America, Australia and South Africa. The factory supplied boots and accoutrements not only for the armies in India but for the British Army in England and it is no idle fancy to picture some of the British troops at Waterloo wearing boots made in Madras.

From this small beginning the factory system has expanded in Madras during the past hundred years until there are to-day no less than 1876 institutions in the province which come under the Indian Factories Act. Of these, 120 are situated within the borders of Madras City itself, including 2 Spinning and Weaving Mills, 2 Aluminium Works, 3 Electrical Works, 1 Pencil Factory, 2 Condiment Works, 8 Foundaries, 6 General Engineers, 1 Rice Mill, 1 Tobacco Factory, 5 Oil Mills, 1 Glass Works, 1 Brick and Tile Works, 1 Enamel Works, 2 Match Works, 3 Cabinet Makers, 5 Jewellery Works and 47 Printing Presses.

* * * * * *

The control of the whole of the trade from and to the port of Madras was of course, originally in the hands of the East India Co.,—though their servants, from the very early days, engaged in private trade themselves. Gradually, however, free merchants began to make their appearance and were licensed by the Company to trade so long as they did not infringe the Company's monopoly of trade between India and Europe. By 1710 when, as we have seen, Madras trade was in a thriving condition, there were 29 free merchants among the residents at Fort St. George, and, before the end of the century, the foundation had been laid of some of the firms still trading in Madras to-day—notably Messrs. Parry & Co., and Messrs. Binny & Co. The original personnel of these firms consisted for the most part of free merchants in partnership with servants of the East India Company.

But the Charter of 1793 drove the thin edge of the wedge into the Company's monopoly and they were thenceforward obliged to provide 3000 tons of cargo space annually for free merchants between India and London. And by 1800 all servants of the Company were forbidden to trade privately—or rather the order to that effect which had been passed much earlier was for the first time effectively enforced.

Thus the free merchants were able to strengthen their position and were strong enough to compete successfully for the home trade when, under the 1813 Charter, the Company finally lost its trade monopoly.

The Company, however, continued as a trading body for another twenty years, until under the Charter of 1833, they became for the first time an administrative body only and the whole of the trade was finally thrown open to private enterprise.

* * * * * *

It must not be thought that with the steady expansion of the trade of Madras, the original handloom weaving industry has died. On the contrary, it still provides a substantial proportion of the total exports from Madras, and affords a means of livelihood, on much the same old cottage industry lines as of yore, to hundreds of families in and around Madras.

Whereas in 1639 the population of Madras was only 7000 and could not have supported more than a few hundred looms; there are to-day, in Madras City and the immediate neighbourhood, more than 5000 looms working, for the most part, on much the same class of goods as they have done for centuries past.

Indeed many of the looms to be seen in Madras today differ only slightly from those in use in olden days, and even the methods employed in dyeing and printing are much the same as they have been from time immemorial. The chief differences today are that the flying shuttle has replaced the old hand shuttle—a process which was only completed about twenty years ago—and that many of the dyes used are synthetic in place of the old natural dyes of the country. Some of these latter, however, are still in use, notably vegetable turmeric, a yellow dye, which has continued in demand because people insist on its peculiar smell.

The annual production of these looms is estimated at 5,760,000 yards of cotton goods, 210,000 yards art silk, 36,000 yards silk and 24,000 yards of druggets. And whereas in 1639 the total exports of piecegoods were valued at Rs. 25,000, the total value today reaches the formidable figure of Rs. 1,20,00,000 annually comprised as follows:—

	Rs.
Lungis and Sarees (mainly to Ceylon and the Straits).	48,00,000
Madras Handkerchiefs (mainly to the U. K. and Nigeria).	45,00,000
Other Cotton goods	27,00,000
Total	1,20,00,000

Nowadays, of course, this represents a comparatively small percentage of the total exports from the port of Madras, which altogether amount to about Rs. 16,00,00,000 annually.

* * * * * * *

Perhaps the two most important factors in the more recent development of Madras trade and commerce have been the building of the present Madras Harbour and the opening of the Madras Railway system.

The idea of a breakwater to protect shipping from the dangers which attended it in the open roadstead off Madras, and to obviate the risks attendant upon landing goods and passengers through the treacherous surf, had long exercised the minds of the local merchants; but it was not until 1875 that the final project, which resulted in the present fine harbour, was sanctioned; nor was it until 1895 that the work was completed.

Over 700 vessels now enter the port annually with a total net tonnage of 2,500,000; figures which may be compared with the 150,000 net tonnage which entered the Madras Roads in 1796, comprised as follows:—

191	..	3 masted ships.
46	..	2 „ „
707	..	1 masted donies, sloops, etc.

The existing Railway system was inaugurated in 1856 when the original Madras Railway Company opened the line from Madras to Arcot.

Since then progress has been rapid, and the two Madras Companies (The Madras and Southern Mahratta Railway Co., and the South Indian Railway Co.) now operate a total of 5750 miles of open line track.

* * * * * * *

It will have been noticed that the history of Madras commerce, as thus briefly outlined, divides itself into three more or less even periods of a century each. From 1639 to about 1739 the advance of general trading prosperity was very rapid. From 1739 to about 1839 it was appreciably slowed down ; and from 1839 to the present day a further steady advance, gathering momentum with the years, has taken place.

Some indication of this more recent progress may be given by recording once more the turnover of the port of Madras at the beginning and end of each century.

		Rs.
1639	..	25,000
1739	..	25,00,000
1839	..	1,15,00,000
1939	..	35,00,00,000

This latter figure, be it noted, is only 39 per cent of the total foreign trade of the Province.

* * * * * * *

And so the stage is set for the next act.

The industrial progress of Madras has been seriously handicapped in the past by the lack of coal within economic distance of the raw material in the Province, a fact which has not hitherto enabled her to keep pace with the north of India. But the recent extensive hydro-electric schemes in the Province have made cheap power available, with the result that new industries are springing up with great rapidity.

There will, of course, be some inevitable set backs and disappointments ; and, just as in 1732 the directors " despaired of ever seeing Madrass retrieve her ancient glory," and just as, in 1807, a leading free merchant described the main trade of the port as being " nearly at an end ", so there will be pessimists in the future.

But Madras does not lack either brains or the will to apply them, and she may well have faith in herself and look forward to her industrial and commercial future with a sturdy optimism.

A Short History of the Madras Chamber of Commerce

By

G. H. Hodgson, M.L.A.,

Chairman, M. C. C.

The East India Company had lost their trade monopoly with Europe in 1813, but they continued for another twenty years to combine trade with their administrative functions.

By the Charter of 1833, however, they became a governing body pure and simple and the trade of the country was, for the first time in nearly 200 years, thrown open, without Government competition, to those who had previously been known as the free merchants, and who as such had traded under considerable restrictions.

Commercial firms at the three main Indian ports were not long in realising that to benefit thoroughly from these changed circumstances it would be advisable to form associations which could speak with the united voice of the merchants on any matters affecting the trade and commerce of the country.

Accordingly on the 29th September 1836 a meeting of the merchants of Madras was held at the office of Messrs. Binny & Co., Armenian Street, Madras, when it was unanimously resolved :—

> "That an Association be formed in Madras under the designation of the Madras Chamber of Commerce."

Mr. John Alves Arbuthnot of Messrs. Arbuthnot & Co., was elected Chairman and a committee was formed consisting of Messrs. J. W. Dare (Parry & Co.), J. Line (Line & Co.), J. Scott (Binny & Co.), J. Ouchterlony (Ouchterlony & Co.), D. Pugh (Parry & Co.) and J. Barrow (Barrow & Co.). Mr. W. H. Hart (Binny & Co.), accepted the office of Honorary Secretary, and Messrs. Binny & Co., undertook the office of Honorary Treasurers, which they held till 1905.

The remaining founder members were Messrs. Fischer & Co., Guichard & Co., Seth Sam & Co., G. Sidloo Chetty and J. C. Tulloch.

The following well known firms also became members during the first half century of the Chamber's existence.

Dymes & Co. (1850), Bank of Madras (1855), Madras Railway Co. (1856), Walker & Co. (1856), P. & O. S. N. Co. (1865), Gordon

Woodroffe & Co. (1868), Best & Co., (1872), Wilson & Co. (1872), Messageries Maritimes (1877), T. A. Taylor & Co. (1878), National Bank of India (1880).

Another Bank called the Chartered Mercantile Bank joined the Chamber in 1856 and was later absorbed by the Mercantile Bank of India, Ltd.

At the time of the formation of the Chamber no permanent arrangements were made respecting a room for the meetings of the Chamber, but it was in contemplation in 1837 to take, and suitably furnish a portion of the old Court House which was then undergoing thorough repair. In 1869 the Chamber entered into possession of a room which had been specially built at No. 6, First Line Beach, for its accommodation. This room was leased to the Chamber from that date till 1920 and formed part of the old "Madras Mail" office.

From 1921 to 1924 the offices were located for varying short periods in the premises of the Imperial Bank, Beach, the Imperial Bank, Mount Road, Messrs. Best & Co., Ltd., and Messrs. Parry & Co., Ltd., and in 1924 they were removed to their present premises on the First Floor of the Mercantile Bank Buildings.

At the monthly General Meeting held on the 27th January 1920, it was unanimously resolved to convey to the Editor of "The Madras Mail" the appreciation and sincere thanks of the Committee and members for the very valuable assistance which he and his predecessors had rendered to the Chamber for no less than fifty years. During that lengthy period not only had the office of the Chamber been located in "The Madras Mail" building, but the duties of Secretary had been discharged by a member of "The Madras Mail".

At the first meeting of the Committee of the Chamber in 1836 it was resolved to address the Bengal Chamber of Commerce which had been established the previous year, and on the 6th December, 1836, correspondence was opened with the Bombay Chamber of Commerce which had been established a week before the Madras Chamber.

In the letters addressed to these bodies the Madras Chamber "looked forward with great satisfaction to the probability of the united voice of the Chambers at three Presidencies forming the organ of the whole commercial interests in India, effecting much towards the removal of the restrictions on Trade which has long been denied to individual representations."

On the 10th May, 1839, the proposed co-operation of the Ceylon Chamber of Commerce was gladly accepted by the Madras Chamber, and, on the 12th February, 1856, the Chamber was informed of the establishment of the Madras Trades Association, and at once assured that body of its cordial co-operation in all matters connected with the commercial interests of the Presidency.

The Government of Madras was informed on the 11th October, 1836, of the establishment of the Madras Chamber, and was asked to allow the Chamber to correspond direct with the different public Departments, and to permit the heads of those Departments to furnish information. A Government Order was accordingly published in which it was stated that "much public good" was anticipated "from the proceedings of the institution". But permission to correspond direct with the different public Departments was not granted, it being considered preferable "that the information required by the Association should be supplied through the medium of Government."

The Madras Chamber celebrated its centenary in 1936 and H. E. the Viceroy in conveying to the Chamber his congratulations, referred to its long and honourable record of public service.

Slave Trade in Madras

By

B. Natarajan, M.A.

Lecturer in Economics, M. D. T. Hindu College, Tinnevelly.

Agristic and domestic slavery existed in India from times immemorial. The export trade in human lives, however, was a later growth. The Arabs began it and the European powers expanded it. Neither the Hindu nor the Muslim rulers of India had tolerated the foreign traffic in slaves.

Originally the East Indian slave trade centred round Mozambique, Johanna, St. Lawrence and other African ports. The Negroes were sent to toil on the plantations at Bantam, Jambi, Banjarmassin, etc. Slaves formed a part of the cargo of almost every boat that rounded the Cape of Good Hope on its way to the East Indies. Repeated orders went out to the agents at several factories to buy 'lusty young blacks' at 'cheap rates' for Bantam plantations. Complaints such as one merchant undid the other, 'in body and pursue by cheating evill conversacion especially in one badd bargayne of selling him a light wench for 40 heavy dollars' are found in the archives of the Company.[1]

Peter Mundy found a convenient justification for the traffic. The Negroes were a lawful prize for the injuries the English nation had received 'att divers parts of the iland, especially at Asada, where many of the English were slaughtered by the natives aboutt anno 1645'.[2] But slave traffic was older than the attempt at colonization of Asada. It was not confined to the Negroes either. From the blacks to the browns was an easy transition. On January 5, 1641, the English boat *Michael* arrived at Bantam with a cargo of calicoes and '14 slaves taken in a small vessell on the coast of Malabar'[3]. The real cause of the trade was economic. It was believed that slave labour was thrice as cheap as free labour.[4]

1. From Henry Greenhill and William Gurney at Fort St. George to President Baker, 25 November, 1652 (Original Correspondence Series, 2293).
2. *The Travels of Peter Mundy* (1608-67), Vol. V, p. 46.
3. From the Court to Surat, 29th November, 1641, in Factory Records, Mis. Vol. XII, p. 39.
4. E. B. Sainsbury: *Court Minutes of the East India Company* (1644-49), p. 68.

Madras offered peculiar facilities for the trade. The custom duties here were lower than in the other settlements. Domestic slavery was officially recognised at Madras. Slaves had to be licensed and purchase and sales had to be registered at the Choultry.[5] These were done by the *Adhikari* or the Indian Governor of the town. In 1711, the registration fee was 6sh. 9d. for every slave. The fee was 'afterwards divided betwixt the Company, justices and servants.'[6] A factory record of the period gives it as 8 annas per head.[7] The trade was run mainly by the Dutch at Pulicat who employed brokers at Madras for slave catching. The shipping was done at Madras port itself.

A.D. 1646 was a critical year in the history of the Madras city. A disastrous famine ravaged the city. The Portuguese settlement of San Thome suffered most. Men preferred bondage to black death. Export trade in slaves became brisk. The cargo of a Portuguese vessel that arrived at Acheen from Negapatam in October of that year is described as follows:

> Ther came uppon this smale vessel uppward of 400 slaves, so hunger starved that they were scarce able to crawle when they brought them ashoare, and are now sould for 5 and 6 tale per heade, whereas at other tymes the (y) yield 10 and 12 tale. They report a very strang famine to have been for 13 months past, and yett doth continue in those parts, insoemuch as the people give themselves for slaves to any man that will but feede them, all kinds of provisions, especially graine, beeing att excessive rates.[8]

The famine and the consequent quarrel between the Portuguese and the English being over, peace and prosperity once again smiled on Madras. The treaty drawn up between the European settlers in 1651 laid down that fugitive slaves of either party were to be surrendered. Clause 4 of the agreement reflects the conception of human values prevalent at the period. The runaway slave was to be returned to his master, 'for hee is part of his goods, the right and property whereof flight cannot take from him.'[9]

Apart from this voluntary entry into servitude, there was an illicit trade which involved the most iniquitous practice of stealing children

5. The Choultry stood near to, and just outside of, the Choultry Gate (now bricked up) of the present Fort St. George. Love: *Vestiges*, Vol. I, p. 127 *n.* 2.

6. Charles Lockyer: An account of the trade in India, containing rules for good government in trade, price courants, and tables, etc., (1711), p. 7.

7. Public Letters to England, 9 October 1714, Vol. IV.

8. British Museum Additional Manuscripts, 14037, *f* 46.

9. Agreement between the Agent at Fort St. George and Gomes Freire Andrade, Captain-General of San Thome, December 30, 1651 (O. C. 2238).

and unprotected women. It was sometimes practised by foreigners, but the worst offenders were the Indian brokers who often for a few paltry silver bartered away the freedom and happiness of hundreds of their innocent compatriots. Nicholas Manucci, the Venetian traveller gives a harrowing account of a transaction in which an Italian priest at Tranquebar engaged himself. At his connivance the wife and four sons of an Indian Christian of Madura was treacherously sold away for a sum of 30 pagodas and shipped off to Manilla. The frantic efforts of the husband to recover his dear ones and the pitiless treatment he received at the hands of the vicar and the Danes are too pathetic to be told.[10]

A slave transaction at San Thome contrasts favourably with the heartless ways of the Hollanders. A man in Lord Bishop's service sold a slave girl to a ship's captain for 26 pagodas. The girl absconded and took shelter in the Bishop's house. The buyer claimed the girl. The Lord Bishop turned him out saying that she was in no way a slave. As for compensation, 'the cleric had spent the money and had nothing wherewith to pay.'[11]

On the English side of the settlement, illicit trade in slaves had an unhampered course at this period. In 1653, Venkati, the Chief Merchant of the Company and his brother Kannappa were accused of the crime. The Chief Merchants 'being Linguists in the Fort, Governors of the Towne and haveing the Taliars office' wielded great power. 'By reason of the influence of an office to another' they created havoc in Black Town, fomenting caste quarrels and extorting illegal dues. Kannappa acted as a slave-baiting broker for the Dutch.

On learning this, the virtuous indignation of the Councillor Mr. John Leigh flared up in a language worthy of a Wilberforce or Abraham Lincoln.

> That he hath taken many Bribes in Licensing stolne children in this Towne to the great Dishonour of Hon'ble Company, to the shame of the Governor and Councill here, that Madras, the Companys Towne, should bee a Baud to procure the Hollanders with slaves. Why were not the children first carried to Pulicatt? Noe, they durst not, but come to the English Towne. They will venture their necks for 9d; for the custome is but 18d. and the Nabob hath 9d. of it...... Some of us has children; it would grieve our soules to have them stolne and sould for slaves; and these People have as much right to their children and Love to them as wee.[12]

10. Manucci: *Storia Do Mogor* (1653-1708), Vol. IV, pp. 127-9.

11. *Ibid.*, p. 179.

12. Declaration against the Bramony Connapa concerning the Choultry (O. C. 2369). Love says the document is undated (*Op. cit.*, Vol. I, page 131)

Leigh therefore pleaded that the heavy hand of Justice must unsparingly alight on these 'Trators, Manstealers and Depeoplars of the country' lest the world should accuse the English of complicity or knowledge in this criminal affair. Were he permitted to take the law into his own hands, he would suppress the traffic in no time. It was no ordinary crime. Punishment ought to be commensurate with its iniquity. 'In all parts of Europa it is Death; in Turkey it is Death, and in this Country it is Death. And by the Law of God it is Death'. Mr. Henry Greenville, a brother Councillor[13] and a number of Indian residents[14] of the town joined Mr. Leigh in his vehement denunciation of Kannappa.

But Kannappa was the prize-boy of President Baker. For a crime which involved death according to all the laws of God and man, he was let off with a fine of 16 pagodas. Disappointed, Leigh writes in his diary, 'I was informed by the old Talliar that hee knew of 27 children for which hee (Kannappa) had received pagodas; but 16 pagodas cleared his life. It covered the greatest scandall that ever was brought upon the Hon'ble Company.' Leigh contrasts this with the firm manner in which the Nawab of Arcot dealt out justice. 'The Nabob sent for the first stealer of them and made him a slave for ever to carry stones for a great ffort. Hee had better been hanged, but the Law is staking through theire Bodies and the receaver Death likewise; and we covered this for 16 pagodas.'[15]

The fact that Baker, the President of the Council, did not see eye to eye with his colleagues indicates that whatever the offence was in the eye of law, in practice it was treated with great indulgence. Economic forces had asserted themselves over moral and humanitarian considerations. In 1662 an incorporated[16] company for slave trading was started in England with the Duke of York at the head. In October of the next year a warfare over slave traffic began between the English and the Dutch. A squadron under Captain Robert Holmes was sent to attack the Dutch settlements in Gambia and America. The avowed object of the English attack on the Guinea coast was to leave a clear field for slave trading.[17] Where Africans could not be had the next best

and he assigns the year 1653 to it (p. 545). Foster gives the date March 1654 (vide *English Factories*, 1651-54, p. 244).

13. Remonstrance to President Baker concerning the two Brahmans, 1 March 1654 (O. C. 2367).

14. Declaration of the Painters, weavers, etc., inhabiting Chenapatam against the Braminees, Vincaty and Connapa (O. C. 2542, Anno 1654).

15. O. C. 2384, *Cir.* July 1654.

16. Cawston and Keane: *Early Chartered Companies*, p. 231.

17. Peter Mundy: *op. cit.* p. 166n.

were Indians and Burmese. In 1668 directions were sent by the Court of Directors to the 'Fort' (St. George) for four 'Gentues (Indians) or Arracans (Burmese) with their wives to be procurred in the Bay for the Company's service at Helena and sent there by the next shipping.'[18]

Thirty years rolled by after the 'sentimental' John Leigh had raised his ineffectual protest against this inhuman practice. Complaints grew louder and louder until at last, in 1682, the authorities at Madras 'considering the scandal that might accrue to the government and the great loss that many parents may undergo' prohibited the export of slaves of any age whatsoever.[19] A notification to the effect was published in four languages—English, Portuguese, Gentoo (Telugu) and Malabar (Tamil)—and ordered to be put up in four prominent places in the town. It said that the law breaker would be fined fifty pagodas on every slave exported, the sum to be 'recovered of him in the Choultry of Madraspatnam; one-third for the use of the Honourable East India Company, one-third to the poor, and one-third to the informer'.[20]

This law remained on the statute book barely for five years. Another great famine occured in 1687 and with it the traffic in slavery revived. Men again preferred the bonds of slavery to the jaws of death. The Government noted that the trade in slaves was 'growing great from this port by reason of the great plenty of poor, by the sore famine and their cheapness.' The English legal system would rather have an indifferent law observed than a good law violated. Despairing of ending a traffic into which the victims voluntarily bowed their necks, the Government relaxed their prohibitory regulation. Incidentally the Company availed themselves of the opportunity for augmenting the customs revenue of the settlement. One pagoda was charged on each slave sent off the shore.[21]

A month later, the Council themselves did a stroke of business on their own account, although not by export. The 'Muckwaes' or fishermen of Madras deserted the Company's service and dispersed to Pulicat and Sadras. Attempts to recall them proved futile. The Company therefore decided to have their own staff of Masulla boatmen. Slaves would eminently suit the purpose. Mr. Fraser, who being Land Customer had the best opportunity for it, was ordered to buy 'fforty young Sound Slaves for the Rt. Hon'ble Company, and dispose them to

18. From the Court to Fort St. George, 27 November 1668 in Court Book, Vol. XXVI, p. 349, vide *Court Minutes*, 1668-70.

19. Public Consultations, 1 September 1682, Vol. VII; also 18 September 1683.

20. Public Consultations, 13 November 1683.

21. Public Consultations, 1 August 1687.

the severall Mussulaes, two or three on each, in charge of the Chief man of the boat, to be fed and taught by them.'[22] With a view to have better care and better command over them, it was ordered to distinguish them by red coats with the Company's mark and numbers.

The relaxation of the prohibitory law, however useful, gave rise to complaints from unhappy parents. The law was therefore made more stringent in 1688, although reversion to complete prohibition was not thought of. No slaves were to be exported until they were duly examined by the Justices of the Choultry and their names registered in a book kept for the purpose. The first offender was liable to a fine of five pagodas, but when repeated was to lose his ears in the pillory.[23]

Even this did not go far enough. The traffic in children became open and scandalous. A number of Muslim children were kidnapped. A class of crimps arose who made it a profession of combing the rural parts and spiriting away innocent children. The enormity of the crimes 'reached the ears of the Emperor at Delhi. The Company received great complaints and troubles from the country Government.' Aurangazeb would not tolerate the traffic. He had not only prohibited it in his dominion, but also had expressed his displeasure against the Dutch who were carrying it on at Masulipatam. That put the English on the alert. The business itself was dull and brought little 'advantage' to the Company. Therefore, 'to prevent prejudice and mischief for the future', it was ordered that after the 20th May 1688, no person belonging to the City of Madras 'do directly or indirectly buy or transport slaves from this place or any adjacent port (whereby the Government may be anyway troubled or prejudiced)'.[24] Penalty for the infringement of the law was pitched at fifty pagodas for each slave. However, consideration was shown to those who had already stocked slaves for export. In their case, permission was to be granted for shipping them off but not until the Justices had satisfied themselves by public proclamation that none came to claim the slaves. The penalty of losing the ear in the pillory for second offence remained on the statute book for several years after. Thomas Salmon writing in 1724 refers to it.[25]

The prohibitory enactment, strong as it was, could not put an end to a lucrative trade that had entrenched itself in vested interests built through decades. Where economic forces reign supreme,

22. Public Consultations, 29 September 1687, Vol. XIII.

23. *Ibid*, 2 February 1688.

24. Public Consultations, 14 May 1688, Vol. XIV.

25. Thomas Salmon : *Modern History or the Present State of All Nations* (1724) quoted in *Vestiges*, Vol. II, p. 76.

moral regeneration cannot take place overnight. The crusade against slavery did not become effective in the West till the close of the 18th Century and perhaps not until it was realised that it was even unsound economy to employ slave labour. These ideas had their echo in the distant City of Madras. In 1790, Mr. Taylor, the Acting Justice, came to know that several children had been decoyed to Madras from upcountry places in a country vessel, with a view to export. The benevolent judge ordered them to be landed and taken charge of by the *kotwal*. The victims numbered 41 in all, 20 boys and 21 girls.[26]

On Mr. Taylor's report, the Government definitely resolved to prohibit the traffic. With a view more effectually to prevent a practice so detrimental to the country, and injurious to the rights of humanity', the Madras Government proclaimed a reward of 30 pagodas for the discovery of every offender, to be paid on conviction, and of 10 pagodas for each person of either sex who should be delivered from slavery in consequence of such discovery'.[27]

The children, so timely redeemed by Justice Taylor, continued to enjoy the hospitality of the Company for over two and a half years. Afterwards, Mr. Popham, an enterprising public spirited barrister of Madras, proposed to apprentice them for a term of years in his experimental cotton farm. The philanthropist promised to clothe and feed them. The Government objected to the system of apprenticeship presumably on the ground that it meant a relapse into the state of bondage. Mr. Popham was therefore permitted to employ them on condition that he would restore them when they were claimed back.[28]

Thus Madras eventually succeeded in suppressing the traffic. It was the earliest port to do it. In the Dutch, French and Portuguese settlements, the practice persisted long after it had fallen into abeyance in British ports.[29] The English had to contend with many difficulties before they could efface it from the empire.

The great part played by South Indian slave labour in the economic development of the East Indies is little recognized to-day. In the early part of the 18th century, Sumatra and Java were humming with activity thanks to the large labouring population from Tamil land working as slaves of 'great men and merchants'. It is known to very few that it was these Tamils that first introduced the cultivation of paddy into

26. Public Consultations, 5 March 1790, Vol. CLXI.
27. Public Letters to England, 18 September 1790, Vol. XXXII.
28. Public Consultations, 15 March 1793, Vol. CLXXXII.
29. Census Report (1871), Madras Town, p. 64.

those distant lands. To them, says Charles Lockyer, 'the Acheens owe the greatest part of their Husbandry in managing their Crops of Paddy or Rice which was hardly known on this part of the Island, till these were driven hither by Famine'.

Their contribution to the commercial prosperity of the islands is no less important. Contemporary accounts give a glowing tribute to the qualities of their head and heart. Though of weaker build than the natives of the East Indies the Tamils were 'a sharper, wiser People in general, and more addicted to Trade than the Mallayans......They keep a just Account of all their Dealings and the Master comes in for a part of the profit'. Genius finds its level even under vile servitude. The slaves of the Coromandal Coast, consequently, were treated 'rather like Friends and Companions, than Servants by their Masters, who value themselves on their Justice to and Number of them'. Their condition was so much beyond reproach that foreigners found it impossible to distinguish them from native freemen. The masters had great confidence in them and vested them with full powers to use their discretion and talents, 'every one as his genius leads him without Molestation or Hindrance'. Nay more; the native owners even encouraged them by assisting them with cash and credit. The slaves did not live in the household of the master, but 'up and down the Town and Country in Houses and Plantations of their own'. There they tasted little of slavery but the name. Only those who proved incurable idiots or incorrigible knaves, 'little differing from beasts of burden', were treated as slaves. It is even doubtful if those Muslim masters ever compelled their slaves to change their religion.[30] Perhaps it is these slaves of South India that kept the torch of Indian culture burning in those far-off islands, feeding it with the marrow of their incessant toil.

30. Lockyer: *op. cit.* pp. 54-6.

Three Hundred Years of Banking in Madras

By

S. T. Sadasivan,

General Manager, The Indian Overseas Bank Ltd., Madras.

Joint Stock Banking as we know it to-day had its origin in relatively recent times. The earliest beginnings were made at the commencement of the 19th century and a fair measure of progress was attained in the latter half of that century. Indigenous banking, however, is of very ancient growth although very little is known of its origin and development. Recent researches have thrown considerable light on the nature of business transacted by the indigenous bankers from the earliest times; and the valuable information collected by a band of research workers has been summarised in the Report of the Indian Central Banking Enquiry Committee. Records in which detailed references are made to indigenous banking are available from the middle of the 17th century onwards, the most important book in this connection being J. B. Tavernier's "Travels in India." The later records, published and unpublished, of the East India Company and of the various enquiries into the affairs of the East India Company, such as the Reports of the Committees of Parliament and the proceedings of the Court of Directors of the East India Company in the early days of the 19th century, contain valuable information relating to trade and banking in the early days, of which only a part has been extracted by the researches of Economists like L. C. Jain and H. Sinha.

The system of indigenous banking which was in vogue from the earliest times was very well suited to the requirements of the country. In this connection, the following remarks of Mr. W. E. Preston, some time Chief Manager of the Chartered Bank of India, Australia & China and member of the Royal Commission on Indian Currency and Finance, 1926, who had made a careful study and shown keen appreciation of the services of indigenous bankers in India, are significant: "It may be accepted that a system of banking, eminently suited to India's then requirements was in force in that country many centuries before the science of banking became an accomplished fact in England. It is true that the methods of old in force in India were vastly different from the European ideas of banking to-day and partook more of money lending, money changing and later of the hundi business; nevertheless as applied to the conditions then existing in India, they admirably acted their part and must be recognized as having rendered immense services to the country as a whole, particularly when we keep in view the enormous agricultural interest of India."

In those early days, money changing was an important part of the indigenous banker's business. There were such a large number of mints and so many different metallic currencies of varying silver content that exchange of one form of currency for another provided the indigenous banker with an important source of banking profit.

In the 17th century, foreign traders came from the West to establish trade relations with the East. How these traders financed their commerce with India in the days when the West had no banking relations with the East, how credit links were forged, what shape they took and how the indigenous banking system was affected by the arrival of the foreign traders in those early days of their settlement in India, are subjects of great interest and importance. One thing is clear that when these people arrived in India, the indigenous system was already well established and was functioning along three lines namely: money lending, money changing and bill discounting. The European traders could not, however, make use of this credit system as they were not conversant with the language of the indigenous bankers, while the bankers had no knowledge or experience of the financing of Western trade and the credit risks associated with it. In order to overcome these two-fold difficulties, two remedies were adopted. In the first place, the early English merchant houses took upon themselves the business of banking in addition to their commercial and trading activities. At the same time, the importance of forming connections with indigenous bankers who held a high place in the financial and political activities of the country was not ignored; and the directors of the East India Co. as early as 1677 wrote to Fort St. George authorities that, by the offer of rewards, they should encourage their servants to learn the language of the indigenous bankers and learn their arithmetic.

The political upheavels and the wars of the 17th and 18th centuries dealt a severe blow to indigenous banking system.

With the decline of indigenous banking and the gradual progress of English trade the need was keenly felt for the establishment of banks which would meet both administrative requirements and the demands of trade. These two-fold needs led on the one hand to the creation of Government Treasuries and Sub-Treasuries and on the other hand to the foundation of early European banking institutions. As a result of this, the indigenous bankers lost must of their money changing business, particularly after 1835 when a uniform currency was established in the whole of British India, with the adoption of the Madras rupee, approximately equal in value to that of Bombay and Farukabad, weighing 180 grains, out of which 165 grains were pure silver, as a standard for the whole of the East India Company's dominions in India. Consequent on this important currency reform, one profitable department of the indigenous banker's business had almost entirely to be curtailed.

The Nattukkottai Chettiars are the indigenous bankers of South India, about whose activities the Madras Provincial Banking Enquiry Committee and the Burma Banking Enquiry Committee have given very detailed accounts regarding their capital, private wealth and extent of public business done. What has not been sufficiently emphasised is that the Nattukkottai Chettiars are the one class of indigenous bankers who had developed deposit banking as understood in the West and for very long time accepted both current and fixed deposit accounts from the public just as any other joint stock bank run on Western lines. The Nattukkottai Chettiars with their flair for banking felt that opportunities for profitable operations lay in overseas countries in primitive stages of development rather than in the highly developed agricultural area of South India. In the early days they started as traders and established themselves in Calcutta and Colombo over 120 years ago. Very soon, however, they shed their trading functions and became pure bankers. The order of their establishment in overseas countries would appear to be first Ceylon, then Malaya, and later Rangoon. The Chettiars' connection with Malaya dates back to over a century. Coral Merchant Street is the headquarters of Chettyar bankers in Madras.

Turning to the development of joint stock banking in Madras, the earliest joint stock bank to be established was the Bank of Madras in 1843 with a share capital of Rs. 30 lakhs, of which the Government subscribed Rs. 3 lakhs and this was followed later in that year and in the following year by the establishment of branches of the Agra and United Services Bank and the Simla Bank. The Bank of Madras has had an unbroken career of success. The Presidency Banks' Act of 1876 clearly defined the business that the Bank of Madras in common with the Bank of Bengal and the Bank of Bombay was authorised to transact. In 1921, the individuality of the Bank of Madras was merged into that of the Imperial Bank of India, the giant which dominates Indian banking at the present day.

Of the Exchange Banks carrying on business in Madras, the Chartered Bank of India, Australia and China was established in 1853 with a modest capital; but years of successful operation in India, China, Japan, Siam, Malaya and Dutch East Indies has brought the bank an enormous measure of prosperity, as the following figures of capital and reserve will show:

		Capital £	Reserve £
1863	..	644,000	10,000
1900	..	880,000	325,000
1925	..	3,000,000	4,000,000
1938	..	3,000,000	3,000,000

A decline of £1 million in the Reserve Fund occurred in 1931 when exceptionally heavy losses in foreign exchange arising from England's abandonment of the gold standard were written off to the debit of the Reserve Fund. Apart from its European connections in Madras, the Bank is very closely associated with the Mohammedan merchants carrying on hides and skins business.

The Mercantile Bank of India Ltd., was established on the 2nd December 1892 to take over the business of the Chartered Mercantile Bank of India, London and China. The original institution was the Mercantile Bank of India, London and China which was formed on the 30th November 1853 as an Indian Company with its Head Office and Directorate in Bombay. It opened for business on the 3rd January 1854 and a branch was opened in Madras about that time. In November 1857 the business was transferred to the newly formed Chartered Mercantile Bank of India, London and China which was a Sterling Company. The first premises occupied in Madras were in Moore Street but later the branch was moved to McLean Street in premises which have since been acquired by Messrs. Binny & Co., (Madras) Ltd. In 1875 the Bank moved into No. 8, First Line Beach where its business was carried on until December 1923 on which date it transferred to its own building at 16, First Line Beach known as Mercantile Bank Buildings.

These imposing buildings overlooking the Madras Harbour were commenced in March 1922 and consist of two blocks, the front being of four storeys and the rear of three. The front block elevation to First Line Beach has been designed in a conventional English Renaissance style, is dominated by two towers 91 feet high and is one of the first buildings to meet the eye when arriving at Madras by sea.

Two outstanding personalities in the Bank have been William Gordon who was in charge of the branch from 1876 to 1899 and to whose memory there is a monument in the Scots Kirk in Madras. He was the uncle of Lady Catto, Lord Catto being a present Director of the Bank.

The other personality referred to was H. L. Padday who was in charge from 1903 to 1919 but who was in Madras for many years prior to that as a subordinate officer in the Bank. He will be remembered by many of the present residents of Madras, especially so as he is still Secretary of the Madras Dinner in London.

The following figures show the capital and reserve of the Bank at different periods.

	Capital	Reserve
	£	£
1863	500,000	60,000
1900	561,500	30,000
1930	1,050,000	1,500,000
1931	1,050,000	1,050,000
1937	1,050,000	1,075,000

The fall of £450,000 in the Reserve Fund in 1931 was due to the necessity of providing for non-recurring exchange losses arising from the suspension of gold standard, for writing down investments to market prices, and for writing off bad and doubtful debts.

The National Bank of India was first established in 1863 in Calcutta under the name of the Calcutta Banking Corporation with a capital of about Rs. 31 lakhs, but the domicile was later shifted to London and the name was changed to its present one in 1866. The capital was then increased to £466,500. Four out of the seven first directors of this bank were Indians but after its transfer to London it assumed the character of an entirely British bank. A Branch of the National Bank of India Ltd., was first opened in Madras in Armenian Street in the year 1877 under the management of the late Mr. John Kyd. The office was subsequently transferred to the premises on 1st Line Beach at present occupied by Messrs. Best & Co. Ltd., where the business was conducted until the opening of the new building of the Bank's present premises at the south end of 1st Line Beach in 1916.

Prior to 1877 the Bank was represented through its Agents, Messrs. Binny & Co., until 1871 and the Bank of Madras from 1871 to 1877. The capital and reserve of the Bank at various stages of its growth are given below :

	Capital	Reserve
	£	£
1866	466,500	—
1900	500,000	330,000
1929	2,000,000	3,000,000
1931	2,000,000	2,200,000
1938	2,000,000	2,200,000

The bank has extensive connection in India, East Africa, Ceylon, Zanzibar and Aden. The Reserve Fund of the bank in 1931 was, as shown above, £2,200,000. The reduction of £800,000 in the Reserve Fund in that year was due to the writing down of investments, which suffered exceptional depreciation in 1931. The investments, no doubt, appreciated later but no adjustment was made of balance sheet valuation.

The Eastern Bank is comparatively a new-comer to the field of exchange banking. It was founded in 1909 and has offices in India, Iraq, Singapore and Colombo. The figures of the capital and reserve of the Bank are set out below:

	Capital	Reserve
	£	£
1922	1,000,000	300,000
1932	1,000,000	500,000
1938	1,000,000	500,000

The P & O. Banking Corporation, which was founded in 1920, established a branch in Madras in the following year, but the early expectations of the sponsors of the institution were never realised and the control of the bank passed into the hands of the Chartered Bank in 1927. The continued absence of opportunities for profitable trading led to the decision to wind up the institution in February this year by sale of its assets to the Chartered Bank.

Of the Indian joint stock banks operating in Madras, the premier South Indian institution is the Indian Bank which was founded in 1907 after the collapse of Arbuthnot & Co., in which such a large number of South Indians lost their money. The Bank has had a uniformly successful career and is rightly held in high esteem in South India. Its capital at present is Rs. 12,79,280 and the Reserve Rs. 13,00,000. The total working resources exceed Rs. 4,15,00,000. Of the other banks, the Bank of Hindustan was established in 1929 with a capital of Rs. 10,00,000 and the Indo-Commercial Bank Ltd., in 1932 with a capital of Rs. 2½ lakhs, subsequently raised to Rs. 18,75,000. The latest entrant in the field of banking is the Indian Overseas Bank Ltd., which was established in February 1937 with a subscribed capital of Rs. 25,00,000 and a paid-up capital of Rs. 12,50,000 and within the short period of 2½ years it has been in existence has attained a remarkable degree of success. This bank made a departure in South Indian banking by establishing branches in Burma and Malaya and catering to the banking needs of Indians overseas. Among other banks carrying on business in Madras are the Nedungadi Bank, the Palai Central Bank and the Nadar Bank.

Of Indian banks incorporated outside the Presidency of Madras, the most successful institution operating in South India is the Central Bank of India Ltd. The Bank owes its inception in Madras to the enterprise of the Tata Industrial Bank who opened an office here in 1920 but on the absorption of this Bank by the Central Bank of India Ltd., in 1923, the Madras Branch of the Tata Bank became the Central Bank of India, Madras. The branch was closed in 1929 but was revived in 1935 and has since extended its operations in the mofussil districts of South India.

The Madras Provincial Co-operative Bank, which is the apex bank of the co-operative movement in the Presidency was established as the Madras Central Urban Bank in 1906 and has had a remarkable and successful career. Within the 33 years of its existence, it has been able to accumulate a Reserve Fund of Rs. 16,00,000 against its paid-up capital of Rs. 6,63,950. The Bank, although the apex bank of the co-operative movement, has always conducted its business on the lines of a commercial bank and has maintained a very strong liquid position.

In April 1935 the Reserve Bank of India was established to take over the government accounts, the management of the currency, and the custody of bankers' balances.

The year 1938 was marred by the failure of the Travancore National & Quilon Bank Ltd., an institution formed by the merger of the Travancore National Bank and the Quilon Bank, in the previous year.

With the inauguration of the Reserve Bank of India and the contacts which it has established with the different kinds of banking institutions, the stage has now been set for a more rigorous control over the business of banking, and it is permissible to hope that a new Bank Act would be enacted in the near future.

Some Business-Houses in Madras

By

V. Venkatarama Aiyar, M.A.,

Asst. Professor of History, The Presidency College, Madras.

Sir Thomas Ainscough, His Majesty's Trade Commissioner for India and Ceylon in a message to the Madras Chamber of Commerce on the occasion of its Centenary Celebrations in 1936 wrote: "The remarkable commercial industrial and agricultural development of the Presidency is attributable in a marked degree to the courage, foresight and imaginative energy of three generations of members. While regulating their business activities on sound lines, they have not only advanced their own interests but also have contributed in a generous measure to the welfare, and prosperity of the peoples of South India." No truer words could have been written. It sums up the results of the work of the merchants for about 2½ centuries and represents a work of which the Madras merchants may feel justifiably proud. In the present day Indian atmosphere charged with nationalistic and socialist ideas, the part played by European merchants in the later 18th and early 19th centuries in the industrial development of the country and in laying down standards of business management has not naturally received sufficient attention. An examination of the early history of business firms in Madras from the days of the East India Company shows that the early European merchants did a lot of pioneering work and laid the foundations of sound organisation and integrity universally acknowledged as fundamental to the growth of trade and commerce in any country in the world. Madras is one of the oldest cities and from the days of the East India Company has occupied a prominent place in the development of trade between Europe and South India. Thanks to the excellent traditions set up by the European business firms of the later 18th century, and the Indian business firms of the later 19th century, Madras has been making rapid strides in industrialization in recent years. It is well-known that Englishmen came over to India at first for purposes of trade. Their first settlements like Madras, Calicut, Masultipatam, Cassimbazaar, Patna etc.; were all ware-houses and factories and mostly situated on the sea coast. But this commercial character did not last long. The political circumstances of the country and also the advancement of the company's commercial interests forced the company to make wars and acquire territories as well. The interests of commerce led to territorial expansion.

In the early days of the history of the company, right down to the end of the 18th century, the company's traders were themselves the public officers of the Company as well. They employed influential and capable 'Natives' as the company's merchants, to supply cloth for export to England and to serve as channels of distribution for the European goods imported by the company. In the records of the Court of Directors and in Despatches from the company's servants, we have frequent references to the purchase and export of longcloth, broadcloth, selampore, calico, arrack, precious stones like diamonds, rubies, and coral. Cloths of various kinds seem to have been in great demand for export and so, money was distributed by the company to those merchants to be advanced to the weavers, painters, dyers, etc., and the merchants were held responsible for the money advanced until the delivery of the finished goods. It was also part of their work to find suitable market for the disposal of the European goods. One of the merchants was named the Chief Merchant. These chief merchants ought to be distinguished from Dubashes who seem to have been "the agents employed by individual factors in connexion with their private trade."

The office of the Chief Merchant of the Company appears to have been a very coveted post and carried much influence. In the early days, only one or two persons were nominated as Chief Merchants. But in 1688, as the result of the varied nature of the work done by them, an agreement was made between the then Governor, E. Yale and the free merchants to the effect that twelve men should hereafter be nominated as chief merchants and with specific duties assigned to them. They in their turn selected twenty of the junior members of the joint stock "to go up country and make purchases." One of the most important of these chief merchants was one *Verona* alias Kasi Viranna who was the head of a joint stock named Cassa Verona Company about 1678-1680. All the company's orders were given to him who executed them through his agents and all imported merchandise was also purchased by him to be disposed off up country by his agents. Sunkurama, Tomby (Thambu) Chetti, Allingal Pillai alias Alangada Pillai were all chief merchants whose memories have been perpetuated by the names of certain important streets in Madras. All goods for export and of import were stocked in various godowns in the Fort Area. The names of the streets in the Fort with the exact nature of the godowns have been given in the Company's records. Mention is made of 'the cloths godowns at the south end of Charles street' 'The Import Ware-house keepers,' 'Copper godown beneath the Court House,' 'The Broad cloths

THE SOUTH SEA GATE

godown in the Fort Square', 'Merchants godown in James street etc'., where the cash chest was lodged, coir or rope godowns and grains godowns, situated not in the Fort area but a little away from it nearer the gentoo or the Black Town. Kasi Viranna and Thambu Chetti as influential chief merchants had their godowns also in the Fort. But considerable difficulty seems to have been experienced by the merchants in the transport and disposal of goods from these godowns and also on account of the fact that they had no common meeting place to meet, discuss matters and strike bargains.

A note by Dr. John Fryer who visited Madras in 1673 says that the merchants met perhaps twice a week in the Black Town. Without a common meeting place for the merchants, not only did concerted action as the result of joint deliberation become impossible but was it also not possible for them to develop a spirit of *esprit de corps* and promote a feeling of brotherhood among them. Later, the Sea-gate at the Fort was used for the purpose. Captain Alexander Hamilton a Master Mariner who visited Madras in 1718 wrote that "there was no ditch on the sea front,—that boats were drawn up close to the walls of the Fort,—(a factor corroborated also by pictures of old Fort St. George); and that all the merchants usually met at 11 o'clock at the sea gate to treat of business in merchandise." This was going on for some time, but we hear of complaints made frequently that great inconvenience was caused to the merchants by the unnecessary and vexatious impositions of the ship dubashes in the disposal of investments given to them. The "Investment" referred to the practice of the Company whereby a part of its revenues was set apart for purchase of goods locally, to be exported to England in order to make up for the unfavourable trade balance against them. The custom hitherto was to make it up by import of specie or bullion which for some reason was given up after 1765. As Mr. M. Rutnaswami has pointed out, "the investment played a celebrated part in the history of the company and influenced the course of the development of its policy and administration." The immediate effect of it however was to give a fillip to local trade and exports. In 1787, at the instance of Mr. Peter Massey Cassim, a scheme for the construction of a pucca exchange was approved by the Government and steps were directed to be taken towards the achievement of that end. An exchange company with a capital of 25,000 pagodas was at once formed. A private building in the Fort owned by one Mr. Hughes was purchased and a new building was planned to be built. The funds for the building were realized by floating a number of lotteries. One of them was for a sum of 100000 Pagodas of which 9/10ths were to be distributed as prizes, 1/20th was to be given to the lottery agent and 1/20th was to go to the Exchange Fund. We do not know when the subsequent lotteries were held but by 1795 it is on record that the Exchange had been completed to be used as a meeting place for the merchants. The men of the time and foreign visitors alike were very much impressed with this new building which was so designed as to serve not merely as a meeting place for merchants but also as a place to be used for public meetings, lottery drawings, entertainments etc. This is the building now used as the officers' Mess in the Fort. On the groundfloor of this building were offices and warehouses. In the records of the company mention is made of firms having their warehouses therein. For example, Gaudoin and Ranken had their auction rooms under the Exchange between 1796-1802. Mention is made of a firm known by the name of Messrs Waddel Inverarity and Co., renting a warehouse in it.

In passing, it may also be of some interest to note that the light house was first erected on the roof of the Exchange "carrying a lantern reflectors and 12 lamps burning cocoanut oil." It continued to be there till 1842 when it was removed to its present site. It is said that it was visible from the docks of the ships for 17 miles or from the mastheads for 26 miles. In 1826 the Exchange was leased to Government for an annual rent of 800 pagodas and was used to house the Board of Revenue till 1861 until its removal to its present site at Chepauk that year. Ten years later it was, that is, in 1836, that a meeting of the merchants of Madras held at the offices of Messrs. Binny and Company resolved to have an association that has continued to the present day as the Madras Chamber of Commerce, whose offices are at present located in the Mercantile Bank Buildings.

Another point of interest to be noted in this connexion is the fact that whenever funds were needed for public works of common good of this kind, they were raised by lotteries. This method was resorted to in 1781 by Governor Macartney whose Government was hard put to for money to carry on the administration. It was again attempted in 1790-1791. The following notes in the "*Madras Courier*" will be of interest in this connexion.

16th March 1791. A Native Inhabitants 'Merchants' Lottery Fund of 50000 pagodas was advertised under the management of Charles Drake. The profits were to be devoted to the Male Asylum and to the relief of the poor, lame and blind natives of Madras.

27th December 1791. The European inhabitants nominated David Haliburton and others—(names mentioned)....to be the managers of a lottery fund of 50000 Pagodas the profits of which were to be devoted to the repair of such roads in the environs of the English Settlement as do not come under the particular case of Government.

We are also informed that in 1797 a proposal was made for the establishment of a 'hospital and dispensary for the native poor of Madras and that funds were to be raised by organising lottery and private subscriptions.' A causeway across the river at the site of the present Commander-in-Chief bridge was built out of the profits of the lottery fund. In 1799, the Committee of the Male Asylum and Road Lotteries made a liberal contribution to the construction of Kerr's Chapel in Georgetown, which since has been identified with the church situated at the north end of Popham's Broadway. The total profits on these lotteries between 1797 and 1818 amounted to about 14½ lakhs of Rupees which were all devoted to such charitable and public causes as have been outlined above. We have the statement of accounts furnished by the Lotteries Committee to the Government in 1799 and the resolution of the Government thereon, which show not only the extraordinary care taken by the merchants who were the members of the Lottery Committees and subscribers thereof, for economic management but also the variety of objects of public good for which the funds were used.

Statement of the 1st, 2nd, 3rd, 4th and 5th Male Asylum and Road Lotteries held from 1st August 1795 to 24th November 1799 showing Profits appropriation.

To amount paid for the construction of the cause way ..	2917	Pagodas.
To amount paid for the construction of the bridge near the Burial grounds ..	2806	"
To amount paid towards the construction of a Protestant Church in Black Town ..	1500	"
To amount paid in aid of the Mother country ..	5000	"
To amount paid towards the repairs of roads in the vicinity of the settlement ..	12170	"
Balance ..	1209	"

The Government considered the above statement and passed the following resolution; "The Board so entirely approve the appropriation of the produce of the Lottery under the management of the Commissioners that it is resolved to permit them to continue it for the various purposes of Public good."

These lotteries were taken over by Government in 1807. The great amount of public spirit shown by the merchants in organizing lotteries for promotion of schemes of public good is particularly significant at the present day. That such widely divergent duties and responsibilities should have been cast on them and very willingly borne are worthy of appreciation and regard. Much of the development of the city of Madras in various directions in those days was in a large measure due to the initiative taken by the merchants. They took a great deal of interest not only in their own advancement but also in the advancement of the people around them. They welcomed opportunities of service and in most cases the initiative came from them. In the great famine of 1781, for example, when food was scarce and when people were dying of starvation, the Madras Merchants showed a commendable public spirit in subscribing liberally towards the relief of the famine stricken people. They not only subscribed among themselves 800 pagodas monthly but managed also to raise a sum of 5000 pagodas among the Calcutta merchants. They regretted that the response from the 'Natives' was very poor and that their total contributions amounted only to about 742 pagodas—lump sum. They also complained that even these payments were irregular. The letter written by the Relief Committee to Government pathetically described the condition of the poor and appealed to Government to use all their influence to increase the Natives' subscriptions and also themselves to afford assistance from the company's stores such as Palmyrahs to enable them to erect a few "sheds to cover these miserable wretches from the heat of the sun."

Public entertainments were also organised for collection of funds. There is a note to the following effect in a Madras letter to the India Gazette of 9th December 1782. 'The Comedy of the provoked wife and the comic opera of the Padlock are now in rehearsal and will be performed early in the month of January for the relief of the poor native inhabitants of Fort St. George. Tickets will be delivered as usual at the Theatre.' About the same time on the initiative of a large number of leading merchants, a public meeting was held at the Town Hall to request Government to adopt more rigorous measures for combating the famine. The meeting was attended among others by Sir George Ramsay a partner in Cuthbert Ramsay & Co., Charles Binny, Moses D'Castor of the firm of Decastro Pelling & DeFries. This aspect of their work must be considered as an important and glorious chapter in the history of the Madras merchants in the 18th century.

Towards the close of the 18th century a prohibitory order was issued by the Government absolutely forbidding the Company's officers from engaging themselves in private trade and asking them to choose between resignation of their public offices and withdrawal from commercial pursuits. About the same time also, all the houses of business in the Fort were directed to be transferred to the New Black Town in order that the Fort might be exclusively used for the military. In a letter of the merchants to Lord Clive in 1800, many of the merchants having houses in Fort St. George expressed their readiness to dispose them off at reasonable rates. As a result of these circumstances a number of independant European mercantile firms came into existence from the later half of the 18th century. The names of a few mercantile firms about 1790 are mentioned viz., Pelling & De Fries, Chase a Parry, Balfour Spalding & Colt, Roebricks and Abbot Amos and Borden Francis Lautor, Shamier & Sons & Sarquis Satur. The *Madras Courier* mentions many more, such as J. J. Durant & Sons, Messrs Beggle and Heefke, Lancy & Co., Burn & Co., etc. There are several notices in the *Madras Courier* relating to advertisements for these firms which testify to the variety of the business transacted by them.

"16th January 1790—Large pearls to be sold by Messrs D'Fries in the Black Town on Monday for ready money.

15th December 1790 Messrs. J. J. Durand & Sons beg leave to acquaint their friends and these public that they have fitted up a separate apartment for the purpose of carrying on trade in jewellery and watch making.

27th January 1791—Mr. J. Burn begs leave to acquaint his friends and the public that he is now selling at his godown in the Passage his China Investment consisting of Tea, Sugar candy, Nankeen, Chinaware, Hams etc. at reasonable terms.

23rd March 1791 Messrs. Beggle and Heefke have for sale at their godown the last nearest the Bandicoot Alley in the Fort St. George coniac Brandy of a special quality.

13th July 1791 Mrs. Laney presents her respectful compliments to all Ladies and gentlemen and begs to inform them that she continues to carry on the Millinary business in all its branches and has also opened a shop at her house where she has a variety of European articles for sales."

We do not know what happened to all these firms—Most of them appear to have subsequently amalgamated, changed their designation flourished for some time, and disappeared. Mention for example is made of the fact that in 1827 a certain property was conveyed to George Lys. trustee of the *late* firm of John D'Fries & Co. What happened to John D'Fries & Co., must also have happened to most of the other mercantile firms. But in the list of firms mentioned as having existed in 1790 there are two with a continuous existence and one has continued to the present day, the firms of Chase & Parry and the firm of Francis Lautor. Messrs. Parry & Co., are one of the leading commercial houses in Madras at the present day. The firm of Francis Lautor had a very interesting history. In the list of inhabitants of Madras in 1780 whose names have been recorded in the records occur two names those of De Latour and Joseph Latour. The former was a French merchant who arrived in Madras from Pondicherry in 1777 and the latter was a Swiss who also came to Madras about the same year. De Latour referred to here was no other than the person referred in to the list of firms of 1790 as Francis Latour. In 1800 he was joined by George Arbuthnot and in 1810 by John De Monte, the firm being known at first as Arbuthnot De Monte & Co., and ultimately as Arbuthnot & Co., who carried on a flourishing business and who was one of the most important commercial houses in Madras till the early years of the present century. They established several industries and were responsible e.g. for the Madras Portland Cement works, Bangalore Bricks & Tile works the Reliance Engineering works, the Chittalsvasal Jute Mills etc. Later they formed a joint Stock Coy. styled Arbuthnot Industrials Limited. Soon after the establishment of this limited concern occurred one of the greatest and the most appalling financial crises that have ever occurred in recent times and the Company went into liquidation. Credit suffered a rude shock and it took a long time to recover. The shares of the company were taken over by Fakir Mohamed Sait and Hajee Ismail Sait and the title of the firm changed to South India Industrials Ltd.

The other name in the list is the firm of Chase and Parry known for some time as Parry Dare and Co. and now as Messrs. Parry and Co., Ltd.

They owe their name to Thomas Parry, third son of Edward Parry of Leighton Hall, near Welshpool, who arrived in Madras in 1788 and commenced business under that name, having been licensed immediately on his arrival to trade as a free merchant.

Since that date the firm has had an unbroken record of commercial and industrial enterprise in the Madras Presidency.

The Head Offices of the Company covering over an acre of ground are situated on a valuable site at the southern end of First Line Beach, Madras, known as "Parry's Corner." This site was purchased from the Nawab of the Carnatic in the year 1775 and was subsequently sold to the founder of the business in 1803.

The Company are to-day erecting a modern six storey office building on the corner site, but the older portions of the Madras Offices still stand and are probably very little altered from what they were in the Napoleonic era in which the business was founded.

THOMAS PARRY : FOUNDER OF PARRY AND CO.

—By Courtesy of Messrs. Parry & Co., Ltd., Madras.

The Company possesses portraits of all the retired senior partners of the firm commencing with that of Thomas Parry, a reproduction of which is given here.

Pictures of old Madras now in possession of this commercial house show the immense changes that have taken place opposite Parry's Corner since work was started on the Port, and the great accretion of the foreshore as a result of the building of the present Harbour. In the old days the sea washed against the walls of Parry's Buildings, and the following account of a cyclone in 1807 is extracted from a letter written by Thomas Parry that year:

> "The surf broke over the ramparts of the Fort and so high that the Coffee Room at the Exchange was filled with salt water. It gained so much on the Black Town that it came up into the verandah of the new houses on the Beach. All the works in the front of the Customs House are blown up. A part of the foundation of the verandah of the Naval Office gave way, and the south end of the verandah fell in. Harrington's house was nearly gone, when the Gale luckily abated; the whole of the foundation is exposed. All the front line of the Banksalls is destroyed and the property on them carried away by the seas. Clive's Battery is rendered useless. Every tiled house in the place unroofed in some degree and numbers of people killed. Scarcely a building that has not suffered in doors and windows.
>
> Our buildings on the Beach have been damaged but not much. The sea carried away the end of one godown with some of the Company's rice.
>
> You would be distressed to witness the wreck of our friend Doctor Anderson's Gardens—all his fine mango trees have suffered and many of them are entirely destroyed."

Thomas Parry died in 1824 after 36 years residence in Madras during which he never returned to Europe. On the 14th of August that year when travelling with a nephew, aged only 10, between Porto Novo and Cuddalore, both were attacked by cholera and died the same day. They were buried in Christ Church, Cuddalore Old Town, where there is a stone to Parry's memory; and a tablet was erected at the same time in St. George's Cathedral, Madras. This tablet is adorned with a figure by W. Baily, R.A. of a native of South India mourning against a pillar inscribed with the words '*Nihil Humani Ab Illo Alienum*' and bears the following graceful eulogy so typical of the age in which it was written:—

"In memory of Thomas Parry Esq., who died at Porto Novo on the 14th August 1824 aged 56 years.

"In him were happily united those qualities which elevate and adorn the human character, whether in the exercise of liberal and enlightened principles, or in the practice of the social virtues to which his urbanity and extensive attainments gave a grace and attraction beyond the ordinary reach of men. During a residence of thirty-seven years in Madras his unblemished reputation had justly obtained for him the respect, esteem and veneration of all classes of the Community, and alike endeared him to the Native and European inhabitants. His loss is irreparably felt, and unfeignedly deplored.

His remains are interred in the Missionary Church at Cuddalore."

A full account of Thomas Parry's life is given in a book published last year by one of the directors of the firm, Mr. G. H. Hodgson, entitled "Thomas Parry—Free Merchant, Madras, 1768-1824."

Parry's principal business was the export of South Indian produce to Europe. But he was the pioneer in Madras of the Tannery Business and owned many indigo concerns besides engaging in shipping, both Coastal and to the Straits and the Far East for which purpose he owned several vessels.

INDUSTRIAL ENTERPRISE

After Thomas Parry's death the Company developed in all branches of industrial work more particularly the manufacture of Sugar, Heavy Chemicals, Agricultural Fertilisers, Timber, etc. Their interests are perhaps more varied than those of any other commercial firm in South India and they may be regarded as the pioneers of industrial enterprise in this part of the country. From the early years of the nineteenth century they have been intimately connected with the Sugar Industry and are Managing Agents of The East India Distilleries and Sugar Factories Ltd., The Deccan Sugar & Abkhari Co., Ltd., and The Travancore Sugars and Chemicals Ltd.

The Heavy Chemical and Pottery works of the East India Distilleries & Sugar Factories Ltd., are situated at Ranipet, North Arcot District, where also are established the Company's Fertiliser Works.

The Manure Works are of particular interest as an industrial enterprise, now that so much attention is being paid to scientific agriculture, and the Company has for many years devoted considerable money, time and attention to the instruction of the ryot in this important part of the country's development.

The conversion of this business house into a Private Limited Company in 1928 is but a step in its steady progress and development. Some 50 years ago there were two partners and about four assistants attending to the firm's business; whereas to-day the covenanted staff in Madras and up-country totals nearly a hundred, and the business is controlled by three Directors—G. H. Hodgson, C. Elphinston and G. B. Gourlay. The London Agents are Messrs. Parry Murray & Co., Ltd., Broad Street, managed by Mr. A. F. Buchanan, a late senior partner of Messrs. Parry & Co.

Another important firm that can trace its history to the early 18th century is Messrs. Binny and Co. The Binny family have been connected with India for over 2½ centuries. They have been the pioneers in textile trades and the Buckingham and Carnatic Mills of which they are the Managing Agents represent one of the largest textiles manufacturing concerns in India supplying every kind of cloth required for the civil and military departments alike. The exact date of the establishment of the company is not known though it was almost certainly prior to 1798. The *Centenary Hand-book of the Madras Chamber of Commerce* mentions that "records exist of the marriage of Thomas Binny to Elizabeth Rozario on 2nd February 1682 and of John Martyn to Catherine Binney on 16th April 1791." One Charles Binney came out to India in 1769 and was Secretary to Nawab Wallajah from about 1779 to 1782. Having come out without a license, Charles Binney was forced to go back home but he managed to return to Madras in 1778, along with Governor Rumbold who came to succeed Lord Pigot. In fact in the list of the names of passengers who arrived in the Company's ship "Bessborrough" which brought Governor Rumbold, Charles Binney is mentioned as the Governor's Secretary. Charles was also one of the signatories to a memorial sent to Government in 1785 by 203 European residents of Madras" for a redress of various grievances. Another member of the family by name Alexander Binny was pursar of one of the ships belonging to the Nabob. Yet another by name George Binny was a Surgeon at Ganjam in 1779. The firm of the Binneys owed its foundation, however, to one John Binny who arrived in Madras in 1797 and entered the Nawab's service as a Surgeon which place he kept on till 1801, when he was appointed as a Sheriff of the East India Company. His name finds a place in the list of sheriffs from 1727 to 1801. The place now occupied by Messrs. Spencer and Co. and the Connemara Hotel was the site of his residence which he was occupying till 1820—a place known as Binney's Street. He had a brother by name Thomas Binney also a Sea Captain like John-Binny, who founded a firm of the same name at Calcutta. The Madras firm was in the year 1803, known as Binney and Dennison and Company. No information is available as to the identity of Dennison but by 1814, the firm came to be known definitely as Binny and Company. In the early days, they were occupying some rooms in Fort St. George but transferred themselves to their present site about 1812. The two brothers appear between themselves to have been running two galleys between Madras and Calcutta perhaps belonging to the Nawab, known as success galley and surprise galley which names 'are still retained in the two tugs owned by the company at the present day.' At present Binnys occupy a very high place among general merchants at Madras. Besides general business, they are also shipping and general agents for a number of other companies. Their business-activities are very varied. The Buckingham and Carnatic Mills are self sufficient in all respects, with their own spinning, weaving and dyeing departments. The Buckingham Mill was established in 1877 and the Carnatic Mill in 1882 and they were amalgamated in 1920 with Binny and Company as Managing Agents. It is said that their Dyehouses are the best and most completely equipped in all respects and that the mills contain "the largest Khadi Dyeing plant under one management in the whole world." Binnys are also one of the earliest growers of coffee. They started coffee-growing even as early as the fifties of the last century. In the matter of promoting social welfare and providing medical, educational and other facilities for the men working under them, they have been almost the pioneers.

Among other important European firms established more recently in the latter half of the 19th century may be mentioned Messrs. Spencer & Co., Addison & Co., Simpson & Co., Best & Co., and the Burmah Shell Oil Storage and Distributing Company of India, Ltd. Spencer's were started from very humble beginnings in 1863 as an unpretentious little firm of auctioneers, wines and general merchants in the building of the present Bosottos with a small capital of Rs. 25,000 by one Charles Durrant who was joined later by J. W. Spencer. Between 1863 and 1897, a number of changes in its personnel took place and finally in 1897 it was registered as a Limited Liability Company. Their business has subsequently expanded in all directions. Apart from being general merchants, and cold storage specialists, they have Refreshment Room contracts with the Madras and Southern Maharatta Railway, Mysore State Railway, South Indian Railway and the North-Western Railway. They have a Tobacco factory at Dindigul, one of the best equipped in India, supplying cigars to different parts of the world. They are also proprietors of hotels like Connemara at Madras and West-end at Bangalore.

Messrs. Addison & Co., were established in 1873 by one Mr. Hawkings as small printing works. In 1886 the concern was purchased by the late Mr. Tom Luker and developed. Addison's pioneered the low price watches by introducing the "Waterbury with the 6 foot spring." Tens of thousands were sold in a few months. In 1890, it pioneered the Cycle industry in Madras, while in 1901 at a time when perhaps, there was only one motor car seen in Madras owned by Sir Francis Spring they took up the import of cars and set up repair shops etc. of their own. These works now cover several acres. They were one of the leading firms in high class printing and stationary. Their business is now confined to type-writers and office equipment. Messrs. Best & Co., are well known as one of the largest exporters of hides and skins besides being Managing Agents for a large number of shipping and industrial companies. It was in 1879 that it was established by Mr. A. V. Best and Mr. John McLintock as a partnership concern taking over the business of one Aspinwall and Coy, established in the city ten years earlier. In the course of the next few years, others also joined as partners and the firm was duly registered in 1911 under the Indian Companies' Act of 1882. Of the firms founded in the 19th century, perhaps the oldest is Simpson and Co. It was established in 1840 by the late Mr. Simpson. Then it has passed through the hands of Messrs. Seaton, Cuddon, Green and Sir Alexander Macdougall, who all joined the firm as ordinary assistants and became managers and proprietors in turn. It was converted into a private limited liability concern in 1926 and a Public Limited Company in 1939.

No account of big business in Madras will be complete without a reference to the impetus given to the industrial development of the city and the Presidency by the Burmah Shell Storage and Distributing Company, Limited. Though recent in origin and dating only from January, 1928, the company has been responsible for the rapid development of transport in all parts of the Presidency. A succinct account of the growth of this company has been given in the *Centenary Number of the Madras Chamber of Commerce.* As has been mentioned therein, there is hardly a motorable road in the Presidency where petrol is not available and hardly a place even in the jungles where kerosine is not sold. They have got excellent facilities and their own installations at Tondiarpet for storage of kerosine and petrol. Other concerns in the same line are the Standard Vacuum Oil Company of New York and Caltex Oil Company. By mutual agreement, competition has been eliminated with the result that fairly steady prices prevail. The Burmah Shell Company have also their own factory capable of manufacturing tins on a large scale for storage of oil. Besides, they have got branch and divisional offices in different parts of the Presidency which facilitate the transaction of business. Kerosene oil was first marketed to Madras in 1889 through Best and Company and in 1893 the first oil tanker arrived in Madras to discharge its cargo into the installation at Royapuram constructed in the same year. At the same time another company known as the Royal Dutch Oil Company commenced its operations through their managing agents the late Arbuthnot and Company. In 1906 the business of both these firms was taken up by the Asiatic Petroleum Company, Limited, whose managing agents were Best and Company. In 1903 imports of oil from Burmah began and two years later storage tanks were also installed. The first agents for Burmah oil were Binny and Company and later Shaw Wallace and Company. In 1916 a petrol storage tank was also added to the installation. On 1st January 1928 the Burmah Shell Company was formed to act as agents for all the existing oil companies. As importers of Burmah oil, the Burma Oil Company, had an advantage since the excise duty they had to pay was far less than the import duty which the other oil companies had to pay. The difference in rates was nearly one anna to the advantage of the Burmah Shell.

Passing on to Indian Mercantile exporting and importing houses, not much information is available. In the first place the establishment of some of these firms has been very recent. For a long time most of the Indians were content to be Dubashes and contractors and serve the needs of the European merchants. Indian business further suffered from serious handicaps. The idea of Joint Stock or Limited Liability Concern has never appealed to Indian businessmen whereas Europen firms were mostly limited concerns. Most of the business was conducted more or less on an individual or family basis. With frequent partitions, the bane of the joint family system, the old business did not thrive and gradually died out. Further, Indian business had no proper encouragement. The control of the major ports, railways, shipping companies, etc., was all exclusively in the hands of Europeans. The want of exchange banks and an equal want of branches in foreign countries through which there can be a steady flow of trade, was also a serious handicap. The European companies had also a good deal of Government patronage. Under these circumstances, Indian Mercantile firms were very slow to rise and establish themselves. It is a matter for satisfaction however, that matters have improved considerably and that in many spheres business has been passing out of European hands. The skins and hides trade has almost completely passed into Indian hands. Messrs. Jamal Moideen Saib and Sons, Roshan N. M. A. Carim Oomar and Company are all leading in this line. Among the partners of the Roshan N. M. A. Carim Oomar & Co., mention may be made of Kaka Haji Mohamed Umar Saheb and Jalal Haji Abdul Kareem

Saheb who have built up the firm. They have their own direct agents in other countries. The Malang Trading Company which came into existence as late as 1932 have been successfully assisting in the promotion of the tanning industry in Madras. Piecegoods is another trade which has also been taken away from the European merchants. Godown street almost exclusively consists of Exporters and Importers of piecegoods. Japan is now the greatest competitor and Indian merchants have been able to establish direct dealings with her. The firm of Ahmed Abdur Karim Brothers, Ltd., may be mentioned in this connection. Iron and steel is another field which has also been almost lost to European firms. Imports of these commodities have been considerably reduced. Trading in them is almost exclusively in the hands of the Borah merchants and another important dealer in the same line is Rasappa Chetti. Bunder street merchants deal exclusively in provisions and oilman stores such as coffee, tea, tinned fruits etc.

The same holds good of paper, stationary and sugar. The managing agencies for the Bengal and Titagur Paper Mills are in the hands of foreign firms, but other kinds of papers both foreign and indigenous are stocked largely by Indian concerns such as M. Akbar and Brothers, M. Husson Ali and Sons, and P. Singaravelu Chetti. Sugar is entirely controlled by Indian firms like Hajee Habib Peer Muhammad, with head office at Kathiawar, Hajee Jamal Noor Mohamed Sait with head office at Bombay and others. These have a number of branches all over India and even outside. The establishment of the Indian Stores Department and the adoption of the Rupee Tender system since 1930-31 have also given a great fillip to the indigenous firms, as purchases are made as far as possible locally. Government has ceased to act as direct purchasers when alone there was room for Government patronage. It will not be long before Indian Mercantile firms will come to dominate the whole field of industry and commerce. It is a welcome sign that Indian merchants like their European brethern recognized the need for concerted action and evolution of a common policy and for that purpose established the South Indian Chamber of Commerce in 1909. Its first habitation was at Rattan Bazaar and in 1910 it was shifted to the Mercantile Bank buildings which by a strange coincidence is now occupied by the sister institution of the Madras Chamber of Commerce. The present site of the Chamber in the North Beach Road was occupied in 1913. The work of this chamber is found best summarised in the Silver Jubilee Souvenir of the Chamber. The jubilee was celebrated under the presidency of His Excellency, the Governor on 7th December 1935. That Indian and European merchants should join hands and work for the economic uplift of the Presidency, is the devout wish of all, Indian or European. If this happy co-operation is achieved on a larger scale in India, there can be no doubt of the birth of an economically contented and prosperous New India and both Indian and European merchants can claim with justifiable pride that they have contributed in no small measure to the evolution of that New India.

The Andhra Chamber of Commerce

By

V. Venkateswara Sastrulu,
Hon. Secretary, A.C.C., Madras.

The Andhra Chamber of Commerce, Ltd., was started in the year 1927 by some prominent citizens among whom mention may be made of Dewan Bahadur Kommi Reddi Suryanarayanamurti Naidu, the Hon'ble Mr. Narayandas Girdhardas, Mr. C. Ranganayakulu Chetty, Mr. K. Sreeramulu Naidu, Mr. K. Nageswara Row Pantulu and Mr. Vavilla Venkateswara Sastrulu, with a view to organise and safeguard the commercial and industrial interests of the Telugu districts of the Madras Presidency.

Some of the objects for which the Association is established are:

(a) To promote and protect the trade, commerce and industries of India, in the Presidency of Madras and in particular in the Andhra country.

(b) To aid, stimulate and promote the development of trade, commerce and industries in India or any part thereof with capital principally provided by Indians or under the management of Indians.

(c) To watch over and protect the general commercial interests of India or any part thereof and the interests of the Andhras in particular engaged in trade, commerce or manufacture in India and in particular the Andhra-desa.

(d) To bring about a friendly feeling and unanimity among commercial Andhras, irrespective of caste, colour or creed, on all subjects involving their common good.

(e) To consider and formulate opinions upon all questions connected with trade, commerce and manufactures, and initiate or support necessary action in connection therewith.

(f) To collect, classify and circulate statistics and other information relating to trade, commerce and industries.

(g) To urge or oppose legislative and other measures affecting trade, commerce or manufactures and to procure change of law and practice affecting trade, commerce and manufactures and in particular those affecting trade, commerce and industries in which (Andhras) Indians are concerned and obtain by all acknowledged means the removal as far as possible, of all grievances affecting merchants as a body and mercantile interests in general.

(h) To communicate with the Chamber of Commerce and other commercial and public bodies throughout the world and concert and promote measures for protection of trade, commerce, industries and manufactures in which Andhras are engaged.

(i) To maintain a Library of books and publications of commercial interests so as to diffuse commercial knowledge and information amongst its members and concert measures for advancing commercial and technical education and such study of different branches of Art and Science as may tend to develop trade, commerce and industries in India.

It has on its roll of members all the leading merchants in the Telugu country, as well as in the city of Madras. It has been affiliated to the Federation of Indian Chambers of Commerce and Industry. It has been recognised by the Government of Madras and the Government of India as a representative of the Commercial, Industrial and Banking interests of the Telugu districts. It has obtained statutory representation in the Madras Corporation, the Madras Excise Licensing Board, the Madras Industries' Board and the Government Royapuram Hospital Committee etc.

SECTION V

GEOGRAPHY

The Problem of Water in Madras

By

V. D. Krishnaswami, M.A., Dip. Arch. (Cantab.)

The settlement of the English at Madras was a haphazard affair. From the first water supply was one of its chief problems; and when after a century rolled by a capital city developed there, the state of things as regards water went on deteriorating for another century until a partial solution was obtained in 1872. It is only in the present year that a final solution can be glimpsed on the horizon.

Alexander Hamilton, a trader in the East Indies writing in 1718 (79 years after the commencement of the English settlement), says "Fort St. George or Chennapatnam is situated in one of the most incommodious places I ever saw. It fronts the sea which continuously rolls impetuously on its shore—more here than in any other place on the coast of Coromandel. The foundation is sand with a salt water river on its back which obstructs all springs of fresh water, so that the Fort has no drinkable water within a mile."

Morphology.—The present city has grown up on a strip of land of very tame topography about 9 miles along the coast and from 3 to 4 miles broad, presenting a uniformly flat appearance, the highest points being only 40′ above sea level in Kilpauk and Mylapore. The bulk of it was at the time of the settlement and for long after, paddy fields irrigated from tanks like the Vyasarpady tank, the Spur tank, and the Long tank (Nungambakkam and Mylapore tanks combined) which could be recognised even now by their stagnating pools in monsoon time menacing the public health. Perambur, Choolai, Purasapakam, Vepery and Basin Bridge as also a part of George Town and the Broadway (where Attapallam or Pedda canal ran to empty itself in the 'Northern River') were all low lying swamps. The principal villages inhabited at the time of the settlement were Madraspatam somewhere north of the Fort and Mylapore on the south. Beyond Mylapore in the south, the ground was again swampy and estuarine.

The geological structure of the town as revealed by the earliest official borings in 1832 on the site of the Land Customs House (the present Museum), and later on by numerous bore wells sunk during successive drought years and by the trenches recently dug for the underground drainage, shows alternating layers of fluviatile sands and clays to an average depth of 12′. Along the coast Mylapore is on a dune hill and north of the Fort, Peddanaickenpet, Muthialpet, Washermanpet, and Kaladipet are situate on a well-defined dune ridge bifurcated along its north-south axial line by the Broadway. The structure of these shows dune sands intercalated with bog clays. Below 12 feet anywhere there is a stratum, 15 feet thick, of black, stiff buttery clay with recent shells, passing down into coarse marine sands. Gneissic bed rock is struck everywhere at about 57 feet.

The rainfall has been scarcely 40″ on the average. Under the above hydrographic and geological conditions, the obtaining of safe drinking water from the open porous subsoil was obviously out of the question. The location of the English settlement of 1639 cannot therefore be described from the health point as anything but a blind one that has resulted in a perpetual groping for water which has not yet found its goal.

Quest for Water.—The only lure to the English settlers was the thriving indigenous trade in 'Calico' (muslin) at this place. The Fort gave rise to a New Town around it. This was called Chennapatnam which as it grew soon joined itself to the northern Madraspatam and came to be christened 'Black Town' by the settlers. The nearest source of good drinking water to the residents of the 'White Town' (Fort) consisted in wells in the northern part of Peddanaickenpet, the western portion of the New Town. It was sold by water-bearers in pots and by others who brought it on cattle and carts. This water appears to have been relished for its cool and sparkling character and when particularly good, it was compared to 'Mountain Water,' apparently the water of St. Thomas Mount. A pot of water is said to have cost two *duddus* (10 copper cash each). The water was stored for the garrison in cisterns of timber and masonry.

The Fort was captured by the French in 1746 and one effective step taken by the besiegers is said to have been to cut off the water supply. It was restored in 1749 and within a decade we find a Select Committee arranging through an engineer, Mr. Call, for making provision for water storage enough for a garrison of 1500 Europeans, 3000 sepoys and 1000 native non-combatants for 6 months at a ration of ½ a gallon per man per day. But quite within a few years of this time the English supremacy became assured and there was no longer the need for enlarging the cisterns to the magnitude of siege requirements.

The aspect of drinking had been but one—and that a minor one—of the two sides of the need for good water, that had presented itself from the commencement. The East India Company gave employment to a large number of washers, bleachers and dyers of calico, and the Company was driven to the necessity of finding plenty of open space and good water for these men to carry on their business. The first settlement of these workers took place in Peddanaickenpet but soon, it appears, the area proved inadequate. During the time of Governor Collett (1717-20) a complaint was made to him to the effect that the water of the 'Northern River' (portion of the Buckingham Canal west of George Town and south of the General Hospital) had become much spoiled. This was evidently due to the very operations of these men —not to speak of accumulating sewage among an increasing population not alive to their sanitary necessities and having no provision for drainage. Accommodation was then found north of the town where the ground abounded in fresh springs. Even to-day it is so. This new settlement acquired the occupational name of 'Washermenpet.' And about the same time a new petta was encroached on without the consent of the Nawab of Arcot and it was called after the Governor's name as 'Colletpet,'—corrupted into its present name 'Kaladipettai.' Both the places are on the axis of the dune ridge and rich in fresh water. The necessities of these professional men and the limited extensions available, led, in Governor Pitt's time (about 1735), to the founding of a new weavers' settlement at Chintadripet. The Governor is said to have cast 'covetous eyes' on an extensive garden in this area enjoying a good supply of water owned by one Sunkurama, a local merchant, under a *cowle* from Governor Collett. He was ousted without any regard for his *cowle* and the garden was converted into a new weavers' village as, here the people of that calling were alone permitted to settle down. Thus Chintadripet, Washermenpet and Colletpet are clearly seen to have been the necessary accretions of a trading settlement where the principal occupation was the manufacture of calico dependent on a good water supply.

A turn of events.—It is a matter of history how in about two decades from Sunkurama's affair the company rose to sovereign power before which all dangers disappeared. With this turn in their fortunes the calico trade too was abandoned. Madras henceforth became the capital city of a rising state and the cause of its expansion though changed in nature continued to operate with unabated force. In 1792 the defeat of Tippoo removed all internal dangers in South India and about this time we find the municipal affairs entrusted to a separate body. An Act of Parliament of 1793 states the object of municipal administration to be that the streets should be regularly and effectively cleansed, watched and repaired and that scavengers should be appointed for the purpose. Organised drainage came only with the organised water supply to the city in 1872.

The Fort Scheme.—The population estimated in 1639 at 7,000 had considerably increased and in a letter from the 'principal inhabitants' (apparently to the Company) of 1791 the population was put at 3 lakhs. All estimates from sight have tended on the side of exaggeration and having regard to the fact that the 'Madras Justices' put the population of 'Black Town' at 60,000, we may safely put the population of the city at about three times this figure or say, two lakhs. Long before this time, the drinking water supply to the Fort had become an acute problem and had to be placed on a reasonably satisfactory basis having regard to the new proportions assumed by the Fort. The native population around had from habit paid no heed to the fundamentals of organised sanitation and there was serious danger of contamination of the drinking water. Except perhaps the main roads there must have been a most appalling disregard of sanitary morals. Cholera epidemics broke out in the hot months and there was water scarcity during and after the poor monsoons which were not by any means infrequent. All this had occasioned serious apprehensions in the minds of the military authorities and a scheme was eventually devised and secured their approval. It was executed in 1772 under a contract with Captain Baker. The scheme was called the "Seven Wells Government Waterworks" the wells being situate in an area two miles from the Fort and at a distance of near a mile from the sea, north of Peddanaickenpet.

These wells are situated on the crest of the dune ridge and with the tests then available the water must have appeared particularly good in quality. The wells are ten in number and not seven, 16′ in diameter with varying depths from 23 to 29 feet. Water was raised by picotahs into cisterns and passed through a filter measuring 48′ × 30′ × 6′. From the filter the water was raised into two main cisterns from which it was conveyed by gravitation in 5 to 3½ inches cast iron pipes to the various points of distribution to the military in and outside the Fort. The supply of the wells has been put at 140,000 gallons a day or nearly 10 mil. c.ft. per annum, at an annual cost of about £1200. The number of men for whom the supply was estimated in Baker's contract was substantially the same as that worked out by the 'Select Committee'. During the century that elapsed before Madras came to be served from the Red Hills reservoir, the wells showed no signs of exhaustion, and indeed on one occasion, early in 1885, when a cyclone had breached the Red Hills reservoir, the city had a partial supply for 10 days from these wells in addition to the Red Hills water led in by other means. Between 1783 and 1787 the service was sought to be extended to private houses in and out of the Fort but the proposal did not receive encouragement at the hands of either Europeans or Indians. The Indians appeared to have preferred their accustomed wells for drinking purposes and their own wells for other domestic uses.

SEVEN WELLS

An appalling situation.—The Fort having been thus provided for and the surrounding population being contented to move in their own grooves from habit, things went on without a change for nearly a century. But the evils of the situation went on accentuating themselves until they were felt to be intolerable in the sixties of the last century. The city was now an agglomeration of 16 villages with teeming populations loosely knit together and dependent for water on shallow wells among which potable water was a mere chance. Their cohesion was being brought about by the filling up of the vacant spaces in between through the practice of the European administrators, settlers and merchants, who had no need to care for distances, of building carefree 'Garden houses'—a practice which the introduction of a general protected water supply for the city, was to further accentuate. The census of 1871 showed an actual population of very nearly 4 lakhs and the administration report of the Madras Municipality of 1871-72, when the new supply scheme was to place an abundance of good wholesome water within the easy reach of all the inhabitants for a reasonable outlay, describes, the evils under which the city had till then, been suffering. It says that nothing had been done to improve the drainage of the city and that the open porous nature of the sandy soil of the city had hitherto in great measure mitigated the evils arising from damp. The people of the city more especially the poor had been compelled in several localities to drink the water of the tanks and ponds fed by the sewers of the town. Mr. Standish, the executive engineer writes : "it was but very recently that I discovered how excessively filthy are the tanks attached to the several pagodas which were resorted to principally by high caste people. In the Kachaleswara temple, a green fermenting crust had formed on the surface worse than anything I had ever seen in our worst drains and yet there were people who resorted to it for bathing purposes." The report goes on to point out the crying need for a comprehensive drainage scheme as "it cannot be expected that 32 mil c. yds. of water (the quantity proposed to bring into Madras) could be poured year after year over this soil with impunity and it is simply a matter of time when the subsoil water will rise so high as to render the ground floor of houses damp and unwholesome." This gives a tolerably fair idea of the state of water supply and drainage in the century that followed the establishment of the Company as a ruling power.

Organised supply of 1872.—For the first practical step towards meeting the growing menace we have to come down to 1861. It followed up an idea originated six years before for enlarging and combining certain large irrigation tanks, one of which was only eight miles from the town, as part of an extensive irrigation scheme. Mr. Fraser, an engineer who was deputed for the purpose, elaborated a scheme for the enlargement of the Red Hills and the Cholavaram irrigation tanks both for irrigation and for providing an abundant and wholesome water supply to the city. Fears were also entertained about the quality of the 'Seven Wells' water and a report made by Mr. Meyer and Dr. Wyndow, who had been appointed to analyse the water of the Wells said that the smallest amount of impurity found was double that which 'the authorities at home considered possible' and that the natural and only sound inference from the conditions of the soil was that it would be necessary for Government to look for water beyond this polluted area (the area of the 'Wells'). The scheme submitted by Mr. Fraser secured the consent of the Government of India in 1866 and was executed in the next six years. The essence of it may be said to be that local water was discarded and recourse had to the water of the Kortalayar river i.e., from twenty miles away.

The hopes, whatever they might have been, as to the possibilities of the underground water came to be abandoned in 1885 when careful boring conducted by Government under the advice of Mr. King of the Geological Survey assisted by a French engineer with experience at Pondicherry, upon a site chosen in the People's Park as the most favourable, showed that any artesian supply was a thing not to be hoped for, as granite occurred everywhere at a very shallow depth.

Under the scheme in question, the Kortalayar river was dammed at Tamarapakkam (*vide* map) from which place a supply channel was constructed to divert it to the Cholavaram tank. It intercepts two minor tributaries, Boosikal and Katankal, of the river and absorbs their content. The other supply channel connected the Cholavaram tank with the Red Hills tank, which was to be the immediate water reservoir for the city. The 'Red Hills' are no hills at all but an elevated laterite area. Besides the channel supply, the tanks themselves have a combined catchment area of 34 sq. miles while the intercepted tributaries have a catchment area of 106 sq. miles. The cost of the weir and of the channel as also of the improvements to the tanks by way of enlarging their capacity, coming up to 18 lakhs of rupees, was borne by the Government, and their upkeep and maintenance are the charge of the Public Works Department.

The waterworks necessary for conveying the water of the Red Hills to Madras by gravitation were constructed and maintained by the Corporation. They comprised a 'Valve-house,' situated at the S. E. corner of the tank for drawing up water and an open earth supply channel which had a bottom width of 6 feet and steep sides having a depth of 7½ feet. The channel was 6½ miles long with a gradient of 3 inches per mile. Except for a short length at the upper end, where the channel is in cutting, it was carried upon an embankment. At the Madras end the channel delivered the water into a circular well 22 feet in diameter and 21 feet deep, from where the cast iron mains of the distribution system ramified. This well with its distributary apparatus, known as the 'Madras Municipal City Waterworks' is situated at the highest available point 44 feet above sea level at Kilpauk. These works have, with reference to later works, been designated the *Old Works,* and their cost as also subsequent expenditure in extending and cleansing the distribution pipes came to Rs. 23 lakhs. The supply scheme was inaugurated by Lord Napier and the first supply to the city was on the 13th May 1872.

Defects disclosed.—It was soon found that the supply system was far from satisfactory in many points and that the works needed considerable remodelling. The Red Hills Lake had been tapped at so high a level that for considerable periods the water surface in the lake went lower and had to be pumped. This always synchronised with a cholera epidemic in the city and a rise in the mortality caused by intestinal troubles which pointed to the pumping as having a fouling effect on the water. The open earth channel caused a serious loss of water through evaporation and percolation. The capacity of the channel itself proved insufficient for the requirements as its maximum capacity proved only about 7 or 8 mil. gallons a day, while the estimated capacity had been more than double the amount. It was liable to contamination on its way by human beings and was continually liable to breaches. There were no filters nor was there any provision in the distribution system for delivery at adequate pressure while it became frequently choked with organic matter.

New Works.—To remedy the above defects New works had to be constructed at a cost of Rs. 62 lakhs between 1907 and 1924 by Mr. Madeley, the Corporation Engineer. He has given a fine description of the New works in a memoir entitled '*Madras City Water Distribution Scheme—Reports and Estimates*' 1911. The bulk of these works was finished by 1914 when they were opened for use by Lord Pentland. Among these may be mentioned (1) [at the tank] an intake tower, located where the water is deep, which by going 10 feet below the intake of the old method added 58 per cent to the water previously available, so that the lake can be almost entirely emptied,—besides a screening chamber and roughing filters, (2) an arched masonry culvert 5 feet wide and 4 feet high which replaced the old open channel and trebled the previous supply besides avoiding pollution in transit, (3) [at Kilpauk] sand filters, filtered water tanks, pressure pumps, and an elevated tank to ensure a steady pressure in the mains and (4) a remodelling and extention of the Distribution System. A chlorinating plant added later on chlorinates the water before it is let into the filters.

But all the same it was soon pronounced that the effluent from the slow sand filters was bad, though 'safe' from an epidemiological point of view. This was due to the fact that though the immediate effluent had no sulphuretted hydrogen, the water contained sufficient organic matter to putrify and produce this gas in the pipes. The matter is still undergoing consideration and remedial measure at the hands of a Government Filtration Committee and Rs. 5 lakhs have been sanctioned for the purpose. Even in 1936 the water was considered to be far from satisfactory in this respect.

Unreckoned factors.—These works were designed and constructed on an estimated basis of rain and population which unfortunately belied the forecasts. Mr. Madeley expected a population of 7 lakhs in 1941 but in 1931 itself it came to 6½ lakhs showing a phenominal boom of 22·8 per cent during the previous decade ; while it was only in the decade 1891 to 1901 that the increase went beyond 10 per cent (with a growth of nearly 13 per cent). The figures for the daily consumption of water show 2½ million gallons in 1878, 10 to 12 mil. gallons in 1910-1915, 12 to 15 mil. gallons in 1915-23, rising year after year by a million gallons except during drought years. At present it is 28 million gallons per day. Besides all this we have to reckon with the fact that the city itself has been growing, of which the most conspicuous instance has been the Mambalam extension. Commerce and industry of various kinds have been taking root in the city with improved railway communications and the erecting of the New harbour ; and the latest sanitary improvements, chief among which has to be mentioned the underground drainage, are vast consumers of water. With the city, its population and the rate of consumption growing side by side, the scarcity of rains that has been the feature of the last two decades has made the fact increasingly evident that we have to look for something to replace the year to year storage beyond which the architects of the present system did not envisage.

The measures so far possible namely, the widening of the supply channels, improvements to the dams etc., did not go beyond the fringe of the matter.

The present water-famine.—The outlook necessary has come as the result of the very acute water famine that has followed the complete failure of the monsoon of last year,—water being now supplied with an intermittency of an unprecedented character and the weir at Tamarapakkam is being raised with mud and turfed over to catch the effects of possible summer showers, and yet it is said that 16 mil. gallons are being consumed per diem in place of the normal 28 mil. gallons. Brains of all sorts of training were set racking as the daily press has made evident. Wells were everywhere getting dry and a campaign that in former years led to closing down of a large number of wells has again given place to a campaign of self-sufficiency through reopening them. Tube wells and bore wells are becoming the order of the day.

The writer has personally taken logs of a large number of wells and attended the excavations of the new underground drainage scheme, to study the hydrographic character of the strata. In the dune area in the north of George Town there are good underground springs that would give a large yield for local supply, showing that the early move for water that brought into existence Washermanpet and Kaladipet, were moves in the right direction. The new Mambalam extension built on an original tank bed has also some good springs; but they are all, as has to be expected, undergoing deterioration as the result of the numerous wells now coming into being. There has been nowhere any evidence to upset the conclusion of Mr. W. King and after him of Mr. Cornet that no hopes need be entertained of tapping an artesian supply. As a whole it can be safely said that the entirety of the underground sources within the city is a factor only to be ignored in any scheme not proceeding with purely private ends; so that the only direction in which the question has to be thought out, is storage by leading in surface water, which to all outward appearance has been exploited already.

A bright spot.—In this dilemma, there has occurred a bright spot. So long ago as 1909 Sri. C. Velayudha Mudaliar, a mirasdar of Karikalavakkam near Trivallur suggested to the Government that a dam across the Kortalayar, some 19 miles up the Tamarapakkam weir, where the river was joined by the Nagari river, was likely to vastly improve its irrigational potentialities. The Government investigated this matter for irrigational purposes in 1924 and the reports made thereon suggested a dam at Pundi some 5 miles lower down. After this, in 1927, when the city was suffering acutely from one of its periodic water scarcities, Government appointed a Commission to examine the various possibilities for improving the water supply of the Red Hills tank, but the recommendations made related only to the addition of head sluices and the widening of the supply channel and the like, which has already been referred to. The question of damming up the river has again been before the present Government since the middle of last year. In April last the hon. Mr. Yakub Hassan, Minister for Public Works, visited the Pundi locality and a scheme appears to be occupying the attention of the Government having for its object a solution once for all of the water supply problem of the city.

In all normal years the Kortalayar has been losing a large volume of water to the sea over the last of its anicuts at Vallur, often to a height of 10′. An engineer who happened to see the flow is said to have ex-

MAP OF MADRAS WATER SUPPLY SOURCES

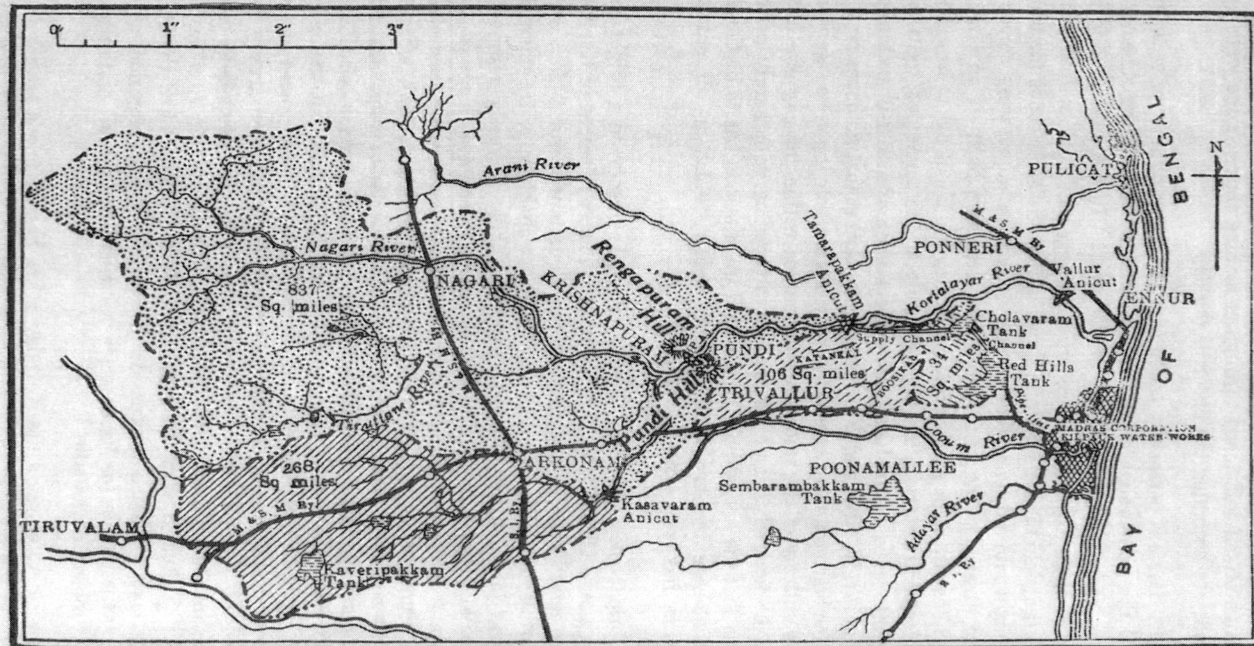

Shaded portions indicate catchment areas supplying Red Hills Tank. (P.A.)=Proposed Anicut at Pundi. Scale: 1"=6 miles.

claimed 'to impound this water, would be to create a new tank, Red Hills and Cholavaram combined.' The scheme is one for the erection of a dam 40 feet high above the bed level to a length of 2000 feet between the Rengapuram and Pundi hillocks on either side of the river so as to create a large reservoir of 11·8 sq. miles. The entire cost is said to come to 50 lakhs including about 10 lakhs for acquiring the villages that would get submerged. The capacity of the Red Hills and Cholavaram tanks is given at 2700 mil. c. ft. of which annually 2200 is issued, out of which again 900 go to the town and 500 for irrigation and the rest gets lost by evaporation and percolation from tanks. If the capacity of the new reservoir is going to be 2500 mil. c. ft., as estimated, after allowing for the present rights of irrigation lower down, the addition will indeed solve for ever the water problem of the city—which at present consumes only a third of this amount,—whatever the threatening drought and however the city and its population may expand. The bed of the river at the dam site is sandy with lateritic boulder conglomerate resting on Sriperumbudur shales which again rests on granitic gneiss, and it is well adapted for the dam ; the country between Krishnapuram and Pundi is funnel shaped and constricted at the dam and widening out rapidly up the river, the left bank being steeper than the right. With the estimated data the work promises to be of such a character that its benefits would far outstrip the initial cost. The writer's geological work in the area around Pundi and Madras points to the scheme in question as being the only sound one in the circumstances of the city, as it will confer lasting benefit on it by securing for it a perennial supply of water of the quality that it is now enjoying.

It is to be hoped that the year 1939 would by bringing in this benefit prove to be a landmark in the history of the human progress in the city, by solving once for all the problem with which it has started in a rather blind way. One is strongly tempted to think here of the circumstances in which the present harbour in Madras came into being. It was planted on a surf beaten beach as a challenge—so to say—to nature by Sir Francis Spring. It was built in the face of great opposition and prognostics of evil. But it has triumphantly justified itself, and the greatly augmented sea-borne trade of the city bears eloquent testimony to the usefulness of its being. But the scheme in question no way partakes of the utopian character that the harbour presented at its inception. There is no going against nature in this scheme and the blessing it is likely to confer will be many sided in its character and the impetus it will give for the growth of the city will be of that nature that long before its sexcentenary its people will not be able to realise how it had happened that Madras had ever to put up a fight for mere water.

SELECT REFERENCES

The following books and reports have been consulted by the author. The writer has to thank the Commissioner of the Madras Corporation for kindly allowing him access to his records and maps among which the last of the undermentioned papers was found. The writer has also to thank the Industrial Engineer of the Department of Industries for kindly permitting him access to his records.

1. *Vestiges of Old Madras* by H. D. Love—1913.
2. *Ways and Works in India* by MacGeorge—1894.
3. *Records and Memoirs of the Geological Survey of India.*
4. *Records of the Industries Department.*
5. *Administration reports and other records of Madras Corporation.*
6. *Madras Journal of Literature and Science*—1866 III Series, pt. 2.
7. '*History of Madras*' by Prof. C. S. Srinivasachari.

Growth of the City of Madras

By

George Kuriyan, B.Sc.,
Lecturer, University of Madras.

The Site. When Francis Day got the first grant for Madras from Damarla Venketapati, the Governor of all the coast country from Pulicat to San Thome, the name of Chennapatnam was given to the settlement at the desire of the Naik after his father Chennappa,[1] but "when Day and Cogan founded the settlement in 1639, it was Hobson's choice for them, and they had to choose a site which nobody else would conceivably want".[2] Day could probably have chosen San Thome, 'a fortified town of wealth and importance', but he chose in preference a narrow strip of land north of San Thome which seemed to him likely to prove an easier and more permanent holding. A shallow lagoon-like river running parallel with the sea for a short distance formed the protection needed on the land side, but otherwise, the river was useless. To Day it must have been the ease of defence which could have weighed as the most important factor in the location of the settlement.

The village offered was settled by a small expedition which reached the place on the 20th February 1640.[3] The erection of the Fort commenced on the 1st March (about 8 days later), and perhaps the inner fort was completed by St. George's Day (23rd April)). This possibly accounts for the name Fort St. George.[4] The fort was situated on the

1. C. S. Srinivasachari's article on *The Stages in the Growth of the City of Madras* in the Journal of the Madras Geographical Association, Vol. II, No. 3, p. 80. Also Love, *Vestiges of Old Madras*, Vol. I, p. 17 and W. Foster '*Founding of Fort St. George,*' p. 16. "To the new settlement was given at the desire of the Naik, the name of Chennapatnam after his father Chennappa."

2. G. H. Hodgson: *T. Parry—Free Merchant*, p. 13.

3. 'Official Handbook of Madras' ed. F. E. James, p. 33.

4. W. Foster: *Founding of Fort St. George*, p. 13. From the proceedings taken against Cogan, it is found that the fort was completed by 30-6-1643 costing 9,250 pagodas. See also the Journal of the Madras Geographical Association, Vol. II, No. 3 page 95. "The original fort was only a fortified enclosure begun by Day and continued by Cogan. It measured 100 yards by 80 yards and was roughly co-terminus with the Fort Square of a later period. Buildings and streets rose up round it and constituted the White or Christian Town." See also Love, Vol. I, page. 28. "The fort was lined out nearly square in plan with a bastion at each angle. It was 108 yards north to south, and 100 yards east to west."

southern extremity of the strip and therefore commanded the town and land extending about 3 miles in one direction, viz., north.[5]

Two streams flowing from the west and north respectively had a common outlet to the sea about a mile south of the village of Madraspatam. The first which was then known as the Triplicane river and now as the Cooum, followed a winding course through the villages of Chetpet, Nungambakkam and Triplicane. The other, a smaller stream called the North or Elambore river[6] flowed parallel to and about a mile distant from the coast, along the west side of Madraspatam till it reached the present site of the General Hospital. It then bent sharply to the east and when near the sea turned southwards again for ¾ of a mile (see Langle's and Pitt's maps) and met the Triplicane river at its outlet. The first bend by the existing General Hospital was within 300 yards of the Triplicane river and at that point a cut was made at some period before the end of the 17th century[7] between the two streams, with the object of probably equalising the flood levels. The low lying marshy tract of land between the two rivers was consequently surrounded by water and it was known as early as 1643 as the island.[8] The two streams formed a wide backwater and communication with the sea was open only during the rains. The site chosen for the Fort was a point on the surf bank of sand which lay between the Elambore river and the sea, ¾ of a mile north of the outlet and just south of the village of Madraspatam. At or near the site were a few huts forming a small kuppam or fishing hamlet, which Lockyer calls the 'Maqua town'.[9]

5. Love: Vol. I, p. 89.

6. Thomas Pitt's map of 1710-11 shows that the present Cochrane's Canal combined with what is now the northern branch of the Cooum was formerly called the Elambore river, notwithstanding that the western branch or the Triplicane river flowed nearer the village of Elambore or Egmore. The North river flowed through or close to the villages of Pursewauka, Pudupauka, Vepery, etc., which were then tributary to the village of Egmore. Again Pitt's map shows the position of 'Eggmore and the Company's Wilderness' very near the bend of the river on its western bank, practically opposite the Company's garden.

7. Love, Vol. II, p. 123. a bridge had been built across the artificial cut which connected the Elambore and Triplicane rivers; it is shown on Pitt's map and was probably erected in 1703.

8. Lockyer in his description of Madras about 1702 states that the island then was a peninsula. See also Love, I, p. 585. 'Orders were issued in 1696 that the cutt river be cleared,' i.e., the artificial channel between the Triplicane and Elambore rivers. It is therefore probable that Lockyer's description is not accurate.

9. See Map of Madras of 1710/1 by Pitt and Talboys Wheeler's Map of Madras in 1733.

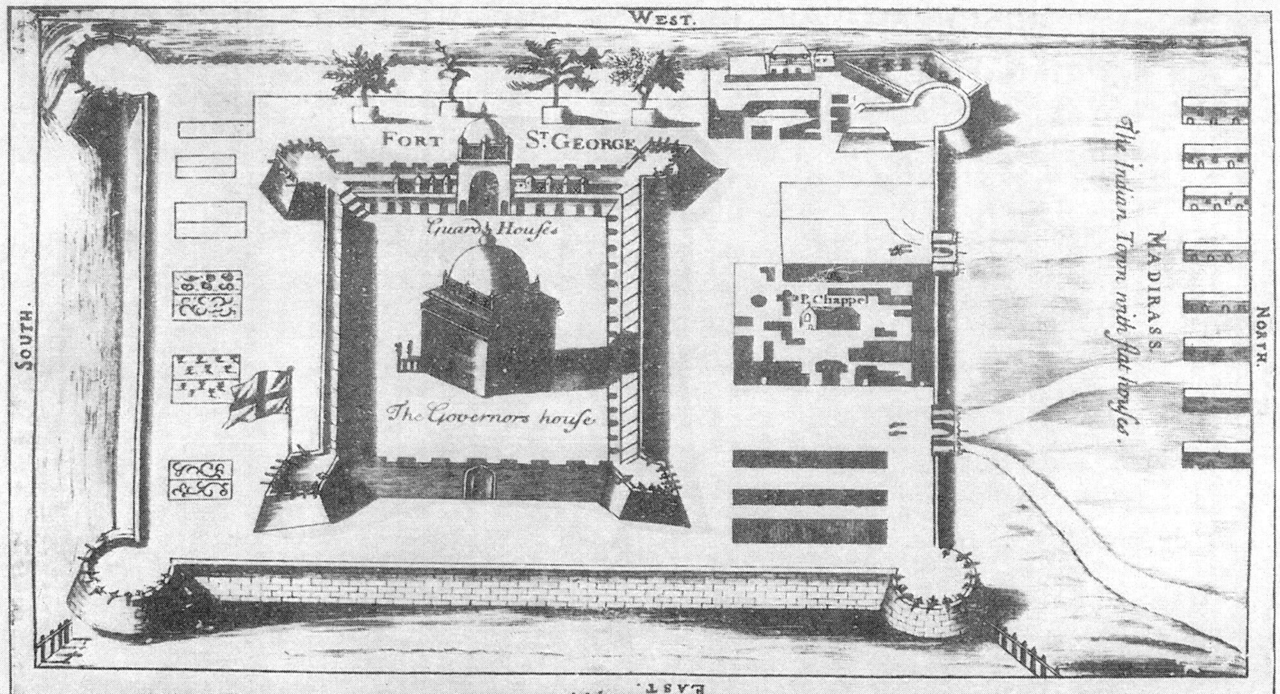

FRYER'S MAP OF MADRAS (1673)

On the basis of these facts, it is inferred (1) that the site of 'Chinapatam' was that of modern Fort St. George and (2) that the original village of Madraspatam lay north of, and proximate to, 'Chinapatam.'[10] Fryer's Map (reproduced here) (1673 ?) though not accurate is the oldest map available[11] and it shows "Madirass the Indian town with flat houses" immediately to the north of the European walled town. Hence the original site of the village of Madraspatam was probably on the northern Esplanade of modern Fort St. George. The interval of space between 'Chinapatam' and 'Madraspatam' was rapidly built over so that the two places became virtually one town; and a single designation being required for the united towns, the English preferred Madraspatam with which they had from the first been familiar, while the Indians elected to adopt 'Chinapatam.'

Extent of Madras. Although the extent of the territory granted by the Naik is nowhere specified,[11a] yet, because it conferred the right to collect the revenue of the town, it probably was the whole area contained within the village limits of Madraspatam. Talboy Wheeler's Map of Madras in 1733[12] shows the circumjacent villages and as subsequent grants of villages are those whose limits are clearly shown on this map (except Narimedu), there is no reason to suppose that the village boundaries had varied since 1640.

The boundary passed through a point on the coast 300 yards north of the river outlet and travelled across the islands to the cut uniting

10. Journal of the M.G.A., Vol. 3, No. 3, pages 85 and 86 and *Love*: Vol. I, page 281 "Moving towards the shore we left St. Thomas which lies three miles but south of Maderas and Fort St. George." Hence Madras and Fort St. George are two places. See also Love, Vol. I, page 83. "The Rajah Sri Ranga Raya in his cowle discriminates between the village of Madraspatam and the new town growing up around the Fort which he calls Zera Ranga Raya patam—my towne. Neknam Khan distinguishes the place called Madrassapatam from the Fort and town of Chinnapatam. From these it can be inferred that Zera Ranga Rayapatam and Chinnapatam are different names for the new town while Madrassapatam is the separate, though probably contiguous old town."

11. Love: Vol. I, page 539. "The earliest map of Madras which has been traced is one of 1688 published in Langle's 'Monuments ancients et modernes de l' Hindoustan.' The source is not given and the plan is far from being accurate. It bears a curious resemblance to Paradis' plan of 1749 which is also wanting in accuracy. This plan has been reproduced for this paper. Prof. C. S. Srinivasachari dates Fryer's Map at 1673, while Col. Love dates it at 1691.

11a. Love Vol. I. Page 27. Foster: Founding of Fort St. George page 17. See also *contra* Talboys Wheeler, Madras in Olden Times, Vol. I, page 57 and Hamilton's Gazetteer.

12. Talboys Wheeler's Map of Madras in 1733, redrawn for Col. Love is reproduced here from this drawing a copy of which is kept in the Madras Record Office.

the two rivers. It then followed the Elambore river for a distance of nearly 1000 yards, curved inland but subsequently met the river again at the northwest angle of the present George Town. Bending due east till about 1000 yards from the coast, it then turned north for a distance of some 2000 yards. Finally it travelled east again to the sea, thus enclosing a compact area except for a small projecting strip at its northern end. The total length of the tract from north to south was about 3¼ miles and its mean width about a mile. This was probably the extent of territory granted by the Naik in 1639.[13]

"At the company's first beginning to build a fort, there was here but only the French Padres and about 6 fishermen's houses; so as to entice habitants to people the place, proclamation was made in the Company's name that for the term of thirty years, no customs of things to be eaten or worn should be taken from any of the town-dwellers."[14] Although the Company claimed ownership of all the territories included within the boundaries of Madras, the earliest agents in their anxiety to obtain settlers made liberal grants of land to private persons without limitation of time or exaction of ground rent. In a letter dated the 25th October 1639, "Madraspatnam" is mentioned as a fair-sized place and hence the paucity of settlements must be with reference to the new area. The Dutch records of 1641 say that the English settlement which formerly consisted of about 15 to 20 fishermen's huts, had now about 70 or 80 houses. In a letter dated 9th October 1647 by Ivy and Gurney, an account of the great ravage of the famine of 1647 is given. "The famine was so violent that during the last five months 4000 died in Madraspatam, 15,000 in Pulicat and about the same number in St. Thome."[15] It is very doubtful if these estimates of the dead are accurate, probably they are not; but nevertheless, an indication is given regarding the respective sizes of these settlements. By 1647, Madraspatam including the new and old towns had nearly ¼ the total population of St. Thome and by 1648 the estimated population of Madraspatam was as high as 15,000. Apparently therefore Madraspatam grew up at an extremely rapid rate within the first few years of its founding.[16]

13. The limits of the territory are believed to be those shown on the original map of 1733 by a red line.

14. *Foster*: "Founding of Fort St. George," Page 16.

15. *Ibid*, p. 36.

16. Attempts were made to determine the population of the City as early as 1639 when it was estimated that the total population of the City was 7000. By 1646 the estimated population was as much as 19,000 and in 1669 Thomas Bowrey estimated the total population to be 40,000. Dr. Fryer in 1673 stated that there were 33,000 inhabitants exclusive of Europeans and Sir William Langhorne calculated that the total population was 50,000 in 1674. There certainly had been

The native town situated close to the north of the Fort was originally built in the form of a square and was in 1700 about a mile and a half in circumference. Fryer in 1698 stated that the native city like the Christian Town[17] was quadrangular. "Its boundaries were:—*north*, the present China bazaar, *south* the inner north wall of modern Fort St. George, *east* the sea, and *west* a line parallel to the shore extending from Popham's Broadway to a point near the present sally port on the north west glacis where it struck the then course of the river. This river has now degenerated into a drain."[18] One of the earliest attempts to delimit the boundaries of Madras was by the construction of a wall by Ivie, sometime between 1644 and 1648, the extent of which is a matter for surmise, but details of later date lead to the belief that the rampart bounded the north and part of the west side of the town and probably the south side also. The northern wall probably ran from the sea along the present China Bazaar road to the end of Popham's Broadway, and the western rampart, from this point southwards till it encountered the river. The south wall would be a short length traversing the spit of sand south of the inner Fort. That part of the town which was bounded by the sea and the river was probably sufficiently protected by natural obstacles. The space thus enclosed included both the White and Black Towns of Thomas Pitt's Map of 1710/1. It is true to assume that this wall delimited the boundaries of the city then. The suburbs to the north and west of the town were Muthialpetta to the east of Broadway and Peddanaickpettah to the west which continued south down to the Company's garden by the river.[19] During the occupation of Madras by the French, nearly half of Black Town was demolished to a distance of nearly 400 yards from the south wall of the Fort. Old Black Town was at first unfortified, subsequently it was walled with mud with two gates of brick opening into the White Town. From time to

no enumeration and these were nothing more than estimates. In 1681 the Company estimated the total population to be 200,000 and by 1691, in the estimation of the Company the population of the City had risen to 400,000. That no reliance of any sort could be placed on these estimates, is shown by the subsequent Census Statistics. According to the Census of 1871 the City had a population of only 397,552; by 1881 it had increased to 405,848; in 1891 it was 452,818; in 1901 it was 509,346; in 1911 it was 518,660; in 1921 it was 526,911 and in 1931, 647,228. The only phenomenal growth of population of the city was during the last census decade. If this growth has been maintained, the next Census may show that Madras is fast approaching the millionaire standard! See also Pharoah & Co., *Gazetteer of South India* (1855), page 183, *Love*, Vol. I, Page 547, *Maclean* "Manual of Administration," Vol. 2, page 279 and *Love*, Vol. 2, page 132.

17. *Love*, Vol. 2, page 73; Vol. 1, page 207.
18. *Love*, Vol. 1, page 284.
19. See Thomas Pitt's map of 1710/1.

time proposals were made to build a masonry rampart in place of the mud walls, but it was only Governor Thomas Pitt (1698-1709) who built a brick wall about the town, regularly fortified with bastions and outworks and mounted with artillery.[20]

After the disappearance of the old Black Town, the name Black Town came to be applied to Muthialpetta and Peddanaickpetta jointly. Pitt's map shows that Peddanaickpetta was the first area to be used for residential purposes outside the White Town by the English Factors. It also contained the Company's New Garden House. Between the two pettas was an open space containing gardens and a portion of the Company's paddy fields. Much of the north western part of Peddanaickpetta continued to be cultivated land even as late as 1755.[21] Gradually this petta ceased to be the fashionable European quarter that it was about 1700. Attapollam,[22] the lowlying region between the two pettas was reclaimed and developed by the enterprising solicitor Stephen Popham. Earth was brought from Hog hill (Narimedu (?) perhaps shown as low hills in the background in the Prospect of Fort St. George attached to Pitt's map) and gradually the whole area was built over.

History of the fortifications. In 1693 to 94 the court of Directors despatched recruits with orders to strengthen the fortifications of Fort St. George, but no indication as to what was done is to be found in the records. In 1706-07 Governor Pitt represented to the Court of Directors about the weakness of the Fort, but nothing was done till 1742 when more troops arrived and the Directors instructed the Governor 'to put the fort in the best posture of defence'. In 1743 Engineer Smith submitted plans for strengthening the Fort and increasing its area from 15 to 30 acres and he defined this additional area by a wet ditch which he dug and faced with bricks. He traced out 4 new bastions. "All these works were carried on as high as the berm, but from financial reasons were then discontinued and Orme states that 'the

20. *Maclean* Manual of Administration, Vol. 2, Page 91. "As early as 1690, some attempt had been made to protect Black Town by a mud wall. The necessity of improving this was brought home in 1702 when Daud Khan threatened a siege of Madras and a tax was raised for this purpose. From time to time, when danger threatened, this tax was repeated, but in times of peace it was found difficult to collect these taxes. The result of these imposts was a masonry wall or boundary hedge round the north and west sides of the town with 11 bastions. Many traces of the wall still exist and some of them have been converted into Police Tannahs. A monument of this former defence is preserved in the name of the street lying within the line of the west wall which is popularly known as Wall tax road to this day."

21. See *Conradi's* Map of Madraspatnam in 1755.

22. See *Ravenshaw's* map of Madras in 1822.

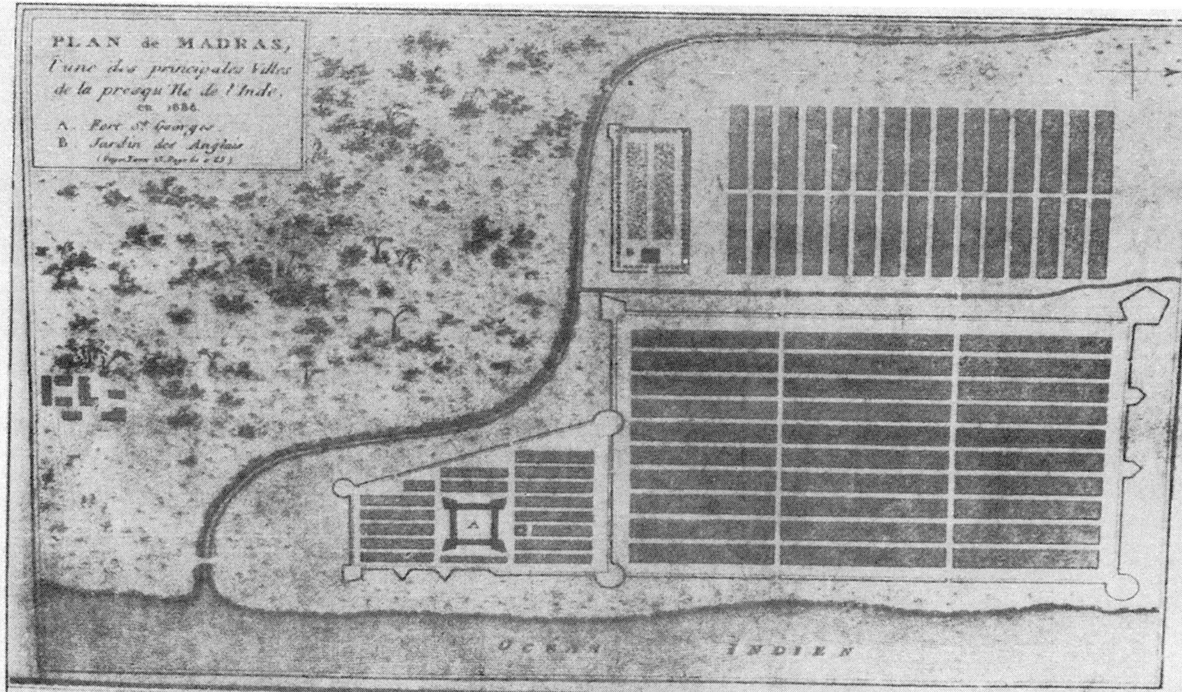

Madras in 1688.
(from L. Langlès)

naked ditch remained neither an obstruction nor defence.' The French during their possession of the Fort improved its fortifications considerably. The bastions and the batteries had been enlarged and strengthened; part of Black Town had been destroyed and with its ruins an excellent glacis on the north side had been formed and palisades and covert ways in front of the two north gates had been constructed. A glacis on the south had also been commenced, but still the defences were very inferior and incapable of resisting a strong European enemy."

The apprehension of another attack from the French in 1756 compelled the Governor to strengthen the fortifications. The main modifications were :—

(1) the river bed was filled up and its course deflected[23]

(2) the northern face was strengthened; buildings within 400 yards of the covered way of the north front in Old Black Town were ordered to be demolished and in October 1757, it was actually carried out.[24]

(3) the western wall and glacis were rebuilt so that the face had its covered way palisaded and it contained 3 ravelins after the improvements.

The year 1782 saw the accomplishment of the reform of Fort St. George which was begun by J. Brohier in 1756. Its first phase was Cogan and Day's castle, the second the quadrangular bastioned enclosure of the White Town which converted the original castle into a citadel; third the development of the walled town into a fortress planned as a half decagon and the fourth the entire reconstruction of the Fort as a half decagon with ample out-works.[25]

Absorption of the surrounding villages. "Outside the bounds of Madraspatam was a group of villages, comprising Tandore[26] on the North,

23. *Love*, Vol. 1, page 534. The idea of enlarging the White Town by diverting the course of the old river and filling up the old bed appears to have originated with Yale before he became Governor, i.e., before 1687. The proposal was not carried into effect however till nearly three fourths of a century later. See also *Love*, Vol. 2, page 492. "Fortifications on the west front closed the channel of the river which swept in a curve along the old curtain. As Smith's ditch could not safely carry the freshes, Brohier in 1755 diverted the Elambore river into a passage across the island, which had been cut by a flood five years before." This diversion is shown in *Conradi's* map of Madraspatnam in 1755.

24. *Love*, Vol. 2, Page 530.

25. *Love*, Vol. 3, Pages 275 and 276.

26. Tandore. *Love*, Vol. 3, Page 385. 'Tandore on the road to Trivetore.' Tandore is Tandavoor and marked in Talboys Wheeler's map of Madras in 1733. It is clearly the present Tondiarpet.

Perembore to the Northwest, Vepery and Pursewaukam on the West, Egmore and Nungambaukam to the Southwest and Triplicane on the South."[27] In 1645 " the English factor Greenhill visited Raja Sri Ranga Raya either at Vellore or Chandragiri and obtained a cowle securing some new privileges in addition to what had already been got under the earlier grant, viz., the right to administer justice and an additional piece of ground known as Narimedu which was probably the northern bank of the Elambore (North) river, near the present General Hospital and was known as Hog hill ".[28] In 1672 Nabob Yeknam Khan (Neknam Khan) granted a cowle to Sir William Langhorne. " I do grant that the English shall enjoy the same ancient priviledges as well of the ground belonging to the place called Madraspatam as Narimedu and all other priviledges, which they have hitherto enjoyed from the time the town of Chinapatam was first situated." Neknam Khan's cowle implies that Madras territory remained the same in 1672 as it was in 1639, except for the addition of Narimedu. It is therefore presumed that Narimedu was added to the territories under Fort St. George in 1645 and subsequently recognised by the Nabob in 1672.

" The first suburban village to be acquired was Triplicane; there is no certainty about the exact date of its acquisition by the English, but the year 1658 seems the likeliest date on account of several reasons.[29]

27. *Love*, Vol. 1, page 82.

28. Journal of the M.G.A., Vol. 2, No. 3, page 80; also *Love*, Vol. 1, pages 345 and 346. "It appears probable that Madraspatam covering the limits of a pre-British town or village of that name may have included the whole territory originally assigned by Naik Damarla Venketappa; that Chinnapatam was the specific name of the new fort and town which the English erected within those limits, but south of the original village, and that Narimedu was ground adjacent to the native town on its west side which was thrown in by the Raja of Vizianagar when he confirmed the Naiks grant in 1645." No mention is made of Triplicane. See also foot note 43.

29. Journal of the M.G.A., Vol. 2, No. 3, Page 86 and *Love*, Vol. 1, Pages 346 to 350. A lease of Triplicane was granted on the 12th July 1672 by Nabob Mussa Cawricana, successor to Nabob Neknam Khan, but there is good reason to conclude that this village was temporarily under the control of Fort St. George for a short period anterior to 1662. A firman from His Highness the 'Ollumpana' King of Golconda dated the 23rd February 1676, recited and confirmed Neknam Khan's Cowle. The only modification was the addition of the town of Triplicane to the territories granted to the English. In 1673 de la Haye occupied Triplicane to secure passage for his supplies on the pretext that it was still under the control of Golconda. Sir William Langhorne protested (5th March 1672/3) Langhorne added that Triplicane was not one of the villages dependent on St. Thome. See also Talboy Wheeler, Vol. 1, Page 117, where Triplicane is mentioned by the Governor on 9-4-1681 as our own village and the neighbouring villages are distinguished.

In 1678 Master entered into negotiations with Golconda for renting the outlying villages of Egmore, St. Thome and Trivetore but they fell through.[30] Early in 1693, Sir John Goldsborough received a purwannah dated the 10th February from Nawab Asad Khan, the Moghul Vizier. "by which the towns Tandore, Persewacca, and Yegmore were granted to the company in the name of President Higginson, the English Governor of Chinnapatnam. Goldsborough decided however that no attempt should be made to improve the revenues until the gift was confirmed."[31] There were some difficulties about the actual British occupation of these villages and 'the trouble of having the occupation entered in the books of the Moghul Kanungos was compounded by the

Ibid, Page 119. "The Governor sent peons to Trivetore, Egmore, St. Thome and the other villages about us, declaring to the inhabitants that if they did not send in provisions and fuel as heretofore, they would suffer the same fate as Condore had done......"

30. *Love* Vol. 1 pages 402, 408, and 410. Master was prepared to pay the following rents:—San Thome with its villages of Pallacawrana, Nanmangalam, Olandur, Nandambawca, Mambalam and Sattevido for 1300 to 1500 pagodas; Trivetore and its dependent villages of Sattangawdo, Chedayamcuppam, Tandore, Yerradalacherry, Ernoar and Cartiwack for 900 pagodas and Egmore and its villages of Porishawaca, Pudupawca, Vepery, Keepawca, Chettypatta, Omanjacca, Lungabawca, Roshana, Buduro and Agaram for 670 pagodas. Pallacawrana is Pallavaram, Nanmangalam lies about 1¼ miles to the south east of Pallavaram (*vide* Lawford's map of 1861) Olandur is Alandur near St. Thomas Mount; Mambalam is the present Mambalam. Sattevido is not Satyavedu and is not identifiable. Sattangaudo is Sattangud about a mile to the south west of Thiruvettiyur. Chedayamcuppam lies 2 miles to the North West of Thiruvettiyur. Tandore is Tondiarpet. Yerradalacherry is very probably Aleundacherre mentioned in the purwanna which Dr. Browne obtained from Kasim Khan. Its present name is Elandacherry to the west north west of Sadayamcuppam at a distance of about 1¼ miles away from it and about 2½ miles to the north west of Thiruvettiyur. Ernur is Ernavur, a village about 2 miles to the north of Thiruvettiyur and about 2 miles south of Ennore. Kuttewaukam lies close to Ennore. Chettypatta is Chetpat; Omanjacca is Amjikere and Lungumbawca is Nungumbaukam. Agaram is on the Poonamalle High Road immediately to the west of Aminjikara, where the road crosses the river Couum. Roshana (bakkam) is marked on the 1 "map of Madras between the Teacher's College and the Collector's Office." (?) Buduro cannot be easily identified.

See also *Maclean* "Manual of Administration" Vol. 2 Page 274. Ernavoor is Yeravanore and Shaudium Cuppam is Shadayan Cuppam; both lie in the Saidapet taluk to the south of Madras. It is surprising why Maclean identifies them to the south of Madras inspite of the grant being for five northern villages and when there are places having the same name to the north of Madras near Trivetore and very probably, its dependent villages. If Maclean's identification is to be accepted, then how and why they are tributary to Trivetore would have to be accounted for. See also *Love,* Vol. 2, pages 285 and 289.

31. *Love* Vol. 1 Page 578; and Vol. 2 Page 105.

promise of an annual payment.'[32] After the British had entered into possession, Arasama Nayak basing his claims on a grant by Zulfikar Khan, son of the Vizier demanded the rendition, not only of Egmore and Pursewaukam but also of Triplicane. The Council resolved to resist this demand by force and applied to the 'Grand Vizier' who made a grant in 1693-4 over-riding that given to Arasama Nayak. It was as late as June 1720 when the Government undertook the administration of the three old villages of Egmore, Pursewaukam and "Tonderwood."

On the 7th August 1693, Dr. Brown on behalf of the Company obtained from Kasim Khan the Carnatic Nawab designate a purwanna for six villages to the north of Madras, viz., Trivetore, Sautungaud Shaudium, Cuppum, Ernavoor, Cuttewacaw and Aleundacherre. The Council thought it undesirable to enter into possession and though Cuttewacaw was separately granted by the Nawab in 1695, it was soon voluntarily relinquished. These northern villages did not pass into British hands until 1708.[33] Nawab Saadat Ullah Khan declined to restore the five villages, but the president resolved to take them by force. "On the 23rd September 1717 the President (Collet) took Trivetore and two other villages and on the following day Mr. Horden secured the remaining two. These five villages were subsequently let to Sunkurama for 12 years at 1200 pagodas per annum."[34] By promise of special concessions, Governor Collet, some time during the period 1717 to 1719, encouraged the immigration of weavers and painters to Trivetore. The settlers built themselves a new village on the south side of the town and named it Colletpetta (now disguised under the name Kalatipetta). When completed it consisted of 104 houses, 10 shops and a temple and contained 489 adult inhabitants.[35]

32. Journal of the M. G. A., Vol. 2, No. 3, pages 89 and 90.

33. *Love* Vol. 1 Page 578, and Maclean Vol. 2 Page 274 *Trivetore, Shattancawd and Kuttewaukam.* Sep. 25th 1708. Purwannah from Davood Khan. In Oct. 1713 Resumed by Nawab Saadat Oollah Khan, Jan. 5th, 1716, Firman from the Emperor cancelling the resumption and confirming the grant. 12th August 1765 General Moghul Firman. See also *Love* Vol. 2 Page 289. *Love* Vol. 2 Page 105. "From various indirect allusions, it appears that the possession of the five new villages (Lungumbauc, Varsalavada, Trivetore, Sautungudda, and Cuttevauca) was actually resumed by the native government in 1711. They passed permanently to the British however, under the Moghul's firman dated the 21st July 1717 and proclaimed on the 24th July 1717." It is interesting to note that the firman was first read in English and afterwards in Urdu and Telugu by the chief Dubash. It was not read in Tamil!

34. *Love* Vol. 2 Page 154.

35. Among these five villages it was only Vysurpady and Nungumbaukam which were ceded to the French as a part of the city of Madras. Trivetore, Shattancaud and Cuttivaukam were not so ceded. *Maclean*, Manual of Administration, Vol. 2,

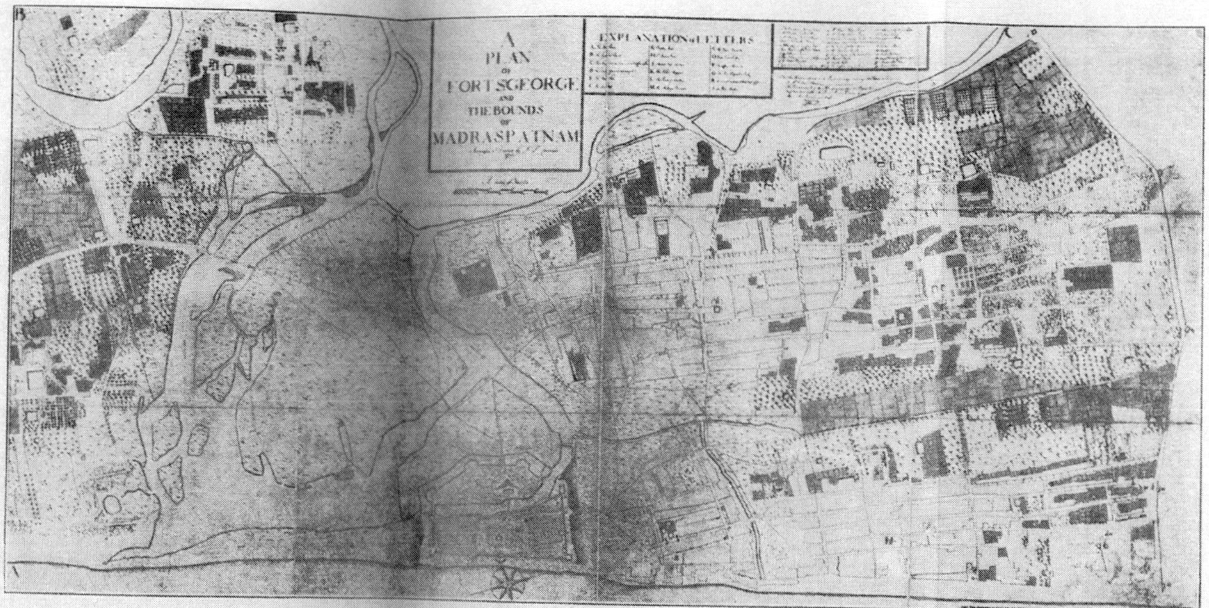
A
PLAN
OF
FORT S.GEORGE
AND
THE BOUNDS
OF
MADRASPATNAM
EXPLANATION of LETTERS

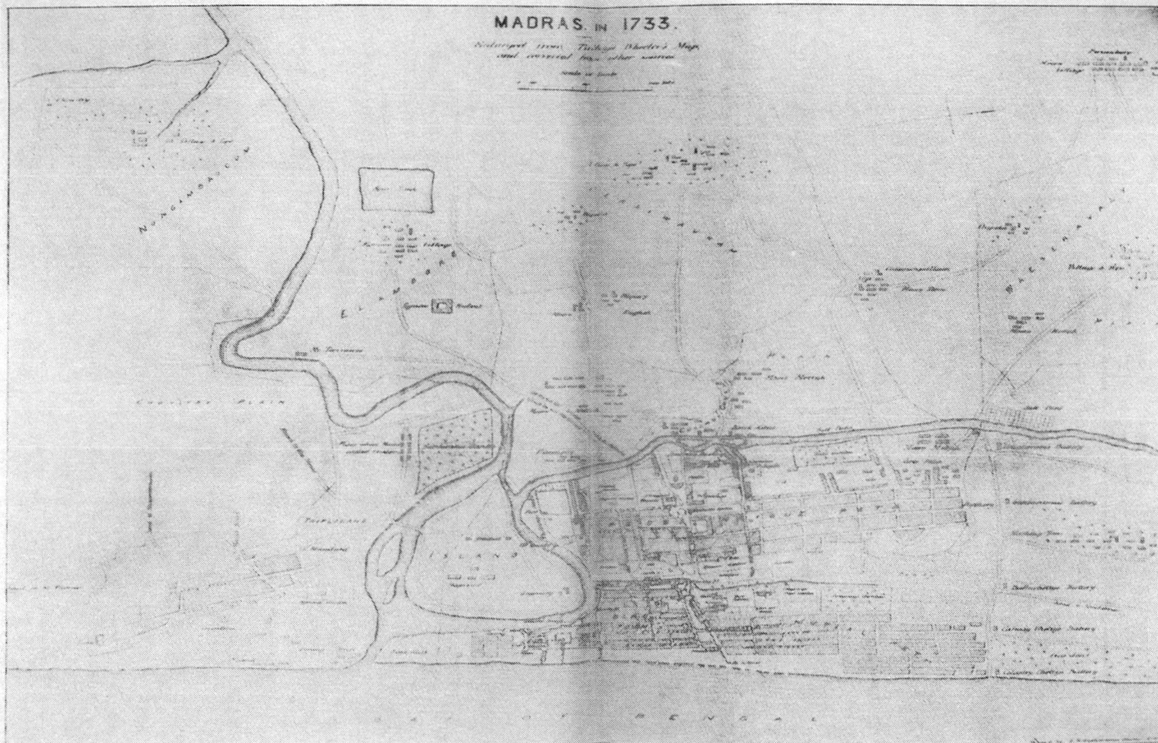
MADRAS. IN 1733.

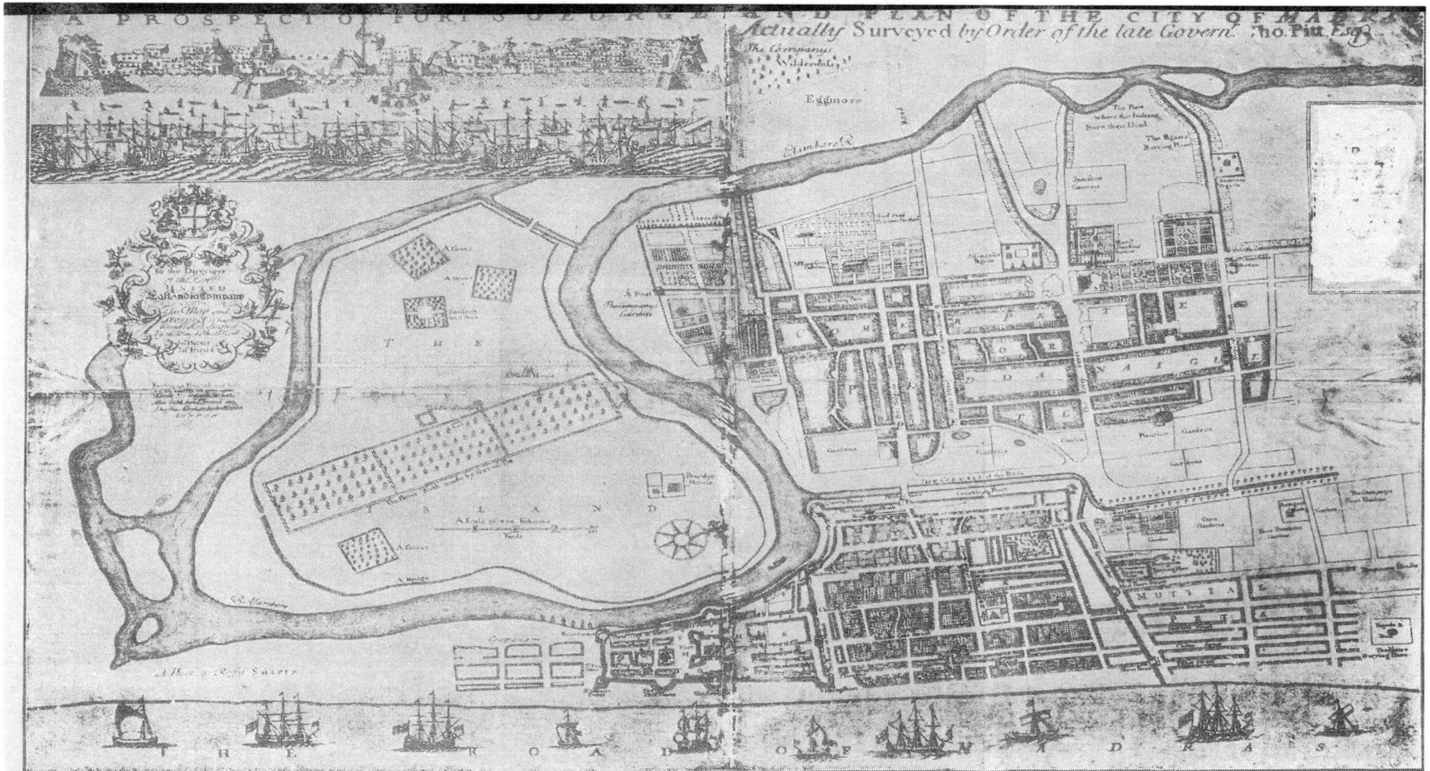
A PROSPECT OF FORT S GEORGE AND PLAN OF THE CITY OF MADRAS
Actually Surveyed by Order of the late Govern. Tho. Pitt Esq.
The Companys Wilderness
Eggmore
Elambore R
THE ISLAND
Eastindia Company
THE ROAD OF MADRAS
MUTTIAL
A Grove
A Scale of one Mile

The suburb of Chintadrepettah was founded as a weaver's village during the Governorship of Morton Pitt (1730-35). The Directors were complaining of the diminishing export of calicos from Madras and consequently Governor Morton Pitt determined to improve Calico printing in Madras by importing spinners and weavers. A site was chosen for their settlement in the peninsula formed by a loop of the Triplicane river which was originally the garden of Sunku Rama, the Company's Chief merchant (1724-31). The Governor felt that Sunku Rama's title to the garden was bad as the grant was made by Governor Collet without the consent of the Council, and without consideration. Only spinners, weavers, painters, washers and dyers were admitted to the new village and the inhabitants had to settle their disputes by arbitration. It was estimated that by the beginning of 1737, the population had nearly doubled itself as a consequence of immigration.

Wedged in between Pursewaukam on the North and West and Egmore on the South and Peddanaickpetta on the East was the village of Vepery (Ypre, Vipery) which still belonged to the Moghul Government. In 1695 the Council requested that the village may be granted on a rental basis, but the application was unsuccessful. "But it was only in 1742 that they received it from the young orphan Nawab Muhammad Said of Arcot."[36]

page 274. *Vysurpaudy* and *Nungumbaukam*, Sep. 25, 1708. Purwanna from Davood Khan, in October 1713 they were resumed by Nawab Saadat Oollah Khan. On January 5th, 1716, the Emperor cancelled this resumption and confirmed the grant. On September 10th 1746, they were surrendered to the French as a part of the City of Madras and on the 15th August 1749, they were delivered up under the treaty of Aix la Chapelle. On August 12th, 1765, the original grant was confirmed by the general Moghul firman.

[It is interesting to note that among these five villages, it was only Vysarpaudy and Nungumbaukam which were ceded to the French as a part of the city of Madras. Trivetore, Shattancaud and Cuttivaukam were not so ceded].

36. Journal of the M. G. A. Vol. 2 No. 3 Page 91 "...... by granting the English the five villages of Ernavore; Sadian Cuppam (both near Thiruvottiyur), Vepery, Perembore and Pudupauk as well as the right of coining Arcot Rupees and Pagodas." See also *Love* Vol. 2 Page 284.

Vepery, Perembore and Pudupauk. Sannad from Nawab Saadat Oollah Khan on 4th November 1742 granting by way of inam to the Company the three villages. They were surrendered to the French on Sep. 10th 1746 and were returned in August 1749. The grant was subsequently confirmed by the General Moghul Firman of 1765. Thus among the British possessions, Trivetore, Shattangaud, Cuttewaukam, Ernavur and Sadayan Cuppam were not surrendered to the French as they were probably not construed as a part of the city of Madras. Even to-day they are not.

It is conjectured that "a monastic settlement was formed at San Thome about 1522, that a town gradually grew up around the church, and that down to 1550, the place possessed little importance."[37] The rise of San Thome must have been very rapid, for it was a prosperous town by the time Caesar Fredrike visited it (1567) and within fifteen years Gasparo Balbi reported the existence of fortifications and several churches. Its golden age lasted only for a short spell due to foreign aggressions and domestic strife; and when the English settled at Fort St. George, "a large number of Portuguese, both home and country born deserted San Thome for Madras." In 1662, it came under the Sultan of Golconda and 10 years later came under French control. "The French occupation of San Thome which lasted a little over two years was one long period of beleagurement." It capitulated in August 1674 and was delivered by the Dutch to the Sultan of Golconda from whom the English subsequently tried to get a grant in perpetuity of the place. "When the Sultanate of Golconda was extinguished by Aurangazeb, they resumed negotiations for securing the place; and they had come very near to possession; but the fruit was snatched away from their hands at the last moment (1688)"[38] Daud Khan, the Moghul ruler of the Carnatic, who was generally hostile to the English proposed to develop San Thome at the expense of Madras and even constructed an earthern rampart around the town. Fortunately for the English, the Moghul Emperor would not give his assent to this scheme which thus ended in nothing. That the English looked upon San Thome with jealousy is evidenced by the persecution of a few Armenians who were suspected of a plan to establish a mercantile centre there; Coja Saffur, an Armenian was even confined in the Fort. San Thome continued to be under the Nawab of Carnatic until Boscawen hoisted the English colours on the 11th October 1749. The adjacent village of Mylapore is an old one and as early as the time of Governor Pitt, the English wanted to acquire it, but it was finally acquired only in October 1749. On August 12th 1765 the grant was confirmed by the general Moghul firman.

37. *Maclean* Manual of Administration Vol. 2 Page 91. "The town of San Thome now an integral part of the Madras City was founded and fortified by the Portugese in 1504 and was held by the French from 1672 to 1674. Sacked by Zoolfar Khan in 1698, it was occupied by the English in 1749 who expelled the French priests as political emissaries. See *Love* Vol. 1 pages 289-291. "It would appear that the Portuguese settlement of San Thome could not have been formed earlier than 1522. The erection of the neighbouring Franciscan Church of the Luz in Mylapore is attributed to 1516 on the authority of an inscribed stone......".

38. Journal of the M. G. A., Vol. 2, No. 3, Page 88.

Pitt's map of Madras.—The preceding account narrates in a more or less chronological order, how from very small beginnings, the city of Madras has grown up. The earliest reliable map is that of Pitt,[39] drawn about 1710/1 " which displays the true form of Cogan and Day's square bastioned fort, (the inner fort) and the shape of the White Town." Adjoining White Town is Black Town lying to the north of it and surrounded by walls on all sides except the East. The Cannal of the Pedda separated Black Town from 'Peddanaiguepetta,' otherwise called 'Comerpete' on the West and Muttialpetta on the north. Peddanaickpetta had several garden houses. The island surrounded by a hedge of thorny bushes[40] was then much larger than now and it contained the famous Pitt's Avenue leading to the Company's Garden with a fort in it. The map bears every indication of being the result of an accurate survey and it proves Fryer's conventional plan of 1691 (?) to be inaccurate. It also shows that no reliance can be placed on Langle's plan of Madras in 1688.[41] The Mint is shown in the position to which it was transferred in 1711 so that the map was drawn probably in 1711 or towards the end of 1710 when the new site of the Mint had already been chosen. In the Prospect of Fort St. George attached to the map low hills are shown in the back-ground. These probably are exaggerated indications of the higher ground in Peddanaickpetta which was subsequently called Hog Hill. Dr. Edward Bulkley died in 1714 and his tomb is (even now seen) at the edge of the present western Esplanade of Fort St. George, opposite the entrance to the Medical College Grounds. A comparison of Pitt's Map with a modern map shows that the doctor was buried in his own garden. This fact enables us to fix with precision the position of the Company's Garden House. It must have been located partly on the General Hospital Road and partly on the Medical College grounds. Further measurements show that the bank of the river, south of the garden House was at the beginning of the 18th Century, about 160 yards north of its present position. It is also interesting to note that

39. The title of the map is "A Prospect of Fort St. George and Plan of the City of Madras, actually surveyed by Order of the late Governor Thomas Pitt Esq." and therefore the map must have been drawn after 1709, as Pitt's Governorship was during the period 1697 to 1709. See *Love* Vol. 2 Page 89.

40. Official Hand Book of Madras, edited by F. E. James page 41. "It was during the period of Pitt's Governorship that the island ground was embanked, drained and improved." The embanking of the island was undertaken in 1705 and the garden was acquired by weavers for building purposes in 1706.

41. Langle's Plan of Madras (reproduced from *Love* Vol. 1 Page 540) can be compared to Pitt's map. The shape of the inner fort and of White town is true. Black Town has a surrounding hedge or wall and part of Paddanaickpetta is also shown. The details of the streets are inaccurate.

Black Town was entirely surrounded by a wall, the northern arm of which ran up to the sea.

In 1710/1 when the plan of the city was drawn, its limits were the 'Coupang' (Cuppam) to the south of the Fort, the river Elambore to the west, (the area lying further west being only the Company's wilderness) the outer hedge of the Island to the south-west while the northern boundary was indefinite. In the map, Elephant Street is the northernmost street in Peddanaickpetta and the northern bounds of the city did not extend beyond 200 yards of this street. Apparently Muthialpetta extended slightly further north—for about 500 yards north of Elephant street as is indicated by the Company's fruit garden. The eastern boundary was the sea represented by the Roads of Madras with 10 ships. The sea was close to the Fort and there was very little of the beach. Within the boundaries of this map would have been included every portion of the city and it is therefore correct to presume that these then were the City limits.[41a] Madras in 1711 was therefore very small and it had not absorbed into itself the outlying suburbs, even Triplicane, which on historical evidence is considered to have been under the possession of the Company from 1658 onwards.[42]

Talboys Wheeler's Map of Madras in 1733. [The original of this map was drawn on a scale of 2″ to a mile and it was enlarged and

41a. *Love*, Vol. I, Page 444. *Maclean*, Manual of Administration, Vol. II, Page 93, and Talboy Wheeler *Madras in Olden Times*, Vol. I, Pages 137-139 and 153. Even as early as 1698, a Corporation was established in Madras by Royal Charter. Its limits were:—"Our town of Fort St. George and City of Madrasapatam upon the Coast of Coromandel in East Indies and all territories thereto belonging, not exceeding a distance of ten miles from Fort St. George to be a Corporation under us ...." Although the limits are thus defined as early as 1698, it is interesting to see that the Corporation exercised no effective control over this region. On the contrary the Map of 1710/1 (also Maps of 1733, 1755, 1798, etc.) suggests that the City was much smaller.

42. See *Love* Vol. 2 Page 73. Salmon in 1699—1700 describes Madras as follows:—"The Fort stands pretty near to the middle of the White Town where the Europeans inhabit. The White Town is about ¼ mile in length and about half so wide. On the west part of the town runs a river close to the buildings, on the east, the sea comes up close to the Town and no large vessels can ride within 2 miles of the place. There is a little suburb to the south of the White Town inhabited only by the black waterman and the fishermen. Black Town lies to the north of the White Town and is more than 1½ miles in circumference; it has a river on the west (the Elambore river was further west) and the sea on the east and to the northward a canal is cut from the river to the sea. Beyond Black Town are gardens for half a mile together planted with mangoes, coconuts, guavas, orange trees (?) etc." The accuracy of the description is testified by the map.

redrawn for Col. Love on the scale of 1" to 800 yards, a copy of which is kept in the Madras Record Office. This reproduction is from Col. Love's map.] Its chief value lies in its indication of village boundaries. 'Muttaialpetta,' 'Pedda Naiguepeta,' 'the Choultry Plain,' 'Nungambaucum,' 'Elambore,' 'Persiwaukum,' 'Choonga Chuly plain,' 'Waseravaly,' 'Triplicane' and the Island are all marked. A comparison with Pitt's map of 1710/1, shows that (1) both Peddunaickpetta and Muthialpetta have extended northwards for a distance of nearly 1500 yards and the washing town has developed still further north ; (2) a boundary line is seen across the Island separating Fort St. George from Triplicane ;[43] (3) the Great Walk or Pitt's Avenue is omitted, but there is a Garden bridge connecting the Company's garden to the island.[44]

The various out-batteries of the defence of Black Town like Colastri Chetty's battery, Calway Chetty's battery, Balla Chetty's battery, Gonguerama's battery, Badriah's battery are all marked and these were connected together by a bound hedge of prickly pear and thorn bushes. In the map is also marked a number of Moors Mettahs—and the line joining these Mettahs could be construed as the outermost limits of the City in 1733. Nevertheless residences of the English are found outside the Mettahs, e.g., in Vepery, in Elambore, in Pudupet, in Puduppakkam etc., suggesting that the English had by then begun to move outside the limits of the city for residential purposes. The western portion of Muttialpetta and a good portion of Peddanaickpetta continued to be occupied by the garden houses of Europeans. Thus 200 years ago Madras existed on a scale far smaller. The Fort less than half its present size was the European town ; the native city since swept away,

43. *Love* Vol. 1 Page 382. The village boundary of Madras on the south embraced the greater part of the island. A portion of the Island belonged to the Company during the Governorship of Sir Edward Winter (1668). In the absence of a specific grant it is true to assume that it was included in the Naik's Cowle of 1639, because Neknam Khan's Cowle of 1672 implies that Madras territory remained the same in 1672 as it was in 1639 except for the addition of Narimedu.

44. *Love* Vol. 2 Pages 116 and 203. The Island bridge is marked connecting the fort with the Island grounds. This was first projected by Yale in 1690, but was not carried into execution ; and until 1715 the passage was made by boat. The original Island bridge was built in 1715, it was repaired in 1722 and was removed soon after the middle of the 18th century in consequence of the diversion of the stream. The Triplicane bridge linking the Island with Triplicane is marked on the map and was probably constructed along with the Island bridge (1715) and was rebuilt in 1721. The garden bridge was built on the 21st July 1718 across the Elambore river near the Company's garden house. It carried the direct road from Triplicane and the south to Peddanaickpetta. It was rebuilt in 1720 and it was removed some time subsequent to the siege of Madras.

was contiguous to it on its northern side. George Town was a sparsely populated suburb occupied by gardens and garden houses, the districts to the westward were marked by tiny villages, centres of agricultural areas, held by the company on precarious grants from the Government of the country, while everything south of Triplicane was native territory over which the British had no dominion.

Plan of Fort St. George and the bounds of Madraspatam by Conradi. [1755. Scale 60 yards to the inch or 29" to a mile approximately. Reproduced from a copy kept in the Madras Record office.]

A new survey of Madras was made in 1755 as a result of which this map was produced. It 'repays careful study as it marks the transition from ancient to modern Madras.'[45] The North river has a new channel connecting it with the Cooum where it bends to the east round the corner of the present General Hospital grounds thus making the Island ground truly an island. Its former course has been dammed up at either end of the White Town so that Smith's ditch has become the true western boundary of the fortifications and the old river bed forms a pond (clearly brought out in the map) in the middle of the Fort. The Company's garden house and other buildings in the Island have disappeared, but the Company's garden itself is shown as surviving in a portion (marked 8) with the note 'garden formerly of the Governor'. The map shows clearly the part of old Black Town destroyed by the French to a distance of 400 yards from the northern rampart. There is also an esplanade between old Black Town and Muthialpetta.[46] The Triplicane Bridge is marked clearly, but it is noteworthy that the highway from this bridge does not follow the present alignment of Mount Road. It actually passes 'behind the back of the Governor's new garden house'[47] just acquired from Mrs. Madieros.[48] The south bank of the river to the north west of Triplicane Bridge is devoid of buildings; it is in fact a marshy area intersected by streams. The houses in Napier Park are thus not of very great age as is commonly supposed. The Company's servants were acquiring building sites both in Egmore and in Vepery, but by 1755 Triplicane was the favourite suburb. Several garden houses are seen in Triplicane and the adjoining area; and

45. *Love* Vol. 2 Page 471.

46. Created by the demolition of houses at the time of the threatened Maratha incursion of 1740.

47. Governor's new garden house is marked 1 in the map.

48. *Love* Vol. 2 Page 463. On the 28th August 1753 the present site of the Government house was purchased, as the original garden house was demolished by the French. See also Asylum Press Almanack of 1936 Page 532.

Peddanaickpetta has ceased to be the fashionable European quarter. The only garden houses marked are those of Walsh and Franco. The southern boundary of Madras as depicted in the map is rather arbitrary; it is shown by a line running from west to east at a distance of about 1000 yards south of the mouth of the river Cooum in which sand bars are seen. The map clearly shows the northern boundaries by depicting the hedges. The western boundary is shown by the Elambore river in the northern half of the city, but in the southern half it is indefinite. Chintadripetta has become a part of the city. This map therefore indicates clearly that even as late as 1755, Purusawalkam, Vepery, Choolai and Vyasurpady had not yet been assimilated into the town; only a portion of Triplicane has become a part of the city.

In 1775 it was proposed that a bound hedge be planted right round the limits of Madras beginning from the Redoubt at San Thome along the borders of the San Thome river (Adyar) to Morse's Choultry (on Mount Road near Lushington Gardens) through the Long Tank round the village of Chittapet (Chetpet) to the Octagon (?) and Vepery and from thence to be continued to the sea at about a mile distant from the northern wall of Black Town. This project was then not carried out, but was revived by Popham 11 years later.[49] The extent of this projected hedge shows probably the limits of Madras in 1775.

Limits of Madras fixed on the 2nd of November 1798 by the Governor in Council when the Recorder's Court was established. (Drawn in 2 scales, 1″ to 1800′ and 1″ to 900′. Reproduced from the copies kept in the Madras Record Office.).

The limits of the city are very clearly shown in this map. The "southern limit shall be the southern bank of the 'Saint Thome' river (Adyar) as far as the road leading to the long tank, that the limits shall then be continued in a northern direction along the bank of the long tank and from thence along the bank of the Nungambaukam tank[50] as far as the village of Chettapet on the banks of the Poonamalle river (Cooum); that the limits shall be continued in the same direction to the villages of Kilpaukam and Perembore, and from the latter village it do take an eastern direction to the sea, so as to include the whole village of Tondiar; also that no lands situated to the south of 'Saint Thome' river or to westward of the bank of the long tank or of the

49. *Love* Vol. 3. Page 32. During the period 1755 to 1775, Madras territory got considerably enlarged to include within its limits, not merely Triplicane, but also, Mylapore and San Thome. Official Hand book of Madras. Page 134.

50. The tank of Nungambaukam was subsequently included in the city when Mambalam was acquired in 1923.

Nungumbaukam tank shall be considered within the limits of the said town of Madras; but that all the lands included in the said villages of Chettapet, Kilpaukum, Perembore and Tondiar shall be considered within the said limits."[51] These limits are more extensive than those depicted in the proposed bound hedge of 1775, (mainly towards the north). On a comparison with the maps of 1733 and 1755 it is seen that the limits have extended very considerably and the boundaries of the City of Madras as depicted in the map of 1798 very nearly correspond with those of the present day.[52] Thus at the beginning of the 19th century Madras City came almost to its present shape and extent even as the Presidency came to be finally formed. Black Town (the present George Town)[53] possessed almost the same limits as at the present day and its ramparts on the north and west are indicated. The North river was outside the ramparts and it has dwindled into a streamlet. The west wall of Black Town was skirted by a defensible tract of ground half a mile wide providing field for fire. There was no highway along the sea front; first and second line beach roads were nonextent. All the suburbs like Chintadrepetta, Triplicane, St. Thome, Mylapore etc. are shown. Chetpat and Kilpauk are dotted with residential quarters, but Nungambaukam and Teynampet extending as far south as the Adyar, were wholly under wet cultivation. In Triplicane the palace of the Nabob is seen and the suburb of Wallajapettah has grown up. The Triplicane High Road was the chief thoroughfare of Triplicane leading to San Thome. The Government House park was much smaller than at present and Mount Road is seen in its present alignment. The area between Triplicane and San Thome was filled with gardens and coconut groves. The acquisition by Europeans of land to the south west of the Fort for country houses and gardens was going on steadily. *Prima facie,* it may appear peculiar that these mansions lie inland and not on the shore. The Company's servants of the 18th Century longed for a change of scenery. They lived and toiled in the White Town where they saw enough of sea and sand. Originally a country house was not a permanent residence for its owner. It was designed for week-ends and holidays and its great feature was its garden. On the beach, fruit and flowers would not flourish. A second-

51. Gazetteer of Southern India published by Pharoah & Co., (1855), page 149; also *Love*, Vol. 3, Page 531 *et seq.*

52. Except that Theagarayanagar (Mambalam) has been included within the Municipal limits since 1923. The western limit of this extension is the South Indian Railway Line.

53. *Love* Vol. III Page 533. The name Black Town has now been changed to George Town in memory of the visit of His Majesty King George V then Prince of Wales and in deference to the sentiment of some of the inhabitants.

ary reason for the selection of the interior must have been the ease of communication. Along the sea shore there was no highway;[54] the thoroughfare from Triplicane to San Thome was half a mile from the shore. The principal highways from the Fort were Mount Road[55] leading to Chingleput and the south; and the road from Egmore to Poonamallee and the west.[56] From the early days of Madras, St. Thomas Mount had been a sanatorium and holiday resort and the route thither from the fort was a great thoroughfare.[57] As the British acquired the suburban villages, Peddanaickpetta lost popularity and Triplicane rose in favour as a residential quarter. Prior to the capture of Madras a group of country mansions had arisen on the south side of the Triplicane Bridge and when the Company purchased one of them for the use of the Governor, the area traversed by Mount Road was marked as the building ground for the future. The Company's servants were acquiring building sites both in Egmore and in Vepery, but by 1755 Triplicane became the favourite suburb.[58] From the first half of the 18th century Choultry plain became the favourite resort of the Europeans,[59] and by the beginning of the 19th century it became the

54. See F. E. Penny 'On the Coromandel Coast' Page 23. "As late as the beginning of the 19th century, the spray of the waves fell upon the old walls of Fort St. George and there was no driving road between the beach and the sea gate. In 1877 (?) the road had been made. As the building of the southern arm of the harbour progressed, the sea retreated throwing up broad stretches of sand behind it until now in the present day, the waves break more than half a mile from the spot where I passed through the surf."

See also 'T. Parry, Free Merchant' by *Hodgson*. Page 14. "All landings of both passengers and cargoes in those days were made opposite the sea gate of Fort St. George, the sea at that period (1787) breaking quite close to the fortification. It has now receded several hundreds of yards owing to the sand accretion caused by the southern arm of the Madras harbour. Twining in 1792 records that the water gate was not more than 50 yards from the sea.

Official hand book of Madras Page 55. The Marina was constructed by Sir M. E. Grant Duff (Governor 1881—86) and completed in 1885.

55. Mount Road was widened and remade in 1796. See Asylum Press Almanack for 1936 Page 531 and Official hand book of Madras Page 94.

56. "Poonamalle High Road and Mount Road were built mainly for military purposes. Official hand book of Madras, Page 51.

57. *Love* Vol. 2 Page 614. See also p. 231.

An Armenian merchant Petrus Uscan in 1724 rebuilt the great Marmalong Bridge which spans the Adyar River betwéen Madras and the Mount. Egmore bridge afterwards called the Metta bridge was built in 1703, it was washed away in 1716 and was rebuilt in 1728, now known as St. Mary's bridge.

58. *Love* Vol. 2 Page 493.

59. Pharoah's Gazetteer of Southern India, page 179. Choultry plain was to the west of Mount Road and it extended from Government House to just beyond the Cathedral. See "Parry, Free Merchant" by *Hodgson* Page 17. "Choultry plain

most fashionable residential area about Madras.[60] In 1780 Innes Munro estimated that there were between 500 to 600 garden houses in the Choultry Plain[61] but this is certainly an exaggerated statement. Thomas Twining in 1794, estimated that there were about 200 garden houses in the Choultry plain. This seems to be a fair estimate.

Plan of the Town of Madras and its Limits as surveyed in 1822 for the use of the Justice in Sessions by W. Ravenshaw. (Scale 8″ to the mile. Copy preserved in the Madras Record Office.)

The boundaries of Madras as depicted in this map are identical to those shown in the map of 1798. Hence it is true to assume that during the period 1798 to 1822 the City limits remained the same. It is interesting to notice that the Island has a much smoother outline. There is as yet no marina, Poonamalle High Road has become an important thoroughfare, but the bulk of Nungumbaukam and Teynampet continue to be under wet cultivation. An exhaustive list of buildings is given in a corner of the map. The Sea Custom house is marked in the position to which it was recently shifted.

Madras and Its Suburbs exhibiting the following limits, Medical, Police, Supreme Court, Collector of Land Customs, Taxing limits of the Municipal Commissioners. (Drawn originally on a scale of 4″ to the mile and copy preserved in the Madras Record Office.).

The limits of the Supreme Court correspond with the boundary of the city as delimited in Ravenshaw's map. (and thus also of 1798) and beyond these are the taxing limits of the Municipal Commissioners almost at the 10 mile limit from Fort St. George[62] and still further out is the Abkari limit, about 15 miles from the fort. It is interesting to note that these limits are more or less concentric around Fort St. George.

was that area lying between the Triplicane—San Thome road on the east and the Long Tank on the west and included the villages of Egmore, Nungumbaukam, Teynampet and Royapetta." See also *Hamilton* 'East India Gazetteer' (1815) Page 506 and 507.

60. This is evidenced by the construction of the Cenotaph the position of which is marked in the maps of 1798 and 1822. It was on Mount Road, just south of its junction with Eldham's Road practically opposite the R. I. A. S. Bakery. See Asylum Press Almanack of 1936, Page 535.

61. "T. Parry, Free Merchant" by *Hodgson* Page 17.

62. The charter of 1698 delimits the boundaries of the City as an area within a radius of ten miles of Fort St. George. Curiously the Madras University Act also defines the limits of the University in an identical manner. Maps before 1861 do not depict this boundary at all; even to-day the Municipal limits fall short of this.

The harbour is not shown on the original map though Prof. C. S. Srinivasachari makes a statement to that effect.[63] He would apparently date it after 1870. But the internal evidence of the map is conclusive in determining the date accurately. This map was prepared when Lt. Col. Lawford was the officiating Chief Engineer (see signature on the map) and when Calder, O'Heefke, Clinton, Suares and Winchester were lithographers in the Survey office. Lt. Col. Lawford retired in 1862 and acted as Chief Engineer in 1861. In addition, the Civil List of 1861 shows the lithographers in the same order of seniority as is shown in the map. (After 1862, it is seen that some of them have gone out and new officers have been recruited). It is therefore quite clear that the map was drawn in 1861. Again no feature is shown on the map which on other evidence is known to have come into existence after 1861.

The city of Madras has not grown up considerably since 1800; actually present-day Madras is larger than the Madras of 1798 only by the extent of territory it has acquired in 1923 in Mambalam. Nevertheless its population has grown up enormously. In 1763 it was estimated that Madras was a million city[64] but the Census of 1871 showed that the previous estimates were heavily erroneous. Accurate records of population are only available since 1871 and it is found that the city has been growing steadily in numbers since 1871, mainly through immigration. The next Census of 1941 may show that it is fast approaching the million limit, if it has not already reached it.

Although the City limits have remained more or less the same during the last 150 years, its urban development has not been the same in every direction. The City has developed much more towards the south and southwest rather than in any other direction due mainly to the better facilities of communication to the south and southwest. Nevertheless it is surprising that Basin Bridge is still unbuilt upon while Mambalam with identical conditions have become an important residential unit of the city.[65]

63. Journal of the M. G. A. Vol. 3 Page 106.

64. *Maclean*, Vol. 2, Page 92.

65. I wish to express here my most sincere thanks to Dr. B. S. Baliga, Curator, Madras Record Office and his staff, for their unfailing courtesy and promptness in placing at my disposal all the old maps of Madras; and to the Chief Secretary to the Government of Madras for kindly permitting me to reproduce some of these maps to illustrate this paper.

The Growth of the Population of Madras

BY

REV. C. W. RANSON, B.LITT.,
Kellet Institute, Madras.

SIR WILLIAM FOSTER described the earliest chapters of Madras history as " little better than blanks relieved by a few meagre facts and a number of doubtful statements." Careful and industrious research has since been devoted to filling in the blanks and correcting doubtful statements and there is now a fairly extensive literature on the general history of old Madras.

For the first two hundred and fifty years of its life, however, Madras did not concern itself overmuch with population questions. It was not until the late nineteenth century that census operations were seriously undertaken in India and for the period prior to 1871 we are dependent for our knowledge of the growth of the population of Madras upon estimates which, at their best, represent only informed guesswork and, at their worst, the wildest conjecture.

EARLY ESTIMATES OF POPULATION (1639-1871).

Within eighteen months of its foundation, Madras had become the chief factory and the headquarters of the East India Company on the Coromandel Coast. By the end of the seventeenth century it had achieved sufficient importance to be regarded as the chief British Settlement in India and the principal port for European and Indian goods. This striking commercial development suggests a rapid growth in the population around the Fort. Large scale trading operations are dependent upon the existence of a commercial community and there can be little doubt that as soon as the East India factors established themselves in Fort St. George they attracted the settlement of India traders, weavers, painters and dyers. The incentive provided by the prospect of trade was reinforced by the granting of a thirty years' exemption from taxes to those who settled near the Fort. It has been estimated that by the end of 1640 there were seventy or eighty substantial houses, presumably occupied by traders, on the northern and southern sides of the Fort, while a permanent settlement of about four hundred families of weavers had developed in the village of Madraspatnam.[1]

1. See Foster: *The Founding of Fort St. George,* note p. 16.

About thirty years later Thomas Bowrey (c. 1670) wrote an account of "the Countries Round the Bay of Bengal"[2] and described the "native inhabitants" of Madras as "for the most part Gentiles (commonly called Gentues) and Mallabars, many of which live within the outermost walls of this place called Fort St. Georg's." Then follows an interesting estimate of their numbers: "I have heard it reported and can well give credit thereto, that there are noe lesse than forty thousand of them, viz., men, women and children that live under St. Georg's flagge and pay customes for all sorts of goods they buy and sell within the compasse or command of our guns."

Another contemporary account of Madras has been given by a Cambridge man called John Fryer who visited Fort St. George about 1673. His travels are described in a "New account of East India and Persia" (1698). The number of English residents in Madras he calculated to be three hundred. The Portuguese, "who made Fort St. George their refuge when they were routed from St. Thomas by the Moors," he estimated at three thousand, and the Indian population at thirty thousand. Fryer has left an interesting description of the Settlement. After mentioning "the limits and conditions of the English town," he invites his readers to "pass the Pale[3] to the Heathen town." This is described as "dividing itself into divers long streets," which are "chequered by as many transverse." The houses "of less note" are "low and decent."

"Without the town grows their rice which is nourished by the letting in of water to drown it. Round about it is bestrewed with gardens of the English, where besides gourds of all sorts for Stews and Pottage, Herbes for Sallad, and some few flowers as Jassamin, for beauty and delight, flourish pleasant Topes of Plantains; Cocoes; *Guiavas,* a kind of Pear; *Jawks,* a coat of armour over it like an hedghog's guards its weighty fruit, oval without for the length of a span, within in fashion like squils parted; Mangos, the delight of India; a Plum, Pomegranets, *Bonanoes,* which are a sort of Plantain, though less, yet much more graceful, Beetle, etc."

It is to be noted that these descriptions of Madras belong to the period before the authority of Fort St. George extended to the numerous villages and small towns which surrounded it. Not until 1693 were Tondiarpet, Pursawalkam and Egmore granted to the Company. In 1708 and 1742 other villages, including Veysarpadi, Nungambakkam,

2. Ed. by Sir Richard Temple: 1905.

3. This seems to have been the name given to "the North Curtain of the Outer Fort". (See Love: *Vestiges of Old Madras,* Vol. I, p. 284, note 1.).

Pudupakkam, Vepery and Perambur were added to the jurisdiction of Fort St. George. But it was only in 1765 that the possession of these and other tracts by the Company was confirmed by a "firman" of the Mughal emperor.[4]

The population estimates of Bowrey and Fryer must, therefore, be taken as applying only to the Fort itself and the areas like Blacktown immediately adjoining it. This conclusion is confirmed by an examination of the map known as "Pitt's Prospect." The discovery by Colonel Love in the Bodleian Library at Oxford of an engraved copy of this early drawing of Fort St. George has added greatly to our knowledge of the early topography of the Settlement. Thomas Pitt was Governor from 1698 to 1709. His map indicates that by that time a fairly populous though compact town had developed to the north and west of the Fort, and from this built-up area a series of roads radiated to link up the satellite, but, as yet, detached villages of Triplicane, Nungambakkam, Egmore, Pursawalkam, Vysarpadi and Perambur.

By about 1683, Joseph Hearne, the Governor of Fort St. George, estimated the population of Madras at 400,000. There is no indication as to whether or not he included the population of the satellite towns and villages in this figure. But, however it was reckoned, this calculation was probably grossly inflated. In 1791 the population, which by then included the adjoining villages, was estimated at 300,000[5] and when the first scientific census was taken in 1871 the city had not reached the 400,000 mark.

Prior to 1871, quinquennial enumerations of population had been undertaken by the Government of Madras, but the accuracy of these calculations cannot be relied upon. In 1822 the estimate was 462,051, and of this figure the author of the 1871 Census Report remarks: "Probably the conicopolies (enumerators) were paid by the number of persons they were supposed to enumerate." As late as 1863, an ex-Governor, Sir Charles Trevelyan, informed the Royal Sanitary Commission that the people of Madras City numbered "not less than a million."!

THE CENSUS PERIOD (1871-1931)

The first scientific census was taken in 1871, and not until that date have we any population statistics on which it is possible to place reliance.

The 1871 Census Report on the City of Madras is the fullest and most detailed account of the city to be found in the whole series of

4. *Imperial Gazetteer of India,* Madras, Vol. I. p. 504.
5. See Love: *Vestiges,* Vol. III, p. 434.

these Reports. It is a matter for regret that the results of subsequent enumerations have not been presented with the same fulness.

In 1871 the population of Madras was found to be 397,552 and each subsequent decennial census has shown an increase in the population of the city.

GROWTH OF POPULATION (1871-1931)

Date	Population of Madras City.	Absolute decennial increase.	Per Cent decennial increase.
1871	397,552	..	..
1881	405,848	8,296	2·1
1891	452,518	46,670	11·5
1901	509,346	56,828	12·6
1911	518,660	9,314	1·8
1921	526,911	8,251	1·6
1931	647,230	120,319	22·8

Over the whole of this sixty-year period the growth of the city has been continuous, though the rate of growth has varied from decade to decade. This development has been the result, not of a natural increase in the population (i.e., an excess of births over deaths), but of migration to the city from other areas. Vital statistics in India are notoriously unreliable. But the figures, such as they are, show that in Madras city between 1891 and 1930 there was a total natural defect in the population (i.e. an excess of deaths over births) of 55,159, while during the same period the city increased by approximately 200,000 persons. It thus appears that something like 250,000 persons migrated to the city from other areas during the forty years prior to the 1931 census.

REASONS FOR THE CITY'S GROWTH

The rapid expansion of the urban areas around Fort St. George in the earliest days of the Settlement was, as we have already mentioned, due to the attraction of trade with the Company to Indian merchants and craftsmen. Contributory factors may be found in the thirty-year exemption from taxation which was offered to those who settled near the Fort, and in the civil security which the Fort afforded at a time of upheaval and disorder.

With the gradual assumption by the East India Company of governmental and judicial functions, the number of officials and their clerical assistants increased proportionately. Thus there grew up, in connection with the courts and the executive administration, a new professional class and a petty *bourgeoisie* distinct from the traders and craftsmen.

The nineteenth century brought to India the marvels of mechanical power and the methods of western education and both these factors exerted some influence upon the character of urban development in Madras.

The demand for the new education produced the Anglo-Vernacular schools from which the modern educational system, with the University at its apex, subsequently grew. This development of academic life added further diversity to the population of the city. The schools and colleges attracted a large student community and the profession of teaching grew proportionately in size and in importance.

The introduction of mechanical power brought about a change in the relative importance of Madras as an industrial and trading centre. The industrial revolution inflicted serious injury upon the indigenous industries on which Madras had flourished. The geographical position of the city and the absence of any convenient supply of fuel handicapped Madras in its industrial development under modern conditions. While Bombay and Calcutta forged ahead industrially, Madras lagged behind and soon yielded her former supremacy to these younger but more favourably situated cities. In the latter half of the nineteenth century large textile mills were established in the north west of the city. The growth of modern transport made Madras a port and a railway centre of importance, but the city has never become (and shows few signs of becoming in the near future) a highly industrialised unit. Whether the increasing use of electrical energy will result in any change in Madras' relative industrial backwardness it is impossible to predict.

It is clear that Madras, as a city, is not easy to classify. It is a seat of government and a centre of commerce. It is a sea-port and a university town. It contains modern large-scale factories and traditional handcraft industries. And it is not dominated by any one form of activity. The occupational distribution of the population is varied and, in the major occupations, remarkably even. Of every thousand male earners in the city in 1931, 32 were engaged in the service of the state and 32 in the textile industry, while 59 were employed in hotels and trade in foodstuffs and 41 in miscellaneous trade. 26 per *mille* were occupied in printing, 24 in making and selling jewellery and 23 in carpentry. While it is clear that trade-Madras' original *raison d' etre*—

occupies a majority of those citizens who are engaged in specialised activities, the work and interests of the city are notably diverse.[6]

The growth of modern cities is usually attributed to the centripetal influence of developing industry and trade, but in the case of a city of such varied character as Madras a single generalisation of this kind does not adequately account for the increase in population. The forces which have operated in the development of the city are, as we have seen, diverse and Madras clearly attracts many different types of migrant.

Since 1871 the percentage increases per decennium have varied from 1·6 to 22·8, and the student of urban problems is constrained to seek for reasons for this erratic growth in the population of the city. Why, for example, should the city have increased by only 8,251 between 1911 and 1921 and by 120,319 between 1921 and 1931? The former period included the war years with their stimulus to urban and industrial activity. The latter period covered the dramatic post-war slump in prices, the tentative recovery and the beginnings of the devastating "economic blizzard" which started to blow in 1930. We are here faced with a set of facts which do not support the conventional generalisation that the growth of cities is conditioned by industrial and commercial expansion. The volume of migration to Madras city appears to have been determined by factors other than the fluctuations of trade and industry within the city.

In this connection it is important to remember that the driving motives behind the migration to the city of large numbers of people may vary considerably. On the one hand, those who seek higher wages or ampler opportunities, facilities for education or the amenities which life in a highly organised urban community affords, may be *attracted* to the city. On the other hand, those who suffer unemployment and privation in periods of agricultural depression may be *driven* city-wards by sheer economic necessity and perhaps with only vaguest notions of what awaits them there.

An examination of the census figures in relation to economic conditions, as reflected in the movement of prices, reveals that, in general, migration towards the city has tended to accelerate during periods marked by low or falling prices and to slow up when prices are high or moving upwards.[7] The Census of 1931 revealed a phenomenal increase

6. See Census Tables: City of Madras, 1931, p. 16.

7. A detailed statement of this theory is to be found in *A City in Transition* by C. W. Ranson (C.L.S. Madras), pp. 57-74.

in the population of Madras. About the same time there was an alarming increase in the number of slums, hutting-grounds and *cheris* in the city, and in the number of homeless labourers and vagrants in the streets.[8] There is thus reason to believe that the rapid increase in the population of the city since 1921 has been, to a large extent, the result of the migration of despair. Depressed agricultural conditions induced by the precipitous drop in prices between 1921 and 1931 appear to have driven large numbers of landless Adi-Dravida labourers towards the city.

DISTRIBUTION OF POPULATION WITHIN THE CITY

Madras is sometimes described as "the city of magnificent distances," and is indeed unusually fortunate in the possession of many open spaces. There has been no geographical or administrative barrier to the horizontal expansion of the city and it has spread itself, with a lavish use of space, over an area of about 29 square miles. Madras has thus been happily spared the vertical, sky-scraping tendencies of some other large cities; and, given intelligent foresight and planning, there is no reason why lateral expansion should not continue without undue sacrifice of the city's precious heritage of abundant space.

The population is, at present, very unevenly distributed within the city boundaries. The most congested areas are immediately to the north and west of the Fort and are the older parts of the city. There is, on the other hand, an enormous semi-circular belt around these crowded areas where the density of population is exceptionally low. More than half of the area of Madras had less than 25 persons per acre in 1931. In five municipal divisions, excluding the Fort, the density did not reach 15 persons per acre. The census tables indicate a welcome tendency towards a decrease in those excessively congested divisions where there is a density of over 150 persons per acre and there is obvious need and abundant scope for a gradual redistribution of population within the city. It is certain that such a redistribution will not be confined to the present municipal limits. During the past twenty years or so there has been an increasing readiness to settle outside the city margins. This tendency has been encouraged by the growth of rapid and efficient transport. The advent of the motor bus and the electrification of the suburban portion of the South Indian Railway have greatly facilitated access to the city from outlying areas

8. The official census figure for "Beggars and Vagrants" was 1578 in 1931. A Corporation Census in 1933, discovered a total of 10,749 vagrants, beggars and homeless labourers.

and consequently stimulated suburban residence. In 1931 "the effective urban population of the Cooum and Adyar lower valleys" was "almost a lakh above the numbers confined within the actual city boundaries."

PLANNING A GROWING CITY

The facts recorded in the preceding paragraphs raise many practical problems which do not lie within the scope of this essay. But it may be permissible to conclude this brief record of the past with an even briefer plea for the future. The city of Madras has grown to immense proportions and its growth has been largely uncontrolled and unplanned. What Kipling wrote of Calcutta is, at least, equally true of Madras "chance directed, chance erected." The city, as it stands, is a product of *laisser faire*. There is much in the heritage of this city for which its citizens may well give thanks. But it seems certain that if what is worth preserving in that heritage is to be saved for the future there must be a resolute and carefully planned attack on the problems created by a growing population.

There are tens of thousands of citizens compelled to live in filthy and insanitary hovels. There are multitudes crowded in narrow and noisome streets. The housing developments of recent years have been mainly in the hands of the speculative builder and he has been subject to little restraint. The results do little credit to a great city.

A former Director of Town Planning, the late Mr. Reginald Dann, once said that he knew of no large city in India or the East where the problems of development and improvement were systematically and effectively attacked except through a special planning or development authority. The provision for a growing population, the preservation of Madras' most valuable amenities and their exploitation in the interests of the health and well-being of the city call both for intelligent and comprehensive planning by a special authority and unwearying vigilance and co-operation by the citizens.

The Site and Situation of Madras

By

B. M. Thirunaranan, B.A., Hons.,
Lecturer, University of Madras.

The foundation of Fort St. George was decided no less by geographical factors than by historical circumstances. The physical setting has profoundly influenced the entire history of human occupation of the site of Madras; but this has never been recognised properly, in spite of the fact that Madras has been, in the past, foremost in developing the geographical knowledge of the country.[1] This is mainly due to the neglect which geography has suffered in later years: that it was possible to complain, as recently as last year (1938), that "because of an inexplicable dearth of maps, we do not possess a reliable account of the topography of old Madras,"[2] only shows how low the subject has fallen from its former high estate.

The site now occupied by the city stretches nearly nine miles along the coast, from the River Adyar in the south to within a mile of the village of Tiruvottiyur on the north; it has a maximum width, east to west, of nearly three and a half miles, west of the mouth of the River Cooum, and covers an area of about twenty seven square miles. The town stands on a sandy plain, the lowest parts being from 2 to 6 feet, and the highest from 16 to 24 feet above mean sea level.[3] The average

1. See the Appendix to this paper on "Early Geographical Work at Madras".
2. C. W. Ranson: A City in Transition, 1938.
3. Mean Sea Level at Madras was originally taken from a bench mark on a stone fixed in the Escarp of the North Ravelin of Fort St. George. On the stone is the following inscription: "Mean Level of the Sea from May to October, six feet ten inches below this Line which answers to the Tide Gauge mark. Ascertained in 1821 by Major de Havilland, Acting Chief Engineer." These tidal observations were among the earliest to be made in India.

The Office of the Tidal Observations of the Survey of India have redetermined sea level values at Madras by means of Tidal observations made between 1880-'89, and 1895-1920. As a result of these, Indian Spring Low Water, which is a compromise between the heights of the lowest tides of the dry and wet seasons, is now stated to be 16·57 feet below a bench mark cut on the 3rd step on the east side of Lord Cornwallis's fountain, and Local Mean Water Level is 14·63 feet below the same bench mark. A comparison of the observations at Madras during 1880-89 with those of de Havilland in 1821 has shown that the mean sea level at Madras in 1881 was

level of the whole of Madras may be taken at from 8 to 12 feet above this datum. In some places the strata consist almost entirely of sand, but are generally of alternate layers of sand and clay. Water is found in all parts at a few feet above or below mean sea level, and during the rainy season all those areas less than 8 feet above the datum are liable to be flooded.[4]

Except the western part of the city, no single neighbourhood is altogether elevated above others. In each there are high and low portions which differ from each other in height from 8 to 16 feet, but in all the districts the lowest parts are nearly on a dead level with each other. The lowest streets in San Thome, Triplicane, Chintadripet, Egmore, Vepery, Purasawakkam, George Town, Royapuram and Tondiarpet, are, in each instance, from 4 to 7 feet above mean sea level. Each district, however, has its ridges and valleys, and the surface relief of Madras is best described by treating them separately.[5]

The area included within the city's limits may be divided in the first place into two parts separated by the Cooum river. The northern part may be sub-divided into three sections, *viz.,* (i) north of the M.S.M. harbour branch railway line and east of the Buckingham Canal; (ii) south of the railway and east of the Canal; and (iii) the area west of the Canal. The Island in the Cooum and the adjacent Chintadripet area lying within the loop of the river are quite distinct in many ways and may therefore be described separately. The part of the city lying south of the Cooum river can also be sub-divided into three sections. There is first a strip along the coast about a mile or a mile and a quarter in width from the

about 1 foot lower relatively to the land than it was sixty years previously. It may also be noted here that there is a seasonal change in sea-level, ranging from 0·5 of a foot below I.S.L.W., in March to 0·6 of a foot above I.S.L.W., in November and December.

The datum adopted for the drainage levels is 20 feet below the G.T.S. datum.

4. Statement by the Commissioner of the Madras Corporation, based on a report by the Chief Engineer for Irrigation, Madras.—*Madras Mail*, 28th October 1938.

The main outlet to the sea of the surface drainage of the city is the Cooum; the water-level in the river rises, whenever its mouth in open, to a height of more than 4 feet above mean sea level, as a result of the inflow of sea-water during high tides; the large inflow of water during spells of heavy rain is apt to raise the water-level still further, sometimes nearly 3 feet above what the level was before the rainfall. It will thus be evident that areas less than 8 feet above mean sea level are liable to flooding because the combined effect of high tides and heavy rainfall raises the water-level to that height.

5. The description of the surface relief is based mainly upon the contour map. Much help was also derived from the excellent account of the physical features of the area covered by the city, in Captain H. Tulloch's "Report on a Project for the Drainage of the Town of Madras", 1865.

shore line: between this coastal strip and the Mount Road beyond the Cathedral, where it runs more or less parallel to the shore, is another belt also about a mile in width, where the ground rises gradually towards the west. Beyond this, west of the Mount Road, is the recently developed Mambalam area; here the principal feature is the extreme flatness of the ground, which was formerly the bed of a large tank.

The first section comprising Royapuram and Tondiarpet, is that part of the city which lies north of the M.S.M. railway line running from Basin Bridge Junction to the Harbour, and between the Buckingham Canal and the sea. A ridge half a mile broad, and from 12 to 15 feet above sea level, runs north to south, midway between the canal and the sea, and slopes gradually down on either side. The sea has eroded the coast north of the Harbour and has cut into this ridge, forming a sandy cliff about 8 to 10 feet in height at Casimode, just beyond the revetment which has been built along the coast to check the erosion. The rate of erosion has been greatest here, averaging about thirty feet inwards annually, since the harbour was built in 1881. Nearly four hundred acres of land have thus disappeared during the last 58 years; but this is offset by the accretion of sand at the rate of a million tons yearly, which has added an area of about 450 acres on the southern side of the harbour.[6]

The next section, bounded by the railway line on the north and the Cooum river on the south, is also between the Canal and the sea, and comprises George Town and the Fort. In George Town there are two ridges running parallel to each other and almost due north and south; Popham's Broadway, 6 to 8 feet above mean sea level, is the valley line between these ridges. From the First Line Beach, which is 11 to 12 feet above the datum, the ground rises to the west for about a quarter of a mile until the crest of the first ridge is reached, which is over 20 feet high at its northern end, where the Katchaleswarar Temple is situated, at the end of Thambu Chetty Street. From this ridge the ground slopes downwards to the west for another quarter of a mile as far as the Broadway. The ground then rises westwards for about a third of a mile until the second ridge is reached; the Mint Street runs

6. These details concerning the erosion and accretion along the coast were given by Mr. G. P. Alexander, the Madras Port Trust's Engineer, from a paper which he is preparing on the problem of the sand accretion in relation to the Madras Harbour. Previous discussions of this problem as it affected the harbour are found in

(i) Official Papers concerning the Construction of the Madras Harbour, arranged by A. T. Mackenzie, 1902, and

(ii) Sir Francis Spring's papers in the Proceedings of the Institute of Civil Engineers, Volumes 190, 194, 205, 206, and 210.

along its crest, which varies in height from 13 to 20 feet. From the Mint Street, the ground slopes more steeply to the west towards the Canal, for about a quarter of a mile.

The Fort is situated at the southern end of the ridge facing the sea, and the area enclosed by it has a general slope towards the west, i.e., towards the Cooum. This ridge has a cliff-face along its eastern seaward side, varying in height from 3 to 4 feet in front of the Fort. The cliff can be traced south of Cooum also; the Marina Road runs on top of the cliff, and the footpath parallel to it (the Lover's Walk) is just east of the base of the cliff-face, which ranges from 3 to 5 feet in height.

These cliffs show that the sandy ridges along the coast have been eroded by the sea to some extent. This eroding tendency of the sea is further substantiated by the fact that groynes and revetments had to be built along the sea-face of Black Town and the Fort as well as along the Triplicane Beach to protect the coast from erosion. Major de Havilland built one such revetment along the coast at the beginning of the 19th century, running the entire length of the sea-face of the Fort and Black Town, and this structure was called after him "de Havilland's Bulwark": the present Beach Road in front of the Fort runs on top of it in places. A number of groynes are also found marked on some of the old maps of Madras, e.g., in the Illustrated Map of Madras, 1866 (Higginbotham's), five such groynes are shown south of the Cooum, and in another map dated 1869, several groynes are shown in front of the Fort also.[7] Some of these structures are still visible in front of the Fort and the Senate House, where they project above the sand accretion.

Two distinct phases in the development of the shore-line are revealed by these physical features. In the first phase the sea withdrew, and on the beach which thus emerged the sand was piled up into ridges and hillocks by the action of wind and waves. In the next phase the sea attacked the ridges and partly eroded them; the low cliffs facing the sea are evidence of this destructive phase. It must not, on this account, be assumed that the level of the sea has altered relatively to that of the land at every phase. The destructive and constructive phases show mainly that the form of the shore is not yet adjusted to the physical forces at work upon it; in other words, the shore-line is still in an immature stage of evolution.

7. The originals or exact copies of these and other old maps of Madras are preserved in the Madras Record Office. Several of these old maps have been published on a much-reduced scale in Love's "Vestiges of Old Madras", Talboys Wheeler's "Madras in the Olden Time", and in the Journal of the Madras Geographical Association, Vol. 8.

In the western portion of the city which lies north of the River Cooum, the surface relief is so different in its northern and southern sections that we can conveniently divide the whole area into two parts lying north and south of a line drawn westwards from the Custom House facing the Harbour. The larger part of the northern section is so low that it is periodically submerged; hence this is also the least populous part of the city, and the large vacant areas have attracted factories to this part of the city. The ground is less than 12 feet above mean sea level over most of this area, and it is only in the extreme west that there is a narrow strip less than half a mile broad in which the level increases westwards.

In the southern section there is a steady rise westwards from the People's Park adjoining the Buckingham Canal, and the surface is also more uneven, compared to the northern section already described. Only a small area adjoining the Park is so low as to be liable to flooding, and elsewhere the uneven surface combines with the increasing elevation to make drainage easy. The surface drainage divides into two main streams, separated by a ridge whose crest is marked by the Purasawakkam High Road. North of this ridge the surface drainage collects in a valley which runs south-west to north-east and eventually reaches the Buckingham Canal. This line of drainage is quite distinct from the Oteri Channel which lies north and west of it. The surface drainage of the area lying between the Purasawakkam ridge on the north, the Spur Tank on the west and Egmore on the south, collects together in the Vepery division and flows into the Cooum at the north-western part of the meander enclosing Chintadripet.

The Island in the River Cooum, and the area west of it occupied by Chintadripet in the loop of the river, are both very low-lying and more or less liable to flooding. The Island is extremely flat and is less than 5 feet above mean sea level, except in the extreme western part where the European cemeteries are situated. It is nearly always converted into a sheet of water during the spells of continuous and heavy rain which are common during the rainy season. A large part of Chintadripet is also very low-lying, especially the northern portion adjoining the Cooum, and the neck of the peninsula.

The river used formerly to cut across the neck by overflowing its eastern bank near where the Harris Bridge is now, and then following a course roughly parallel to the Mount Road and west of it, more or less along the line of Narasingapuram Street. The soil is consequently unstable in this locality and hence many of the older buildings in this street have become tilted and cracked as a result of the subsidence of their foundations. The diversion of the Cooum across the neck of the meander which encloses Chintadripet was greatly aided by the inflow of the surface drainage of Vepery at the north-western part of the loop. This tended to hold up the water in the river above this point, and the impounded waters used to overflow readily across the low-lying neck. There was a well-defined channel across the neck about the middle of the 18th century, as is shown in Conradi's map of Madras, dated 1755. This channel was the chief means of escape for the waters of the Cooum during the last quarter of the 18th century, when the meander became silted up just below the bend where the Vepery drainage entered it, as is shown in Dalrymple's map dated 1778, and also in the map of the Limits of Madras in 1798, when the Recorder's Court was established. By the beginning of the 19th century, the river banks seem to have been raised and strengthened, and the waters confined to the bed of the main stream; but the channel across the neck of the meander continued to exist as a stagnant ditch (Ravenshaw's map, 1822).

In the southern part of the city the most varied relief is found in the coastal belt, which consists of a series of three sand-hills alternating with depressions. At the northern end of the belt is a low, flat-topped ridge which extends along the Marina, from near the mouth of the Cooum, as far south as the Presidency College. Adjoining it on the south is a depression, which is now occupied by the Presidency College sports ground and the Wenlock Park, but was formerly the bed of a small stream which had been the outlet to the sea for the drainage of this part of the city.

South of this depression is the second ridge, which culminates in the hillocks on both sides of the Ice House. This ridge turns inland at its northern end and runs in a northwesterly direction for more than half its length; and it is on the western side of its northern end that the Parthasarathy Temple in Triplicane is situated. This ridge overlooks the wide depression between Triplicane and Mylapore which was drained by two other minor streams. Their former courses can still be traced, one between the Ice House ridge and the Queen Mary's College, and the other further south, in the burial ground at the south end of the Marina. None of these three depressions drain to the sea any longer, because the city has a system of underground drainage; besides, it was impossible for these small streams to keep their outlets to the sea open across the rapidly growing sand accretion, for they used to be shut off from the sea for about ten months in the year, by the sand bars which closed their mouths even before the harbour was built[8].

The third and southernmost of the sand-hills is the ridge on which a large part of Mylapore and San Thome have been built. It rises to a

8. W. Clark: Drainage of Madras, 1875.

maximum height of 24 feet, and runs inland almost east to west: in both these respects it is very different from the other two hillocks of this coastal belt. The crest of the ridge corresponds more or less to the line of the Luz Church Road, and ends abruptly in a sandy cliff east of the San Thome Cathedral, about 6 to 8 feet in height. This cliff is further evidence of the coastal erosion already pointed out. The old Luz Church is situated at the western end of this ridge, and the Mylapore temple is nearly midway between these two churches and on the southern side of the ridge, overlooking the valley of the Adyar.

Adjoining the coastal belt on the west is a tract ranging from 8 to 20 feet above mean sea level and rising uniformly and gradually westwards. Most of this tract was under cultivation till recently, and large parts of it are still agricultural. The soil is clayey in most of this area, and clay beds occur at various depths everywhere in this belt, in the same way as they do in several other parts of Madras.

The sand ridges along the coast and the lower level of this inner clayey lowland suggest that this area must have been a marsh originally, which has been filled up and reclaimed by the sand and clay beds deposited in it, under alternately wet and dry seasonal conditions similar to those prevailing now—the sand being blown in from the shore by the wind during the dry season, and the clay being brought down during the rainy season by the streams flowing into the marsh. Organic remains are found abundantly in some of the clay beds, and pockets of marsh gas have also been discovered[9]. Marshy conditions favourable to their formation very probably existed in the past, when this part of the coast was occupied by a lagoon similar to those existing even now at Pulicat and Ennore. The former existence of a lagoon is conclusively proved by the fossil shells found in these clay beds, which belong to living species characteristic of estuarine conditions[10].

9. These pockets of marsh gas are probably formed by the decomposition of organic matter in the clay. They have been pierced by well-borings occasionally, and the resulting escape of gas has revealed the existence of the pockets. One such instance in Mylapore was reported in "The Hindu" a few years ago, and there were many wild speculations about it in the local papers; but the escape of gas stopped in a few days.

10. These fossils were collected from a bed of exceedingly sticky, black clay about 2 feet thick, occurring at a depth of 18 to 20 feet below the surface, in wells sunk in houses in Haddow's Road, Nungambakkam. Seven different species are represented by the specimens collected, of which six were provisionally identified by Mr. P. G. Dowie, Assistant Professor of Geology, Presidency College, Madras, as living forms, one of which (Arca sp.) prefers salt water, and all are marshy or estuarine species, i.e., capable of living in fresh and salt water alike.

The lagoon must have existed in geologically recent times to enable these living forms to become fossilised in the clay beds deposited in it. The marshy conditions seem to have persisted well into historic times, as is suggested by the relatively late human occupation of the whole of this area, and specially by the nature of the land utilisation. The lagoon must have come into being only after the formation of the off-shore bars, which became coastal ridges when the lagoon was filled up and reclaimed. The disappearance of the lagoon may have been brought about by any or all of the following causes; (a) uplift of the land, and consequent draining of the lagoon into the sea; (b) deposition of material in the lagoon, raising its bottom ultimately to the same level as the adjacent dry land; (c) diminution of the water flowing into it, causing the lagoon to dry up eventually. If there had been any uplift of the land after the formation of the lagoon, it would have led to (i) the formation of a more or less wide beach east of the sandy ridges which separate the lagoon from the sea, and (ii) the rejuvenation of the streams in this area, and consequent deepening of their channels. There is no such evidence, but instead, we find that the Cooum has been raising its bed level in the lower reaches by depositing sediment: it is therefore very unlikely that there has been any local regional uplift of the land in this part of the coast. The deposition of material in the lagoon has been described already as the chief cause of its disappearance. There was also a decrease in the volume of water flowing into the lagoon, when the Palar shifted its course from the Cooum channel to its present more southerly course, less than a thousand years ago.[11]

Lastly there is the Mambalam area west of the Mount Road, which has been included within the municipal limits and developed as an extension of the city within the last twenty years. This area was formerly a tank, and possibly the water of the Cooum used to overflow across it southwards from near Aminjikarai, into the Adyar. In fact, a proposal was once made many years ago, to take advantage of the favourable slope of the ground in this area to connect the two streams by a channel, and by this means divert the floods in the Cooum. This tract is extremely flat, and is therefore difficult to drain, even though it is more than 20 feet above mean sea level. The heavy clay soil, deposited formerly

11. The evidence of this change in the course of the Palar and the probable date of its occurrence have been discussed in "The Rivers of the Palar Basin", Journal of the Madras Geographical Association, Vol. 13. The Cooum is known as "the old Palar" at Tiruverkadu, a village two miles north of Poonamallee and close to the river (p. 227, *Sivasthala Manjari*, in Tamil, edited by V. T. Subramanya Pillai, Madras, 1931). This recognition of the change by local tradition seems to corroborate the relatively late date suggested for it.

when this area was the bed of a tank, makes the problem of drainage even more difficult by not allowing the rain-water which collects on the surface to soak into the soil.

The main features of the site of Madras are therefore typical of an immature emergent coast-line, and four stages can be distinguished in its development. In the first stage, the sea withdrew, and the off-shore bars and other sand-hills and ridges were formed. The lagoon came into being in the next stage, when the offshore bars had grown sufficiently to separate it from the sea. The filling of the lagoon forms the third stage; the end of this stage possibly overlapped the beginning of the fourth, *i.e.*, the latest stage, in which the sea has tended to destroy and thus remove the coastal ridges formed during the earlier phases.

The swampy conditions seem to have persisted long enough to restrict all early human settlements to the relatively higher sites provided by the sand-hills. All the old and important temples have been built on them[12]; and since temples are generally placed in conspicuous or focal positions in relation to the neighbouring human habitations, the early settlements must have also been on these sandy ridges. This is further borne out by the close network of narrow streets in these higher areas; the alignment, along the ridge of each locality, of its main thoroughfare, *i.e.*, its High Road, which is therefore literally a "high" road[13]; and the name of Triplicane, which perpetuates the earlier marshy conditions.[14]

The first inhabitants of these early settlements on the sandy margins of the lagoon must have lived mainly by fishing, and agriculture probably came later, when the lagoon had been filled up and drained sufficiently to allow the exposed parts of its clayey bed to be cultivated. But since these cultivable areas were at lower levels and therefore

12. The Kapaleeswarar temple in Mylapore, the Parthasarathy temple in Triplicane, the Perumal temple in Egmore, the Gangadhareesvarar temple in Purasawakkam, and the temples of Ekambareesvarar, Kandaswamy, and Katchaleesvarar in George Town are all built on such elevated sites. The original site of the Chennakesava or Town Temple was also of this type, and overlooked the valley of the stream which formerly flowed along the Broadway.

13. The High Roads of Vepery, Purasawakkam, Egmore, Nungambakkam, Triplicane and Royapettah are all of this character, and may be compared to the High Streets of English towns. The Poonamallee, Perambur and Tiruvottiyur High Roads are the main roads leading to those places and are comparable to the highways of England, such as the Dover Road and the Bath Road.

14. "Triplicane" is the corrupt Anglicised form of the Tamil name, Tiruvallikkeni = Tiru+alli+keni, which may be translated as "Beautiful water-lily pond".

liable to floods during the rainy season, the farmer folk must have also made their dwellings on the same sand-hills on which the fisher folk had already settled. In the early days of the spread of agriculture in this area, the farmers must have been in a minority in these settlements and therefore obliged to get the consent of the fisher folk, who were not only older inhabitants of the settlement but also in a majority, for building their temples and celebrating their festivals. It is likely that this consent was more readily obtained when it was made profitable for the fishermen to give it. The fishermen of this part of the coast have probably derived in this way their right to participate in the festivals of some of these important temples.[15]

As the lagoon dried up further, the farmers probably grew in numbers and influence: at the same time the fishermen were forced more and more to seek their "harvests" in the sea, and in some cases they abandoned their houses in the old villages and settled themselves nearer to the sea. These new "fishing" villages or "kuppams" were naturally named after the original villages from which their inhabitants came, *e.g.*, Tiruvottiyur and Tiruvottiyurkuppam, and Triplicane and Parthasarathy Kuppam, named after the temple of Parthasarathy in Triplicane.

Till European advent brought with it two other new occupations, *viz.*, trade and industry, the site of Madras remained in the occupation of these small, more or less separate communities of farmers and fisherfolk. The fishermen lived by the sea, while the farmers cultivated the clayey lowland tracts; and thus the extensive sandy ridges in the northern part of the town remained unoccupied till Fort St. George was built. The narrow sandy strip between the sea and the northern arm of the Cooum river was selected as the site of the Fort, because of the natural facilities for defence which it possessed, in having water on three sides. The easiest access to the Fort was from the north, and hence the many merchants and weavers, who were attracted by the prospects of trade with the English factory to settle near the Fort, found it most convenient to establish themselves on the adjacent sandy tract. And thus it has happened that this area, which had been, till then, the least populous and least important part of the

15. During the festivals at the Katchaleesvarar temple in George Town, the Parthasarathy temple in Triplicane and the Tiruvottiyur temple, the gods are carried in procession by the fishermen, and they are entitled to certain "honours" on such occasions.

This mingling of the communities can, however, be explained quite differently, as another example of the widely prevalent tendency in South India, of originally distinct religious customs and beliefs of different communities to merge into a common celebration of the same festivals and common worship of the same deities.

site of Madras, became the most populous part of all soon after the Fort was built, and eventually the heart of the city.

The growth of Madras into one of the major cities of India is more clearly understood when it is considered in relation to its geographical situation. The factory at Madras was built by the English merchants who had already settled at Masulipatam and experienced there the disadvantages of having a too powerful and extortionate neighbour. The site was fixed after several trials elsewhere on the Coromandel coast, between Masulipatam and Madras. These attempts were doomed to failure, because this part of the coast, between the deltas of the Kistna river and the Palar[16], is narrow, infertile, thinly populated and backed by several parallel mountain ranges which greatly hinder communications with the interior. The success of the factory at Madras was doubtless due to the fact that the English found here more favourable conditions for peaceful trade than had existed at Masulipatam. It is clear, from the terms of the grant made to the English and the letters which Day wrote to explain his action, that the establishment of the English factory and the growth of their trade were as ardently desired by the local chieftain, Damarla Venkatadri, for his own benefit, as the factors at Masulipatam did for theirs. Nevertheless, the English trade at Madras would not have grown any more than it did at Armagaon, if Madras had not been situated on the seaboard of the Palar delta.

The lower Palar basin is one of the principal subdivisions of the Tamil region, and by virtue of its regional individuality, it has been traditionally known as Tondaimandalam[17] among the people of the Tamil region. Many towns have flourished in this fertile region in the past, as capitals of the early Tamil kingdoms, pre-eminent among them being Conjeevaram. The city-sustaining capacity of this region is also illustrated by the growth of Arcot and Vellore in later times, under the Vijayanagar and Muhammadan rulers. Madras has inherited these potentialities for city growth which Tondaimandalam possesses, and has

16. The term "Palar delta" is used here to include the delta proper as defined in the "Rivers of the Palar Basin" and also the younger coastal plain which has been formed east of the former seaboard of the delta as a result of the emergence of the land.

17. The traditional use of the term Tondaimandalam and the extent of this region are discussed in the "Traditional limits and Sub-divisions of the Tamil Region", Proceedings of the 26th Indian Science Congress, 1939.

The situation of Madras in Tondaimandalam is very precisely stated in a gift deed (1640 A.D.) executed by Bari Thimmanen, who was employed as Native Head in the affairs of the Company, in which he is described as residing at "Chenna Puttanem alias Navyer Nattoo, attached to Pulul Cottai of Sholavala Nattoo, under Thondamundalum."

grown in recent times even at the expense of the older towns of this region. The population statistics of Madras, Conjeevaram and Vellore, since the first census in 1871, show a continuous and large increase at Madras, while both Vellore and Conjeevaram have declined in numbers, especially during the last thirty years. Their decline can be attributed more definitely to the growth of Madras, because some of their trade was diverted thither, and their industries declined *e.g.*, the weaving and metal-working at Conjeevaram, because they were unable to face the competition of the cheap mass-produced articles imported by way of Madras. These imports which were harmful to the local industries of these towns benefited Madras by adding to its trade.

The rise of Madras as a political capital is also explained by its situation. It is a "port of entry" of a maritime power, *i.e.*, the point where the naval power gained a foothold on the mainland. The other European trading posts on this coast, such as the Dutch factory at Pulicat, the Portuguese settlement at San Thome, and the English, French, Dutch and Danish settlements along the seaboard of the Kaveri delta, are all similar "ports of entry." Such ports are distinguished from other seaports by their purpose and function; the "port of entry" is intended primarily as a means of access to a region, and is established and maintained by a maritime power for exploiting the potentialities of that region; on the other hand, a seaport can also arise as an outlet of a country, as a means of expansion of its trade or its people. This distinction is illustrated by the difference between Madras, on the one hand, and the modern port of Vizagapatam and the ancient ports Mylapore and Mahabalipuram, on the other. The port of entry can always be reached by ships, and is therefore held by a maritime power by means of its naval forces, which also ensure a safe withdrawal when necessary. The "port of entry" represents the most advanced or "forward" position which the principal fighting forces of the maritime power, viz., its navy, can hold securely; hence the capitals, that is the bases from which the political control and organisation of the regions have to be maintained, are located at these ports so long as the hold on the regions is dependent on seapower.

If we compare the position of Madras on the seaboard of the Palar delta with the positions of the other towns of this delta which have served as capitals in the past, it becomes apparent that each of these centres has served as a capital under different circumstances. The political unification and control of a delta can be achieved from within or from outside; the control from outside can be either from the sea or from inland. The capital has necessarily to be a seaport when the external control is based upon seapower; and any site along the seaboard of the delta will do equally well, because all parts of the seaboard are more or less equally accessible from the sea. Every such capital will, however, suffer from the disadvantage of not being a natural focus of routes in the delta, and such a "nodality" has to be achieved artificially by focussing the means of communication on the capital. The greatest natural advantage in this respect is possessed by the apex of the delta, and this is generally the site of the capital from which external control based upon "land" power is achieved. In the Palar delta Arcot has served this purpose under Muhammadan rule. Woriyur and Trichinopoly at the apex of the Kaveri delta have served in the same way under the Cholas and the Muhammadan rulers; and later, when the East India Company took possession of the Kaveri delta, its control was again organised from Trichinopoly, because by that time the East India Company had acquired extensive territorial possessions and becomes a "land" power, whose hold on the Kaveri delta was based upon land forces. When the political unity of the delta is attained from within, the strategic considerations which are paramount when the control is from outside cease to be so important, and other factors, such as the force of tradition, prevail in determining the site of the capital, *e.g.*, Conjeevaram in the Palar delta and Tanjore in the Kaveri delta.

Madras was therefore a proper site for the capital of a power which gained access from the sea. The main factors in its situation which account for its growth are the fertility and the extent of its hinterland, and the accessibility of this hinterland which was greatly improved by the later growth of railways. During the earlier stages of the growth of Madras from its small beginnings, the relative seclusion which the lower Palar basin enjoys, by virtue of being almost surrounded by much drier, less fertile and thinly peopled tracts which repel invaders, was a specially important factor. This circumstance was as responsible as the general political disintegration of the country for making this part of South India politically a backwater, in which it was possible for the small beginning of the East India Company at Madras to take root and establish itself sufficiently firmly to attain its present vastness.

APPENDIX

EARLY GEOGRAPHICAL WORK IN MADRAS

The earliest recorded surveys of India are the coast surveys made by the sea captains of the East India Company around their chief ports of call, and they date from the first decade of the 17th century. Unfortunately most of the log books of voyages prior to 1855 were either burnt in Calcutta about that year, or were similarly destroyed in 1860 at the India Office. Major James Rennell made surveys in Bengal and Bihar and published them in 1781 in his *Bengal Atlas*: this and his

Memoir of a Map of Hindustan" (1788), have rightly earned for him the title "the Father of Indian Geography."

The real beginnings of the survey of India "on a scientific and methodical system," are only to be found towards the end of the 18th century, when the first proposal for a trigonometrical survey of India was made. It came from Captain Lambton, and owing to the interest which Lord William Bentinck, then Governor of Madras, and Major-General James Stuart, then Commander-in-Chief of Madras, took in surveying, it resulted in the commencement of the trigonometrical survey of South India which became later the Great Trigonometrical Survey of India. The first base was measured near Madras in 1802, and the survey remained under the Government of Madras till 1815 when it was placed under the Surveyor-General of India. As the work of the trigonometrical survey progressed, many errors were detected in the maps based on older surveys, *e.g.*, the difference in the width of the peninsula between Mangalore and Madras. The longitude of Madras is the secondary meridian or substitute for the Prime meridian of Greenwich Observatory, because the trigonometrical survey of India started from Madras and also because the Madras Observatory was one of the earliest in India to fix its longitudinal position by means of astronomical observations.

Topographical surveys also had their origin in the Madras Presidency. The earliest topographical maps were compiled by the Officers of the Madras Quarter Master General's department from military route surveys and independent surveys. Colonel Colin Mackenzie, who was the first Indian Officer to use the plane table and to employ triangulation for topographical surveys, organised the Military Institution at Tripassore in the Chingleput district, in 1795, for the scientific education of military officers. This institution existed till 1816 and contributed largely to develop the geographical knowledge of India, its students surveying 1600 square miles in detail every year. It supplied many officers to the Madras Topographical Survey, *e.g.*, Lieutenants Garling and Connor who surveyed the West Coast of the Peninsula from South Kanara to Travancore between 1811 and 1829; and Turnbull, Keyes and Ward who surveyed Tinnevelly, Madura, Dindigul, Trichinopoly and Coimbatore districts in the south and the Telugu districts later on. Many maps of the several parts of the Presidency were available by 1840, as a result of the work of these officers trained at Tirupassore; each of these surveys was accompanied by a descriptive memoir. When the Directors of the East India Company decided to publish the Indian Atlas on 1″ = 4 miles, the Madras surveys supplied the earliest sheets.

The Madras Observatory has also contributed notably to the growth of geographical knowledge. It was instituted in 1792 but it originated from a small private observatory started in 1787 by one Mr. William Petrie, who, upon leaving India, presented his instruments to the Government for the use of the new observatory. The astronomical work of the observatory helped to make Madras the fixed point of departure of the trigonometrical survey of India. The longitude of Madras was redetermined more accurately towards the end of the last century when telegraphic communication with England was first established. For the same reason Madras time has been adopted as standard time for the greater part of India for railway and other purposes, and the Madras Observatory has performed the work of keeping correct time for all India. Magnetic and meteorological observations have also been made at the observatory and on its behalf at various inaccessible and distant places in South India, *e.g.*, Doddabetta, and even as far as Singapore, and the results published.

The decline of scientific activities in general at Madras in subsequent years is due chiefly to the shifting of the East India Company's head-quarters in India from Madras to Calcutta. This transfer also involved the shifting of many of the scientific activities from Madras to Bengal, as has been noted in the case of the trigonometrical survey.

(A detailed account of the early surveys in the Madras Presidency is given in McLean's Manual of Administration of the Madras Presidency, Vol. I. The early history and growth of surveys in India are dealt with in the Imperial Gazetteer of India Vol. IV., in the Chapter on Surveys, and in Markham's and Black's Memoirs on the Indian Surveys. The history and work of the Madras Observatory are dealt with in McLean's Manual, Vol. I).

NOTES ON THE MAP:—(1) The contours are based on the levelling done up to 1914, since when some of the low-lying areas have been filled up and the ground-level of those localities raised four to five feet above their former levels. (2) The sites of the temples mentioned in footnote 12 are marked on the map by means of symbols. (3) The several streets and localities to which detailed references are made, have not been shown in this map because they can be readily located by referring to the town maps of Madras on the scales of 3" and 5" to a mile. (4) The changes in the coast-line are shown only approximately in the map, and are those that have occurred between 1865 and 1939.

SECTION VI

RELIGION

Protestant Missions in Madras

By

Rev. C. H. Monahan, M.A.,

Madras.

The first Protestant missionary in Madras was a German Lutheran, Benjamin Schultze, who had come to Tranquebar in 1719. When invited to Madras, to avoid the exactions of the Tanjore Kingdom, he sailed in a little boat to Cuddalore and journeyed thence on foot. After months on the road he arrived in July 1726, "bare-foot, limping and sick. But in fourteen days his giant like nature had recovered." He began work in Black Town, teaching children and conversing in Tamil with adults who came to his lodgings. Being a gifted linguist he also was able to use Telugu, Portuguese and Hindustani. The first Church of the Mission was near the old lighthouse at the N. E. extremity of the glacis of the Fort. After 23 years of arduous toil in India this most abstemious, unselfish and energetic missionary returned to Germany in broken health.

In 1742 Fabricius became head of the Mission. He was a sincere lover of peace and of a kindly disposition, but not so firm in discipline as Schultze. His great work was a Tamil Version of the Bible, still used by many Lutherans. He also translated German hymns into Tamil. It is said that "many of his translations are even better than the originals." His lot was cast in troublous times. Between 1745 and 1760 Madras was often the scene of war. In 1745, when the French under Labourdonnais destroyed half of Black Town including the Mission House and School, Fabricius had to take refuge at Pulicat, where the Dutch Governor received him kindly. Between 1746 and 1749 Fort St. George was captured and held by the French for 3 years. They dismantled the Church and Mission premises and took the spoil to Pondicherry. When the English Admiral Boscawen recaptured the Fort in 1749 he handed over to the Protestants a Church and Mission premises in Vepery in compensation for that taken by the French Roman Catholics.

Coja Petrus Uscan, an Armenian, who in 1726 had built the Marmalong (Mambalam) Bridge, claimed that "the Chapel......at Viparee" was his personal property. When he died in 1751 his body was buried in the Chapel yard. However the Government by deed dated November 24, 1752 formally conveyed it to the Mission. But in 1770 the

Directors in England recognized the validity of Petrus Uscan's will and paid compensation for the Church in Vepery.

In 1757 the French again came to Madras, led this time by the Irishman, Count de Lally. Fabricius had to go again to Pulicat in February 1758. He was often reduced to great straits during the wars. He gave nearly a third of his modest salary of Rs. 500 per annum to the Mission and lived on the coarsest Indian diet, drinking only water. Even after General Coote defeated the French at Wandiwash in January 1760 the troubles of Fabricius were not at an end. A devastating hurricane and a severe outbreak of cholera in 1763 carried off 44 of his people.

In 1767 the Mahrattas made a raid towards Madras but were driven off by the English troops before they reached Vepery. But in 1780 Hyder Ali threw Madras into consternation by his invasion of the Carnatic. The Vepery Mission premises were commandeer'd as quarters for British troops fetched from Bengal. The calamities of all the former wars were trifling compared with this one. Capt. Innes Munro tells of the horrors he witnessed which beggared description; villages blazing on every side—immense droves of fugitives whose cries were distinctly heard a mile off—the Mahratta troopers brandishing bloody swords—bodies wantonly mutilated—roads strewed with slaughtered infants and decrepit old people—some women were outraged—others committed suicide to escape such indignity. As if this disaster were not enough, in 1782 an awful storm broke on Madras. It was followed by appalling famine—in Black Town the stench of unburied corpses filled the air, while crows, vultures and jackals preyed upon the dead.

In such conditions the late years of Fabricius were spent. His unselfishness led him to help those in need. But in his lack of worldly wisdom he acted very injudiciously. Money that he had borrowed or obtained on trust he lent to people at higher interest hoping thereby to increase the income needed for meeting the distress of the poor. Some whom he trusted proved false and he was unable to meet his obligations. One of his creditors put the poor old man in the debtors' jail, where the famous Schwartz visited him. In 1788 having "lost his faculties by age, labour and trouble" he signed his act of resignation. Soon after he died "worn down by infirmities and grief." The sad close of his life must not blind us to the long and noble service he rendered to the Tamil Church which is gratefully remembered to this day especially in Vepery as witness the name of the Fabricius High School.

In 1788 Gericke, who had private means, which he generously used in the service of the Mission, succeeded Fabricius and did valuable work in spite of much family affliction.

After his death in 1808 Dr. Rottler came from Tranquebar to take charge of the Mission. He was an admirable scholarly man of a peaceful disposition but there were others who were contentious. Thus at the beginning of the 19th century owing to internal dissensions the once vigorous Vepery S.P.C.K. work had sunk to comparative insignificance.

Why did the East India Company in the 18th century admit French Roman Catholic and German Protestant Missionaries whilst they refused admission to British Missionaries? Partly through fear that the Company might be compromised with its subjects, if Missions of the same nation as the Government engaged in Christian propaganda. But the chief reason was commercial fear, lest under the guise of Missionaries British free traders or "interlopers" might break the Company's monopoly of trade between Great Britain and India. In the new India Charter of 1813 Parliament opened the door to all Missionaries. The great evangelical revival of vital Christianity in England had led to the foundation of great Missionary Societies in the last decade of the 18th century. In 1785 Methodist Missions in the West Indies had begun even without a Society. The London Missionary Society (L.M.S.), founded in 1795, sent out men in 1804 but no boat of the East India Company was allowed to carry them. They took passages in a Danish vessel from Copenhagen to Tranquebar and so reached Madras. One of them was the first L.M.S. Missionary in this City—Wm. C. Loveless—He arrived in 1805 but was only allowed to minister to Europeans and Eurasians. He opened two large schools, and founded the Madras Bible and Tract Societies. The great B. & F. Bible Society had been founded in 1804 in London. Loveless was a man of great simplicity and charming humility of character. He was given charge of the Male Orphan Asylum and so lived without cost to the Mission. Through him the L.M.S. Church in Davidson Street, Black Town, was built and opened in 1810. In 1812 Loveless resigned from the Orphan Asylum and with his excellent wife carried on a high class Boarding School in Vepery. It was at his suggestion that Traveller of the same Mission built the L.M.S. Church in Vepery in 1819.

The Church Missionary Society (C.M.S.), founded in 1799, sent two missionaries in 1814, Rhenius and Schnarre, both German Lutherans. Rhenius, a Prussian, was a very capable and strong-willed man. He bought a site in Black Town near the Mint and in 1817 began building a Church. In October the Hindu residents sent a petition against the building to the Governor in Council. The Superintendent of Police enquired into the matter and the work was stopped by December 1817. Government indemnified the Society and erected a new Church "for the Native Protestants of Madras," now known as "Tucker's Church" in Popham's Broadway.

A Wesleyan Missionary was the next to reach Madras, James Lynch, an Irishman. He was one of six who on December 30, 1813 sailed with Dr. Thomas Coke, a Clerk in Holy Orders, friend of John Wesley founder of Methodist Missions and, according to a British Officer "the holiest little devil I ever met." Coke never reached India. At the age of 66 he died at sea. Lynch after 3 years in Ceylon was invited to Madras by five "serious persons" who had been reading Wesley's writings. He held his first service in Black Town on March 2nd, 1817. All his work was in English. He was a keen evangelist, simple, unassuming and courageous. "His talent for reproving sin was extraordinary."

The first competent Tamil scholar of the W. M. S. was Elijah Hoole. He arrived in Madras in 1820 after a terrible experience on the "Tanjore" which caught fire and had to be abandoned east of Trincomalee. He was "quite a remarkable man" according to Penny, well able to converse on equal terms with such a scholar as the Abbe Dubois. A few days after landing he heard the venerable Dr. Rottler preach in Tamil to an overflowing congregation at the opening of "Tucker's Church" on October 11th, 1820.

In the same year there was a violent explosion of caste prejudice among some members of the Vepery Mission Church. The following covenant made in July 1820 by a deposed Catechist and others is painfully revealing: "Covenant made among us, members of the English Mission congregation—Because Mr. Haubroe on the 23rd day of this month permitted a child of a Pariar to take his seat in the Church alongside of the Tamil school-boys, which is a great disparagement to our caste" (sic) "be it covenanted that we neither (with our families) will come to Church more, nor send our children to school; but if anyone shall break this covenant, he is bound to pay 12 pagodas to the police office as a person guilty before the congregation." It was to the credit of the Missionary that he refused to countenance such unchristian feelings.

James Lynch with the help of his L.M.S. friends Loveless and Traveller opened on 25th April 1822 the English Church in Popham's Broadway, where the tradition of effective English preaching was established by him, which has been continued in the Methodist Mission to the present day in its Churches at Egmore, Georgetown and Perambur. After ten strenuous years in the East Lynch returned to Ireland in 1824 and many years after as a venerable old man laid his hands on the head of Wm. Butler and inspired him with an interest in India which found expression when he became the first Missionary of the M. E. Church in N. India.

In 1826, exactly a hundred years after Schultze reached Madras the S.P.C.K. Vepery Mission was taken over by the S.P.G. The fact that all the previous missionaries of the S.P.C.K. had been men with Lutheran orders, whilst the principles of the S.P.G. required Episcopal Ordination, caused some difficulties in adjustment at first.

The same year (1828) that Hoole (W.M.S.) departed, Rev. J. Smith (L.M.S.), the brother of Mary Moffat, began a great ministry in Davidson Street during which several young men of promise joined the Church. Amongst them were John Bilderbeck and Henry Bower, the Chief Reviser of the Tamil Version of the Bible. Smith set himself to train these and other men for the Ministry. After attending in 1843 the ordination of one of his young friends at Masulipatam he embarked in a coasting boat for Madras, which was lost at sea. He was never heard of again.

For 30 years the American Board worked in Royapuram and Chintadripetta but retired in 1866 in order to concentrate on their Mission in Madura. The C.M.S. in 1865 took over Zion Church and Parsonage in which Dr. Winslow has completed his Tamil Dictionary in 1862.

In 1837 Madras was invaded by a very vivid and masterful personality from Scotland, John Anderson. The historic speech of Alexander Duff in the General Assembly of the Church of Scotland in 1835 thrilled the house. The report of it read in a newspaper "Kindled a spirit within us" says Anderson "that raised us up from our bed and pointed as if with the finger to India as the field of our future labours." He came as a missionary teacher and was a man of prodigious energy lavishly expended. He had a heart filled with zeal for God, a buoyant spirit and vigorous body which he drove unmercifully. On April 3rd 1837 "with firm faith in God and in the power of His Word and Spirit" he opened a school in Black Town with an attendance of 57. When the hot weather holiday began he must needs start a school in Conjeevaram on the 29th of May with a shade temperature of 110° to 111°! Such was the zeal of this remarkable man. By October 1838 the school in Madras had 270 pupils, when his first struggle with caste occured. Most of the pupils were caste Hindus, but three Pariahs had been admitted. Hindu parents demanded their dismissal. Anderson refused and thereby lost 100 pupils for the time. But in the end he won and the Mission had no need to fight that battle again. As to his method of teaching he said: "The animating soul of the system is a thorough Bible instruction." Robert Johnston his "True-Yoke-Fellow," joined Anderson in 1839. When P. Rajagopal and A. Venkataramiah were baptised in 1841 a storm of fury burst upon the missionaries: "Slanders on every side, falsehoods and monstrous lies in regard to us and our schools." When it was suggested to Rajagopal in Court that the missionaries must have offered him some unworthy inducements, he answered "No, nothing but Jesus Christ Crucified." The school survived this and other such storms and greatly increased both in numbers and influence. Anderson and his colleague had come out as missionaries of the Church of Scotland, but at the time of the Disruption in 1843 they sided with the Free Church and withdrew from the Established Church of Scotland, which in 1845 opened on the Esplanade a School which David Sinclair in 1887 raised to a College. After a long and useful career this Institution was amalgamated in 1911 with the Madras Christian College some twenty years before the two Churches were happily re-united in 1931.

As congregations increased in size and number the need of an indigenous Ministry was acutely felt. John Anderson had a quaint and utterly impracticable theory about the support of the Indian Ministry: "Your......Native Preachers will stand on the firmest and best footing, if they derive their support exclusively from the Church in Scotland." No Society seriously followed that plan. But efforts to train and ordain suitable candidates for the Indian Ministry were greatly hindered about the middle of the century by the old obstacle of caste. Bishop Spencer invited a candidate for ordination to dinner. He accepted the invitation but feigned illness rather than break his caste. His brother confessed to a missionary that he could not have eaten with Luther or Baxter or even with the Lord Jesus when on earth. Two men trained for the Wesleyan Ministry could not be ordained as they refused to eat with any of their Christian brethren who were not of their caste. Unfortunately Ziegenbalg and Schwartz had reluctantly admitted caste in the Church in the hope that as the people grew in grace they would leave it behind. That hope proved vain as the other Missions realized vividly. Bishop Corrie had clearly seen that "If we refuse to receive the sacrament because another has partaken before us, we lose sight of the Saviour." More and more the different Missions came to realize that they all had to face the same problems. So they founded the Madras Missionary Conference in which they met from month to month. In 1850 that Conference issued a strong manifesto against caste in the Church which is supposed to have been drafted by Johnston, colleague of John Anderson. The manifesto was accepted by all except the "recently formed" German Mission in Vepery, which since 1845 had a Church in Tannah Street for its Tamil congregation, having separated from the S.P.G. when St. Paul's was built that year.

A. R. Symonds long connected with the S.P.G. in Sullivan's Gardens, where he was Principal of their Theological College, had to deal with a case in which the preposterous claim was made that even if a convert's wife was willing to live with him, her family had a right to claim her from him, as they argued that the husband, by becoming a Christian, had forfeited all civil rights. This had been the case prior to 1850 when the Lex Loci Act was passed by which liberty of conscience was guaranteed to all. Sir W. Burton of the Supreme Court declared that this Act had been passed, not to encourage a change from one religion to another, but *to secure liberty of conscience and equal rights to all.* "This Act of 1850" he said "is the great Charter of Religious Freedom."

We have now reached the time (1851) when the example of Anderson as a pioneer of Higher Education was followed by other Societies than his. As a result there have been created the following High Schools for boys: Wesley in Royapettah of which James Cooling (1876 to 1915) was for many years the Principal, whilst also for 30 years the General Superintendent of his Mission, St. Paul's and Fabricius in Vepery and Kellet in Triplicane. The L.M.S. started one in 1851 in Georgetown, but gave it up after many years of successful work. In 1855 Harris School in Triplicane was begun by the C.M.S. Cannon E. Sell a great authority on Islam was for years its Principal. A few years ago it was handed over to another body. The High Schools for girls in the City owe much to the labours of such women as Mrs. Porter of the L.M.S., Mrs. Anderson of the Church of Scotland, Mrs. Roberts and Mrs. Cooling of the Methodist Mission and others. As an outcome of their labours we now have Boarding High Schools for girls: Bentinck in Vepery, Northwick in Royapuram, another C.S.M. High School in Georgetown, Methodist Girls' High School, Royapettah and St. Ebba's, S.P.G., in Sullivan's Gardens.

It is not possible within the compass of this paper to give anything like an adequate account of Women's Work by the Societies. Girl's High Schools have been mentioned. Many Elementary Girls' Schools have been carried on. Teaching women in the Zenanas and visitations of the girls' parents engage the time of many women missionaries. In the Church of Scotland, Kilpauk, besides a very interesting school for girls and little boys, valuable industrial teaching has for long been given, as is done in the Mylapore Home Industries for women by the Methodist Mission. In San Thome the beautiful work done by the C.E.Z.M. ladies in the School for the Deaf and Dumb must not be overlooked.

But perhaps the greatest service to women by missionaries in Madras has been in medical work. The name of Dr. Anna Macphail of the Church of Scotland will not soon be forgotten. She was for many years warmly welcomed in multitudes of homes until her retirement.

She and her colleagues laboured for long in cramped quarters in Main Road, Royapuram, until the fine buildings of the Christian Rainy Hospital were erected in Tondiarpet. Diwan Bahadur N. Subrahmanyam, Judge of the Small Cause Court and later Administrator General of Madras, founded a hospital in Mylapore and named it after his mother "Kalyani." He handed it over to the Women's Department of the Methodist Mission which still carries it on. They have enlarged it considerably more than once.

Better than all missionary institutions, has been the growth of indigenous Christian congregations, some of which we have already mentioned. There remain to be noted the Tamil congregations of the Methodist Church in Georgetown, Perambur, Purasavalkam, Royapettah, Triplicane and Mylapore; of the Anglican Church Sullivans Gardens, Egmore, Washermenpet and Perambur, of the Methodist Episcopal Churches (English and Tamil) in Vepery, the congregations of the Telugu Baptists in Vepery and Perambur, of the Strict Baptists at Kilpauk and the S.I.U.C. at Royapuram.

In 1878 the Danish Missionary Society began work in Madras when Jensen came. With the help of Hay of the L.M.S. and Alexander of the Christian College he ordained Dr. J. Lazarus in 1883 as a Missionary of the Society. Jensen's work was chiefly that of preaching in the open air, in which knowledge of Tamil proverbs made him apt at repartee. Dr. L. P. Larsen came in 1889. He was an exceptionally gifted linguist, who after service both in his own Mission, in the Y.M.C.A. and in the United Theological College, spent some nine years as one of the chief Revisers of the Tamil Bible.

United effort has for many years been seen in the work of the Y.M.C.A. with its great premises on the Esplanade built when David McConaughy was Secretary. It also has Centres of Work in Royapettah and Vepery. In the latter place the Y.W.C.A. does much noble service for women. St. Margaret's Hostel and Mithrabhavanam, as well as the central buildings provide for the religious and social welfare of many young women.

We have seen how the first Protestant missionaries who were Germans were supported by the British S.P.C.K. During the war between England and France in the middle of the 18th century, on the capture of Pondicherry a small printing press was found there and brought to Madras. It was given by Government to the Vepery Mission, as was also a small plot of land presumably the site of the Diocesan Press. In 1815 a Diocesan Committee was formed that retained its Book Depot and small press, when S.P.G. took over the Mission; they printed Tamil prayer books etc. About the middle of the 19th century they sold the Press to the American Board in Chintadripetta. When that Mission in 1866 withdrew from Madras the S.P.C.K. Diocesan Committee bought back the Press for Rs. 40,000. In 1899 a lay printer was brought from England. Canon Sell became Hon. Secretary and held the office for 31 years. Out of profits new machinery was bought and new buildings started. Work came in from all parts of India and from England. In 1930 the C.L.S., which had been at work for many years in publishing and circulating Christian literature and school books, bought the Diocesan Press and still carries it on under expert management. Now the Press does all the printing work while the C.L.S. attends to circulation and distribution, the two rendering inestimable service in matters of Christian education and social service of many kinds.

From the days when William Miller of the Madras Christian College and A. R. Symonds of Sullivan's Gardens would come to examine the classes at Wesley High School, Royapettah, there has been a tradition of Mission comity and co-operation in Madras that has in our own days led to signal and world-wide developments. This spirit found its first concrete expression in the formation of the Madras Christian College in 1876, in which from the first a number of Missions co-operated.

In 1862 William Miller came to Madras and became the controlling spirit of the School, which he raised to a College. He has the glory of being the pioneer in creating union institutions among the Missions. From the first the (Wesleyan) Methodist Mission has paid an annual contribution and supplied a Professor on the staff. F. W. Kellett, Fellow of his College at Cambridge and University prizeman, succeeded George Patterson and was followed by F. E. Corley, also a Fellow of his College at Oxford. Kellett was deeply interested in students, and worked not only in the Christian College but also in Triplicane where the Kellett High School and the social service centre in the Kellett Institute keep alive his memory. The C.M.S. from the first, later the Church of Scotland, the American Baptist, the S.P.G. and the Arcot Missions have taken a share in supporting the College. The spirit of co-operation seen in the Madras Christian College from 1876 found fresh expression in a series of great Missionary gatherings, the third of which was held in Madras in 1900. This was a notable gathering, for its business was conducted on a new model, which was repeated in the Shanghai Conference and in the Edinburgh, Jerusalem and Tambaram World Missionary Conferences. Preparation of the topics to be discussed was given to groups which for many months beforehand worked on the agenda. When the Conference met each group made its report that was discussed and, if necessary, amended by the full Conference, whose decisions were final. The Conference appealed for greater unity in the Church. This bore fruit in 1908 when the South India United Church was formed out of Presbyterian and Congregational elements of international origin. Prof. Kellett was the Secretary of the Conference. He had toiled terribly for many months beforehand in organizing it, whilst doing his College work as well. He had been associated in Triplicane with G. Gower Cocks and Duncan G. M. Leith. Cocks, Principal of Wesley High School, one day in his Scripture lesson spoke of Christ as the Resurrection and the Life. He was led to state his own faith that through Christ he would certainly meet his mother again. That very morning he had a heart seizure in class, was carried on a stretcher to the Mission House where he died after a short interval. His students, Brahmin, Muhammadan and Christian, vied with one another for the honour of bearing his coffin. Duncan Leith laboured for many years both in Kellett High School and Institute, Triplicane and became one of the best known Social Reformers of the City. In December 1926 he was drowned while bathing at Ennore. The City was deeply moved by this tragic event. He had for many years been one of the chief Promoters of Christian unity and co-operation between the Churches.

The great Edinburgh Missionary Conference in 1910 was followed in Madras by a visit from Dr. J. R. Mott in which missionary co-operation was greatly strengthened by the formation of a united council now known as the Madras Representative Christian Council (M.R.C.C.) which is affiliated with the National Christian Council (N.C.C.). Even before that the Missionary Educational Council had been organised with headquarters in Madras. Both these bodies have greatly facilitated the work of common planning and mutual help between Missions. One of the most signal examples of international missionary co-operation is the Women's Christian College, Madras of which Dr. Eleanor McDougall was Principal for 23 years from 1915 to 1938. It is supported by twelve European and American Missions. Both in the life of the University and in the Schools served by women graduates of the College its influence has been very far-reaching. The need of a Christian Training College for woman graduates and secondary students soon came to be keenly felt, with the result that St. Christopher's Training College was founded in Vepery by a group of Missions with Bentinck as its practising school through the kindness of the L.M.S. At the invitation of the N.C.C. Dr. Lindsay, Master of Baliol, presided over a Commission on Christian Higher Education in India, which on its visit to Madras urged that the Intermediate classes of Wesley College be closed and the premises used for the first Christian Training College for Men in India. After five years of negotiation the Meston Training College, Royapettah was opened in July 1937. Five Missions and the Tinnevelly Diocesan

Council co-operate in aiding the College, much the largest share of the cost being supplied by the Methodist Mission and by the College Appeal Fund in Great Britain.

The International Missionary Council met in December 1938 in the new premises of the Madras Christian College at Tambaram opened in 1937, than which no more suitable place for such a united Christian gathering could have been found in Asia. The very College symbolized the spirit of co-operation. It is little wonder that when delegates of the Protestant Churches throughout the world, representing 71 different countries and areas met there, they experienced a wonderful unity transcending national differences and conflicts, so much so that the brotherly spirit uniting Chinese and Japanese delegates at a time when their countries are at war, made *MADRAS* 1938 an inspiration and challenge to the world.

Around the City Pagodas

BY

V. R. RAMACHANDRA DIKSHITAR, M.A.,

Lecturer, University of Madras.

EVEN in the centuries that preceded the Christian era, there flourished the town of Mylapore. The tradition that Saint Thomas was buried here in the first century A.D. and that the Sage Tiruvalluvar was born here or at least lived here a good part of his life—and Tiruvalluvar may be assigned with great probability to the first century B.C.—confirms the view that in the centuries preceding and following the Christian Era Mylapore must have been a prominent locality. The tradition again as recorded in the *Divyapprabandam* of the Vaishnava Alvars gives the hint that Mylapore was the town to which the hamlet of Triplicane was attached. For does not the *Prabandam* speak of Mayilaittiruvallikeni? Triplicane was a suburb of Mylapore until it shot to prominence in the time of the Pallavas who, it is plausible, were the founders of the present Parthasarathy shrine. Mylapore is much celebrated in literature and legend. While the spurious *Kapilar Ahaval* makes it the birth-place of Valluvar, still other grounds are there to show that it was the residence of Valluvar, if not his birth-place. There is a separate shrine dedicated to this Sage in the present Kapalisvarar temple. There is some reason to conjecture that originally the shrine stood near the Mylapore beach and had been either overwhelmed by sea or pulled down by fanatics of alien faith. According to the *Tirunurrantati* attributed to Avirodhi Alvar and the *Neminatham*, Ten Mayilai or South Mylapore was celebrated also on account of its Jain pagoda which is now lost. It was the birth-place of Peyalvar, one of the earliest Alvars, in whose honour a shrine exists even to-day. It is evident that the Saiva Samayacharya Sambandar visited this ancient place and established it as a leading Saiva centre. Here it is said that this Acharya wrought the miracle of calling to life a Chetti girl from her cremated bones. This ancient shrine contains many sculptural images commemorating certain local legends, of which two are note-worthy. One, the penance of Parvati in the form of a mayil (peacock), and the other the miracle wrought by Saint Sambandar referred to above. Mylapore is also noted for its association with the sixty-three Saiva devotees called in popular Tamil Arupattumuvar belonging to different castes and communities. There are bronze statuetes enshrined in the Kapalisvarar temple for all these sixty-three

Nayanmars. Even to-day a big festival is got up annually in honour of all these Saints, attracting thousands of people from all parts of the city and the suburbs.

Apart from such religious traditions which have centred round the town, Mylapore played an important part in the heyday of the Pallavas as a port of considerable significance. Mylapore port was as much a centre of trade as the Mamallapuram port under the Pallavas. It is probable that much sea-borne commerce was carried on in this port, as can be testified from the treatise *Nandikkalambakam.* Nandivarman III is known as Mallaivendan. Being advantageously situated, Mylapore kept up its prominence until the beginning of the 16th century when the Portuguese took possession of it and beautified the shore part with churches and chapels. The Portuguese settlement got the name San Thome. Under them it became a commercial place, and it was administered separately from the Indian town of Mylapore. By 1640, the Portuguese power had begun to decline. The political history of the town, generally known as San Thome de Meliapur from this time until it was acquired by the Government of the East India Company in 1749, need not detain us. Many a vicissitude in her political life did not diminish its prominence as a Saiva centre, nor did the cultural influence of the temple suffer to any appreciable extent. Additions have been made to the shrine, including beautiful sculptures, and its festivals are being celebrated on a grand scale. On the north-western corner of the temple tank there is a figure of Jyeshthadevi or the Goddess of Misfortune facing the tank and reckoned to be an image of the Pallava period.

Triplicane, as has been stated above, began as a small suburban village of Mylapore. If we can credit the tradition recorded by Tirumalisai Alvar, the original shrine was the Ranganatha one now on the north-eastern part of the Parthasarathy shrine. The date of its original construction is not known. Important Alvars like Peyalvar and Tirumangai Mannan have composed songs in its praise and Tirumangai even refers to Tellisingar after which the present Tolasingasvami Perumal Koil Street was named. The temple contains within its precincts a Pallava inscription of Dantivarman, fragments of Chola records and a few inscriptions of Vijayanagar times. The main shrine dedicated to Parthasarathi was probably the gift of Pallava Mallan on the basis of two facts: (i) The Dantivarman inscription clearly shows that he only made a gift of land and therefore it existed already in his time, (ii) Tirumangai attributes definitely the construction to a Pallava and he must be one of the predecessors of Dantivarman. Among them Pallavamalla was a staunch Vaishnava and hence he might have been the founder. Along with this big temple the village also grew and

THE KAPALISWARA TEMPLE, MYLAPORE

soon became separated from Mylapore. An inscription in the temple shows that a pious citizen added to the structures and repaired the old ones in 1564 A.D. There are a number of fine carvings and beautiful images in the temple. People say that no fish can live in the tank Kairaveni in front of the temple because of the curse of a Sage who was disturbed by a fish in his penance on the banks of the tank. With its acquisition by the Company about 1676, the management of the temple was taken by the Company and its chief merchants like Beri Timmanna. The influence of the temple grew under the fostering care of the Company's merchants. We shall refer to this later.

Mention may be made of the ancient temple of Tiruvorriyur, sacred to Thyagaraja, which is again a celebrated Saiva shrine, about five miles to the north of Madras. Three of the four Samayacharyas have sung in its praise. These were Appar, Sambandar and Sundaramurti. Here also is situated the tomb of Saint Pattinattu Pillaiyar. The temple was also a centre of learning and in its mandapa were held discourses on Vyakarana and other subjects. There was a mutt attached to this about the 9th century A.D. presided over Caturanana Panditas. There are a number of inscriptions beginning with Pallava times recording gifts of land and other endowments to the temple. Sri Sankaracharya is said to have visited this shrine and put down the power of an evil goddess who was devouring anything that came before her. There is a tradition that associates the Durga Devi on the northern side of the main shrine with Kannaki, the Pattinidevi of the *Silappadikaram*. An annual festival lasting for 15 days is celebrated in her honour even to-day. On the last day the pandal is burnt down as a symbol of Kannaki burning down Madura city.

Tiruvorriyur was acquired by the English only in the beginning of the 18th century, and became a separate suburb of the city; and the Company's government had not much occasion to interfere in its growth and progress. There is a single record of 1785 describing the disturbances in this pagoda between the Left Hand and Right Hand castes, when the Company's government had to interfere and bring about an amicable settlement. But this old shrine continues to maintain its prestige and is visited by a number of pilgrims even to-day. As a piece of architecture and for its fine sculpture, the temple is unsurpassed in beauty and excellence.

Mention may also be made of the Puzhal Jain temple. About nine miles to the north-west of the city of Madras on the road from Madras to the Red Hills, there is a very ancient Jain temple dedicated to Sri Rishaba Deva or Sri Adinatha Bhagavan. Tradition says that it was built by a Jain Saint who had a vow not to take food before doing puja to a Jain image. When he came to the village Puzhal, he was invited by a Grahasta for food. But the ascetic said that he could take his food only after worshipping God in the form of a Jain image. The Grahasta at once ordered a sculptor to make an image according to the rules laid down in the Jain scriptures. On seeing the image the ascetic was exceedingly glad in heart; he performed puja to it and broke his fast. While departing from the village he asked his host to build a temple for the image and for the expenses to be paid to the workmen he asked him (the Grahasta) to pay every man a handful of mud in the evening. This is a strange and cheap way of paying for hard labour! The work of building the temple began and in the evening of the day when the workmen came to their master for the wages, he gave every one of them a handful of mud. Lo! when the mud touched the hand of the labourer it was changed into coins worth the labour he turned out. In this way the temple was built. The temple is now under the management of an Upadhyaya who resides in the village. It is not possible to assign a date to the origin of this pagoda.

For ages together, the ground that lay between Tiruvorriyur and Mylapore was no man's land, interspersed with primitive hamlets of fishermen and country sailors, until 1639 when Francis Day, a factor of the East India Company, obtained this vacant site and built a fortified town which is the great and wonderful city of which we all feel proud to-day. The following pages will deal with the growth of the Hindu pagodas in this city.

Notwithstanding the rise of cults of different religious persuasions from time to time and the countless invasions of alien cultural waves, the Hindu religion has held its own. This unalterable character in the life of this religion is due to the special genius of Hinduism for tolerance and appreciation of differing points of view. Madras under British rule was no exception to this long established practice. It was the policy of the Company's government to patronise the Indian faiths, Hindu and Moslem, sometimes undertaking the direct management of the temples and sometimes supporting native enterprise. In pursuance of this policy, the Government of Madras, as we shall see in the sequel, took over the management of the Madras Town Temple, and also of the Triplicane temple, among others, as well as of a mosque or two. Duties were levied on merchandise for the maintenance of the mosques and the temples. Both the communities, Hindu and Moslem, were subjected to this taxation, and this practice continued for a long time. But in 1707 the Moghul and Pathan Moormen, merchants in the city, showed their unwillingness to pay for the Hindu shrines. Thomas Pitt who was then the Governor decided in favour of the continuation of the old practice. The Pathan merchants, however, seemed to have threatened at this to desert the city and settle in San Thome. As this would have led to the ruination of trade, the Company's government ultimately yielded to their wishes in 1716. Some time later the Bengal merchants were also exempted from payment of taxes to support both Hindu and Muslim institutions.

We shall pass in review some of the temples that rose to prominence during the days of the Company and see in what ways the government of the day and its chief merchants helped in the growth and development of Hindu religious institutions. We are reminded of the philanthropist and chief merchant of the Company Alangada Pillai who flourished at the end of the 17th century. Most probably the street that bears his name in Triplicane is after this generous citizen of Madras. Alangada Pillai founded a new Saiva temple, known in the Records as Allingall's Pagoda. This pagoda now goes by the name of Ekambaresvarar temple and finds mention in the map of Madras drawn by order of Thomas Pitt dated 1710. This pagoda is located in Mint Street which was originally known as the Washers Street, being a street primarily of calico washers. It may be recalled that Alangada Pillai who founded this institution was a colleague of Pedda Venkatadri who succeeded Verona (Kasi Viranna) on the latt^r's death in 1680. We are told that Alangada Pillai died in 1685; and was succeeded by Beri Timmappa, son of Pedda Venkatadri as chief merchant. Beri Timmappa did not properly acquit himself in his new office, and had to flee from Madras even within a year of his office. Chekka Serappa succeeded Beri Timmappa as chief merchant in 1696. This temple was long regarded as the common property of the Right Hand and Left Hand castes, the troubles arising out of quarrels between them causing frequently unrest and trouble to the government. It was later recognised as the possession of the Right Hand castes.

Much more important than this Ekambaresvarar temple, and very much in the eyes of the Company was the Madras Town temple also called the Chennakesava temple. This account of this temple has an historical interest to the student of Madras history. It figures prominently as the Great Pagoda in Thomas Pitt's map of 1710. It was located, as the map would show, in the present High Court Park. Nothing definite is known about the original foundation of this shrine. The earliest notice about this pagoda is by Dr. Fryer who was on a visit to the city in 1673. His impressions are worth quoting as they shed some welcome light on its architecture and sculpture, though his remarks thereon show colossal ignorance of the symbols represented by them.

> "Maderas divides itself into divers Long Streets, and they are checquered by as many transverse. It enjoys some CHOULTRIES for Places of Justice; one Exchange, one PAGOD, contained in a square Stone-wall; wherein are a number of Chappels

(if they may be comprehended under that Classis, most of them resembling rather Monuments for the Dead than Places of Devotion for the living) one for every tribe ; not under one Roof, but distinctly separate, though altogether, they bear the name of one intire PAGODA. The work is inimitably durable, the biggest closed up with Arches continually shut, as where is supposed to be hid their Mammon of Unrighteousness (they burying their Estates a here when they dye, by the persuasion of their Priests, towards their VIATICUM for another State) admitting neither Light nor Air, more than what the Lamps, always burning are by open Funnels above suffered to ventilate : By which Custom they seem to keep alive that Opinion of PLATO, in such a Revolution to return into the World again, after their Transmigration according to the Merits of their former living. Those of a minuter dimension were open, supported by slender straight and round pillars, plain and uniform up to the top where some Heiroglyphical Portraiture lends its assistance to the Roof, flat, with stones laid along like Planks upon our rafters. On the walls of good sculpture were obscene Images, where ARETINE might have furnished his Fancy for his Bawdy Postures: The Floor is stoned, they are of no great altitude ; stinking most egregiously of the Oyl they waste in their Lamps, and besmear their Beastly Gods with: Their outsides shew Workmanship and cost enough, wrought round with monstrous Effigies ; so that OLEUM AND OPERAM PERDERE, Pains and Cost to no purpose may not improperly be applied to them. Their gates are commonly the highest of the Work, the others concluding in shorter Piles."

With the acquisition of suburban villages perhaps the last of which was San Thome in 1749, the Company's government felt the need for the expansion of their army. The question of defence against their rivals and enemies assumed proportions of enormous importance. According to the Military Consultations of the year 1757, this pagoda had to be razed to ground owing to military exigencies. The government which was fully wedded to the support and patronage of Hindu institutions would not dare to desecrate the hallowed ground. In consideration of this act on their part, the Company generously offered in 1762 an area equal to that occupied by the old shrine in Peddunaikenpetta, to the south of China Bazaar Road, and helped the merchants and the local Hindu residents to put up a new structure, and the result was the new Town Temple erected in 1766. It is said that the Hindus being of Saiva and Vaishnava persuasion built two shrines—Chennai Kesava Perumal and Chennai Mallikesvarar. And the two shrines together are known as the Town Temple in the Records available, and seem to have existed in close association from the very beginning.

PANORAMIC VIEW OF THE TOWN TEMPLES OF CHENNA KESAVA PERUMAL AND MALLIKARJUNA

It may be noted in passing that from a letter addressed to Fort St. George in 1752, five years before its demolition, the pagoda is claimed to be the Company's Pagoda, and official recognition had been obtained to that effect. Col. H. D. Love who quotes this letter has an interesting observation to make. On account of this official recognition the temple servants of the New Town Temple continued to wear until recently badges marked with the words "East India Company." This only goes to confirm the view that was taken at the outset that the Town Temple was the Company's Pagoda and most probably the management of the temple was at one time vested in the Company. This means that a high percentage of tolls collected in the city for the maintenance and upkeep of temples and choultries were devoted to the expenses of the Town Temple. Mention can be made of two civil suits regarding the proper heir to the management of the temple. From these suits one can gather some important materials concerning the temple, its foundation and upkeep. One suit was in 1831, filed by the son and the grandson of Muthukrishna Mudaliar, who is claimed to be the founder-patron of the temple. Muthukrishna Mudaliar was Dubash to Governor Pigot (1755-63 and 1775-77). In those days the Dubashes wielded enormous powers and influence. So Muthukrishna opened a subscription list to erect the new Town Temple in place of the demolished one, and himself subscribed 5202 pagodas, while the Company's government paid a compensation price by contributing 1173 pagodas. The total amount collected including that realised from the public amounted to 15652 pagodas, and a fine structure was put up in the China Bazaar Road. Consequently the government appointed him as the First Warden of the shrine. He died in 1792 and as a result of the suit in 1831, his grandson Manali Muthukrishna Mudali (Junior) was recognised as Warden. According to the figures available during this early period, the income of the temple was from three sources: the Company's contributions being 500 pagodas, tolls and customs 800, and Raja of Kalahasti as the representative of the old Damarla family contributing 100 pagodas. In the second civil suit filed in 1898, some original documents were produced and these show that Naga Battan who was a gun-powder maker in the Company's service and Beri Timmanna a broker who came along with Day to Madras granted endowments to the Chennai Kesava Perumal temple in 1646 and 1648 respectively. Both the donors executed their documents in favour of one Narayanappa Ayyar or Narayana Ayyar.

[1]A Gift executed to Narrainappyer by Bari Thimmanen, who was employed as Native Head in the affairs of Moserinjour, an English Agent

1. Mr. K. Venkatasami Naidu, the Mayor of Madras, furnished me with this information from a record in his archives. We have the authority of Beri Thimmanna here to say that Madras (Chennapatam) formed a part of the Chola Kingdom

and Captain, residing at Chenna Puttanem alias Nawyer Nattoo, attached to Pulul Cottai of Sholavala Nattoo, under Thondamundalum, which had thereto been remarkably successful; dated Monday, Thriyodasee or the 13th (of either the bright or dark fortnight), the 28th of Chitri month in Sarvathari year of Salivahana Era, 1569.

(To say)

"Whereas at (this) Chenna Puttanem I have built the Chenna Casava Perumaul Covil, and have endowed it with Manyam, a piece of ground, and other privileges, which all I do (hereby) transfer now to you, and which you are to hold and enjoy from son to grandson, as long as the duration of (both) the sun and moon performing the divine services to their utmost extent. Should any one act prejudicially towards the charity, he would incur the guilt of having massacred a black cow on the bank of the Ganges. It is the gift to Narrainappyer by Bari Thimmanen through his consent."

(Signed) THIMMANEN.

"And as dictated written by Arnachellam on the part of Gooroovaputtem, Carnum of Chenna Puttanem."

As if to corroborate this, B. Ramaswami Nayudu, who published a *Memoir on the Revenue system of Madras,* in 1820, calls himself a descendant of Beri Timmappa (Timmanna) whom he refers as the builder of the Madras Temple. If the statement of Ramaswami Nayudu could be credited, then Beri Timmanna should have substantially added to the existing structure, as it undoubtedly stood before from the fact that only two years before Naga Battan had endowed it.

There were several other shrines put up in Madraspatam, thanks to the munificance of private merchants and generous public. Thomas Salmon who served as an Ensign of Madras garrison in 1699 has left behind an account of the city at the time and has occasion to refer to the existence of a number of temples, big and small, and points to the institution of female choristers or songstresses and priests. It was then a custom for these Choristers to form part of the equipage of a man of status and of some early governors of Fort St. George whenever they went out. For Salmon himself notes that governors of his time did not encourage that practice. About 1796 George Parry, Superintendent of Company's

in the greater division of Tondamandalam, which, according to the celebrated Naccinarkiniyar, was one of the divisions of the Tamil Nadu.

Lands reporting on collection due to the pagoda makes mention of ten temples and a water pandal, maintained by public funds.

It is not possible in a paper like this to furnish an account of the various temples that grew up rapidly in the growing city. Mention however may be made of the great Kachchali pagoda or the Kachchalesvarar temple built *circa* 1725 in Armenian Street beyond the Company's Old Garden by the members of the Left Hand caste in a Garden which originally was owned by one Kalavai Chetty. When it was found that the structure encroached upon the preserves of the Right Hand castes the latter objected and dissensions ensued. An arbitration board was set up and it was decided to open a new approach to the temple. There was the Mallikarjunar pagoda situated in the north of Muthialpet, between Thambu Chetty Street and the Linga Chetty Street. It is said to be an ancient foundation, and referred to as the "Mally Carjuns Old Pagoda" in the Company's records of the 17th century.

Another was Kalyana Varadarajasvami temple erected at Collett's pettah, the suburb that took the name of Governor Joseph Collett (1717-20). The latter vested in one Viraraghava, a Brahmin, the management of the shrine. The Governor is said to have helped the growth of this pagoda by lavish gifts. A part of the funds from the exports and imports of the city was allowed to this, and it is said that the Church Warden Viraraghava bestowed all his estate to the shrine. In this pettah weavers and painters from Tiruvorriyur settled in 1719.

The next pagoda of importance was Krishnaswami temple built about 1787, also in Muthialpetta. Three years had hardly passed since its foundation when dissensions between the Left Hand and the Right Hand castes set in. The members of the Right Hand caste hoisted their white flag during the festival in 1790, thus replacing the flag of five colours which was the ensign of the Left Hand group. The riot took a serious turn, and led to the arrest and imprisonment of the caste headmen at the Main Guard at the inner Fort Gate. The Government had to interfere and ordered that caste flags should be pulled down and the ensign of St. George alone be used. It was the custom to use these flags at Hindu festivals. The Government released the prisoners and instructed the Town Major to be the medium of communication between the Governor and the military garrison to maintain peace.

A similar case of Government arbitration is noticed when there was trouble between Komatties and Beri Chetties concerning the Chintadri Pillaiyar temple, erected probably in 1717, not far from the present Chennai Mallikesvarar shrine in Muthialpetta. In this locality one of the early pagodas seems to be Kalahastesvara shrine built in the heart of the present Coral Merchants Street, the date of its foundation coinciding with the commencement of Fort St. George.

The Kandaswami shrine situated in George Town near the Big Bazaar is a very wealthy and richly endowed temple, founded in the 18th century, with the help of the Beri Chetty community of the city. The image is said to have been taken from the Tirupporur shrine. It has a beautiful stone-faced and stepped tank and very costly and jewelled *vahanas*. The tower of the temple was renovated in recent times by a rich merchant, Kali Ratna Chettiyar. A grand festival is celebrated every year in the month of Tai (January-February) which attracts a vast concourse of people from every part of the city.

In the early part of the 18th century a piece of ground called the Komatla Thota (Cutwal Chawadee) otherwise called Kooragayala Thota (a vegetable garden) situated in Audiappa Naick street was dedicated by the then owner for the benefit of the Bania community. Its income was to be spent for their festivals and charities. This charity was managed by Sunku Chinna Krishnama Chetty in 1784. It was during the church wardenship of Colla Ravanappa Chetty, that the pagoda Kanyiakaparameswari and a number of bazaars were built in 1803-4 in Kotwal Bazaar by raising public subscriptions, himself contributing a liberal donation. The charities are now being managed by a committee of Vysiyas and are being devoted, among other purposes. to the education of Vaisya pupils. They are running two hostels, a dispensary and two elementary schools, one for boys and the other for girls. The present Kotwal market forms property of the Devasthanam.

Passing on to the suburbs of the Madraspatam side by side with foundations and annexations, the growth of Hinduism is distinctly marked. The village of *Chinna-tarai-pettai* is largely due to the enterprise and initiative of Adiappa Narayana the Dubash of Governor Benyon. The village of weavers which goes by the name of Chintadripettah today thus came into being. The residents being mainly Hindus, Adiappa erected new temples and for the benefit of the Muhammadans a mosque was also put up. About 1740 with the gradual loss of the estate of Adiappa, an appeal was preferred to the Company's Government for funds for the upkeep of the temple. Adiappa died in 1743. But the Chintadripet temple was later used as a powder magazine when the city was besieged in 1758-9 and as hospital in 1785.

Among the additions to the city, on an appeal to Emperor Aurangazeb, the Governor E. Yale, got Tandore (Tondiarpet), Persewacca (Purasawakkam) and Yegmore (Egmore) as free gift. The Emperor's son granted Nungambacca (Nungambakkam) and four adjoining vil-

KANDASWAMY TEMPLE, GEORGE TOWN

lages for an annual rent of 1500 pagodas. These were villages much more ancient than Fort St. George, and had their little pagodas like the Gangadharesvarar shrine of Purasawakkam. But the Iswaran temple in Nungambakkam deserves some attention. It contains a dated inscription and records a grant of lands to the Brahmans for its maintenance. Nungambakkam with Egmore is mentioned in epigraphy of the 11th century A.D. Egmore was known as Elumur and had a shrine dedicated to Telliyasinganayanar. Perhaps it is the present Perumal Koil adjoining the Gangu Reddy Road and facing the Chinna Reddy Road. It is interesting that Saint Appar refers to it. There was again probably a temple at Tirucharator near the end of Mint Street, and its only vestige is a slab (preserved in the Madras Museum) containing a fragment of inscription of Parthivendravarman's time.

The Muhammadan residents of the city were comparatively few. They figure as Moors in the Company's records. Their chief residences were in Moors Street. A mosque was built for their welfare in this street in Old Black Town by a chief merchant Cassa Verona (Kasi Viranna) who died in 1680 on behalf of the Company. When Yale was Governor, another mosque was put in Muthialpet. Both these served the Muhammadan population of Madraspatam in the first century of its existence. It is interesting to see how the Hindus of the city were tolerant and respected the religious teachings of their Muhammadan brethren. They founded mosques for them and in some cases continued to manage such foundations.

Thus it is seen that by donations, endowments and funds collected from a tax on exports and imports being a voluntary payment, and with customs dues, the Company's government made ample provision for the maintenance and upkeep of Hindu pagodas and Moslem places of worship. Whenever there were communal troubles between the Left Hand and Right Hand castes, government effectively interfered and settled their differences either by arbitration or by order in Council. In some cases the riots were of a serious nature and the government was hard put to keep order and peace. On one occasion the aged and children of the caste were imprisoned, but Government released them. It is not possible to find out the origin of the rise of the twc groups, the Left Hand and the Right Hand. But they already figure in the time of the imperial Colas and seem to be peculiar to South India. On what basis this division was made it is not yet possible to say definitely. One explanation may be that one group represented the native inhabitants and the other emigrants to the land. Though both professed a common faith and common beliefs, the disputes were about the particular street through which a festival or a funeral procession was to pass, and matters of such trivial interest. Even to-day remnants of these groups survive in parts of Chingleput district. Whatever be their origin and views, the Company's government took timely and bold steps to compose their differences then and there, and bring about communal unity and peace. For under these conditions alone trade and commerce would flourish and prosper.

The accounts of the pagodas were properly kept. It was then a custom to pay a fee of ten cash to the Town Conicoply (Kanakku Pillai or accountant) by every pagoda. It was not paid out of the funds of the Company, but it was a voluntary payment made by the native merchants, probably in charge of charities and charitable institutions, like temples, watersheds and other religious and quasi-religious institions. A certain Kanakku Pillai Periya Aiyan claimed this fee when it fell in arrears for a long time. This office of Conicoply served the purpose of auditing the accounts so that the funds allotted would not be misused.

While it was largely a case of communal riots between Left and Right Hand castes in the temples established at Madraspatam, there were similar troubles between Tengalai and Vadagalai sects among the Vaishnavas, concerning the management of the Parthasarathy temple at Triplicane. The chief differences centred round the form of the prayer and the service in the temple. Up to 1676 when Triplicane was granted to the Company, they did not interfere in its politics. But when it became a part of the city, the temple was placed in charge of the Company's chief merchants. In 1736, an interesting case before the Mayor's Court was launched to the effect that two merchants refused to take certain oaths, as they 'were contrary to their religion and the Rules of their caste.' The Mayor's Court committed them to jail. But a great crowd of people entered the Fort on behalf of these merchants and petitioned to the President of the Council. The President observed that the Natives might not be disturbed in their religious Rites and ceremonies, and instructed the Mayor and the Sheriff to release these two merchants.

The next dispute between the two sects of Brahmans broke out in 1780 and engaged the attention of Governor John Whitehill. It was a petition from the Tengalai sect against the new prayer of the Vadagalai Brahmans who had been authorised to use their prayer by Lord Pigot and who were assisted in that by the Town Major and a number of Sepoys. The Government decided in favour of the petitioners. This evoked a counter-petition from the Vadagalai sect. Sadlier, a member of the Council, confirmed the decision of the Board taken in 1754 and

THE PARTHASARATHI TEMPLE, TRIPLICANE

1766 and ordered that 'neither of the Prayers named Streesyla Diapatrom (Sri Sailesa Daya Patram) be allowed to be said in future.' A similar outbreak is reported in 1790. As in the case of the Town temple the Company's government managed the Triplicane temple by means of their chief merchants and continued to maintain communal concord and harmony allowing freedom of conscience as far as possible.

In pursuance of the policy established by precedent and custom the officials of the East India Company patronised the pagodas in different ways. Lord Clive (Earl of Powis) Governor of Madras (1798-1803) presented jewels to the Conjeevaram and Madras pagodas from the loot of Seringapatam. The patronage of Joseph Collett has already been referred to. Lionel Place, Collector of Chingleput (Jaghir District) (*circa* 1794-1800), who had his headquarters at Karunguzhi is said to have made several gifts to the temples at Madurantakam, now a Railway Station not far from Madras.

In addition to gifts and patronage of the temples and their festivals by the Company's government, it was customary to send out troops on the occasion of the celebration of Indian festivals and of the ceremonial visits of the Nawabs of the Carnatic. It once happened that a Private of the 40th Native Infantry was killed by a fireworks explosion, when he escorted two women carrying bundles of rockets during the great Conjeevaram festival in June 1836. On this Sir Robert O'Callaghan, Commander-in-Chief in 1836, ordered that such escorting troops should be "kept in a collected body as a military guard for the maintenance of order, and......not on any account to be permitted to join or take part in the procession or ceremony, nor to act as escorts either to persons or property."

This order was construed by Brigadier Fane, commanding at Trichinopoly, as an absolute prohibition, and he refused the honorary escort for the Hindu festivals at that place. He quoted, in support of action, a previous circular that the employment of military drums and bands should not be allowed in the cantonments as was usually permitted on certain festival days, and at places of worship, except when required for the service of the Established (Anglican) Church. In this way began the protest of the Company's servants against participating in Hindu festivals.

The whole question was considered by the Governor-in-Council, the Commander-in-Chief adhering to his own view. A Government order was issued in March 1837 that the previous order of June 1836 of the Commander-in-Chief was not to make any change as to the occasions on which troops should attend native festivals, but only to regulate the manner of their employment when required to attend at such festivals according to custom; and they should not participate in the ceremonies or processions, nor detached individually, but only employed as soldiers for the maintenance of order. It was not to interdict their attendance as guards or escorts at festivals and to compliment native princes.

The Commander-in-Chief who was not satisfied with the order of the Madras Government kept it in abeyance and forwarded all the papers to the Government of India. The reply received from the Government of India on 21-6-1837, regretted the ambiguous wording of the Madras Commander-in-Chief's General Order of 21st June 1836, and also his habit of issuing letters having all the force of a general order, on questions involving general policy or innovations in long-established customs. It approved of the resolution of the Madras Government and recommended that the circular orders of the Commander-in-Chief varying with it, should be allowed to fall gradually into desuetude, without being formally cancelled. Attendance of troops at native festivals and in honour of native princes was to continue as usual; only Christian drummers should not be compelled to be present at the religious festivals of the Sepoys except when on duty with their Company. The Madras Commander-in-Chief appealed against this to the Court of Directors stating that the compulsory attendance of officials and soldiers at festivals might be offensive to their conscience and deprecating the allowing of orders to fall into desuetude. The reply from the Court of Directors was unfavourable as it led to the resignation of Sir Peregrine Maitland, the then Commander-in-Chief of Madras Army in December 1838. The immediate cause of his resignation was his refusal to punish a European soldier who did not attend a native festival contrary to practice. The practice of troops attending festivals, etc. however gradually ceased.

At this time Bishop Corrie of Madras again submitted to the Madras government a memorial signed by 150 civil and military servants and by 50 clergymen and missionaries protesting against official patronage of idolatry. The Secretary of the Madras Government in the course of his reply wrote; "that he was directed to inform the Bishop that the sentiments of the Governor were not in accordance with the sentiments of the memorialists, that the Governor was sorry the Bishop did not attend to his own particular duties in moderating the zeal of overheated minds, instead of agitating questions that were calculated to endanger the peace of the country." The Bishop was thus censured. When the memorial ultimately reached the Directors, they sent a despatch that was "ambiguous and faint-hearted." This was another ground which weighed with Sir Peregrine Maitland in his resignation. Lord Auckland who became Governor-General in 1836 was perplexed by this episode in Madras.

But 'the tender dry-nursing' of Hindu and Moslem religious institutions continued to be shown by the Company's Government. It is recorded that in 1837 the Order of British India was bestowed on Kilpauk Chittaldroog for his splendid organisation of the procession of Jagannath. At the same time the agitation on the part of Christian officials and non-officials also continued with the result that in 1840 the pilgrims' tax was abolished. The gradual withdrawal of Company's patronage was viewed with suspicion by the natives of India. Confidence was however restored by the proclamation of Her Imperial Majesty Queen Victoria in 1858, assuring of religious neutrality due regard being paid 'to the ancient rights, usages and customs of India.' From this time the temples in the city were placed under the management of a trustee or trustees and continue to function with satisfaction. During this period again a number of small temples have been built, and the old ones renovated.

BIBLIOGRAPHY

H. D. Love: *Vestiges of Old Madras* (1913).

Rev. William Cambell: *British India in its relation to the Decline of Hinduism and the Progress of Christianity* (London, 1858) Chapter XXV.

F. Penny: *The Church in Madras*, Vol. III.

A. Mayhew: *Christianity and the growth of India*, pp. 144-45.

Buckland: *Dictionary of Indian Biography* (1906).

Wilson: *History of the Madras Army.*

Madras Epigraphy Reports.

Epigraphia Indica, Vol. VIII.

John Fryer: *East India and Persia* (Hakluyt Society).

Records relating to the Town temple (in the possession of Mr. K. Venkataswami Naidu).

MacLean: *Manual of the Madras Administration* (1881).

The Aryan Path, Vol. VI, Nos. 10-12 (1935).

Divyappirabandam.

Tevaram.

Kapilar Ahaval.

Tirunurrantati.

Neminatham.

Fort St. George and St. Mary's Church

By

H. C. Stagg

Messrs. Macmillian & Co., Madras.

Madras for a city of its size and importance is singularly lacking in buildings or sites of any great historical importance, mainly because the original settlement was a creation of the East India Company, purely as a trading centre.

In the early part of the seventeenth century, it was essential that any overseas trading centre was fortified against possibility of attack, and when Francis Day, on behalf of the Company, obtained from the Naik of Chandragiri the grant of a strip of land at Madraspatam as a site for a Factory, permission to build a fortification to protect the same was also obtained. This original settlement and Fort was the basis of the present Fort St. George.

Compared with the present Fort, the settlement was quite small, consisting of only sufficient buildings to house the Company's staff and 'Factory', or trading quarters. It was surrounded by a fortified wall, with bastions at each corner, the whole area comprising only about 100 yards square.

This settlement, completed in 1650, ten years after the commencement of building, soon become the Company's Headquarters on the Coromandel Coast. As trade increased, extensions were needed, and these being erected outside the walls of the original Fort, had to be enclosed by a new wall, and by 1666 the Agent of the Company—at that time Aaron Baker—had completed an outer Fort, with bastions, batteries and a moat. This new fort was the basis of the present Fort, but of the old inner fort no traces are left. The Fort contains within its walls, St. Mary's Church, the first Anglican Church to be built in India, which with its wealth of monuments, tombs and records, gives us a picture of the development of the British in Madras.

The Indian servants of the Company took up their residence mainly to the North of the Fort, the settlement being named Blacktown, and in due course this area was also enclosed by ramparts to afford protection for the residents. Only a small portion of these outer ramparts at Royapuram is now in existence as they were demolished by the French during their occupation of Fort St. George in 1746-9. The name Blacktown was changed to Georgetown in 1906, in commemoration of the visit of the Prince of Wales, the late King George V to Madras.

Of the buildings of historical interest inside the Fort, St. Mary's Church is of most importance. This Church was built entirely by the result of local effort, the Governor of Fort St. George, the Hon. Streynsham Masters, heading the subscription list with a donation of 100 pagodas (£33). The work of building was started in 1678 and the Church was completed and opened for worship in 1680. Apart from the Vestry, Sanctuary and Spire, the Church remains unaltered to the present day.

The Church was designed and built by William Dixon, who was the Chief Gunner and Designer of Bastions to the East India Company, a peculiarity of the design being the bomb-proof roof, which was made five feet thick.

The burial ground was originally the site now occupied by the Law College; but the tombstones erected there being used by the French during the siege of Madras as cover for the besiegers, were, when the siege was raised, dismantled and the inscribed stones moved to the Fort, where they now form a pavement round the North Side of the Church Compound. Among them also are a few taken from the Old Capuchin Church of St. Andrew, destroyed in 1749. The oldest stone, dated August 5th 1652, is to the memory of Elizabeth Baker, wife of the first Governor of Fort St. George. Many of the stones appear to have served as gun platforms at various times and have been recovered from the Fort walls. Two memorials were left standing on the site of the old cemetery, one being the obelisk to the memory of David Yale, the son of Elihu Yale, one-time Governor of Madras, 1682, especially famed by the Yale University in America being named after him. Yale was an American colonist by birth, but had been educated in England, and had come first to Madras in the East India Company's service as a Writer. After his return to England, being approached to help in founding a place of learning in America, he forwarded a gift of books worth then over £500 to the infant University, which was subsequently known as the Yale University.

St. Mary's contains the burial places and monuments of many famous Europeans who have served in India—statesmen and missionaries, soldiers and sailors. Six Governors of Madras lie buried below the Chancel steps, all men of renown and of marked uprightness of character, and a detailed examination of the various inscriptions on these and other memorials in the Church well repays the time so spent.

The Church records and registers date from the consecration of the Church in 1680 and form a complete record of the Church, with the exception of the three years 1746-9 during which Madras was in the pos-

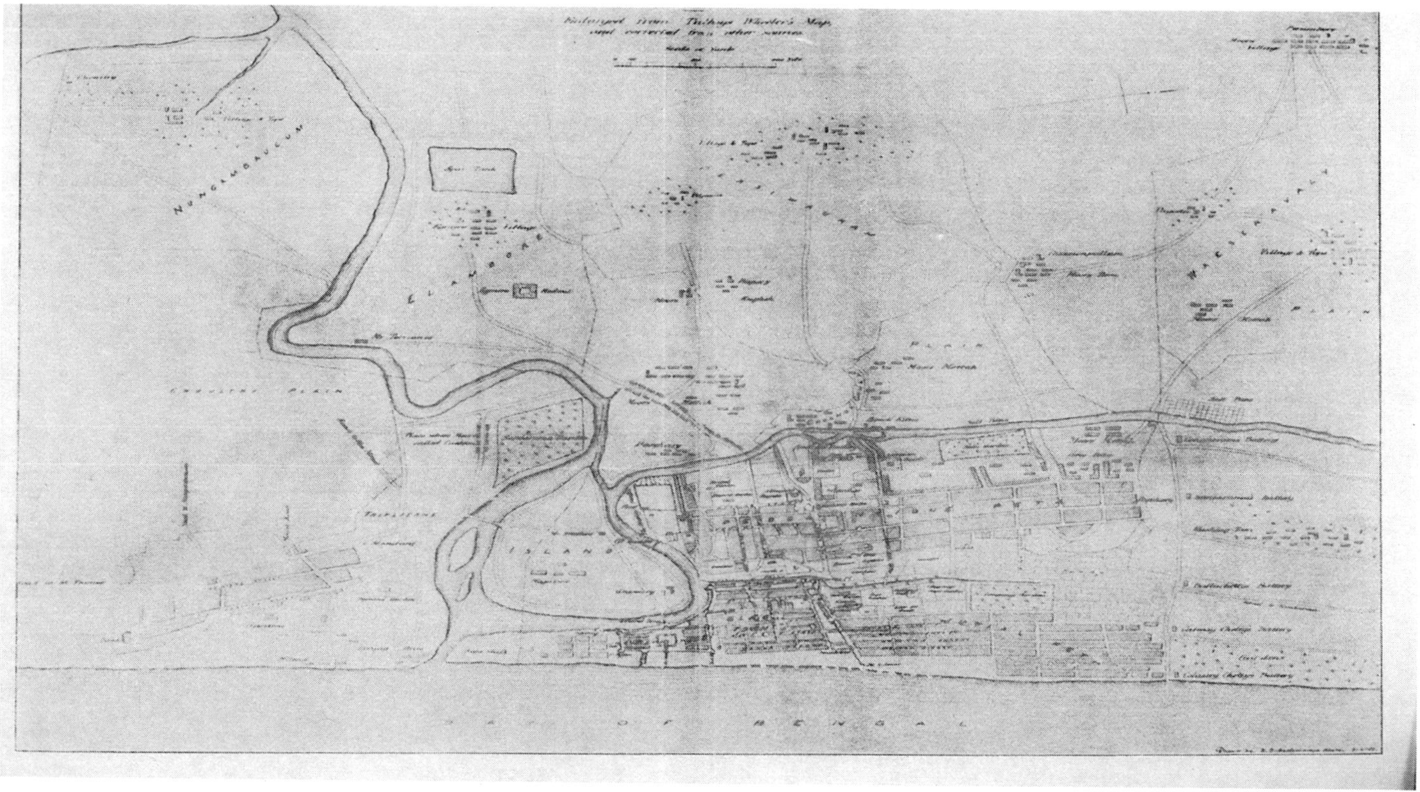
NUNGUMBAUKUM
ISLAND
BAY OF BENGAL

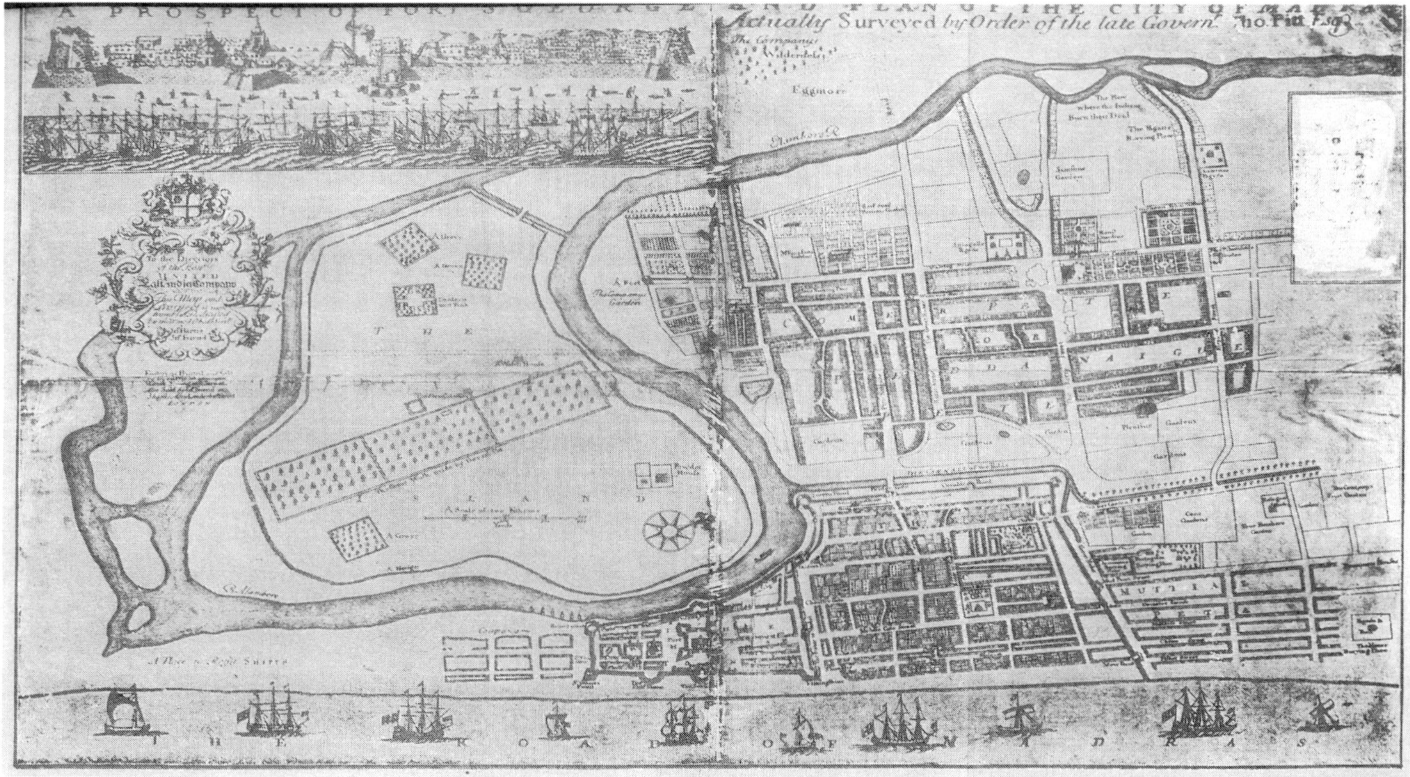
A PROSPECT OF FORT S.T GEORGE AND PLAN OF THE CITY OF MADRAS
Actually Surveyed by Order of the late Govern.r Tho. Pitt Esq.r
The Companys Walderdole
Eggmore
Ellambore R.
The Place where the Indians Burn their Dead
The Moors Burying Place
Garden
A Port
The Company's Garden
Powder House
Gardens
A Grove
A Scale of one Mile
THE ISLAND
A Place to Repair Shipps
Company
COM
PE
DA
TE
NAIG
MUTTIA
PETTA
Company's Burying Place
The Companys Great Gardens
THE ROAD OF MADRAS
To the Directors of the Honble United East India Company
This Map and Prospect

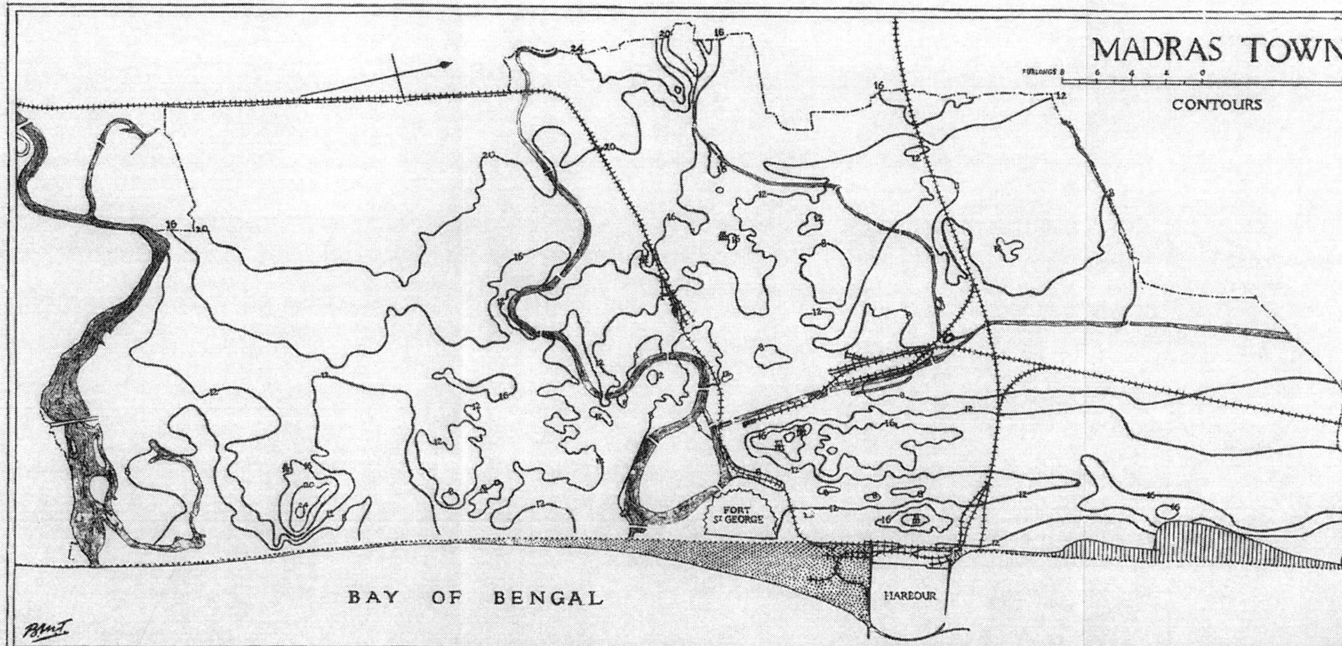
MADRAS TOWN
FURLONGS 8 6 4 2 0 1 MILE
CONTOURS
FORT St GEORGE
HARBOUR
BAY OF BENGAL

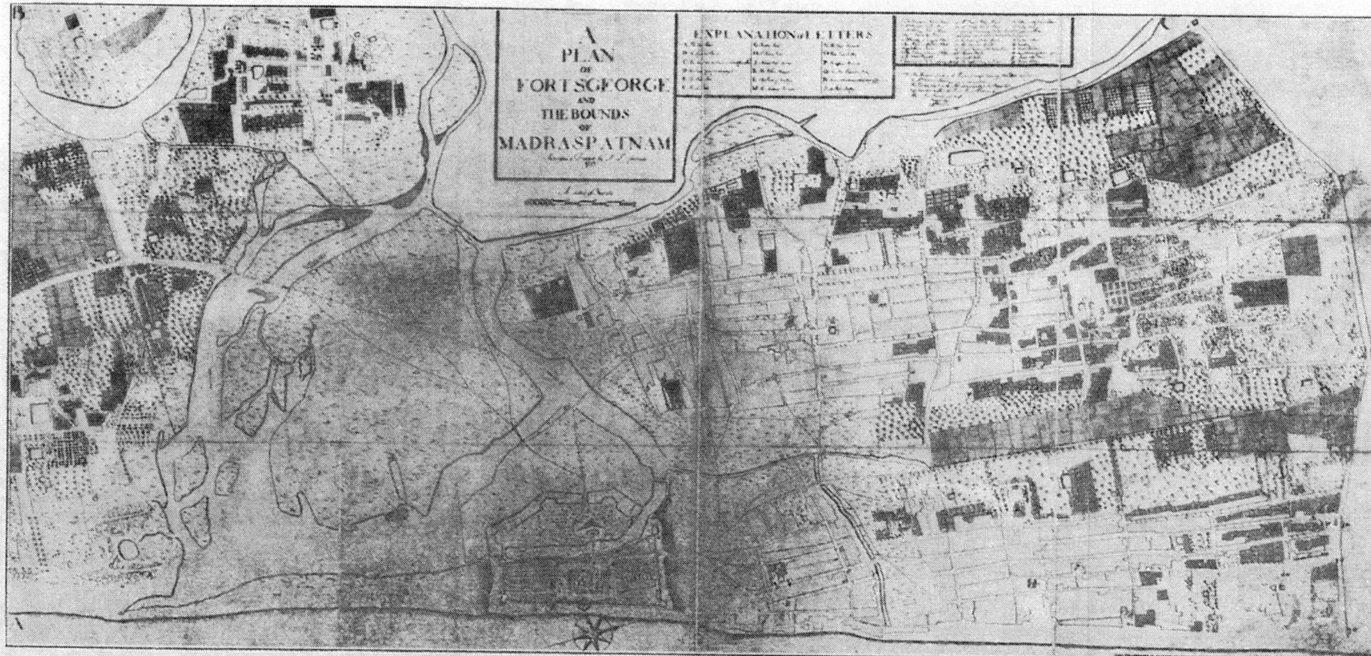
A
PLAN
OF
FORT S.GEORGE
AND
THE BOUNDS
OF
MADRASPATNAM
EXPLANATION of LETTERS

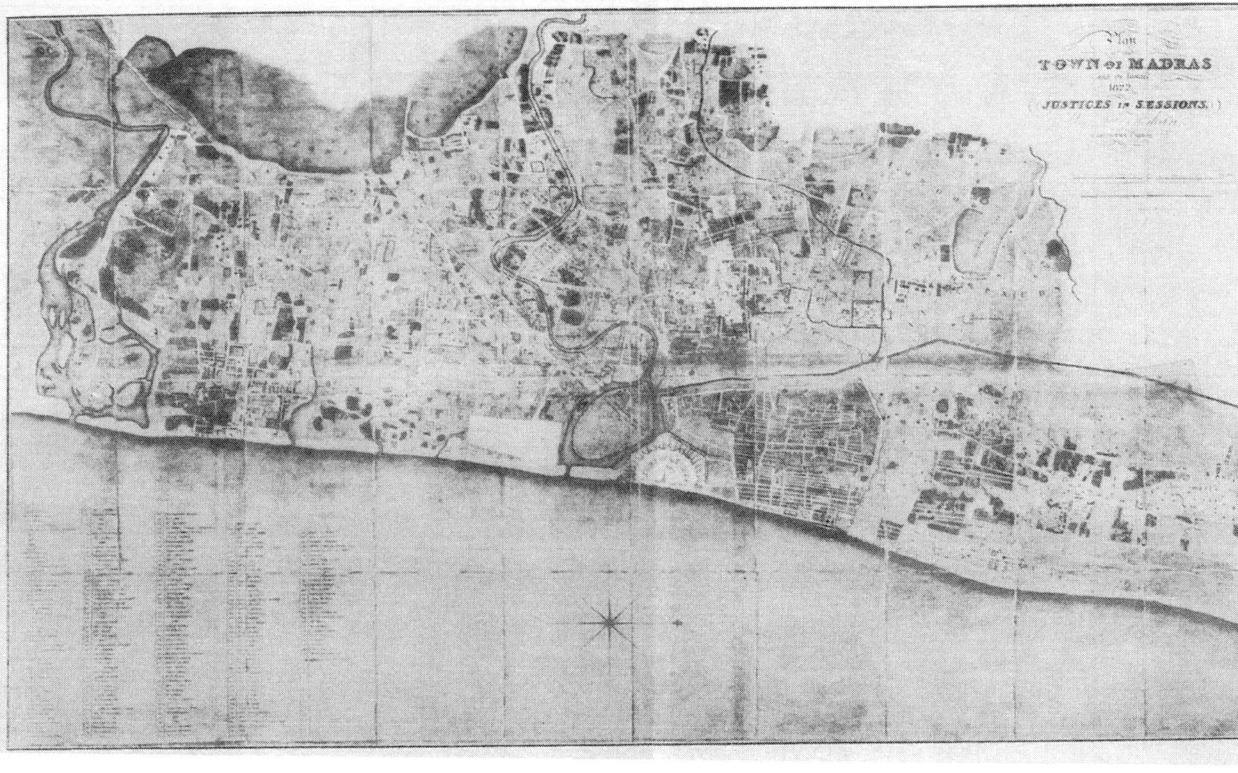
Plan
TOWN of MADRAS
1822
JUSTICES in SESSIONS.

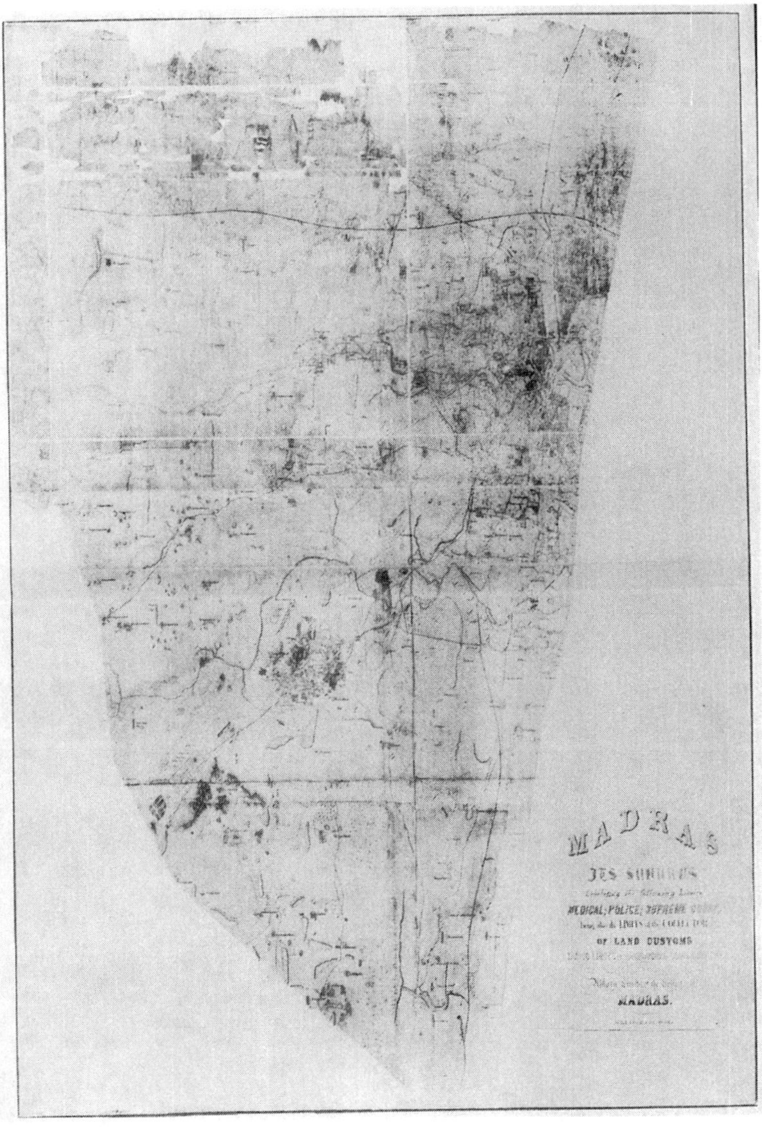
MADRAS
OF LAND CUSTOMS
MADRAS.

ST. MARY'S CHURCH, FORT ST. GEORGE

session of the French. The first marriage entry is that of Elihu Yale to Catherine Himmers on Nov. 4th 1680. Another record of great interest is the marriage of Robert Clive to Margaret Maskelyne on Feb 18th 1753. A reference in the records is also found to Job Charnock the founder of Calcutta, whose three children were baptized in St. Mary's Church.

The Church has in its possession many valuable and historical articles. The large picture over the Altar depicting the Last Supper, is dated by experts as sixteenth century work and is ascribed to the School of Raphael. Tradition says that the Chalice in the picture was painted by the great Raphael himself. No authentic record can be found of the origin of the picture but it is supposed to have been taken from a church in Pondicherry when this town was captured by the British in 1761. Altar rails were presented to the Church by the Princess of Tanjore, who desired thus to commemorate her love and friendship for Lady Hobart, wife of Lord Hobart, who was Governor from 1794 to 1798. The carved teakwood railings of the West Gallery are of beautiful Oriental design and workmanship, and date back to the 17th century. Of considerable historical value is a Bible printed in 1660, once the property of the Hon. Streynsham Masters. St. Mary's also possesses many pieces of Church Plate of historic interest, the most important being:—the Yale Plate, presented in 1687 by Elihu Yale; a large silver alms-dish, embossed with the Yale family coat-of-arms; the Goldsborough Plate, a plate and Flagon presented in 1689 and embossed with the Goldsborough coat-of-arms; a plate of heavy beaten silver, engraved with the crown of the King of Denmark, originally in use in the Danish Mission at Tranquebar, and entrusted to St. Mary's when this mission was closed down. With this came an alms-bag mounted on a rod which bore a silver band dated 1687.

Two other pieces of Danish workmanship are a graceful Wine Flagon dated 1712 and a small individual Communion set of silver, dated 1689. A composite Chalice undated, is of special interest as the stand is a chased silver French candlestick, the bowl of beaten English silver work, while the lid is of Indian design and workmanship.

Adorning the walls of the Church are many old Regimental Colours deposited here on the disbanding of the regiments; the pair of greatest interest being those of the 102nd Royal Madras Infantry, originally Neill's Blue Caps 1688, and carried through the Burmese war of 1852/3 and the Indian Mutiny.

Besides the Church there are few buildings of historical interest in the Fort. The present office of the Accountant General, West of the Church, was at one time the residence of the Governor of the Fort and was occupied by Clive at the time of his marriage. The Officer's Mess (North of the Secretariat) was originally built as the Public Exchange Hall, and it is of interest that the money for its construction was raised by a series of lotteries, and that the first lighthouse erected in Madras was built on its roof. In the centre of the present block of buildings comprising the Secretariat and Council Chamber is the site of the original official residence of the Governor. The black pillars of the present structure have a peculiar interest in being part of a colonnade erected by Governor Sir Thomas Pitt in 1734, which extended from the Fort Square to the Sea Gate. These were removed by the French to Pondicherry when they captured Madras in 1746, and brought back again in 1771 when the British successfully stormed Pondicherry. The best preserved ones were incorporated in the present Council buildings in 1910.

The Catholic Mission in Madras

By

THE RIGHT REV. MGR. P. THOMAS,
Madras.

WHEN Francis Day acquired the strip of land on which Fort St. George now stands and the English established themselves in Madras, there were many Catholics and churches in the neighbouring Portuguese settlement of San Thome but none in the city proper. Some of these Catholics were of pure Portuguese origin while others were of mixed blood with Portuguese names. They were well acquainted with the language, customs and manners of the inhabitants of the country and the agents of the East India Company realised their importance and value as subordinates, interpreters, clerks, tradesmen and soldiers. They were invited to settle in the new township; plots of land were given to them for houses outside the Fort and they were allowed the free exercise of their religion with the services of a priest of their own faith. The Portuguese settlers in the Fort were ministered unto by a Portuguese priest. Within a year of the foundation of Fort St. George, the Portuguese missioners built a church on the outskirts of the British settlement. That was the Church of the Assumption of Our Lady situated in Portuguese Church street, North Georgetown;—thus a building of historic importance.

Jealousies and disagreements soon arose between the English and the Portuguese and the Company's representatives began to dislike the idea that Portuguese priests should be the spiritual directors and advisers of Catholics in their territory. In the meantime, it happened that a French Capuchin Fr. Ephraim de Nevers arrived in Madras on his way to Pegu, Burma. A native of Auxerre and a brother of Monsieur de Chateau des Bois, Councillor of Paris, he made his journey by land across the peninsula from Surat to Masulipatam in order to reach his destination. But he could not get a ship in Masulipatam, the English settlement there having been in the meanwhile broken up. He was advised to go to Madras and accordingly Fr. Ephraim came here to look for a vessel that would take him to Burma. As there was no ship sailing immediately, Fr. Ephraim made himself useful by ministering to the Catholic settlers in Fort St. George. A polished linguist, he was able to converse in English, Portuguese and Dutch, besides his own native tongue, French. He was also conversant with Persian and Arabic. As already stated the ministrations of Portuguese priests to the Catholic inhabitants of Madras did not find favour with the Company's representatives. The English merchants, therefore, invited Fr. Ephraim to remain in the city and take charge of the Portuguese settlers, promising him support and protection. They thought it prudent to have clergymen different in nationality from, and independent of, the Portuguese Bishop of San Thome, to minister to Catholics in their settlement. Fr. Ephraim himself was unwilling to stay being under orders to proceed to Pegu, and besides, as Madras was within the diocese of San Thome, the Bishop was not likely to approve of a scheme in which the ministrations of his own priest would have to be set at nought in favour of a stranger. But the East India Company was influential. Reference was made to Fr. Ephraim's superiors in Paris and another to the Holy See. The Pope was requested to separate ecclesiastically the British portion of Madras and Pope Urban VIII issued a decree to that effect and erected the Prefecture Apostolic of Madras.

Though the English at Fort St. George and the Portuguese at San Thome seem to have lived on friendly terms, there was an under-current of distrust on both sides. The Portuguese resented the establishment of a Prefecture Apostolic in Madras. And in 1649 when Fr. Ephraim visited a Portuguese factory in San Thome, he was seized by some officers and carried off to Goa in a small frigate which was ready to sail. He was lodged in prison but it was two years before he was released and returned to Madras at the intervention of Coota Khan, the King of Golconda, as well as that of the Governor of Fort St. George.

Catholics were so numerous in the White Town around Fort St. George as also in the Black Town (now George Town) close by that within three years of the foundation of Fort St. George the Governor permitted a French priest to build a chapel in the town. It was indeed somewhat strange and was an index of the broad and tolerant spirit of the local representatives of the East India Company at the time that in the British settlement founded, under the auspices of such a notorious anti-Catholic as Queen Elizabeth, a Catholic church should have been built but not an Anglican church. And when the church was blessed and solemnly opened for service in 1675, the Governor ordered salutes to be fired (Penny, The Church in Madras p. 219) Another church was built in Hunter's Road, Vepery, on the very spot in which St. Mathias' (Anglican) is situated. In 1746 Fort St. George and the walled town of Madras surrendered to the French naval and military force under Admiral La Bourdonnais. The rendition of Fort St. George and Madras to the English Company was arranged in the treaty of Aix-la-Chapelle of 1748 and carried out in August 1749. The capture of Madras was partly attributed to the information reported to have been given to their countrymen in Pondicherry by the French Capuchin priests. The Catholic churches in the Fort and in Vepery were confiscated and destroyed under orders from the Directors of the Company in England. In a despatch to Fort St. David, the Directors wrote: "Having suffered greatly by the number of priests and popish inhabitants at Madras, who have acted a very treacherous part to us continually in that place, especially when it was attacked, therefore, we strictly forbid your suffering any Romish Church within our bounds, or of any of their priests to dwell among you, or that religion to be openly professed; and in case any papists have crept into places of trust in our service, they must be immediately dismissed;"—Dated December 24, 1747 (Penny op. cit., 323-324). Father Rene, on whom the suspicion rested most heavily, was deported to Europe and others expelled from the Fort.

Fabricius and Breithaupt, royal Danish missionaries who entered the services of the S.P.C.K. and who had retired to Pulicat with some of their orphans and converts after the fall of Madras, wrote to the Governor of Fort St, David requesting that they might be given possession of the Catholic churches in Madras and deprecating the grant of the free exercise of the Catholic religion. This letter was written two months before the local Government decided to adopt a policy of confiscation and partial expulsion. The chapel at Vepery together with the mission house and garden were handed over to Fabricius and the S. P. C. K. Mission.

In 1767 Fr. Bernard, the Superior of the Capuchins, sent a petition to the Directors in England asking for compensation for the churches and houses confiscated and destroyed. The Capuchins sent also a deputation to England two years later for the redress of their grievances. In 1787 Sir Archibald Campbell took a census and found that there were 17,000 Roman Catholics within the walls of Madras. In the meantime, the power of the French had declined, the French having been defeated in various engagements and the fortifications in Pondicherry destroyed. The English became gradually more tolerant of the religion of Frenchmen and a few years later paid the Capuchins Rs. 50,000 as compensation for the destruction of the church in White Town and that in Vepery. Efforts were, however, made to exclude French priests and to replace them by Portuguese and Italians. The Government interfered constantly with the appointment or exclusion of priests so much so that in 1802 the Catholic inhabitants of Madras petitioned the Government not to interfere in matters of appointment of priests or of ecclesiastical discipline and detail. From the 19th century onwards, the Government left the Catholic Church alone and allowed it to live its own life. The

Capuchins built the Cathedral in Armenian Street in 1775, but inscribed the date 1642 on the gates as a public record of their first establishment in Madras and later when the Church was enlarged and the gates widened, the date was preserved at the request of the oldest inhabitants. The Capuchins carried on their work bravely in spite of many vicissitudes and trials till the year 1832 when a Vicariate Apostolic was erected in Madras. St. Andrew's Church, Vepery was built by a Capuchin.

According to a time-honoured local Indian tradition, corroborated by collateral evidence, St. Thomas, one of the twelve Apostles, preached on the West Coast in Malabar, founded churches and established Christian communities and came finally to Mylapore, which was then a flourishing city. The number of converts he made roused the wrath of the Hindu priests who drove him from his cave in Little Mount and pursued him to St. Thomas Mount, about a mile away, and pierced him with a lance as he prayed kneeling on a stone in A.D. 68. His remains were brought to Mylapore and buried in a house in which he had lived and which was used as a place of worship.

Thus it was that there were Catholics and churches in Mylapore before the English settled in Madras. No record is available of the subsequent history and progress of Christianity in the city till the arrival of the Portuguese when a settlement grew up round the shrine of St. Thomas and was given the name of San Thome.

St. Francis Xavier, the great apostle of Mylapore in 1545 prayed at the grave of St. Thomas. The first church built in the city of which evidence is available is that of the Luz in 1516 about a mile due west of San Thome Cathedral. When the Portuguese first came to the Coromandel Coast and were struggling against a gale seeking a landing place, they made a vow to the Blessed Virgin Mary. Suddenly they discerned a light on the shore. They decided to land. The light moved on and disappeared in a jungle. The Portuguese stopped where the light had vanished and built a church in honour of Our Lady of Light, "Luz", after Nossa Sanhorada Luz (Our Lady of Light). This story is supported by the fact that the Church is even now called in the vernacular 'Kattu Kovil' or "Jungle Church" and the whole locality round it is known as "The Luz". The road and the street and many houses are also named "Luz". The locality is no longer a forest, but a wealthy residential quarter with many graceful buildings. The Franciscans, and the Dominicans established missions in San Thome and the Ausgustinians and the Jesuits followed in their wake. At the request of Philip II, King of Portugal, Pope Paul V erected the diocese of San Thome. The present Bishop of Mylapore is the twentieth to rule over the diocese of San Thome from the year 1606. There were many periods

ST. ANDREW'S, VEPERY

—By Courtesy of the Rt. Rev. Mgr. P. Thomas.

during which the See of Mylapore remained vacant, the longest and most notable of them being from 1637 to 1693 when no less than nine personages were selected by the Crown of Portugal for the honour; but they either declined the appointment, or were promoted or died before the election was confirmed by the Holy See. Its territory at the time was vast comprising as it did the Fishery Coast, the Coromandel Coast, Bihar and Orissa, Bengal and the ancient Pegu. The present magnificent Cathedral was built and completed by Bishop Henry Reed de Silva, who was the first to assume the title of the Bishop of Mylapore in order to avoid confusing San Thome in Madras with San Thome de Principe (on the West Coast of Africa), an important possession of Portugal.

In 1832 Madras was erected into a Vicariate Apostolic and on July 3 of the same year, Fr. John Polding, an English Benedictine, was appointed the first Vicar Apostolic but he declined the appointment and eventually became the Archbishop of Sydney. The Mission was then taken charge of by Pedro D'Alcantara, of the Carmelite Order, Vicar Apostolic of Bombay. In August 1835 Dr. Daniel O'Connor assumed government of the mission and was succeeded by other Irishmen till the death of Dr. Colgan in 1911. Dr. Patrick Joseph Carew became the Vicar Apostolic in 1840 but was transferred to Calcutta two years later; then came Dr. John Fennelly 1842-68; his brother Stephen Fennelly, 1868 to 1880; Joseph Colgan 1882 to 1911; John Aelen, coadjutor since 1902 and Archbishop from 1911 to 1928. On his resignation Archbishop Eugene Mederlet of the Salesian Society was appointed Archbishop of Madras. He died suddenly while on a mission tour in December 1934 and was succeeded by the present Archbishop Louis Mathias in July 1935.

It was during the administration of Irish Bishops, chiefly, Dr. John Fennelly, that the status of the Catholic community was raised and the legitimate claims of British Catholic subjects in both military and civil service adequately recognised by the Government. They and the other Irish missioners, almost all of who were doctors of divinity and had a perfect knowledge of the English language, were socially and intellectually on a level with the best British talent. When Dr. O'Connor first came out, he brought letters of introduction to the Government House. On the first occasion when he drove to the Church of St. Mary of the Angels in Armenian Street, wearing a cocked hat and buckled shoes, long coat and knee-breeches, the old ladies protested that he could be no Catholic bishop but an emissary of the Government to make them all Protestants. One of the outstanding features of the episcopate of Dr. John Fennelly was the tremendous influence he exercised over the European residents of the city and in particular over the Irish Catholic soldiers, who were numerous in those days. An indefatigable worker, he never spared himself but laboured continuously for his flock. He was also a great writer and an able controversialist, and made the Catholic religion, against which the prejudice of Englishmen was deep-seated, respected and its adherents accorded equal rights with those of the Protestant faith, especially in the matter of promotion of Catholics from the ranks in the Indian army.

The progress of the Catholic Church in Madras was not a little hampered by the continual bickerings and misunderstandings between the Propaganda and Padroado. The local ordinaries in San Thome insisted on the Capuchins acknowledging their jurisdiction, a claim which the latter rejected relying on the papal brief. Church was built against church and altar raised against altar. The Concordats of 1857 and 1886 between the Holy See and Portugal gradually improved matters and the diplomatic convention of June 29, 1929, completely abolished the system of double jurisdiction. The river Cooum was made the boundary between the diocese of Mylapore and the Archdiocese of Madras, the territory south of the river with the Catholics and churches therein being exclusively assigned to the former, and those north of the river to the latter.

Catholics in the city of Madras are fairly numerous and form a strong body. Scattered in various parts of the city and with 18 churches to serve their needs (12 of which belong to Madras and 6 to Mylapore) they number approximately 40,000 at present. According to the Government census of 1931, the number of Catholics was 32,622 against 21,109 Protestants of all denominations taken together. There are a few churches of good proportions and striking beauty, as the San Thome Cathedral, St. Anthony's Church, Pudupet, St. Joseph's Church, Vepery, and the Church of Christ the King, Loyola College. There are nineteen convents belonging to different congregations, engaged in educational and charitable work. The Presentation Order, the oldest in the city introduced in 1842, is represented by six houses. A number of elementary and secondary schools are conducted by both European and Indian nuns for Anglo-Indian and Indian pupils and are also attended by hundreds of non-Catholic children. Catholic life is thus vigorous as evidenced by the activities of educational and charitable institutions and various organisations for the promotion of the spiritual and corporal works of mercy. The Loyola College established in 1925 ranks among the foremost colleges in the city and the uniformly brilliant results it has thus far secured has rendered it famous throughout the Presidency.

LUZ CHURCH, MYLAPORE

No account of the history of the Catholic Mission in Madras can be complete without some reference to the glorious pageant of Catholic faith and piety during the last three days of December 1937. The various functions and ceremonies of the National Eucharistic Congress gripped the attention of the whole city, revealing as it did the splendid unity of spirit and purpose of tens of thousands of Catholics of all races and languages. They served to strengthen on the one hand the consciousness and prestige of Catholics and on the other to impress non-Catholics of the tremendous importance of spiritual values and standards in the lives of Catholics. The whole of Catholic India, and even distant Burma and Ceylon participated in it with one mind and one heart. Nearly all the Archbishops and Bishops of India and heads of missions, over 50 in number, in their picturesque scarlet robes, and nearly 1000 priests, mostly Indian, and the laity in their thousands in small groups and large pilgrimages poured into Madras, unmindful of inconvenience or expense, displaying the keenest interest and enthusiasm from start to finish.

His Excellency the Most Rev. Leo P. Kierkels, titular Archbishop of Salamis Apostolic Delegate of the East Indies, was appointed Papal Legate for the Eucharistic Congress, and his arrival in Madras was marked by scenes of great enthusiasm.

He was accorded a Civic Reception by the Corporation of Madras on December 29, 1937. The Council Chamber presented a most impressive spectacle with Archbishops and Bishops filling rows after rows of the seats attired in their bright purple robes. The reply of His Excellency Mgr. Kierkels was as memorable as it was splendid and made a profound impression on the Councillors, who enthusiastically cheered parts of that memorable utterance. Taking his cue from the Mayor's reference to religion, His Excellency pointed out that religion was the most efficacious safeguard of public authority and a mighty power in the lives of nations. The Catholic Church was an international institution transcending the boundaries of race and language. As St. Paul quoted Athenian poets to the Areopagus, so did the Papal Legate pass on from an apposite saying of Swami Vivekananda to a declaration of the mission of the Catholic Church as voicing not Europe nor politics but as being "the voice of religion which from a small country of Asia hath gone forth into all the earth, being to-day the loudest call to ethical and spiritual values and the widest rallying cry to all believers in God to unite in warding off atheism and unbelief." The voice of Catholicism "is neither of the East nor of the West; it is the voice of the spirit, independent of climes, nowhere alien any more than the voice of science and truth." The address was listened to with rapt attention.

It went to the heart of the Corporation Councillors and Aldermen not one of whom was a Catholic. It was replete with quotations from classical authors and revealed the great sympathy of the representative of the Pope for India and the deep knowledge he possessed of Indian affairs. His Excellency reminded the Councillors, to their amazement, that the following day would "mark the 250th anniversary" of their original Charter, issued on December 30, 1687.

It is not possible to speak more at length of the many other great functions held in connection with the Congress, such as the Garden Party which was attended by the Prime Minister and other members of the Cabinet and the leading official and non-official gentlemen of the city of every creed and community; the meetings on the Island grounds with their picturesque settings when an official reception was accorded to the Papal Legate and striking addresses were delivered by Archbishop of Mathias of Madras, the Papal Legate, Archbishop Sylvester Mulligan of Delhi and Simla, Bishop Rossillon of Vizagapatam, Bishop Leonard of Trichinopoly and Bishop Roche of Tuticorin.

Catholics, though small in number, have played a notable part in the public life of the city. The influence exercised by Catholic thought and action has been surprisingly effective and out of all proportion to its numerical strength. The memorable campaign organised and carried out by Catholics in 1933 scotched the attempt for the introduction of birth control clinics. The work of the League of Decency in the following year for the cleaning of the films of indecencies found considerable support from leading citizens of all creeds.

Chaplaincy Work in Madras in East India Company Days

By

Rev. W H. Warren,
Secretary, C.L.S., Madras.

The history of chaplaincy work can be traced back to the beginning of the seventeenth century. At that time the Company owned no land in India, but from 1607 chaplains were employed on the Company's ships coming East. They were engaged for the whole period of the voyage, which might last from three to four years while the vessel cruised from port to port in the tropics seeking trade.

After the building of Fort St. George, there is no record of any chaplain's visit before 1647, but it is likely that occasional services may have been held by a chaplain coming ashore from one of the Company's ships. A desire for a resident chaplain was expressed by the Factor and soldiers in the Fort in the year 1644. The request was sent to Surat, at that time the Company's headquarters in India, and the President and Council there forwarded the request to London in a list of various wants of the Company's servants in the East. The tenth paragraph of the letter runs: "A minister is needful at Fort St. George, unto which place Mr. Isaacson from Suratt was designed."

Isaacson was the first resident chaplain in India, having been at Surat since 1644. He arrived at Fort St. George at the end of 1647, but the appointment was only temporary, and he returned to Surat at the end of the following year. He was succeeded by Robert Winchester. Winchester was a ship's chaplain who had been badly treated by his captain, and had chosen to stay on shore at Surat. From there he appears to have travelled on another ship which touched at Fort St. George. The people were so impressed by his preaching ability that they applied for permission to retain him on the establishment. He remained for a year, and then had to return to England on account of ill health.

The following year Joseph Thompson arrived from Bantam in Java. During the following years mention is made of Thompson at Masulipatam, and of the return of Isaacson to Madras. It would seem that the chaplains at that period moved periodically from one of the Company's settlements to another, there probably being not enough chaplains for the number of settlements. A petition of June 1658 to the Agent and

Council at Fort St. George contains a reference to "Padre Isaacson", and it is interesting to find how early this familiar designation came into use for chaplains. During his second period, Isaacson was involved in a dispute with the Roman Catholic priest. When the Fort was built, some of the Portuguese settlers of San Thome were invited to settle as traders and soldiers. They brought their wives and families, and some of the English factors and soldiers married girls from among them. Some of the children born of these marriages were baptised by the priest, and complaints were also made that some of the soldiers had been converted. There was a strong party in the Fort in favour of the expulsion of the priest, but the Agent, Mr. Thomas Chamber, would not agree to this, and his action was approved by the Company. The activities of the priest, however, were limited to work among the Portuguese.

Another chaplain, William Whitefield, brought to the notice of the Agent and resident merchants in the Fort the fact that there was no library in the settlement, and that he himself had a personal and professional need of one. The merchants collected among themselves a sum of money which they invested in a bale of calico. They sent this to London with the request that it be sold, and the money realised used to purchase books mentioned in the covering letter. In their general letter to Fort St. George of February 20, 1662-3, the Directors wrote: "On our last year's shipping came to our hands a bale of morees; sent for account of your Minister, to be sold and returned in books; the said calicoes are accordingly sold, and amounted to £85 sterling, in which sum we have bestowed in several books (as per list herewith sent to you) the sum of £58 10s. 0d., the remainder, being £26 10s. 0d., deducting thereout for several charges, we have given to Captain Charles Wyld in 23½ pieces of gold to be delivered to your said Minister." A year later the Directors, on their own initiative, sent out books to the value of £20 which they directed to be kept in the Fort for the use of Ministers. These supplies of books were the origin of the Company's library at the Fort.

In the year 1677, Streynsham Master was appointed Governor of Fort St. George, and it was during his term of service that St. Mary's Church was built. The Governor and his Council proceeded on their own initiative without consulting the Directors in London or asking for financial assistance. The work of excavating was begun on Lady Day, 1678, and the building was completed in 1680. There is no record of the name of the architect, but the credit is usually assigned to Edward Fowle, the Master Gunner at the Fort. The chaplain at this time was Richard Portman, to whom the Bishop of London issued a commission to consecrate the Church and a licence to officiate in it. These documents arrived in October 1680 with the ships of that season, and on October 28, in the presence of the Governor and Council and the residents in the settlement, the service of dedication and consecration was performed. Streynsham Master, in his own name and in the names of the principal residents, presented a petition to Portman as Bishop's Commissary in which they asked him to accept " this our freewill offering ", and prayed him to consecrate it. At the conclusion of the service salutes were fired by the garrison.

The traveller Lockyer visited Fort St. George in 1703, and left an account of the place as it was at that time. After describing the Fort and the fortifications round Blacktown (now Georgetown), he goes on: " The Church is a large pile of arched building, adorned with curious carved work, a stately altar, organs, a white copper candlestick, very large windows, which render it inferior to the churches of London in nothing but bells, there being only one to mind sinners of devotion; though I've heard a contribution for a set was formerly remitted to the Company. Prayers were said twice a day. On Sundays religious worship was strictly observed, the bell beginning between 8 and 9." He then describes the Governor, no doubt looking very imposing in perriwig and laced coat, going to Church in state between lines of soldiers drawn up, to the number of 200, between the gate of the inner fort and the Church door. The residents awaited his arrival at the Church, and followed him into the sacred edifice while the organ pealed out the voluntary.

The building of St. Mary's brought about a change, not only in the status of the chaplains, but also in the whole philanthropic and social side of the settlement. Ecclesiastically the Fort and the surrounding neighbourhood constituted the Parish of St. Mary's Church, and that remarkable institution, the St. Mary's Vestry, came into existence. The Company was still a trading concern, and officially held itself responsible only for the preservation of law and order in its settlements. The Vestry, which consisted of the Governor and the Council, the chaplains, and British residents, became responsible for all the social welfare and philanthropic activities of the settlement. Its direct concern was always with the British residents and those of mixed descent, now called Anglo-Indians, but as we shall see it was not unmindful of the needs of others. In the intervals that elapsed between the departures and arrivals of chaplains, the churchwardens conducted services at the Church, maintained the registers, and sometimes officiated at funerals.

The work of the Vestry was financed from a number of funds known collectively as the Church Stock. It was built up in various ways, by legacies and church collections, by fines which the Company levied on its servants for breaches of its rules, and at one period by double boat hire charged for Sunday journeys to and from the ships. From it the Vestry administered poor relief, provided for orphans, and undertook medical and educational work. The loss of the old Vestry books during the occupation of the Fort by the French from 1746 to 1749 makes it impossible to give any detailed account of all the various activities of the Vestry, but the main outlines of its work can be indicated.

Poor Relief. This was administered by the chaplains and churchwardens to the destitute residents, British and Anglo-Indians, and there was a special fund for the benefit of widows and orphans. In 1696 another fund was established for the relief of the Indian poor, who had hitherto been allowed to beg in the Fort. This Fund was placed in the hands of the Mayor and Aldermen, who were ordered to distribute it at the Choultry, just outside the Choultry Gate, every Monday morning.

Education. As far back as 1670 the Directors of the Company commenced to make enquiries about the education of children in the Fort, and expressed themselves very strongly as to how they should be brought up. Two years later a Mr. Pringle, who had been taken prisoner by the Dutch, on his release arrived at the Fort and was appointed schoolmaster. He went home a year later, and was succeeded by Mr. Ralph Ord, who remained for four years. Ord in turn was succeeded by Mr. John Barker, who worked for twenty-five years till his death in 1707. The work then appears to have been neglected for some years till 1715, when new arrangements were made by the then chaplain, the Rev. William Stevenson. A charity school, after the English model, was formed for English and Anglo-Indian children, and the Tamil children and those of Portuguese descent were entrusted to the care of the S. P. C. K. missionaries in Blacktown. The S. P. C. K. mission, afterwards transferred to Vepery, was on part of the ground now occupied by the High Court Buildings. The St. Mary's Charity School was managed by a body of seven persons, consisting of two ministers, two churchwardens, and two overseers elected by the Vestry. It began with eighteen boys and twelve girls, who received both education and board. These appear to have been orphans, but it is probable that other children attended also as day scholars. At a later date the Vestry assisted the formation of the Male and Female Orphan Asylums, and the present Civil Orphan Asylums are the outcome of an amalgamation of the St. Mary's Charity School and the Civil Male and Female Orphan Asylums in 1872.

Medical work. The Vestry was responsible for founding the first hospital in Madras. It was built in the Fort near the Church by private subscriptions, and in 1688 a suggestion was made to the churchwardens that it should be removed outside the Fort to a situation by the river. The old building was sold to the Company, and new premises erected. Towards running expenses the Vestry contributed fifty pagodas yearly, and part cost of furniture, clothing of patients and medical supplies, the remainder being borne by the Company. It was considered to be a charitable institution, in part at any rate, up to 1698. As the population increased the support of the hospital gradually became too great a strain on the resources of the Vestry, and in 1698 the Vestry petitioned the Council to be relieved of financial responsibility. The hospital then became a Company institution and the civil side developed into the present General Hospital. The Vestry continued to pay the expenses of the patients it sent.

In addition to these activities the Vestry acted as trustee for the property of orphan children till they came of age. Under certain circumstances it had to act as the local bank! If a merchant died without leaving local heirs, the Company would realise the estate and pay over to heirs or assigns in Britain; but if left to heirs in Madras, or for local charitable purposes, the Company would take no responsibility, so the Vestry had to act as bankers or trustees as the case might be. It is perhaps not surprising that from time to time the Vestry found itself involved in administrative difficulties. It was one of these that led to dissolving the Vestry in 1805. In 1757 it had taken charge of a legacy left by Peter Uscan for various charitable purposes, among them the keeping in repair of the Marmalong Bridge. At the time it was agreed that the interest should be paid over to the Fort Paymaster who would carry out the repairs as necessary, but for some reason which is not clear, it appears that shortly afterwards the Vestry took direct responsibility for the repairs, and continued this work for nearly fifty years. In 1803 a dispute arose over plans for widening the bridge, the then chaplain, Dr. Kerr, being of opinion that the interest on the legacy could be used only for repairs. The matter was referred to the High Court, and the resultant proceedings called into question the whole legal status of the Vestry. The verdict was that the ecclesiastical law of England did not govern the case; that there was no legal Vestry, nor Churchwarden, nor corporation of any kind capable of holding property, and that the Uscan Fund must therefore be paid into Court. In 1805 a resolution was passed by the Vestry to the effect that the whole of the Church Stock be placed under the direction and control of the Supreme Court of Judicature. This was done, and the work of the Vestry came to an end, after a useful and honourable career of over 120 years.

Among the chaplains of the eighteenth century, the name of Robert Palk is conspicuous. He came out as a naval chaplain in Admiral Boscawen's fleet, and was appointed chaplain at the Fort in 1748. He made himself useful to the Governor and Council in many ways, and although the Directors in London made various efforts to transfer him, excuses were found each time for keeping him at Madras. Two chaplains were sent out from England, so Palk was given the post of Military Paymaster. The Directors ordered that he be sent as chaplain to Tellicherry, and at another time he was applied for by Bombay; the death of one of the chaplains enabled the Council to evade both demands. The fight went on for five years, the Council determined to make use of his exceptional ability as an administrator and diplomatist, and the Directors trying to transfer him to chaplaincy work elsewhere. Palk acted as one of the Peace Commissioners at the conference with the French at Sadras, and successfully carried out negotiations with the Court of Tanjore. The Council also appointed him a member of the Select Committee for the general management of the political and military affairs of the coast. A final order came from the Directors that he should be transferred as Junior Chaplain to Fort St. David. When the Governor informed Palk of this, he applied for leave to return to England, and permission was given. It was not till over a year later, however, that Palk gave up his offices and went home. The impression he made on the Directors was such that in the following year they wrote to the Fort St. George Council that they had determined to appoint him Governor when the vacancy should occur. He returned to Madras with Col. Stringer Lawrence, and commenced his civil and political life as Export Warehouseman and Commissary in dealing with the country powers. When he became Governor in 1763 the office of Commander-in-Chief of the Forces was omitted from his commission, he being in Holy Orders, and bestowed upon Col. Lawrence.

Another celebrated name is that of Andrew Bell. He arrived at Fort St. George in 1787, and his scientific lectures attracted attention. He became Chaplain of the Fort in 1789, and was made a member of the Asiatic Society. He was the first Superintendent of the Male Asylum, and it was here that he made his famous experiment in education by the use of pupil-teachers. He returned to England in 1796 having suffered by over-exposure to the sun during the siege of Pondicherry where he was acting as chaplain to the troops. A few years later he became famous for his efforts to promote elementary education in England on what was known as the Madras system.

The name of Dr. Kerr has previously been mentioned. He came out as chaplain of a frigate in 1792, but fell ill and was left behind. With the assistance of a friend he started a school in Blacktown. The following year he was appointed a military chaplain and sent to Ellore. He succeeded Dr. Bell at the Fort and at the Male Asylum in 1796. He built St. Mark's church, set up the Government Press at the Male Asylum, and established the Charitable Committee for the relief of the poor which afterwards became the Friend-in-Need Society.

In 1813 the British territories in the East Indies were placed under the superintendence of a Bishop and three Archdeacons. It is interesting to note that the diocese of the new bishop consisted of the whole of India, Ceylon, the Straits Settlements, China, Australasia, St. Helena and the Cape of Good Hope. Except for one visit of Bishop Wilson to Borneo, the Bishops of Calcutta did not attempt to visit districts outside India and Ceylon. Travelling was slow, and at times had its adventures. On one occasion Bishop Wilson, after taking nine days to come from Trincomallee to Madras, attempted to land in a surf boat. A large and unexpected wave swept bishop, chaplain and doctor from their seats and their hats and books were seen floating in the boat. "Dignity agrees not with drenched clothes, and while the guns were firing, bands playing and troops presenting arms, the Bishop was hurrying away to find shelter and dry clothes in Government House."

Up to the time of the new ecclesiastical arrangements, it had been customary for the local Government to appoint one of the senior chaplains to the Presidency Church, (St. Mary's), and to make him the channel of all communications with other chaplains. In 1814 the Rev. Edward Vaughan occupied this post, but in the event a chaplain junior to him was selected as the first Archdeacon of Madras, the Rev. John Mousley. The following year the Archdeacon took over the correspondence work, but the Presidency Chaplain continued to receive all copies of register books and other returns which had to be made by the chaplains of the various inland stations. This continued till 1831, when the duties and records were transferred by order of Government to the Registrar. Thus by degrees the Archdeacon became the head of the Ecclesiastical Department, and so continued till the formation of the Madras Diocese in 1835.

After 1871 garden houses began to extend over the Choultry Plain, and in Egmore and Vepery. This led to the erection of more churches. St. George's Church, (afterwards the Cathedral) was built in 1815, and St. Matthias' at Vepery in 1827. In 1835 Daniel Corrie was enthroned at St. Mary's as the first Bishop of Madras. In the following year he opened a Grammar School near Tucker's Church which continued there till its amalgamation with Doveton College in 1929. He was succeeded by Bishop Spencer in 1838, and he in turn by Bishop Dealtry in 1849, who continued in office till 1861, and thus outlived the rule of the Company in India.

During this period, the work of the chaplains in Madras gradually became more of a routine character, but some of them were responsible for outstanding developments. Morgan Davis (1810-22) had charge of St. Mark's, and with it the Male Asylum and the Press. He helped to establish the Civil Female Orphan Asylum nearby, and for nearly twelve years watched over these institutions, and helped to place them on a sound financial footing. In 1817 the spiritual charge of the Hospital and Jail was added to his duties. Marmaduke Thompson (1809-25) founded the Friend-in-Need Society when the St. Mary's Poor Fund came to an end. Charles Church (1817-22) founded the Madras Auxiliary Bible Society, and was its first honorary Secretary. An idea of the duties of a chaplain at that time may be gained from a list of the offices held by F. J. Darrah (1826-37) : while chaplain of St. Mark's, he was also chaplain of the Military Female Orphan Asylum, Secretary of the S. P. G., President of the Philanthropic Association and of the Friend-in-Need Society, chaplain and manager of the Male and Female Asylums. It is perhaps little wonder that of the fifty-seven chaplains appointed to the Madras Presidency between 1805 and 1835 twenty-two died in India

The work of the Company's chaplains, as distinct from that of missionaries, was officially limited to the European and Anglo-Indian communities, but as the Rev. Frank Penny has shown in his *Church in Madras,* there was little that went on in those days in which they were not actively interested in some way or other. In the history of Madras City they stand out as instrumental in providing the first library, the first school, the first hospital, the first orphanage, the first poor relief, the first bank, and the Government Press. It is a record to which it would be difficult to find any parallel in the annals of the city.

SECTION VII

ARTS AND LETTERS

Dravidic Studies in Madras

By

Dr. C. Achyuta Menon, B.A., Ph.D. (Lond.)
Lecturer, University of Madras.

INTRODUCTORY

If the division of India on a linguistic basis is decided on, what will happen to Madras? Some have a ready answer to this question. They argue thus: "The Cooum river bisects Madras into two; give one half to Tamils and the other to Andhras." One is not sure whether such a mathematical precision will help us in the matter. What about the innumerable business places including coffee-hotels and restaurants of Madras where Malayalam and Kanarese have come to stay? What about the China Bazaar Road which is a real epitome of India where all Indian languages are spoken. We will leave the problem to the modern politicians to solve and endeavour to know how the main languages of the Presidency were faring for the last two or three centuries in this city.

It may be stated at the very outset that with the erection of the Fort St. George at Madras by the English, a new chapter in the history of the city was opened. The coast-town began to give up gradually its parochial character and assume the importance of a common centre for North and South based on its position between the two—a position which it maintains even to-day. The British East India Company changed its headquarters gradually from Masulipatam to Madras from which directions were issued from time to time for the conduct of the factories established under it in the various ports of South India. Their operations brought them into contact with the chief powers ruling different parts of the province and their subjects. In their dealings with them they realised that the knowledge of the main languages of the Presidency, viz., Tamil, Telugu, Malayalam and Kanarese was of the utmost value. Nay, it was an absolute necessity. The realisation of this fact may be regarded as the primary cause that inspired the voluminous and laborious literary efforts in the languages of this Presidency which will be described in the course of this article.

In this connection, we have to take into consideration the activities of the missionaries who came to India for religious service and propaganda. In fact, so far as literary ventures are concerned, missionary enterprise must be given precedence to commercial or political expansion. Although we hear of Christian and Jewish Saints visiting South India at an early period, say, soon after the commencement of the Christian era[1], systematic missionary propaganda, dates only after the arrival of Vasco-de-Gama. Western merchants that belonged to his camp and succeeded him were in need of religious service by their own priests when their journey to and stay in India became protracted and assumed a permanent character. While their merchant brethren were carrying on their commercial transactions with the native inhabitants their priests endeavoured to do a bit of religious preaching with them. Portuguese were notorious for this and it was when their propaganda took an aggressive turn that the Zamorin of Calicut—which was by the way, the first city to receive a foreigner in modern times—declared war against them which ultimately led to the giving up of all their ambitions in India.[2] Other nations as the Dutch, the French and the English took a lesson from this and conducted their propaganda later through inoffensive and diplomatic channels.

It is obvious that no religious propagandist can do justice to his work without an adequate knowledge of the language of the people with whom he is dealing. It is no wonder then, that the European missionaries realised this sufficiently early and directed their energies and efforts to this end. Problems of grammar and translation are the main difficulties that a foreigner engaged in the study of a new language has to face and an analysis of the works done by European missionaries and administrators will disclose that they devoted themselves mainly to the production of grammars and lexicons. It must be, however, gratefully acknowledged that missionaries when once they started their self-imposed task were impressed with the inherent worth of the languages they were studying and they accomplished their work with an amount of thoroughness which is the envy and despair of modern Indian scholars. It is not for us to question their motives as neither religious zeal nor a spirit of venture which raised many a nation to the pinnacle of its glory is a reprehensible thing in itself. When that materialises into solid contributions which the western missionaries and administrators can very well take credit for, they are even beyond praise.

1. (*a*) Solomon's agents visited Malabar first in 1000 B.C. Then again in 70 A.D. *Cochin Tribes and Castes,* L. K. Ananta Krishna Iyer, p. 401. (*b*) Apostle St. Thomas visited Mylapore (52 A.D.); and died there. His body was entombed in the Church at St. Thome. Page 402-3. *Ibid.*

2. K. M. Panikkar. *Malabar and Portuguese,* pages 182-196.

We will now proceed to examine the achievements of the two agencies mentioned above, making the city of Madras the nucleus of our analysis. Most of the linguistic work that stands to the credit of the foreigners during the period, was done in the moffussil stations[3] but they attained fruition at Madras which became a centre of all provincial activities in various fields. The first notable event in this connection is the establishment of the S. P. C. K. Press in Madras (now known as the Diocesan Press) in the year 1761, which is the first press to start printing books in Indian languages. The Press authorities took a good deal of interest in the literary activities of the Protestant Mission at Tranquebar and brought them to light. The first Manager of the Press, Fabricius (1761-9) was the author of "Malabar (Tamil) English Dictionary" which was printed in this press. It is curious that in the title of the work 'Malabar' is used in the sense of Tamil. He was also the author of a Tamil Grammar. Among the publications printed in this press during 1805-1812 mention is made of "The Tamil New Testament, The Tamil Catechisms, Fabricus' Tamil Hymn Book, the 2nd edition and other works on religion, morals, education not excepting the classics and the sciences in English, Latin, Tamil, Teloogoo, Hindustani and Malayalam."[4]

A Catholic Mission at Madura had by this time, done some pioneer work, in the field of Tamil. Two outstanding names attached to this Mission deserve special mention, viz., Robert-de-Nobili and Constantius Beschi (1680-1747). The former is said to have spent his last days (1656) in Mylapore and if so Madras has every right to claim the scholar as one of its alumni. He seems to have combined in his person "the sanctity of the Sanyasi and the erudition of the Pandit."[5]

[6]Fr. C. Beschi belongs to that rare type of scholars who are born to achieve something great. The following account of his work will give an idea of the man and his genius:—

"As a great Tamil scholar and poet, Beschi has always attracted the attention of all Tamils and has served as the model of Protestant missionaries engaged in Tamil studies like Rottler, Caldwell and Pope. Of Beschi's works on the grammar of the Tamil languages and of his dic-

3. There were five big missionary centres, three in the East Coast, Serampore, Madura and Tranquebar, and two in the West Coast, Mangalore and Kottayam.

4. From a note of Mr. W. H. Warren, the present Secretary of the Press.

5. Prof. C. S. Srinivasachari, page 147, Indian Historical Records Commission, proc. Vol. VIII p. 147.

6. A list of his numerous works in prose and verse both in Tamil and Latin was published in *The Madras Journal of Literature and Science* (1840).

tionaries one writer admiringly points out that they "have proved invaluable aids to his successors and to Protestant missionaries indeed, to all students of Tamil after him."[7]

There was indeed a previous manuscript 'Life of Beschi' in Tamil written about 1790 which probably served as the basis for the scholar's life which was published in Tamil in 1822 by A. Muthuswami Pillai, Manager of the College of the Fort St. George, who had previously undertaken a tour in the southern districts of the Presidency for the purpose of securing a collection of Beschi's works at the instance of F. W. Ellis a celebrated scholar civilian who wrote numerous papers on the Tamil, Telugu and Malayalam Languages. The memoir was enriched with a catalogue of Beschi's works with extracts taken from some of them. In 1840 the author gave, at the request of Sir Walter Elliot, then Member of the Board of Revenue, an English version of the biography. There is a translation into French of the Tamil notice of Muthuswamy Pillay made by Father Lones du Ranquet, S.J., in a letter of the Fishery coast 1st March 1841. A manuscript French notice of Beschi by a contemporary Catacleum Missionary, who wrote in 1731 is said to have been in the library of the Church of Surat and is now in the Calendrier des Missionaries jesuitas dans 1' Inde (Publ: Nationale Fords Fancais No. 9777, Paris).[8]

Beschi was an all-round scholar and poet of Tamil and his works cover a wide field, (1) Grammars, (2) Lexicons and (3) Literary works.

(*a*) *Grammar*: There are two books under this category, one *on High Tamil* and another on the *Common dialect* of the Tamil language. Both were originally written in Latin and later translated into English,[9] the former by B. G. Babington and the latter by G. W. Mahon (of the S. P. C. K. Press, Madras 1848). Two other books on literary topics, viz., (3) Tonnul Vilakkam (in Tamil) (ancient

7. Though the scene of activities of Father Beschi was not Madras he has a right to be mentioned among the scholars who worked in Madras in view of the fact that two of his famous works, viz., "Grammar of the Common dialect of the Tamil Language" and "Sadur Aharadi" were published here by the College Press. Besides, his life and productions were the main inspiration for the literary ventures undertaken in Madras after him by scholars like Mr. A. Muthuswamy Pillai who was on the staff of the College. In fact the first vernacular publications issued by the College Press were the popular works of Beschi including his grammar.

8. Prof. C. S. Srinivasachari. Proceedings of the Indian Historical Records Commission, Vol. VIII, p. 148.

9. A grammar of High Tamil, Latin Test and Translation by B. G. Babington, Trichy, 1917. The 2nd was first printed at Tranquebar in 1739. It was reprinted at the College Press at the instance of the Madras Government in 1813. Another edition of it appeared in 1843 at Pondicherry.

scientific treatise)' and (4) The clavis—Latin—(doubtful) are assigned to him. These deal with Tamil Prosody, Rhetoric, Composition, Orthography and Etymology. Tonnul Vilakkam has undergone several editions. A Telugu grammar also is included by some among the works of Beschi. But lack of evidence makes us hesitate to accept the view.

(b) *Lexicon*: (1) 'Sadur Aharadi' (Quadruple Dictionary) is the most important in this group. It was composed in the years 1732-47 and was first published in Madras under the auspices of the College of the Fort St. George. According to one admiring critic this work discloses the author's vast erudition and astonishing knowledge of the Tamil language and its classics.

(2) 'Tamil-Latin Dictionarium' is another work of Beschi. It contains a long preface in Latin and has been the basis of subsequent efforts by other scholars.

(c) *Literary Works*: Among his literary works (1) 'Tembavani' stands foremost. It is an epic in Tamil on St. Joseph in 36 cantos and may be regarded as a work of a high order which, for several years, Tamils could not believe was written by a foreigner.

(2) His translation in Latin of the Sacred Kural though not printed was made use of by later editors, like Ellis[10] and Pope,[11] of the work.

Soon after the death of Beschi the Jesuit Society and mission (Madura) with which he was associated were suppressed and for long this famous Tamil scholar remained in oblivion.

In the same century similar endeavours were made in Malayalam, Kanarese and Telugu by Portuguese, Italian and Spanish missionaries. But their activities were confined to Kottayam[12], Mangalore[13] and Serampore[14] and did not attract attention in Madras and as such do not come within the province of this survey.

OFFICIAL ACTIVITIES: UNDER THE EAST INDIA COMPANY

With the starting of the College of the Fort St. George by the company linguistic studies in South India passed from individual attempts to a more systematic channel under official control. The College was founded in the year 1812[15] with a press, a depot and a library attached

10. Ellis, *Kural*, Madras (1822).
11. Pope, *Sacred Kural* (1886).
12, 13 and 14. Indian Historical Records Commissions, Proceedings, Vol. VIII, page 151.
15. Literary Life of C. P. Brown, p. 22.

to it. A Board also was constituted to look after its affairs. The Library of the Oriental Manuscripts which originally belonged to the Madras Literary Society[16] was after some time transferred to the custody of the Board. The College and other organisations connected with it developed into full working order by the year 1820 when the Rules for the conduct of the Board and the College were framed.[17] Though the College was originally meant for training the Civil Servants in the languages of the Province, its aims had a wider scope and application. We learn from a consultation[18] that "the acquirement of a knowledge of the general grammar and connection of the several languages of Southern India and of some acquaintance with the sources whence they spring is the chief object" of the Institution which a Board consisting of eminent scholars like F. W. Ellis, A. D. Campbell, was called upon to serve. The Board distributed its patronage equally to all the main languages of the Presidency and for convenience sake it is proposed to review their activities under each language. Certain works were undertaken by the Board itself. Private enterprise was encouraged by financial assistance by Government on the recommendation of the Board, which examined the merits of individual cases.

TAMIL

The Board commenced its literary activities by purchasing the copyrights at the instance of the Government of "several elementary works of first utility in the High and Low Dialects of the Tamil Languages," including Beschi's grammar of low Tamil, and "A brief exposition of Tamil by Chidambara Pandaram, the head Tamil master of the College.[19] Pandaram soon after began to work on the Tamil translation of 'Vignaneswariyam' and 'Vyavahara Kandam'[20] comprising the 8th and 9th books of the translations of the 'Institutes of Manu' by Sir William Jones. In the year 1815 the Government asked the Board to review the Translation of the English Liturgy[21] by Rev. Mr. Rottler and the Tamil translation of Beschi's 'Grammar of Sen Tamil' by B. G. Babington. The former was ultimately recommended for purchase in 1825 although the Government was not quite satisfied with the quality of the work. It was however, thought that it would serve as a foundation for

16. Started in 1817 by Sir Thomas Newbolt, the then Chief Justice of the Supreme Court.

17. Rules for the Colleges of the Fort St. George (1820).

18. Manuscript of Public Consultations, 1812 (Madras Record Office).

19. Consultations, 1813 (Set).

20. *Ibid* 1814. Vol. VIII. The author received 1000 Pagodas for these works which he utilised for the erection of a public choultry.

21. Consultations, 1815.

subsequent attempts. In the same year a reward was given to Thandavaraya Vadhyar for the writing of 'Amarakosa' and three other works in Tamil and the translation of the 'Arabian Nights' in Tamil by Thana Mudaly, was patronised by the Government by purchasing a few copies of it.

From 1825 to 1834 there is a lull in the literary activities of the College Board. In 1834 however, Rottler's work, Vol. I Part I was taken up for publication. The 2nd and 3rd parts of the work revised by Messrs. Taylor and Venkatachala Mudaly (certified teacher of the College) followed in the years 1837-41. Again there is a gap till the year 1853[22] when the question of compiling a catalogue of the Mackenzie Collections in Tamil engaged the Board's attention. Mr. Taylor was put in charge of the work.[23] In the year 1854, an American missionary, Rev. Miron Winslow came forward with a prospectus of 'A comprehensive Tamil and English Dictionary' of High and Low Tamil and sought Government support. The work was published in 1862 and contained this remarkable testimony about Tamil "in its poetic form, the Tamil is more polished and exact than Greek and in both dialects with its borrowed treasures more copious than Latin." It is interesting to compare this picture with the one which emanated from the brain of the late T. B. Macaulay, " a single shelf of a good European Library was worth the whole native Literature of India and Arabia.[24] In the same year Dr. Caldwell's 'Dravidian Affinities' received Government help and was published. Ellis's 'Mirasi Tenure' and Robertson's glossary of Tamil and English words used in Law Courts are the contributions to the legal lore of the period.

TELUGU

In the field of Telugu the Board's work is by no means inconsiderable. The first work that came up for the consideration of the Board was a Telugu dictionary called 'Andhra dipika' compiled by Mamudi Venkayya of Masulipatam. The copyright of the work was purchased for 1,000 pagodas. This was followed by 'a Grammar of Teloogoo

22. But the missionaries of the period were not idle. They produced a 'United Tamil Version of the Bible" which was planned by the Madras S.P.C.K. and Jaffna Auxiliaries Bible Society in 1845. It was printed in 1850. (—*Promotion of Tamil Studies*, C. S. Chari. C. R. N. Commemoration Vol. p. 86).

23. Mr. C. P. Brown who was by this time known as a great Telugu scholar was not quite satisfied with the work of Taylor.

24. His minute dated the 2nd February, 1835. Selections from Educational Records, Part I, page 109. (Govt. of India, 1920).

language commonly termed the gentoo '[25] by A. D. Campbell, which was printed[26] at the College Press and dedicated to the Governor-General. In this work Campbell had the assistance and co-operation of the famous orientalist, F. W. Ellis and two Indian scholars,—Messrs Udagiri Venkatanarayana Iyah, the head English master of the College and Pattabhirama Sastri, Head Sanskrit and Telugu master of the College, who also produced at that time another book called 'Dhatu mala' (Telugu roots) In the same year the College Board secured the manuscripts collected by Col. Colin Mackenzie and one of his assistants. The need of a comprehensive Telugu dictionary was keenly felt at this time and the work of Mr. T. Dalziell was examined in this connection and the year after Mr. Campbell was asked to compile one. He was allowed to have two Indian assistants and live in Bellary for the purpose. In 1819, the Government ordered the publication of the 'Tales of Vikramarka '[27] written by Mr. K. Gurumurthi, a master in the College and the 2nd Edition of Campbell's 'Telugu Grammar.' Mr. C. P. Brown, the great Telugu scholar was now coming to the forefront. In 1827, he brought out at the instance of the college Board 'An analysis of Telugu Prosody,' for which he was paid 1000 pagodas. In 1835, Mr. Morris whose elementary work on Telugu language had already received support, prepared the "English and Telugu Dictionary" at the instance of the College Board with the assistance of the Telugu master, Mr. K. Gurumurthi Sastri. It was published in the same year.

In Telugu the works of T. C. Morris supplemented by his brother, H. Morris and C. P. Brown are of a very high standard. We have already commented on Morris' attempts. Mr. Brown was a versatile and prolific writer. His works include grammar, prosody, cyclic tables of Hindu and Mohammadan Chronology, Nistara Ratnakaram (Ocean of Salvation) and translation of the verses of Vemana, to mention a few. His own account of the state of Telugu learning in his own time gives us a picture of the conditions under which he worked. Says he :—

"When I began these tasks Telugu literature was dying out, the flame was just glimmering in the socket; the Madras College founded in 1812 preserved a little spark."[28] His remarks seem to have roused the native scholars from their slumber and provoked them to an outburst of literary activity. English synonyms (Carpenter) with

25. Consultations, '1813.'
26. 1816, First Edition; 1849 3rd Edition.
27. Copies of this were sent to England.
28. Prof. C. S. Srinivasachari, Indian Historical Records Commission, Proceedings, Vol. VIII, p. 157.

Telugu explanation by B. Subbarayalu is another notable work of the period.[29]

KANARESE AND MALAYALAM

Compared to the volume of output in Tamil and Telugu, the attention bestowed on Kanarese and Malayalam is meagre. Perhaps the Malayalis and Kanarese people in the city were a minority.

(a) *Kanarese*: Correspondence commenced about the Karnataka grammar by M. C. Kerrel (M.C.S.) even so early as 1815[30]......when the Government asked the Board to judge its merits. It dragged on till 1820 when it was decided to purchase the copyright thereof and publish it. After some years the need for a better Dictionary was felt when Mr. Reeve of the London Mission Society came forward with his English-Kannada and Kannada-English Dictionary which was recommended by the Board for purchase. It was published in four quarto volumes in the year 1832. He took 14 years to finish his work and he speaks with feeling the difficulties he had to face in the course of it. "The rareness of ancient manuscripts, the endless blunders of drivelling and hireling transcribers, the paucity of duplicates for collation, and comparatively smaller number of men to be found among the natives possessing appropriate philological information, soundness of judgment or zeal for literary research[31] and improvement have occasioned no inconsiderable suspense, annoyance and embarrassment."

With this the activities of the Board with regard to Kanarese seems to have come to a standstill till 1849 when we find from the Records that certain works of Rev. Mr. Moegling were recommended for help. We do not know what the works were. But the 'Basava Purana' and the 'Chenna Purana' produced by the same writer were granted aid sometime later. The Court of Directors do not seem to have been quite happy over this donation as is evident from the observations they have made in that connection. "The aid of government should be confined to original works or to publications calculated to be useful to junior civil servants and the expense of which is moderate."[32]

(b) *Malayalam*: Rev. Mr. Whish's 'Malayalam Grammar and Dictionary' was the first work in Malayalam to receive the attention of the Board and Government during the period. What exactly happened to

29. It is not possible to say whether this work received any assistance from the Board.

30. Consultations, 1815.

31. Preface. Page 11 of the work, *A Karnataka English Dictionary* (1894), p. 7-8.

32. Public Department Proceedings, dated 16th December 1852.

this work is not definitely known although the records show that the author was encouraged to compile it.[33] Correspondence on the subject began so early as 1815. In the year 1834 the Royal Asiatic Society of Great Britain and Ireland made an enquiry and in reply to that the Government informed them of the works in vernacular languages done by the late Mr. C. M. Whish. A notable scholar who took an interest in Malayalam at that time was Mr. F. W. Ellis who as has been stated already, was a member of the Board associated with the College. He had written several articles on Malayalam and was struck with the abundance of Sanskrit derivatives in the language. He has also a few comments to offer about Ezuttaccan, the celebrated epic poet of Malayalam.[34] Their accuracy is, not however, beyond question in the light of subsequent research.

In 1847, Rev. I. Reek's proposed grammar of the Malayalam language received help from the Government. Two more grammars of the language, one by Mr. Spring of the Madras Civil Service and another by Rev. Peet of the Church Mission Society[35] appeared at this time. The dictionaries, (Malayalam-English and English-Malayalam) by Rev. Bailey of the C. M. S. Mission were by far the most substantial production of the age. In 1842, Government help was sought for their publication. They were printed at the C.M.S. Press, Kottayam, Travancore and are two voluminous works. The author apparently knew more of Sanskrit and less of Malayalam and as such his dictionaries contain more Sanskrit words than Malayalam. Dr. Gundert mentions this defect of the work in the preface to his Malayalam-English Dictionary.

"It is one of the chief defects of that otherwise valuable work that it does not discriminate between Malayalam and Sanskrit terms and leaves the student entirely in the dark, both as regards etymology and the proportional importance of words."[36] It should not be inferred from this account that the period was poor of productions in Malayalam.[37] The activities of Western scholars (Missionaries) in this

33. It is also significant that Dr. Gundert in the preface of his magnificent work (Malayalam-English Dictionary) makes no reference to this work but he mentions the works of Rev. Bailey.

34. Logan's Manual of Malabar, Vol. I, p. 94.

35. These were replaced by the works of Dr. Gundert and Dr. Garthwaite later. It is doubtful whether they have seen a second edition.

36. Page vi, Preface to Gundert's 'Malayalam-English Dictionary.'

37. (a) A Malayalam translation of the Bible was printed in Rome in 1639. A copy of this is available in the India Office Library (London).

(b) A book on the plants of Malabar was prepared by Portuguese in the early part of the 17th Century.

(c) Portuguese and Italian Missionaries of Virapoli compiled a Malayalam Dictionary in the 16th Century. Preface, Page iv. Gundert's Dictionary.

respect were mostly in the West Coast, and they were directed by two agencies, viz., the Basel German Mission (with Head-quarters at Mangalore) and the C.M.S. (with Head-quarters at Kottayam).

AFTER THE COMPANY'S DAYS

The preceding survey has shown that during the first half of the 19th century linguistic studies were making considerable headway although evidence of original talent was not forthcoming. Both the College of the Fort St. George and private enterprise, combined to produce works in various languages to suit the needs and requirements of the times. There was a regular stream of scholars coming one after the other, willing to continue what their predecessors had done. This flow of scholarly genius was however arrested when the College was abolished by the Company in the year 1854 and a Board of Examiners took its place. It was a period of transition in every respect. Different interests and ideals began to grow and it became impossible to bring them under one focus. Many institutions with more or less identical objects sprung up in place of one. Though their activities cover a wider field they lacked the original unity and solidarity, which the central institution of the Company maintained. The Company was preparing to hand over the administration to the British Government as its responsibilities increased day by day. The dual role, i.e., commercial and administrative, it was playing hitherto was too much for one organisation to bear and division of functions became an imperative necessity. The few years that followed the closure of the College were indeed momentous. I am not referring to the great sensation of 1857. Already there were signs in Madras of varied educational activities which very often went with literary enthusiasm. The Madras Christian College originally called the 'General Assembly's Institution' was started in 1837[38] by Rev. John Anderson, the first missionary of the Church of Scotland who came to Madras. Three years after the city witnessed the beginning of the present Presidency College as the outcome of a joint enterprise of "leading Europeans and Indians in Madras[39] in the form of a High School. In the year 1857, the Madras University came into being with this "High School of the Madras University" as its nucleus.[40] The year after saw the birth of Pachaiyappa's College which again started life as a High School.

38. Glyn Barlow *The Story of Madras*, page, 95.

39. *Ibid.*

40. The College was housed in its present building in 1870. (*The Story of Madras*, page 96).

These Arts Institutions had South Indian languages as part of the course provided in them and made a central Institution like the College of the Fort St. George a superfluity. As these were in course of time affiliated to the University the latter assumed by degrees the position of the College at the Fort in maintaining the standard and level of instruction in Indian languages and English. Second languages had a chequered history under the University. In the beginning they were included under the compulsory items of study; but in the early years of the present century they were relegated to the background as optionals, with a nominal compulsory Syllabus. This experiment fortunately did not last long and a return to the old position was effected in about twelve years. With this development the enthusiasm for the individual languages grew and the Madras University undertook in 1912 as a first step in the direction of promoting the vernaculars, the compilation of the Tamil Lexicon which attained completion three years ago. It may be considered the *magnum opus* of the University. The latest phase of the University's interest in South Indian languages is represented by the Oriental Research Institute in which original research in more than six Indian languages is being done by well known scholars. In recent years educational expansion of the Presidency necessitated the creation of new Universities and each main language of the Presidency has now a University of its own.[41] The University of Madras being the oldest still retains its original representative character.

It is not possible within the space of this paper to give even a brief survey of the varied literary achievements of eminent scholars of the time[42] of whom only a small proportion was connected with the above-mentioned institutions. There was a healthy fusion in them of the old and new traditions of scholarship which inspired a large variety of literary effulgence.

THE TYPE OF WORKS PRODUCED

As I have indicated in the beginning of the paper the activities of European scholars were mainly directed towards the production of bi-lingual dictionaries. Since 1854 considerable progress has been made in this direction the later scholars taking full advantage of the works of the pioneers in the field. The most outstanding foreign scholar of the period was Dr. G. U. Pope whose translation of Kural, Naladiar and Tiruvasagam are magnificent works in Tamil. Except in Tamil, dictionaries produced in Telugu, Kanarese and Malayalam in this period were

41. Andhra University for Telugu, 1926.
    Annamalai University for Tamil, 1929.
    Mysore University for Kanarese, 1916.
    Travancore University for Malayalam, 1938.
42. C. P. Brown's work in Telugu-English Dictionary, 1852.

a decided improvement, on the existing ones.[43] But they were compiled outside Madras.

COMPARATIVE PHILOLOGY

Though the College Board had as one of its aims "the knowledge of the connection of the several languages of South India" very little has been accomplished in this respect subsequently. Dr. Caldwell's 'Comparative Grammar of Dravidian Languages[44] is the only solid contribution to the subject. Though it was not produced in Madras, the University of Madras gave due recognition to the work by approving it as a text-book for Higher Examinations and to the author by inviting him to deliver the Convocation address in 1879 and making him a Fellow of the University.

Either leisurely scholars were getting rarer and rarer or the labour and trouble involved in a work of the kind which demanded an intimate knowledge of at least half a dozen languages, Comparative Philology has been a much neglected field. The Oriental Research Institute of the Madras University has unique opportunities to do research in this line and it is hoped that the facilities afforded thereby will be amply utilised.

SUBSIDY TO AUTHORS

The present century is far behind the previous one in another important function which the College of Fort St. George was serving. Its Board very often recommended and secured help to authors either through granting them subsidy for the publication of their works or purchasing the copyright thereof. Since the abolition of the College this useful act of philanthropy which considerably helped Linguistic Studies has been a desideratum. The Government also made provision for such an endowment and regarded it as a legitimate item of expenditure to be incurred ungrudgingly. The only institution that does something of its kind in Madras is the School Book and Literature Society. Though it was instituted as early as 1820, it seems to have begun to function actively only when it was registered under the Act XXI 1860. Its primary object was "to promote the cause of education by the preparation, publication, purchase, and sale at a moderate price of English and Vernacular school books of the best quality, without regard to commercial profit, books bearing directly on religion or theology being excluded.[45]

43a. Kittel's *Kanarese-English Dictionary* in Kannada, 1894.

43b. Dr. Gundert's Malayalam-English Dictionary (1872) in Malayalam.

44. First Edition, 1861. Second Edition, 1875. Third Edition, 1913 (Revised and Edited by Rev. Wyatt, M.A., and T. Ramakrishna Pillay).

45. Memorandum of the Association, Clauses 1 & 2

It was also to engage itself in the dissemination of "Vernacular literature of a healthy moral tone (a) by the production...... (b) purchasing copyrights or otherwise encouraging the publication of really useful works the authors of which may not themselves have the means of publishing them." In recent times the Society is giving prominence to the second object and grants pecuniary help to vernacular publications that are declared useful by the expert committees they appoint now and then to advise them. It looks like the direct descendant of the Board attached to the College of the Fort St. George. But the connecting links in its history are now forgotten.

S.P.C.K. PRESS

Another surviving institution to which reference has already been made, that links us with the past, is the Diocesan Press (originally known as S.P.C.K. Press). Its present name shows the culmination of its long and interesting history[46] during which it changed many hands and saw diverse conditions. It is now under the management of the Christian Literature Society and has become its chief instrument for its literary and religious activities.[47]

Shall we now make a prophecy! It is common knowledge that in recent years nationalism with its immense driving power has given a fresh impetus to the study and cultivation of the languages of India. Its champions have realised their power of appeal to the people at large. External pressure under which they were groaning is now being gradually lightened and the languages are coming to their own, fully conscious of their newly attained freedom though slightly tending to rivalry and conflict,—which are often the first fruits of independence and constitute but a passing phase. South India has fully shared this new awakening. National consciousness has created the inner urge to get at the root of our heritage and has unearthed many forgotten literary treasures laying bare the inestimable value of our age-long culture. Are not these signs of a new light dawning upon us, a new literary renaissance heralding its arrival?

46. It owes its origin to the exploits of Sir Eyre Coote, who brought from Pondicherry to Madras as part of his loot "a hand-press and some cases of type and other printing equipment." Fabricius, the great scholar was at that time in charge of the S.P.C.K. Mission at Vepery and at his request the plant was handed over to him on the understanding that it should be at the service of the government when required. (Consultation, 1761). (From a letter of Mr. W. H. Warren, the Present Secretary of the Press).

47. This article shows only one side of the picture, the other side still remains in the dark.

The Madras Libraries

By

R. Janardhanam Naidu,

Librarian, Connemara Public Library.

It was in the year 1661 that the English colonists at Madras first realised the need for a library for their use. Chaplain William Whitefield prevailed upon the then Governor of Madras and the Factors and some other resident members to collect a sum of money and invest it in a bale of calico-cloth which they sent by the home-bound ships to be exchanged for books in London. The following resolution is found in the Court-Minute book of the East India Company, dated 20th February 1662-63 :—" It was ordered that the remainder of the proceeds of the calicoes sold by the Governor, which was given (to) the Minister at the Fort (of Madras) by the Factors and sent home to buy him books, should be sent (to) him in the rialls of 8 (a then current coin) after the books are paid for. " It is gathered that books were purchased to the value of £28-10-0 and forwarded to the Chaplain probably to serve as the beginning of an official library. A year later the Directors purchased and despatched to Madras books of the value of £20 directing them to be kept in the Factory House for the use of succeeding Ministers. The Rev. Frank Fenny would regard the above two presentations as the origin of the company's Library at the Fort. In 1663-64 Governor Sir Edward Winter wrote that " His (Whitefields) books we have thought requisite to buy of him, to be continued as a standing library in your Fort, for the better convenience of such as shall succeed in case they bring them not with them." The books were re-purchased from the company's funds. A similar purchase was made from another Minister, Walter Hooke, who died at Masulipatam and were added to the Fort Library in 1671. In their annual letter dated 24th December 1675, the Directors required the Madras Council to send them " a perfect catalogue of all our books, both with you at Metchlepatam and the Bay." The collection of books thus acquired at Fort St. George were largely theological suiting the needs of the time. The Chaplain was in charge of the lending of books to persons who were obliged to return them when demanded, under the penalty of paying one pagoda each. This is probably the earliest time when the system of lending books was tried in this Presidency. It is seen in traveller Lockyer's account that when he visited Fort St. George in 1703 he saw the library in it with a collection of books to the value of £438 with a free school in a large room under the library conducted by Chaplain Lewis.

From Lockyer's Account of Madras the Directors came to know of the Fort St. George Library which had in the meantime increased in size thanks to the presents of books from several persons and from S.P.C.K. They wanted their chaplains "to sort the said books into proper classes, and to take a catalogue of them to be kept in the library, of which they shall deliver a copy to our President (Governor) and to send a copy home to us; and we desire our President to order two of our servants together with our Ministers to examine the books by the catalogue once a year,... and make their report at the Vestry...." A catalogue was got ready in 1716 but the Directors were not satisfied with it and concluded that the books were a confused irregular heap. A satisfactory catalogue was prepared in 1720 by a new Chaplain for which the Governor and the Council gave him a palanquin allowance.

Mr. H. Dodwell writes in his books "The Nabobs of Madras" that among the acts of kindness shown to Clive, he was admitted into an excellent library belonging to the Governor, which was indeed the public library. Though the collection of books had been scattered by the French yet in 1754 the Madras Council prevailed upon the Directors to renew their practice of sending out periodically consignments of books from home in order to induce their servants to employ their leisure hours in reading and study. This request was not complied with, thus leaving Madras to develop its library facilities in other ways.

There are at present a fairly large number of libraries at Madras to serve the needs of its residents though indeed attempts will have to be strenuously made for increasing this number. A knowledge of the materials available in these libraries and the facilities afforded by them would naturally prove to be of great value to the citizens of Madras and this Presidency, and the following is a brief account concerning them.

The Government of Madras is maintaining the Connemara Public Library, situated within the Museum compound at Egmore, for the benefit of the residents of Madras and its immediate vicinity and also for the whole of this Presidency. It was opened in the year 1896 as a free consulting Library but from the beginning of 1930 it has also been lending books to the residents of the city and its immediate neighbourhood and to well organised libraries in the moffussil districts which may apply for affiliation to this library to borrow books from it. Those who wish to consult books in the library are allowed to do so provided they are seventeen years old and are willing to abide by certain rules such as, that they will not cause damage to the books used by them or disturbance to any reading in the library.

Those who wish to become borrowing members will, in addition to satisfying the condition of age mentioned already have to be guaranteed by one of the following *viz.*, Principal or Professor of a college, a Corporation Councillor, an Hon. Presidency Magistrate, or a Government Gazetted officer, and will also have to remit a deposit of rupees twenty each. Each member is allowed to borrow 3 books at a time which he can retain for a period of a fortnight and can renew them for a further period provided no other member applies for the same. No subscription is charged, but if a member loses a book he will have to replace it forthwith. When he ceases to borrow, his deposit will be returned to him on receipt of an application for it.

The library contains books on all subjects, Literature, Histories, and Sciences and in addition there is a large number of literary, historical and scientific periodicals, sets of which from very early years to the present day are available. Books are being constantly added to the library generally selecting such of permanent value and also answering the demands of the public.

The library practises the open access system that is, when a visitor enters it, he can directly go either to the catalogue cabinet or to the book shelves to select a book or books for himself. He can go through the books at the shelf and select those that he considers will be of much value to him. In the course of his regular study in the library, if he needs some other books for reference, he can forthwith go to the shelf and pick them up for himself. If he finds any difficulty in doing so he can at once apply to the library staff for the required help and they will instantly render him the necessary service. The periodicals that arrive week after week or every fortnightly or monthly are assembled on the tables and are directly accessible to the public.

There is also a portion of the library set apart for research workers where all facilities needed by such workers are most willingly given by the members of the staff. Those who wish to prepare theses or lectures or write books can most profitably make use of this portion of the library.

The library is open on all days in the year including public holidays, except Fridays, between 7 a.m. and 5-30 p.m. from October to March and between 7 a.m. and 6 p.m. for the rest of the year. By constant care and supervision a congenial atmosphere for study is maintained in the Library Reading hall and it is hoped that larger and larger numbers will make use of it.

The Madras University Library is maintained by the University of Madras and with the help of a substantial grant from the Government of Madras and is at Chepauk within the University buildings. It was opened in the year 1914 and is rapidly growing in size and is open on all days

52

in the year between 7 a.m. and 8 p.m. It restricts its admission to consult books free in it to those who are students in the colleges affiliated to the University of Madras and to those who are graduates of Madras University. Only students of senior status reading in the affiliated colleges and graduates of the University can borrow books from it provided they are recommended by the Principal or a Professor of a college or by the authorities of the University, and also pay a deposit of Rs. 20 each. No subscription is charged and the terms for the loan of books are similar to those of the Connemara Public Library. There is a good collection of standard works and periodicals in this library which the students and graduates of the University may make the best use of. Graduates of the University from the moffusil stations may also borrow books from this Library if they satisfy the conditions laid down by it.

The Government Oriental Manuscript Library is located in the University Library buildings, Chepauk, and was opened in the year 1847. It contains numerous manuscripts in Indian languages and also printed books. It is primarily a free consulting Library but also lends books and manuscripts on special conditions. There is an exceedingly valuable collection of manuscripts in this library most useful to research workers and scholars. It is open on all days in the year except on Fridays and on public holidays between 11 a.m. and 5 p.m. and on Saturdays till 4 p.m.

Adyar Library opened in the year 1886 is situated within the Theosophical Society buildings at Adyar and is a free consulting library. It contains books and periodicals besides valuable manuscripts. It is open between 7-30 a.m. and 5-30 p.m. and has only 15 annual holidays. Books also can be taken on loan by furnishing cash securities.

Ranade Library at Mylapore is again a free consulting library but books can be borrowed by subscribing members. It is maintained from the proceeds of an endowment. It has a fine collection of books.

Corporation of Madras maintains a library which is in a part of the Ripon Buildings and is called Sunkuwar Municipal Library. It contains mainly books on civics and is free to public only for consultation. It is open on all days in the year beween 11 a.m. and 5 p.m. except on Sundays and on public holidays.

The Registrar of Books has a very large collection of books printed within this presidency in different languages from the year 1870 and they are kept in a portion of the office of the Director of Public Instruction, Nungambakam. They are not freely accessible to the public, but if any citizen of Madras or this presidency wishes to consult any of the books he can do so by obtaining the permission of the Registrar which is usually freely given. On special conditions loan of books can also be had from the Registrar. The office of the Registrar is open on all days in the year, except on Sundays and on public holidays between 11 a.m. and 5 p.m. and on Saturdays till 4 p.m.

Among the subscription Libraries, Madras Literary Society founded in the year 1812 ranks the foremost. It is at Nungambakam and has an excellent collection of books in Fiction. It is open on every week day from 7 a.m. to 7 p.m. and on Sundays and holidays between 8 a.m. and 12 noon. Resident members pay a quarterly subscription of Rs. 10 or a monthly subscription of Rs. 4. Non-resident members pay Rs. 10 quarterly, and carriage charges for books supplied to them.

Among the recent institutions mention may be made of the Young Men's Christian Association and Young Men's Indian Association which have their own libraries and they are open to members of the respective associations for consultation and loan.

Madras is a city of distances and therefore it is in need of more libraries to serve the growing needs of the public. A library for every ward of the city is a necessity. It should consist of a reading room with journals and newspapers, a section with reference books, a section for lending books, a lecture hall and a book section exclusively for children. There should be a consolidated catalogue of all the libraries in the several divisions so that a book available in a particular division may be known to the whole of Madras to enable a resident of one part to borrow a book from another part through the library of the division of which he is a member. In other words the libraries of different divisions should not unnecessarily duplicate ordinary books and should freely borrow from one another to satisfy their respective clients.

Apart from the capital cost the maintenance of these libraries will involve a good deal of recurring cost. It will be too much to expect all this to be met by the Madras Corporation Philanthropists should come forward to co-operate with the Corporation to start libraries in different parts of the city. In the West, in the United States of America and in Great Britain, it is due to the substantial contributions of benefactors like Andrew Carnegie that many libraries have come into existence throughout the length and breadth of those countries. Quite recently Rockefeller of America gave a mighty contribution to the extent of 50% of the cost, to the Cambridge University Library of Great Britain, which is one of the most typical libraries in the world. Benefactors will have to come forward with substantial donations to help the Corporation of Madras in a cause like this which will lead to a happy and everlasting benefit to the residents of the city.

Madras city is also very badly in need of an important commercial libary where up-to-date books and periodicals on Trade and Commerce should be stocked which will be of very great value to people engaged in commerce. It will render an enormous service to the trades and industry of this presidency. A library like this should be maintained by the private benefactions of the merchant princes of this province. This library will not only serve the merchants of Madras but also the floating merchant population who so frequently visit Madras in connection with their trade and industry. The benefit coming from this can never be overestimated.

Madras has to set an example to the province and therefore if it, in time, introduces in its body politic, the required number of libraries for its residents and proves the beneficial results of such institutions, the district boards and municipalities of the province will soon follow the lead. The benefits of the compulsory elementary education in Madras city can be made to yield its lasting value only if facilities are given to its residents to prevent themselves from lapsing into illiteracy.

Sanskrit Study in Madras

BY

DR. C. KUNHAN RAJA, B.A. HONS., D.PHIL. (OXON),
Reader, University of Madras.

THE city of Madras comprises within itself some of the old seats of religious and literary activities in South India, namely the ancient towns of Mylapore and Triplicane. It is in the fitness of things that the University is located in the latter place although such location was more the effect of chance than of any design. The temples in these two places have been centres of religious worship and have been intimately connected with Tamil and Sanskrit Literature from very early times. This paper deals only with the advancement of Sanskrit Study in modern Madras.

The environments of Madras and Districts connected with Madras, had one of the earliest connections with the modern phase of Sanskritic studies in India as introduced by modern scholars. In the second half of the eighteenth century there lived at Pulicat, very near Madras, a scholar named John Phillip Verdin, better known as Bartolomeo Fra Paolino de San. He had his education at Prague and he joined the Carmalites at Rome where he learned Oriental Languages. He was for fourteen years in Malabar, now within the Madras Presidency; he was Vicar General and Apostolic Visitor. He returned to Rome to superintend the printing of religious books for the use of Indian Missioneries. He wrote a Sanskrit grammar and wrote largely of his Indian travels and experiences. He was born in 1748 and died in 1806.

But the most important and interesting figure in Sanskrit fields in the eighteenth century, so far as Madras was concerned, is Col. Colin Mackenzie. He was the Surveyor-General of the East India Company and in that capacity he had opportunities of visiting the various parts of South India. He studied the Indian languages and he had the assistance of able Pundits. The collections made by him during his stay in India in the field of South Indian history and culture are something stupendous. These collections consist of maps, drawings and sketches, of inscriptions copied, of information about the history of various places and customs and manners collected through oral evidence from various persons, of manuscripts of ancient works in various languages and of such kinds.

His collections had an unsettled career for a long time, and now are distributed in different centres. A detailed account of his work in this field is given by H. H. Wilson in his catalogue of the Mackenzie Collection published at Calcutta in 1828, and also in the Journal of the Royal Asiatic Society of Great Britain and Ireland for the year 1834. His collections were purchased by the East India Company for a large sum. There is the Mackenzie Collection now deposited in the Government Oriental Manuscripts Library, Madras, on which the Department of Indian History in the Madras University is doing splendid work. Part of the original manuscripts collected by Col. Mackenzie formed the nucleus of the present immense collection of Sanskrit manuscripts now known as the Government Oriental Manuscripts Library, Madras. A part of the Collection is in the India Office, London. The collection had migrated from place to place, Madras, Calcutta and London. It had suffered neglect and consequently loss and decay.

The activities of Col. Mackenzie were only an accident in the history of Sanskrit studies in Madras. A systematic attempt for organising the study in Madras was made only about half a century after the death of Col. Mackenzie. I have to deal with this subject under the different heads of (1) collection of manuscripts and their publication along with original research associated with it, (2) provision for advanced study of Sanskrit along what are called modern lines and (3) provision for such advanced study on what are called the traditional or Pundit lines.

One of the most notable events in the history of modern Sanskritic studies in India was the writing of a letter by Pandit Radhakrishna, Chief Pandit of the Lahore Durbar before the Panjab was annexed to British India after the defeat of Ranjit Singh, to the Viceroy and Governor-General of India, dated 10th May 1868. In this letter he indicated the lines on which a catalogue of Sanskrit works available in Palace collections and in public libraries and also in private possessions could be prepared. The Viceroy had already given orders for the preparation of such a catalogue. The Government of India had been taking a great interest in the undertaking and had made financial provision for the successful fulfilment of the undertaking. All the information on the subject is available in a work called "Papers relating to the collection and preservation of the records of ancient Sanskrit literature in India", edited by the order of the Government of India by A. E. Gough. Calcutta, 1878. Information about what the Government of Madras did on the matter is contained from page 139 to page 158 of the book.

Fortunately for the Madras Government, there was at that time a great scholar in the Indian Civil Service in the Madras area in the person of A. C. Burnell (1840-1882). His father was in the East India Company's marine service. Educated at Bedford and King's College, Cambridge, he passed the Indian Civil Service examination and joined Madras in 1860. He was for a long time at Tanjore until 1880, when his health gave way. He prepared the catalogue of the rich collection of manuscripts in the Palace of the Maharaja of Tanjore. He had himself collected many valuable manuscripts and presented them to the India Office. He had also edited some rare works. He sacrificed his health for scholarship and died while still in his youth.

For scholarship and erudition, for devotion to work, for mastery of the subject, and for the accuracy of information, this catalogue cannot be surpassed. Recently a new set of Descriptive Catalogues has been prepared and published.

The original manuscripts collected by Col. Mackenzie, after some stray wanderings, had found their way back to Madras. They were catalogued by Rev. Taylor. At a later stage, when Gustav Oppert was Professor of Sanskrit in the Presidency College, the Government of Madras organised a Manuscripts Library. As time advanced, the collection increased and now it is one of the biggest collections of Sanskrit Manuscripts in the world. The collection was first located in a small extension to the Museum in Egmore. The arrangement was to transfer the custody of the Collection to the Madras University when the University would have its own Library Building. The Professor of Sanskrit in the Presidency College has been the Curator of the Library. Now when the University has finished its own immense Library Building, the manuscripts have been transferred to that buildings, still under the control of the Government, with the Professor of Sanskrit in the Presidency College as its Curator. Under the auspices of this Library, some works of great importance have been published, and the collection in the Library has been the basis of many publications by scholars who are not directly connected with the Library. All lovers of Sanskrit learning owe a deep debt of gratitude to the Government of Madras for the continued interest it has taken in advancing the cause of this collection and in providing the necessary funds for its upkeep and progress. There is a good descriptive Catalogue of the collection running up to over fifty volumes.

Although not in the City of Madras, just beyond the river which forms the southern boundary of the city, there are the beautiful Estates of the Theosophical Society in which are located the international Headquarters of the Society. Among the many useful activities of the Society at its Headquarters, the most important is the maintenance of the great Oriental Library known as the Adyar Library. This

Library was founded about the same time when the Madras Government established its own Manuscripts Library. The Library was opened on the 28th December 1886. This Library is kept up by the Theosophical Society out of its own funds, and this too has one of the most important collection of Sanskrit Manuscripts in the world, both in point of the number of manuscripts and in point of the rare works available in it. Prof. F. O. Schrader now of the University at Kiel in Germany was its Director for about ten years. The Library has published a catalogue of the manuscripts, and a descriptive catalogue is in the course of preparation. Many books have been published from the Library. The Library is now running a Bulletin, which has become within two years of its life, one of the foremost Oriental Periodicals in the world. The manuscripts collection is made use of by scholars in all the parts of the world.

Besides the catalogues of these three big Manuscripts Libraries much information about manuscripts in the Madras Presidency is contained in the two catalogues by Oppert in two volumes and Hultsch in three volumes. These two catalogues give information about the various private libraries in the different parts of the Presidency. Most of the manuscripts noted in these catalogues must have been recently collected for the Government Oriental Manuscripts Library or for the Adyar Library. Still there must be many that lie hidden in private libraries and these two will be of great help for manuscripts hunters.

In 1927, the Madras University established a Department for advanced study and research in Sanskrit. The Department has published a large number of rare works in the different branches of Sanskrit learning, Veda, Grammar, Lexicography, Mimamsa, Vedanta etc. The Department has also given training to many students in modern methods of research. The work of the Department including the students has been well appreciated by scholars all over the world who had occasion to know of the work. The University has made provision for the study of modern European languages as an aid to advanced study in the various subjects and the students of the Department have always taken advantage of the provision and have profited thereby. The Department has also made provision for giving the students facilities for the study of Avesta, Tibetan and other allied languages.

The Presidency College, Madras, was constituted in its present form with a Principal and Professors, under the control of the Director of Public Instruction in 1855. In the next year was instituted a professorship for vernacular studies. But for over twelve years there was no provision for the teaching of Sanskrit. In 1868, J. Pickford was appointed the first Professor of Sanskrit, followed by Gustav Oppert, in whose time it was that the Madras Government started the Oriental Manuscript Library. The place has since been occupied by scholars of great distinction. The college has always made provision for imparting instruction in Sanskrit to the highest standard prescribed by the University. The old students of the College now fill almost all the places in the Sanskrit Department of the college. This is the only college where there is provision for the teaching of Sanskrit upto the highest examination in the Madras University, and it may also be mentioned that Sanskrit is the only Oriental Language for which there is such provision in any institution within the University. In nearly all the colleges within the University, the Sanskrit Chair is occupied by an old Student of the Presidency College. In the University Research Department all the posts are held by the old students of the College. Many ladies also have been students of the Sanskrit section of the college. Most of them had passed the University examination with great distinction, though all of them have languished into obscurity later.

While the Presidency College provides for the advanced study of Sanskrit on what are called modern lines, provision for the study of Sanskrit on what are called traditional or Pundit lines is provided in the Mylapore Sanskrit College, founded by the late V. Krishnaswami Ayyar. The Madras University has included Sanskrit as one of the subjects in the Arts Faculty. Sanskrit also forms a part of the Faculty of Oriental Learning. University distinctions designated the Title of Siromani are awarded in this Faculty. Mimamsa, the three Vedantas, Nyaya, Vyakarana, Sahitya, Ayurveda and Jyautisha are the subjects in Sanskrit in which there is a course of study prescribed and the Title of Siromani conferred on those who pass the examination at the end of the course. The Mylapore Sanskrit College is the only college in the City which makes provision for this course. The subject of Ayurveda is taught in another institution (under the same management) adjacent to this college. This college is one of the best among the many institutions approved by the University for imparting instruction in the course. The other institutions are all in moffusil stations.

Madras can be proud of its achievements in the field of Sanskrit in point of manuscripts collection and advanced research and also in point of provision for advanced study for University Degrees. The Presidency College makes provision for undergraduate course and is maintaining a very efficient staff. The University has included the subject for the various degrees including research degrees. Many persons have taken research degrees in the subject. There is ample facility by way of well equipped libraries (the University Library, the Library attached to the Government Oriental Manuscripts Library, the Presidency College Library and the Adyar Library). There are periodicals of established reputation devoted to Sanskrit and allied subjects. The University has a whole-time research staff for Sanskrit. This research staff has now undertaken the compilation of a New Catalogus Catalogorum giving information about Sankrit and Sanskritic Manuscripts in the whole world, in Public Libraries, in Palaces and Temples, and in private collections.

Artistic Development in Madras

By

Dewan Bahadur K. S. Ramaswami Sastri, B.A., B.L.

The rise and consolidation of a set of detached villages on the eastern sea-board of India into the great metropolitan city of Madras form one of the romances of modern times and are described elsewhere in this Volume. An endeavour will be made here only to describe and evaluate the growth of Art in the city of Madras during the last three hundred years. As J. T. Wheeler says in his interesting work,* " Old Madras! What a multitude of associations are called up by the simple words! What curious pictures of the past flash before our eyes......Members of Council rode about in bullock bandies and the guards of the President were armed with bows and arrows, swords and shields .... Gentlemen wore large loose preposterous breeches and hats with conical crowns and bunches of feathers......" Let us try to lift the curtain of the past and have a peep into the many-sided artistic changes in Madras since its humble birth.

The Art of Town-Planning.—The art of town-planning is the mother art, and without it the arts, including the fine arts and the useful arts, cannot thrive and attain perfection. The ancient Indian cities grew around great temples and were better planned than modern cities about which Professor Radha Kamal Mookerjee says well: " A planless muddle of factories, warehouses, railways and slums has led to terrible congestion."

The ancient cities of India were not only temple cities but were also garden cities. The modern sight of rows of constructions of of brick and mortar, interspersed with crowded and insanitary slum dwellings in thatch, was unknown before. India must not lose her love of gardens and avenues, specially because she is a tropical country. The planting of gardens and avenues has always been considered a pious and meritorious act in India. It is a matter for congratulation that Madras, unlike Bombay and Calcutta, has grown up as a garden city, though this was more due to historic accidents than to conscious planning. There is no need to convert Madras from a Paleotechnic city into a Neo-technic city. It has evolv-

* *Madras in the Olden Time* (1640-1748), published in 1861.

ed from a military station into a Neo-technic city by a stroke of luck.' The newest suburb, viz., Tyagarayanagar, has sprung up on the site of the old Mylapore lake. The city is capable of considerable expansion westwards and to a less extent northwards and southwards, and is a vigorous tree throwing out new branches crowned with new and lovely flowers and fruits.

It would seem that much of the luck of Madras in being a garden city is due to the hobby of some of the early Governors of Madras in that direction. Governor Pitt wrote to his friend Samuel Onglay of London on 23-1-1702 : " My leisure time I generally spend in gardening and planting." He took steps to embank, drain and plant the hitherto marshy Island. He made the fine double avenue known as " the Great Walk " across the Island so as to form a vista for the Company's Garden House on the north bank of the Elamboore (now called Egmore) River (North River) which flows into the Cooum river. Though the rivers running through Madras have little beauty and less sanctity, yet Madras must be thankful to them for some amenities. Even the " silvery Cooum " as it is called—probably by way of raillery at its unsilveriness—fills a place of its own in the amenities of Madras. It is called also the Poonamalle River and the Triplicane River, and probably Cooum is a contraction of Komalam or Komaleswaram. H. D. Love's *Vestiges of Madras* gives us much information about the many garden houses in Madras. For instance he refers to Niccolao Manucci's Garden House. "Elephant Garden " or Maria Pois's Garden which was north of it was taken on lease by the Company in 1675. The road running west from it was called Elephant Street, a name still preserved towards its western end as Elephant Gate Road.

The clearing up of the slums has been taken up of late by private effort as well as by the activity of the Madras Corporation, because the civic sense is growing keener day by day. The Government has been most keen and eager and sympathetic in this direction. There is thus a fair prospect of Madras being rid of her slums in the near future.

The art of architecture.—In 1699 Thomas Salmon refers to the Fort St. George thus : " It was built in the form of a square and is better than a mile and a half in circumference, being surrounded with a brick wall 17 feet thick, with bastions at proper distances " and that " it has also a river on the west and the sea on the east." Governor Thomas Pitt took up the fortification of Black Town (now called George Town) in 1700 and completed it in seven years. In the Black Town were the English Burial Ground, the Armenian Church, the Great Pagoda, and the Mosque. It may be mentioned also that in the India Office there is a series of six views of Eastern Forts painted by Lambert and Scott about 1732. These comprise Fort St. George, Fort William, Bombay Castle, Tellicherry, Cape of Good Hope and St. Helena. Neither artist visited India. The East India Company bought them at 15 guineas per picture. The picture of Fort St. George shows ships in front and houses and the fort at the back. In 1735 John Bowles made a print of it. In 1735 Gerard Vandergucht engraved the paintings.

It may be mentioned here that Mr. George Norton Pitt who was a Governor of Madras erected the South Sea Gate colonnade, an avenue of four rows of pillars covered with terraced roof, which formed a sheltered approach from the Sea Gate to the Fort Square. The sea was very near the walls of Fort St. George then and the eastern gate of the Fort—the sea gate—opened directly into the sea. The colonnade consisted of thirty-two columns of black Pallavaram gneiss. The French carried them off in 1746 to adorn Pondicherry. After the fall of Pondicherry, the English brought them back and reerected in their original position. In the 19th century the colonnade was converted into a covered building by walling up the spaces between the pillars. Later on the building was used for the Government Press and Record Room. In 1910 it was dismantled to make room for the new Legislative Council Chamber in the construction of which the best preserved of the columns were incorporated.

Reference may be made here to a few other public buildings which have grown up in Madras. The earliest hospital was kept in Cogan's House in 1664 to treat sick soldiers. In 1688 a double-storyed house near the Church was used for that purpose, and later yet a hired house in James Street was so used. There was a garden in the place where the Medical College and the General Hospital are now situated. A special mention should be made of the Chepauk Palace. The Nawab Muhammad Ali, Wallajah, wanted to build a palace in Madras and wrote to Mr. Palk who was then the Governor of Fort St. George : " Besides the Fort of Madras, in such times, I know no other place of security." A site 18000 square yards in area was thereupon granted to him. The Chepauk (Chepauk means a lovely village) was built by him in two blocks—the southern called Kalasa Mahal consistir.g of two floors and the northern building which consisted of one floor and consisted of Humayun Mahal and Dewankhana. These stately and spacious buildings were in the Saracenic style and have got small and big domes peculiar to that style of architecture. On the death of the last Nawab in 1855 the buildings were acquired by the Government. The southern building housed the P.W.D. Secretariat as well as the College of Engineering till the College was recently shifted to Guindy. The northern building is used as the office of the Board of Revenue. The styles of Dravidian architecture are represented by the gopuras of the city temples. Some aspects of this style of architecture combined with the Indo-Saracenic style are noticeable in the New University Buildings on the Marina.

It is not possible to go here into details about other buildings in Madras. But it may be stated that Madras has specialised in a style of building which combines elegance and comfort. What is called 'Madras terrace' is well-known. It is only now that ferro-concrete work is superseding it. Madras plastering also is famous. Mrs. Kinderesley said in 1777: "What gives the greatest elegance to the houses (in Madras) is a material peculiar to the place: it is a cement of plaster called *channam* made of the shells of a very large species of oysters found in this coast; these shells when burnt, pounded and mixed with water, form the strongest cement imaginable; if it is to be used as a plaster, they mix it with whites of eggs, milk and some other ingredients; when dry it is as hard and very near as beautiful as marble."

But it must be said that of late there has been much deterioration in the artisic construction of public as well as private buildings in Madras, judging from the point of view of the beautiful art of architecture. The old skill in carving ornamental wooden pillars or fashioning ornamental stone pillars culminating in floral designs seems to be no longer wanted. Curves seem to be taboo. We have oceans of straight lines unrelieved by an iota of curvature or ornamentation. The race of the old master builders (sthapatis) is almost extinct. The Manai Sastras (Silpasastras) are almost forgotten. The ubiquitous Maistri is an expert in the quick construction of cheap and ugly buildings constructed in an odd medley of styles! What John Summerson says of London is equally true of other towns: "London is being rebuilt, but not, as we are all painfully aware, in the interests of order or magnificence."

Mention may also be made about the fountains in Madras. There is a fountain south of the Victoria Hall. Another is at the junction of the Police Commissioner's Road and the Pantheon Road. A third is at the southwest approach of the Government House Bridge or the Mount Road. A fourth is at the junction of the Beach Road and Edward Elliot Road. It is this last fountain that has been charmingly lit up by coloured electric lights for a few months past. But Madras is far behind Mysore in the matter of public fountains.

The Arts of Sculpture and Painting.—The various statues in Madras are by themselves a special study. We may mention the bronze statue of Queen Victoria (1887) in Chepauk Park near the Senate House; the statue of the King-Emperor Edward

SIR THOMAS MUNRO

VII in front of the Government House (1903); the statues of King-Emperor George V (1914) at the Pachaiyappa's Corner; the statue of Lord Cornwallis in marble in the Connemara Library; the statue of Brigadier-General Neill (1860) which was in the Mount Road before and has as the result of popular demand been shifted to the Museum; the equestrian statue of the noble and beloved Governor Sir Thomas Munro in the Mount Road; and the white marble statue in the Presidency College of E. B. Powell (the first Principal of the College and Director of Public Instruction); and the statue of Dr. William Miller (1901) at the Esplanade. The statues of Sir T. Muthuswami Iyer and Sir V. Bhashyam Iyengar in the High Court, the statues of G. K. Gokhale and Sir S. Subramania Aiyar and Mr. V. Krishnaswami Aiyar (1911) in the Senate House are other interesting relics.

Indian painting, like other Indian arts, has had its own ideals and objectives and methods. The European painter gets his effects by juxtapositions of light and shade and colour but the Indian painter does so by the significance of definite lines. The former has specially excelled in landscape painting. India is taking to it now more than before.

In the field of painting the two modern schools in the Madras Presidency are the Ravi Varma school at Trivandrum and the Rama Rao school in Rajahmundry. Ravi Varma was indebted to the western school of oil-painting and learnt his first lessons from the English artist Theodore Jansen who went to Trivandrum to paint the portraits of the Maharaja and the members of his family. He excelled in portraits as well as subject pictures and won Lord Hobart's gold medal at the Madras Art Exhibition in 1874. Assisted by his brother he executed the painting of Sir Arthur Havelock now in the Banqueting Hall.

Many artists visited Madras in the 18th and 19th centuries. Mention may be made of George Chinnery who came in 1802 and stayed until 1808. It is said that he painted the Madras picture of Stringer Lawrence and Nawab Walajah. Thomas Hickey was another artist who lived in Madras between 1800 and 1806. Earlier came Robert Home who arrived in Madras in 1790 and painted a portrait of Sir Eyre Coote. Tilly Kettle who was in India from 1770 to 1776 painted a picture of Nawab Walajah and his five sons, exhibited at the Society of Artists in 1771. These and others have been responsible for the picture gallery in the Banqueting Hall and other halls in the Government House. (See Love: Portraits in Government House).

The oldest portraits there are those of King George III and Queen Charlotte. It is strange to learn that in the letter sent on 6-2-1768 by

King George III when sending some pictures to the Nawab that the king is described as "George III, by the Grace of God, King of Great Britain, France and Ireland." Most of the portraits are full length and life size and are 8 feet by 4 feet, while some are three quarter length and life size and are 4 feet by 3 feet. The pictures are those of several former Governors and Viceroys and Commanders-in-Chief. We find among the pictures there the pictures of Major Lawrence and Nawab Walajah as well as the emblazoned mouldings of the royal arms and those of the East India Company. Though comparatively a recent art, photography in Madras has become very popular, and is associated with almost every function. Photography and oil painting have become the fashion in modern Madras.

Madras and the arts of Literature and Drama.—Among the ancient achievements of Madras in the field of literature must be mentioned the works that came into existence in Mylapore which was a civilised and distinguished town long ago. It was perhaps the birth-place of Tirukkural, one of the classics of the world. It is said also that Mylainathar wrote there a great commentary on the famous Tamil Grammar Nannool. The renowned Mahomedan scholar and poet Masthan Sahib wrote his poems there.

A passing mention may be made of the high achievements of English journalism in the Madras city. The growth of unity and modernity and patriotism in the Province is due in the main to the radiation of news and views from the city through the *Hindu*, the *Madras Mail* and the *Indian Express* among the dailies and through various weeklies and monthlies.

The most noteworthy features in the development of literature and drama in the local languages in Madras in recent times are the rise of journalistic prose and the rise of dramas and novels and short stories. The role played by *Swadesamitran* (a Tamil Daily) for six decades and by various other Tamil dailies and other papers and by the *Andhra Patrika* (a Telugu Daily) and by various other Telugu dailies and other papers is noteworthy. The *Ananda Vikatan*, a bright Tamil weekly, has recaptured the note of humour and brought it into the field of journalism and has slowly perfected the short story as a literary form. The *Kalaimagal* has brought the note of combined ancient and modern knowledge and scholarship.

A special mention must be made here of the great work done by the Suguna Vilas Sabha in the city of Madras by way of uplift and purification of the stage during the last forty years. Rao Bahadur P. Sambanda Mudaliar is a landmark in South Indian dramaturgy and has done work of high quality both as an author and as an actor. The Telugu stage also has achieved many notable triumphs in Madras. But the most outstanding fact in the realm of literary work in Madras is the peerless work done by Mahamahopadhyaya V. Swaminatha Iyer. Prominent and special mention should be made also of the wonderful songs of patriotism and Swaraj written by the late poet and patriot Subramania Bharati.

The Cinema and the Radio have come like conquering heroes in recent times and have taken the public mind by storm. It remains to be seen whether they will steam-roll and macadomise art, or will, in their turn, submit to the enchantments of the enchantress. To-day the Cinema artists are wildly exploring all life—puranic, historical, social—to provide stunts and thrills. The plethora of song which harmed the Tamil stage seems to persist in the Tamil Cinema also. Impossible and outlandish love scenes abound and almost rival the impossible and outlandish scenes of stunt fights. The Radio appeals only to the ear and has to charm by a shower of many-coloured sparks and is hence vitiated by a restless and often futile hunt after variety. What will happen when television arrives no one can now forsee.

The Art of Music and Dancing.—The greatness of the Karnatic system of music lies in its purity of type, in its excellence in *Alapana* and *gamakas* (graces), and in its vital touch with devotion. In Madras city Paidala Gurumurti Sastri who lived in the 18th century and Veena Kuppier who lived in the 19th century were outstanding figures in the realm of South Indian music. The temple music always continued unbroken through the ages, especially the music of the Nagasvaram.

Madras city has done signal service to the cause of South India Music by its discerning patronage of the great masters of Karnatic music through the medium of many musical sabhas including the Music Academy, the Fine Arts Society, etc. The musicians also are beginning to organise themselves and the Vainika Gayaka Mahasamajam is a pioneer organisation in that direction.

A special mention should be made of the splendid pioneering work of Krishna Bhagavathar in the field of the Harikatha in Tamil. The Harikatha is a wonderful blend of scholarship and dramatic narrative and high class music, and combines the finest and most powerful objectives of the literary art (love and humour and pathos and devotion). It was discovered and refined as an artistic instrument in Maharashtra but Krishna Bhagavathar and following him the late Panchapakesa Bhagavathar and Chidambara Bhagavathar of Mangudi and others refined it still further and filled its rifts with ore till it became most popular and most educative. Many ladies have taken to it of late and among them the name of Gayanapatu Keertanapatu Sangeeta Ratnam C. Saraswati Bai stands unique because of her marvellous music and her excellent exposition.

The art of Dance (Bharata Natyam) has had a chequered career in India. Of late, a new movement has come in which bids fair to improve the *morale* of the community which had devoted itself to the art of dance, and at the same time an artistic surge has brought the art of Bharata Natyam into favour once again. Nay, the swing of the pendulam is in the direction of teaching the art of dance to girls in the schools and respectable women look upon the art with favour.

Decorative and Industrial Arts.—From time immemorial the rich productions of India have been eagerly desired by the civilised world. India's cotton, spices, perfumes and jewels were welcome everywhere. Even more than the rare natural products of India were the productions of India's skill in industrial art. A Department of Industries is now actively at work. There are many tanneries, textile mills, printing presses, railway workshops, etc., in Madras. The Indian Aluminium industry was begun in Madras in 1898. There are a Pencil Factory at Washermanpet and Match Factories in Tondiarpet and Tiruvottiyur. We have got also a glass factory at Tondiarpet, and enamel works at Chetpet. Mr. Rajah D. Mawney has started a drug factory. Among other industries must be mentioned the manufacture of brass and copper, and German silver vessels, of gold and silver ornaments, and jewellery, of galvanised buckets and tin cans, of iron safes and locks and steel trunks and of furniture and rattan work and kuskus and bamboo thattis and cane baskets and artificial flowers. There are also rice mills and beedi manufactories. We have also button manufacture, soap manufacture, manufacture of scents and scented sticks, ink manufacture, paper manufacture, pottery manufacture, etc. But in every industry there is much need of up-to-date methods and better marketing facilities and elimination of middlemen if the industries are to attain real improvement and prosperity.

Industry passes into industrial art only when utility is supplemented and sublimated by beauty. A sword can cut equally well whether it has a plain handle or an artistic handle. A cloth can hide nudity whether it is plain or embroidered. The Indian skill added beauty to utility. Swords and shields and helmets and armours were made beautiful by Art. We find many examples of these in the Madras Museum. Among other achievements of Indian industrial art should be mentioned brass ware with silver incrustation, encrusting gold and silver wire on the surface of iron or bronze, encrusting of precious stones on jade, the weaving of kincobs with gold or silver thread, etc.

A BIRD'S-EYE VIEW OF MADRAS

Two excellent examples of pith work are found in the Madras Museum. One of them is a wonderful representation of the Brihadeesvara temple at Tanjore. The pithwork was done at Trichinopoly. I find also in the Madras Museum some excellent and elaborate pieces of wood carving such as door-pieces, pillars, ceiling pieces, etc., brought from the house which was occupied by Count de Lally during the siege of Madras in 1758. In the school of Arts at Madras is to be found a collection of rare images in various metals, specimens of paintings with gold leaf work, tapestry work, etc., gathered from various portions of the Presidency.

Thus on the whole the growth of Art in Madras during the last three centuries has been unregulated and sporadic just like the growth of the city itself. The essential ideals of Indian Art have not been kept in mind and there has been an odd medley of styles in every direction. Art must come into its own in education before it can come into its own in life.

Madras as a Seat of Musical Learning

By

P. Sambamoorthy, B.A., B.L.,
Lecturer, University of Madras.

Madras has the distinction of being one of the bright spots on the map of South Indian music. Herein lived and flourished some of the great scholars (lakshanakaras), musicians and composers who have shed lustre on Karnatic music. All the important seats of musical learning in South India were either capitals of States wherein the Rajahs patronised music or were Zamindaries, wherein the Zamindars, themselves musicians, maintained Samasthana Vidvans in their courts. Tanjore, Mysore, Travancore, Pudukottah, Ramnad, Sivaganga, Ettiyapuram, Udayarpalayam, Karvetnagar, Venkatagiri, Vijayanagaram and Bobbili were the chief seats of musical learning during the last two hundred years and more. If Tanjore is the brightest spot on the map of South Indian music, it is due to the fact that for a period of over two and a half centuries it had as its rulers (Nayaks and Mahrattas) men who were genuine lovers and patrons of the art. Though Madras was neither the capital of an Indian State nor a Zamindari, still it gradually developed into an important seat of music as many prominent musicians and composers took up their residence here. The stream of Vidvans that came from the north and went to Tanjore to win laurels invariably halted at Madras on their way. It is said that the renowned singer Bhuloka Chapa Chutti (the man who rolled the world into a mat) Bobbili[1] Kesavayya during his stay in Madras used to go every morning to a place near the present Napier Bridge, Marina and sit under the shade of the trees and carry on his strenuous vocal practices. The Bhuloka Chapa Chutti found this spot, far removed as it was from the

1. There are many legends about this Bobbili Vidvan. He always rode on horse-back—very unusual for musicians. In his thirst for fame, he went to many Royal Courts and defeated the Samasthana Vidvans there in musical contests. The vanquished musicians were compelled to surrender their tamburas and costly presents they had received from their patrons. When he came to Tanjore during the reign of Sarabhoji it is said that cartloads of these tamburas, shawls and other valuable articles surrendered by the defeated musicians, followed him. The Bobbili musician sang to the accompaniment of a majestic tambura bedecked with flag. Ghanam Krishnier, the eminent composer of Tamil padas learnt the intricacies of *madhyamakala* style of singing from Bobbili Kesavayya.

busy town, quite congenial for his vocal practices. The temples at Mylapore, Triplicane and Tiruvottiyur were visited by distinguished musical luminaries and songs were composed by them in praise of the presiding Deities of those shrines. Generous patrons of music also lived in and around Madras and many a musician and composer came from distant places to exhibit his skill before them. All these circumstances helped Madras to gradually rise in musical importance and become an important seat of music.

One of the earliest composers to settle down in Madras was Paidala Gurumurti Sastri (18th century). He is the greatest composer of gitas after Purandara Das (1494-1564). He is referred to as *Veyigita* Paidala Gurumurti Sastri, i.e., who composed a 1000 *gitas* and also as *Naluvadi vela ragala* Gurumurti Sastri, i.e., who had knowledge of 40,000 ragas. He has composed *lakshana gitas, sanchari gitas, prabandhas* and *kirtanas* and signed them with his name. Whereas earlier *gita* composers like Venkatamakhi and Ramamatya wrote in *bhandira bhasha,*[2] Gurumurti Sastri composed his *gitas* in Sanskrit. He was a renowned Lakshana-lakshya Vidvan of his time and was held in great esteem. In recognition of his musical scholarship, the then Rajah of Tanjore presented him a palanquin. Gurumurti Sastri's brother Subbaraya Sastri was also a brilliant singer and has composed many varnas.

Vina Kuppier, the Samasthana Vidvan of Kovur[3] during the time of Sundaresa Mudaliar was the central figure in the musical life of Madras during the first half of the 19th century. He was a direct disciple of Tyagaraja and was intimately associated with him for more than two decades. The great composer had a profound regard for his disciple on account of his rare musical attainments and scholarship in Sanskrit and Telugu. Kuppier was a brilliant composer of *kritis, kirtanas, varnas* and *tillanas.* His *kritis* bristle with many technical beauties. He was called Narayanagaula Kuppier in recognition of his extraordinary skill in handling this rare *raga.* Even now his Ata tala Varna in this *raga* beginning with the words *Maguva ninne kori* stands

2. Bhandira bhasha is a corrupt form of Sanskrit and is best suited for musical sahitya. This language received an impetus during the time of Bhoja and Somesvara. There is a Manuscript in the Saraswati Mahal Library, Tanjore, dealing with the grammar of this language.

3. Kovur is a village about 14 miles from Madras and is near Poonamalle. It lies on the bus route. It has a Saivite temple and Tyagaraja visited this temple about a hundred years ago. It was here that he sang the famous *Kovur Pancharatnam,* five kritis in praise of Sundareswara Swamy, the Deity of the temple. The 5 kritis are:—*Sambo Mahadeva* (Pantuvarali), *Nammi vacina* (Kalyani), *E vasudha* (Sahana), *Kori Sevimpa* (Kharaharapriya) and *Sundaresvaruni* (Sankarabharana). The place is also known as Gopuram.

as the best *lakshya* (example) in this *raga*. His *Group-kritis*: *Kalahastisa Pancharatnam*, *Venkatesa Pancharatnam* and *Chamundisvari Pancharatnam* are a class by themselves. Besides being a Vainika, he was also a brilliant Violinist and Vocalist. He had a number of disciples and followed his Master in giving them free food and tuition in music. Prominent amongst his disciples may be mentioned his son Tiruvottiyur Tyagayyar, Kottavasal Venkataramier, Sitaramayya and Fiddle Ponnuswami Pillay. For his mastery in the different branches of the art of music, Kuppier was called *Gana Chakravarti*. He left his native home in Tiruvottiyur early in the 19th century and came to Madras and settled down in Muthialpet. He attended the concerts of the European Band given at the Fort and was fascinated by the beauty of European music. The last solfa passage in the *Bilahari raga*, Adi tala varna of his, beginning with the phrase P d r S is definitely suggestive of this European influence.[4]

It was at Kuppier's request that the great composer of Tiruvadi consented to include Madras in his itinerary, when he started on his pilgrimage to Tirupati and Conjeevaram. In Madras, Tyagaraja stayed as the honoured guest of Kovur Sundaresa Mudaliar at the latter's palatial residence in Bunder Street. It was on this occasion that the great composer sang[5] the *Devagandhari raga* for six days—an achievement which he alone was capable of. On his way to Madras, he halted at Tiruvottiyur and there sang the *Tiruvottiyur Pancharatnam*—five *kritis* in praise of Tripurasundari, the Goddess of the shrine. Tyagaraja honoured Kuppier by paying a visit to the latter's house and there sang a song in praise of Venugopalaswami, the family deity of the Gana Chakravarti.

4. It will be interesting to note in this connection that Tyagaraja himself wrote songs like *Pahi Rama Chandra* and *Vara lilo gana lola* (both in Sankarabharana); *Sara Sara Samari* (Kuntalavarali) and *Raminchuva revarura* (Suposhini) which bear influences of European music. The sage of Tiruvayar had occasion to listen to European music from Baluswami Dikshitar, the first to learn Violin playing under a European Violinist and a few others. Muthuswami Dikshitar also was enamoured of European music and he wrote some melodies after the style of European music. It will be interesting to note that for the tune of the English National Anthem "God Save the King" Muthuswami Dikshitar has written a Sanskrit Sahitya beginning with the words *Santatam pahi mam*.

5. Devagandhari is a raga with a limited scope. That is, it will not be possible for a musician relatively to make an alapana of this raga for a considerable length of time. But to Tyagaraja's genius, it mattered little whether a raga was of an *apurva* (rare) type or a common one. Only a few composers have attempted melodies in this raga and that too only one or two. But Tyagaraja has given us ten scholarly compositions in this raga.

Vina Kuppier celebrated the Chitra Pournami and Vinayaka Chaturthi festivals in his house with great eclat. In connection with these festivals, leading musicians from all over South India came to his house and gave concerts. It was a rare honour for a musician to get an opportunity to perform before the Gana Chakravarti and his circle of musical luminaries, who adorned Madras.

Tiruvottiyur Tyagayyar, the worthy son of Vina Kuppier, carried on the noble traditions of his father. Many people learned music at his feet and some of them became eminent musicians. His house in 89, Ramaswamy Street, George Town, became a veritable place of pilgrimage for musicians and music-lovers. By his works *Pallavi Svara Kalpa Valli* and *Sankirtana Ratnavali*, Tiruvottiyur Tyagayyar has placed the music world under a deep debt of gratitude to him. He has composed 108 kritis and many beautiful varnas and ragamalikas.

The versatile musical genius Tachur Singaracharlu (1834-1892) took up residence in Madras in the latter part of the 19th century. Madras as a seat of music turns a new chapter from his time. His proficiency in Sanskrit and Telugu, his intimate knowledge of the theory and history of music, his extensive repertoire and scholarship, his compositions in common and rare ragas, all these helped him to become the chief figure in the musical life of Madras during the latter half of the 19th century. Ably assisted by his younger brother Chinna Singara Charyulu, he published a series of graded text-books on music in Telugu. The brothers lived in No. 3, Thambu Naicken Lane near the present " Soundarya Mahal ", Govindappa Naicken Street, George Town. The concerts that they organised in the Rama Mandiram in connection with the Rama Navami festival every year were attended by thousands of people. Every new musician who came to Madras and who wanted to make a name had first to go and perform before the Singaracharlu Brothers and get their appreciation. They trained a number of disciples and a few[6] of them are surviving even now.

Vadivelu who was honoured with the present of an ivory violin by His Highness the Swati Tirunal Maharaja of Travancore, visited Madras in 1828. Vina Kuppier heard Vadivelu's music and admired the talents of the young musician who was then only 18 years of age.

Of the composers that took up their residence in Madras in the last century may be mentioned Patnam Subramanya Iyer and Pallavi Seshayyar. The former lived only in Tiruvadi but came to Madras to give training in music to the daughters of Salem Minakshi, a prominent

6. Vina Krishnamachariar, the eminent contemporary composer living in Bangalore, is a disciple of Tachur Singaracharlu.

songstress of that time. He lived in Krishnappa Naicken Agraharam, Peddunaickenpet. Because of his long stay in Madras he came to be called (Chenna) Patnam Subramanya Iyer by the people of Tanjore and that name has passed into history. It was during his stay in Madras that he composed many of his *kritis, varnas* and *tillanas*. Pallavi Seshayyar, an adept in handling *pallavis* was the son of Neykkarappatti Subbier, a disciple of Tyagaraja. Seshayyar has composed beautiful *kritis, tillanas* and *varnas*. Once during the festival in Tiruvottiyur Tyagayyar's house, he broke all previous records by singing *Saveri raga* for eight hours. One of his illustrious disciples was Vidvan Manattattai Duraiswamy Iyer, who also lived in Madras.

Of the prominent musicians that lived in Madras in the past mention may be made of Pandit Lakshmanachariar (the eminent Harikatha Performer), Palghat Anantarama Bhagavatar, Nadukkaveri Vaidyanatha Iyer, B.A. Varadachariar, Kalahasti Vina Venkataswamy Raju, Thenmatam Narasimhachariar, Photograph Masilamani Mudaliar (the first to specialise in Photography), Addaganti Virasami, Sabhapati (brother of Violinist Ambayiram), Harmonium Kandasami Mudaliar, Venu (a gifted singer), Gurumurti Nattuvanar, Muthuswami Nattuvanar and Veena Dhanammal. Almost all the lady singers of eminence, that South India has produced during the last century and the present century lived in Madras.

Madras was also a centre of sacred music. Numerous Bhajana mandirams have been functioning in the different parts of the city from a long time. Every pettah even now has at least two or three bhajana mandirams from where one can hear recitals of sacred music on Fridays, Saturdays and other festival days. The great devotee Alluri Venkatadri Swami lived in Triplicane. Adi Narayana Das, a member of the line of Bhadrachala Ramadas lived in Mambalam and his Rama Navami utsavams were attended by thousands of people. Tevaram and Tiruppugazh sabhas giving training to youngsters and adults in the recital of Tamil sacred music have been in existence from the last century. The Dhanur masa bhajanas in Mylapore and Peddunaickenpeta have been an annual feature in the religious life of Madras for many decades. The Mylapore Bhajana was inaugurated by Tyagaraja's disciples and is still being carried on. B.A. Varadachariar (the first Graduate of the Madras University to become an eminent singer), Erriah Bhagavathar and Balasubrahmanya Iyer have been associated with the Dhanur masa bhajanas in Peddunaickenpeta. T. P. Kodandarama Iyer, B.A., the founder of the Panduranga Mandiram and the author of "Bhagavat Bhajana Paddhati" and other works on sacred music lived in Triplicane. Ramalingaswamy of *Arutpa* fame visited Madras frequently. His famous Tamil *Viruttam* beginning with the words 'Orumaiyuda ninadu' was composed in praise of the Deity in the Kandaswamy temple, Park Town. Mint Street was and still is literally the Musical Grub Street of Madras.

Madras has also a proud record for its musical endowments. Juttur Subrahmanya Chetty, in the last century created a handsome endowment and from the proceeds of this fund, a decent honorarium is given to an eminent Nagasvaram player every year. The invited Nagasvaram player comes with his party and gives concerts for ten days in the Chenna Kesava Perumal temple during the Periyalwar festival in the month of June. It is the tradition for the invited Nagasvaram players to take one *raga* for each evening and elaborate the same for about two hours and finish the concert with a *pallavi*, *ragamalika* and some light pieces. All the leading Nagasvaram players of the past like Sembanarkoil Ramasami, Mannargudi Chinna Pakkiri, Sivakolundu and Madura Ponnuswami and of the present like Tiruvadamarudur Viruswami were recipients of this honour. The S. K. P. D. in Kotwal Bazaar maintains a concert party (since 1860) consisting of a Vocalist, Violinist and a Mridangam player. This party provides concerts of sacred music in the temple on Fridays and other sacred days a bhajana ghoshti[7] is maintained by the Pachaiappa's Trust and daily bhajanas are performed by this party in their mandiram in Mint Street.

Kirtanas in praise of Parthasarathi, the presiding Deity of the temple in Triplicane, have been composed by Mysore Sadasiva Rao (*Sri Parthasaradhe*—Bhairavi), Subbaraya Sastri (*Ninnu sevinchina*—Yadukulakambhoji), Subbarama Dikshitar (*Parthasaradhini*—Yadukulakambhoji) and Tyagaraja *svari vedalina Parthasaradhi*. The first one is in Sanskrit and the other three are in Telugu.

It is usual for Sthala Vidvans and other prominent musicians to celebrate certain annual festivals in their houses. On such occasions eminent musicians used to come and give concerts. Since the audiences on such occasions consisted mostly of Vidvans and *rasikas*, the performers invariably exerted their best and the concerts in such festivals were of a scholarly character and invariably proved real musical treats. The festivals conducted by Vina Kuppier and his son Triuvottiyur Tyagayyar in Muthialpet and the Ramanavami festival conducted by Tachur Singaracharlu Brothers have already been referred to. The Krishna Jayanti utsavam conducted by Josyer Nallasubbier, the Arudra utsavam conducted by Guruvapathan (a goldsmith and a disciple of Tiruvottiyur Tyagayyar), the Navaratri utsavam conducted by Tiruvengadachariar, the Ramanavami utsavam conducted by Jalatarangam

7. This Institution owes its origin to Govindappa Naicker's Charities and is sixty years old.

Ramaniah Chettiar and Sesha Iyengar are a few of the other important festivals conducted in the past.

Nathamuni Band was the first organised band of players of wind instruments (wood and brass) to perform Indian music in Madras. Many Nagasvaram players and professional dance parties lived in Madras from the 18th century onwards. Regular Sangita Sabhas which organised periodical concerts by eminent musicians for the benefit of their members were also formed first in Madras. The Krishna Gana Sabha, the Parthasarathi Swami Sabha, the Bhagavath Katha Prasanga Sabha and the Bhakti Marga Prasanga Sabha played not a little part in elevating the musical taste of the citizens of Madras in those days.

Of the patrons of music that lived in and around Madras, prominent mention must be made of Manali Muttukrishna Mudaliar, Manali Venkatakrishna (Chinniah) Mudaliar, Kovur Sundaresa Mudaliar and Pachiappa Mudaliar. The bounty of the Manali family was well known for centuries. Arunagirinathar (the author of the *Tiruppugazh*), Arunachalakavirayar (the author of the Tamil opera—*Rama Natakam*), and Ramaswamy Dikshitar the author of the monumental composition[8]—the Hundred and Eight Raga Tala Malika, were honoured with Kanakabhishekam (anointment with gold) by the members of this family. It was Manali Chinnayya Mudaliar that placed Balaswamy Dikshitar under the tutelage of a European Violinist. It was Dikshitar's proficiency in Violin playing that gained for him admission into the Ettiyapuram Samasthanam. It was at the suggestion of Mr. Chinnaswami Mudaliar, M.A., that Subbarama Dikshitar undertook to write the great work *Sangita Sampradaya Pradarsini*. The Ettiyapuram Samasthanam is entitled to the perennial gratitude of the music world on having published this great work.

It was in Madras that almost all the important works on Music were printed and published. Mr. A. M. Chinnaswamy Mudaliar, M.A., with the help of Tyagaraja's disciples published his great work 'Oriental Music in European notation' in 1892. The first edition of Tyagaraja's collected works was printed in Madras. Captain C. R. Day of the Oxfordshire Light Infantry and the author of the standard work "Music and Musical Instruments of Southern India and Deccan" (1891) lived in Madras for some time. The activities of the Madras Gayan Samaj drew his praise. In his book he says "Societies such as the Gayan Samaj of Poona and Madras have recently sprung up and are doing much to encourage popular music . . ." In another place in the book he pays a tribute to

8. This composition is longer than the longest symphony of Beethoven. In it, each section is not only in a different raga but also in a different tala.

Mr. T. M. Venkatesa Sastri as a well-known authority on the theoretical music of South India.

Mr. C. Tirumalayya Naidu, the author of the brilliant monograph on Tyagaraja and who also wrote the pamphlet "Music and the Anti-Nautch Movement" and the Telugu book "Gana Vidya Sanjeevini" lived in Madras. He was a noted critic and did much to interest the elite of the city in high class music.

The first Journal exclusively devoted to music "Sangita Satsampradaya Dipika" was published in Madras.

Madras was again the scene of two famous musical contests. The one between Maha Vaidyanatha Iyer and Venu took place in the eighties of the last century and the other between two eminent Nagasvaram players in 1906. Venu was a powerful singer and an adept in the intricacies of the tala system like his Master Photograph Masilamani Mudaliar. He challenged Maha Vaidyanatha Iyer to come to Madras. The eminent Vidvan from the south accepted the challenge. A day was fixed for the contest and Mr. Masilamani Mudaliar was chosen as the umpire. On the appointed day, crowds of musicians and music lovers had gathered in the Tiruvannamalai Matam hall, Nattu Pillaiar Koil Street, George Town (the place of the contest). Maha Vaidyanatha Iyer came with Fiddle Venkoba Rao. At the time appointed for the contest, there was dismal silence in the assembly. Venu had already prepared some very difficult pallavis bristling with all types of intricacies in the common ragas. His plan was to give the option of singing the raga first to his opponent (thinking that he would after all sing only common ragas) so that when his turn came he could easily stupefy him by releasing one of these intricate pallavis. When the question was asked "Who is to begin the raga?" Venu straightaway suggested that Maha Vaidyanatha Iyer might begin. Maha Vaidyanatha Iyer without saying anything just prepared to sing *Sankarabharana.* But the shrewd Violinist Venkoba Rao read something in the suggestion of Venu and immediately pulling Vaidyanatha Iyer hinted to him to sing the *raga Narayanagaula.* The hint was given in their private dialect so that its purpose was not understood by any one. The singer took the clue and developed this *raga.* He sang and sang beautifully well. But Venu was dismayed for he was not able to identify the raga. When he could not identify the *raga,* how was he to set his previously prepared pallavi in that raga and confound his opponent? Eventually Maha Vaidyanatha Iyer was declared victorious and it was the intelligence and presence of mind of Venkoba Rao that saved his reputation.

The Nagasvaram contest between two players by name Krishnan and Kuppan took place in the Krishnaswamy Temple, Coral Merchant Street

Muthialpet and Tiruvottiyur Tyagayyar was the umpire on this occasion. A Nagasvaram set with precious stones was donated by Dubash Mukunda Naidu and was offered as the prize to the winner. The prize was carried off by Kuppan.

Compared with other places, the city of Madras has the largest number of Music Sabhas and the largest number of professional musicians (concert performers and music teachers) practising. The Music Academy Festivals which have been held annually for over twelve years have now become an important feature of the city life. When Music was introduced in the S.S.L.C. curriculum, it was a Madras Girls' High School that sent up candidates first for the Examination. Again when music was introduced in the University curriculum, it was a Madras College that first got affiliated to impart instruction in this subject. The facilities given for the advanced study and practice of music by Samasthanas in former times are now given by the Madras University which has recently established a permanent Department of Music and instituted a Diploma Course in Music. The University aims at the spread and diffusion of South Indian music in all its aspects.

History of Education in Madras

By

Dr. P. J. Thomas, M.A., D.Phil.,

Professor, University of Madras.

It is generally admitted that Madras is intellectually one of the most advanced cities in India; the progress of education has perhaps been more rapid here than in any other Indian city. This may be due partly to the racial qualities of the South Indian, but the early start he had in English education must have contributed largely to this. It may therefore be worth while recounting the history of education in Madras. Incidentally it will be seen that another centenary equally important is ahead of us.

Soon after their settlement at Madras, the East India Company seem to have interested themselves in education. We find from the records that as early as 1678, that is, 38 years after the founding of the settlement, a schoolmaster called Ralph Ord drew from the Company's treasury the then high salary of £50 per annum, equal to that of the junior Member of Council. Unfortunately we have no information about the location of his school and the nature of the instruction provided there. In 1687 the Court of Directors, in a letter to the Governor of Madras on the draft scheme of a Municipality for this city, suggested that the Court of Aldermen, when established, might "assess and levy a rate upon the inhabitants for the building of one or more free school or schools for teaching the English tongue to Gentoos or Moors or other Indian children, and for salaries to the schoolmasters." But nothing seems to have been done; for, in 1691 Governor Yale[1] reminded the Corporation that they had as yet done nothing by way of providing schools, and demanded that the funds set apart for the purpose should be restored to Government. The Court of Directors also wrote disapproving of this policy of neglect. The citizens of Madras were, however, more alert. At a public meeting held on 28th October 1715, it was resolved to establish a charity school for European and Eurasian children, giving them diet and education gratis. Thus came into being the St. Mary's Charity School in the Fort, with a boys' and a girls' branch. "While they are entertained in the school, the boys shall be

1. Elihu Yale, Governor of Madras (1687-92), better known as the founder of the Yale University, U.S.A.

taught to read, write, cast accounts or what they may be further capable of, and the girls shall be instructed in reading and the necessary parts of housewifery." Apparently the school was worked on a fairly broad curriculum and was not merely literary in scope.

MISSIONARY EFFORTS

Thus State efforts were necessarily slow; even in England, Government did little for education in those days. But the missionaries were more energetic. In 1711, the Society for Promoting Christian Knowledge (S.P.C.K.) offered to maintain one or more charity schools at Madras through the agency of the Danish missionaries at Tranquebar, of whom the famous Ziegenbalg was the chief. The missionaries arrived in 1717 and in the same year they were given permission to erect two charity schools in the City—one for the Portuguese in the English town and the other for "Malabars" (Tamils and other local people) in the black Town. Thus the first efforts to educate Indians came from missionaries and not from the Company. The first missionaries taught German chiefly, and this caused disapproval from the Company's officers. At first, the S.P.C.K. was unable to persuade any Englishman to go out to India as schoolmaster, and therefore the German missionaries themselves learnt English and taught it in their schools. Mr. Giester was the first of these teachers, but later the mission itself seems to have become 'anglicised'. However, the school for 'Malabars' established in the Fort soon ceased to exist, as there was not much public appreciation for it, owing chiefly to the fact that the Hindu parents were averse to sending their children to a school definitely Christian in character. The school, however, was reopened in 1726 by the Missionary Schultze and attracted many students. This subsequently became the Vepery Anglo-Vernacular School which has enjoyed almost a continuous existence ever since.

The Catholic mission also began their efforts early, but their progress in the city was slow. Between 1746 and 1748, the French under Dupleix were in possession of Madras and they gave permission to a wealthy Armenian Catholic merchant to build a church and mission house at Vepery. A building was soon erected. When the British regained Madras, the Armenian merchant and his followers were suspected of intriguing with the French and the mission house at Vepery was confiscated by the Government. In 1752, this building was presented to the Protestant Mission. It then stood where to-day St. Mathias Church stands. Compensation was however given to the Catholics, who were allowed to build a church close by (St. Andrew's). The first Catholic School, however, was only founded in 1837—St. Mary's Seminary, Armenian Street.

The first printing press in the city was set up in 1761. When the English in their turn occupied the French town of Pondicherry (1761), they found there a printing press, and they took it as booty to Madras and presented it to the S.P.C.K., then working at Vepery, and thus came into being the well-known S.P.C.K. (later called Diocesan) Press. The Press was not a very profitable concern in the beginning and had to be closed in 1810, as there was no means of paying the workmen; but it was however revived in 1850, owing to the vigorous efforts of the District Committee of the S.P.C.K.

In 1784, the S.P.C.K. established a school for the education of Anglo-Indian children in Madras and maintained a schoolmaster at an annual cost of £50. This developed into the Vepery Grammar School. It was subsequently enlarged several times and was the chief educational agency in Madras till the establishment of the Free Church Mission. Under Bishop Corrie, it became the "Madras Grammar School," The Mission also kept a charity school for girls at Vepery. Subsequently, the London Missionary Society and the Wesleyan Mission established schools in Madras. The Wesleyan Mission dates from 1890 and this was the origin of the College at Royapettah. A school at St. Thomas Mount was also established in 1812.

EARLY STATE EFFORTS

From 1786, several institutions for the education and maintenance of orphans were established under the patronage of Government. First came the Military Female Orphan Asylum, with the Missionary Gerike as Superintendent. The building used was presented by the Nawab of Carnatic who had purchased it at a cost of Rs. 80,000. Two years afterwards, the Military Male Orphan Asylum was established with the famous Dr. Andrew Bell as the Superintendent. Subsequently, a Civil Orphan Asylum was also started in Madras and this institution received a fund by the will of Mr. Gericke who died in 1803. It was in this school that Sarbhojee, son and successor of the Rajah of Tanjore, was educated from 1793 to 1797.[3]

Of Andrew Bell, it is necessary to give more than a passing reference, because he, like Elihu Yale, attained to great fame after leaving

2. This was by no means the first printing press in the Presidency. Cochin takes the credit for the first press in India; the Portuguese set up a press there as early as 1577.

3. Bishop Heber, who travelled in South India in 1826, has spoken very highly about the literary accomplishments of this Prince. Heber writes: "His judgment of the poetical merits of Shakespeare excelled even that of Byron." (*Indian Journals*, 1826, p. 265)

Madras. He is well-known as the founder of the 'Madras' or 'Monitorial' or 'Lancaster' system of education. Under this system, most boys are teachers as well as taught. They teach younger boys, while they are taught by the elder ones. As Mr. Bell was riding past a pial school one morning, he found sharp boys teaching backward ones; the whole school was active although there was only one teacher. Dr. Bell employed this method among the boys in the Orphan Asylum, of which he was superintendent. He improved on the indigenous practice and established a system of mutual instruction which he called the 'Madras System' and claimed this as an 'invention' (as distinguished from discovery). In 1796, he went back home, and carried on an effective propaganda for the "Madras System". He won for it the support of several educationalists and persons of high dignity, including the Queen (Consort of George III) and Czar Alexander I. Although he stayed only nine years in Madras, he gathered a fortune of £25,000, which latter increased by clever investment to £120,000, and part of this he devoted for founding a Madras College in his native town of St. Andrews. This College was long in existence, but seems to have given up the 'Madras System' not long afterwards.[4] Anyway, we must be grateful to Dr. Bell for advertising Madras so widely.

The Charter Act of 1813 did not impose a new policy upon the Company; yet from about that time, Government's angle of vision changed. Not satisfied with the books published by the missionary bodies, a 'School Book Society' was established by Government in 1819 with a view to providing books of a secular nature different from those published by missionary bodies.[5] Sir Thomas Munro, when he was Governor of Madras (1820-27), gave his earnest attention to the subject of education. Not only did he make a survey of the schools in the various districts of the Presidency but drew up a scheme for the maintenance of schools at every Collectorate and Tahsildari (Taluk), and set up a Committee of Public Instruction for carrying it out.[6] The annual budget for education was for Rs. 4,000 of which Rs. 700 went to the Madras School Book Society.

The first effort of the newly-formed Committee of Public Instruction was to establish a Normal School for the training of teachers, and for this, accommodation was provided in the building used by the Col-

4. Lawson: *Memoires of Madras*, pp. 210-18.

5. This Society had by 1827 published several books in English and Tamil for the use of schools. See Reports on Census 1871, p. 68.

6. This was afterwards amalgamated with the College Board and became the Board of Public Instruction. The College Board was responsible for the instruction and examination of junior civil servants in Oriental and Vernacular languages.

lege Board for the examination of the junior civil servants (now the Office of the Director of Public Instruction). An English headmaster was employed on a salary of Rs. 300 per mensem, and the Masters retained by the College Board also helped in the work of the School. Provision was made for the training of 40 teachers, to be sent out to the mofussil schools. Two trainees were to be selected from each district, one Hindu and one Mussalman, and among Hindus preference was to be given to Brahmins.[7] Each student was to be given a stipend of Rs. 15 per mensem. At the same time, 61 Tahsildari schools were also set up, and 9 other schools in Madras and its suburbs.

Meanwhile, the *cause célèbre* of Indian education was being fought, mainly in Bengal. What was to be the medium of instruction through which a knowledge of the sciences was to be spread in India in conformity with the purpose of the Charter Acts of 1813 and 1833? Scholars versed in Oriental literature, T. C. Prinsep and H. H. Wilson in particular, preferred Oriental languages; but practical men like Charles Trevelyan (author of an excellent tract on the education of Indians), who were more concerned with the material improvement of India and the modernization of Indians, and shrewd administrators who wanted efficient clerks in the Government Offices, preferred English; and Macaulay (brother-in-law of Trevelyan) who was then Law Member of the Supreme Government cast his vote with the latter and his famous minute of 1834 decided the policy of Government. On 7th March 1835, the Government of India decided that 'the great object of Government ought to be the promotion of European literature and sciences among the natives of India.' That decision was the most epoch-making in the history of India. 'Never on earth was such a momentous question discussed' wrote Sir John Seeley. And truly.

The intentions of the Supreme Government seem to have been imperfectly understood by the authorities in Madras, and they abolished the Collectorate and Tahsildari schools in 1836.[8] The Board of Public Instruction was also abolished, and in its place was established a Committee of Native Education, consisting of a Member of Council (President), a Presbyterian Chaplain, the Marathi translator to Government, the Deputy Judge Advocate, the Company's Astronomer, and the Company's Solicitor. Government also instructed the Committee to submit proposals for the establishment of a normal school at Madras for the training of English teachers. The Committee submitted a more

7. *Report on the Educational Census*, 1871, p. 69.
8. Selections from Educational Records, Edited by J. A. Richey, Part II, p. 177.

ambitious scheme than contemplated by Government, and proposals were made for the immediate establishment of a college as well as a normal school at Madras and four English schools in different parts of the city. But no action was taken on the proposals until the arrival of Lord Elphinstone as Governor of Madras (1838).

FOUNDATION OF THE 'UNIVERSITY'

Lord Elphinstone was a person of firm character and benevolent disposition. Soon after his arrival, he took steps to carry out the intentions of the Supreme Government in the matter of English education. Availing themselves of such an opportunity, the public of Madras, under the lead of George Norton, Advocate-General, presented to the Governor on November 14, 1839, a petition signed by 70,000 'native inhabitants,' in which they pointed out the need for an English college in the city for imparting higher education. According to Norton, the address indicated 'an excited state of feeling' and gave clear indication of a strong public opinion taking shape in the matter of education. 'We have had occasion to learn the inestimable advantages of education. The natural effects of useful knowledge are fully open to our comprehension. We see in the intellectual advancement of the people the true foundation of the nation's prosperity......' 'We descend from the oldest native subjects of the British Power in India; but we are the last who have been considered in the political endowments devoted to this liberal object'......'Where amongst us are the collegiate institutions which, founded for these generous objects, adorn the two Sister Presidencies?' Yet, it was not for mere spoon-feeding that the petitioners prayed. 'We seek not education which depends on charity. We shall take a pride in contributing according to our means to so noble a work'......The public must have 'some voice and share' in the management of the institutions to be established. They also expressed their pride in that Madras had given the inspiration to certain methods of instruction, (the Madras system) which had since become popular in Britain. This petition is a memorable document and must be treasured.

Lord Elphinstone, after careful deliberation, wrote his minute on December 12, 1838, in which he proposed the establishment of a collegiate institution, or University, for the study of literature, philosophy and science and a High School to prepare students for the University. This division was in conformity with the practice then obtaining in Scotch Universities. In order to carry out this scheme, a University Board was to be set up and this was to take the place of the Committee of Native Education established in 1836.

Accordingly, the University Board called 'the President and Governors of the Madras University' was established. It was presided over by George Norton, and had on it the following gentlemen:—J. Cuddy, J. Morgan, Raghava Chariar, D. Sim, J. Wylle; C. Streenivasa Pillai; L. Dent; Hyder Jung; Nussur-ool-Moolk, K. Narasingha Row, Armoogam Moodaliar, Chocapah Chetty. Later additions were C. Runganadum, Streenivasa Pillai and Venkatapatty.

As a result of the Board's activities, that 'department of the University denominated the High School' was established in 1841, and was located in a rented building, formerly occupied by the General Police Office, now the chief Presidency Magistrate's office. Mr. Eyre Burton Powell, a Cambridge wrangler, was appointed Headmaster on the recommendation of the Hon'ble Mountstuart Elphinstone, and was paid a salary of Rs. 700 a month.[9] Three tutors assisted him, nearly, Mr. White, Mr. McLeish and Mr. Godfrey; and three native teachers taught the Oriental languages, namely, Seetaram Sastraloo, Maha Lingiah and Gunnesh Gungader Shastry. English was to be the medium of instruction in the High School and only those who could read and write that language were to be admitted. 'Such a proficiency is by no means difficult of attainment through the many existing facilities of elementary and other schools founded in the various parts of the Presidency.' This qualification also supplied, according to Norton, 'the test of the respectability of the candidate.' However, a preparatory school had been established for children under 12. As many as 65 pupils were on the rolls of the Preparatory School, and most of these passed to the High School.

Nor was the education to be gratuitous. In comformity with the proud offer made in the petition, it was decided that students should pay a monthly fee of Rs. 4. 'A charitable education is bestowed not only with propriety, but also with benefit to the public at large, on those who are altogether incapable of affording to pay for their instruction themselves. But to proffer altogether from the public funds, from individual benefaction, that superior quality of education which is suitable to natives moving in these higher ranks of life, and to bestow it out of such pecuniary sources on those who are amply competent not only to pay for all their own educational advantages, but contribute towards removing the ignorance of others—would be contrary to all reasonable expectation.' The Board admitted 67 pupils to the High School and they were all 'classed' according to their attainments.

9. Mr. Powell later became the Director of Public Instruction, Madras.

The opening ceremony of the High School took place on 14th April 1841, at the College Hall. H. E. the Governor of Madras presided, and there was present a noble gathering, including H. H. the Nawab of Arcot and suite, Members of Council, Military Officers, Judges, and the President and Governors of the University. In all, there were present about 1,500 persons and the gathering 'presented probably the most numerous and respectable assemblage of the native population witnessed in Madras.'[10] The Fundamental Rules approved by Government were first read, and then Mr. Norton read an address to H. E. the Governor, in which he explained the nature and scope of the institution to be opened.

Lord Elphinstone, in his reply, thanked the President and Governors for their arduous labours and said that the proceedings they witnessed was 'the dawn of a new era, rather than the opening of a new school.'

The High School of the University thus came into being. Among the subjects included in the curriculum were English grammar, arithmetic, morality, history, geography; algebra; mechanics; natural philosophy and the vernaculars. Subsequently, political economy also came into the curriculum. The text-books prescribed in history were "History of Greece" by S.D.U.K., Sympathe's 'Lectures' and Goldsmith's "History of England." In political economy, Marcets' 'Political Economy', and Norton's 'Rudimentals' were prescribed. Newton's 'Principia' was a favourite text-book in science. Successful pupils were called "Proficients." Year after year, the Reports of the University Board give the names of "Proficients" and copies of some of the best answers. Among the persons who distinguished themselves at the time were: (Sir) T. Madhava Rao, (Sir) A. Seshiah Sastri, B. Lovery (later Principal, Pachaiayappa's College), Thinathialoo Naidu, M. Sadasivam; V. Ramanujam; (Sir) T. Muthuswami Aiyar and Runganatha Sastri.

Lord Elphinstone had hoped to start a collegiate institution also. This idea had to wait till 1854, when the Presidency College was founded. The institution still continued to be located in Egmore. The number of students gradually increased and among the professors were famous men like J. B. Norton, J. D. Mayne, Talboys Wheeler (the historian) and Mr. Ranganatha Mudaliar.

Nor were professional studies neglected. Plans were soon made for converting the Medical School (founded 1835) into a College and for the promotion of a College of Civil Engineering. A Survey School

10. *The Opening of the Madras University* (1841), Vepery Mission Press, p. 1.

was started in 1840 and a School of Arts in 1850. A Law Class and a teachers' training Class were begun in the Presidency College soon after its foundation.

Two important private institutions came into being in the City about this time. The Scottish Mission headed by Mr. John Anderson opened a school at Madras in 1837. The school was first located on the spot where the Ophthalmic Hospital now stands, but was later shifted to the City, in order that it might cater for the needs of the large Indian community close by. At first a storied building in Armenian Street was hired. This school later developed into the Madras Christian College, which was destined to play a creditable rôle in the higher education of the Presidency.

The Pachiappa's School dates from 1842. It has an interesting history behind it, but this need not be told here. Pachiappa Mudaliar, who died about the year 1778, had bequeathed by will a lakh of pagodas for certain religious and charitable purposes. But, for 60 years, the executors had neglected their duty in this matter. This was discovered by Sir Herbert Compton, Advocate-General, and he brought the matter before the Supreme Court and obtained a decree permitting the utilization of part of the funds for the establishment of schools. Accordingly a school was founded in Black Town in 1842 and this later grew into the Pachiappa's College.

After 1850, doubts began to be entertained about the soundness of the theory that education should begin from above and then descend to the masses. The responsibility of the State in regard to education was being realized more fully. Sir Charles Wood's Despatch of 1854 took this into account and prescribed reform on the following lines:—(1) The constitution of a separate Government Department of Education; (2) the institution of universities in the Presidency towns; (3) the establishment of an institution for training teachers for all classes of schools; (4) the increase in the number of Government colleges and schools; (5) increased attention to vernacular schools; and (6) the introduction of a system of grants-in-aid. Accordingly in 1855, a Department of Education was established in the Government of Madras and Mr. (later Sir Alexander) Arbuthnot, Secretary to the University Board, became the joint Director of Public Instruction and sanction was given for the appointment of Inspectors of Schools.

The 'University of Madras' was incorporated by an Act dated September 5, 1857 "for the purpose of ascertaining by means of examinations, the persons who have obtained proficiency in different branches of literature, science and art, and of rewarding them by academical degrees as evidence of their respective attainments and marks of honour proportioned thereunto." The first entrance examination was held in September 1857 and the first examination for the B.A. degree was held in February 1858. The institution thus started was not for teaching but for conferring degrees. At first it was not distinct from the Presidency College; in fact, till 1874, when the Senate House was built, the university office was located at the Presidency College. At first all teaching was confined to that college; later the Christian and the Pachiappa Colleges came to share in that work. It is well to recognise in this connection that although the degree-giving authority of the University dates only from 1857, the real University of Madras was inaugurated on April 14, 1841. Therefore its centenary falls due on April 14, 1941.

SUBSEQUENT PROGRESS OF THE UNIVERSITY

Between 1857 and 1904, the University of Madras grew rapidly in strength and influence. In 1857, there were only 47 students. By 1904, the number rose to 15,434. Since then; the new Universities of Mysore, Andhra and Annamalai branched off. Yet in 1937, the number of students in the Madras University was 17,500. As many as 35,000 graduates have left the portals of the university till 1938. Under the Act of 1904, the University had jurisdiction not only over the Madras Presidency but over the adjoining Indian States. In 1923, the University was provincialised by the Amendment Act of that year. Nevertheless, colleges in Hyderabad, Travancore, Cochin and Pudukottah continued to be affiliated to it.

The principal events in the history of university education in Madras in recent times are: (1) The foundation of Loyola College, thanks largely to the genius of the late Father Bertram, (2) The migration of the Madras Christian College to Tambaram, outside the University boundaries. The Pachiappa's College is also proposing to migrate to Chetput, not far from the Loyola College.

There are to-day 76 institutions affiliated to the University. Of these, 15 are constituent colleges (situated within the territorial limits of the University, viz., within a radius of ten miles from the Fort St. George); 40 affiliated colleges and 21 Oriental institutions. Of the 55 colleges, 16 are second grade (preparing for the Intermediate Examination), 20 first grade (preparing for Intermediate and B.A. Examinations), 8 are affiliated up to the Honours standard and 11 are professional colleges. The 11 professional colleges include two in Law, two in Medicine, one in Engineering, four in Teaching, one in Agriculture and one in Veterinary Science. Of the 76 institutions mentioned above, 7

PANORAMIC VIEW OF UNIVERSITY BUILDINGS

—*By courtesy of the University of Madras.*

institutions, (viz., six Arts Colleges and one Law College) which are situated in Travancore will cease to have connection with the University after 1940.

Originally, all teaching was confined to the colleges. After 1904, the need for advanced studies was felt and, thanks to a special grant made by the Government, new University Departments in Economics, Indian History and Archaeology, and Dravidian Philology were started. Since 1923, Departments in Mathematics, Philosophy, Sanskrit, Tamil, Telugu, Kannada Malayalam Arabic ; Persian and Urdu; Botany, Zoology, Bio-chemistry; Politics and Public Administration, Geography and Indian Music were established. These Departments are engaged chiefly in research work, but some of them give regular instruction for University Diplomas (Economics, Geography, Politics and Indian Music).

In September 1936, the University completed a building scheme at a cost of over Rs. 20 lakhs, and Madras University is now housed in an imposing structure, known as the University Buildings on the Marina, which contains accommodation for not only the large administrative office but also for the various teaching and research Departments of the University, and the Library. The three research Laboratories are situated to the South-West of the University Buildings and are accommodated in three separate Laboratories, one for Zoology, one for Botany, and one for Biochemistry. The University has also erected its own Examination Hall, situated on the Marina to the South of the Wenlock Park. Some idea of the provision made in these buildings may be realised from the following: The University buildings are divided into two separate buildings connected with a corridor,—(1) the Library building and (2) the Departmental building. The administrative offices of the University are housed on the first floor of the Library building. The University Library which is also housed in this building is the finest in South India and contains over 1,00,000 volumes. About 5,000 volumes are added every year, and in addition there are numerous periodicals, some of which are not available in any other library in India.

Thus the University has grown with the march of time. It not only caters for the needs of the undergraduate but has made liberal provision for post-graduate study and research. It has to-day a large number of research workers, and their publications are steadily growing in number and magnitude. We may legitimately hope that this university will play a noble part in the great work of intellectual and economic uplift before the country under the Reforms of 1935.

A History of Journalism in Madras

BY

K. P. VISWANATHA IYER, M.A.,
Asst. Editor, 'The Hindu,' Madras.

NEWSPAPERS in Madras had their origin in the needs of the small but growing European Colony of the Presidency. They were l te in coming so that in the first century of the city's life it had no newspapers, as newspapers even in England had not then developed. The earliest of these were three weeklies, the *Government Gazette*, the *Madras Gazette* and the *Madras Courier*. The bill of fare provided by them related to the social life of the community and to 'home' news. The news from Europe consisted of extracts from European papers of reports of Parliamentary proceedings. Owing to the infrequency of, if not irregularities in, steamer service—ships had to come in fleets under convoy—and particularly lack of service from October to December, the extracts given related to periods which had long passed by.

"For a Madras Newspaper to please," says a writer[1] of the sixties of the last century, "It must be wise in moral essays (Johnsonian in type) or witty in flippant correspondence or the respective editors must be witty or wise. The two *Gazettes* elected to be wise; the *Courier* thought it would pay best to be witty. The *Madras Gazette* was perhaps the oldest of the three, but the *Government Gazette* claimed precedence." The best known editor of the *Government Gazette* was J. Goldingham, Esq., "who of course had to exercise discretion in its Europe extracts and for the rest seemed to be guided by three rules: first, to write as little editorial matter as could consist with being an editor; secondly, to make that little contain as little meaning as possible; and thirdly not to forget that the use of language is to conceal a meaning." The *Government Gazette* was patronised by the 'services' first because it was the official organ, secondly because it was etiquette, and thirdly, because it was a charity." The *Madras Gazette* was printed at the Exchange in the Fort. It had an able man for many years as editor, but "to write editorials then was condescension; Madras was not then literary."

The *Madras Courier* was a different paper; it was the result of the enterprise of a Mr. William Urquhart who had set up a printing

1. W. T. Munro in his *Madrasiana*.

office in Stringer street where he began with an advertising half sheet in large types known as the *Commercial Circulator.* The *Courier,* born of this advertising sheet, was made famous by its young editor C. H. Clay of handsome mien and of easy manners who was clerk to the Chief Justice and Court Sealer. "His legal associations," says Munro, "were useful to him. He had the entry of good society and was backed by military officers. To quiz and quibble, praise and quote Byron (who just then burst like an aerolite), to quarrel with ceremony and to grumble because not to be allowed to appear in it were among the attributes of the Madras brilliant. In one column was a dead set against heavy and late Madras dinners, in one adjoining the mourn of a sub because not invited. The *Madras Courier* was thus in fact the *Tatler* and the *Spectator* of the Anglo-Indian community in the Presidency at the time." Local journalism of the time appears to have had its own amenities. There were frequent quarrels between the *Gazette* and the *Courier.* "The *Gazette,*" to quote Munro again, "set up an essayist with the title of the 'Trifler,' while the *Courier* came out forthwith exhibiting the 'anti-Trifler.' The 'Trifler' bore the Union motto *tria juncta in uno.* 'Anti-Trifler' maintained that the last word should be *una* or three old women rolled into one. Apart from the Trifler's exhibiting a few signs of help and vigour, it was chocked by the petulance and persevering and pasquinades of 'anti-Trifler' so that the 'Trifler' did not survive the fourth or the fifth issue."

The press of those times was kept under strict censorship by the Government. The Damocles' sword was over the journalist's head. Metcalfe's Act did away with deportation of the journalist and is said to have established liberty of the press. But conditions really continued difficult long after. Now and then some signal lights (asterisks to wit) appeared, but says our historian of the times, "the editor's legal knowledge kept him within bounds. Only once was the *Courier* editor at fault. The second page conceded to correspondence was filled throughout by the headmaster of the College of Fort St. George with a detailed panegyric of his own phase of the Hindu religion. Next week two columns and a half were planted with lights like a page in *Tristram Shandy.* We got at the secret in five words 'expunged by the Chief *Secretary.*' Some fellow had questioned the soundness and solidity of Seshiah's positions and the editor did not know that to do so was counter to a recent Bengal Regulation." Another specimen of the sort of letters that used to appear in these early papers may be mentioned. Under the guise of a gouty civilian, we are told, a letter was written complaining bitterly of his better half and asking very seriously if he might not be allowed to put her in chains. Someone replied equally seriously advising the writer of the letter to do no such barbarous thing but rather to consider Socrates and his Xantippe and take comfort!

One of the influences which went to the building up of a special type of newspaper press in the second century of the life of the city was the foreign Christian Missions. The missionaries were the first to cast types in the vernacular languages and to employ Indian compositors. The earliest vernacular newspaper was issued in Bengalee by the Baptist Mission at Serampur. Many of these papers, based on the activities of the missionaries, bore the marks of their origin, being limited almost exclusively to theological controversies. The Brahma Samaj and the orthodox Hindus followed the example of the missionaries and founded their own papers. In these controversies, some of the European laymen also interested themselves. The missions in Madras, the Malabar Jesuit Mission, the C. M. S., the S. P. G., the Wesleyan Mission and so on were the patrons of the printing press and they had their own associations and newspapers, of which the *Athenium* and the *Crescent* were the most notable. In this period, the lay papers also evinced a lot of interest in religious matters. Thus the *Neilgherry Excelsior* and the *Madras Observer* contained a number of articles on religious and quasi-religious subjects. Many aspects of the religion of the Hindus also came in for notice in these journals as also many phases of their culture. The *Neilgherry Excelsior* was in fact an organ of the European community settled on the Blue Mountains.

An offshoot of the missionary movement which had also a contribution to make to journalism in Madras was the foundation of the Free Thinkers Association in the seventies of the last century and of the Theosophical Society. With the growth of English thought, it began to exercise a potent influence on the minds of Indians and this influence formed the basis of three distinctive lines of development. One was the growth of Rationalism with the establishment, as indicated before, of the Free Thinkers Association and the social reform movement; the other was the Revivalist Movement which found expression in the support given to the Theosophical Society; a third which also effected a profound change in the political outlook of Indians was the rise of Nationalism. The journalistic product of Rationalism in Madras was the *Free Thinker*. This, however, was short-lived, theosophy having successfully absorbed the Free Thinkers. Till late in the last century, the vernacular press of Madras was politically unimportant, being for the most part devoted to religion; but in English there were political papers.

Modern journalism in Madras is really a by-product of politics. Towards the middle of the last century, political papers strictly so called came to be founded. The *Spectator* (1836), the *Madras Times* (1860) and the *Madras Mail* (1867) were all papers established with the object of furthering the general and certain particular interests of the European community. The *Madras Times,* till it was absorbed by the *Mail,* had a notable, at times stormy career. It represented the humbler section of the European community, the trader, the planter, and the smaller merchants. It became a power late in the century under George Romilly who was an uncompromising upholder of the European interests in the narrow sense. Its affiliations were with the Trades and the Planters' Associations as those of the *Mail* were with the Chamber of Commerce and the Madras Club. The *Madras Mail,* unlike the *Times* was aristocratic. It was the paper of the European members of the Services and the Nabobs of the business world. It was suave and sedate and under the Lawsons and Mr. Henry Beauchamp accurately reflected the mind of the European intellectual. It was modelled on the serious daily papers of England.

Corresponding papers on the Indian side were late in coming. The first Indian newspaper conducted by an Indian was the *Crescent,* an organ of the Native Association formed under the leadership of the late Lakshminarasu Chettiar to make known the grievances of the Indian population to the Viceroy and the Governor. For lack of support from educated Indians, who were few in number at the time, it soon became defunct. Thanks, however, to the late Raja Sir T. Madhava Rao and his compeers Dewan Bahadur Raghunatha Rao and Ranganatha Mudaliar, a new paper was launched, the *Native Public Opinion.* Some time later, Mr. A. Ramachandra Iyer, who later became Chief Justice of Mysore, founded the *Madrasee.* There being no scope for two Indian journals, the *Native Public Opinion* was amalgamated with the *Madrasee.* The amalgamated journal soon however fell into the hands of men who were opposed to the general current of educated Indian opinion. One of the achievements of this journal was the opposition it offered to the appointment of T. Muthuswami Iyer to the High Court Bench. No wonder it ceased ere long to enjoy public confidence and became defunct. Another paper of the time, the *People's Friend,* suffered a similar fate.

The result of the failure of these journals was the founding of the *Hindu* in September 1878 by a group of Madras publicists—G. Subramania Iyer, T. T. Rangachariar, P. V. Rangachariar, D. Kesava Rao Pant, N. Subba Rao and M. Viraraghavachariar. The actual work of running the paper fell to G. Subramania Iyer and Viraraghavachariar who had entered life as school masters. The *Hindu* began as a weekly paper but soon became a tri-weekly (1883) and was six years later converted into a full fledged daily. With it was associated in the beginning gentlemen who in after life distinguished themselves in Indian journalism—C. Karunakara Menon, K. Natarajan, C. Y. Chintamani.

The founding of the *Hindu* is a landmark in the history of journalism in Madras; its growth, with that of Indian newspapers in other Provinces, marked the growth of Indian Nationalism. A comparison of the state of the press in Madras in the early years of the present century with what it was in the seventies of the last century will be of interest. In 1875-76 there were in Madras city nine English and seventeen Indian newspapers. Two of these, the *Madras Mail* and the *Madras Times*, were edited by Englishmen and had a daily circulation of about 3,000 to 4,000 copies. These were chiefly read by Europeans and Eurasians, but the *Mail* had a large number of Indian readers also. The Government and the commerce of the country being in the hands of Europeans, the *Mail* had considerable influence with the authorities and had access to official information such as Indian newspapers had not. It maintained a high standard of literary excellence and a news service ahead of that of other papers. The Indian papers were too poor to pay for news services and their circulation too was small, the number of educated Indians being then very limited. Official records show that in 1900 the circulation of the *Hindu* was about 1800. With the increase in the number of educated Indians, the demand for Indian newspapers also improved. When, therefore, Mr. Karunakara Menon resigned the editorship of the *Hindu*, owing to personal reasons, when the *Hindu* was taken over by Mr. Kasturiranga Iyengar, he was able to start a paper of his own, the *Indian Patriot*, which became the organ of moderate opinion and of the Indian States. A little earlier another newspaper had also come into being—The *Madras Standard*—which under the editorship of G. Parameswaran Pillai, assisted, by friends like the late Eardley Norton, exerted an influence with the Indian community for a time unsurpassed by its contemporaries.

The growing strength of the Indian National Congress, in which was focussed Indian public opinion, and its success in securing for Indians a rapidly increasing share in the administration of the country, contributed to the growth of the influence of the Indian press as well. In 1905, when Mr. Kasturiranga Iyengar purchased the *Hindu* from its owners, Mr. G. Subramania Iyer and Mr. Viraraghavachariar, its influence had been established. What it lacked was organisation and financial independence. Mr. Iyengar contributed these essentials. He established the truth of the proposition that the secret of the success of a newspaper was unbending independence, accuracy, efficient service, thoroughly business-like methods and unsullied character on the part of the conductors. The enterprise of the *Hindu* under his successors was equal to the great burden thrown on the press by the War. The opportunity which the War gave for revolutionising methods of production and organisation of news service was fully availed of by the *Hindu*. The volume of news received, it was found, could not be handled adequately by handcomposing, while the increase in circulation imposed a strain on the printing machines, which they could not stand. It was found that even if the machines were run all the twenty-four hours, the number of copies required could not be printed. Linotype machines and rotary presses were a necessity; and the *Hindu* mechanised its printing. Earlier, *New India*, a reincarnation of the old *Madras Standard* under Mrs. Besant, had been faced with the same problem; its circulation in the Home rule agitation days, having increased considerably more than that of any other paper in the province, could not be coped with by the ordinary flat-bed presses. The *Hindu* learnt the lesson and went in for rotary presses.

The mechanical development and changes in circulation had a tremendous influence on the press of the province. Newspapers with limited capital resources or which had fallen from public favour because of their editorial policy dropped out. The *Patriot* became defunct; the *Standard* was dying and survived as *New India* for a time only because of the stimulus of a dominating and resourceful personality whose views for a time coincided with public opinion. The *Madras Times* was absorbed by the *Madras Mail* because it was found that there was no scope for two papers to serve the European community. Another important factor which also came into operation at the time was the growth of the Non-Brahmin movement and the need for a paper to express the opinion of the non-Brahmins. The founding of the Justice Party led to the starting of *Justice*, the organ of that community. The growth of parties and their crystallisation threw up as a precipitate party papers like *Justice* and later *Swarajya*. The idea of a morning newspaper to meet the needs of that section of the public which had no strong party affiliations was taken up and successfully worked out by Mr. R. W. Brock Editor of the *Madras Times*, who, after its amalgamation with the *Mail* founded the *Daily Express*. It began well, showing signs of success, but the intrusion of the control of financiers in the sphere of editorial policy and other factors led to the complications which eventually killed the paper. *Justice*, with the decline of the party, dwindled into a weekly for lack of adequate support. Its fate as well as that of *Swarajya* shows that mere party journals have little scope in the country.

In the field of vernacular journalism, the most noticeable development is the trend towards a tabloid type of paper. The idea of a pice paper in English had been tried out. *To-day*, the pioneer, met with an early death, while the *Indian Express* had to increase the price from half-anna to three quarters of an anna. Vernacular papers, however, lowered the price, the competition of *Dinamani* having forced *Swadesamitran*, another successful venturc of the late G. Subramania Iyer, to reduce its pricc likewise to half an anna and enjoyed increased circulation.

After the commencement of this century, and especially after the War, there have been a very good number of weeklies, monthlies and quarterlies not only in the vernaculars, but also in English. Mention may be made of important Telugu papers like *Andhra Patrika*, the *Bharati*, and *Trilinga*. Among English journals mention may be made of the Indian Review, Educational Review, Journal of Indian History, Journal of Oriental Research, Journal of the Madras Geographical Association, the Triveni, and others. Some of these are high class research journals, and maintain very high standards.